An Introduction to International Criminal Law and Procedure

SECOND EDITION

ROBERT CRYER
HÅKAN FRIMAN
DARRYL ROBINSON
ELIZABETH WILMSHURST

CAMBRIDGE
UNIVERSITY PRESS

CAMBRIDGE UNIVERSITY PRESS
Cambridge, New York, Melbourne, Madrid, Cape Town, Singapore,
São Paulo, Delhi, Dubai, Tokyo

Cambridge University Press
The Edinburgh Building, Cambridge CB2 8RU, UK

Published in the United States of America by Cambridge University Press, New York

www.cambridge.org

Information on this title: www.cambridge.org/9780521119528

First published 2007
Second edition 2010

Printed in the United Kingdom at the University Press, Cambridge

A catalogue record for this publication is available from the British Library

Library of Congress Cataloguing in Publication data
An introduction to international criminal law and procedure / Robert Cryer ... [et al.]. – 2nd ed.
   p.   cm.
ISBN 978-0-521-11952-8 (hardback)
1. International offenses.   2. Criminal procedure (International law)   3. International criminal
courts.   I. Cryer, Robert.   II. Title.
K5301.I587   2010
345–dc22

                                                                                    2010015483

ISBN 978-0-521-11952-8 Hardback
ISBN 978-0-521-13581-8 Paperback

1006259952

Contents

Preface to the Second Edition

Our intention for this second edition is the same as it was for the first: to provide an accessible yet challenging explanation and appraisal of international criminal law and procedure for students, academics and practitioners. We focus on the crimes which are within the jurisdiction of international courts or tribunals – genocide, crimes against humanity, war crimes and aggression – and the means of prosecuting them. We also briefly discuss terrorist offences, torture, and other crimes which are not (yet) within the jurisdiction of an international court or tribunal.

International criminal law is now a vast subject, even in our circumscribed view of what it contains. This book is intended as a manageable and useful introduction to the field, and therefore does not attempt to delve into the entirety of the subject in the full detail it deserves. We welcome comments on possible improvements that could be made, and are grateful for those that we received on the first edition. We have sought to be succinct rather than simplistic in our presentation. We have included references to academic commentary, both in the footnotes and in 'further reading' sections at the end of each chapter. However, there is a great deal of writing on international criminal law, and we could not refer to it all. We hope that this book piques the interest of those new to the subject to further investigations including into the considerable and insightful literature which the developments in international criminal law have engendered.

While we hope that this book will appeal to practitioners as well as to students, the chapters are intended to cover the subjects which can be dealt with during a university Masters course in international criminal law. Part A is introductory. Following a discussion in Chapter 1 of what we mean by international criminal law and of some of its most fundamental principles, we consider in Chapter 2 the objectives of this body of law. Part B is concerned with prosecutions in national, rather than international, courts. Chapter 3 discusses the principles of jurisdiction as they relate to international crimes, Chapter 4 describes some instances of national prosecutions and Chapter 5 concerns extradition, transfer of information and other means by which States cooperate to assist in bringing suspects to justice before national courts. Part C, which concerns international prosecutions, begins in Chapter 6 with a history of the trials following the Second

World War and Chapters 7 and 8 respectively discuss the ad hoc Tribunals and the International Criminal Court. Chapter 9 describes in brief other courts with an international element which have been established to investigate and prosecute international crimes. Part D discusses the substantive law of international crimes. Chapters 10 to 13 cover genocide, crimes against humanity, war crimes and aggression; Chapter 14 introduces the subject of 'transnational' crimes, and takes as examples terrorist offences and torture. Chapters 15 and 16 introduce the principles of liability and defences respectively. Part E is concerned with the processes of international prosecutions: Chapter 17 focuses on the procedures, Chapter 18 on the role of victims, and Chapter 19 on sentencing. Part F considers various aspects of the relationship between the national and international systems: State cooperation with the international courts and tribunals (in Chapter 20) and immunities, in relation to both national and international jurisdictions (in Chapter 21). Amnesties and other alternatives and complements to prosecutions are considered in Chapter 22. We end with our conclusions in Chapter 23, which contains our assessment of the development of international criminal law and its institutions and our forecast for the future.

The authors have all taught, to a greater or lesser extent, in international criminal law courses. Three of us took part in the negotiations on the International Criminal Court and participated at the Rome Conference. Some of the comments in this book rely directly on our experience in this capacity.

We have all had an input into each chapter. Each of us drafted a number of chapters, which were circulated and commented upon by the other three. Each chapter has been the object of intensive discussion amongst all of us to achieve as much coherence among our views as possible. We have attempted to produce a book which reads as a coherent whole, rather than as a collection of separate papers from different writers. Of course, with four authors, complete consensus on every matter of substance was neither possible nor expected and the views expressed in individual chapters are therefore those of the author of that chapter, and not necessarily of the group as a whole.

In the first edition the responsibility for Chapters 2, 3, 6, 7, 15 and 16 rested with Robert Cryer, for Chapters 4, 5, 9, 17, 18 and 19 (the latter two now Chapters 19 and 20) with Håkan Friman, for Chapters 11, 12 and 20 (now 21) with Darryl Robinson and for Chapters 8, 10, 13, and 14 with Elizabeth Wilmshurst. Chapters 1 and 21 (now 23), which express the views of us all, were written by Rob and Elizabeth (Chapter 1) and by Rob (Chapter 21(23)).

The responsibility for updating has largely remained the same with each person updating their own chapters. The only changes are that Robert has taken over Chapter 4, written Chapter 22 and updated Chapter 1. Håkan has written the chapter on victims (new Chapter 18), and Elizabeth has taken over Chapter 9. Elizabeth has also had the responsibility of keeping us all together and seeking a consistent text.

We express particular thanks to Finola O'Sullivan and Sinead Moloney of Cambridge University Press. It would be remiss of us to fail to note the contributions of Professor Claus Kreß and Charles Garraway to the conceptualization of the first edition. We remain grateful to them.

Robert Cryer
Håkan Friman
Darryl Robinson
Elizabeth Wilmshurst
January 2010

Table of Cases

ICJ

ICTR

ICTY

SCSL

Table of National Cases

United States

Table of Treaties and other International Instruments

Table of Abbreviations

A. Ch.	Appeals Chamber
ACHPR	African Charter of Human and People's Rights
ACHR	American Convention on Human Rights
AJIL	*American Journal of International Law*
All ER	All England Reports
AP	Additional Protocol to the Geneva Conventions
ASEAN	Association of Southeast Asian Nations
ASP	Assembly of States Parties to the International Criminal Court
AU	African Union
BFSP	British and Foreign State Papers
BYBIL	*British Yearbook of International Law*
CARICOM	Caribbean Community
CAT	UN Convention against Torture and other Cruel, Inhuman and Degrading Treatment
CIS	Commonwealth of Independent States
CLF	*Criminal Law Forum*
CMR	Court Martial Reports
CPA	Coalition Provisional Authority
ECCC	Extraordinary Chambers in the Courts of Cambodia
ECHR	European Convention for the Protection of Human Rights and Fundamental Freedoms
ECOSOC	UN Economic and Social Council
ECOWAS	Economic Community of West African States
ECtHR	European Court of Human Rights
EJIL	*European Journal of International Law*
EOC	Elements of Crime
ETS	European Treaty Series
EU	European Union
FRY	Federal Republic of Yugoslavia
F. Supp.	Federal Supplement
GA	General Assembly
GC	Geneva Convention

Hague Recueil	*Recueil des cours de l'Academie de droit international*
ICC	International Criminal Court
ICCPR	International Covenant on Civil and Political Rights
ICJ	International Court of Justice
ICLQ	*International and Comparative Law Quarterly*
ICLR	*International Criminal Law Review*
ICRC	International Committee for the Red Cross and Red Crescent
ICTR	International Criminal Tribunal for Rwanda
ICTY	International Criminal Tribunal for the former Yugoslavia
IFOR	Implementation Force (NATO)
IGC	Interim Governing Council
IHL	international humanitarian law
ILC	International Law Commission
ILM	International Legal Materials
ILR	International Law Reports
IMT	International Military Tribunal
JICJ	*Journal of International Criminal Justice*
KFOR	(NATO) Kosovo Force
LJIL	*Leiden Journal of International Law*
LNTS	League of Nations Treaty Series
London Charter/ Nuremberg Charter	Agreement for the Prosecution and Punishment of the Major War Criminals of the European Axis
LRA	Lord's Resistance Army
LRTWC	Law Reports, Trials of War Criminals
MONUC	UN Organization Mission in the Democratic Republic of the Congo
NJIL	*Nordic Journal of International Law*
OAS	Organization of American States
OAU	Organization of African Unity
OHR	Office of the High Representative
OIC	Organization of the Islamic Conference
OJ	Official Journal
OSCE	Organization for Security and Cooperation in Europe
OTP	Office of the Prosecutor
PAUTS	Pan-American Union Treaty Series
PCIJ	Permanent Court of International Justice
PT. Ch.	Pre-Trial Chamber
RPE	Rules of Procedure and Evidence
SAARC	South Asian Association for Regional Cooperation
SADC	Southern African Development Community
SC	Security Council
SCR	Supreme Court Reports
SCSL	Special Court for Sierra Leone
SFOR	Stability Force (NATO-led force deployed in Bosnia)
SICT	Supreme Iraqi Criminal Tribunal

SOFA	Status of forces agreement
STL	Special Tribunal for Lebanon
T. Ch.	Trial Chamber
UKTS	United Kingdom Treaty Series
UN	United Nations
UNAMID	African Union/United Nations Hybrid operation in Darfur
UNMIK	UN Interim Administration Mission in Kosovo
UNTAES	United Nations Transitional Administration for Eastern Slavonia, Baranja and Western Sirmium
UNTAET	United Nations Transitional Administration in East Timor
UNTS	United Nations Treaty Series
WTO	World Trade Organization
YIHL	*Yearbook of International Humanitarian Law*
ZaöRV	*Zeitschrift für ausländisches öffentliches Recht und Völkerrecht*

Book titles and their abbreviations as used in the text

Antonio Cassese, Paolo Gaeta and John R. W. D. Jones (eds.), *The Rome Statute of the International Criminal Court: A Commentary* (Oxford, 2002): Cassese, *Commentary*.

José Doria, Hans-Peter Gasser and M. Cherif Bassiouni (eds.), *The Legal Regime of the International Criminal Court: Essays in Honour of Professor Igor Blishchenko* (Leiden, 2009): Doria, *Legal Regime*.

Jean-Marie Henckaerts and Louise Doswald-Beck, *Customary International Humanitarian Law* (Cambridge, 2000), vol. I: Henckaerts and Doswald-Beck, *ICRC Customary Law*.

Roy Lee (ed.), *The International Criminal Court – The Making of the Rome Statute: Issues, Negotiations, Results* (The Hague, 1999): Lee, *The Making of the Rome Statute*.

Roy Lee et al. (eds.), *The International Criminal Court – Elements of Crimes and Rules of Procedure and Evidence* (New York, 2001): Lee, *Elements and Rules*.

Göran Sluiter and Sergey Vasiliev (eds.), *International Criminal Procedure: Towards a Coherent Body of Law* (London, 2009): Sluiter and Vasiliev, *International Criminal Procedure*.

Carsten Stahn and Göran Sluiter (eds.), *The Emerging Practice of the International Criminal Court* (Leiden, 2009): Stahn and Sluiter, *Emerging Practice*.

Otto Triffterer (ed.), *Commentary on the Rome Statute of the International Criminal Court: Observers' Notes*, 2nd edn (München/Oxford/Baden-Baden, 2008): Triffterer, *Observers' Notes*.

PART A

Introduction

1

Introduction: What is International Criminal Law?

1.1 International criminal law

International law typically governs the rights and responsibilities of States;[1] criminal law, conversely, is paradigmatically concerned with prohibitions addressed to individuals, violations of which are subject to penal sanction by a State.[2] The development of a body of international criminal law which imposes responsibilities directly on individuals and punishes violations through international mechanisms is relatively recent. Although there are historical precursors and precedents of and in international criminal law,[3] it was not until the 1990s, with the establishment of the ad hoc Tribunals for the former Yugoslavia and Rwanda, that it could be said that an international criminal law regime had evolved. This is a relatively new body of law, which is not yet uniform, nor are its courts universal.

International criminal law developed from various sources. War crimes originate from the 'laws and customs of war', which accord certain protections to individuals in armed conflicts. Genocide and crimes against humanity evolved to protect persons from what are now often termed gross human rights abuses, including those committed by their own governments. With the possible exception of the crime of aggression with its focus on inter-State conflict, the concern of international criminal law is now with individuals and with their protection from wide-scale atrocities. As was said by the Appeal Chamber in the *Tadić* case in the International Criminal Tribunal for the former Yugoslavia (ICTY):

> A State-sovereignty-oriented approach has been gradually supplanted by a human-being-oriented approach ... [I]nternational law, while of course duly safeguarding the legitimate interests of States, must gradually turn to the protection of human beings ...[4]

---

1 See, e.g. Robert Jennings and Arthur Watts (eds.), *Oppenheim's International Law* (9th edn, London, 1994) 5–7.
2 Glanville Williams, 'The Definition of Crime' (1955) 8 *Current Legal Problems* 107.
3 See Chapter 6 and e.g. Timothy L. H. McCormack, 'From Sun Tzu to the Sixth Committee, the Evolution of an International Criminal Law Regime' in Timothy L. H. McCormack and Gerry J. Simpson (eds.), *The Law of War Crimes: National and International Approaches* (The Hague, 1997) 31.
4 *Tadić* ICTY A. Ch. 2.10.1995 para. 97.

The meaning of the phrase 'international criminal law' depends on its use, but there is a plethora of definitions, not all of which are consistent. In 1950, the most dedicated chronicler of the uses of 'international criminal law', Georg Schwarzenberger,[5] described six different meanings that have been attributed to that term, all of which related to international law, criminal law and their interrelationship, but none of which referred to any existing body of international law which directly created criminal prohibitions addressed to individuals; Schwarzenberger believed that no such law existed at the time. 'An international crime', he said in reference to the question of the status of aggression, 'presupposes the existence of an international criminal law. Such a branch of international law does not exist.'[6]

Cherif Bassiouni,[7] on the other hand (and writing almost half a century later), listed twenty-five categories of international crimes, being crimes which affect a significant international interest or consist of egregious conduct offending commonly shared values, which involve more than the State because of differences of nationality of victims or perpetrators or the means employed, or which concern a lesser protected interest which cannot be defended without international criminalization. His categories include, as well as the more familiar ones, traffic in obscene materials, falsification and counterfeiting, damage to submarine cables and unlawful interference with mail.

Different meanings of international criminal law have their own utility for their different purposes and there is no necessary reason to decide upon one meaning as the 'right' one.[8] Nevertheless, it is advisable from the outset to be clear about the sense in which the term is used in any particular situation. In this chapter we will attempt to elaborate the meaning which we give to the term for the purposes of this book and compare it with other definitions.

1.1.1   Crimes within the jurisdiction of an international court or tribunal

The approach taken in this book is to use 'international crime' to refer to those offences over which international courts or tribunals have been given jurisdiction under general international law. They comprise the so-called 'core' crimes of genocide, crimes against humanity, war crimes and the crime of aggression (also known as the crime against peace). Our use thus does not include piracy, slavery, torture, terrorism, drug trafficking and many crimes which States Parties to various treaties are under an obligation to criminalize in their

---

5 Georg Schwarzenberger, 'The Problem of an International Criminal Law' (1950) 3 *Current Legal Problems* 263.

6 Georg Schwarzenberger, 'The Judgment of Nuremberg' (1947) 21 *Tulane Law Review* 329 at 349.

7 M. Cherif Bassiouni, 'International Crimes; The Ratione Materiae of International Criminal Law' in M. Cherif Bassiouni (ed.), *International Criminal Law*, 3rd edn (Leiden, 2008) vol. I, 129, 134–5.

8 But omnibus uses of 'international criminal law' risk implying that there is a structural unity to what is being referred to, and thus treating very different things as having similarities. For an example, see Barbara Yarnold, 'Doctrinal Basis for the International Criminalisation Process' (1994) 4 *Temple International and Comparative Law Journal* 85.

domestic law. But because a number of the practical issues surrounding the repression of these crimes are similar to those relating to international crimes (in the way we use the term), they are discussed in this book, although only terrorist offences and torture will be discussed in any detail. Some of them (terrorist offences, drug trafficking and individual acts of torture) have been suggested as suitable for inclusion within the jurisdiction of the International Criminal Court (ICC)[9] and may therefore constitute international crimes within our meaning at some time in the future.

Our approach does not differentiate the core crimes from others as a matter of principle, but only pragmatically, by reason of the fact that no other crimes are currently within the jurisdiction of international courts. However, it is clear that since these crimes have a basis in international law, they are also regarded by the international community as violating or threatening values protected by general international law, as the preamble to the Rome Statute of the International Criminal Court makes clear.[10]

'International criminal law', as used in this book, encompasses not only the law concerning genocide, crimes against humanity, war crimes and aggression, but also the principles and procedures governing the international investigation and prosecution of these crimes. As we shall see, in practice the greater part of the enforcement of international criminal law is undertaken by domestic authorities. The principle of complementarity, which is fundamental to the whole of international criminal law enforcement, shows that national courts both are, and are intended to be, an integral and essential part of the enforcement of international criminal law.[11] In this book therefore we shall cover not only the international prosecution of international crimes, but also various international aspects of their domestic investigation and prosecution. However, as mentioned above, this is only one way of conceiving of international criminal law; below we evaluate some of the other approaches to defining the subject.

1.2   Other concepts of international criminal law

1.2.1   Transnational criminal law

Until the establishment of the international courts and tribunals in the 1990s, the concept of international criminal law tended to be used to refer to those parts of a State's domestic criminal law which deal with transnational crimes, that is, crimes with actual or potential

---

9 See Final Act of the Rome Conference A/CONF.183/10, Res. E.

10 See, in particular, preambular paragraphs 3–4, which affirm that such crimes threaten the 'peace, security and well-being of the world', and as such, must be prosecuted.

11 See Arts. 17 and 18 of the ICC Statute. As to the situation generally, Judges Higgins, Kooijmans and Buergenthal have stated: 'the international consensus that the perpetrators of international crimes should not go unpunished is being advanced by a flexible strategy, in which newly established international criminal tribunals, treaty obligations and national courts all have their part to play'. *Case concerning the Arrest Warrant of 11 April 2000 (Democratic Republic of Congo* v. *Belgium)* 14.2.2002 Separate Opinion para. 51.

transborder effects. This body of law is now more appropriately termed 'transnational criminal law'. A similar terminological distinction between 'international criminal law' (criminal aspects of international law) and 'transnational criminal law' (international aspects of national criminal laws) can also be found in other languages, such as German ('*Völkerstrafrecht*' compared with '*Internationales Strafrecht*'),[12] French ('*droit international pénal*' and '*droit pénal international*') and Spanish ('*derecho internacional penal*' and '*derecho penal internacional*').

Transnational criminal law includes the rules of national jurisdiction under which a State may enact and enforce its own criminal law where there is some transnational aspect of a crime. It also covers methods of cooperation among States to deal with domestic offences and offenders where there is a foreign element and the treaties which have been concluded to establish and encourage this inter-State cooperation. These treaties provide for mutual legal assistance and extradition between States in respect of crimes with a foreign element. Other treaties require States to criminalize certain types of conduct by creating offences in their domestic law, and to bring offenders to justice who are found on their territory, or to extradite them to States that will prosecute. While international law is thus the source of a part of this group of rules, the source of criminal prohibitions on individuals is national law.[13]

Until recently, there was not a clear distinction in the literature between international criminal law with its more restricted meaning and transnational criminal law. Transnational criminal law, with its focus on domestic criminal law and on inter-State cooperation in the sphere of criminal law, remains the body of 'international criminal law' with which national lawyers are most familiar. Providing full coverage of this body of law would require a volume in its own right. Our discussion of it will address only issues of State jurisdiction, such obstacles to national prosecution as immunities, and State cooperation in national proceedings relating to international crimes; we deal with 'transnational crimes' only in so far as they raise cognate issues to international crimes.

1.2.2   *International criminal law as a set of rules to protect the values of the international order*

Another, and more substantive, approach to determining the scope of 'international criminal law' is to look at the values which are protected by international law's prohibitions.[14] Under this approach international crimes are considered to be those which are of concern to the international community as a whole (a description which is not of great precision), or acts

---

12 Kai Ambos, *Internationales Strafrecht*, 2nd edn (Berlin, 2008).
13 See generally, Neil Boister, 'Transnational Criminal Law?' (2003) 14 *EJIL* 953 at 967–77.
14 For discussion in relation to the core crimes, see Bruce Broomhall, *International Justice and the International Criminal Court: Between State Sovereignty and the Rule of Law* (Oxford, 2003) 44–51.

which violate a fundamental interest protected by international law. Early examples include the suppression of the slave trade. The ICC Statute uses the term 'the most serious crimes of concern to the international community as a whole' almost as a definition of the core crimes,[15] and recognizes that such crimes 'threaten the peace, security and well-being of the world'.[16]

It is of course true that those crimes which are regulated or created by international law are of concern to the international community; they are usually ones which threaten international interests or fundamental values.[17] But there can be a risk in defining international criminal law in this manner, as it implies a level of coherence in the international criminalization process which may not exist.[18] The behaviour which is directly or indirectly subject to international law is not easily reducible to abstract formulae. Even if it were, it is not clear that these formulae would be sufficiently determinate to provide a useful guide for the future development of law, although arguments from coherence with respect to the ambit of international criminal law can have an impact on the development of the law (as has occurred, *inter alia*, in relation to the law of war crimes in non-international armed conflict).[19]

1.2.3   Involvement of a State

Another approach to defining 'international crimes' relies upon State involvement in their commission.[20] There is some sense in this. For example, aggression is necessarily a crime of the State, committed by high-level State agents. War crimes, genocide and crimes against humanity often, perhaps typically, have some element of State agency. But the subject matter of international criminal law, as we use it, deals with the liability of individuals, mostly irrespective of whether or not they are agents of a State. In the definition of the crimes which we take as being constitutive of substantive international criminal law, the official status of the perpetrator is almost always irrelevant, with the main exception of the crime of aggression.[21]

---

15 Arts. 1 and 5(1). The International Law Commission framed its investigation into international criminal law in the broad sense as being one into the 'Crimes against the Peace and Security of Mankind': Draft Code of Crimes Against the Peace and Security of Mankind, in Report of The International Law Commission on the Work of its Forty-Eighth Session, UN Doc. A/51/10. See also Lyal Sunga, *The Emerging System of International Criminal Law* (The Hague, 1997).

16 ICC Statute, para. 3 of the preamble.

17 M. Cherif Bassiouni, 'The Sources and Content of International Criminal Law' in M. Cherif Bassiouni (ed.), *International Criminal Law*, 2nd edn (New York, 1999) 3, 98.

18 See Robert Cryer, 'The Doctrinal Foundations of the International Criminalization Process' in Bassiouni (ed.), *International Criminal Law* 107.

19 On such developments, see Chapter 12.

20 See, e.g. M. Cherif Bassiouni, *Crimes Against Humanity In International Criminal Law* (2nd edn, The Hague, 1999) 243–6, 256.

21 The reference in Art. 8(2)(b)(viii), ICC Statute, to the transfer of population 'by the Occupying Power' would also seem to require that the perpetrator is a State agent.

1.2.4 Crimes created by international law

An international crime may also be defined as an offence which is created by international law itself, without requiring the intervention of domestic law. In the case of such crimes, international law imposes criminal responsibility directly on individuals. The classic statement of this form of international criminal law comes from the Nuremberg International Military Tribunal's seminal statement that:

> crimes against international law are committed by men, not abstract entities, and only by punishing individuals who commit such crimes can the provisions of international law be enforced … individuals have international duties which transcend the national obligations of obedience imposed by the individual state.[22]

The definition of an international crime as one created by international law is now in frequent use.[23] But this criterion may lead to unhelpful debate as to what is and what is not 'created' by international law.[24] The more pragmatic meaning used in this book, which we do not claim to be authoritative, excludes from detailed discussion certain conduct which has been suggested to be subject to direct liability in international criminal law but which others dispute, such as piracy and slavery,[25] a general offence of terrorism,[26] and individual acts of torture.[27]

Occasionally the *sui generis* penal system of the international criminal tribunals and courts is described as 'supranational criminal law' in process of development.[28] This term, to the extent that it has a determinate meaning, is somewhat misleading since it is normally reserved for law imposed by supranational institutions and not treaty-based or customary international law;[29] the ICTY, International Criminal Tribunal for Rwanda (ICTR) and ICC

---

22 Nuremberg IMT: Judgment and Sentences (1947) 41 *AJIL* 172 at 221.

23 Broomhall, *International Justice and the International Criminal Court*, 9–10; Robert Cryer, *Prosecuting International Crimes: Selectivity in the International Criminal Law Regime* (Cambridge, 2005) 1; Hans-Heinrich Jescheck, *Die Verantwortlichkeit der Staatsorgane nach Völkerstrafrecht* (Bonn, 1951) 9; Otto Triffterer, *Dogmatische Untersuchungen zur Entwicklung des materiellen Völkerstrafrechts seit Nürnberg* (Freiburg im Breisgau, 1966) 34; Gerhard Werle, *Principles of International Criminal Law* (The Hague, 2005) 25.

24 A slightly different criterion of an international offence, one with a 'definition as a punishable offence in international (and usually conventional) law', leads to the inclusion of a much wider category of crimes, including hijacking, injury to submarine cables and drugs offences (Yoram Dinstein, 'International Criminal Law' (1975) 5 *Israel Yearbook on Human Rights* 55 at 67). Many of these would fall, under our taxonomy, to be considered under the rubric of transnational criminal law.

25 See, e.g. Broomhall, *International Justice and the International Criminal Court*, 23–4.

26 See, e.g. Antonio Cassese, *International Criminal Law*, 2nd edn (Oxford, 2007) ch. 8.

27 *Ibid.*, 149–52. For a counterpoint see Paola Gaeta, 'International Criminalization of Prohibited Conduct' in Antonio Cassese et al. (eds.), *The Oxford Companion to International Criminal Justice* (Oxford, 2009) 63, 68–9.

28 E.g. Roelof Haverman, Olga Kavran and Julian Nicholls (eds.), *Supranational Criminal Law: A System Sui Generis* (Antwerp, 2003).

29 See, e.g. Werle, *Principles of International Criminal Law*, 38–9.

are not supranational in nature, neither as regards the laws they enforce nor, largely, as institutions.

1.3 Sources of international criminal law

As international criminal law is a subset of international law, its sources are those of international law. These are usually considered to be those enumerated in Article 38(1) (a)–(d) of the Statute of the International Court of Justice, in other words, treaty law, customary law, general principles of law and, as a subsidiary means of determining the law, judicial decisions and the writings of the most qualified publicists.[30] As will be seen, all of these have been used by the ad hoc Tribunals. They are available for use by national courts in so far as the relevant national system concerned will allow. The ICC Statute contains its own set of sources for the ICC to apply, which are analogous, although by no means identical, to those in the ICJ Statute.[31]

1.3.1 Treaties

Treaty-based sources of international criminal law, either directly or as an aid to interpretation, include the 1907 Hague Regulations, the 1949 Geneva Conventions (and their additional protocols) and the 1948 Genocide Convention. They form the basis for many of the crimes within the jurisdiction of the ad hoc Tribunals and the ICC. The Statute of the ICC, which sets out the definitions of crimes within the jurisdiction of the ICC, is, of course, itself a treaty. Security Council resolutions 827(1993) and 955(2004), which set up the ICTY and ICTR respectively, were adopted by the Security Council pursuant to its powers under Chapter VII of the UN Charter, and thus find their binding force in Article 25 of the Charter. The source of their binding nature is therefore a treaty. The Statutes of the Tribunals have had an important effect on the substance of international criminal law both directly, as applied by the Tribunals, and indirectly as a source for other international criminal law instruments;[32] the influence of the ICC Statute has so far largely been through its impact on national legislation.

It has been suggested that treaties might not suffice to place liability directly on individuals[33] and as such cannot be a direct source of international criminal law. Such arguments run up against long-standing practice in international humanitarian law, which has been to apply to individuals the 'laws and customs of war' as found in the relevant treaties, as well as

---

30 See generally Dapo Akande, 'Sources of International Criminal Law' in Antonio Cassese et al. (eds.), *The Oxford Companion to International Criminal Justice* 41.

31 Art. 21 of the ICC Statute.

32 See Theodor Meron, 'War Crimes in Yugoslavia and the Development of International Law' (1994) 88 *AJIL* 78.

33 Guénaël Mettraux, *International Crimes and the Ad Hoc Tribunals* (Oxford, 2005) 7–9.

in customary law. As the Permanent Court of International Justice noted over eighty years ago, treaties can operate directly on individuals, if that is the intent of the drafters.[34] The International Committee for the Red Cross and Red Crescent (ICRC) study on customary humanitarian law reports that 'the vast majority of practice does not limit the concept of war crimes to violations of customary international law. Almost all military manuals and criminal codes refer to violations of both customary law and applicable treaty law.'[35] That does not mean that every provision of the Geneva Conventions, for example, imposes direct criminal responsibility on individuals. Breach of some of them, for example those regarding the finest details of the treatment of detainees, would probably not constitute a war crime.[36]

It is only those treaties or provisions of a treaty which are intended to apply directly to an individual that can give rise to criminal responsibility. The 'suppression conventions', for example, which require States to criminalize conduct such as drug trafficking, hijacking and terror bombing[37] are not generally regarded as creating individual criminal responsibility of themselves; the conduct covered by those treaties will be incorporated in national law by whatever constitutional method is used by the State concerned. Further, if a court is to apply the terms of a treaty directly to an individual, it will be necessary to show that the prohibited conduct has taken place in the territory of a State Party to the treaty or is otherwise subject to the law of such a Party.[38] The practice of the ICTY has been, with occasional deviations,[39] to accept that treaties may suffice to found criminal liability. This began with the *Tadić* decision of 1995 and the position was reasserted in the *Kordić and Čerkez* appeal.[40] In the *Galić* case the ICTY Appeals Chamber noted that the position of the Tribunal is that treaties suffice for criminal responsibility, although 'in practice the International Tribunal always ascertains that the relevant provision is also declaratory of custom'.[41] This is to adopt a 'belt and braces' approach rather than to require a customary basis for war crimes. The proposition that treaties may found international criminal liability is inherent in the Statute of the ICTR, which criminalizes violations of Additional Protocol II (not all of which was at the time considered customary).[42]

---

34 *Jurisdiction of the Courts in Danzig* Case 1928 PCIJ Series B. No. 15, p. 17.

35 Jean-Marie Henckaerts and Louise Doswald-Beck, *Customary International Humanitarian Law* (Cambridge, 2005) 572.

36 See Chapter 12.

37 See Chapter 14.

38 This problem will no longer arise in regard to crimes derived from the four Geneva Conventions which now have universal State participation.

39 *Galić* ICTY T. Ch. 5.12.2003 Separate and Partially Dissenting Opinion of Judge Nieto-Navia, paras. 109–12; *Milutinović, Sainović and Ojdanic* ICTY A. Ch. 21.5.2003 paras. 10 ff. See further Héctor Olásolo, 'A Note on the Principle of Legality in International Criminal Law' (2007) 19 *Criminal Law Forum* 301.

40 *Kordić and Čerkez* ICTY A. Ch. 17.12.2004 paras. 41–6, clarifying *Tadić* ICTY A. Ch. 2.10.1995 para. 143.

41 *Galić* ICTY A. Ch. 30.1.2006 para. 85.

42 ICTR Statute, Article 4, Report of the Secretary-General Pursuant to Paragraph 5 of Security Council Resolution 955 (1994) S/1995/134, para. 12.

1.3.2 Customary international law

The ICTY has accepted that when its Statute does not regulate a matter, customary international law, and general principles, ought to be referred to.[43] Customary international law, that body of law which derives from the practice of States accompanied by *opinio iuris* (the belief that what is done is required by or in accordance with law),[44] has the disadvantage of all unwritten law in that it may be difficult to ascertain its content. This is not always the case, however, when the customary law originates with a treaty or other written instrument, for example a General Assembly resolution, which is accepted as reflecting custom, or has been recognized by a court as such.[45] Nevertheless the use of customary international law in international criminal law has sometimes been criticized on the basis that it may be too vague to found criminal liability[46] or, even, that no law that is unwritten should suffice to found criminal liability. These claims will be discussed below at section 1.5.1 in relation to the principle of *nullum crimen sine lege*. Suffice it to say for the moment that this was not the position of the Nuremberg or Tokyo IMTs, nor is it that of the ad hoc Tribunals.

1.3.3 General principles of law and subsidiary means of determining the law

The ICTY has resorted to general principles of law to assist it in its search for applicable rules of international law. Owing to the differences between international trials and trials at the national level, the ICTY has been chary of uncritical reliance on general principles taken from domestic legal systems and acontextual application of them to international trials.[47] That said, the ICTY and ICTR have both resorted to national laws to assist them in determining the relevant international law through this source. As was said in the *Furundžija* decision, however, care must be taken when using such legislation, not to look simply to one of the major legal systems of the world, as 'international courts must draw upon the general concepts and legal institutions common to all the major legal systems of the world'.[48] In relation to criminal law, general principles of law are not ideal. After all

---

43 *Kupreškić* ICTY T. Ch. II 14.1.2000 para. 591.

44 An alternative description of customary international law dispenses with the need for *opinio iuris*, relying on the constant and uniform practice of States (Maurice Mendelson, 'The Formation of Customary Law' (1998) 272 *Hague Recueil* 159).

45 E.g. para. 3(g) of the Definition on Aggression in GA res. 3314(XXIX) of 14.12.1974; see section 13.2.3; and see Mendelson, 'The Formation of Customary Law', ch. 5.

46 Vladimir Djuro-Degan, 'On the Sources of International Criminal Law' (2005) 4 *Chinese Journal of International Law* 45 at 67. See also Olásolo, 'A Note' 301.

47 *Erdemović* ICTY A. Ch. 7.10.1997 Separate and Dissenting Opinion of President Cassese, para. 5.

48 *Furundžija* ICTY T. Ch. II 10.12.1998 para. 178.

they are, by their nature, general, and thus tend to be a last resort. Also, as the *Erdemović* case showed, at times there simply is no general enough principle to apply.[49]

As regards the ICC, it is to apply, where the first two categories of law do not provide an answer:

> ... general principles of law derived by the Court from national laws of legal systems of the world including, as appropriate, the national laws of States that would normally exercise jurisdiction over the crime, provided that those principles are not inconsistent with [the] Statute and with international law and internationally recognized norms and standards.[50]

The ICC may also apply 'principles and rules of law as interpreted in its previous decisions'.[51] The ICC is not, however, bound by its previous decisions; it has no equivalent to the common law principle of *stare decisis.* The ICTY has frequently had recourse to judicial decisions for determining issues of law, and has constructed a system of precedents for dealing with its own jurisprudence.[52] The ICTY and ICTR have had reference to domestic, as well as international, case law.[53] Domestic case law is a major material source of evidence about international criminal law. However, a caveat must be entered in this regard. The assertions of international law in domestic cases can be affected by local idiosyncrasies. These can arise from the domestic statutes that are being evaluated or applied, or from a court seeing international criminal law through a distinctly national lens.[54]

Finally, although the writings of scholars are not, in themselves, sources of international criminal law, it is possible to have recourse to the views of scholars, which at times, have been highly influential.[55] However, care must always be taken to ensure that the statements relied on are accurate statements of the law as it stands, rather than a statement of how the author would like the law to be; this is important, not least because of the *nullum crimen sine lege* principle.[56] Also, selection of scholars from only one, or a limited set of, legal tradition(s) can lead to a skewed view of what an inclusive approach to international criminal law would require.

---

49 *Erdemović* ICTY A. Ch. 7.10.1997 Opinion of Judges McDonald and Vohrah, paras. 56–72.
50 Art. 21(1)(c) of the ICC Statute. This and all other sources of law available to the ICC are qualified by Art. 21(3) which requires application and interpretation of the law to be consistent with internationally recognized human rights, and without adverse discrimination.
51 *Ibid.,* Art. 21(2).
52 *Alekšovski* ICTY A. Ch. 24.3.2000 paras. 89–115. See Robert Cryer, 'Neither Here nor There? The Status of International Criminal Jurisprudence in the International and UK Legal Orders' in Michael Bohlander and Kaiyan Kaikobad (eds.), *Law, Perspectives on Legal Order and Justice – Essays in Honour of Colin Warbrick* (Leiden, 2010) 155.
53 See, e.g. *Tadić* ICTY A. Ch. 15.7.1999 paras. 255–70.
54 See Leila Sadat Wexler, 'The Interpretation of the Nuremberg Principles by the French Court of Cassation: From Touvier to Barbie and Back Again' (1994) 32 *Columbia Journal of International Law* 289.
55 E.g. *Krštić* ICTY A. Ch. 19.4.2004 para. 10; *Stakić* ICTY T. Ch. II 31.7.2003 para. 519; *Katanga and Chui* ICC PTCh. 30.9.2008 paras. 482, 485, 501.
56 See section 1.5.1.

1.4 International criminal law and other areas of law

International criminal law relates to other areas of international law. The three areas for which an understanding is the most important are human rights law, international humanitarian law and the law relating to State responsibility.

1.4.1 International criminal law and human rights law

The development of crimes against humanity and the law of human rights was partially inspired by a wish to ensure that the atrocities that characterized Nazi Germany were not repeated. Thus the modern law of human rights and a considerable part of international criminal law have a common base.[57] More recent developments in the enforcement of international criminal law, in particular the creation of the two ad hoc Tribunals, were introduced in response to mass abuses of human rights by States against their own citizens or others within their territory. Hence, parts of international criminal law have developed in this context to respond to egregious violations of human rights in the absence of effective alternative mechanisms for enforcing the most basic of humanitarian standards.

Human rights obligations are imposed primarily on States, and it is frequently State agents who are the transgressors; where States are not implementing their human rights obligations, the principles of international criminal law are a useful and necessary alternative to State responsibility. The similarities in the objectives of both bodies of law are clear; both seek to provide a minimum standard of humane treatment. Both, unlike most other branches of international law, have a direct impact on individuals, albeit in somewhat different ways.

The international instruments on human rights played an obvious part in the drafting of the Statutes of the two ad hoc Tribunals and in the Statute of the ICC.[58] And the ad hoc Tribunals have used human rights law, and decisions of international bodies applying that law, to assist them in their interpretation of substantive international criminal law and in establishing new procedural concepts of law. For example, the ICTY in *Kunarac*[59] explained its past practice thus:

> [b]ecause of the paucity of precedent in the field of international humanitarian law, the Tribunal has, on many occasions, had recourse to instruments and practices developed in the field of human rights law. Because of their resemblance, in terms of goals, values and

---

57 See, e.g. R. Emilio Vinuesa, 'Interface, Correspondence and Convergence of Human Rights and International Humanitarian Law' (1998) 1 *YIHL* 69, 70–6; William A. Schabas, 'Criminal Responsibility for Violations of Human Rights' in Janusz Symonides (ed.), *Human Rights, International Protection, Monitoring, Enforcement* (Aldershot, 2003) 281.

58 See, e.g. the provisions on the rights of the accused in Art. 21 of the ICTY Statute and Art. 20 of the ICTR Statute, largely reproducing Art. 14(1) to (3) and (5) of the International Covenant on Civil and Political Rights; the procedures in the ICC Statute are very heavily influenced by human rights instruments, but see in particular Arts. 55 and 67.

59 *Kunarac* ICTY T. Ch. II 22.2.2001 para. 467.

terminology, such recourse is generally a welcome and needed assistance to determine the content of customary international law in the field of humanitarian law.

The ICTR (particularly at trial level) has used human rights jurisprudence on hate speech and freedom of expression to assist it in drawing the boundaries of the offences of direct and public incitement of genocide and the crime against humanity of persecution in the cases of the Rwandan Radio Station RTLM,[60] and the musician Simon Bikindi.[61] In the area of international procedural law and, in particular, the right to a fair trial, the Tribunals have been especially ready to draw from human rights law. In *Dokmanović*, for example, the ICTY affirmed that an arrest must be made 'in accordance with procedures prescribed by law', as indicated in Article 5(1) of the European Convention for the Protection of Human Rights and Fundamental Freedoms and Article 9(1) of the International Covenant of Civil and Political Rights.[62] In *Tadić*, the Appeals Chamber recognized that a general principle of law may have its source in human rights instruments, in that case the principle that the Tribunal had to be 'established by law'.[63]

Nonetheless, although there are overlaps between human rights law and international criminal law, they are not synonymous, and there are dangers in treating them as being so. Almost every international crime would be a violation of human rights law, but the converse does not apply. The use of human rights standards by the Trial Chamber in the case of the Rwandan Radio Station RTLM with respect to direct and public incitement to genocide was upheld by the Appeals Chamber, but on the basis that the Trial Chamber was careful to distinguish hate speech, that may be a matter for human rights bodies, and that offence.[64] International criminal courts and tribunals do not exist to prosecute violations of the whole panoply of human rights. Further, human rights obligations are primarily imposed upon States, not individuals, and it is for States to decide how they will enforce them on their own agents; except in the case of the most serious abuses, this will not often be by criminalizing the activity concerned. Finally, whereas human rights norms may be given a broad and liberal interpretation in order to achieve their objects and purposes, in international criminal law there are countervailing rights of suspects that are protected through principles requiring that the law be strictly construed and that ambiguity be resolved in favour of the accused.[65]

---

60 *Nahimana, Barayagwiza and Ngeze* ICTR T. Ch. 3.12.2003 paras. 983–1010.

61 *Bikindi* ICTR T. Ch. III, 2.12.2008, paras. 378–97.

62 See *Mrkšić*, et al. ICTY T. Ch. II 22.10.1997 paras. 59–60.

63 *Tadić* ICTY A. Ch. 2.10.1995 paras. 42–7.

64 *Nahimana, Barayagwiza and Ngeze* ('*RTLM* Appeal'), AC 28.11.2007, paras. 692–6, 972–88 (although they were more circumspect on crimes against humanity of persecution). See also Partially Dissenting Opinion of Judge Shahabuddeen, paras. 18ff. Although see Partially Dissenting Opinion of Judge Meron, paras. 3–20 in relation to crimes against humanity of persecution.

65 See, e.g. Darryl Robinson, 'The Identity Crisis of International Criminal Law' (2008) 21 *LJIL* 925; Allison Marston Danner and Jenny Martinez, 'Guilty Associations: Joint Criminal Enterprise, Command Responsibility and the Development of International Criminal Law' (2005) 93 *California Law Review* 75. *RTLM* Appeal, Partially Dissenting Opinion of Judge Meron, para. 8.

As the case law of the two Tribunals and, in time, the ICC grows, it is likely that there will be less of a need for these courts to have recourse to human rights jurisprudence to supplement the sources of international criminal law.

1.4.2 International criminal law and international humanitarian law

International criminal law also shares common roots with international humanitarian law, the body of law designed to protect victims of armed conflict. Large areas of international humanitarian law are now criminalized as war crimes. Thus, international humanitarian law serves as a point of reference in understanding and interpreting the corresponding war crimes provisions. As with human rights norms, care must be taken before transposing all humanitarian law standards directly into international criminal law; the latter has distinct principles of interpretation. These issues are discussed further in Chapter 12.

1.4.3 International criminal law and State responsibility

International criminal law in the sense in which we use it concerns the criminal responsibility of individuals, not States.[66] The responsibility of a State under international law is a matter for a separate branch of international law, and is not dependent upon the legal responsibility of an individual. If an agent of a State is convicted of an international crime the act in question may, depending upon the circumstances, be attributable to the State, in which case that State may also be internationally responsible.[67] The same act therefore can give rise to both individual criminal responsibility and State responsibility.[68] For example, an agent of Libya was convicted of offences in relation to the aircraft explosion over Lockerbie in 1988, and the governments of the United Kingdom and the United States separately made claims for compensation from Libya.[69] The question of State responsibility for international crimes was dealt with directly in the *Bosnian Genocide* case where, having determined that genocide had occurred in Srebrenica, the International Court of Justice decided that Serbia was not responsible for the perpetrators of that crime. Controversially, it

---

[66] See generally André Nollkaemper, 'Concurrence Between Individual Responsibility and State Responsibility in International Law' (2003) 52 *ICLQ* 615; Andrea Bianchi, 'State Responsibility and Criminal Liability of Individuals' in Antonio Cassese et al. (eds.), *The Oxford Companion to International Criminal Justice* 16.

[67] *Case Concerning the Application of the Convention on the Prevention and Punishment of the Crime of Genocide (Bosnia and Herzegovina* v. *Serbia and Montenegro) (Bosnian Genocide* case), 26.2.2007, paras. 377–415. See generally Marko Milanović, 'State Responsibility for Genocide – A Follow-Up' (2007) 18 *EJIL* 669. For a critique see Paola Gaeta, 'On What Conditions May A State be Responsible for Genocide?' (2007) 18 *EJIL* 631; Antonio Cassese, 'On the Use of Criminal Law Notions in Determining State Responsibility for Genocide' (2007) 5 *JICJ* 875.

[68] E.g. *Furundžija* ICTY T. Ch. II 10.12.1998 para. 142.

[69] See section 9.5.

rejected the standard for attributability of conduct to a State used by the ICTY, asserting that the relevant test may not always be the same between international criminal law and general international law.[70] However, given the State's relationship with the perpetrators, the ICJ determined that Serbia was separately responsible under Article I of the Genocide Convention for its own failures to prevent and punish that crime.[71]

The question of whether acts of a State can be categorized under international law as *criminal* acts is one of some controversy. Draft articles on State responsibility prepared by the International Law Commission in 1976 used the term 'international crime' to refer to an internationally wrongful act by a State which results from the breach by that State of an international obligation so essential for the protection of fundamental interests of the international community that its breach is recognized as a crime.[72] But there were objections to the concept of criminal responsibility, many being based on the nature of the State. It is difficult, although not completely impossible, to apply elements of criminal liability such as *mens rea* to States. There is also the problem of punishment. In practice no international court or tribunal has ever provided for punishment of States different in kind from the law concerning tortious or delictual wrongs of a State. The final version of the draft articles of the ILC on State responsibility no longer uses the concept of State crime, but characterizes the relevant acts as 'serious breaches of obligations under peremptory norms of general international law'.[73]

1.5   A body of criminal law

The two bodies of law that make up international criminal law (international law and criminal law) are compatible, although the relationship between the two can be fractious. International criminal law should be appraised from the standpoints of both bodies of law. Its sources are those of international law, but its consequences are penal.[74] As a body of international law it requires an understanding of the sources and interpretation of international law. But it is also criminal law and as such needs substantive provisions that are clear and exact rather than the often more imprecise formulations of international law.[75] Further,

---

70 *Bosnian Genocide* case, para. 405. See, e.g. Antonio Cassese, 'The *Nicaragua* and *Tadić* Tests Revisited in the Light of the ICJ Judgment on Genocide in Bosnia' (2007) 18 *EJIL* 649; Marina Spinedi, 'On the Non-Attribution of the Bosnian Serbs' Conduct to Serbia' (2007) 5 *JICJ* 829.

71 *Bosnian Genocide* case, paras. 425–50.

72 Art. 19.2 of the 1976 draft articles.

73 Arts. 40 and 41 of the draft articles on Responsibility of States for Internationally Wrongful Acts (A/CN.4/L.602/Rev.1).

74 See, e.g. Cassese, *International Criminal Law*, 6–10. On the nature of criminal law, see Glanville Williams, 'The Definition of Crime'.

75 For a discussion of this, and a critique of the lack of attention paid by international criminal lawyers to this aspect of international criminal law see George P. Fletcher, *The Grammar of Criminal Law, American, Comparative and International: Volume I: Foundations* (Oxford, 2007).

the relevant international courts and tribunals require methods and procedures proper to a criminal court, with due regard to the rights of the accused at all stages of the investigation and court procedures. At a more abstract level, the sophisticated philosophical analyses of the appropriate ambit of criminal liability that have been developed at the domestic level ought to be borne in mind whenever international crimes or their principles of liability are being appraised.[76]

Certain fundamental principles of national criminal law systems have now become entrenched in international law, and more particularly, in human rights law. As we have seen in section 1.4.1, international criminal law has been influenced strongly by human rights law. One aspect of human rights law with a close analogue in criminal law theory is the prohibition of retroactive criminal prohibitions and penalties (sometimes referred to together as the principle of legality or *nullum crimen, nulla poena, sine lege*).[77] As shown below, this principle is important both in the application of the law and in the drafting of the instruments of the international courts and tribunals. Due to the relative imprecision of the nature and content of international law, the principle has greater prominence in international than in national courts.

1.5.1 Nullum crimen sine lege

This principle has two aspects: non-retroactivity and clarity of the law, both of which seek to ensure that the law is reasonably publicized, so people can know whether their planned course of action is acceptable or not. It is a fundamental principle of criminal law that criminal responsibility can only be based on a pre-existing prohibition of conduct that is understood to have criminal consequences. Article 15 of the International Covenant on Civil and Political Rights (ICCPR) states that:

> No one shall be held guilty on account of any act or omission which did not constitute a criminal offence, under national or international law, at the time when it was committed ... Nothing in this article shall prejudice the trial of any person for any act or omission which, at the time it was committed, was criminal according to the general principles of law recognised by the community of nations.[78]

Claims that prosecutions for international crimes violated this principle predate the ICCPR. The Nuremberg and Tokyo IMTs both faced claims that prosecution of crimes against peace involved violations of the *nullum crimen* principle. The Nuremberg IMT, with

---

[76] For useful examples see, e.g. Mirjan Damaška, 'The Shadow Side of Command Responsibility' (2001) 49 *American Journal of Comparative Law* 455; Claus Kreß, 'The Crime of Genocide Under International Law' (2006) 6 *ICLR* 461.

[77] See generally, A. P. Simester and G. R. Sullivan, *Criminal Law: Theory and Doctrine* (3rd edn, Oxford, 2007) ch. 1.

[78] International Covenant on Civil and Political Rights, Art. 15.

which the Tokyo IMT agreed, responded by asserting that crimes against peace were already criminalized in international law[79] and that, anyway:

> The maxim *nullum crimen sine lege* is not a limitation of sovereignty, but is in general a principle of justice. To assert that it is unjust to punish those who in defiance of treaties and assurances have attacked neighbouring States without warning is obviously untrue, for in such circumstances the attacker must know that he is doing wrong, and so far from it being unjust to punish him, it would be unjust if his wrong was allowed to go unpunished.[80]

At the time, which was before the modern law of human rights, the Nuremberg IMT may have been correct about the law on point. On the other hand, it is possible that the prohibition of retroactive criminal laws was a general principle of law by then,[81] and the retroactive nature of liability for crimes against peace has been used to criticize the Nuremberg and Tokyo IMTs.[82]

When drafting the Statute of the ICTY, the UN Secretary-General was sensitive to such critiques, stating that:

> [T]he application of the principle of *nullum crimen sine lege* requires that the international tribunal should apply rules of international humanitarian law which are beyond any doubt part of customary law so that the problem of adherence of some but not all States to specific conventions does not arise. This would appear to be particularly important in the context of an international tribunal prosecuting persons responsible for serious violations of international humanitarian law.[83]

This statement emphasizes the fact that if a rule reflects customary law it will not be necessary for the relevant court to establish whether the parties to the conflict were parties to the relevant treaty. But it is misleading in its formulation. The important issue from the perspective of the *nullum crimen* principle is whether the treaty was applicable to the relevant armed conflict, not whether it reflected customary international law. There is nothing in the *nullum crimen* principle in general or in Article 15 of the ICCPR[84] that requires that any particular source of international law provide the prohibition.[85]

Suggestions that customary international law does not suffice to found criminal liability[86] are based on a strict construction of the *nullum crimen* principle (*nullum crimen sine lege*

---

[79] See section 13.1.2.

[80] Nuremberg IMT Judgment (1947) 41 *AJIL* 172 at 217.

[81] See Gordon Ireland, 'Ex Post Facto From Rome to Tokyo' (1946) 21 *Temple Law Quarterly* 27; *contra* Susan Lamb, '*Nullum Crimen, Nulla Poena Sine Lege* In International Criminal Law' in Cassese, *Commentary*, 733 at 740.

[82] See sections 6.3.2 and 6.4.2.

[83] Report of the Secretary-General Pursuant to Paragraph 2 of Security Council resolution 808, UN Doc. S/25704, para. 34.

[84] Nor in the ECHR, Art. 7.

[85] Machteld Boot, *Genocide, Crimes Against Humanity, War Crimes: Nullum Crimen Sine Lege and the Subject Matter Jurisdiction of the International Criminal Court* (Antwerp, 2002) 127–87.

[86] Djuro-Degan, 'On the Sources of International Criminal Law' 67; and see Olásolo, 'A Note' 301.

scripta),[87] which, whilst applicable in some domestic legal orders, is not the principle applicable in international law.[88] There is no reason in principle why customary international law cannot be used to form the relevant criminal law[89] and the ICTY has consistently taken this view.[90]

The general practice of the ICTY has been to adopt a fairly relaxed standard to the *nullum crimen* principle.[91] However, in the *Vasiljević* case, a Trial Chamber asserted that:

> [f]rom the perspective of the *nullum crimen sine lege* principle, it would be wholly unacceptable for a Trial Chamber to convict an accused person on the basis of a prohibition which, taking into account the specificity of customary international law and allowing for the gradual clarification of the rules of criminal law is either insufficiently precise to determine conduct and distinguish the criminal from the permissible, or was not sufficiently accessible at the relevant time. A criminal conviction should indeed never be based upon a norm which an accused could not reasonably have been aware of at the time of his acts, and this norm must make it sufficiently clear what act or omission could engage his criminal responsibility.[92]

Owing to their view that customary law did not provide a sufficiently clear definition of the offence of 'violence to life and person', the Chamber refused to convict the defendant of that charge.[93] It is true that excessively vague offences can violate the *nullum crimen* principle, but it is questionable whether in this particular case, the Tribunal's finding that the international law on the subject was excessively vague was correct.[94] This is particularly the case as clarification of the ambit of offences through case law does not inherently fall foul of the *nullum crimen* principle.[95] Judicial creation of crimes, which some have claimed the ICTY has done,[96] would. It must be said, however, that when human rights courts have come to deal with the question of international crimes and the *nullum crimen* principle, they have been decidedly generous when appraising State action. For example, in the *Jorgić* case[97] the European Court of Human Rights was willing to accept convictions in Germany for genocide on a broader interpretation of that crime than was later adopted by the

---

87 'No crime without written law'.

88 Alain Pellet, 'Applicable Law' in Cassese, *Commentary* 1051 at 1057–8.

89 *Ibid.*

90 See, e.g. *Tadić* ICTY A. Ch. 2.10.1995 para. 94.

91 William Schabas, *The UN International Criminal Tribunals: The former Yugoslavia, Rwanda and Sierra Leone* (Cambridge, 2006) 63–7.

92 *Vasiljević* ICTY T. Ch. I 29.11.2002 para. 193.

93 *Ibid.*, paras. 203–4.

94 See Antonio Cassese, 'Black Letter Lawyering vs Constructive Interpretation: The Vasiljević Case' (2004) 2 *JICJ* 265.

95 See Mohamed Shahabuddeen, 'Does the Principle of Legality Stand in the Way of Progressive Development of the Law?' (2004) 2 *JICJ* 1007; Ben Emmerson and Andrew Ashworth, *Human Rights and Criminal Justice* (London, 2001) 281–92.

96 Mettraux, *International Crimes*, 13–18.

97 *Jorgić* v. *Germany*, Application No.74613/01, Judgment, 12.7.2007, paras. 89–116.

International Criminal Tribunals, on the basis that it was at least arguable at the time that the German courts' interpretation was correct.

The *nullum crimen* principle played an important role in the drafting of the ICC Statute. The ILC draft Statute with which the negotiations began[98] did not contain definitions of the crimes within the jurisdiction of the ICC, the ILC maintaining that the Statute should be 'primarily an adjectival and procedural instrument'.[99] There was soon, however, a move to define the crimes in the Statute with the clarity and precision needed for criminal law and it was with that objective that the definitions of crimes and, later, the elements of crimes were set out. The wish of the negotiating States to ensure that they knew exactly what they were signing up to may have been at least as strong a motivating factor as the principle of *nullum crimen* in this regard.

The Statute itself contains a strong restatement of the *nullum crimen* principle. Article 22 reads in part:[100]

1. A person shall not be criminally responsible under this Statute unless the conduct in question constitutes, at the time it takes place, a crime within the jurisdiction of the Court.

2. The definition of a crime shall be strictly construed and shall not be extended by analogy. In the case of ambiguity, the definition shall be interpreted in favour of the person being investigated, prosecuted or convicted.

The first sentence of the second paragraph was intended, rightly or wrongly, to prevent the ICC from engaging in expansions of criminal liability not mandated by the States Parties.

1.5.2   Nulla poena sine lege

This, related, principle requires that there are defined penalties attached to criminal prohibitions.[101] In customary law, the punishment for international crimes may include the death penalty[102] though many States have undertaken international obligations not to impose such a penalty, or may not permit that sentence in their domestic law.

It appears that concerns about the *nulla poena* principle also caused the Secretary-General, when drafting the ICTY Statute, to require the Tribunal to 'have recourse to the general practice regarding prison sentences in the Courts of the former Yugoslavia'.[103] The ICTR Statute has a similar provision, but with reference to Rwandan sentencing

---

98 See section 8.2.
99 Report of the International Law Commission on the work of its forty-sixth session, UNGAOR 49th session Suppl. No. 10, A/49/10 (1994) at 71.
100 On which see Bruce Broomhall, 'Article 22' in Triffterer, *Observers' Notes*, 713.
101 See Chapter 19 and Kai Ambos, '*Nulla Poena Sine Lege in International Criminal Law*' in Roelof Haveman and Olaoluwa Olusanya (eds.), *Sentencing and Sanctioning in International Criminal Law* (Antwerp, 2006) 17.
102 *Klinge* III Law Reports of Trials of War Criminals 1 at 3.
103 ICTY Statute, Art. 24. Lamb, '*Nullum Crimen*' 758–9.

practices.[104] The fact that both States provided for the death penalty at the time of the offences, but the Tribunal cannot impose that sentence, has made this difficult to apply. The Rome Statute also contains an article entitled '*nulla poena sine lege*': Article 23. This states, uncontroversially: 'A person convicted by the Court may be punished only in accordance with this Statute.'[105]

Further reading

Dapo Akande, 'Sources of International Criminal Law' in Antonio Cassese et al. (eds.), *The Oxford Companion to International Criminal Justice* (Oxford, 2009) 41.

Gary J. Bass, *Stay the Hand of Vengeance: The Politics of War Crimes Tribunals* (Princeton, 2000).

M. Cherif Bassiouni, *International Criminal Law*, 3rd edn (Leiden, 2008) vol. I.

Machteld Boot, *Genocide, Crimes Against Humanity, War Crimes: Nullum Crimen Sine Lege and the Subject Matter Jurisdiction of the International Criminal Court* (Antwerp, 2002) 127–87.

Bruce Broomhall, *International Justice and the International Criminal Court: Between State Sovereignty and the Rule of Law* (Oxford, 2003) ch. 1.

Antonio Cassese, 'The Influence of the European Court of Human Rights on International Criminal Tribunals – Some Methodological Remarks' and Erik Møse, 'Impact of Human Rights Conventions on the two *ad hoc* Tribunals' in Morten Bergsmo (ed.), *Human Rights and Criminal Justice for the Downtrodden* (The Hague, 2003) chs. II and VIII respectively.

Robert Cryer, *Prosecuting International Crimes: Selectivity in the International Criminal Law Regime* (Cambridge, 2005) Introduction, chs. 1 and 5.

Vladimir Djuro-Degan, 'On the Sources of International Criminal Law' (2005) 4 *Chinese Journal of International Law* 45.

George P. Fletcher, *The Grammar of Criminal Law: American, Comparative and International: Volume I: Foundations* (Oxford, 2007).

Nina H. B. Jørgensen, *The Responsibility of States for International Crimes* (Oxford, 2000).

Timothy L. H. McCormack, 'From Sun Tzu to the Sixth Committee, The Evolution of an International Criminal Law Regime' in Timothy L. H. McCormack and Gerry J. Simpson (eds.), *The Law of War Crimes, National and International Approaches* (The Hague, 1997) 31.

Alain Pellet, 'Applicable Law' in Antonio Cassese, Paola Gaeta and John R. W. D. Jones (eds.), *The Rome Statute: A Commentary* (Oxford, 2002) 1051.

Alfred P. Rubin, *Ethics and Authority in International Law* (Cambridge, 1997).

Georg Schwarzenberger, 'The Problem of an International Criminal Law' (1950) 3 *Current Legal Problems* 263.

---

104 ICTR Statute, Art. 23.
105 See William Schabas, 'Article 23' in Triffterer, *Observers' Notes* 730.

2

The Objectives of International Criminal Law

2.1 Introduction

The assertion of criminal jurisdiction over a person is amongst the most coercive activities any society can undertake. Punishing a person involves conduct towards them which requires a deprivation of some form of their liberty or a setting-back of their property interests.[1] Such a deprivation of liberty or property requires justification.[2] Furthermore, criminal law is not, in itself, a good or a bad thing. It is a tool, designed to achieve certain ends. Some of those ends may be better pursued by means other than prosecutions.

It has been suggested by some that the justifications for punishment may differ, or at least be differently interpreted, between international criminal law and domestic criminal law.[3] It is true that the general situations in which international criminal law is invoked are those of mass criminality, which are not the normal case in domestic criminal law enforcement.[4] In addition, certain additional aims for international criminal law tend to be grafted onto those which are postulated for domestic systems of criminal law. These include the telling of the history of a conflict, distinguishing individual from group responsibility, reconciling societies and capacity building in domestic judicial systems.[5]

It is also true that international society is not the same as domestic society. Nonetheless, much of the implementation of international criminal law is intended to be at the domestic level, therefore it is questionable whether the objectives of punishment ought to differ that significantly between international and municipal criminal law. It has also been suggested

---

1 Indeed, in certain cases, unlawful imprisonment is, itself, an international crime. See, e.g. ICC Statute, Arts. 7 (1)(e), 8(2)(a)(vii).

2 See, generally, Lucia Zedner, *Criminal Justice* (Oxford, 2004) 84–111.

3 See, e.g. Mark Drumbl, 'Collective Violence and Individual Punishment: The Criminality of Mass Atrocity' (2004–2005) 99 *NorthWestern Law Review* 539; Frederick Harhoff, 'Sense and Sensibility in Sentencing – Taking Stock of International Criminal Punishment' in Ola Engdahl and Pål Wrange (eds.), *Law at War: The Law as it Was and the Law as it Should Be: Lieber Amoricum Ove Bring* (Leiden, 2008) 121.

4 Although not all instances where international criminal law is relevant occur against this background: isolated, or relatively isolated war crimes remain international crimes.

5 Antonio Cassese, 'Reflections on International Criminal Justice' (1998) 61 *Modern Law Review* 1 at 6–7.

that the justifications for punishment at the international level are inconsistent, and at times incoherent.[6] Even if this were the case (and it may well be), it would not necessarily undermine international criminal law. The same criticism could be made about the justifications for punishment at the domestic level, yet this has not led to widespread calls for the abolition of criminal law there.[7] It is true however that international criminal lawyers and the ad hoc Tribunals have at times been profligate in their assertions about the benefits and purposes of prosecutions. There is a risk in doing so of setting unreasonable expectations for what criminal law can do. If international criminal law is set impossible tasks 'disenchantment and depression will set in when these goals are not being met'.[8]

It must also be remembered, at the outset, that the turn to criminal justice has not occurred in a vacuum. It has occurred in part as a response to dissatisfaction with the other methods of dealing with international criminals, which were either extrajudicial executions, or ignoring them. The first of these is clearly unlawful now.[9] The second, which was said by Robert Jackson to 'mock the dead and make cynics of the living'[10] is one which is rarely lawful.[11]

It is the purpose of this chapter to introduce some of the justifications for punishment and the purposes it seeks to achieve.[12] It will also consider the wider goals which are claimed for international criminal law and discuss whether those goals can be met, alongside some of the challenges to international criminal law that have arisen.

2.2　The aims of international criminal justice

Broadly speaking, there are two approaches to justifying punishment: forward-looking (teleological); and those that focus on the crime itself (deontological).[13] In practice, most criminal justice systems tend to be defended on the basis of a mixture of the two.[14] There are

6 See, e.g. Immi Tallgren, 'The Sense and Sensibility of International Criminal Law' (2002) 13 *EJIL* 561; Mirjan Damaška, 'What is the Point of International Criminal Justice' (2008) 83 *Chicago-Kent Law Review* 329 at 331–5; but see Paul Roberts and Nesam McMillan, 'For Criminology in International Criminal Justice' (2003) 1 *JICL* 315.

7 Although see, e.g. J. G. Murphy, 'Marxism and Retribution' (1973) 2 *Philosophy and Public Affairs* 217; Stanley Cohen, 'Alternatives to Punishment – The Abolitionist Case' (1991) 25 *Israel Law Review* 729; Philip Allott, *The Health of Nations* (Cambridge, 2003) 62–9.

8 Iain Cameron, 'Individual Responsibility under National and International Law for the Conduct of Armed Conflict' in Engdahl and Wrange (eds.), *Law at War*, 58; Damaška, 'What is the Point', 331.

9 Additional Protocol I, Art. 75, which represents customary international law. See *Hamdan* v. *Rumsfeld* 126 S Ct 2749, 2997 (2006); Geneva Conventions 1949, common Art. 3; ICCPR Art. 6; *Suarez de Guerrero* v. *Colombia* (Human Rights Committee 45/79); ECHR Art. 2.

10 Robert Jackson, 'Report to the President' (1945) 39 *AJIL* 178, 182.

11 See section 4.3.

12 For more general surveys of the justification of punishment see, e.g. David Garland and Anthony Duff, *A Reader on Punishment* (Oxford, 1994); David Garland, *Punishment and Modern Society* (Oxford, 1990).

13 For a useful introduction at the domestic level see Stanley Cohen, 'An Introduction to the Theory, Justifications and Modern Manifestations of Criminal Punishment' (1981–1982) 27 *McGill Law Journal* 73.

14 Which is acceptable, see Herbert L. A. Hart, *Punishment and Responsibility* (Oxford, 1968) ch. 1.

a number of different aims that have been postulated for punishment in international criminal justice. The primary place in which the ICTY (and ICTR) has discussed the aims of punishment is in relation to its sentencing practice.[15] The two main aims that the ICTY has asserted for its practice are retribution and deterrence.[16] It has also at times asserted the relevance of rehabilitation of offenders,[17] and other objectives.

2.2.1   Retribution

Retributive theories have a long history in criminal law, but are now often associated with Immanuel Kant.[18] They focus on the necessity of punishing those who have violated societal norms, irrespective of the possible future benefits of prosecution, on the basis that the offenders deserve punishment for what they have done. The specific focus of this approach is the perpetrators themselves, on the basis that to treat them as a means to another end (as teleological approaches are wont to do) is to fail to respect them as full persons (i.e. reasoning moral agents). In other words, such theories claim that to refuse to focus on the autonomous actions of the perpetrators by holding them responsible for those actions, is to treat them as less than people, as responsibility is the concomitant of autonomy and full personhood.

Modern retributive theorists are careful to distinguish their position from that of simple vengeance. It is clear that the international criminal tribunals, when dealing with retributive justifications for punishment, have tried to avoid conflating the *lex talionis* and retributive justifications of punishment.[19] For example the ICTY in the *Aleksovski* case asserted that retribution:

> is not to be understood as fulfilling a desire for revenge but as duly expressing the outrage of the international community at these crimes. This factor has been widely recognised by Trial Chambers of this International Tribunal as well as Trial Chambers of the International Criminal Tribunal for Rwanda. Accordingly, a sentence of the International Tribunal should make plain the condemnation of the international community of the behaviour in question and show 'that the international community was not ready to tolerate serious violations of international humanitarian law and human rights'.[20]

Analogously, albeit in a passage that appears to place rather a lot under the rubric of retribution, the *Nikolić* case stated that:

---

15 On which, see section 19.2 and William Schabas, *The UN International Criminal Tribunals: the former Yugoslavia, Rwanda and Sierra Leone* (Cambridge, 2006) 554–61.
16 See, e.g. *Aleksovski* ICTY A. Ch. 24.3.2000 para. 185. See also SC res. 827 (1993) on the ICTY.
17 *Momir Nikolić* ICTY T. Ch. I 2.12.2003 para. 85.
18 See generally R. A. Duff and D. Garland, 'Thinking About Punishment' in Duff and Garland, *A Reader on Punishment*, 1, 2–3.
19 The *lex talionis* of the Biblical Old Testament is often expressed through the maxim 'an eye for an eye, a tooth for a tooth' (Deuteronomy 19:21).
20 *Aleksovski* ICTY A. Ch. 24.3.2000 para. 185.

[i]n light of the purposes of the Tribunal and international humanitarian law generally, retribution is better understood as the expression of condemnation and outrage of the international community at such grave violations of, and disregard for, fundamental human rights at a time that people may be at their most vulnerable, namely during armed conflict. It is also recognition of the harm and suffering caused to the victims. Furthermore, within the context of international criminal justice, retribution is understood as a clear statement by the international community that crimes will be punished and impunity will not prevail.[21]

One positive aspect of retributivism was pointed out by the Trial Chamber in the *Todorović* case: it 'must be understood as reflecting a fair and balanced approach to the exaction of punishment for wrongdoing. This means that the penalty imposed must be proportionate to the wrongdoing, in other words, that the punishment be made to fit the crime.'[22] One difficulty with this is that it has been questioned whether punishments for international crimes can be proportionate to what can be enormous levels of wrongdoing and culpability.[23] A strong counterargument to such assertions is given by Mark Osiel, 'There is a sense in which this argument is true, but trivial. After all, many ordinary offenders commit multiple offences for which they cannot "repay" … in fitting measure, within their remaining lifespan.'[24]

More specifically, though, a distinction between cardinal and ordinal proportionality ought to be recognized. Cardinal proportionality sets out the basic level of severity of response, such as minimum and maximum punishments, that a system can give for any crimes. Ordinal proportionality sets where a crime sits on the level of severity within that system. It may simply be that international criminal law and domestic criminal law have different cardinal points, and retributive theory is as much about ordinal proportionality as cardinal proportionality, which also differs between States. That is not to say that it cannot throw up oddities, particularly between national jurisdictions and between national courts and international courts, but again that the problem is not one which is unique to international criminal law.

Still, there are problems with a purely retributive approach. Some claim that it is important, for example, to move beyond a culture of blame.[25] Critics of retributivism can argue that, as it appears to demand punishment without regard to cost, it sets impossibly high standards, particularly in relation to disadvantaged societies, and requires punishment even where it is pointless. There may be merit in this position, although a pure Kantian could respond that it misses the point in that the question is not what is practicable, but what is

---

21 *Momir Nikolić* ICTY T. Ch. I 2.12.2003 paras. 86–7.

22 *Todorović*, ICTY T. Ch. I 31.7.2001 para. 29. See also *Plavšić* ICTY T. Ch. III 27.2.2003 para. 23.

23 Harhoff, 'Sense and Sensibility', 125.

24 Mark Osiel, 'Why Prosecute? Critics of Punishment for Mass Atrocity' (2000) 22 *Human Rights Quarterly* 118, 129.

25 See, e.g. Desmond Tutu, *No Future Without Forgiveness* (London, 1999).

morally necessary. Even so, there is a risk of moral absolutism and insensitivity to context in such a position.

2.2.2   Deterrence

Deterrence is perhaps the best known of the justifications of punishment. Such theories were championed in particular by utilitarian political theorists such as Jeremy Bentham, who, in distinction to retributivists, focused on the future-related benefits of prosecution. It is a commonplace that punishment ought to be imposed to prevent both the offender and the population more generally from engaging in prohibited conduct. Equally, there are risks involved in deterrence. The first is that there is nothing inherent in utilitarianism that prevents exceedingly heavy punishment, and indeed punishment of the innocent, to achieve its goals. After all, it is likely that punishing close family members of a criminal for their misdeeds would quite possibly give a greater degree of deterrence than punishing criminals directly. Also, threatening torturous punishment for even minor violations of the law could prevent such breaches. But that is the logic of the police State.

There are two other more general critiques of deterrence-based theories in international criminal law. The first is a philosophical one. Retributivists, in particular those of a Kantian persuasion, are right to point out that deterrence theories, especially those that look to general deterrence (i.e. deterrence of others, who see the punishment of others and decide not to engage in criminal conduct)[26] see people merely as a means to an end, which is inconsistent with their moral worth as human beings. The second is that deterrence-based approaches treat people as rational calculators, who carefully weigh up the costs and benefits of their actions, and this does not reflect the reality of the type of decision-making that often precedes decisions to commit crimes.[27] It is thought by many that the idea of fighting for a 'higher good', bigotry or more pressing concerns than possibly, at some point, being brought before a court or tribunal, are the determinative factors in the minds of those who commit international crimes.[28] This may be true in some situations, but the point probably underestimates the rational calculations of many high-ranking leaders who are not blinded by other considerations.[29]

Whatever their merits, such critiques have led the ICTY to accept deterrence as a justification for punishment, but only within limits. For example, in the *Tadić* sentencing appeal the Appeal Chamber, when referring to deterrence, said that 'it is a consideration that

---

26 The other type of deterrence, particular deterrence, is based on preventing particular offenders engaging in such conduct again, as they become all too aware of the costs of such behaviour.

27 David Wippman, 'Atrocities, Deterrence and the Limits of International Justice' (1999) *Fordham International Law Journal* 473; Drumbl, 'Collective Violence and Individual Punishment', 590–1.

28 E.g. Harhoff, 'Sense and Sensibility', 127.

29 Stephen Roach, 'Justice of the Peace? Future Challenges and Prospects for a Cosmopolitan Court' in Stephen Roach (ed.), *Governance, Order and the International Criminal Court* (Oxford, 2009) 225, 226–9.

may legitimately be considered in sentencing ... Equally, the Appeals Chamber accepts that this factor must not be accorded undue prominence in the overall assessment of the sentences to be imposed on persons convicted by the International Tribunal.'[30]

Furthermore, the Appeals Chamber in the *Nikolić* case attempted to deal with some of the critiques of unmodified deterrence theories as follows:

> During times of armed conflict, all persons must now be more aware of the obligations upon them in relation to fellow combatants and protected persons, particularly civilians. Thus, it is hoped that the Tribunal and other international courts are bringing about the development of a culture of *respect* for the rule of law and not simply the *fear* of the consequences of breaking the law, and thereby deterring the commission of crimes. One may ask whether the individuals who are called before this Tribunal as accused are simply an instrument to achieving the goal of the establishment of the rule of law. The answer is no. Indeed, the Appeals Chamber has held that deterrence should not be given undue prominence in the overall assessment of a sentence.[31]

Although the reasoning it contains is not a complete answer to the critiques above, as this quote implies, more sophisticated deterrence-based theories work on a more subtle level than some of their critics acknowledge. Those theories do not assert that deterrence works at the level of rational calculation, but at a preliminary stage, where people are (consciously or otherwise) setting up the available options. Where people simply think that certain options are not (in part, morally) open to them, they do not enter the second calculation of their costs and benefits, perhaps similarly to the way that now people simply do not think of settling disputes by duelling. This is linked to the denunciatory/educative function of punishment, which will be discussed below.[32]

Like most criminal theorists, the ICC Statute accepts that there is some role for deterrence in international criminal law.[33] Preambular paragraph 5 of the Statute asserts that the parties are '[d]etermined to put an end to impunity for the perpetrators of these crimes and thus to contribute to the prevention of such crimes'. It might be noted that, in the past, the absence of enforcement of international criminal law, and the small number of offenders that international criminal tribunals have prosecuted, undermined the goal of deterrence, as people do not think that they are likely to be punished.[34] Those doubting the possibility of deterrence in international criminal law have pointed to the fact that the creation of the ICTY did not stop crimes being committed in former Yugoslavia between 1993 and 1995. In that instance however, it might be noted that the Tribunal was a fledgling institution, with very few people

---

30 *Tadić* ICTY A.Ch. 26.1.2000 para. 48.

31 *Momir Nikolić* ICTY T. Ch. I 2.12.2003 paras. 89–90.

32 See Mark Drumbl, *Atrocity, Punishment and International Law* (Cambridge, 2007) 174.

33 See also, more generally Payam Akhavan, 'Can International Criminal Justice Prevent Future Atrocities?' (2001) 85 *AJIL* 7.

34 See Tom Farer, 'Restraining the Barbarians: Can International Law Help?' (2000) 22 *Human Rights Quarterly* 90 at 92–3.

in custody. Moreover, it was often thought that the Tribunal would be likely to be bargained away in a peace deal. Thus the example may not be transferrable to international criminal law in general.[35] If a culture of accountability is created, and domestic courts play their part in prosecution of international crimes as the drafters of the ICC Statute intended, then this critique may become blunted over time.[36] There is already some anecdotal evidence of deterrence operating in relation to the international criminal tribunals, although there is no cause for complacency.[37]

2.2.3   Incapacitation

Incapacitation is another utilitarian justification of punishment. It has links to individual deterrence, in that it seeks to prevent crimes by keeping the person in detention.[38] This has not had a great influence on international criminal law,[39] although Judge Röling, in the Tokyo IMT, asserted that the justification for prosecuting aggression, in spite of the fact that it was not previously criminal, was that the defendants were dangerous and their influence on Japan had to be excluded by their imprisonment.[40] Some of the arguments against amnesty, that rely on the idea that those who seek amnesties will not quietly retire, are linked to this justification of punishment. Incapacitative theories of punishment are controversial, as they rely on the imprecise science of determining who will reoffend and who will not. They do not focus on what has been done but, in effect, punish people for what they might do in the future.[41]

2.2.4   Rehabilitation

Rehabilitation is a theory of punishment which can trace its history back to the eighteenth century,[42] and is based on the idea that the point of criminal sanctions is reformation of the offender. It is a theory of punishment that has many advocates in the human rights community at the domestic level, in particular those who are supporters of restorative justice.[43] It has not made great advances in international criminal law, in part because the

---

35 Paul Williams and Michael Scharf, *Peace With Justice: War Crimes and Accountability in the Former Yugoslavia* (Oxford, 2003) 21–2.

36 Harhoff accepts that the risk of prosecution is higher now than ever before, 'Sense and Sensibility', 128.

37 *Ibid.*

38 See, e.g. Zedner, *Criminal Justice*, 98–101.

39 Drumbl, 'Collective Violence and Individual Punishment', 589.

40 Dissenting Opinion of the Member from the Netherlands, 10–51; see Neil Boister and Robert Cryer, *Documents on the Tokyo International Tribunal* (Oxford, 2008) 684–703.

41 Zedner, *Criminal Justice*, 100.

42 *Ibid.*, 95–8. See also Andrew von Hirsch and Andrew Ashworth, *Principled Sentencing* (Oxford, 1998) ch. 3.

43 Interestingly many such advocates at the domestic level are often far more retributivist when it comes to international crimes.

main perpetrators of international crimes are not thought to be the appropriate beneficiaries of rehabilitation. Nonetheless, there are occasions upon which the international tribunals have mentioned rehabilitation in relation to lower level offenders. Most notable in this regard is the decision of the Trial Chamber in the *Erdemović* case. Erdemović was a young Bosnian Croat who took part in the Srebrenica massacre under duress. In sentencing him to a relatively short five-year period of imprisonment, the Trial Chamber noted his 'corrigible personality' and that he was 'reformable and should be given a second chance to start his life afresh upon release, whilst still young enough to do so'.[44] The ICTY's practice seems to be that those who plead guilty ought to have their punishment carried out with a view to rehabilitation, although this is contingent on genuine remorse, and the rehabilitation may be more to do with that, and the admission of guilt, than the sentence itself.[45]

2.2.5 Denunciation/education

One of the more modern theories designed to justify punishment, and one which has considerable support, is that of communication/denunciation.[46] Some of the most sophisticated defences of international criminal law adopt this defence of punishment for international crimes.[47] In other words criminal procedures and punishment are 'an opportunity for communicating with the offender, the victim and wider society the nature of the wrong done'.[48] This is designed to engage offenders, and attempt to make them understand what was wrong with what they have done,[49] whilst also reaffirming the norm in the community and educating society about the unacceptable nature of the conduct condemned. Others add that it reaffirms faith in the rule of law.[50]

Some doubt this approach to punishment, criticizing the idea that international criminals are part of a relevant normative community with whom punishment is meant to communicate, on the basis that their acts or attitudes make it impossible or unlikely that they can or will heed the message. This contention is similarly applicable to domestic crimes, and a strong argument can be made that in international crimes the relevant normative community to

---

44 *Erdemović* ICTY T. Ch. 5.3.1998 para. 16.

45 Harhoff, 'Sense and Sensibility', 131.

46 Antony Duff, *Punishment, Communication and Community* (Oxford, 2001); Andrew von Hirsch, *Censure and Sanctions* (Oxford, 1993) ch. 2; William Wilson, *Central Issues in Criminal Theory* (Oxford, 2002) 61–5.

47 For example, Damaška 'What is the Point', 343; Antony Duff, 'Can We Punish the Perpetrators of Atrocities?' in Thomas Brudman and Thomas Cushman (eds.), *The Religious in Responses to Mass Atrocity* (Cambridge, 2008) 79.

48 Zedner, *Criminal Justice*, 109.

49 See Wilson, *Central Issues*, 62–3; Klaus Gunter, 'The Criminal Law of "Guilt" as a Subject of a Politics of Remembrance in Democracies' in Emilios Christodoulidis and Scott Veitch (eds.), *Lethe's Law: Justice, Law and Ethics in Reconciliation* (Oxford, 2001) 3.

50 Drumbl, *Atrocity*, 173.

which a person has to belong is humanity, rather than any thicker conception of community, and that the possibility of rejection of the message does not mean that it should not be attempted to be inculcated.[51] Also, those accused of international crimes are not the only audience for the message, which is also partly aimed at the wider community, to achieve general deterrence. There have though been suggestions as well that there are difficulties relating to what the moral message is when broad principles of liability, which stretch individual culpability, such as joint criminal enterprise, are used.[52]

The ICTY has asserted the relevance of the didactic function in the *Kordić and Čerkez* case, referring to 'the educational function ... [which] ... aims at conveying the message that rules of international humanitarian law have to be obeyed under all circumstances. In doing so, the sentence seeks to internalise these rules and the moral demands they are based on in the minds of the public.'[53]

The fact that there are lively debates over whether the term genocide may be applied to certain events implies that the expressive function of punishment and labelling is important in international criminal law.[54] The importance of the expressive function of punishment was seemingly accepted by the ICTY Appeals Chamber in the *Krstić* appeal when it said that:

> Among the grievous crimes this Tribunal has the duty to punish, the crime of genocide is singled out for special condemnation and opprobrium. The gravity of genocide is reflected in the stringent requirements which must be satisfied before this conviction is imposed. These requirements – the demanding proof of specific intent and the showing that the group was targeted for destruction in its entirety or in substantial part – guard against a danger that convictions for this crime will be imposed lightly. Where these requirements are satisfied, however, the law must not shy away from referring to the crime committed by its proper name.[55]

2.3   Broader goals

2.3.1   Justice for victims

There are certain other goals which have been suggested for international criminal law, all of which have a utilitarian focus, and relate in some ways to the future of the societies in which international crimes are committed. The first of these is that prosecutions may engender a sense of justice having been done, or 'closure' for victims, either on the basis that seeing

51 Duff, 'Can We Punish', 85–100.
52 Damaška, 'What is the Point', 350–6.
53 *Kordić and Čerkez* ICTY A. Ch. 17.12.2004 paras. 1080–1.
54 Diane Marie Amann, 'Group Mentality, Expressivism and Genocide' (2002) 2 *ICLR* 93; see also Robert Sloane, 'The Expressive Capacity of International Punishment' (2007) 43 *Stanford Journal of International Law* 39.
55 *Krstić* ICTY A.Ch. 19.4.2004 paras. 36–7.

their persecutors prosecuted will have that result, or that the process of testifying will do so. Such a role in relation to victims was noted by the ICTY in the *Nikolić* case, which asserted that 'punishment must therefore reflect both the calls for justice from the persons who have – directly or indirectly – been victims of the crimes'.[56]

It can also be questioned whether criminal trials and punishment of offenders can have the suggested cathartic effects for victims.[57] It is doubtful, given the focus in international criminal tribunals on higher level offenders, that many victims will have an opportunity to see those people who committed the particular offences against them come to trial (although national courts have a large role here). Evidence that the experience of testifying is helpful is mixed, with some victim-witnesses reporting that they were glad they had testified, whilst others did not.[58] The extent to which victims may be helped by prosecutions depends, inter alia, on the role they are permitted to play in the proceedings.[59] There have been suggestions that the ICTY and ICTR have not always been exemplary in their treatment of victim-witnesses. Nonetheless, the ICC Statute has various provisions providing for victims' participation in proceedings and for reparations.[60]

2.3.2   Recording history

The next postulated goal is that of truth telling. The claim is that the process of subjecting evidence to forensic scrutiny will set down a permanent record of the crimes that will stand the test of time.[61] Some go further to suggest that trials should be structured to create a narrative which will be useful to a post-conflict society.[62] The judgments of international criminal tribunals have been lengthy, and have engaged in detailed discussion of the background of the conflicts which have led to the crimes, and have been criticized for doing so.[63] In the *Krstić* judgment the intention of the tribunal to counter denial and create a record of the Srebrenica massacre was clear, and similar things can be said about the ICTR's characterization of the Rwandan genocide as being such.[64] The practice of the Tribunals is not entirely consistent; sometimes the Chambers of the Tribunals have disavowed an

---

56 *Momir Nikolić* ICTY T. Ch. I 2.12.2003 para. 86.
57 Jamie O'Connell, 'Gambling With the Psyche: Does Prosecuting Human Rights Violators Console Their Victims?' (2005) 46 *Harvard International Law Journal* 295.
58 Eric Stover, 'Witnesses and the Promise of the Hague' in Eric Stover and Harvey Weinstein (eds.), *My Neighbour, My Enemy: Justice and Community in the Aftermath of Mass Atrocity* (Cambridge, 2004) 104.
59 Harhoff, 'Sense and Sensibility', 131, see Chapter 18.
60 See Chapter 18.
61 See, e.g. Cassese, 'Reflections on International Criminal Justice', 6.
62 Mark Osiel, *Mass Atrocity, Collective Memory and the Law* (New Brunswick, 1997).
63 José Alvarez, 'Rush to Closure: Lessons of the Tadić Judgment' (1998) 96 *Michigan Law Review* 2061; José Alvarez, 'Lessons from the Akayesu Judgment' (1998–1999) 5 *International Law Students' Association Journal of International and Comparative Law* 359.
64 Drumbl, *Atrocity*, 175.

intention to write history. In the *Karadžić* case, the defendant sought to persuade the ICTY to find, if not for the purposes of legal evaluation then for the purposes of history, that he had been promised immunity from prosecution if he left politics. The Trial Chamber gave short shrift to such a suggestion, stating that 'The Trial Chamber rejects the Accused's submission that not having an evidentiary hearing at this stage would be a disservice to history. The Chamber's purpose is not to serve the academic study of history.'[65]

The idea that criminal trials ought to serve truth-telling functions has been criticized. Some think that criminal trials are not always the best place to seek to write history.[66] There are various aspects to this claim. In relation to the Nuremberg and Tokyo IMTs the claim, which was made, inter alia, by one of the judges of the Tokyo IMT, was that 'distortions of history did take place' for, at times, political reasons.[67] For the most part such comments relate to the findings on conspiracy and aggression, rather than war crimes and crimes against humanity.

There are more general points that may be made about criminal tribunals writing history. It is difficult to write the whole history of a period without straying beyond the bounds of the criminal trial, which is to try a specific person for specific conduct.[68] This gives rise to the concern that the trial may resolve into a political debate about the validity of the different historical accounts that are being told. It is indeed strange that in long-running conflicts which are the context to the commission of many atrocities, a court should be the arbitrator between competing historical accounts.[69] Such events are not easily cognizable or interpretable through the medium of criminal law.[70] The rule-bound nature of criminal trials is not one designed to ensure a full discussion of history. As Judge Röling put it, there is a difference between the 'real truth' and the 'trial truth'.[71]

Nevertheless, the contextual elements of international crimes, in particular of crimes against humanity and genocide,[72] make it necessary that the larger context in which a person's actions must be placed is an issue at trial in which the defence is entitled to

---

65 *Karadžić* ICTY T. Ch. III 8.7.2009 para. 46.

66 Martha Minow, *Between Vengeance and Forgiveness* (Boston, 1998) 46–7.

67 B. V. A. Röling, 'The Nuremberg and Tokyo Trials in Retrospect' in M. Cherif Bassiouni and Ved Nanda (eds.), *A Treatise on International Criminal Law* (Springfield, 1973) 590 at 600. See Donald Bloxham, *Genocide on Trial: War Crimes Trials and the Formation of Holocaust History and Memory* (Oxford, 2001); Richard Minear, *Victors' Justice* (Princeton, 1971); but see also Yasuaki Onuma, 'Beyond Victors' Justice' (1984) 9 *Japan Echo* 63 at 66.

68 Osiel, *Mass Atrocity*, ch. 3; although see Ruti Teitel, *Transitional Justice* (Oxford, 2000) 74–5.

69 See Martti Koskenniemi, 'Between Impunity and Show Trials' (2002) 6 *Max Planck Yearbook of United Nations Law* 1. Of course, sometimes a court itself is split over the history, as was the case, for example, in the Tokyo IMT. See Gerry Simpson, 'War Crimes: A Critical Introduction' in Timothy McCormack and Gerry Simpson (eds.), *The Law of War Crimes: National and International Approaches* (The Hague, 1997) 1 at 26–8.

70 Koskenniemi, 'Between Impunity', 12–13.

71 B. V. A. Röling and Antonio Cassese, *The Tokyo Trial and Beyond* (Cambridge, 1992) 50. Many would query whether there is one form of 'real truth'.

72 Both in customary law and in the ICC Statute and its concomitant Elements of Crimes, see Chapters 10 and 11.

introduce evidence too. Furthermore, the nature of a fair trial process is that it gives those responsible for international crimes the opportunity to raise political propaganda and to attempt to delegitimize the prosecution.[73] This may be a necessary aspect of such trials, since the alternative, that of silencing the defence, is unacceptable, but balancing the competing interests here is difficult.[74] The temporal, geographical and subject-matter jurisdiction of international criminal tribunals means that the story they can tell is by no means the full one,[75] even though some of the international criminal tribunals have used evidence of events outside their jurisdictional reach.[76]

While such critiques do not substantially undermine the work done by those Tribunals in collecting and making public primary evidence such as documents and witness testimony, they do cast aspersions on the role of courts as presenters or interpreters of history. The evidence brought before some tribunals can, however, be very useful in combating later denial of such crimes (as has occurred in relation to the practice of the Nuremberg IMT and the ICTR). The practice of 'plea bargaining' in the Tribunals has been said by some Trial Chambers of the ICTY to assist in the process of truth-telling,[77] but other chambers have doubted that the full story can be told without full trials.[78]

2.3.3 Post-conflict reconciliation

Linked both to the satisfaction of victims and the telling of truths about international crimes, which has been said to form the basis of a society moving beyond its schisms, it has been claimed that providing a sense of justice through prosecutions for international crimes can facilitate societal reconciliation and provide the preconditions for a durable peace.[79] This is often expressed in the aphorism 'no peace without justice'.[80] Evidence from Latin America, where policies of amnesty were rife in the 1970s but where prosecutions have continuously been sought and are now beginning to occur, provides some support for that position.[81]

---

73 See generally Gerry Simpson, 'Politics, Sovereignty, Remembrance' in Dominic McGoldrick, Peter Rowe and Eric Donnelly (eds.), *The Permanent International Criminal Court: Legal and Policy Issues* (Oxford, 2004) 47 at 49.

74 See generally, Koskenniemi, 'Between Impunity'.

75 José E. Alvarez, 'Crimes of Hate/Crimes of State: Lessons from Rwanda' (1999) 23 *Yale Journal of International Law* 365 at 375.

76 *Nahimana, Barayagwiza and Ngeze* ICTR T. Ch.I 3.12.2003 paras. 100–4.

77 *Jokić* ICTY T. Ch. I 18.3.2004 para. 77. See Mark Harmon, 'Plea Bargaining: The Uninvited Guest at the ICTY' in José Doria, Hans-Peter Gasser and M. Cherif Bassiouni (eds.), *The Legal Regime of the International Criminal Court: Essays in Honour of Igor Blischenko* (Leiden, 2009) 163, 177–9.

78 *Dragan Nikolić* ICTY T. Ch. II 18.12.2003 para. 122. See also Schabas, *The UN International Criminal Tribunals*, 427–8; Drumbl, *Atrocity*, 181–2.

79 See, e.g. Cassese, 'Reflections on International Criminal Justice', 6.

80 Indeed, this is the name of one well-known NGO working in the area of international criminal law.

81 The politics of impunity, on the other hand, are often thought to inspire later crimes, even decades later, see e.g. Harmon, 'Plea Bargaining', 179–82; Jens Ohlin, 'Peace, Security and Prosecutorial Discretion' in Carsten

There is, however, no clear empirical proof of this, and other societies have managed without trials[82] (although some would say that those societies are not reconciled[83]).

The Security Council provided significant support for the interconnection of peace and justice when it determined that in the situations in former Yugoslavia and Rwanda, prosecutions would assist in reconciliation and a return to peace in the area.[84] It is interesting that in the *Tadić* jurisdictional appeal, the Appeals Chamber of the ICTY simply said that such a decision was within the competence of the Council to make, rather than entering into any discussion of the substantive merits of the point.[85] Later, in the *Nikolić* case, the ICTY gave the idea more direct support.[86]

The high tide mark of support for the link between criminal justice and peace in the ICTY came in the *Plavšić* case. Biljana Plavšić was co-President of the Republika Sprksa during 1992. She surrendered to the Tribunal and pleaded guilty to crimes against humanity, expressing her remorse and stating that in doing so she wished to 'offer some consolation to the innocent victims – Muslim, Croat and Serb – of the war in Bosnia and Herzegovina'.[87] In sentencing Plavšić to eleven years imprisonment, the Tribunal noted 'that acknowledgement and full disclosure of serious crimes are very important when establishing the truth in relation to such crimes. This, together with acceptance of responsibility for the committed wrongs, will promote reconciliation.'[88] The ICTY's practice on point has been characterized as 'incoherent', on the basis that, in other cases, the ICTY has refused to reduce sentences on the basis of contributions to the peace process.[89]

Some of the most serious doubts that have been expressed about international criminal law relate to the claim that it promotes peace and reconciliation.[90] It has been suggested that to require prosecutions will simply cause parties to conflicts to fight to the last.[91] On the other hand there is anecdotal evidence of the ICC's deterrent effect in the Democratic Republic of Congo.[92] It is simply too early to say whether the optimists or pessimists are

---

Stahn and Göran Sluiter (eds.), *The Emerging Practice of the International Criminal Court* (Leiden, 2009) 185, 203–5.

82 See, e.g. Priscilla Hayner, *Unspeakable Truths: Confronting State Terror and Atrocity* (London, 2001) ch. 12.

83 See Richard Wilson, *The Politics of Truth and Reconciliation: Legitimizing the Post-Apartheid State* (Cambridge, 2001).

84 Although such a determination was necessary to invoke Chapter VII of the UN Charter to create the ICTY and ICTR.

85 See section 7.2.4.

86 *Momir Nikolić* ICTY T. Ch. I 2.12.2003 para. 60.

87 *Plavšić* ICTY T. Ch. III 27.2.2003 para. 19.

88 *Ibid.*, para. 80.

89 Drumbl, *Atrocity*, 62.

90 Anthony D'Amato, 'Peace v. Accountability in Bosnia' (1994) 88 AJIL 500; Ian Ward, *Justice, Humanity and the New World Order* (Aldershot, 2004) 131.

91 Anonymous, 'Human Rights in Peace Negotiations' (1996) 18 *Human Rights Quarterly* 249.

92 William Burke-White, 'Complementarity in Practice: the International Criminal Court as part of a system of Multi-level Global Governance in the Democratic Republic of Congo' (2005) 18 *LJIL* 557 at 587, 588.

correct. The parties to the ICC Statute affirmed, in the preamble of that treaty, that the commission of international crimes threatens the 'peace, security and well being of the world'.[93] The ambivalent relationship between international criminal justice and peace is perhaps shown by the fact that the Security Council, using its powers to restore and maintain international peace and security under Chapter VII of the UN Charter, may not only refer a situation to the International Criminal Court, but also defer the activity of that court in certain circumstances.[94]

2.3.4 Further asserted benefits of international trials

Certain benefits have also have been postulated, not of international criminal law in general, but of international trials. One of the most powerful of these is that international tribunals, with international judges, operating at a distance from the events themselves, are not as open to political manipulation or influence from actors in those societies, or unconscious bias on the part of the judges.[95] Nonetheless, there have been a number of claims before the ICTY, ICTR and the Special Court for Sierra Leone (SCSL) that judges are biased.[96] Also, it is an often-made critique that the international tribunals are too distant from their primary audience, the victimized community.[97] It is also sometimes claimed that international judges are the best judges of international crimes.[98] There are two possible bases for these claims, the first being that international judges and tribunals are representative of the relevant community affected by international crimes, which is the community of all humanity. The second basis is more prosaic: that international judges are more familiar with the relevant law. It is true that domestic judges are less likely to be fully aware of the intricacies of international criminal law than some of their international counterparts. Indeed, some eminent and experienced international lawyers have sat on the international criminal tribunals. However, not all judges who have sat on international criminal tribunals go to them professing expertise in international criminal law; an in-depth knowledge of the workings of a criminal trial is an equally useful background for an international criminal judge.[99]

It has also been suggested that international tribunals are better able to investigate and prosecute offences which occur across State borders than domestic courts.[100] This may be the case, but the extent to which it is true depends on the extent of the tribunal's jurisdiction

---

93 ICC Statute, Preambular para. 3.
94 Arts. 13 and 16 of the ICC Statute; see further sections 8.6, 8.8.
95 Cassese, 'Reflections on International Criminal Justice', 4, 7.
96 See section 17.2.2.
97 See below, section 2.4.
98 Cassese, 'Reflections on International Criminal Justice', 7.
99 The late ICTY judge Sir Richard May was a judge in the UK, and an acknowledged expert on (UK) evidence law prior to his appointment to the tribunal.
100 Cassese, 'Reflections on International Criminal Justice', 8.

and investigatory powers, which differ between the various courts. Finally it has been suggested that an international criminal court would provide for uniformity in the process and law for punishing international crimes.[101] There is some truth in this. Although there have been a number of different international criminal tribunals, with different procedures and different substantive law, the ICC Statute has promoted harmonization of the law at the domestic level. Equally, the value of uniformity is strongly linked to the merits of the law which becomes the standard.[102]

2.4   Other critiques of criminal accountability

Despite the functions which prosecutions may serve, there are also many critiques of criminal accountability, and international tribunals in particular. International tribunals are expensive. The ICTY and ICTR have, between them cost more than $2 billion and the ICC has so far cost about €0.5 billion. These are unquestionably huge sums of money, and the ICTR has been accused of financial irregularity.[103] To gain some perspective though, it might be noted that the annual base military budget in the US in 2009 was $515.4 billion. In addition, the international criminal courts prior to the ICC were set up almost completely from scratch, and international tribunals, unlike their domestic counterparts, are almost entire criminal justice systems in themselves.

International tribunals are also (with the exception of the SCSL) located far away from the places where the crimes occurred.[104] This means that they are inaccessible to many of the victims and seen as responding more to an international audience than the purported beneficiaries.[105] This gives succour to those who argue that the creation of the tribunals was more a sop to the conscience of those who failed to prevent or bring an end to the crimes now being punished.[106] Where trials are held further from the *locus delicti* they often encounter domestic resistance there, in part because of misrepresentation of their work and allegations of bias.[107] There is also a lack of 'ownership' of international tribunals at the local level. Given that such tribunals tend to focus on those most responsible, it is also the case that most victims will not see their immediate oppressors punished. In situations of large-scale commission of crimes, however, it is difficult to

---

101 *Ibid.*
102 Robert Cryer, *Prosecuting International Crimes: Selectivity and the International Criminal Law Regime* (Cambridge, 2005) 167–84.
103 See section 7.3.3.
104 Alvarez, 'Crimes of Hate'. Even the Special Court in the Taylor case has moved the trial away from Sierra Leone, on security grounds.
105 *Ibid.*
106 See Gary John Bass, *Stay the Hand of Vengeance: The Politics of War Crimes Tribunals* (Princeton, 2000) ch. 6.
107 Patrice McMahon and David Forsythe, 'The ICTY's Impact on Serbia: Judicial Romanticism Meets Network Politics' (2008) 30 *Human Rights Quarterly* 412.

imagine any criminal justice system that could fulfil the task of ensuring that all international criminals were punished.[108]

More generally, it has been questioned whether criminal law is an adequate mechanism to comprehend events involving international crimes, particularly large-scale international crimes like genocide. The critique was perhaps most strongly made by Hannah Arendt,[109] but others have also made similar points. Martti Koskeniemmi, for example, has said that 'sometimes a tragedy may be so great, a series of events of such political or even metaphysical significance, that punishing an individual does not come close to measuring up to it'.[110] It could be queried whether trials are any worse at 'measuring up to it' than the other methods that have been suggested for dealing with such events, and Arendt was not against the prosecution of international crimes as such, although she was critical of aspects of some proceedings.[111] Still, it is true that most international crimes occur against the background of 'system criminality', where individual and collective responsibility is mixed. As such, individual liability can only be part of the answer.[112] Since individual criminal liability and State responsibility are largely separate, this need not be such a problem, as the existence of one does not negate the existence of the other.[113] The difficulty is finding ways that adequately express both the individual and collective contributions to international crimes.[114]

More generally, prosecutions of international crimes are open to the criticism that they are designed to legitimate those that create them. For example, the creation of the ICTY and ICTR may have allowed powerful States to cover their unwillingness to take more decisive action.[115] Prosecutions can also be used by States and successor governments to attempt to make the point that they are morally different from those on trial, even where there are international crimes that can be laid at their door too.[116] In addition, substantive international criminal law fails to deal with conduct very worthy of censure, thus providing some form of legitimacy for it.[117] International trials and international criminal law ought not to

---

108 William Schabas, 'The Rwanda Case: Sometimes It's Impossible' in M. Cherif Bassiouni (ed.), *Post Conflict Justice* (New York, 2002) 499.

109 Lotte Kohler and Hans Saner (eds.), *Hannah Arendt/Karl Jaspers: Correspondence* at 54, cited in Osiel, 'Why Prosecute?', 128.

110 Koskeniemi, 'Between Impunity', 2.

111 Hannah Arendt, *Eichmann in Jerusalem: A Report on the Banality of Evil* (Harmondsworth, 1994) epilogue.

112 See André Nollkaemper and Harmen van der Wilt, 'Introduction' in André Nollkaemper and Harmen van der Wilt, *System Criminality in International Law* (Cambridge, 2009) 1 at 4.

113 Beatrice Bonafé, *The Relationship Between State and Individual Responsibility for International Crimes* (Leiden, 2009), although on the overlaps and difficulties in entirely separating them see also Gerry Simpson, 'Men and Abstract Entities' in Nollkaemper and van der Wilt, *System Criminality*, 69; Andrea Gattini, 'A Historical Perspective: From Collective to Individual Responsibility and Back' in *ibid.*, 101.

114 Gattini, 'A Historical Perspective', 126.

115 See section 7.2.

116 Simpson, 'War Crimes: A Critical Introduction', 19–26.

117 Simpson, 'Politics, Sovereignty, Rembrance', 56.

serve as an excuse to the international community for not dealing with other more difficult and deep-seated problems.

International criminal justice, and international tribunals, reflect inequalities in the selection of cases. Selective justice is a problem from the point of view of the rule of law, and it can undermine many of the justifications of punishment.[118] For example, deterrence is unlikely to be possible if potential offenders take the view that they may be able to obtain exemption from prosecution. Retribution is not served well by selective punishment, and it causes the lessons that may be taught by international criminal law to be confused and equivocal.[119]

Some would go further than this, to argue that international criminal law is in some ways a Western construct, and that it is imposed on other societies.[120] With respect to the norms themselves, of genocide, crimes against humanity and war crimes, this is almost certainly overstated, in that genocide, crimes against humanity and most war crimes are considered contrary to universal norms. As has been said, 'modern writers on the subject correctly point to Chinese, Islamic and Hindu traditions that underscore the universal values enshrined in the prohibition of ... crimes that shock the conscience of mankind'.[121] The treaties establishing the core of war crimes, the Geneva Conventions, have been ratified by probably every State in the world,[122] and the General Assembly has repeatedly and unanimously condemned genocide, crimes against humanity and war crimes.[123] Some scholars, however, have taken the view that by using custom rather than treaties, the ad hoc Tribunals have preferred the interests of large States, which may have more weight in the creation of custom.[124]

When it comes to enforcement, selectivity arguments can take on a post-colonial aspect, i.e. that 'international prosecutions are instituted mainly against citizens of states that are weak actors in the international arena or fail to enjoy the support of powerful nations'.[125] It has also been claimed that decisions about what to do about international crimes are better left to national authorities.[126] The issues involved are not simple, but it might be noted that a number of post-colonial States (such as Rwanda, Uganda and the Democratic Republic of

---

118 Drumbl, 'Collective Violence and Individual Punishment', 593.
119 See, e.g. Damaška, 'What is the Point', 361.
120 Steven Ratner, Jason Abrams and James Bischoff, *Accountability for Human Rights Atrocities in International Law: Beyond the Nuremberg Paradigm*, 3rd edn (Oxford, 2009) 26.
121 Leila Sadat, 'The Effect of Amnesties Before Domestic and International Tribunals: Law, Morality, Politics' in Edel Hughes, William Schabas and Ramesh Thakur (eds.), *Atrocities and International Accountability* (Tokyo, 2007) 229.
122 Kosovo is a controversial case, given the disagreements that surround its asserted statehood.
123 E.g. GA Resolutions 47/131 (7.4.93) 63/303 (23.7.09).
124 Anthony Anghie and B.S. Chimni, 'Third World Approaches to International Law and Individual Responsibility in Internal Armed Conflict' (2003) 2 *Chinese Journal of International Law* 77, at 92–5.
125 Damaška, 'What is the Point', 361; Charles Chernor Jalloh, 'Regionalizing International Criminal Law?' (2009) 9 *ICLR* 445.
126 Anghie and Chimni, 'Third World Approaches', 91–2.

Congo) have asked for international prosecutions of international crimes. Again, a synergistic relationship between national and international approaches to international crimes is probably the most helpful way forward.[127] On the former critique, selectivity is a large problem in international criminal law, although the critique is decreasing in potency.[128] The answer to such critiques is not to abandon punishment altogether, but to work towards nonselective application of the law. Even some enforcement is probably better than none, and powerful States are finding it more difficult to resist claims for criminal accountability of those who commit international crimes on their behalf.[129]

Further reading

José E. Alvarez, 'Crimes of Hate/Crimes of State: Lessons from Rwanda' (1999) 23 *Yale Journal of International Law* 365.

Anthony Anghie and B. S. Chimni, 'Third World Approaches to International Law and Individual Responsibility in Internal Armed Conflict' (2003) 2 *Chinese Journal of International Law* 77.

Antonio Cassese, 'On the Current Trend towards Criminal Prosecution and Punishment of Breaches of International Humanitarian Law' (1998) 9 *EJIL* 2.

Mark Drumbl, *Atrocity, Punishment and International Law* (Cambridge, 2007).

Mirjan Damaška, 'What is the Point of International Criminal Justice' (2008) 83 *Chicago-Kent Law Review* 329.

Frederick Harhoff, 'Sense and Sensibility in Sentencing – Taking Stock of International Criminal Punishment' in Ola Engdahl and Pål Wrange (eds.), *Law at War: The Law as it Was and the Law as it Should Be: Lieber Amoricum Ove Bring* (Leiden, 2008) 121.

Martti Koskenniemi, 'Between Impunity and Show Trials' (2002) 6 *Max Planck Yearbook of United Nations Law* 1.

Jens Ohlin, 'Peace, Security and Prosecutorial Discretion' in Carsten Stahn and Göran Sluiter (eds.), *The Emerging Practice of the International Criminal Court* (Leiden, 2009) 185.

Paul Roberts, 'Restoration and Retribution in International Criminal Justice' in Andrew von Hirsch et al. (eds.), *Restorative Justice and Criminal Justice: Competing or Reconcilable Paradigms?* (Oxford, 2004) 115.

Robert Sloane, 'The Expressive Capacity of International Punishment' (2007) 43 *Stanford Journal of International Law* 39.

Immi Tallgren, 'The Sense and Sensibility of International Criminal Law' (2002) 13 *EJIL* 561.

---

127 See Ratner et al., *Accountability*, 26. Alternatives to criminal prosecutions are evaluated in Chapter 22.
128 See Cryer, *Prosecuting International Crimes, passim.*
129 Damaška, 'What is the Point', 363.

PART B

Prosecutions in National Courts

3

Jurisdiction

3.1 Introduction

Jurisdiction is the power of the State to regulate affairs pursuant to its laws. Exercising jurisdiction involves asserting a form of sovereignty. This fact causes difficulties when jurisdiction is exercised extraterritorially. Where extraterritorial jurisdiction is asserted sovereignties overlap, and general international law has not yet developed any principles to determine any hierarchy of lawful jurisdictional claims.[1] This chapter discusses the principles of jurisdiction as they relate to international crimes. In some instances the extent to which international law allows jurisdiction over international crimes is broader than the jurisdiction which it offers over other crimes. Therefore this chapter must be read with the caveat that it is not a general discussion of the law of jurisdiction, but an explanation of jurisdiction over international crimes, a topic which is not coterminous with the general international law of jurisdiction, although it forms part of it.

3.2 The forms of jurisdiction

There are three ways in which jurisdiction may be asserted: legislative, adjudicative and executive. The extraterritorial assertion of legislative jurisdiction is less controversial than that of adjudicative jurisdiction, and, in the absence of consent, claims of extraterritorial executive jurisdiction almost inevitably infringe the sovereignty of the relevant territorial State.

3.2.1 Legislative jurisdiction

This is the right of a State to pass laws that have a bearing on conduct. Some States take the view domestically that they are entitled to pass legislation covering matters which take place throughout the globe: hence the aphorism that the UK Parliament could pass a statute making it a crime for a French person to smoke on the streets of Paris. However,

---

1 See section 3.5.4.

enforcement of such a statute would be difficult from a practical point of view, as well as problematic in international law, owing to the principle of non-intervention. States are entitled to protest assertions of legislative jurisdiction which are unwarranted under international law, and there is an increasing trend towards them doing so. However, other States do not always consider their rights to be heavily affected by those claims until a specific case arises in which they are relied on.

3.2.2   Adjudicative jurisdiction

This is the extent to which domestic courts are able to take action to enforce their State's laws and pass judgment on matters brought before them. At this point other States may, rightly or wrongly, be more assertive in expressing their concerns about the exercise of jurisdiction. By passing judgment over offences abroad it is possible that courts, hence States, are intervening in the domestic jurisdiction of the State in which the offences were committed. In criminal cases, 'jurisdiction to prescribe and jurisdiction to adjudicate in criminal matters are generally congruent in scope'.[2]

3.2.3   Executive jurisdiction

Executive (or enforcement) jurisdiction is the most intrusive of jurisdictional claims. Executive jurisdiction is the right to effect legal process coercively, such as to arrest someone, or undertake searches and seizures. In the vast majority of cases, this is done by domestic law enforcement agencies such as the police. The *Lotus* case,[3] which is generally accepted to reflect current international law on executive jurisdiction accurately, stated that:

> The first and foremost restriction imposed by international law upon a State is that – failing the existence of a permissive rule to the contrary – it may not exercise its power in any form in the territory of another State. In this sense jurisdiction is certainly territorial; it cannot be exercised by a State outside its territory . . .[4]

In the *Eichmann* case, it was accepted by Israel that, irrespective of the moral rectitude of its action in bringing Adolf Eichmann out of hiding in Argentina to Israel for trial, doing so without the consent of Argentina violated its sovereignty.[5] Care must be taken, however, to distinguish the exercise of executive jurisdiction over a person and the later exercise of adjudicative jurisdiction over them. That an arrest is illegal does not necessarily mean that a court cannot proceed against a person brought before them unlawfully. The maxim is often

---

2 Claus Kreß, 'Universal Jurisdiction over International Crimes and the *Institut de Droit International*' (2006) 4 *JICJ* 561 at 564.
3 *SS Lotus* (France v. Turkey) (1927) PCIJ Rep., Ser. A, No. 10.
4 *Ibid.*, at 18.
5 *Attorney-General of Israel* v. *Eichmann* 36 ILR 5 paras. 40–50 (District Court). For comment see, e.g. Helen Silving, 'In re Eichmann: A Dilemma of Law and Morality' (1961) 55 *AJIL* 307.

expressed as *male captus bene detentus* (roughly, bad capture, good detention). The ICTY has come close to adopting this approach, by claiming that, in relation to its own jurisdiction:

> Apart from such exceptional circumstances [egregious human rights violations, not abduction *simpliciter*] however, the remedy of setting aside jurisdiction will ... usually be disproportionate. The correct balance must therefore be maintained between the fundamental rights of the accused and the essential interests of the international community in the prosecution of persons charged with serious violations of international humanitarian law.[6]

As the quote shows, though, the ICTY left itself some elbow room in extreme cases to refuse jurisdiction. Some national courts have adopted the position that abduction or human rights violations may vitiate jurisdiction,[7] but, in spite of a trend towards such a position, it is not clear that there is an established principle of international law requiring them to do so.[8]

3.3   Conceptual matters

3.3.1   The question of proof

It is often said that States are entitled to exercise jurisdiction unless there is a specific rule of international law that prevents them from doing so. The basis for this belief is the *Lotus* case's pronouncement that 'far from laying down a general prohibition to the effect that States may not extend the application of their laws, and the jurisdiction of their courts to persons, property and acts outside their territory, [international law] leaves them in this respect a wide measure of discretion which is only limited in certain cases by prohibitive rules'.[9] However, even if that was the position in 1927 (which is doubtful), it does not reflect State practice since, which is to assert a positive ground for the exercise of jurisdiction, rather than to rely on the absence of a prohibition.[10] When the separate opinions in the *Yerodia* case came to deal with the '*Lotus* presumption' they could not agree on its continued relevance.[11]

---

6 *Nikolić* ICTY A. Ch. 5.6.2003 para. 30. See also *Barayagwiza*, ICTR A. Ch. 19.11.1999; *Barayagwiza*, ICTR A. Ch. 31.3. 2000.
7 See, e.g. *R* v. *Horseferry Road Magistrates ex parte Bennett* [1993] 2 All ER 318 (UK); *State* v. *Ebrahim* (1992) 1 South African Criminal Law Reports 307.
8 See, e.g. the Decision of the Bundesverfassungsgericht (1986) *Neue Juristische Wochenschrift* 3021, denying the existence of an 'established principle of international law'; the arguments to the contrary are in Stephan Wilske, *Die völkerrechtswidrige Entführung und ihre Rechtsfolgen* (Berlin, 2000) 338–40.
9 *SS Lotus*, at 19.
10 See Michael Akehurst, 'Jurisdiction in International Law' (1972–1973) 46 *BYBIL* 145, 167; Vaughan Lowe, 'Jurisdiction' in Malcolm Evans (ed.), *International Law*, 2nd edn (Oxford, 2006) 335, 341–52.
11 *Case Concerning the Arrest Warrant of 11 April 2000* (Democratic Republic of Congo v. Belgium) ICJ General List 121, 14.2.2002 (hereinafter '*Yerodia*'); see Separate Opinion of President Guillaume, paras. 13–14; Joint Separate Opinion of Judges Higgins, Koojimans and Buergenthal, paras. 49–51; Dissenting Opinion of Judge ad hoc Van den Wyngaert, paras. 48–51.

3.3.2   Treaties and jurisdiction

It is important to note that States are entitled to pass jurisdiction to one another. The treaty-based transnational crimes are usually examples of where States have agreed between themselves that they may exercise jurisdiction on each other's behalf.[12] An example of this is Article 5(1)(2) of the 1979 New York Convention Against the Taking of Hostages.[13] Such treaties include obligations on (or permissions to) State parties to criminalize certain conduct on quite broad jurisdictional bases, and either to extradite or prosecute suspects. These treaties are often seen, albeit somewhat inaccurately, as creating universal jurisdiction. The jurisdiction conferred, strictly speaking, is only a matter of concessions between the parties, who agree that other States may exercise their jurisdiction on their behalf. There is nothing unlawful about this. States are entitled to pass jurisdiction to one another.[14] However, if a State were to assert a right to prosecute someone on the basis of a treaty which is not referable to a concession of one of the accepted forms of jurisdiction by a State Party to the convention, it would violate international law, unless the convention can be regarded as reflective of custom.[15] Such claims of customary status are easier to make than prove. In the following sections, this chapter will concentrate on the jurisdiction States have pursuant to customary international law.

3.4   The 'traditional' heads of jurisdiction

3.4.1   The territoriality principle

The territoriality principle is the least controversial basis of jurisdiction. Under this principle, States have the right to exercise jurisdiction over all events on their territory. This includes ships and aeroplanes which are registered in those countries. A State has jurisdiction over a crime when the crime originates abroad or is completed elsewhere, so long as at least one of the elements of the offence occurs in its territory. If it is the former, it is said to be 'objective' territorial jurisdiction, if it is the latter, then it is 'subjective' territoriality. An example is Article 14(2) of the Armenian Criminal Code, which provides that:

> [A] crime is considered committed in the territory of the Republic of Armenia when:
>
> 1. it started, continued or finished in the territory of the Republic of Armenia;

---

12 See section 14.1.2.

13 1316 UNTS 205.

14 Some doubt this, see e.g. Madeline Morris, 'High Crimes and Misconceptions: The ICC and Non Party States' (2000) 64 *Law and Contemporary Problems* 131, but there is considerable practice to support its legality, see, e.g. Dapo Akande, 'The Jurisdiction of the International Criminal Court over Nationals of Non-Parties: Legal Basis and Limits' (2003) 1 *JICJ* 618, 620–34.

15 See Lowe, 'Jurisdiction', 349–51; Anthony Colangelo, 'The Legal Limits of Universal Jurisdiction' (2006–2007) 47 *VJIL* 149, 166–9.

2. it was committed in complicity with the persons who committed crimes in other countries.[16]

An example of objective and subjective territoriality in international criminal law would be where a rocket is fired from one State at a civilian object in another. The State in which the rocket was fired would have jurisdiction over the event on the basis of subjective territoriality, whilst the State in which the rocket landed would have jurisdiction over it on the basis of objective territoriality.

The problem for international criminal law with the territoriality principle is not its existence, but the reluctance of many States to prosecute offences which occur on their territories, or, conversely, the extent to which fair trial guarantees are offered where such prosecutions occur. Examples of trials for international crimes based on territoriality include the Rwandan *gacaca* trials,[17] and the trials ongoing in the Bosnian War Crimes Chamber. These latter examples include cases originally investigated by the ICTY, but referred by it to the War Crimes Chamber.[18]

3.4.2 The nationality principle

The second generally accepted principle of jurisdiction is nationality (sometimes known as 'active nationality').[19] States are entitled under international law to legislate with respect to the conduct of their nationals abroad. Many States adopt this head of jurisdiction quite broadly. Article 12(2) of the Bosnia/Herzegovina Criminal Code, for example, states that '[t]he criminal legislation of Bosnia and Herzegovina shall be applied to a citizen of Bosnia and Herzegovina who, outside the territory of Bosnia and Herzegovina, perpetrates a criminal offence . . . '.

Nationality is an important basis of jurisdiction in international criminal law, in particular in relation to armed forces stationed overseas who, in the legislation of most States, 'carry the flag' abroad with them.[20] The principle, nonetheless, applies beyond the armed forces, and also covers civilians. An example of this is section 9 of the UK's Offences Against the Person Act 1861, which, as an exception to the usual preference of common law countries for territoriality jurisdiction, also asserts jurisdiction over murders committed by British nationals irrespective of the place of commission.

---

16 Available at http://www.nottingham.ac.uk/shared/shared_hrlcicju/Armenia/Criminal_Code_English_.doc.
17 See Erin Daly, 'Between Punitive and Reconstructive Justice: The Gacaca Courts in Rwanda' (2001–2002) 34 *New York University Journal of International Law and Politics* 355.
18 E.g. *Stanković* ICTY T. Ch. 17.5.2005; *Rašević and Todović* ICTY T. Ch. 8.7.2005.
19 For some of the benefits of nationality jurisdiction, see Paul Arnell, 'The Case for Nationality Based Jurisdiction' (2001) 50 *ICLQ* 955.
20 This is important as often, under Status of Forces agreements, territorial States agree to waive their jurisdiction over foreign forces in their territory.

Nationality jurisdiction relies on the link between a national and the State to which he or she owes allegiance. For the most part the question of who is a national is relatively uncontroversial and dealt with by the legislation of the State granting nationality. Equally, the extent to which other States are required to accept that nationality (and thus any jurisdiction based on it) is limited by international law.[21] One test for nationality in international law was given in the *Nottebohm* case: that the person with the purported nationality must have a 'genuine connection' with the State of which he or she is an alleged national.[22] Some doubt that the *Nottebohm* test is the appropriate test for nationality jurisdiction. They do so on the basis that the *Nottebohm* case was dealing not with a jurisdictional matter, but with the extent to which a State could rely on its own grant of nationality to exercise diplomatic protection with respect to a person who had sought that nationality.[23] These are strong reasons, although it must be noted that where jurisdiction is being asserted on the basis of the nationality of the offender, the *locus delicti* is being required to accept the jurisdiction of a foreign State over events on its territory, so there are some analogies that may legitimately be drawn. Nonetheless, the broad jurisdiction accepted by international law in relation to international crimes (when compared to ordinary domestic crimes) means that this will rarely be an issue, unless a person who denies nationality is being prosecuted on the basis of legislation that does not adopt those broader jurisdictional claims.

For nationality jurisdiction, it is often required that the person over whom that jurisdiction is being asserted was a national at the time of the offence rather than after. Otherwise, it has been claimed, a violation of the *nullum crimen sine lege* principle could occur.[24] Nevertheless, some States provide for jurisdiction in the situation where suspects later acquire their nationality.[25] Those States tend to view such an exercise of the jurisdiction as being a vicarious use of the authority of the *locus delicti*.[26] As a result, the lawfulness of any such use depends on whether the conduct for which the suspect is prosecuted was criminal in the *locus delicti* (or in international law) at the time of its commission,[27] or if that State makes its opposition to the 'borrowing' of its jurisdiction known.[28]

A number of States assert jurisdiction over the activities of their permanent residents even when they are abroad. This is an expanded form of nationality jurisdiction, but one which is acceptable under international law, as those who have chosen to reside permanently in a

---

21 Lowe, 'Jurisdiction', 346–7.
22 *Liechtenstein* v. *Guatemala* (1955) ICJ Reports 4.
23 Lowe, 'Jurisdiction' 346–7. More generally see Chittharanjan Amerasinghe, *Diplomatic Protection* (Oxford, 2008) 92–6, 113–6.
24 See Roger O'Keefe, 'Universal Jurisdiction: Clarifying the Basic Concept' (2004) 2 *JICJ* 735, 742–3.
25 See, e.g. Swedish Penal Code ch. 2 s. 2.
26 This is justified on the basis that many States adopting such a position refuse to extradite their nationals.
27 If it was not, then a violation of the *nullum crimen* principle would result.
28 As we will see, however, in relation to international crimes, States can exercise their own jurisdiction over international crimes wherever they occur anyway.

State are clearly analogous to its nationals. A similar consideration applies to non-nationals who serve a State's armed forces.

Perhaps the most famous example of nationality jurisdiction was the US prosecution of Lieutenant William Calley for his role in the My Lai massacre in Vietnam.[29] This case also provides an example of one of the criticisms often laid at the door of nationality jurisdiction, that prosecutions by States of their own nationals for war crimes may tend to be overly lenient.[30]

3.4.3   The passive personality principle

Passive personality jurisdiction is jurisdiction exercised by a State over crimes committed against its nationals whilst they are abroad. In most instances the assertion of such jurisdiction is controversial. All of the judges who expressed an opinion on the matter in the *Lotus* case took the view that customary international law does not accept such a principle.[31] There has been an increase in the use of passive personality jurisdiction, particularly by the US, in relation to terrorist offences.[32] However, considerable disagreement remains surrounding the lawfulness of its application.[33] There are fears that passive personality jurisdiction favours powerful States at the expense of weaker States. Concerns have also been raised that passive personality jurisdiction could lead to people being subjected simultaneously to the laws of many different States, which would include prohibitions of which they were understandably unaware.[34]

The latter problem only arises where the law differs between States. The problem ought not to apply to international criminal law, as its prohibitions apply across States rather than reflecting national oddities. One of the few areas in which passive personality jurisdiction has traditionally been accepted is in relation to war crimes.[35] Thus States have the right to prosecute war crimes committed against their nationals. One of many examples is the *Washio Awochi* trial,[36] in which a Japanese national was prosecuted by a Netherlands Court Martial for forcing Dutch women into prostitution in a club in Batavia. International law goes beyond this, however, to permit prosecution of offences committed against the nationals of co-belligerent States. For example, in the *Velpke Baby Home* case

---

29 *US* v. *Calley* (1969) 41 CMR 96; (1973) 46 CMR 1131; (1973) 48 CMR 19.

30 See Timothy L. H. McCormack, 'Their Atrocities and Our Misdemeanours: The Reticence of States to Try Their "Own Nationals" for International Crimes' in Philippe Sands and Mark Lattimer (eds.), *Justice for Crimes Against Humanity* (Oxford, 2003) 107.

31 See, e.g. David J. Harris, *Cases and Materials on International Law*, 6th edn (London, 2005) 281; the judgment itself, however, does not contain a ruling on the matter.

32 One example is *US* v. *Yunis* (1991) 30 *ILM* 403.

33 See Lowe, 'Jurisdiction', 351–2.

34 James L. Brierly, 'The "Lotus' Case"' (1928) 44 *Law Quarterly Review* 154, 161.

35 E.g. *Rohrig, Brunner and Heinze* (1950) 17 ILR 393.

36 XII LRTWC 122.

the UK prosecuted German nationals for neglect and mistreatment of Polish children which took place in Germany.[37]

Where passive personality jurisdiction is asserted over international crimes the same questions arise in relation to determining nationality as for nationality jurisdiction. The relevant time for determining nationality is generally considered to be the time of the offence. Consequently, the fact that a person later gains the nationality of a State that wishes to prosecute offences against him or her does not grant that State passive personality jurisdiction. As with nationality jurisdiction, however, the broader jurisdiction applicable to international crimes means that this will not normally be a problem. For example Israel sought to assert passive personality jurisdiction in the *Eichmann* case on behalf of Eichmann's Jewish victims. Its claims on this basis, in relation to the victims, who were not Israeli nationals at the time of Eichmann's offences, has been severely criticized,[38] although Israel's right to try Eichmann on the basis of the universality principle was generally accepted.

3.4.4   The protective principle

A State is entitled to assert protective jurisdiction over extraterritorial activities that threaten State security, such as the selling of a State's secrets, spying or the counterfeiting of its currency or official seal. Although the principle could be used to justify the assertion of jurisdiction over aggression, and was asserted by Israel as one of the bases of jurisdiction over Adolf Eichmann,[39] practically all its imaginable uses in relation to international criminal law overlap with territorial, nationality or passive personality jurisdiction. The assertion of the protective principle in *Eichmann* was criticized on the basis that, irrespective of its right to prosecute him, the State of Israel did not exist during the Holocaust.[40]

3.5   Universal jurisdiction

3.5.1   Introduction

Universal jurisdiction is probably the most controversial principle of jurisdiction in international criminal law. It is certainly the most talked-about.[41] The term 'universal jurisdiction' refers to jurisdiction established over a crime without reference to the place of perpetration, the nationality of the suspect or the victim or any other recognized linking point between the

---

37 George Brand, *Trial of Heinrich Gerike* (London, 1950). Lauterpacht ('Foreword', *ibid.*, at xv) went further, to assert that the trial was based on universality, but see George Brand, 'Introduction', *ibid.*, at xxix.
38 James E. S. Fawcett, 'The Eichmann Case' (1962) 38 *BYBIL* 181, 190–2.
39 *Attorney-General of Israel* v. *Eichmann* 36 ILR 18, 54–7, 304.
40 David Lasok, 'The Eichmann Trial' (1962) 11 *ICLQ* 355, 364.
41 For a useful overview of the voluminous literature on the subject at the turn of the millennium, see A. Hays Butler, 'The Doctrine of Universal Jurisdiction: A Review of the Literature' (2000) 11 *CLF* 353.

crime and the prosecuting State. It is a principle of jurisdiction limited to specific crimes. There are those who deny that universal jurisdiction exists at all.[42] However, the view more consistent with current practice is that other than piracy, which is subject to universal jurisdiction owing to it occurring, by definition, on the high seas,[43] States are entitled to assert universal jurisdiction over war crimes, crimes against humanity, genocide and torture,[44] as those crimes are defined in customary law.[45] There are no examples of universal jurisdiction prosecutions for aggression.[46]

Jurisdiction tends to inhere in States for the purpose of protecting their own interests. The purpose of universal jurisdiction, on the other hand, is linked to the idea that international crimes affect the international legal order as a whole.[47] Owing to the recognition that such offences affect all States and peoples, and awareness that territorial and nationality States do not always respond fairly and effectively to allegations of international crimes, international law grants all States the right to prosecute international crimes. The precise conditions under which a State may do so, however, are controversial, and matters are not helped by a tendency to roll together the issues of whether universal jurisdiction exists and whether or not there is a duty to exercise such jurisdiction. This is compounded by a conflation of two other questions: if States may exercise universal jurisdiction and whether they ought to do so. The discussion below relates to whether States are entitled to assert universal jurisdiction as there is no real evidence that, outside of treaty obligations, States are obliged to do so.

3.5.2   Approaches to universal jurisdiction

Universal jurisdiction has often, at least since the ICJ's decision in the *Yerodia* case[48] if not before, been separated into two questionable sub-categories. These are what is often termed

---

42 See, e.g. Alfred Rubin, 'Actio Popularis, Jus Cogens and Offences Erga Omnes' (2001) 35 *New England Law Review* 265; Marc Henzelin, *Le Principe de l'Universalité en Droit Pénal Interntionale* (Brussels, 2000).
43 Some question whether piracy is an appropriate analogy for modern assertions of universal jurisdiction: see Eugene Kontorovich, 'The Piracy Analogy: Modern Universal Jurisdiction's Hollow Foundation' (2004) 45 *Harvard International Law Journal* 183. Even if this is the case, it does not, however, undermine State practice in the area.
44 See *Institut de Droit International*, Seventeenth Commission, Universal Jurisdiction Over Genocide, Crimes Against Humanity and War Crimes, Krakow, 2005, 2. See Kreß, 'Universal Jurisdiction'. On torture see *Furundžija*, ICTY T. Ch. II 10.12.1998 para. 156.
45 Colangelo, 'Legal Limits'.
46 Attempts to persuade German prosecutors to take on the question of aggression with respect to Iraq have failed, see, e.g. Claus Kreß, 'The German Chief Federal Prosecutor's Decision Not to Investigate the Alleged Crime of Preparing Aggression Against Iraq' (2003) 2 *JICJ* 245.
47 Rosalyn Higgins, *Problems and Process: International Law and How We Use It* (Oxford, 1994) 56–63; Andreas Zimmermann, 'Violations of Fundamental Norms of International Law and the Exercise of Universal Jurisdiction in Criminal Matters' in Christian Tomuschat and Jean-Marc Thouvenin (eds.), *The Fundamental Rules of the International Legal Order* (Leiden, 2006) 335.
48 *Case Concerning the Arrest Warrant of 11 April 2000* (Democratic Republic of Congo v. Belgium) ICJ General List 121, 14.2.2002.

'absolute' or 'pure' universal jurisdiction (also known as 'universal jurisdiction *in absentia*') and 'conditional' universal jurisdiction, (sometimes known as 'universal jurisdiction with presence'). Pure universal jurisdiction arises when a State seeks to assert jurisdiction over an international crime (usually by investigating it and/or requesting extradition of the suspect) even when the suspect is not present in the territory of the investigating State. Conditional universal jurisdiction is universal jurisdiction exercised when the suspect is already in the State asserting jurisdiction.

The distinction has gathered considerable acceptance in academic literature,[49] Nonetheless, and although the matter is not entirely not beyond controversy, the better view is probably that the distinction is non-existent at a conceptual level.[50] Although a number of States have limited their use of universal jurisdiction to where a person is present on their territory, this can, at least in part, be explained on the basis that adopting pure universal jurisdiction 'may show a lack of international courtesy'.[51] Where States have adopted such a limit it appears that some of them have done so as a matter of practical prudence, or as the result of political pressure, rather than as a matter of law.

The resolution on universal jurisdiction of the *Institut de Droit International* attempts to tread a middle path between the approaches by providing that 'Apart from acts of investigation and requests for extradition, the exercise of universal jurisdiction requires the presence of the alleged offender in the territory of the prosecuting State … or other lawful form of control over the alleged offender.'[52] However, the *Institut*'s resolution appears to mix questions of jurisdiction and whether States are entitled, under human rights law, to try people *in absentia*.[53] It is also questionable whether adjudicative jurisdiction can be split up between extradition and trial in the manner the *Institut* suggests,[54] in particular as those asserting the distinction between absolute and conditional universal jurisdiction in *Yerodia* were discussing an arrest warrant, which was intended as a precursor to extradition.[55]

---

49 See, e.g. Antonio Cassese, 'Is the Bell Tolling for Universality? A Plea for a Sensible Notion of Universal Jurisdiction' (2003) 1 *JICJ* 589, 592–3; Georges Abi-Saab, 'The Proper Role of Universal Jurisdiction' (2003) 1 *JICJ* 596, 601.

50 O'Keefe, 'Universal Jurisdiction: Clarifying the Basic Concept', is a particularly powerful argument to this effect. See also Thomas Weigend, 'Grund und Grenzen universaler Gerichtsbarkeit', in Jörg Arnold et al. (eds.), *Festschrift für Albin Eser* (Munich, 2005) 955; Kreß, 'Universal Jurisdiction' 576–8.

51 *Yerodia*, Separate Opinion of Judge ad hoc Van den Wyngaert, para. 3.

52 *Resolution*, para 3(b).

53 Kreß, 'Universal Jurisdiction', 578–9.

54 *Ibid.*, 576–8.

55 The position for non-coercive acts of investigation, such as requests for information, however, may be differentiated, on the basis that they can be refused at will. The ICJ in the *Certain Criminal Proceedings* Case (Djibouti v. France) paras. 170–1 considered a request for information to a person who was immune not to violate international law, as it was not a coercive measure.

3.5.3   The rise of universal jurisdiction

The possibility of universal jurisdiction being exercised over war crimes was mooted during the Second World War.[56] A number of cases prosecuted after the Second World War could be justified or explained on the basis of universal jurisdiction.[57] The United Nations War Crimes Commission[58] took the view that 'the right to punish war crimes … is possessed by any independent State whatsoever'.[59] Equally those cases could be justified on the basis of the expanded passive personality jurisdiction which international law accepts for war crimes.

In 1949 the Geneva Conventions provided a treaty-based analogue to universal jurisdiction in relation to their grave breaches provisions. Article 49 of Geneva Convention I (to which the other three conventions have similar provisions) reads:

> Each High Contracting Party shall be under the obligation to search for persons alleged to have committed, or to have ordered to be committed, such grave breaches and shall bring such persons, regardless of their nationality, before its own courts [or hand them over to another High Contracting Party].[60]

The grave breaches regime is often considered a paradigmatic case of universal jurisdiction, and in practice is exceptionally similar to it. Still, it should be noted that the Conventions speak of 'grave breaches' of their own provisions. Given that (other than common Article 3) the Conventions only apply to conflicts between High Contracting Parties,[61] by their own terms the grave breaches provisions only have *inter partes* effect as a matter of treaty law.[62] Still, the fact that every State in the world has ratified the Conventions makes this a distinction of form rather than substance.[63]

Probably the most famous exercise of universal jurisdiction was the Israeli prosecution of Adolf Eichmann. Eichmann was abducted from Argentina in 1960 by the Israeli Security Service, Mossad, and flown to Jerusalem to be tried.[64] The District Court, in affirming Israel's right to prosecute him, stated that:

> The abhorrent crimes defined under this Law are not crimes under Israeli law alone. These crimes, which struck at the whole of mankind and shocked the conscience of

---

56 Willard Cowles, 'Universality of Jurisdiction Over War Crimes' (1945) 33 *California Law Review* 177.

57 E.g. *Tesch and Others* (the *Zyklon B Case*) I LRTWC 93.

58 Which, for clarity's sake, it should be noted was an inter-Allied body, rather than the (practically) universal international organization.

59 XV LRTWC 26 (Commentary).

60 See Richard van Elst, 'Implementing Universal Jurisdiction Over Grave Breaches of the Geneva Conventions' (2000) 13 *LJIL* 815.

61 The Geneva Conventions, Common Article 2.

62 Their prohibitions, however, clearly reflect customary law.

63 The situation with respect to grave breaches of Additional Protocol I is a little more complex, as it is less (although still broadly) ratified. Most if not all of the grave breaches provisions of Additional Protocol I, however, reflect customary law.

64 Israel originally claimed that the 'rendition' (in modern terminology) was undertaken by public-spirited private Israeli citizens, but its assertion was not widely believed. See also section 3.2.3.

nations, are grave offences against the law of nations itself (*delicta juris gentium*). Therefore, so far from international law negating or limiting the jurisdiction of countries with respect to such crimes, international law is, in the absence of an international court, in need of the judicial and legislative organs of every country to give effect to its criminal interdictions and to bring the criminals to trial. The jurisdiction to try crimes under international law is universal.[65]

It might be noted that in spite of its comments about an international criminal court which, in the light of the principle of complementarity, now seem anachronistic, the District Court's opinion is a strong affirmation of a right (and perhaps even a duty) to establish universal jurisdiction over international crimes. Israel did rely on other bases of jurisdiction, but its primary jurisdictional claim was universality, as the Supreme Court explained:

> if in our judgment we have concentrated on the international and universal character of the crimes ... one of the reasons for our so doing is that some of them were directed against non-Jewish groups.[66]

After *Eichmann*, there was little evidence of any political will to engage in universal jurisdiction prosecutions until 1985, when Israel requested the extradition of John Demjanjuk from the US. Demjanjuk was suspected of being a notorious camp guard in Treblinka known as 'Ivan the Terrible'. The US agreed to extradite Demjanjuk,[67] who stood trial in Israel, but was acquitted on the basis that although he was a guard at Sobibor and Trawniki camps, he was not 'Ivan the Terrible'.[68]

The next possible examples of assertions of universal jurisdiction were Acts such as the UK's War Crimes Act 1991,[69] and Australia's War Crimes Amendment Act 1988,[70] both of which dealt with offences committed in the Second World War by those acting on behalf of the Axis but who later became residents of those two countries. As jurisdiction crystallizes at the time of the offence, these Acts and the (limited) prosecutions under them, are best seen as based on universal jurisdiction.[71] This is because later residence per se is not a head of jurisdiction, and the basis of jurisdiction is not territoriality or nationality.[72]

---

65 (1968) 36 ILR 5 at para. 12 (DC).

66 (1968) 36 ILR 277 at para. 12 (SC).

67 *Demjanjuk* v. *Petrovsky* 776 F. 2d 571 (USCA 6th Cir. 1985); cert. den. 475 US 1016 (1986), 628 F. Supp. 1370; 784 F. 2d 1254 (1986).

68 See Jonathan M. Weinig, 'Enforcing the Lessons of History: Israel Judges the Holocaust' in Timothy L. H. McCormack and Gerry J. Simpson (eds.), *The Law of War Crimes: National and International Approaches* (The Hague, 1997) 103, 115–18.

69 War Crimes Act 1991, s. 1(a). On the Act see Christopher Greenwood, 'The War Crimes Act 1991' in Hazel Fox and Michael A. Meyer (eds.), *Armed Conflict and the New Law: Effecting Compliance* (London, 1993) 215.

70 War Crimes Amendment Act 1988, s. 5. See generally Gillian Triggs, 'Australia's War Crimes Trials: A Moral Necessity or Legal Minefield?' (1987) 16 *Melbourne University Law Review* 382.

71 See Chapter 4.

72 It would be possible to argue that jurisdiction could be co-belligerent (or passive personal jurisdiction), but the Acts do not limit themselves to victims who were nationals of the Allied powers.

The conflicts in Yugoslavia and Rwanda (which notably gave rise to the ICTY and ICTR) led to a number of prosecutions, in particular of people who had come to countries such as Germany and Switzerland as refugees.[73] A number of prosecutions were undertaken in Belgium, pursuant to its Law of 16 June 1993 Relating to the Repression of Grave Breaches of the Geneva Conventions of 12 August 1949 and their Protocols I and II of 8 June 1977,[74] which criminalized certain violations of those treaties without regard to the place of their commission.[75]

By 1999 it appeared that universal jurisdiction was developing considerable momentum. The *Pinochet* litigation throughout Europe,[76] for example, was thought by careful commentators to represent 'the globalization of human rights law through the affirmation that the consequences of, and jurisdiction over, gross violations are not limited to the State in which they (mostly) occur, or of that of the nationality of the majority of the victims'.[77] In the same year Belgium revised its 1993 legislation on grave breaches to add to it jurisdiction over genocide and crimes against humanity 'irrespective of where such breaches have been committed'.[78] The presence of the suspect in Belgium was not required for the initiation of proceedings, which could be brought by private parties. The 1999 law also declared that immunities were inapplicable in proceedings relating to the Act.[79]

3.5.4   The decline of universal jurisdiction?

Although the 1993 statute gave rise to a number of proceedings relating to Rwanda, which did not upset the Rwandan government,[80] the Belgian law proved to be politically controversial. Proceedings were brought though never completed against, amongst others, Ariel Sharon, Yasser Arafat, Fidel Castro and Hashemi Rafsanjani.[81] These proceedings all led to political embarrassment for Belgium. The case against Abduldaye Yerodia Ndombasi led to a challenge to the Belgian law in the International Court of Justice.

---

73 Andreas Ziegler, 'International Decisions: In re G' (1998) 82 *AJIL* 78; Luc Reydams, *Universal Jurisdiction: International and Municipal Legal Perspectives* (Oxford, 2003) 196–200.

74 *Moniteur Belge*, 5 August 1993.

75 See Reydams, *Universal Jurisdiction*, 109–16.

76 See the comments on the various cases in (1999) 93 *AJIL* 690–711.

77 Christine Chinkin, 'R v. Bow Street Stipendiary Magistrate, ex parte Pinochet (No. 3) [1999] 2 WLR 827' (1999) 93 *AJIL* 703 at 711. The precise bases of jurisdiction were made more complex by the fact that jurisdiction under general international law was supplemented in a number of States with arguments based on the Torture Convention.

78 (1999) *ILM* 921, Art. 7. For an overview see Damien Vandermeersch, 'Prosecuting International Crimes in Belgium' (2005) 3 *JICJ* 400.

79 (1999) *ILM* 921, Art. 5(3).

80 See Luc Reydams, 'Belgium's First Application of Universal Jurisdiction: The Butare Four Case' (2003) 1 *JICJ* 428.

81 See Steven R. Ratner, 'Belgium's War Crimes Statute: A Postmortem' (2003) 97 *AJIL* 888, 890.

The Yerodia case

Yerodia, then Foreign Minister of the Democratic Republic of Congo, was the subject of an international arrest warrant issued by Damien Vandermeersch, a Belgian investigating judge on 11 April 2000. Six months later the DRC brought a suit against Belgium in the ICJ, alleging that Belgium had acted unlawfully by asserting universal jurisdiction over Yerodia and ignoring his immunity as a Foreign Minister.[82] Late in the proceedings the DRC dropped the claim relating to universal jurisdiction, and concentrated on the issue of immunities, on which the ICJ eventually found in its favour.[83]

Owing to the DRC's litigation strategy, the majority decided that the ICJ did not need to determine the lawfulness of Belgium's assertion of universal jurisdiction. The majority was criticized for this by a number of the judges, including the President of the Court, Gilbert Guillaume,[84] Judges Higgins, Koojimans and Buergenthal,[85] and the Belgian ad hoc judge, Christine Van den Wyngaert.[86] Their critiques are telling: logically the question of jurisdiction precedes that of immunity (as there must be immunity from something).[87] Also, the arguments about immunity may have been affected by the arguments about universal jurisdiction (in particular those relating to *jus cogens*).

Unlike the majority decision, a number of the separate and dissenting opinions dealt with universal jurisdiction in detail. They revealed a deeply divided court. Four judges (President Guillaume, Judges Ranjeva, Rezek and Judge ad hoc Bula-Bula) were opposed to the assertion of jurisdiction, whereas six judges (Judge Koroma, Judges Higgins, Buergenthal and Koojimans in their joint opinion, Judge al-Khasawneh and Judge ad hoc Van den Wyngaert) supported it (Judge al-Khasawneh at least implicitly took that view).[88] Although many saw this case as a blow to universal jurisdiction, it must be noted that the majority of judges who expressed a view on the matter upheld the universality principle and only one of the judges questioned the use of universal jurisdiction where the person is found in the territory of the State asserting jurisdiction. Three of the four judges who criticized universal jurisdiction appear only to be referring to such jurisdiction being asserted *in absentia*.[89] Only President Guillaume appeared hostile to any sort of universal jurisdiction outside of treaty regimes.[90]

---

82 *Yerodia*. See Neil Boister, 'The ICJ in the *Belgian Arrest Warrant* Case: Arresting the Development of International Criminal Law' (2002) 7 *Journal of Conflict and Security Law* 293; O'Keefe, 'Universal Jurisdiction: Clarifying the Basic Concept'.

83 See Chapter 21.

84 *Yerodia*, Separate Opinion of the President, para. 1.

85 *Ibid*., Joint Separate Opinion of Judges Higgins, Koojimans and Buergenthal, paras. 3–5.

86 *Ibid*., dissenting Opinion of Judge ad hoc Van den Wyngaert, para. 41.

87 *Yerodia*, para. 46.

88 Judge Oda also seemed sympathetic: *ibid*., Dissenting Opinion of Judge Oda, para. 12.

89 Alain Winants, 'The *Yerodia* Ruling of the International Court of Justice and the 1993/1999 Belgian Law on Universal Jurisdiction' (2003) 16 *LJIL* 491 at 500.

90 *Yerodia*, Separate Opinion of President Guillaume, para. 16.

Limiting universality

Belgium's political problems with its law did not end with the *Yerodia* case. Following attempts to indict ex-President George H. W. Bush, Vice-President Dick Cheney and Colin Powell for war crimes alleged to have been committed by them in the Gulf War 1991, Belgium came under heavy pressure from the United States to alter its legislation.[91] In response, Belgium altered its legislation twice in 2003 to limit its jurisdiction and reintroduce immunities.[92] Some saw the Belgian action as signalling the demise of broad notions of universality.[93] The Belgian law is no longer as wide, but it retains some universal jurisdiction elements. For example, jurisdiction may be exercised if a perpetrator later becomes a Belgian resident.[94] It is also clear that the Belgian position is not that universal jurisdiction *in absentia* is unlawful. Its stated reason for repealing the Act was that it had been abused. After 2003, Belgium sought the extradition of Hissene Habré, the ex-dictator of Chad, pursuant to a complaint made before the Act was amended, on the basis of absolute universality. This implies that its view is that universal jurisdiction remains available in international law, although in the particular case the extradition request was refused and Senegal agreed, following a decision by the African Union, to try Habré itself. The proceedings have moved very slowly, and the matter is now before the ICJ, as Belgium has asserted that Senegal is violating its duty to prosecute under the Torture Convention.[95]

The other State whose use of universal jurisdiction appeared to have been reined in somewhat is Spain. Spain was the first State to ask the UK to extradite General Pinochet.[96] It has, since 1999, also indicted (and in one instance convicted) a number of ex-members of military juntas from Latin America. Although the Pinochet case failed to lead to an extradition owing to the UK Home Secretary's determination that the defendant's ill-health prevented it, Spain has used universal jurisdiction successfully in other cases. It has obtained the extradition of Ricardo Cavallo, accused of torture in Argentina, and convicted Adolfo Scilingo for crimes against humanity for his role in torture and killings in Argentina after he went to Spain to testify about his actions in another case.[97]

A number of cases since 2000 did, however, place a fairly restrictive interpretation on universal jurisdiction, requiring that Spanish universal jurisdiction be 'subsidiary' to the

91 Ratner, 'A Postmortem'.

92 See *ibid*. and see Luc Reydams, 'Belgium Reneges on Universality: The 5 August 2003 Act on Grave Breaches of International Humanitarian Law' (2003) 1 *JICJ* 679.

93 Cassese, 'Is the Bell Tolling'.

94 Criminal Procedure Code, Article 6.1 °*bis*.

95 *Case Concerning Questions Relating to the Obligation to Extradite or Prosecute* (Belgium v. Senegal).

96 Although it ought to be noted that some, but not all, of the victims of the conduct for which Spain sought to extradite Pinochet were Spanish.

97 See Christian Tomuschat, 'Issues of Universal Jurisdiction in the Scilingo Case' (2005) 3 *JICJ* 1074; Alicia Gil Gil, 'The Flaws of the Scilingo Judgment' (2005) 3 *JICJ* 1082; Guilia Pinzanuti, 'An Instance of Reasonable Universality' (2005) 3 *JICJ* 1092.

jurisdiction of the territorial State, with Spain only having jurisdiction if there is no effort to prosecute by that State. This may be a sensible practical limit, but is not required by international law.[98] The Spanish cases also appeared to require the presence of the suspect in Spain, although presence pursuant to extradition, as in the Cavallo case, seemed sufficient.[99] A firm reaffirmation of universal jurisdiction, without any of the limitations suggested in the previous cases, came from the Spanish Constitutional Tribunal in the *Guatemala Genocide* case, which expressly repudiated the earlier, more limited, jurisprudence.[100] However, after a number of controversial attempts to prosecute, inter alia, American officials, similar pressures to those that were brought to bear on Belgium have led the Spanish parliament to take steps to limit the assertion of jurisdiction to where there is a link between the offence and Spain.

Other practice

Having becoming parties to the Statute of the International Criminal Court, a number of countries have introduced international crimes into their domestic law and, when doing so, have also adopted universal jurisdiction over them. Some States, such as New Zealand, have not included any residence or other requirement in their legislation and have thus adopted absolute universality.[101] Germany has adopted similar legislation, although a prosecutor is entitled to dismiss the case if there is no linking point to Germany or it is being investigated by a more closely related State or an international criminal court.[102] The UK and Canada have both included jurisdiction over offences committed by non-nationals who later become linked to them in specified ways. It suffices for Canada's War Crimes and Crimes Against Humanity Act that the person is later present in Canada (s. 8). For prosecution in the UK, the relevant legislation requires the person later to become a resident of the UK.[103] Nonetheless, given that the UK does not extradite to States on bases of jurisdiction it considers to be in excess of international law, by providing (in s. 72) for extradition to States which have broader extra-territorial jurisdiction than it takes over international crimes itself, the UK

---

98 *Guatemalan Generals Case*, Tribunal Supremo, Sala de lo Penal, Sentencia 327/2003. See Hervé Ascensio, 'Are Spanish Courts Backing Down on Universality? The Supreme Tribunal's Decision in *Guatemalan Generals*' (2003) 1 *JICJ* 690, 695–7. For a (persuasive) argument that this has not become customary, even though as a matter of policy it is very sensible, see Cedric Ryngaert, 'Applying the Rome Statutes Complementarity Principle: Drawing Lessons from the Prosecution of Core Crimes by States Acting Under the Universality Principle' (2008) 19 *CLF* 153, 173–7, although see Kreß, 'Universal Jurisdiction' 579–81.

99 Cassese, 'Is the Bell Tolling', 590.

100 Naomi Roht-Arriaza, 'Guatemala Genocide Case' (2006) 100 *AJIL* 207; Hervé Ascenscio, 'The Spanish Constitutional Tribunal's Decision in *Guatemalan Generals*' (2006) 4 *JICJ* 586.

101 International Crimes and International Criminal Court Act 2000, ss. 8, 9, 10, 11.

102 Code of Crimes Against International Law, s. 1; Criminal Code, s. 153f. On practice relating to this see Kai Ambos, 'International Core Crimes, Universal Jurisdiction and §153F of the German Criminal Procedure Code' (2007) 18 *CLF* 43.

103 International Criminal Court Act 2001, s. 68(1).

accepts that international law allows States to adopt universal jurisdiction over war crimes, genocide and crimes against humanity. Owing to the fact that the ICC Statute does not require States to take universal jurisdiction (or even mention it), this acceptance must be based on the position in customary international law.

Other States that have adopted universal jurisdiction legislation include Trinidad and Tobago,[104] the Netherlands (which has engaged in a number of prosecutions on this basis),[105] and Senegal.[106] Even the US, no frequent friend of universal jurisdiction on the basis of customary law,[107] has adopted universal jurisdiction over some war crimes including the use of child soldiers, which is not created by a treaty to which the US is a party.[108] The Peruvian Constitutional Court has also recently affirmed the existence of universal jurisdiction over international crimes.[109]

A particularly notable example of practice is the declaration of the African Union of 2008 on the abuse of universal jurisdiction; in this, the Assembly of Heads of State and Government, in spite of condemning the abuse of universal jurisdiction,[110] 'recogniz[ed] that universal jurisdiction is a principle of international law whose purpose is to ensure that individuals who commit grave offences such as war crimes and crimes against humanity do not do so with impunity and are brought to justice, which is in line with ... the Constitutive Act of the African Union'.[111] This is a significant official statement by 53 States, a number of which have had past (and present) officials investigated on the basis of universal jurisdiction, which recognizes the lawfulness of such jurisdiction. The concern was with the abuse, not the existence, of the jurisdiction.

Turning to the views of the international (and internationalized) criminal tribunals, both the ICTY and ICTR have asserted that States may exercise universal jurisdiction,[112] as has the Special Court for Sierra Leone.[113] Outside this context, the European Court of Human Rights has also accepted that universal jurisdiction exists, at least for genocide,[114] whilst the Inter-American Commission on Human Rights considers such jurisdiction to exist over crimes against international law.[115] Against this background, reports of the death of

---

104 International Criminal Court Act 2006, s. 8.
105 International Crimes Act 2003, s. 2. See Erwin van der Borght, 'Prosecution of International Crimes in the Netherlands: An Analysis of Recent Case Law' (2007) 28 *CLF* 87.
106 Article 2, Loi N° 2007–05 (12.2.2007), Penal Code, Article 431, Constitution of Senegal, Article 9.
107 See John Bellinger, 'US Initial Reactions to ICRC Study on Customary International Law'.
108 Child Soldiers Accountability Act 2007, S2135.
109 Decision 01271-2008-PHC/TC, 8.8.2008 para. 6.
110 In particular the indictment of high-level Rwandan officials by France.
111 Decision on the Report of the Commission on the Abuse of Universal Jurisdiction (Assembly/AU/14/(XI), annexed to Letter from the AU Permanent Observer to the President of the Security Council, UN Doc. S/2008/465.
112 *Tadić* ICTY A. Ch. 2.10.1995 para. 62; *Ntuyuhaga* ICTR T. Ch. I 18.3.1999 (in relation to genocide).
113 *Kallon and Kamara*, SCSL A. Ch. 13.3.2004 paras. 67–71.
114 *Jorgić* v *Germany*, Application No.74613/01, Judgment, 12.7.2007 paras 67–70.
115 Resolution 1/03, 24.10.2003.

universal jurisdiction are greatly exaggerated, even if the status of such jurisdiction being asserted *in absentia* remains controversial.

3.5.5   Universal jurisdiction's practical problems

One of the major problems with undertaking prosecutions on the basis of universal jurisdiction is that the existence of jurisdiction per se does not give rise to any obligations on behalf of the territorial or nationality State to assist in any investigation, provide evidence or extradite suspects.[116] The matter of cooperation falls to treaty obligations or comity.[117] It is perhaps unsurprising that some of the most successful prosecutions on the basis of universal jurisdiction, the Belgian prosecution of the 'Butare four', the Niyontenze case in Switzerland and the UK prosecutions of the Afghan warlord, Faryadi Zardad[118] and Nazi war criminal Anthony Sawoniuk, occurred with the concurrence, if not the support, of the territorial States. Those States permitted investigations and on-site visits, as well as providing witnesses to testify in the forum State. Although in some prosecutions on the basis of universal jurisdiction, witnesses are found in the forum State among the refugee community,[119] the availability of evidence, both human and physical, cannot be presumed. A number of cases based on universal jurisdiction have failed to achieve the standard of proof for a criminal conviction.[120]

Even where witnesses are available, problems of inter-cultural understanding can arise. Translation difficulties, as well as difficulties of appraising the credibility of witnesses testifying through interpretation and from different cultural backgrounds, make the appraisal of witness evidence very difficult. In some cases (the Sawoniuk case being an example), this problem is mitigated by on-site visits by the fact-finders, who can thereby achieve a better understanding of the witnesses' cultural and material context.

There is also the possible problem of 'forum shopping', in which victims or NGOs may seek to initiate prosecutions in multiple fora, to maximize the possibility of a conviction. This can raise the important issue of the rights of defendants, who could be prosecuted (and have to defend themselves) repeatedly in relation to the same facts, something which, if done in one State, would violate the *ne bis in idem* principle.[121] The absence of such a

---

116 See Bruce Broomhall, *International Justice and the International Criminal Court: Between State Sovereignty and the Rule of Law* (Oxford, 2003) 119–23.

117 See Chapter 4.

118 See Robert Cryer, 'Zardad' in A. Cassese et al. (eds.), *The Oxford Companion to International Criminal Justice* (Oxford, 2009) 978–9.

119 Dusko Tadić, who achieved notoriety as the first defendant before the ICTY, was originally proceeded against in Germany, having been recognized by other refugees. The case was dropped after his transfer to the ICTY.

120 E.g. the Dusko Cvetković prosecution in Austria and *In re Gabrez* in Switzerland.

121 George Fletcher, 'Against Universal Jurisdiction' (2003) 1 *JICJ* 580.

principle operating between States makes this a possibility, albeit one which is not unique to universal jurisdiction nor one which has occurred in practice.[122]

3.5.6 Policy-based/political criticisms of universal jurisdiction

There have been a number of arguments of policy brought against universal jurisdiction, which are of varying persuasiveness. The first of these is that prosecutions on the basis of universal jurisdiction may upset the balance struck between prosecution and amnesty in an emerging democracy, where amnesties have been used.[123] This critique has more purchase when applied to processes such as South Africa's than when compared to General Pinochet's self-granted immunity.[124] On the other hand, international crimes are not simply the concern of one State alone. Crimes against humanity, genocide and (probably most) war crimes violate *erga omnes* obligations; therefore all States have some form of interest in the response to such offences.[125] From a purely legal point of view, domestic amnesty legislation does not bind any other State, and the problem is, again, not one unique to universal jurisdiction.

The practical ability of more powerful nations both to assert jurisdiction beyond their borders, and the ability of such States to pressure other countries into leaving their nationals alone has led to claims that universal jurisdiction can be selective in its application. As President Guillaume argued in *Yerodia*, to support universal jurisdiction would be to 'encourage the arbitrary for the purposes of the powerful, purportedly acting for an ill-defined "international community"'.[126]

This argument frequently takes on a neo-colonial twist, as in Judge Rezek's opinion in the same case: '[I]t is not without reason that the Parties before the court have discussed the question of how certain European countries would react if a judge from the Congo had indicted their officials for crimes supposedly committed on their orders in Africa.'[127] As this quote shows, however, this would apply in relation to territorial jurisdiction in a similar manner to universal jurisdiction. Judge ad hoc Bula-Bula, however, made the criticism directly on the basis that the exercise of universal jurisdiction was a form of neo-colonial intervention by Belgium in its former colony.[128]

---

122 See Albin Eser, 'For Universal Jurisdiction: Against Fletcher's Antagonism' (2003–2004) 39 *Tulsa Law Review* 955, 957–8, 963–71; Ryngaert, 'Applying the Rome Statutes', 155–6.
123 Henry Kissinger, 'The Pitfalls of Universal Jurisdiction' (2001) 80 *Foreign Affairs* 86, 90–1; Eugene Kontorovich, 'The Inefficiencies of Universal Jurisdiction' (2008) *University of Illinois Law Review* 389.
124 Kenneth Roth, 'The Case For Universal Jurisdiction' (2001) 80 *Foreign Affairs* 150 at 153.
125 *Furundžija*, para. 156; *Legality of the Threat or Use of Nuclear Weapons Advisory Opinion* (1996) ICJ Rep. para. 79; *Kupreškić et al.* ICTY T. Ch. II 14.1.2000 para. 520 (although this last case goes a little far in asserting that all norms of humanitarian law have this status).
126 *Yerodia*, Separate Opinion of President Guillaume, para. 15.
127 *Ibid.*, Separate Opinion of Judge Rezek, para. 9 (translation in Reydams, *Universal Jurisdiction*, 229).
128 *Yerodia*, Separate Opinion of Judge Bula-Bula.

There is no evidence that universal jurisdiction prosecutions are directed by States for nefarious political reasons (or at least no more than on other heads of jurisdiction).[129] Indeed, some of the suggested prosecutions have caused political difficulties for States in which indictments have been sought[130] and, where non-governmental actors have sought to bring proceedings, they normally have to bring sufficient evidence to persuade a court or a prosecutor to take the matter on.[131] The uses of universal jurisdiction to date have all centred on those who have failed to have been prosecuted in their territorial or nationality States. Selective enforcement, nonetheless, remains a problem in relation to international crimes, whatever the principle of jurisdiction invoked. Some of these problems could be mitigated by the adoption of an international agreement on the exercise of universal jurisdiction,[132] although there are no official proposals for such a treaty at present, and without universal ratification, such a treaty might further muddy the waters of this form of jurisdiction, and call into question the existing customary law on point.

Further reading

Michael Akehurst, 'Jurisdiction in International Law' (1972–1973) 46 *BYBIL* 145.

Derek W. Bowett, 'Jurisdiction: Changing Patterns of Authority Over Activities and Resources' (1982) 53 *BYBIL* 1.

Bruce Broomhall, *International Justice and the International Criminal Court: Between Sovereignty and the Rule of Law* (Oxford, 2003) ch. 6.

Anthony Colangelo, 'The Legal Limits of Universal Jurisdiction' (2006–2007) 47 *Virginia Journal of International Law* 149.

Robert Cryer, *Prosecuting International Crimes: Selectivity in the International Criminal Law Regime* (Cambridge, 2005) 75–101.

Edwin D. Dickinson (Reporter), 'Harvard Draft Convention on Jurisdiction With Commentary' (1935) 29 *AJIL Supplement* 439.

Menno T. Kamminga, 'Lessons Learned From the Exercise of Universal Jurisdiction Over Gross Human Rights Abuses' (2001) 23 *Human Rights Quarterly* 940.

Henry Kissinger, 'The Pitfalls of Universal Jurisdiction' (2001) 80 *Foreign Affairs* 86.

---

129 'Final Report on the Exercise of Universal Jurisdiction in Relation to Gross Human Rights Abuses' in ILA, *Report of the Sixty-Ninth Conference, held in London* (London, ILA, 2000) 403 at 422; Ryangaert, 'Applying the Rome Statutes', 155–6.

130 E.g. Christine Bakker, 'Universal Jurisdiction of Spanish Courts Over Genocide in Tibet: Can it Work?' (2006) 4 *JICJ* 595, 599–601; Jonny Paul, 'Peres Slams UK Law Jeopardizing IDF Officers' *Jerusalem Post* 23.11.2008.

131 Prosecutors frequently have discretion in this regard, even in States where this is not a norm, see, e.g. Salvatore Zappalà, 'The German Federal Prosecutor's Decision not to Prosecute a Former Uzbek Minister: Missed Opportunity or Prosecutorial Wisdom?' (2006) 4 *JICJ* 602.

132 Such a course of action is suggested in Cassese, 'Is the Bell Tolling', 595.

Claus Kreß, 'Universal Jurisdiction Over International Crimes and the *Institut de Droit International*' (2006) 4 *JICJ* 561.

Vaughan Lowe, 'Jurisdiction' in Malcolm Evans (ed.), *International Law*, 2nd edn (Oxford, 2006) 335.

Steven Macedo (ed.), *Universal Jurisdiction: National Courts and the Prosecution of Serious Crimes Under International Law* (Philadelphia, 2003).

Frederick A. Mann, 'The Doctrine of Jurisdiction in International Law' (1964–1) 111 *Recueil des Cours, Academie de Droit International* 9.

Roger O'Keefe, 'Universal Jurisdiction: Clarifying the Basic Concept' (2004) 2 *JICJ* 735.

Kenneth C. Randall, 'Universal Jurisdiction Under International Law' (1988) 65 *Texas Law Review* 785.

Cedric Ryngaert, *Jurisdiction in International Law* (Oxford, 2008).

Luc Reydams, *Universal Jurisdiction: International and Municipal Legal Perspectives* (Oxford, 2003).

4

National Prosecutions of International Crimes

4.1 Introduction

International crimes are primarily intended to be prosecuted at the domestic level. Although the 1948 Genocide Convention foresaw a possible 'international penal tribunal as may have jurisdiction with respect to those Contracting Parties which shall have accepted its jurisdiction'[1] the International Criminal Court regime, through its system of complementarity, clearly sees national courts as the courts of first resort.[2] This has been described as an 'indirect enforcement system' whereby international criminal law is to be enforced through national systems.[3] National prosecutions are not only the primary vehicle for the enforcement of international crimes, they are also often considered a preferable option – in political, sociological, practical and legitimacy terms – to international prosecutions.[4]

But although the world vowed after the Second World War never again to allow such atrocities to occur, they continue to be committed in many places around the world and domestic prosecutions are sparse. Indeed, the international criminal jurisdictions are an answer to the impunity that generally exists domestically. This chapter will address international obligations in this regard and some major legal issues that arise concerning national prosecutions of international crimes. Among the complicating factors, insufficient legislation, *ne bis in idem* (double jeopardy) and statutory limitations are addressed here, while amnesties are dealt with in Chapter 22, state cooperation in Chapter 5 and immunities in Chapter 21.

4.2 National prosecutions

Of the international crimes that are the subject of this book, war crimes have been regulated in domestic law the longest and have been prosecuted most often.[5] Early examples are

---

1 Art. 6, Genocide Convention. See also Art. 5, 1973 Apartheid Convention.
2 See Chapter 10.
3 See, e.g. M. Cherif Bassiouni, *Introduction to International Criminal Law* (New York, 2003) 333.
4 See Chapters 2 and 7.
5 For national case law, see the ICRC webpage: www.icrc.org/ihl-nat.

prosecutions with respect to the American Civil War in the 1860s and Anglo-Boer Wars in the late nineteenth and early twentieth centuries. The quite reluctant prosecutions in Germany and Turkey after the First World War, the Leipzig trials and the Istanbul (Constantinople) trials in the 1920s, related to war crimes and were conducted under domestic laws.[6]

No conflict has generated as many national prosecutions as the Second World War, sometimes for international crimes, but in many instances for 'ordinary' crimes under national penal law. Apart from the (literally) thousands of cases in Germany,[7] many other European States have instituted prosecutions.[8] The most well known are the French cases against Klaus Barbie (head of the Gestapo in Lyons), Paul Touvier (a pro-Nazi militiaman), and Maurice Papon (a high-ranking official of the French Vichy regime), who were convicted for crimes against humanity in 1987, 1994 and 1998 respectively, after very long proceedings plagued with difficulties.[9] Prosecutions have also taken place, inter alia, in Italy (e.g. the *Hass and Priebke* case[10]), Austria, the Netherlands, and former Eastern Bloc countries. In the UK, after the many prosecutions directly after the war, only one Second World War case, *R* v. *Sawoniuk*, has resulted in a conviction for war crimes in the recent past.[11]

Second World War crimes have also been prosecuted elsewhere, most notably by Israel. The seminal *Eichmann* case addressed not only important issues of jurisdiction,[12] including the exercise of jurisdiction upon abduction of the accused from another State,[13] but also criminal defences (superior orders and the 'act of State' doctrine) and the principle of

---

6 See section 6.2. See also Timothy McCormack, 'Their Atrocities and Our Misdemeanours: The Reticence of States to Try Their "Own Nationals" for International Crimes' in Mark Lattimer and Philippe Sands (eds.), *Justice for Crimes Against Humanity* (Oxford, 2003) 121–5.

7 For German judgments concerning Nazi crimes, see Christiaan Rüter and Dick de Mildt (eds.), *Justiz und NS-Verbrechen: Sammlung deutscher Strafurteile wegen nationalsozialistischer Tötungsverbrechen 1945–1999* (Amsterdam and Munich, 1968–c.2011), and Christiaan Rüter (ed.), *DDR-Justiz und NS-Verbrechen: Sammlung ostdeutscher Strafurteile wegen nationalsozialistischer Tötungsverbrechen* (Amsterdam and Munich, 2002–2009).

8 Generally, see Axel Marschik, 'The Politics of Prosecution: European National Approaches to War Crimes' in T. L. H. McCormack and G. Simpson, *The Law of War Crimes: National and International Approaches* (The Hague, 1997) 65–101.

9 See Leila Sadat Wexler, 'The French Experience' in Cherif Bassiouni (ed.), *International Criminal Law*, 2nd edn (New York, 1999), vol. III, 273.

10 Convictions for war crimes and crimes against humanity; Rome Military Tribunal 22.7.1997, Military Court of Appeal 7.3.1998 and Supreme Court of Cassation 16.11.1998. See Paola Gaeta, 'War Crimes Trials Before Italian Criminal Courts: New Trends' in Horst Fischer et al., *International and National Prosecution of Crimes Under International Law: Current Developments* (Berlin, 2001) 751–68. On other Italian trials, see also Pier Paolo Rivello, 'The Prosecution of War Crimes Committed by Nazi Forces in Italy' (2005) 3 *JICJ* 422.

11 [2000] 2 Crim App Rep 220.

12 See Chapter 3.

13 See section 5.4.7.

non-retroactivity of criminal law.[14] Adolf Eichmann stood trial for 'crimes against the Jewish people', crimes against humanity and war crimes. He was found guilty, sentenced to death and executed in Ramleh Prison on 31 May 1962. Jurisdictional issues were also considered when US courts decided to extradite John Demjanjuk to Israel to stand trial for war crimes and crimes against humanity.[15] Before the Israeli courts, however, evidentiary matters came to the forefront, and Demjanjuk was finally acquitted because of doubts in respect of his identity (as the concentration camp guard 'Ivan the Terrible of Treblinka').[16] In 2009, though, Demjanjuk was extradited to Germany to face trial for his wartime activities.

Other interesting cases are the Canadian *Finta* case, where very strict mental and material requirements for crimes against humanity and war crimes were introduced,[17] and the Australian *Polyukhovic* case, where the constitutional validity of war crimes legislation was challenged with respect to jurisdiction and retroactivity.[18] In both cases, evidentiary insufficiency, in part owing to the length of time between the events and the trials, meant that they ended in acquittals.

Conflicts after the Second World War did not produce many national criminal proceedings. A few examples are the US court martials concerning the infamous My Lai massacre during the Vietnam War, albeit for domestic rather than international crimes,[19] some cases in Romania and Ethiopia where reference was made to 'genocide',[20] a show trial in Cambodia of Pol Pot and the Khmer Rouge in 1979,[21] and preparations for prosecutions of crimes committed during the 1971 Pakistan–Bangladesh war.[22]

It was not until the 1990s with the renewed focus on international criminal justice in general, and the establishment of the ad hoc Tribunals in particular, that the frequency of national prosecutions increased. This is particularly true in Rwanda and the States of the

---

14 *A-G of Israel* v. *Eichmann* (1968) 36 ILR 5 (1st DC) and *A-G of Israel* v. *Eichmann* (1968) 36 ILR 277 (SC); see Matthew Lippman, 'Genocide: The Trial of Adolf Eichmann and the Quest for Global Justice' (2002) 8 *Buffalo Human Rights Law Review* 45.

15 *Demjanjuk*, US District Court (N.D. Ohio) 15.4.1985 and *Demjanjuk* v. *Petrovsky et al.*, US Court of Appeals (Sixth Circuit) 31.10.1985; see Jonathan Wenig, 'Enforcing the Lessons of History: Israel Judges the Holocaust' in McCormack and Simpson, *Law of War Crimes*, 115–18.

16 Israel Supreme Court 29.7.1993.

17 Supreme Court of Canada 24.3.1994; see Irwin Cotler, 'Bringing Nazi War Criminals in Canada to Justice: A Case Study' (1997) *ASIL Proceedings* 262, and Leslie C. Green, 'Canadian Law, War Crimes and Crimes Against Humanity' (1988) *59 BYBIL* 217.

18 High Court of Australia 14.8.1991.

19 *US* v. *Calley*, conviction of 29.3.1971 (sentence 31.3.1971), and US Military Court of Appeals decision 21.12.1973. However, Lieutenant Calley's commander, Captain Medina, was acquitted by court martial on 22.9.1971.

20 See William Schabas, 'National Courts Finally Begin to Prosecute Genocide, the Crime of Crimes' (2003) 1 *JICJ* 39; Firew Kebede Tiba, 'The *Mengistu* Genocide Trial in Ethiopia' (2007) 5 *JICJ* 513 at 518.

21 UN Doc. A/34/491 (20.9.1979).

22 See M. Cherif Bassiouni, *Crimes Against Humanity in International Law*, 2nd edn (The Hague, 1999) 549–51.

former Yugoslavia. Rwanda introduced new legislation on genocide in 1996 – dividing genocide into three categories based on the gravity of the crime, carrying different penalties – and started a large number of prosecutions. But with a huge number of detainees awaiting trial, said to be more than 100,000 people, the criminal system had to be reformed and traditional *gacaca* courts were introduced in 2001.[23] Nearly ten years on from the creation of these semi-formal courts, the backlog of cases, and the standards of justice they mete out have caused concern.

In the former Yugoslavia, the Dayton Agreement laid the ground for interaction between the ICTY, having primary jurisdiction over the relevant offences, and national authorities.[24] These relationships have improved over time and the ICTY has referred cases (where no ICTY indictment was issued) to courts in Croatia and Serbia. With respect to Bosnia and Herzegovina, a special scheme applied (called 'Rules of the Road') whereby the ICTY Prosecutor in effect vetted national cases before a domestic arrest warrant for war crimes was to be issued. The latter scheme ended in 2004 when the ICTY stopped issuing new indictments[25] and State authorities in Bosnia and Herzegovina took over the reviews.[26] As part of the completion strategy of the ICTY, cases where the ICTY has issued an indictment can now also be referred to national jurisdictions.[27] A number of cases have been referred to Bosnia, Croatia and Serbia under this scheme, although it now appears to have stalled.[28]

In addition, prosecutions of crimes committed in Rwanda and the former Yugoslavia have taken place in third States, such as Austria, Belgium, Denmark, Germany, Sweden and Switzerland. For example, the *Tadić* case originated as a domestic case in Germany but was taken over by the ICTY,[29] while the Butare Four case in Belgium proceeded after the ICTR had declined to exercise jurisdiction.[30]

The trend has extended beyond these two conflicts. A number of cases, often based on private complaints, have commenced in domestic courts, particularly in Europe,[31] regarding different conflicts all around the world. In some countries, however, for example the United States and Canada, denaturalization and deportation under the citizenship and immigration

---

23 See, e.g. William Schabas, 'Genocide Trials and Gacaca Courts' (2005) 3 *JICJ* 879.
24 See McCormack, 'Their Atrocities', 127–34.
25 See Chapter 7.
26 On the relationship between the ICTY and Bosnian courts see William W. Burke-White, 'The Domestic Impact of International Criminal Tribunals: The International Criminal Tribunal for Former Yugoslavia and the State Court of Bosnia and Herzegovina' (2007–2008) 46 *Columbia Journal of Transnational Law* 279.
27 *Ibid*. See also section 9.3.2.
28 See section 7.2.4.
29 See, e.g. Jan MacLean, 'The Enforcement of Sentence in the Tadić Case' in Fischer et al., *International and National Prosecution*, 727–31.
30 See, e.g. Luc Reydams, 'Belgium's First Application of Universal Jurisdiction: The Butare Four Case' (2003) 1 *JICJ* 428, and Damien Vandermeersch, 'Prosecuting International Crimes in Belgium' (2005) 3 *JICJ* 400.
31 For a survey, see e.g. Human Rights Watch, *Universal Jurisdiction in Europe: The State of the Art* (June 2006), available at www.hrw.org.

legislation have been preferred to criminal prosecution.[32] Specialized domestic courts for international crimes, sometimes referred to as 'inter-nationalized courts', have been established in some countries with international assistance.[33]

National prosecutions of international crimes have been highly selective and, generally, States have been unwilling to prosecute their own nationals.[34] There are examples to the contrary, however, and the numerous post-Second World War prosecutions of nationals in West and East Germany, the more recent prosecutions in the former Yugoslavia[35] and Rwanda, as well as the court martials in the US and UK of a number of soldiers for abusing (and in one case killing) detainees in Iraq[36] are notable exceptions. A high degree of selectiveness within one and the same conflict may project the message that all other activities were legal, or the non-prosecuted parties acted in an irreproachable way.[37] The political willingness to pursue national prosecutions is decisive.[38] A case regarding crimes committed in the prosecuting State may well end up putting the State itself on trial. The Barbie trial, for example, led to embarrassing questions about the French State's collaboration with the Nazis and the commission of international crimes in conflict in Algeria.[39] There are also other political considerations which either prevent national prosecutions altogether or make them highly selective.[40] Serious questions of legality present themselves (selectivity, vagueness of the law, retroactivity and very long time-periods between crime and prosecution).[41] The rather ambivalent feelings that exist also have an impact on legal mechanisms and principles relating to the obligations of States to prosecute or extradite the perpetrators of international crimes.

Another problem is that national courts often expose uneasiness and insecurity when dealing with international crimes. For example, national courts frequently refer to 'customary international law', but without an accompanying attempt to demonstrate the existence of

---

32 See, e.g. Irwin Cotler, 'R v. Finta' (1996) 90 *AJIL* 460, and Matthew Lippman, 'The Pursuit of Nazi War Criminals in the United States and Other Anglo-American Legal Systems' (1998) 29 *California Western International Law Journal* 1.

33 See Chapter 9.

34 See McCormack, 'Their Atrocities', 107–42.

35 E.g. in Croatia, see Ivo Josipović, 'Responsibility for War Crimes before National Courts in Croatia' (2006) 88:861 *International Review of the Red Cross* 145.

36 In the US see Roberta Arnold, 'The Abu-Ghraib Misdeeds: Will There Be Justice in the Name of the Geneva Conventions?' (2004) 2 *JICJ* 999. In the UK see Proceedings of a General Court Martial held at Military Court Centre Bulford in the case of Corporal Donald Payne and others, 7 September 2006 to 30 April 2007.

37 Gerry Simpson, 'War Crimes: A Critical Introduction' in McCormack and Simpson, *Law of War Crimes*, 21–6.

38 Marschik, 'The Politics of Prosecution', 100.

39 See Guyora Binder, 'Representing Nazism: Advocacy and Identity in the Trial of Klaus Barbie' (1989) 98 *Yale Law Journal* 1321.

40 See, e.g. examples regarding Italy after the Second World War, and Pakistan and Bangladesh after the 1971 Cessation War; Bassiouni, *Crimes Against Humanity*, 548–51.

41 See, e.g. Simpson, 'War Crimes: A Critical Introduction', 1–30.

such norms. Also, the legal reasoning in some of the judgments has been criticized as 'lightweight and generally superficial', at least when compared with the ICTY and ICTR judgments.[42]

4.3   State obligations to prosecute or extradite

4.3.1   Treaty obligations

A number of international treaties, which address international (or transnational) crimes, oblige the State Parties to investigate and prosecute the offence in question, or to extradite suspects to another State Party willing to do so: the so-called *aut dedere, aut judicare* ('to extradite or prosecute') principle.[43] Examples can be found in the four Geneva Conventions and Additional Protocol I,[44] covering war crimes that constitute 'grave breaches' under these instruments. The provisions are phrased in the imperative:

> Each High Contracting Party shall be under the obligation to search for persons alleged to have committed, or to have ordered to be committed, such grave breaches and shall bring such persons, regardless of their nationality, before its own courts [or hand them over to another High Contracting Party].

For other serious violations of the Geneva Conventions, which are not 'grave breaches', the principle does not apply under the treaty scheme, but States still have a right, although not a duty, to prosecute such violations.[45]

The principle also exists, inter alia, in the 1984 Torture Convention, the Convention on Enforced Disappearances,[46] and many terrorism-related treaties.[47] Such treaty clauses are often, although not entirely accurately, considered as allowing States to exercise 'universal jurisdiction',[48] and normally phrased in mandatory terms.[49] Newer provisions require States to 'submit' cases of alleged violations to the 'competent authorities for the purpose of prosecution', which is a wording that takes into account modern fair trial rights, such as the presumption of innocence, but which should not be understood to lessen the duty to

---

42 Schabas, 'National Courts', 63.

43 This maxim was originally devised by Hugo Grotius (*De Jure Belli ac Pacis*, 1624) as '*aut dedere . . . aut punire*' ('to extradite or punish'). For an extensive study, see Cherif Bassiouni and Edward Wise, *Aut Dedere, Aut Judicare: A duty to extradite or prosecute in international law* (Dordrecht, 1995).

44 Arts. 49–50 of GC I, Arts. 50–1 of GC II, Arts. 129–30 of GC III, Arts. 146–7 of GC IV, Arts. 11, 85–6, and 88 of AP I.

45 See Theodor Meron, 'Is International Law Moving towards Criminalization?' (1998) 9 *EJIL* 18 at 23.

46 International Convention for the Protection of All Persons From Enforced Disappearances GA Res 61/177 Annex, Articles 9, 11.

47 See Chapter 14.

48 See section 3.5.

49 Exceptions to this, however, are Art. 5 of the 1973 Apartheid Convention, and Art. 105 of the 1982 Law of the Sea Convention (piracy on the high seas), where the exercise of jurisdiction is instead phrased in permissive terms ('may').

prosecute if the evidence is there;[50] one should also note that many civil law jurisdictions provide for compulsory prosecutions when an evidentiary threshold is met. However, the obligations are only applicable between the Parties to the particular treaty.

The 1948 Genocide Convention, on the contrary, includes an undertaking by the States Parties to prevent and punish genocide, but the jurisdictional scope is restricted to the courts of 'the State in the territory of which the act was committed',[51] and there is no explicit *aut dedere, aut judicare* provision.[52] Nonetheless, some argue that the Convention may be read to include an obligation to prosecute or extradite.[53] Support for broader duties than those explicitly set out in the Convention has also been sought in ICJ jurisprudence, but such conclusions have been questioned,[54] and obtained little succour in the Court in the Merits phase of the *Bosnian Genocide* case. The Court expressly saw the obligation to prosecute as territorially limited, although the obligation to cooperate with relevant accepted international criminal tribunals was considered not to be thus limited where fugitives are found on the territory of the State.[55] In the latter situation the Court seemed to accept that prosecution of extra-territorial instances of genocide would suffice to fulfil this duty, probably on the basis that they were thinking of complementarity and the ICC. Domestic prosecution of crimes against humanity is not treaty-regulated except for torture and enforced disappearance (as separate crimes), and apartheid.

4.3.2   Human rights law obligations

As well as treaties explicitly covering international crimes, some have argued that since States have duties to 'respect and ensure'[56] the rights granted in the various human rights conventions, it could be that the latter clause implies a duty to prosecute certain serious violations of human rights. All acts constituting genocide and crimes against humanity would be serious violations of human rights when governments are responsible for them, as

---

50 Michael Scharf, 'The Letter of the Law: The Scope of the International Legal Obligation to Prosecute Human Rights Crimes' (1996) 59 *Law and Contemporary Problems* 41 at 46–7.

51 Art. 6 of the Genocide Convention; see also Arts. 1, 4 and 5.

52 The States Parties do agree, however, to grant extradition and not consider genocide a 'political crime': *ibid.*, Art. 7 (see section 5.4.3).

53 See, e.g. Eric David, *Principes de droit des conflits armés*, 2nd edn (Brussels, 1999) 667–8 (a modern interpretation of the Convention in light of Art. 1), and Lee A. Steven, 'Genocide and the Duty to Extradite or Prosecute: Why the United States is in Breach of its International Obligations' (1999) 39 *Virginia Journal of International Law* 425 at 460–1 (interpretation of Arts. 1 and 4–7).

54 Antonio Cassese, *International Criminal Law* (Oxford, 2003) 302–3, referring to the *Genocide* case ICJ opinion 28.5.1951 para. 23, and the *Bosnian Genocide* case ICJ judgment 11.7.1996 para. 31; cf. William Schabas, *Genocide in International Law* (Cambridge, 2000) 404–6, and Robert Cryer, *Prosecuting International Crimes: Selectivity and the International Criminal Law Regime* (Cambridge, 2005) 102–3.

55 *Bosnian Genocide* case, paras. 442, 449. See Anja Siebert-Fohr, *Prosecuting Serious Human Rights Violations* (Oxford, 2009) 154.

56 E.g. ICCPR, Art. 2.

would most war crimes. This may be supported by some case law from the Inter-American Court of Human Rights, in particular the *Velasquez-Rodriguez* v. *Honduras* case,[57] and more recently the *Barrios Altos* case, which takes a very dim view of amnesties.[58] It is difficult to say, however, that these cases on positive duties under human rights treaties can be read as creating an absolute duty to prosecute all international crimes in all circumstances.[59] Cases from the inter-American system are in advance of the jurisprudence of those of, for example the European Court of Human Rights and Human Rights Committee,[60] and responded to the specific circumstances the Inter-American institutions were dealing with. Therefore, the jurisprudence of the Inter-American Court should not be borrowed directly, in its uncompromising formula and legal reasoning, by other human rights bodies for situations which are structurally different.[61]

4.3.3   Customary obligations and ius cogens *arguments*

Beyond treaty obligations, genocide, crimes against humanity and, at least in part, war crimes are also criminalized in customary international law.[62] As mentioned above, some national prosecutions have taken place, but these are rare and actual State practice does not support the position that States have a general duty to prosecute international crimes. In legal commentary, it has been suggested that a duty to prosecute or extradite nevertheless exists in customary international law; if correct, the duty would bind States regardless of whether they are parties to the relevant treaty. The claim is sometimes made by reference to a particular crime, but sometimes by reference to all international crimes.

There are expressions in support of a customary duty. The 1996 ILC Draft Code of Crime Against the Peace and Security of Mankind, for example, advocated a duty to prosecute or extradite individuals accused of genocide, crimes against humanity and war crimes, as defined in the Code, and to prohibit such crimes regardless of where or by whom the crime was committed.[63] The ICTY Appeals Chamber in *Blaškić* has stated that there is a

---

57 (1989) 28 ILM 291. The classic statement of the argument is Diane Orientlicher, 'Settling Accounts: The Duty to Prosecute Violations of a Prior Regime' (1991) 100 *Yale Law Journal* 2537. See also *Barrios Altos Case (Chumbipuma Aguirre et al. v. Peru)* Judgment of 14 March 2001; Series C No. 75 [2001] IACHR 5.

58 See, e.g. Lisa J. Laplante, 'Outlawing Amnesty: The Return of Criminal Justice in Transitional Schemes' (2009) 49 *Virginia Journal of International Law* 915.

59 E.g. Michael Scharf, 'The Letter of the Law: The Scope of the International Legal Obligation to Prosecute Human Rights Crimes' (1996) 59 *Law and Contemporary Problems* 1; Bruce Broomhall, *International Justice and the International Criminal Court* (Oxford, 2003) 98–100; Cryer, *Prosecuting International Crimes*, 103–5.

60 See the comprehensive review in Siebert-Fohr, *Prosecuting Serious Human Rights Violations, passim*.

61 *Ibid.*, at 109. See further, Chapter 22.2.1.

62 See further, Chapters 10–12.

63 Arts. 8–9. See also the 1996 ILC Report, at 42–50.

customary obligation to prosecute or extradite those who have allegedly committed grave breaches of international humanitarian law, but without developing the argument further.[64] The Preamble of the ICC Statute 'recall[s] the duty of every State to exercise its criminal jurisdiction over those responsible for international crimes', although without clarifying the jurisdictional scope of this 'duty' or being reinforced by any operative provision in the Statute.

In making the case for a customary duty, reference has been made to certain General Assembly resolutions as an expression of *opinio juris*.[65] But close scrutiny of the wording and voting record gives rise to doubts, and the majority of State practice, particularly on amnesties, speaks against an existing customary duty to prosecute international crimes.[66] A strong case can be made, however, that such a duty is emerging concerning prosecutions based on territoriality, and perhaps nationality, jurisdiction.[67]

Another line of argument is that a duty to prosecute follows from the nature of international crimes: the core crimes of international criminal law rest on norms of *ius cogens* (peremptory norms)[68] and as such give rise to obligations *erga omnes* (towards the entire international community).[69] Advocating this position, Bassiouni has argued that the *erga omnes* obligation is not to grant impunity to violators of such crimes and thus to prosecute or extradite, and this argument wins support in ICJ case law so far as genocide is concerned.[70] A linked hypothesis is the existence of an international community (a *civitas maxima*) with a common interest in repressing international crimes which, combined with the right of every State to prosecute international crimes, has led to a duty to prosecute or extradite. Hence, shared moral values have turned into a legal obligation. Taken together, the proponents assert that a customary duty exists in spite of the fact that there is no consistent State practice or *opinio juris* in support of this view. Unsurprisingly, others reject or question this conclusion and many of the underlying assertions.[71]

---

64 *Blaškić* ICTY A. Ch. 29.10.1997 para. 29. Cf. *Furundžija* ICTY T. Ch. II 10.12.1998 paras. 153–7, where the implication of torture being a *jus cogens* crime was discussed, but not with respect to a duty to prosecute or extradite.

65 GA Res. 2840(XXVI) of 18.12.1971 and 3074(XXVIII) of 3.12.1973; see Jordan Paust, *International Law as Law of the United States* (Durham NC, 1996) 405.

66 See, e.g. Cryer, *Prosecuting International Crimes*, 105–10.

67 See, e.g. Darryl Robinson, 'Serving the Interests of Justice: Amnesties, Truth Commissions and the International Criminal Court' (2003) 14 *EJIL* 481, Siebert-Fohr, *Prosecuting Serious Human Rights Violations*, ch. 7.

68 See Art. 53 of the Vienna Convention on the Law of Treaties.

69 See *The Barcelona Traction* case ICJ 5.2.1970 at 32.

70 M. Cherif Bassiouni, 'International Crimes: Jus Cogens and Obligatio Erga Omnes' (1996) 59 *Law and Contemporary Problems* 63. See also the ICJ in the *Genocide* case 28.5.1951 para. 23 and the *Bosnian Genocide* case 11.7.1996 para. 31.

71 See Cryer, *Prosecuting International Crimes*, 110–17. For arguments for and against, see Bassiouni and Wise, *Aut Dedere, Aut Judicare*.

The conclusion that there is a duty to prosecute or extradite does not automatically resolve the scope of criminal jurisdiction to be exercised by States, in particular third States. But as we have seen in Chapter 3, it is widely held that these crimes are subject to permissive 'universal jurisdiction' by States. An argument of mandatory 'universal jurisdiction' (due to the *ius cogens* status of the crimes or otherwise) would in fact result in most States being in constant breach of the obligation, which brings into question whether State practice does indeed indicate the existence of such a custom.

4.4   Domestic criminal law and criminal jurisdiction

4.4.1   *Domestic legislation*

Of course, national prosecutions presuppose that there is applicable criminal law and criminal jurisdiction.[72] The Genocide and Geneva Conventions explicitly require that the States Parties enact necessary legislation.[73] Some States adopt implementing legislation, while others rely upon direct application of international law in the domestic system; hence, not all States will need domestic legislation to meet their treaty obligations. A number of States have enacted special penal law on war crimes and genocide, either in a civil or a military penal system or both. Prior to the ICC Statute, there was no generally accepted convention on crimes against humanity, and thus these crimes were only rarely provided for as distinct crimes in domestic law. Aggression is criminalized in a minority of States.[74]

Most of the underlying offences that can constitute genocide or crimes against humanity have long been criminalized and prosecuted under domestic law, but as ordinary crimes and not in the qualified form of genocide or crimes against humanity. This posed an obstacle to prosecutions in France until the Court of Cassation in *Barbie* established that crimes against humanity, as embodied in the Nuremberg Charter, were directly applicable in France.[75] The ruling paved the way for further prosecutions of Second World War crimes and for subsequent French legislation on genocide and other '*crimes contre l'humanité*'.

Reliance upon 'ordinary crimes' may fall short of criminalization in international law, and thus the State may violate its duty to enact with the manifestation of seriousness that is embedded in the international crimes.[76] In Australia, the approach to rely on ordinary crimes

---

72 On jurisdiction, see Chapter 3.

73 Art. V of the Genocide Convention, Art. 49 of GC I, Art. 50 of GC II, Art. 129 of GC III, and Art. 146 of GC IV.

74 See Chapter 13.

75 Court of Cassation 26.1.1984, rejecting an earlier ruling by the same court in *Touvier* 30.6.1976 where crimes against humanity were considered 'ordinary crimes'; see Sadat Wexler, 'The French Experience', 293–4.

76 This approach has hindered referral of cases from the Tribunals; *Bagaragaza* ICTR A.Ch. 30.8.2006.

in meeting the obligations under the Genocide Convention led a domestic court to the conclusion that genocide was not recognized and could not be prosecuted.[77]

In some cases, the special legislation that is introduced is unsatisfactory. And even if the definitions correspond to those of international law, other aspects such as the modes of liability set forth in the Genocide Convention are sometimes overlooked or inadequately addressed by the application of ordinary domestic criminal law principles.[78] Customary international law is rarely reflected.[79] This will hinder prosecution of crimes that are based on international custom only.[80] Some States (e.g. Germany) do not accept non-written criminal law, due to a strict interpretation of the legality principle. Other States do accept such law (e.g. common law jurisdictions like the United Kingdom), and also direct application of customary international law by national courts, but not that customary international law is capable of creating offences in domestic law;[81] the power to create new crimes should be reserved for the democratic process and elected assemblies.[82]

Moreover, national legislation has sometimes been carefully designed or interpreted to have a selective application. Perhaps the most criticized feature of the *Barbie* case was the imposition by the Court of Cassation of the (additional) requirement that crimes against humanity be committed 'in the name of a State practising a hegemonic political ideology'.[83] This requirement, which also affected subsequent French trials, excluded application to crimes during France's own de-colonialization conflicts in Indochina and Algeria. Likewise, earlier Australian law on war crimes, as interpreted in the *Polyukhovic* case, excluded crimes in East Timor. In Israel, the Nazis and Nazi Collaborators (Punishment) Act of 1950, providing for crimes against humanity, war crimes and 'crimes against the Jewish people', is solely retroactive.[84] Yet another example is the 1991 War Crimes Act in the United Kingdom which was restricted to violations of the laws of war when committed on German or German-occupied territory between 1939 and 1945; an Act that the House of

---

77 *Nulyarimma* v. *Thompson* [1999] FCA 1192.

78 See Art. III of the Genocide Convention; see also Schabas, *Genocide*, 350–2.

79 See, however, the Canadian Crimes Against Humanity and War Crimes Act 2000, s. 4(4), which allows for custom, and the German Code of Crimes against International Law 2002 which incorporates rules of customary international law into the definitions of certain crimes.

80 See Helmut Kreicker, 'National Prosecution of Genocide from a Comparative Perspective' (2005) 5 *ICLR* 313 at 319–20. Note, however, that French courts in *Barbie* and other cases accepted criminal responsibility grounded on customary international law.

81 See, e.g. *R* v. *Bow Street Metropolitan Stipendiary Magistrate ex parte Pinochet Ugarte (No. 3)* [2000] 1 AC 147, and *Nulyarimma* v. *Thompson* [1999] FCA 1192.

82 The UK House of Lords has held that customary international law can no longer create crimes in the UK legal order: *R* v. *Jones* [2006] UKHL 16; see Patrick Capps, 'The Court as Gatekeeper: Customary International Law in English Courts' (2007) 70 *Modern Law Review* 458. A small door may have been left open, however, in relation to war crimes.

83 French Court of Cassation 20.12.1985.

84 See further Wenig, 'Enforcing the Lessons of History', 102–22.

Lords rejected twice with reference to retroactivity and selectivity before it was passed.[85] Even when national courts interpret international law in good faith, there is a significant chance that judges not well versed in international law may misunderstand what it requires.[86] On the other hand, the use of domestic law offences, although more familiar to municipal judges, can sometimes lead to standards being imposed that are narrower than those set by international law.[87]

4.4.2   The ICC as a catalyst for domestic legislation

The fundamental principle that the ICC is to assume jurisdiction only when States fail to do so, the complementarity principle,[88] provides a strong incentive for States to enact the crimes laid down in the ICC Statute and, to a greater or lesser extent, assume jurisdiction over crimes committed abroad.[89] Although not a legal obligation under the Statute, States will want to meet the 'complementarity test'.[90] It is also an opportunity to express a commitment to combating impunity for the most abhorrent international crimes. This has already led to new penal legislation being passed in a number of States, sometimes in spite of having been parties to the relevant conventions for a long time, and the process is under way in others.[91]

The introduction of such laws is a complex task, however, and requires careful political and legal considerations. When it is politically important to ensure a criminalization that coincides with that of the ICC, and thus to prevent the ICC from intervening in future cases, the safest option is to adopt the offences as defined in the ICC Statute. This is the approach taken by, inter alia, Australia, Canada, New Zealand, South Africa and the United Kingdom.[92] Another approach is to transform the offences into the normal legal terminology

---

85 See, e.g. A. T. Richardson, 'War Crimes Act 1991' (1992) 55 *Modern Law Review* 73 at 77, and Marschik, 'The Politics of Prosecution', 87–9.

86 See, e.g. the Italian Lozano case, and Antonio Cassese, 'The Italian Court of Cassation Misapprehends the Notion of War Crimes: The Lozano Case' (2008) 6 *JICJ* 1077.

87 See, e.g. Nathan Rasiah, 'The Court Martial of Corporal Payne and Others and the Future Landscape of International Criminal Justice' (2009) 7 *JICJ* 177. Although, as he notes at 198, elsewhere the converse may be the case.

88 See section 8.6.

89 See, e.g. Katherine Doherty and Timothy McCormack, 'Complementarity as a Catalyst for Comprehensive Domestic Penal Legislation' (1999) 5 *UC Davis Journal of International Law and Policy* 147; Mark Ellis, 'The International Criminal Court and Its Implications for Domestic Law and National Capacity Building' (2002) 15 *Florida Journal of International Law* 215; Broomhall, *International Justice and the International Criminal Court*, 86–93; Darryl Robinson, 'The Rome Statute and Its Impact on National Law' in Cassese, *Commentary*, 1849–69.

90 But see section 8.6.4 for cases of uncontested admissibility.

91 For a collection of such legislation, see www.nottingham.ac.uk/law/hrlc/international-criminal-justice-unit/implementation-database.php.

92 See D. Turns, 'Aspects of National Implementation of the Rome Statute: The United Kingdom and Selected Other States' in D. McGoldrick et al. (eds), *The Permanent International Criminal Court: Legal and Policy Issues* (Oxford, 2003) 337–87.

of the national system as has been done, for example, in Germany.[93] In this process, however, States must also take into account their other international obligations concerning international crimes. Accordingly, the German approach has been to focus on customary international law offences.[94] Yet another approach is to ensure that 'ordinary' domestic offences cover all conduct that also falls within the crimes of the Statute. Neither the 'complementarity test' nor the related *ne bis in idem* provisions (see section 4.7) require that the State and the ICC make the same legal characterization of the underlying conduct (i.e. that national law also includes genocide, crimes against humanity and war crimes as specific offences and relevant conduct is prosecuted as such).

In this process, the scope of national criminal jurisdiction as well as the applicable principles of criminal law and penalties must also be considered. States are free to choose solutions other than those provided for the ICC, but again the choice may affect the capacity to meet the 'complementarity test'; and other international obligations must also be adhered to.

4.4.3   Impact of domestic and international case law

National courts consider foreign case law to a greater or lesser extent. While it is natural in common law jurisdictions to pay attention to decisions from other (common law) jurisdictions, civil law jurisdictions often have a more reluctant approach to jurisprudence as a source of law. But the persuasive effect of court decisions, particularly those of higher courts, is similar. Domestic jurisprudence may also have an impact as a source of law for international criminal courts, as the practice of the ICTY and ICTR shows.[95] Such decisions may serve as tools for the interpretation of treaties, identification and interpretation of rules of customary international law or general principles of law, and perhaps even as independent authorities.

Decisions of international courts are a recognized, but formally a subsidiary, means for determining international law. In practice, these decisions have made very important contributions to the development of international criminal law, from the Nuremberg and Tokyo IMTs to the ICC. Not least, the ICTY and ICTR have made a lasting impact by operating for many years and providing important clarifications of various issues. To what extent international jurisprudence is considered by national courts depends upon how international law is generally integrated into and applied within the domestic legal order. Some domestic legislation, for example in the United Kingdom, explicitly requires that national courts take into account decisions and judgments of the ICC and any other relevant

---

93 See, e.g. Helmut Satzger, 'German Criminal Law and the Rome Statute: A Critical Analysis of the New German Code of Crimes against International Law' (2002) 2 *International Criminal Law Review* 261.

94 However, this approach entails risks of going further than other States would accept, or not going far enough to meet the 'complementarity test'; see Robinson, 'The Rome Statute', 1861–2.

95 See André Nollkaemper, 'Decisions of National Courts as Sources of International Law: An Analysis of the Practice of the ICTY' in William Schabas and Gideon Boas (eds.), *International Criminal Law Developments in the Case Law of the ICTY* (Leiden, 2003) 277–96.

international jurisprudence.[96] In other States which have incorporated international crimes into domestic law, national courts will normally be under an obligation to interpret the domestic provisions in accordance with the interpretation of equivalent international provisions, including that made by international criminal tribunals.[97] A 'bizarre and unfortunate' exception to this is the US Military Commissions Act 2006, section 6(2) of which expressly disavows reliance on non-US interpretations of international legal obligations in relation to war crimes.[98] As domestic legislation this does not, however, affect the international legal obligations of the US.

4.5 Statutory limitations

Most domestic systems know statutory limitations, or prescription (i.e. time limitations on prosecution). While most civil law jurisdictions provide for a general application, most common law jurisdictions exclude murder and other serious crimes. Neither the post-Second World War trials, nor the Geneva Conventions or Genocide Convention, address the issue, but subsequently there has been much debate regarding the application of statutory limitations with respect to genocide, crimes against humanity and war crimes. Statutory limitations aim to prevent unjust delays between the commission of the offence and prosecution (or punishment), but could, if applicable, lead to impunity for the most heinous international crimes. In order to close this possible 'technical' escape from liability, treaties on the non-applicability of statutory limitations to genocide, crimes against humanity and war crimes were adopted under the auspices of the UN and the Council of Europe.[99] Some States have also passed laws which make statutory limitations inapplicable to such crimes, but these laws vary in scope. There is also some municipal and international case law to the effect that statutory limitations shall not apply to international crimes, for example the ICTY ruling regarding torture in *Furundžija*.[100] The ICC Statute explicitly provides that statutory limitations do not apply.[101] The Enforced Disappearances Convention, although stopping short of disapplying statutes

---

96 International Criminal Court Act 2001, s. 66(4) (UK). See generally Robert Cryer, 'Neither Here nor There? The Status of International Criminal Jurisprudence in the International and UK Legal Orders' in Michael Bohlander and Kaiyan Kaikobad (eds.), *International Law and Power: Perspectives on Legal Order and Justice: Essays in Honour of Colin Warbrick* (The Hague, 2010) 183.

97 See, e.g. the *Jorgić* case German Federal Constitutional Court 12.12.2000.

98 S3930. See Michael J. Matheson, 'The Amendment of the War Crimes Act' (2007) 101 *AJIL* 49 at 55.

99 Convention on the Non-Applicability of Statutory Limitations to War Crimes and Crimes Against Humanity of 26.11.1968; European Convention on the Non-Applicability of Statutory Limitations to Crimes Against Humanity and War Crimes of 25.1.1974.

100 *Furundžija* ICTY T. Ch. II 10.12.1998 para. 157. See also the *Barrios Altos Case* IACtHR 14.3.2001 para. 41. A recent domestic decision is the *Sandoval Case* Supreme Court of Chile 17.11.2004 (on enforced disappearances).

101 Art. 29 of the ICC Statute.

of limitation for individual disappearances,[102] provides that any limitation shall take into account the exceptional seriousness of disappearances and shall only run from the end of the offence, given its continuing nature.[103]

But statutes of limitations have been obstacles in national prosecutions.[104] In the *Barbie* case,[105] for example, the French law on non-application of such limitations was strictly interpreted to apply only to crimes against humanity, thus barring prosecution for war crimes. Similarly, prescription concerning war crimes also led to the acquittal by Italian courts in the *Hass and Priebke* case, where the accused had admitted to a massacre of hundreds of civilians during the Second World War. Still, war crimes carrying life imprisonment under Italian law were considered exempt from statutory limitations. In 1976, Swiss authorities had to refuse extradition to the Netherlands of Second World War criminal Pieter Menten due to statutory limitations (and were also prevented from prosecuting the case),[106] as did the lower Argentine courts when considering the extradition of Erich Priebke to Italy, although he was eventually extradited to face trial, and was convicted.

It has been claimed that the non-applicability of statutory limitations to war crimes has developed into a norm of customary international law.[107] Others restrict the claim of a customary rule to genocide, crimes against humanity and torture.[108] While there is clearly a move towards an acceptance that statutory limitations shall not apply, the fact remains that many States still apply such limitations to international crimes in their domestic legal orders and that the two Conventions have a modest number of States Parties.[109] For example, both German and Dutch law retain statutory limitations for the least serious war crimes, even against the general non-applicability of such limitations in the ICC Statute.[110] The assertion of a customary norm may thus be premature.[111] However, it

---

102 Art. 5 of the Enforced Disappearances Convention provides a savings clause for crimes against humanity of enforced disappearance.

103 *Ibid.*, Art. 8(1)(b).

104 See further Christine Van den Wyngaert, 'War Crimes, Genocide and Crimes Against Humanity – Are States Taking National Prosecutions Seriously?' in Cherif Bassiouni (ed.), *International Criminal Law*, 2nd edn (New York, 1999), vol. III, 233–5.

105 French Court of Cassation 26.1.1984.

106 See Andreas Ziegler, 'Domestic Prosecution and International Cooperation with Regard to Violations of International Humanitarian Law: The Case of Switzerland' (1997) 7 *Schweizerische Zeitschrift für internationales und europäisches Recht* 561 at 570–1.

107 Henckaerts and Doswald-Beck, *ICRC Customary Law*, 614–18.

108 See, e.g. Cassese, *International Criminal Law*, 319.

109 In October 2009, the UN Convention had fifty-three States Parties and the European Convention had three Parties (and one signatory).

110 See Harry Verweij and Martijn Groenleer, 'The Netherlands' Legislative Measures to Implement the ICC Statute' in R. S. Lee, *States' Responses to Issues Arising from the ICC Statute: Constitutional, Sovereignty, Judicial Cooperation and Criminal Law* (New York, 2005) 97, and Satzger, 'German Criminal Law and the Rome Statute', 272–3.

111 See also Gaeta, 'War Crimes Trials', 766.

is important to note that domestic legislation does not affect liability under international law, and there is no positive rule of international law providing for prescription of liability for international crimes, and as such, liability under international law is not subject to prescription.

4.6   The Non-retroactivity principle

Related to statutory limitations is the principle of non-retroactivity of criminal law, which in turn forms part of the legality principle.[112] The question of compatibility with the non-retroactivity principle arises when a limitation period is extended or set aside retroactively or when extraterritorial jurisdiction is introduced retrospectively. National courts have accepted retroactive criminality with respect to Second World War crimes, in so far as the crimes were considered covered by conventional or customary international law at the time the offence was committed. Both the Supreme Court of Canada in *Finta* and the High Court of Australia in *Polyukhovic* accepted this regarding crimes committed abroad; the French Court of Cassation in *Barbie* resolved the issue by considering crimes against humanity as directly applicable international crimes. States will consider statutory limitations as either substantive or procedural rules, and the principle of legality is only applicable to the former, but there must in any case be grounds for concluding that the crime existed at the time of its commission.[113]

Some ICC-related legislation addresses the question of retroactivity. According to the Canadian Crimes Against Humanity and War Crimes Act 2000, for example, crimes committed outside Canada may be prosecuted retrospectively, but prosecution of crimes committed before the adoption of the ICC Statute (on 17 July 1998) is allowed only in so far as the crimes correspond to the state of customary law at the time of their commission.[114] The Act also clarifies that the crimes defined in the ICC Statute are deemed to reflect customary law at the latest when the Statute was adopted, possibly earlier, and that crimes against humanity were criminal according to customary international law or general principles of law recognized by civilized nations prior to the Nuremberg IMT Charter or the Tokyo IMT Charter.[115] The New Zealand International Crimes and International Criminal Courts Act 2000 establishes start dates for jurisdiction over genocide and crimes against humanity,[116] which reflect the date when New Zealand ratified the Genocide Convention (for genocide) and the date when the jurisdiction of the ICTY

---

112 See section 1.5.1.
113 See Van den Wyngaert, *National Prosecutions*, 235–7.
114 Crimes Against Humanity and War Crimes Act 2000, s. 6.
115 *Ibid*. The charters were adopted on 8.8.1945 and 19.1.1946 respectively.
116 International Crimes and International Criminal Court Act 2000, s. 8(4).

commenced (for crimes against humanity). Similar provisions are likely to come into force in the UK in 2010.[117]

4.7   *Ne bis in idem* **or double jeopardy**

4.7.1   *Application between States*

The principle that no one shall be tried or punished more than once for the same offence, expressed as *ne bis in idem* or double jeopardy, is reflected in the major human rights treaties,[118] and is an expression of the broader principle of finality and the binding effect of judgments (the doctrine of *res judicata*). Reasons of fairness to defendants and the interest of thorough investigations and preparations of cases by the prosecutorial authorities motivate the principle. The principle also applies in the context of international cooperation in criminal matters.[119]

But these provisions relate only to proceedings in one and the same State.[120] Hence, it is lawful for a State to prosecute a person for an offence for which he or she has been prosecuted, and even punished, elsewhere. Part of this is an outcropping of the principle of sovereign equality. One State's courts cannot bind another. Different States view the effects of a foreign criminal judgment differently. In many common law jurisdictions, for example, the plea of *autrefois acquit, autrefois convict* is not restricted to a previous acquittal or conviction in the same domestic jurisdiction.[121] In other States, the practice ranges from almost complete recognition of foreign judgments to no recognition at all, while most States recognize some foreign judgments to a limited extent. When retrials are allowed, municipal law sometimes demands that a penalty imposed and served abroad is taken into account in sentencing.

Basic differences in the common law and civil law traditions, on issues such as the finality of a judgment, appeals against acquittals and determination of the same act (*idem*), influence the application of the principle.[122] While some States apply a narrow interpretation of *idem*, covering only the conduct in law ('the offence'), other States give it a broader meaning whereby the conduct both in law and in fact is covered. Exceptions may apply, however, and difficult questions arise with respect to conduct that constitutes multiple offences, or

---

117 Coroners and Justice Act 2009. Section 70 provides for jurisdiction over genocide, war crimes and crimes against humanity committed since 1991.
118 E.g. Art. 14(7) of the ICCPR, and Art. 4 of Protocol 7 to the ECHR.
119 See section 5.3.3.
120 See, e.g. Christine Van den Wyngaert and Guy Stessens, 'The International *non bis in idem* Principle: Resolving Some of the Unanswered Questions' (1999) 48 *ICLQ* 779. However, some argue that this is a serious lacuna in the protection of individual human rights, e.g. Alexander Poels, 'A Need for Transnational Non Bis In Idem Protection in International Human Rights Law' (2005) 23 *Netherlands Quarterly of Human Rights* 329.
121 See, e.g. *Treacy* v. *DPP* [1971] AC 537.
122 Christine Van den Wyngaert and Tom Ongena, '*Ne bis in idem* Principle, Including the Issue of Amnesty' in Cassese, *Commentary*, 710–15.

continuing offences. When interpreting the principle, the European Court of Human Rights has arrived at different conclusions,[123] and the European Court of Justice has accepted that the principle is applied differently by different EU member States.[124] There is also no general consensus as to what decisions, apart from convictions and acquittals, may bar new proceedings. Candidates are other decisions which prevent further proceedings, based on abuse of process, 'extinction' of the right to prosecute, certain out-of-court settlements and more controversial plea-bargaining agreements and decisions not to prosecute.[125]

Thus, although the principle applies internally in almost all domestic systems, its cross-border application remains controversial and is not recognized as a customary rule or a general principle of law.[126] It is sometimes argued, however, that a customary rule concerning cross-border application of the principle is evolving, at least with regard to international crimes,[127] as a corollary to the right to exercise universal jurisdiction. Rather than (even more) complex *ne bis in idem* provisions, which provide a 'first come first served' solution, attempts are being made within the EU to find a mechanism that identifies and prioritizes the most appropriate jurisdiction.[128] In support of the evolving norm there, the provisions of the ICTY, ICTR and ICC Statutes all establish that the principle shall apply both ways in the relationship between the international and national courts.

4.7.2 Application vis-à-vis international criminal jurisdictions

The establishment of international criminal jurisdictions adds another dimension to the *ne bis in idem* principle. In line with their primary jurisdiction vis-à-vis States,[129] the ICTY and ICTR Statutes provide that no one may be tried for the same conduct after he or she has been prosecuted at the Tribunal, but the Tribunals are not hindered by domestic proceedings in certain circumstances;[130] the set criteria relate both to the quality of the national proceedings and to the interest of enjoining the seriousness of international crimes. Only finalized

---

123 On Art. 4 of Protocol 7 to the ECHR: see, e.g. *Gradinger* v. *Austria* ECtHR 23.10.1995 and *Fischer* v. *Austria* ECtHR 29.8.2001 (broad interpretations of *idem*), *Oliveira* v. *Switzerland* ECtHR 30.7.1998 (more narrow interpretation).

124 On Art. 54 of the 1990 Convention Implementing the Schengen Agreement see, e.g. *Gözütok and Brügge* ECJ 11.2.2003 paras. 31–3, *Miraglia* ECJ 10.3.2005, and *Van Esbroeck* ECJ 9.3.2006 paras. 25–42 (also applying a broad interpretation of *idem*).

125 In this sense, the ECJ has adopted a quite far-reaching approach, see cases referred to in n. 124.

126 See, e.g. Gerard Convay, 'Ne Bis in Idem in International Law' (2003) 3 *ICLR* 217.

127 See, e.g. Cassese, *International Criminal Law*, 320–1.

128 EC Commission, *Green Paper on Conflicts of Jurisdiction and the Principle of ne bis in idem in Criminal Proceedings* 23.12.2005 (COM(2005)696 final). See also Anke Biehler, Roland Kniebühler, Juliette Lelieur-Fischer and Sibyl Stein (eds.), *Freiburg Proposal on Concurrent Jurisdiction and the Prohibition of Multiple Prosecutions in the European Union* (Saarbrücken, 2003).

129 See Chapter 7.

130 Art. 10 of the ICTY Statute and Art. 9 of the ICTR Statute. The same applies between the SCSL and Sierra Leone, see Arts. 8–9 of the SCSL Statute.

national proceedings can bar prosecution before the Tribunal.[131] The 'deduction of sentence' principle applies in the event that the Tribunal retries the person.

The jurisdiction of the ICC, on the other hand, is complementary to that of States, which calls for a different *ne bis in idem* regime.[132] Apart from barring subsequent ICC proceedings regarding the same (factual) conduct,[133] convictions and acquittals by the ICC preclude the person being tried by a national (or another international) court 'for a crime referred to in Article 5' that was subject to the conviction or acquittal. Interestingly, it seems that owing to the latter provision, although national courts cannot prosecute a person for an international crime after he or she has been prosecuted for it at the ICC, they could prosecute him or her, on the basis of the same conduct, for a domestic crime.[134] It may be understandable that States would want to preserve the right to try a person for murder after an unsuccessful war crimes charge at the ICC, for example when no armed conflict could be established, but as worded the provisions would also allow a subsequent national murder trial in spite of a war crimes conviction on the same facts by the ICC.

The ICC Statute also provides that national decisions concerning 'conduct also proscribed under Article 6, 7 or 8' (of the Statute) hinder prospective ICC prosecutions, but with certain exceptions. Again 'sham trials' do not bar subsequent international proceedings. There is, however, no exception for cases where the national court has dealt with the matter as an 'ordinary crime'; it is the underlying facts, not the legal characterization, that are decisive. Moreover, the ICC is required to assess whether the national proceedings were conducted independently and impartially 'in accordance with the norms of due process recognized by international law'. The ICC Statute does not require the Court to apply the 'deduction of sentence' principle, but provides instead for discretional deduction of time spent in detention 'in connection with conduct underlying the crime'.[135]

4.8   Practical obstacles to national prosecutions

Where national prosecution is of crimes committed abroad, there are special demands relating to security, logistics and international cooperation. Some countries have established specialized police and prosecution units to deal with crimes of this kind, for example Canada, Denmark, the Netherlands, Norway and the United Kingdom.

Where international cooperation is required it may have attendant problems. In many cases, proceedings have been extended due to problems concerning apprehension of the

---

131 *Tadić* ICTY T. Ch. II 14.11.1995; *Musema* ICTR T. Ch. I 12.3.1996 para. 12.
132 Art. 20 of the ICC Statute.
133 This provision is subject to exceptions as provided in the ICC Statute, for example revision of conviction or sentence (Art. 84) and, according to some, appeals against an acquittal (Art. 81).
134 Immi Tallgren, 'Article 20' in Triffterer, *Observers' Notes*, 669; Van den Wyngaert and Ongena, '*Ne bis in idem* Principle', 723.
135 Art. 78(2) of the ICC Statute.

accused.[136] Eichmann was abducted in another State, Barbie was 'expelled' (but not 'extradited') from Bolivia, Touvier was, for a long time, in hiding in France, and many others have escaped justice because of extradition requirements. Documentary and physical evidence are normally difficult to secure and witness evidence is therefore crucial.

National prosecutions have regularly taken place long after the event. This may make live evidence impossible to obtain or may affect the reliability of the statements made; key witnesses may have forgotten critical events and misidentified the accused, as in the *Polyukhovich* and *Demjanjuk* cases. The difficulty of obtaining evidence may also affect fair trial rights and some national courts have applied rules of evidence more liberally to defence evidence as a protection against unjust convictions. Examples are the *Finta* case in Canada and the *Demjanjuk* case in Israel.[137] Furthermore, old defendants may no longer be fit to stand trial or to serve a prison sentence; for example, the *Papon* case and the abandoned UK trial against Szyman Serafinowicz.[138] But domestic prosecutions are the backbone of international criminal law enforcement, since international tribunals cannot undertake prosecution of even a minority of international crimes, and as such one of their major functions is to encourage prosecutions at the domestic level.

Further reading

M. Cherif Bassiouni, *Crimes Against Humanity in International Criminal Law*, 2nd edn (The Hague, 1999).

Horst Fischer, Claus Kress and Sascha Rolf Lüder (eds.), *International and National Prosecution of Crimes Under International Law: Current Developments* (Berlin, 2001).

Roy S. Lee (ed.), *States' Responses to Issues Arising from the ICC Statute: Constitutional, Sovereignty, Judicial Cooperation and Criminal Law* (New York, 2005).

Timothy McCormack and Gerry Simpson (eds.), *The Law of War Crimes: National and International Approaches* (The Hague, 1997).

Steven R. Ratner, Jason S. Abrams and James L. Bischoff, *Accountability for Human Rights Atrocities in International Law: Beyond the Nuremberg Legacy*, 3rd edn (Oxford, 2009) ch. 8.

William Schabas, *Genocide in International Law*, 2nd edn (Cambridge, 2008).

David Turns, 'Aspects of National Implementation of the Rome Statute: The United Kingdom and Selected Other States' in Dominic McGoldrick, Peter Rowe and Eric Donnelly (eds.), *The Permanent International Criminal Court: Legal and Policy Issues* (Oxford, 2003) 337–87.

---

136 See Chapter 5.
137 Richard May, 'The Collection and Admissibility of Evidence and the Rights of the Accused' in Lattimer and Sands (eds.), *Justice for Crimes*, 167–9.
138 See Jane Garwood-Cutler, 'The British Experience' in Bassiouni, *International Criminal Law*, 325–6.

Christine Van den Wyngaert, 'War Crimes, Genocide and Crimes Against Humanity – Are States Taking National Prosecutions Seriously?' in Cherif Bassiouni (ed.), *International Criminal Law*, 2nd edn (New York, 1999), vol. III, 227–39.

Christine Van den Wyngaert and Tom Ongena, '*Ne bis in idem* Principle, Including the Issue of Amnesty' in Antonio Cassese et al. (eds.), *The Rome Statute of the International Criminal Court* (Oxford, 2002) 705–29.

The ICRC collects and makes available national legislation and case law (www.icrc.org), with updates also published in the *International Review of the Red Cross*.

Country reports on legislation and practice are collected in:

Albin Eser, Ulrich Sieber and Helmut Kreicker (eds.), *Nationale Strafverfolgung völkerrechtlicher Verbrechen – National Prosecution of International Crimes* (Max-Planck Institute (2003–05) S 95.1–95.6) vols. 1–6.

5

State Cooperation with Respect to National Proceedings

5.1 Introduction

Criminal law and proceedings are at the heart of state sovereignty and cooperation in criminal matters is a voluntary undertaking; a State is not obliged to cooperate with others in criminal matters unless it has agreed to do so. But over time, the parochial view that criminal law, including its effects, is local in nature has given way to an ever-growing need for and actual regulation of international legal cooperation. Influential factors in this regard are increased cross-border activities, including the commission of crimes, international terrorism and the development of human rights.

International crimes are of concern to all States and therefore lend themselves to efforts at cooperation. A commitment to cooperate, in the form of extradition, is the alternative to prosecution in accordance with the *aut dedere, aut judicare* principle, when applicable.[1] Cooperation is particularly important when the State is exercising jurisdiction over crimes committed abroad, but may also be necessary when a State is investigating and prosecuting crimes committed on its own territory. Prosecution of genocide, crimes against humanity and war crimes is no exception.

But international law, treaty and custom has not (yet) developed a special regime for State-to-State cooperation concerning these crimes.[2] The Geneva Conventions and Additional Protocol I, for example, explicitly refer to cooperation in accordance with domestic legislation.[3] One must therefore resort to general principles and provisions of international and domestic law on international cooperation in criminal matters. In relation to the ICTY, ICTR and ICC, however, State cooperation is subject to separate regimes to which we shall return in Chapter 20.

---

1 See Chapter 4.
2 See, however, e.g. GA res. 3074(XXVIII) of 3.12.1973, which establishes a special regime but does not reflect custom.
3 Art. 49 of GC I, Art. 50 of GC II, Art. 129 of GC III, Art. 146 of GC IV and Art. 88 of AP I.

Traditional forms of legal cooperation[4] are: extradition, mutual legal assistance, transfer of criminal proceedings and enforcement of foreign penalties. In addition, there is an ever-increasing degree of cooperation, at various levels of formality, between police and other law enforcement authorities in different States.

5.2   International agreements

Originally informal, extradition was the first form of legal cooperation to be regulated by international (bilateral and later multilateral) agreements. Other forms of cooperation were subsequently added, first as auxiliary measures to extradition and only later as independent forms of assistance. In the 1960s further steps were taken, especially within the Council of Europe, to extend the cooperation into transfer of criminal proceedings (delegation of prosecution) and post-conviction measures.

Most States require a bilateral or multilateral agreement as a condition for providing cooperation, and thus reciprocity, but States can also grant assistance unilaterally. However, the quantity and quality of international agreements and, even more pronounced, domestic legislation on legal cooperation is unevenly distributed across the world. Some States have concluded a great number of bilateral agreements. Some regions have very advanced multilateral regimes, for example in Europe where both the Council of Europe and the EU are very active in this field,[5] and also within the Commonwealth. But there is no global extradition or mutual legal assistance treaty of general application and many States rely on international and national regimes that are rudimentary, outdated, or restricted to special crimes. In order to assist States, the UN has developed Model Treaties concerning all major forms of cooperation.[6] Assistance with implementing legislation is also provided by the UN, other organizations and individual States.

State cooperation is addressed in various multilateral treaties, the primary function of which is to codify international or transnational crimes and oblige the States Parties to combat them by criminalizing certain acts and provide for criminal jurisdiction. The older treaties, however, address cooperation only in very general terms. For example, the contracting parties to the 1948 Genocide Convention 'pledge themselves … to grant

---

4 The terminology in this field is subject to some controversy. Civil law jurisdictions seem to prefer the term 'international judicial assistance', which reflects the judicial involvement in criminal investigations in these countries, while common law jurisdictions rather refer to 'international or mutual legal assistance'. Other distinctions have been suggested between assistance (to a foreign criminal investigation or trial) and transfer (of proceedings or penalty enforcement), and between extradition and other (lesser) forms of assistance.

5 Regional treaties have also been adopted under the auspices of the Organization of American States, the League of Arab States, and the Commonwealth of Independent States.

6 On 14.12.1990 the UN General Assembly adopted Model Treaties on extradition (res. 45/116), mutual assistance in criminal matters (res. 45/117), transfer of proceedings in criminal matters (res. 45/118), and transfer of supervision of those conditionally sentenced or conditionally released (res. 45/119).

extradition in accordance with their laws and treaties';[7] the 1977 AP I to the Geneva Conventions,[8] as well as the 1984 Torture Convention,[9] require the parties to afford each other 'the greatest measure of assistance'. Nevertheless, many treaties explicitly provide that the relevant crime shall be an extraditable offence and that the treaty may satisfy domestic conditions that a treaty obligation for extradition exists.

More recent treaties, however, elaborate further on legal cooperation in criminal matters and include more or less complete regimes for extradition, mutual legal assistance and sometimes other forms of legal cooperation. Examples of multilateral UN treaties are the 1988 Drug Trafficking Convention,[10] the 2000 Transnational Organized Crime Convention (the Palermo Convention),[11] and the 2003 Corruption Convention.[12] Less detailed, and with a particular focus on extradition (and temporary transfer of detainees and prisoners), are the 1997 Terrorist Bombings Convention[13] and the 1999 Terrorist Financing Convention.[14]

With respect to terrorism, however, there are also some examples where the Security Council has ordered a State to surrender suspects for prosecution in another State, and thereby circumvented the normal requirements for extradition, including that of a treaty base.[15]

Some specialized organizations operate in this area.[16] Most well known is the International Criminal Police Organization (Interpol), originally established in 1923 and with 187 member countries, which provides a police communications system, databases (of criminals and stolen property), and operational police support services. Other examples are the European Police Office (Europol) and the EU's Judicial Cooperation Unit (Eurojust), both created within the EU. In addition, different networks exist, including the European network of contact points for investigation of genocide, crimes against humanity and war crimes.[17]

5.3 Some basic features

Both in law and in practice, cooperation in criminal matters is characterized by a dichotomy between state sovereignty, and hence a preference for one's own system, and a common interest and solidarity among States in combating crimes, which in turn requires trust in the

---

7 Art. 7. See also Art. 49 of GC I, Art. 50 of GC II, Art. 129 of GC III and Art. 146 of GC IV.
8 Art. 88.
9 Art. 9.
10 Arts. 6–11
11 Arts. 13–14, 16–21.
12 Arts. 43–50. In addition, the Convention entails an advanced scheme for cooperation concerning asset recovery, Arts. 51–59.
13 Arts. 8–14.
14 Arts. 9–17.
15 See Chapter 14; see also Michael Plachta, 'The Lockerbie Case: The Role of the Security Council in Enforcing the Principle Aut Dedere Aut Judicare' (2001) 12 *EJIL* 125.
16 See, e.g. D. McClean, *International Co-operation in Civil and Criminal Matters* (Oxford, 2002) 161–2 and 167–8.
17 EU Council Decision 2002/494/JHA of 13.6.2002.

legal systems of others. State-to-State cooperation is horizontal in nature – each State is considered sovereign and equal – which is manifested, inter alia, by reciprocity requirements and extensive grounds to refuse a request for cooperation.

There is also an obvious link between international legal cooperation and the exercise of extraterritorial criminal jurisdiction.[18] The more far-reaching the extraterritorial jurisdiction is, the more problematic the issue of competing, concurrent jurisdictions will be, and this in turn will often hamper cooperation .

5.3.1 Traditional assistance and 'mutual recognition'

Traditionally, the requesting State asks for assistance with a certain measure (or seeks a particular result) and the requested State, if granting the request, takes the measure according to the conditions and the procedures prescribed by its domestic law. Strict formalities and lengthy procedures often plague cooperation and a scheme of this kind does not always produce results that are useful in the requesting State, particularly if the laws are very different or if strict conditions apply regarding, for example, the admissibility of evidence. Efforts have therefore been made to improve this traditional format, inter alia, by allowing the requesting State to prescribe procedural requirements and to participate when measures are taken on its behalf.[19] There is also a move away from the traditional, and often inefficient, diplomatic channel for cooperation requests in favour of specialized central authorities in the States, often located within the Ministry of Justice or Home Office, or even direct communications between the judicial authorities in the different States.

Within the EU a further, and more radical, step has been taken with the introduction of a principle of 'mutual recognition' of foreign judicial decisions as the cornerstone for legal cooperation among the Member States.[20] This development of the horizontal approach to cooperation includes an *ipso facto* recognition and execution of foreign orders or requests with a minimum of formality. The concept rests on a high level of mutual trust and similar, or at least well-known, procedural principles and human rights standards; the 'approximation' of laws (the politically correct term within the EU for 'harmonization') is a closely related issue. First articulated as a general principle in 1999, it has subsequently been implemented in different instruments, most notably regarding the European Arrest Warrant.[21]

---

18 See, e.g. Christopher Blakesley and Otto Lagodny, 'Finding Harmony Amidst Disagreement over Extradition, the Role of Human Rights, and Issues of Extraterritoriality under International Criminal Law' (1991) 24 *Vanderbilt Journal of Transnational Law* 1.

19 See, e.g. Art. 18 of the 2000 Palermo Convention and Arts. 2 and 8 of the 2001 Additional Protocol II to the 1959 European Convention on Mutual Assistance in Criminal Matters.

20 Generally, see Ilias Bantekas, 'The principle of mutual recognition in EU criminal law' (2007) 32 *European Law Review* 365.

21 Council Framework Decision of 13.6.2002 on the European Arrest Warrant and the Surrender Procedures between Member States, OJ L190, 18.7.2002, pp. 1–20. See section 5.4.1.

5.3.2   Double criminality, rule of specialty and statutory limitations

Although cooperation originates from a common interest in combating crimes, international agreements and domestic laws impose strict requirements for cooperation and States retain broad powers to refuse requests from other States.

The principle of 'double criminality' (or 'dual criminality') has long been applied, requiring that the underlying act (or omission) is criminal in both the requesting and the requested State. The principle stems from the principle of legality (*nulla poene sine lege*), but is also closely linked to state sovereignty and reciprocity.[22] It is often asserted that the requirement, although sometimes discretionary, constitutes a major obstacle to effective cooperation and many commentators argue that it is no longer necessary; other grounds for refusal, such as *ordre public*, offer sufficient protection of State interests.[23] But the assertion is not empirically proven and others argue that the double-criminality requirement serves to protect human rights.[24] Many newer instruments, particularly in the EU, seek to abolish the requirement, at least partially; the European Arrest Warrant, for example, does not require double criminality regarding selected crimes, including 'crimes within the jurisdiction of the International Criminal Court'.[25] Some older examples exist too regarding States with similar laws and a long tradition of close cooperation, for example extradition among the Nordic States.[26]

Moreover, the double-criminality rule is applied differently. Some States require identical crimes, while others are satisfied if the underlying facts constitute any crime (of sufficient gravity, if required) in both legal systems. However, this could entail not only a comparison of the definition of the crime (*in abstracto*), but also applicable grounds for excluding criminal responsibility in the case at hand (*in concreto*). A further restriction is the requirement in some countries that not only the conduct but also the applicable criminal jurisdiction of the requesting State must be equivalent to that of the requested State; the exercise of jurisdiction in the requesting State must also have been possible in the requested State.[27] The latter practice hinders cooperation when the requesting State applies extraterritorial jurisdiction and the jurisdiction of the requested State is primarily based upon territoriality, as is

---

22 Generally, see Nils Jareborg (ed.), *Double Criminality – Studies in International Criminal Law* (Uppsala, 1989).

23 See, e.g. Thomas Weigend, 'Grundsätze und Probleme des Deutschen Auslieferungsrecht' (2000) 40/2 *Juristische Schulung* 105 at 107.

24 See, e.g. Michael Plachta, 'The Role of Double Criminality in International Cooperation in Penal Matters' in Jareborg (ed.), *Double Criminality*, 128–9.

25 Art. 2 of the Framework Decision on the European Arrest Warrant; see also the 1996 EU Extradition Convention (Art. 7).

26 As a result of legislative cooperation, extradition laws with substantively the same content have been enacted by Denmark, Finland, Norway and Sweden in 1959–61 (double criminality is not required except concerning extradition of nationals and political offences). Similarly, witnesses are required to give evidence before a court of another Nordic State without any double-criminality requirement. However, this scheme is being replaced by a Nordic Arrest Warrant, established by the Convention on Surrender for Crime between the Nordic States of 15.12.2005.

27 See also the Framework Decision of 13.6.2002 on the European Arrest Warrant, Art. 4(7)(b).

normally the case in common law jurisdictions. In addition to these conditions, the double-criminality rule also has a temporal aspect: the House of Lords in the *Pinochet* case controversially established that the double-criminality requirement must be met at the time of the offence and not (only) at the time of the extradition request.[28]

With respect to genocide, crimes against humanity and war crimes, the ICC Statute and the incentive to enact domestic legislation that the complementarity principle provides, offer hope for improved cooperation even if a double-criminality requirement is retained among States. Many have adopted, or are considering, similar, if not identical, crimes and broader criminal jurisdiction in national law, which should reduce the room for refusals on double-criminality grounds.

The rule of specialty, which is common in extradition treaties,[29] restricts the requesting State to bringing proceedings only with respect to the crimes for which the suspect was extradited; the double-criminality principle and other conditions for extradition, such as the political offence exception, would otherwise easily be defeated. However, the requested State could always consent to prosecution of other offences and within the EU some agreements provide a presumption of consent under certain circumstances as well as a possibility for the suspect to waive entitlement of the specialty rule.[30] For mutual legal assistance, the imposition of conditions on the use or transmission of information and material furnished by the requested State, may serve the same purpose.[31]

Also linked to the double-criminality requirement are statutory limitations, which in some domestic systems apply generally and may bar cooperation; concerning extradition, some agreements, such as the 1957 European Extradition Convention,[32] explicitly allow statutory limitations as a discretionary ground for refusal. In other systems, like the United Kingdom, serious offences are not subject to such limitations, but extradition may still be refused because the passage of time would make it 'unjust and oppressive' (a *habeas corpus* ground).[33] As we have seen in Chapter 4, this also applies to international crimes in many States and no customary rule prevents this practice.

5.3.3   Ne bis in idem *or double jeopardy*

As described in section 4.7, the principle of *ne bis in idem* is a general criminal law principle in most national systems, but one that is normally confined to application within the same

---

28 *R* v. *Bow Street Metropolitan Stipendiary Magistrate ex parte Pinochet Ugarte (No.3)* [1999] 2 All ER 97, HL. See Colin Warbrick, 'Extradition Aspects of Pinochet 3' (1999) 48 *ICLQ* 958.

29 E.g. Arts. 14–15 of the 1957 European Extradition Convention.

30 E.g. Art. 10 of the 1996 EU Extradition Convention, and Art. 27 of the Framework Decision on the European Arrest Warrant. A third protocol to the 1957 European Extradition Convention with waiver provisions is currently being negotiated within the Council of Europe.

31 E.g. Art. 18(19) of the 2000 Palermo Convention.

32 Art. 10 of the 1957 European Extradition Convention.

33 Extradition Act 2003, ss.11, 14, 79 and 82 (UK).

system. But so long as criminal proceedings are not prevented by a judgment (or other final decision) in another State, criminal proceedings concerning the same person and criminal act (or omission) might already be finalized in the requested State when the request is made. This is even more likely regarding offences over which States exercise extraterritorial jurisdiction.

Traditionally, international extradition agreements acknowledge the principle with regard to the requested State by prohibiting extradition if that State has already passed a final judgment against the fugitive. The 1957 European Extradition Convention and, more recently, the European Arrest Warrant provide such grounds for refusal.[34] Similarly, this ground for refusal is provided for other forms of cooperation; while some treaties aim at preventing double punishment only,[35] others seek to prevent double prosecutions too.[36]

Furthermore, there is a trend towards giving the principle a broader application, especially in the EU with the commitment to recognize each other's judicial decisions (mutual recognition). Not only evidence gathering and seizure but also arrests are now subject to such recognition. Consequently, the EU States are allowed, under certain conditions, to refuse execution of a European Arrest Warrant if the fugitive has already been finally adjudged by a third State concerning the same act.[37] This increases the scope for rejecting a request and preserves the common law plea of *autrefois acquit, autrefois convict* without a special reservation to the international instrument.[38] But there is no general rule of international law preventing extradition because of a judgment in a third State.

However, the lack of common standards for the application of the *ne bis in idem* principle (see section 4.7) complicates cooperation and increasingly international courts such as the European Court of Human Rights and the European Court of Justice have had to address how it should be applied to different forms of cooperation.[39]

5.3.4   Human rights and legal cooperation

In criminal law there is often a tension between the fundamental human rights afforded to individuals and the State interest in efficient law enforcement and prosecution; international cooperation in criminal matters is no exception. Extradition laws and treaties have

---

34 Art. 9 of the 1957 European Extradition Convention (and the 1975 Additional Protocol), and Art. 3(2) of the Framework Decision on the European Arrest Warrant.

35 See, e.g. Arts. 35–7 of the 1972 European Convention on Transfer of Proceedings in Criminal Matters (mandatory ground for refusal), and Art. 18(1)(e) of the 1990 European Proceeds from Crime Convention (optional ground for refusal).

36 See, e.g. Arts. 54–8 of the 1990 Convention Implementing the Schengen Agreement (albeit with certain exceptions).

37 Art. 4(5) of the Framework Decision on the European Arrest Warrant.

38 The United Kingdom made a formal reservation to Art. 9 of the 1957 European Extradition Convention.

39 See, e.g. John Vervaele, 'The transnational *ne bis in idem* principle in the EU: mutual recognition and equivalent protection of human rights' (2005) 1 *Utrecht Law Review* 100.

traditionally been interpreted in favour of the request. In common law jurisdictions the 'rule of non-inquiry' has often discouraged the courts from inquiring into the fairness of the proceedings of the requesting State. But while the trend is generally to limit the grounds for refusing cooperation, human rights considerations point in the opposite direction: cooperation, particularly extradition, should not be granted if fundamental human rights of the person concerned would be at risk.

Indeed, one important prerequisite for the more far-reaching cooperation in Europe, and the underlying level of confidence in each other's legal systems, is the adherence to common and well-developed human rights standards. There are calls for better safeguards within the EU, a task that is complicated by the separate system of the Council of Europe, to which all EU Member States belong, but not yet the EU itself. Such efforts are particularly important today when the international fight against terrorism, which includes improved cooperation, is challenged for violating and eroding fundamental human rights.[40]

An early expression of the human rights concerns is the *non-refoulement* principle which applies in refugee law and provides that a refugee should not be returned to a country where he or she is likely to be persecuted, as established in the 1951 Refugee Convention; a principle to which exception is made, however, concerning those who have committed a 'crime against peace, a war crime, or a crime against humanity' or 'a serious non-political crime'.[41]

That domestic human rights protection, constitutional or otherwise, is applicable also to legal cooperation is natural, and established by courts in many States. It was long unclear, however, whether international human rights obligations would apply, and even trump, international cooperation obligations. But in the groundbreaking *Soering* decision of 1989, the European Court of Human Rights established that States Parties to the ECHR have certain obligations to protect individuals against a serious breach of their human rights in another State: 'knowingly to surrender a fugitive to another State where there were substantial grounds for believing that he would be in danger of being subjected to torture', or of inhuman or degrading treatment, would be a violation of the ECHR.[42] Also, 'a flagrant denial of a fair trial' in the requesting country may hinder extradition.[43] The UN Human Rights Committee has followed suit when interpreting the ICCPR.[44]

However, the international human rights bodies only apply the treaties they are established to protect and do not have to choose between conflicting treaty obligations or apply the domestic laws[45] by which these obligations are implemented. The opposite is true for

---

40 See generally, Chapter 14, and Helen Duffy, *The 'War on Terror' and the Framework of International Law* (Cambridge, 2005).
41 Art. 1 of the 1951 Refugee Convention.
42 *Soering* v. *United Kingdom* (1999) ECHR 14, para. 88.
43 *Ibid.*, para. 113.
44 See, e.g. *Ng* v. *Canada* HRC 5.11.1993.
45 The ECtHR has nonetheless assumed certain powers to review the compliance with domestic law, which also applied to detention pending extradition; see, e.g. *Bordovskiy* v. *Russia* (2005) ECHR 66, paras. 41–4.

domestic courts. In some countries the courts can rely upon the constitution, or laws which take precedence over other laws, for example a law incorporating the ECHR, to afford priority to human rights considerations, while in other countries this is reflected in the legislation on international cooperation in criminal matters. From an international law perspective, however, the justification must be sought elsewhere; it has been suggested that certain human rights norms have higher status, based on *jus cogens* notions, and that multilateral human rights conventions have primacy over other international agreements on *ordre public* grounds.[46] But this is controversial and would in any case not go beyond the most serious violations, such as torture, and no general human rights exception from extradition exists today.[47]

Human rights standards do not only play a role in extradition. Material that has been obtained abroad through mutual legal assistance could also be affected by violations, for example evidence obtained by torture,[48] and therefore be inadmissible in the requesting State. Other difficulties relate to data protection concerning transferred information and third party rights in case of the seizure or freezing of property.

5.4   Extradition

Extradition is the surrender of a person by one State to another, the person being either accused of a (extraditable) crime in the requesting State or unlawfully at large after conviction. This is a considerable intrusion in the liberty of the person concerned, but one which is justified by the common interest of States in combating crimes and expunging safe havens for fugitives. The standard term being 'extradition', terms such as 'surrender' or 'transfer' are sometimes used, often with a view to signal a substantive difference.[49]

Extradition is normally subject to strict requirements. The already mentioned principle of double criminality and the rule of specialty apply and the offences must also be extraditable. The requested State may deny extradition with reference to *ne bis in idem*, which sometimes also covers a pardon or an amnesty in that State or a third State.[50]

Additionally, numerous grounds for refusal apply and conditions may be imposed. By allowing States to grant extradition in accordance with domestic law and applicable treaties, as is the case in the 1948 Genocide Convention and in the 1949 Geneva Conventions, the *aut dedere aut judicare* obligation is qualified. Hence, the States may apply the same conditions as for all other crimes. The provisions of the 1984 Torture Convention are different,

---

46 Dugard and Van den Wyngaert, 'Reconciling Extradition', 194–5.
47 *Ibid.*, at 205–6; but see Art. 1(3) of the Framework Decision on the European Arrest Warrant.
48 *A(FC)* v. *Secretary of State for the Home Department (No. 2)* [2005] UKHL 71; [2006] 2 AC 221.
49 See, e.g. Michael Plachta, '"Surrender" in the context of the International Criminal Court and the European Union' (2004) 19 *Nouvelles études pénales* 465.
50 The 1975 Additional Protocol (Ch. II.2) and the 1978 Second Additional Protocol (Ch. IV.4) to the 1957 European Extradition Convention.

however, and it is sometimes argued that a condition such as non-extradition of nationals (see section 5.4.4) may not be invoked to refuse extradition concerning torture; but in practice many States do refuse extradition of nationals even in torture cases.[51] With all these hurdles requests for extradition are not always successful and one may ask what effect the obligation has on the requested State when refusing to extradite. To be meaningful the principle must mean that the requested State shall take domestic action if extradition is denied.[52] But this could entail jurisdictional and practical difficulties and there is little State practice in support of this view to date.[53]

5.4.1   Extradition agreements and the European Arrest Warrant

Many States insist on reciprocity and require an international agreement for extradition. Apart from numerous bilateral agreements, the basic multilateral treaty in Europe is the 1957 European Extradition Convention and its Additional Protocols, adopted by the Council of Europe, which represent a traditional scheme. The EU has followed suit and adopted two conventions in 1995 and 1996, which provide for simplified proceedings and reduced grounds for refusal but they are not widely ratified.[54]

Among the EU Member States, however, the European Arrest Warrant has replaced the traditional extradition scheme and introduced a system whereby a warrant in one State shall be recognized and enforced (arrest and surrender) in all other member States. Building upon the principle of mutual recognition of judicial decisions, the European Arrest Warrant restricts many traditional grounds for refusal.[55] This has prompted amendments to domestic laws, either by special legislation (e.g. Sweden) or amendments to the existing extradition legislation (e.g. the United Kingdom). The scheme is generally perceived as successful. In relation to non-EU States, however, extradition still applies in accordance with multilateral or bilateral agreements and domestic extradition legislation.

As mentioned in section 5.2, global penal law conventions and anti-terrorism conventions include provisions on extradition. A common provision is that States, which make extradition conditional on the existence of a treaty, may accept the convention as the legal basis for such cooperation.

---

51 See, e.g. Arnd Düker, 'The Extradition of Nationals: Comments on the Extradition Request for Alberto Fujimori' (2003) 4 *German Law Journal* 1165.
52 See also Jean Pictet (ed.), *The Geneva Conventions of 12 August 1949: Commentary* (Geneva, 1960), vol. III, 623.
53 See Dugard and Van den Wyngaert, 'Reconciling Extradition', 209–10.
54 The 1995 Convention on Simplified Extradition Procedures (OJ C78, 30.3.1995, p. 2) and the 1996 Convention Relating to Extradition between the Member States of the European Union (OJ C313, 13.10.1996, p. 12).
55 See, e.g. Nicola Vennemann, 'The European Arrest Warrant and Its Human Rights Implications' (2003) 63 *ZaöRV* 103.

5.4.2   Extradition procedures

The extradition procedures follow the law and practice of the requested State and applicable extradition agreements. Traditionally, the requesting State requests the arrest and extradition, or provisional arrest to be followed within a certain time by a surrender request, of the accused or convicted person. The requested State institutes proceedings to execute the request. In most States, both the executive and the judiciary have a role to play in the proceedings: a court considers the formal requirements and the actual surrender is an executive decision. The European Arrest Warrant, on the other hand, is to be recognized and enforced as such in the other Member States with minimal formalities. This scheme is also an example of a general trend towards a primarily judicial process.

The framing of the procedures depends upon the view taken on the extradition process as such.[56] Traditionally, it is seen as exclusively an arrangement between sovereign States, which will check the formal requirements and protect fundamental rights and fairness; the individual will play an insignificant role being merely the object of the proceedings. The opposite view, inspired by the development of human rights, is that the process entails rights that the fugitive may claim individually. Hence, the proceedings can be more or less extensive and time consuming in different States. In common law countries the *habeas corpus* principle extends also to extradition and offers an additional ground to challenge a foreign request.[57] Linked to this, these countries also require that the prosecution evidence against the fugitive justifies the trial for which extradition is sought; supporting evidence is required and a prima facie test is applied. While the United Kingdom has made exceptions to this requirement in recent years – vis-à-vis EU Member States and certain other countries, including the USA[58] – it still applies in many other common law jurisdictions.

In many common law jurisdictions, courts have long applied a rule of non-inquiry regarding the good faith and motive behind the extradition request or the standards of criminal justice of the requesting State;[59] it would conflict with the principle of comity if courts were to 'assume the responsibility for supervising the integrity of the judicial system of another sovereign nation'.[60] Instead, such considerations of justice and international relations form part of the executive decision whether to extradite. A consequence is that the fugitive may not bring evidence concerning discrimination or other possible human rights

---

56 For further discussion, see M. Cherif Bassiouni, *International Extradition: United States Law & Practice*, 5th edn (New York, 2007) 33–47.

57 On UK law see, e.g. Stanbrook and Stanbrook, *Extradition Law and Practice*, 237–48.

58 Extradition Act 2003.

59 For jurisprudence, see Dugard and Van den Wyngaert, 'Reconciling Extradition', 189–91.

60 *Jhirad* v. *Ferrandina* US Court of Appeals 12.4.1976 para. 22; 536 F.2d 478.

violations, and the practice has been criticized.[61] But the rule is not without exceptions[62] and the application varies considerably between different jurisdictions. In the United Kingdom and Ireland, the European Arrest Warrant has prompted mandatory judicial considerations of human rights issues.[63] In civil law jurisdictions as well, the presumption is that the extradition request is made in good faith, but the courts often accept challenges by the fugitive regarding human rights violations.

5.4.3   Extraditable and non-extraditable offences

Extradition is normally restricted to serious offences, often by reference to a minimum level of punishment,[64] which might simplify, but does not do away with, a double-criminality requirement. International and transnational crimes are regularly extraditable, regardless of whether the *aut dedere aut judicare* principle of a particular treaty or a general requirement of gravity applies.

In addition, certain classes of offences are typically excluded from extradition. Most agreements, and thus domestic legislation, provide, as the main rule, that offences of a political nature are non-extraditable;[65] the requested State avoids getting involved in conflicts abroad and preserves its right to grant political asylum. What will be considered a 'political offence' is not internationally defined, however, which leaves room for considerable discretion.[66] It has been criticized as being 'a "blackbox" for cases in which the requested state wants neither to extradite nor to reveal the actual grounds for the refusal'.[67] The scope of application is potentially broad but it has been reduced in some domestic jurisdictions by distinguishing between 'absolute' and 'relative' political offences where only the former will always prevent extradition. Today, however, a number of terrorism treaties explicitly provide that the crimes in question shall not be regarded as a political

---

61 See, e.g. Richard J. Wilson, 'Toward the Enforcement of Universal Human Rights Through Abrogation of the Rule of Non-Inquiry in Extradition' (1997) 3 *ILSA Journal of International & Comparative Law* 751; David B. Sullivan, 'Abandoning the Rule of Non-Inquiry in International Extradition' (1999) 15 *Hastings International & Comparative Law Review* 111.

62 E.g. *R (Saifi)* v. *Governor of Brixton Prison* Court of Appeal 21.12.2000 (extradition denied since evidence of false statements by police officers meant that the accusation was not made in good faith in the interests of justice).

63 See Susie Alegre and Marisa Leaf, 'Mutual Recognition in European Judicial Cooperation: A Step Too Far Too Soon? Case Study – the European Arrest Warrant' (2004) 10 *European Law Journal* 200 at 203–5.

64 Some countries, e.g. the United Kingdom and the US, have instead referred to a list of offences, with the drawback of repeatedly requiring amendments.

65 For example, extradition from the US to the UK was denied in a number of cases involving members of the Irish Republican Army; see Bassiouni, *International Extradition*, 679–701.

66 See, e.g. Bert Swart, 'Human Rights and the Abolition of Traditional Principles' in A. Eser and O. Lagodny (eds.), *Principles and Procedures for a New Transnational Criminal Law* (Freiburg, 1992) 505–34. Generally, see Christine Van den Wyngaert, *The Political Offence Exception to Extradition: The Delicate Problem of Balancing the Rights of the Individual and the International Public Order* (The Hague, 1980).

67 Blakesley and Lagodny, 'Finding Harmony Amidst Disagreement', 46–7.

offence for the purpose of extradition.[68] The 1948 Genocide Convention[69] also has such a clause and, in Europe, the 1975 Additional Protocol to the 1957 European Extradition Convention clarifies that genocide and certain war crimes shall not prevent extradition by being considered political offences.[70] The scope for applying the political offence exception to international crimes is thus restricted and the trend is increasingly to consider 'freedom fighters' as criminal, which is due, not the least, to more ruthless and violent methods being employed. The European Arrest Warrant applies to offences of a certain gravity, including the crimes under the ICC Statute, and does not include a political offence exception.

Another, often excluded, group of offences is military offences.[71] These are offences according to military law, but not ordinary criminal law, and should not hinder extradition for international crimes such as war crimes. Fiscal offences are also traditionally exempt from extradition.

5.4.4   Non-extradition of nationals

Many States, primarily civil law jurisdictions, prohibit the extradition of their own nationals; the principle is based on a historical duty of the State to protect its citizens, sovereignty, and indeed distrust in foreign legal systems, and it is often constitutionally protected.[72] As a counterweight, many of these States provide for extensive criminal jurisdiction over offences committed abroad. This in turn may prevent extradition, however, if the national is in a third State and that State also considers the applied theory of jurisdiction when determining the double-criminality requirement (see section 5.3.2) and takes a restrictive view on jurisdiction, which is often the case in common law countries. This was a key issue in the *Pinochet* case in the United Kingdom where the House of Lords accepted the jurisdiction of the requesting State (Spain) only from the date when the UK had implemented the 1984 Torture Convention (and thus accepted extraterritorial jurisdiction).[73]

Within the EU, efforts have been made to do away with nationality as a ground for refusal.[74] The European Arrest Warrant is an example, which has prompted constitutional discussions and amendments in Member States. As a result the requested State retains a right

---

68 See Chapter 14.
69 Art. 7.
70 Art. 3 of the Additional Protocol.
71 E.g. Art. 4 of the 1957 European Extradition Convention.
72 See, e.g. Michael Plachta, '(Non-)Extradition of Nationals: A Never-ending Story?' (1999) 13 *Emory International Law Review* 77.
73 *R* v. *Bow Street Metropolitan Stipendiary Magistrate ex parte Pinochet Ugarte (No.3)* [1999] 2 All ER 97 at 107 and 135–6. For a critical view, see Warbrick, 'Extradition Aspects of Pinochet 3'.
74 See, e.g. Zsuzsanna Deen-Racsmány and Rob Blekxtoon, 'The Decline of the Nationality Exception in European Extradition? The Impact of the Regulation of (Non-)Surrender of Nationals and Dual Criminality under the European Arrest Warrant' (2005) 13 *European Journal of Crime, Criminal Law and Criminal Justice* 317.

to refuse surrender if it chooses to exercise jurisdiction itself, or it may request the return of the fugitive for service of any custodial sentence or detention order.[75] Similarly, the 2000 Palermo Convention acknowledges the condition that an extradited national of the requested State be returned for the service of any sentence imposed.[76]

5.4.5   Death penalty, life imprisonment and other human rights grounds

Many States that have abolished capital punishment domestically also prohibit extradition when the fugitive may face the death penalty, unless the requesting State undertakes not to impose this penalty in the case at hand or at least not to enforce it.[77] This is in keeping with commitments made in certain human rights treaties and the *Soering* principle that a State is bound by its human rights obligations with respect to extradition. Some international treaties also enshrine this extradition condition.[78] But the penalty as such is not banned under customary international law (see section 19.1), and hence the *Soering* case addressed the matter as a part of the prohibition of torture or inhumane or degrading treatment or punishment.[79]

The 1984 Torture Convention also provides that extradition is not allowed to a country where the fugitive would be in danger of torture.[80] Inhumane and degrading treatment or punishment is a less clear and thus more difficult concept. While the *Soering* case found that 'the death-row phenomenon' falls under the prohibition, the UN Human Rights Commission has not so found and instead attacked the methods of execution.[81] Corporal punishment, poor prison conditions and harsh interrogation methods may also meet the criteria for refusal.[82]

Life imprisonment is also a problematic concept in some States, and even unconstitutional, and there are regional examples where life imprisonment prevents extradition.[83] One solution, provided by the European Arrest Warrant, is to allow States to make the surrender conditional on the issuing State providing for review of life sentences.[84]

---

75 Arts. 4(6) and 5(3) of the Framework Decision on the European Arrest Warrant.
76 Art. 16(11).
77 See William Schabas, 'Indirect Abolition: Capital Punishment's Role in Extradition Law and Practice' (2003) 25 *Loyola of Los Angeles International and Comparative Law Review* 581.
78 E.g. Art. 11 of the 1957 European Extradition Convention.
79 Art. 3 of the ECHR. See also *Öcalan* v. *Turkey* (2005) ECHR 282, paras. 162–75 (also considerations under Art. 2 of the ECHR regarding unfair proceedings and the death penalty).
80 Art. 3(1); see Chapter 14. See also Art. 3(f) of the UN Model Treaty on Extradition.
81 See *Ng* v. *Canada* HRC 5.11.1993 and *Kindler* v. *Canada* HRC 11.11.1993.
82 See, e.g. *Tyrer* v. *United Kingdom* (1978) ECtHR 25.4.1978, *Ireland* v. *United Kingdom* ECtHR 18.1.1978, and *Boudellaa et al.* v. *Bosnia and Herzegovina et al.* Human Rights Chamber for Bosnia and Herzegovina 11.10.2002.
83 E.g. Art. 9 of the 1981 Inter-American Extradition Convention.
84 Art. 5(2) of the Framework Decision on the European Arrest Warrant.

A common clause in international agreements, inspired by the *non-refoulement* principle, prevents extradition when there are substantial grounds for believing that there is a discriminatory purpose behind the prosecution or punishment in the requesting State.[85] The UN Model Treaty on Extradition 1990 extends this prohibition to cases where the fugitive does not receive the minimum guarantees in criminal proceedings according to the ICCPR.[86] But without any qualifications this condition would be difficult to apply and could seriously hamper cooperation. The European Court of Human Rights, beginning with the *Soering* decision, is instead requiring a flagrant denial of a fair trial. Moreover, potential future violations are more difficult to establish than already suffered violations. While a refusal of extradition based upon a judgment *in absentia*, which cannot be appealed, already has support in some extradition agreements[87] and accords with the case law of the European Court of Human Rights,[88] there has been a reluctance to conclude a risk for violations. Increasingly, however, national courts in Europe consider allegations that extradition will result in a serious breach of human rights, at least when the fugitive can support the claim; the mere fact that the requesting State is also party to the ECHR is not sufficient per se for ruling out potential violations.[89] Denying extradition would arguably be consistent with the right to decline cooperation on *ordre public* grounds. Following the European Arrest Warrant,[90] judicial human rights considerations are now mandatory in the extradition proceedings of some countries, for example the United Kingdom and Ireland.

In practice, assurances by the requesting State often make extradition possible in spite of human rights concerns – non-application or non-enforcement of the death penalty, guarantees against torture, the right to a new trial, etc. But such assurances are difficult to follow up and normally without sanctions if breached. Hence, a thorough assessment must be made in each case as to whether they offer sufficient protection and conditional extradition is not always a solution.[91]

In a spate of recent cases, extradition of genocide suspects to Rwanda has been declined by a number of European States (e.g. Finland, France, Germany, Switzerland and the UK)[92] with reference to decisions by the ICTR refusing the referral of proceedings to Rwanda under rule 11*bis* of the ICTR Rules (see Chapter 7). Likely violations of fair trial rights were raised against extradition, particularly with respect to difficulties in securing the attendance of

---

85 E.g. Art. 11 of the 1957 European Extradition Convention, Art. 9 of the 1979 Hostage Convention, Art. 4(5) of the 1981 Inter-American Extradition Convention, and the 1990 Commonwealth Scheme for the Rendition of Fugitive Offenders.

86 Art. 3(f) of the Model Treaty.

87 E.g. Art. 3 of the 1978 Second Additional Protocol to the 1957 European Extradition Convention. Cf. the conditional surrender provided for in Art. 5(12) of the Framework Decision on the European Arrest Warrant.

88 E.g. *Stoichkov* v. *Bulgaria* ECtHR 24.6.2005 paras. 53–8.

89 See Vennemann, 'The European Arrest Warrant', 117–19.

90 See Art. 1(3) of the Framework Decision on the European Arrest Warrant.

91 See Dugard & Van den Wyngaert, 'Reconciling Extradition', 206–8.

92 E.g. *Brown (aka Banyani) & Ors* v. *Government of Rwanda* [2009] EWCA 770.

defence witnesses. But the standard applied by the ICTR is different from that required by the ECHR and Rwanda has reformed its system in order to make ICTR referrals and extradition possible. Hence, in July 2009 Sweden granted extradition to Rwanda in a genocide case.[93]

5.4.6   Re-extradition

In order to observe all the conditions for extradition, and often as part of the rule of specialty, the requesting State is generally not allowed to re-extradite the fugitive to a third State without the consent of the requested State. This is provided, for example, in the 1957 European Extradition Convention concerning re-extradition for offences committed before the surrender to the requesting State.[94] However, the European Arrest Warrant allows re-extradition to another EU State without consent in some cases and also provides that a general waiver from the remaining consent requirement may be made; but re-extradition to a third State will always require consent.[95] In practice this means that the third State seeking re-extradition will have to meet the conditions both in the original requesting and requested States. There are examples, however, where the requirements for re-extradition have, in effect, been circumvented by instead deporting the fugitive under immigration laws (see section 5.4.7).[96]

5.4.7   Abduction, rendition or expulsion

When there are no extradition arrangements, or these are inapplicable (for example the political offence exception) or seen as ineffective, some States will resort to other measures in order to apprehend the fugitive – abduction or 'irregular rendition'. This may be conducted in a particular case, such as the *Eichmann* case,[97] or even as a state policy for certain cases, such as the United States anti-terrorist rendition programme. Such activities can, but do not have to, violate international law, depending on whether the territorial sovereignty of another State and the human rights of the individual concerned are respected or not.[98] Additionally, international humanitarian law may also be invoked in case of an 'armed conflict' (see Chapter 12).

---

93 Decision by the Government of Sweden concerning extradition to Rwanda, 9.7.2009; see also the Decision by the Swedish Supreme Court of 26.5.2009 (Case Ö1082-09). On 20.7.2009 the Government stayed the execution of the decision pending the outcome of proceedings in the ECtHR.
94 Art. 15.
95 Art. 28 of the Framework Decision on the European Arrest Warrant. See also Art. 12 of the 1996 EU Extradition Convention, which removed the consent requirement among the EU States but never entered into force.
96 See, e.g. *Bozano* v. *France* ECtHR 18.12.1986.
97 See Chapter 3; see also P. O'Higgins, 'Unlawful Seizure and Irregular Rendition' (1960) 36 *BYIL* 279.
98 Generally, see the Venice Commission, *Opinion on the International Legal Obligations of Council of Europe Member States in Respect of Secret Detention Facilities and Inter-State Transport of Prisoners*, 17.3.2006 (www.venice.coe.int).

In accordance with the maxim *male captus, bene detentus* national courts have long been prepared to try accused persons regardless of how they came under the jurisdiction of the court, even if the arrest and surrender of the person was unlawful under national or international law. Hence in the *Eichmann* case, the District Court of Jerusalem saw no obstacle to trying the accused although he had been abducted from Argentina, without that State's consent, by Israeli agents. While this principle still applies in some States, notably the United States, it is being replaced in other States by the so-called abuse of process doctrine.[99] Originally established by the House of Lords, the doctrine has been applied by courts, inter alia, in the United Kingdom, New Zealand, Australia, South Africa and Zimbabwe, refusing to exercise jurisdiction due to irregularities when the fugitive was apprehended and transferred. But the case law is inconsistent and different factors have had an impact on the decision whether to decline jurisdiction due to abuse of process: involvement by officials of the forum State, the nationality of the accused, protests by the injured State, the possibility to seek extradition, the treatment of the accused and the gravity of the crimes.[100] In addition, an 'Eichmann exception' has been argued concerning 'universally condemned offences'.[101]

State authorities sometimes choose to deport a fugitive under immigration laws instead of dealing with the matter as extradition.[102] This is usually much faster and the surrender normally unconditional. But as the South African Constitutional Court has stated,[103] deportation and extradition serve different purposes and the former method must not, as in that case, be used unlawfully and with the effect that no undertaking was obtained regarding the non-imposition of the death penalty. As for human rights protection, the European Court of Human Rights has ruled that the *Soering* principle also applies to deportation and other forms of expulsion.[104] Deportation, as a disguised form of extradition when the latter was not possible, may also amount to a violation of the ECHR.[105]

The way in which the fugitive is apprehended and surrendered may also violate his or her right to liberty and to security under international human rights law. It is important to note, however, that instruments such as the ECHR do not regulate extradition or deportation as

---

99 For a survey of national case law, see *Dragan Nikolić* ICTY T. Ch. II 9.10.2002 paras. 79–93. See also, e.g. Silvia Borelli, 'Terrorism and Human Rights', 808–10, and Bassiouni, *International Extradition*, 273–347.

100 *Dragan Nikolić* ICTY T. Ch. II 9.10.2002 para. 95.

101 See Rosalyn Higgins, *Problems and Process: International Law and How We Use It* (Oxford, 1994) 72–3. See also section 17.7.3.

102 Quite apart from such practice in individual cases, some States have opted, as a matter of policy, to deal with war criminals through deportation and denaturalization rather than criminal prosecution and extradition. The most notable example is the US policy concerning Nazi war criminals, see, e.g. Matthew Lippman, 'The Pursuit of Nazi War Criminals in the United States and in Other Anglo-American Legal Systems' (1998) 29 *California Western International Law Journal* 1 at 50–3 (and examples).

103 *Mohamed and Dalvie* v. *President of the Republic of South Africa and Six Others* 2001 (1) SA 893, Constitutional Court.

104 See, e.g. *Chahal* v. *United Kingdom* ECtHR 15.11.1996.

105 E.g. *Bolzano* v. *France* ECtHR 18.12.1986 para. 60.

such, nor do they prevent cooperation in criminal matters as long as such cooperation does not interfere with any specific rights.[106] Hence, atypical measures are not contrary per se to these instruments and the lawfulness of the detention must be assessed against national law and the purpose behind the relevant human rights provision.

5.5   Mutual legal assistance

Mutual legal assistance developed from the so-called 'Letters Rogatory',[107] a comity-based system of requests for assistance with the taking of evidence, but is mainly treaty based today and covers a wide range of measures.[108] These may relate to a criminal investigation, prosecution or trial, and include, for example, the taking of witness statements, search and seizure, service of documents and tracing of persons and information.

The usefulness of such assistance in the requesting State depends in part upon the nature of its criminal procedures. The more adversarial the proceedings, the greater the importance normally attached to witnesses appearing in the courtroom and being subject to cross-examination. Evidence obtained abroad by foreign authorities thus becomes less attractive.[109] In inquisitorial systems, where written evidence is more relied upon, the problem is reduced, although there might be concerns that the evidence was not obtained in a required manner. Consequently, common law jurisdictions were traditionally more hesitant than civil law jurisdictions to make use of mutual legal assistance. But this position has changed and the cooperation is now generally seen as a very important tool for combating crimes; increasingly, the focus is on the proceedings for which the assistance is sought.

In Europe, the basic multilateral instrument[110] is the 1959 Council of Europe Convention on Mutual Assistance in Criminal Matters, to which Additional Protocols have been adopted in 1978 and 2001. The Protocols were developed to improve cooperation and reflect progress elsewhere, particularly in the 2000 EU Convention on Mutual Assistance in Criminal Matters between the Member States of the European Union. This introduced new forms of cooperation and simplified many procedures. Some of the new measures involve both judicial and law enforcement cooperation, for example 'joint investigation teams',[111] and the use of modern technology such as video and audio conferencing. In the

---

106 See *Öcalan* v. *Turkey* ECtHR 12.5.2005 paras. 83–90.
107 Among some States, the practice of sending delegations to another State to conduct its own investigation ('Commission Rogatory') also existed.
108 For a comprehensive survey of multilateral treaties in Europe, see McClean, *International Co-operation*.
109 See Christopher Gane and Mark Mackarel, 'Admitting Irregularly or Illegally Obtained Evidence from Abroad into Criminal Proceedings – A Common Law Approach' (1997) *Criminal Law Review* 720–9.
110 In addition, many States have concluded bilateral agreements with other countries, and there are also sub-regional agreements, for example between the Nordic States.
111 First introduced in the 2000 Palermo Convention, and thereafter adopted in different EU and Council of Europe instruments; see Michael Plachta, 'Joint Investigation Teams' (2005) 13 *European Journal of Crime, Criminal Law and Criminal Justice* 284.

EU, the principle of mutual recognition also applies in this field by, inter alia, the adoption of a Framework Decision on the execution in the EU of orders freezing property and evidence[112] and a (so far weak) European Evidence Warrant.[113] With respect to replacing traditional forms of cooperation with the principle of mutual recognition in the EU, however, mutual legal assistance is so far the least developed area.

Regional conventions on mutual legal assistance also exist among States in America (OAS), the Caribbean (CARICOM), Western Africa (ECOWAS), Southern Africa (SADC), the Commonwealth of Independent States (CIS), Southeast Asia (ASEAN) and South Asia (SAARC).[114] Hence, there is a fairly extensive network of treaties, operating within regions but not between them. However, the 1959 European Convention is also open to non-members of the Council of Europe, and a few such States have adhered to the Convention, and the Commonwealth Scheme on Mutual Assistance (the Harare Scheme)[115] is an example of an arrangement that is not confined to a geographic region. In addition, many bilateral agreements exist. Many States have implemented the treaties by special legislation. A new feature are agreements between the EU and its Member States and third countries; mixed multilateral and bilateral agreements have been concluded with the US[116] and an agreement with Japan has recently been negotiated.

Globally, advanced schemes for mutual legal assistance are provided in more recent treaties on transnational crimes, for example the 1998 Drug Trafficking Convention, the 2000 Palermo Convention and the 2003 Corruption Convention;[117] other treaties such as the 1984 Torture Convention and the 1999 Terrorist Financing Convention mainly contain a general obligation to cooperate.

Mutual legal assistance is circumscribed by conditions, or grounds for refusal, which are similar to those applicable to extradition. Although treaties often phrase such exceptions in facultative rather than mandatory terms,[118] many States have insisted on applying them. But

---

112 OJ L196, 2.8.2003, pp. 45–55.

113 Framework Decision on the European evidence warrant for the purpose of obtaining objects, documents and data for use in proceedings in criminal matters, OJ L350, 30.12.2008, pp. 72–92.

114 Inter-American Convention on Mutual Legal Assistance in Criminal Matters 23.5.1992; Economic Community of West African States Convention on Mutual Assistance in Criminal Matters 29.7.1992; Caribbean Mutual Legal Assistance Treaty in Serious Criminal Matters 6.7.2005; Minsk Convention on Legal Assistance and Legal Relations in Civil, Family and Criminal Matters 22.1.1993; Kishinev (Chishinau) Convention 7.10.2002; SADC Protocol on Mutual Legal Assistance in Criminal Matters 3.10.2002; ASEAN Treaty on Mutual Assistance in Criminal Matters 29.11.2004; SAARC Convention on Mutual Legal Assistance in Criminal Matters 3.8.2008.

115 Scheme Relating to Mutual Assistance in Criminal Matters within the Commonwealth (Harare Scheme) 28.7–1.8.1986, (1986) 12 *Commonwealth Law Bulletin* 1118–24 (later amended in April 1990, November 2002 and October 2005).

116 OJ L181, 19.7.2003, pp. 34–43.

117 An interesting regional treaty is the 2001 Cyber Crime Convention (Council of Europe).

118 See, e.g. the 1959 European Convention on Mutual Assistance in Criminal Matters.

here too there is a trend to do away with, or at least restrict, the various grounds for refusal.[119]

In spite of improvements such as allowing the requesting State to prescribe procedures to be followed, differences in the procedures of the different countries still create problems. Different views as to whether the accused may give testimony or the scope for witness testimonies are two examples. Another shortcoming is that, so far, the accused cannot independently seek assistance from a foreign State; it has to be done between public authorities or courts in the different States.[120] Claims of immunity may also hamper cooperation.[121] But the major obstacle is that the process is slow and cumbersome and fraught by practical problems, often due to ineffective implementation, indirect communications and poor translations and language skills.

5.6   Transfer of proceedings

With diverging views on criminal jurisdiction and all the restrictions and difficulties concerning international legal cooperation, alternative solutions have been considered. One model is the transfer of criminal proceedings from one State to another, both of which have jurisdiction over the offence; a double-criminality requirement always applies and, due to the nature of the cooperation, is often far-reaching. Most well known is a multilateral convention adopted by the Council of Europe.[122] But States tend to insist on reciprocity and the measure is infrequently used since only a few States have ratified the instruments.

Transfer of proceedings is not primarily a device for giving priority to particular jurisdictional grounds; the motive is rather that the accused has ties to the requesting State or that proceedings there would be more convenient. Coordination between the different proceedings is important and many agreements include *ne bis in idem* provisions, albeit often optional instead of mandatory ones. Furthermore, numerous grounds for refusal apply and a transfer of proceedings could be difficult in practice; for example, prosecutorial and judicial decisions taken in the transferring State have little effect, if any, and evidence collected may be inadmissible in the requesting State.

---

119 See, e.g. the 2000 EU Convention on Mutual Assistance in Criminal Matters and its 2001 Additional Protocol; and the 2000 Palermo Convention.

120 The refusal to seek measures abroad at the request of the accused may, however, affect the fairness of the subsequent trial, e.g. *Papageorgiou* v. *Greece* ECtHR 9.5.2003.

121 See, e.g. *Case concerning Certain Questions of Mutual Legal Assistance in Criminal Matters* (Djibouti v. France) ICJ 4.6.2008.

122 The 1972 European Convention on the Transfer of Proceedings in Criminal Matters. See also the 1990 UN Model Treaty on Transfer of Proceedings in Criminal Matters. Transfer of criminal proceedings is also referred to in other multilateral treaties, such as the 1988 Narcotic Drugs Convention (Art. 8).

5.7   Enforcement of penalties

While States have historically been reluctant to recognize foreign criminal judgments formally, cooperation does exist regarding enforcement of foreign prison sentences and other penalties. Apart from humanitarian aspects, this possibility sometimes facilitates extradition: an otherwise reluctant State may accept extradition on condition that the fugitive is returned to serve any sentence imposed.[123]

Both bilateral and multilateral agreements on the point have been concluded. In Europe, the Council of Europe took the lead with the 1970 European Convention on the International Validity of Criminal Judgments and the 1983 Convention on the Transfer of Sentenced Persons (and its 1997 Additional Protocol). The penalty will either be converted into a new penalty in the administering State, after which it is enforced there, or continued enforcement of the sentence will take place. A mandatory double-criminality requirement applies, as do numerous conditions and grounds for refusal. In addition various initiatives have been taken within the EU based on the principle of mutual recognition regarding fines and confiscation orders, as well as custodial and other non-custodial sentences.[124]

Further reading

M. Cherif Bassiouni (ed.), *International Extradition: United States Law and Practice*, 5th edn (New York, 2007).

Rob Blekxtoon and Wouter van Ballegooij (eds.), *Handbook on the European Arrest Warrant* (The Hague, 2005).

Silvia Borelli, 'Terrorism and Human Rights: Treatment of Terrorist Suspects and Limits on International Cooperation' (2003) 16 *LJIL* 803.

Gilles de Kerchove and Anne Weyembergh (eds.), *La reconnaissance mutuelle des décisions judiciaires pénales dans l'Union européenne* (Brussels, 2001).

John Dugard and Christine Van den Wyngaert, 'Reconciling Extradition with Human Rights' (1998) 92 *AJIL* 187.

Albin Eser and Otto Lagodny (eds.), *Principles and Procedures for a New Transnational Criminal Law* (Freiburg, 1992).

Geoff Gilbert, 'Extradition' in Craig Barker and John Grant (eds.), *Harvard Research in International Law: Contemporary Analysis and Appraisal* (Buffalo NY, 2007) 247–74.

---

123 For a general survey, see Michael Plachta, *Transfer of Prisoners under International Instruments and Domestic Legislation. A Comparative Study* (Freiburg, 1993).

124 Council Framework Decision of 24.2.2005 on financial penalties (OJ L76, 22.3.2005, pp. 16–30), Council Framework Decision of 6.10.2006 on confiscation orders (OJ L328, 24.11.2006, pp. 59–78), Council Framework Decision of 27.11.2008 on custodial sentences (OJ L327, 5.12.2008, pp. 27–46) and Council Framework Decision of 27.11.2008 on supervision of probation and alternative sanctions (OJ L337, 16.12.2008, pp. 102–22).

David McClean, *International Co-operation in Civil and Criminal Matters* (Oxford, 2002).

Clive Nicholls & Claire Montgomery, *The Law of Extradition and Mutual Assistance*, 2nd edn (Oxford, 2007).

Wolfgang Schomburg, Otto Lagodny, Sabine Gless and Thomas Hackner, *Internationale Rechtshilfe in Strafsachen*, 4th edn (Munich, 2006).

Ivor Stanbrook and Clive Stanbrook, *Extradition: Law and Practice*, 2nd edn (Oxford, 2000).

PART C

International Prosecutions

6

The History of International Criminal Prosecutions: Nuremberg and Tokyo

6.1   Introduction

International criminal law, or something similar to it, has a very long history.[1] Its closest European precursor before the modern era was the chivalric system that applied in the medieval era.[2] The most notable of the trials that were related to this system was that of Peter von Hagenbach in Breisach in 1474.[3] Although its status as a legal precedent is highly limited, the issues involved at that trial, superior orders, sexual offences, cooperation in evidence gathering, and pleas as to the jurisdiction of the court, have clear present-day relevance.[4] The purpose of this chapter, however, is to introduce the modern history of international criminal prosecutions rather than provide a comprehensive overview of the entire history of the subject. Therefore we will start in the early part of the twentieth century, at the end of the First World War.

6.2   The commission on the responsibility of the authors of the war

After the First World War, the Allies set up a fifteen-member commission to investigate the responsibility for the start of the war, violations of the laws of war and what tribunal would

---

1 See Timothy L. H. McCormack, 'From Sun Tzu to the Sixth Committee, The Evolution of an International Criminal Law Regime' in Timothy L. H. McCormack and Gerry J. Simpson (eds.), *The Law of War Crimes, National and International Approaches* (The Hague, 1997) 31; M. Cherif Bassiouni, 'From Versailles to Rwanda in Seventy-Five Years, The Need to Establish an International Criminal Court' (1997) 10 *Harvard Human Rights Law Journal* 11.
2 See, e.g. Maurice H. Keen, *The Laws of War in the Late Middle Ages* (London, 1965); Theodor Meron, *Bloody Constraint, Crimes and Accountability in Shakespeare* (New York, 1998).
3 See Georg Schwarzenberger, *International Law as Applied by International Courts and Tribunals* (London, 1968), vol. II, ch. 39.
4 See, e.g. Robert Cryer, *Prosecuting International Crimes: Selectivity in the International Criminal Law Regime* (Cambridge, 2005) ch. 1.

be appropriate for trials.[5] It reported in March 1919, determining that the central powers were responsible for starting the war[6] and that there were violations of the laws of war and humanity.[7] It recommended that high officials, including the Kaiser, be tried for ordering such crimes and on the basis of command responsibility.[8]

Further to this, the Commission suggested the setting up of an Allied 'High Tribunal' with members from all of the allied countries to try violations of the laws and customs of war and the laws of humanity.[9] This aspect was criticized by the Commission's US and Japanese members. The US members said that they knew 'of no international statute or convention making violation of the laws and customs of war – not to speak of the laws or principles of humanity – an international crime'.[10] The Japanese representatives questioned 'whether international law recognizes a penal law applicable to those who are guilty'.[11] The majority, however, clearly considered there to be a body of international criminal law, albeit one which did not include aggression as a crime.[12]

As a result, the Treaty of Versailles provided, in Article 227, that the Kaiser was to be 'publicly arraigned' for 'a supreme offence against international morality and the sanctity of treaties' before an international tribunal. It was never implemented as the Netherlands refused to hand the Kaiser over to the Allies on the basis that the offence was a political one.[13] Articles 228 and 229 of the Treaty of Versailles also provided for prosecutions of German nationals for war crimes before Allied courts, including mixed commissions where the victims came from more than one State. These provisions, however, were never put into practice. Some prosecutions, but far fewer than the Allies wanted, were undertaken by Germany itself in Leipzig between 1921 and 1923. The proceedings were characterized by bias towards the defendants, questionable acquittals and lenient sentences.[14] However, two of these cases later formed important precedents in international criminal law.[15]

5 Report of the Commission to the Preliminary Peace Conference, reprinted in (1920) 14 *AJIL* 95.
6 *Ibid.*, 107.
7 *Ibid.*, 114–15.
8 *Ibid.*, 116–7, 121.
9 *Ibid.*, 122.
10 *Ibid.*, 144–6.
11 *Ibid.*, 152.
12 *Ibid.*, 118.
13 See M. Cherif Bassiouni, 'World War I, "The War to End All Wars" and the Birth of a Handicapped International Criminal Justice System' (2002) 30 *Denver Journal of International Law and Policy* 244 at 269–73.
14 Claus Kreß, 'Versailles – Nuremberg – The Hague: Germany and International Criminal Law' (2006) 40 *International Lawyer* 15 at 16–20.
15 *The Dover Castle* (1922) 16 *AJIL* 704; *The Llandovery Castle* (1922) 16 *AJIL* 708. See Kreß, 'Versailles – Nuremberg – The Hague', 16–18.

6.3   The Nuremberg International Military Tribunal

6.3.1   *The creation of the Tribunal*

Although in 1937 a treaty to create an international criminal court to try terrorist offences was negotiated,[16] this was not supported by States, and never came into force. The real leap forward in international criminal law came about at the end of the Second World War. The Allies initially issued a declaration in Moscow in 1943, which promised punishment for Axis war criminals, but stated that this was 'without prejudice to the case of the major criminals whose offences have no particular geographical location and who will be punished by a joint declaration of the governments of the Allies'.[17] After considerable discussion amongst the Allies during the war, Churchill was persuaded by the US and the USSR that a trial of such persons was preferable to their summary execution.[18] As a result, France, the UK, the US and the USSR met in London to draft the charter of an international tribunal. The negotiations leading to the London charter, which formed the basis of the Nuremberg IMT, were tense, in particular as the US and USSR representatives clashed over a number of important issues. The representatives of the USSR thought that the purpose of the tribunal was simply to determine the punishment to be meted out to the defendants, who they thought were to be presumed guilty. This was unacceptable to the US. Differences between the civil law States (France and the USSR) and their common-law counterparts (the UK and US) on the appropriate procedures for the trial also caused considerable difficulties. Nonetheless, on 8 August 1945, the four Allies signed the London Agreement, which created the tribunal.[19] Nineteen other States also adhered to the charter later.

6.3.2   *The Tribunal and the trial*

The Tribunal had eight judges, four principal judges (one for each of the major Allies (France, the USSR, the UK and the US) and four alternates (understudies drawn from the same States). The President of the Tribunal was Lord Justice Geoffrey Lawrence from the UK, who exercised a firm, but largely fair, hand over the proceedings. Each of the main Allies was entitled to appoint a chief prosecutor. The defence was undertaken by a number of German lawyers, the leading lights of whom were Hermann Jahreiss, an international lawyer from Cologne, and Otto Kranzbühler, a preternaturally talented naval judge-advocate.

---

16 1937 Convention for the Creation of an International Criminal Court. See Manley O. Hudson, 'The Proposed International Criminal Court' (1938) 32 *AJIL* 549.
17 Declaration of Moscow 1.11.1943.
18 See Arieh Kochavi, *Prelude to Nuremberg: Allied War Crimes Policy and the Question of Punishment* (Durham, 1998).
19 1945 London Agreement for the IMT.

The indictment was received by the Tribunal on 10 October 1945, at its official seat in Berlin. It contained four main charges, all of which were based on Article 6 of the IMT's charter. Count one was the overall conspiracy, which was handled by the US prosecution team. Count two concerned crimes against peace. This count was dealt with by the UK prosecutors. Count three charged war crimes and count four concerned crimes against humanity. The prosecution of these two offences was split between the French and Soviet prosecutors, the French dealing with the western zone of conflict, the Soviet with the eastern. Twenty-four defendants were arraigned before the tribunal.[20] There were also prosecutions of six criminal organizations.[21] Having received the indictment, the Tribunal moved to the city it is now associated with, Nuremberg.[22]

In the opening session, the US Chief Prosecutor, Justice Robert Jackson (who had represented the US at the London negotiations)[23] began the prosecution case with a stirring speech, embodying many of the ideas that have later been adopted into the ideals of international criminal law. Jackson described the Tribunal as 'the greatest tribute ever paid by power to reason', and sought to deflect concerns about the fairness of the trial and the non-prosecution of Allied nationals by saying that 'while this law is first applied against German aggressors, the law includes, and if it is to serve a useful purpose it must condemn, aggression by any other nations, including those which sit here now in judgment'.[24]

The trial took place over ten months, and 403 open sessions. In the end three of the defendants (Schacht, Fritzsche and von Papen) were acquitted, as were three of the six indicted organizations (the SA, High Command and Reich Cabinet). Of the remaining defendants twelve were sentenced to death and seven to periods of imprisonment ranging from ten years to life. The Soviet judge, Major-General Nikitchenko, dissented from all the acquittals and the life sentence for Rudolf Hess. He would have declared all the defendants and organizations guilty, and sentenced Hess to death.[25]

The judgment of the Tribunal, in addition to its findings on the facts, represented a considerable contribution to international law. The judgment dealt at some length with the defence contention that the prosecution of crimes against peace was contrary to the *nullum crimen sine lege* principle. In spite of the fact that the judgment took the view that the Tribunal's Charter was binding as to what law the Tribunal ought to apply, the judgment

---

20 Karl Dönitz, Hans Frank, Wilhelm Frick, Hans Fritzsche, Walter Funk, Hermann Göring, Rudolf Hess, Alfred Jodl, Ernst Kaltenbrunner, Wilhelm Keitel, Konstantin von Neurath, Franz von Papen, Willem Raeder, Joachim von Ribbentrop, Alfred Rosenberg, Fritz Saukel, Hjalmar Schacht, Baldur von Schirach, Arthur Seyss-Inquart, Albert Speer and Julius Streicher. Martin Bormann was tried *in absentia*, Gustav Krupp was declared mentally incapable of standing trial, Robert Ley committed suicide in custody prior to the trial.
21 See Telford Taylor, *The Anatomy of the Nuremberg Trial* (London, 1993) 501–33.
22 See generally Guénaël Mettraux (ed.), *Perspectives on the Nuremberg Trial* (Oxford, 2008).
23 The Russian judge (Nikitchenko) had also represented his country at the negotiations.
24 1 *Trial of Major War Criminals, Nuremberg* (London, 1946) 85. See Matthew Lipmann, 'Nuremberg Forty-Five Years Later' (1991) 7 *Connecticut Journal of International Law* 1, 39.
25 21 *Trial of Major War Criminals, Nuremberg* (London, 1946) 531–47.

engaged in a detailed, if, in the final analysis unconvincing, review of pre-war developments, in particular the 1928 Kellog-Briand Pact.[26] It used that treaty (which was not intended to create criminal liability) and a number of non-binding sources to create a case that aggressive war was criminalized by customary international law.[27] The Tribunal may have been on more solid ground in relation to positive international law when it asserted that the *nullum crimen* principle was not established as an absolute principle in international law at the time.[28] Probably the Tribunal's most famous holding, however, is its firm affirmation of direct liability under international law, which has become a foundational statement in international criminal law:

> crimes against international law are committed by men, not abstract entities, and only by punishing individuals who commit such crimes can the provisions of international law be enforced ... individuals have international duties which transcend the national obligations of obedience imposed by the individual state.[29]

The 'principles' of the IMT's charter and judgment were quickly affirmed by the General Assembly in its Resolution 95(I).[30] Although some aspects of the Tribunal's decision were controversial in international law,[31] others have proved highly influential, especially its holding that the Hague Regulations represented customary international law.[32]

6.3.3   Assessment of the Nuremberg IMT

The Nuremberg IMT is often accused of being an example of 'victor's justice', although it is not always clear precisely what this concept is. It contains a number of linked, but different allegations. These are that the trial itself was not fair, in particular that the judges were biased against the accused,[33] that the applicable law was designed to guarantee a conviction, and that similar acts were committed by the prosecuting State(s) but were not prosecuted (i.e. a plea of *tu quoque*).[34]

---

26 (1929) UKTS 29.

27 See further, Chapter 13, and Sheldon Glueck, *War Criminals: Their Prosecution and Punishment* (New York, 1944); *contra* Sheldon Glueck, *The Nuremberg Trial and Aggressive War* (New York, 1946). For the Tribunal's views on superior orders, see section 16.8.

28 'Nuremberg IMT: Judgment and Sentence' reprinted in (1947) 41 *AJIL* 172, 217.

29 *Ibid.*, 221.

30 UN Doc. A/64/Add.1.

31 In addition to the debate about crimes against peace, considerable controversy surrounds the determination of the Tribunal that conspiracy existed as a mode of liability in international criminal law. It is doubtful that it did at the time.

32 See, e.g. *Legal Consequences of the Construction of a Wall in the Occupied Palestinian Territory* (2004) ICJ Rep 136, para. 89; *Case Concerning Armed Activities on the Territory of the Congo* (DRC v. Uganda) Merits, ICJ Rep (2005); ICJ General List 116, para. 217.

33 Richard H. Minear, *Victor's Justice: The Tokyo War Crimes Trial* (Princeton, 1971) 74–124.

34 See Cryer, *Prosecuting International Crimes*, ch. 4.

With respect to the first issue, some aspects of the Nuremberg trial were imperfect. There was, for example, a heavy reliance on affidavit evidence,[35] and a huge disparity in resources between the prosecution and the defence. However, given the standards applicable to trials at the time, the proceedings were, basically, fairly run.[36] Even so, a reasonable case can be made that the presence of neutral judges, or a judge from Germany, would have increased the legitimacy of the proceedings.[37] In relation to the critiques of the law, it is true that the law on crimes against humanity and peace was defined by the Allies in London, with the actions of the Nazis in mind,[38] and at least in relation to crimes against peace the charter was, in essence, *ex post facto* legislation. It might be doubted, however, whether the Nazis truly thought that their actions were not criminal according to principles of law recognized by the community of nations, especially after the Moscow declaration of 1943. If this was the relevant standard at the time, the critiques of the Nuremberg IMT on point become less convincing.

The final aspect of the victor's justice critique, that similar acts by the Allies were not prosecuted, has some purchase, although the Allies had not committed mass crimes of the magnitude of the Holocaust. The defence were not permitted to raise the issue of crimes committed by the Allies, although Kranzbüler cleverly raised the *tu quoque* issue as one of law, by alleging that unrestricted submarine warfare was permitted by customary international law, as the US Chief of the Pacific Navy, Chester Nimitz, had admitted that US practice in that sphere was the same as that charged against the naval defendants.[39] The judges did not agree with that proposition of law, but because of the Allied practices they refrained from assessing the sentences of Dönitz and Raeder by reference to the war crimes charges relating to submarine warfare. The *tu quoque* argument also had an interesting effect on the indictments. Owing to the devastation visited upon Germany by Allied (in particular UK) bombing, no charges related to the Blitz over the UK were brought.[40] Russian conduct in the USSR, Poland and, late in the war, Germany made other charges difficult to bring without implicitly inviting *tu quoque* claims.

There are criticisms of the Nuremberg IMT which do not relate to allegations of 'victor's justice'. Particular amongst these, is that the prosecution, in particular the US section, saw the trial as being primarily one of aggression, rather than of the Holocaust.[41] This is supported by the judgment's statement that aggression was the 'supreme international

---

35 Lipmann, 'Nuremberg', 27.

36 *Ibid.*, 39.

37 But see Arthur Goodhart, 'Questions and Answers Concerning the Nuremberg Trials' (1947) 1 *International Law Quarterly* 525, 527.

38 See, e.g. M. Cherif Bassiouni, *Crimes Against Humanity in International Criminal Law*, 2nd edn (The Hague, 1999) 9–10.

39 18 *Trial of Major War Criminals, Nuremberg* (London, 1948) 26–8.

40 Chris af Jochnik and Roger Normand, 'The Legitimation of Violence: A Critical History of the Law of War' (1994) 35 *Harvard International Law Journal* 49, 91–2.

41 Mark Osiel, *Mass Atrocity, Collective Memory and the Law* (New Brunswick, 1997) 225–6.

crime'.[42] However, the Tribunal is primarily remembered now as a trial of atrocities rather than of aggression,[43] and the overall judgment on Nuremberg, and its promised legacy of accountability,[44] tends to be quite favourable.

6.4   The Tokyo International Military Tribunal

6.4.1   The creation of the Tribunal

The Nuremberg IMT's sibling, the International Military Tribunal for the Far East (Tokyo IMT) was set up in January 1946 by a proclamation of General Douglas MacArthur.[45] MacArthur's actions were authorized by powers granted to him by the allied States as Supreme Commander, Allied Powers, to implement the Potsdam declaration,[46] principle 10 of which promised 'stern justice' for war criminals. The declaration had been accepted by Japan in its instrument of surrender. The setting up of the Tokyo IMT on the basis of principle 10 led to a challenge to the jurisdiction of the Tribunal relating to crimes against peace, a challenge which was rejected on the basis that the majority judgment found that, at the time of the surrender, the Japanese government understood that the term 'war criminals' included those responsible for initiating the war.[47]

6.4.2   The Tribunal and the trial

The Tribunal was made up of eleven judges, nine from the signatory States to the Japanese surrender (Australia, Canada, China, France, New Zealand, the Netherlands, the UK, the US and the USSR), together with one each from India and the Philippines. This unwieldy bench was overseen by the Australian Judge, Sir William Webb, whose conduct of the trial has been criticized.[48] The US was entitled to appoint the chief prosecutor, whilst the other countries were only permitted to appoint associate prosecutors.[49] The US choice, Joseph

---

42 Judgment, see (1947) 41 *AJIL* at 186.
43 Osiel, *Mass Atrocity*, 225–6.
44 See M. Cherif Bassiouni, 'The Nuremberg Legacy' in M. Cherif Bassiouni (ed.), *International Criminal Law*, 2nd edn (New York, 1999), vol. III, 195; David Luban, 'The Legacies of Nuremberg' (1987) 54 *Social Research* 779.
45 Special proclamation, Establishment of an International Military Tribunal for the Far East, 19 January 1946, TIAS No. 1589, at 3. See generally Neil Boister and Robert Cryer, *The Tokyo International Military Tribunal: A Reappraisal* (Oxford, 2008); Neil Boister and Robert Cryer (eds.), *Documents on the Tokyo International Military Tribunal: Charter, Indictment and Judgments* (Oxford, 2008); Yuma Totani, *The Tokyo War Crimes Trial: The Pursuit of Justice in the Wake of World War II* (Cambridge, MA, 2008).
46 See *Hirota* v. *MacArthur* 335 US 876; 93 L. Ed. 1903.
47 Judgment of the Tokyo IMT, at 48,440–1.
48 See, e.g. R. John Pritchard, 'An Overview of the Historical Importance of the Tokyo War Trial' in Chihiro Hosoya, Yasuaki Onuma, Nisuke Ando and Richard Minear (eds.), *The Tokyo Trial: An International Symposium* (Tokyo, 1986) 90, 92; Boister and Cryer, *Tokyo: A Reappraisal*, ch. 4.
49 Tokyo IMT Charter, Art. 8.

Keenan, was unsuited to the task, and his professionalism open to serious challenge.[50] The defence was undertaken by a number of Japanese and American lawyers, the most well known of whom were Kenzo Takayanagi, a professor of Anglo-American law from Tokyo, and Ichiro Kiyose, a politician and lawyer.

The huge trial began with the submission of the indictment to the Tribunal on 29 April 1946. The indictment, in fifty-five counts, charged the twenty-eight defendants[51] with crimes against peace and attendant conspiracies, war crimes, and murders, the last on the basis of a prosecution theory that all killings (including those of combatants) in an unlawful war were murders.[52] The trial lasted nearly two and a half years, with the majority judgment being pronounced in November 1948. The judgment found all the accused who remained before the IMT at the time of judgment guilty, although not on all the counts with which they had been charged. It sentenced seven defendants to death, one to twenty years' imprisonment, one to seven years' imprisonment, and the rest to incarceration for life. In addition to this there were three dissenting judgments, one concurring judgment, and one separate opinion.

The majority judgment followed the Nuremberg IMT's opinion on practically all aspects of the law, expressly adopting its reasoning in relation to the binding nature of the Tribunal's charter, the criminality of aggressive war and the abolition of the absolute defence of superior orders.[53] Perhaps the only major difference was that unlike the Nuremberg IMT, which did not find it necessary to deal with command responsibility, the Tokyo IMT discussed that principle of liability in some detail, and applied it to both military and civilian defendants.[54] In relation to the facts, the judgment decided that there was an overarching conspiracy to initiate aggressive wars, and impose Japanese authority over Asia. It also, less controversially, determined that war crimes were committed both against Allied PoWs and civilians, perhaps most notably in the Rape of Nanking in 1937.

The President of the Tribunal gave a separate opinion, in which he gave his own views on the law, in particular that the criminality of aggressive war could be based on natural law.[55] Webb also asserted that as the Emperor was responsible for initiating such wars, his absence ought to be reflected in the sentences meted out to the defendants.[56] Judge Bernard of France

---

50 B. V. A. Röling and Antonio Cassese, *The Tokyo Trial and Beyond* (Cambridge, 1992) 16.

51 Kenji Dohihara, Koki Hirota, Seishiro Itagaki, Heitaro Kimura, Iwane Matsui, Akira Muto, Hideki Tojo, Sadao Araki, Kingoro Hashimoto, Shunroko Hata, Kiichiro Hiranuma, Naoki Hoshino, Okinori Kaya, Koichi Kido, Kuniaki Koiso, Jiro Minami, Takasumi Oka, Hiroshi Oshima, Kenryo Sato, Shigetaro Shimada, Toshi Shiratori, Teiichi Suzuki, Yoshijiro Umezu, Shigenori Togo, Mamoru Shigemitsu. Yosuke Matsuoka and Osami Nagano died during the trial. Shumei Okawa was declared mentally unfit to stand trial. See Tokyo IMT Judgment, at 48,425.

52 These charges were not decided upon, as they were seen as cumulative to the crimes against peace charges. See Boister and Cryer, *Tokyo: A Reappraisal*, ch. 6.

53 Tokyo IMT Judgment, 48,437–9.

54 *Ibid.*, 48,442–7.

55 Separate Opinion of the President, at 6.

56 *Ibid.*, 19–20.

also considered that crimes against peace could be based on natural law.[57] He took a more sophisticated approach to command responsibility than the majority.[58] Nonetheless, he considered the trial to have progressed in such a manner that he was not able to reach a judgment on the responsibility of the defendants.[59]

The two major dissenting judgments were given by the judges from the Netherlands and from India, Judges Röling and Pal. Judge Röling disagreed with the majority (and with the Nuremberg Tribunal) on the question of crimes against peace, taking the view that there was no individual criminal liability for aggression in international law; he was, however, of the view that the occupying powers were entitled to imprison those responsible for initiating wars, as they threatened occupying powers' security.[60] He supported this view by pointing out that the Tribunal had sentenced no one to death for committing a crime against peace alone.[61] While that fact does not prove that the majority saw their sentencing practice in that light, he was right to express doubt about the broad way in which the majority derived a criminal conspiracy from the facts (some of which he contested), and the way they applied command responsibility.[62] He argued that a number of the defendants, most notably Shigemitsu and Hirota, should have been acquitted.[63] He took a stern line on war crimes though, and would have imposed death sentences on more of the defendants found guilty of those crimes.[64]

Judge Pal gave the longest and most well known of the dissenting judgments. He denied that crimes against peace were a part of existing international law and noted that, in the absence of a clear definition, the concept of aggression was open to 'interested interpretation'.[65] Pal also gave an interpretation of the facts completely at variance with that of the majority, largely accepting defence arguments that Japan's actions were only ever ad hoc reactions to provocations by Western powers or explained by fear of communism in China.[66] He gave a lengthy critique of the fairness of the trial proceedings[67] and made clear that he saw the prosecution as hypocritical, owing to the record of many of the prosecuting States in colonialism, and the use of nuclear weapons against Hiroshima and Nagasaki.[68] As a result, he would have acquitted all the defendants, including of the war crimes charges.[69] His opinion was criticized in Judge Jaranilla's concurring opinion. Jaranilla, the

---

57 Dissenting Opinion of the Member from France, at 10.
58 *Ibid.*, 12–18.
59 *Ibid.*, 22.
60 Dissenting Opinion of the Member from the Netherlands, 10–51.
61 *Ibid.*, 48–9.
62 *Ibid.*, 54–135.
63 *Ibid.*, 178–249.
64 *Ibid.*, 178.
65 Dissenting Opinion of the Member from India, at 69–153, 227–79.
66 *Ibid.*, 349–1,014.
67 *Ibid.*, 280–348.
68 *Ibid.*, 1, 231–5.
69 *Ibid.*, 1, 226.

Philippine judge, said that Pal ought to have accepted the charter's provisions on the law, as he accepted an appointment under the charter.[70] He also asserted that the trial proceedings were fair, and that the atomic bombings were justified, as they brought an end to the war.[71] Jaranilla's appointment was controversial, as he had been a victim of the Bataan Death march, and he therefore ought not to have sat, on the basis that he might have been biased against the defendants.[72] His view that the sentences imposed were too lenient did little to dispel this suspicion.[73]

6.4.3   Assessment of the Tribunal

The view of the Tokyo IMT traditionally adopted by most international criminal lawyers was summed up by the title of the most well-known book on the trial, Richard Minear's *Victor's Justice*.[74] There is something to be said for such a view. Where the Tokyo IMT agreed with its Nuremberg counterpart on the law, the same critiques are applicable to both, although in relation to both conspiracy and command responsibility the Tokyo IMT went further, and in the judgment of many, too far. The majority's view of the facts was unsubtle, and the idea of 'an all-inclusive seventeen-year criminal conspiracy involving all the accused strained credulity ... [and] ... betrayed an underlying inability to grasp the dynamics of Japanese politics or a misplaced determination to force, after the fact, unrelated and fortuitous events into a preconceived thesis'.[75] On the other hand, Judge Pal's contrasting view of many of the facts was similarly unconvincing, as he was unduly credulous of the defence's claims that Japan was acting altruistically, to liberate Asia from Western colonialism.[76] In addition, the majority were on stronger ground in relation to the war crimes counts.[77]

In spite of the efforts of some of the judges, there were considerable flaws in the trial process. Also, not only was the *tu quoque* argument given some purchase by the bombing of Hiroshima and Nagasaki, it was also raised by one of the judges themselves. Cultural misunderstandings and insensitivities affected the trial, and some of the judges appeared to be biased. Evidence of Unit 731, the Japanese chemical and biological weapons unit which engaged in human vivisection, was kept from the Tribunal, as the US had promised its members immunity in return for information about their experiments.[78] But simple

---

70 Concurring Opinion of the Member from the Philippines, at 28–32.
71 *Ibid.*, 24–7.
72 IMTFE Paper 141, 10 June 1946, Motion Suggesting the Disqualification and Personal Bias of the Philippine Justice of the Tribunal.
73 Concurring Opinion of the Member from the Philippines, 32–5.
74 R. Minear, *Victor's Justice: The Tokyo War Crimes Trial* (Princeton, 1971).
75 John Piccigallo, *The Japanese on Trial* (Austin, 1979) 212.
76 Boister and Cryer, *Documents*, lxxx–lxxxi.
77 Boister and Cryer, *Tokyo: A Reappraisal*, 202–4.
78 Röling and Cassese, *Tokyo Trial*, at 48–50.

dismissals of the Tokyo IMT as a show trial are unnuanced.[79] There was far too much disagreement between the judges for it to have been as a show trial.[80] Many of the findings on war crimes were accurate, and many of the heavily criticized delays in the trial were occasioned by genuine difficulties, such as difficulties in translating Japanese to English.[81]

It is unquestionable, however, that politics entered into the indictment process and the release policies for those imprisoned. The Emperor was not indicted, on the ground that his immunity was necessary for Japan's post-war stability, and he was deliberately not mentioned by the prosecution nor (with the exception of one slip) the defence.[82] Cold War considerations led to the US (whose views were largely determinative on this matter) acquiescing in the release of all those imprisoned by 1955.[83]

In spite of the acceptance of the judgment by the Japanese government in Article 11 of the 1952 Peace Treaty, it has been questioned whether its findings were accepted by all parts of Japanese society. However, the question of memories and views of the Second World War in Japan is a complex and contested one both inside and outside Japan.[84] In the West the Tribunal has, until recently, been largely ignored,[85] and knowledge of it in Japan is waning. Amongst those in Japan with knowledge of the trial, however, there is less support for Japanese actions in the war,[86] and the Tokyo IMT remains a staple of debate amongst those discussing the question of war responsibility in Japan.[87]

6.5 Control Council Law No. 10 trials and military commissions in the Pacific sphere

In addition to the Nuremberg IMT, the Allied powers occupying Germany also engaged in a large-scale policy of prosecuting war crimes in their respective occupation zones. These were undertaken under the authority of Control Council Law No. 10, which provided for domestic prosecutions of war crimes, crimes against humanity and crimes against peace. Twelve major US trials that took place in Nuremberg after the IMT had concluded its

---

79 See, e.g. Yasuaki Onuma, 'Beyond Victor's Justice' (1984) 11 *Japan Echo* 63; Totani, *The Tokyo War Crimes Trial*, provides a useful counterpoint to Minear, *Victor's Justice*.

80 See, e.g. Totani, *The Tokyo War Crimes Trial*; Boister and Cryer, *Tokyo: A Reappraisal*.

81 Tokyo IMT Judgment, 48,429–30.

82 Herbert P. Bix, *Hirohito and the Making of Modern Japan* (London, 2000) ch. 15.

83 R. John Pritchard, 'The International Military Tribunal for the Far East and the Allied National War Crimes Trials in Asia' in Bassiouni, *International Criminal Law*, vol. III, 142.

84 See Ian Buruma, *The Wages of Guilt: Memories of War in Germany and Japan* (New York, 1994). For a very useful empirical modern study of Japanese views, see Madaoka Futamura, *War Crimes Tribunals and Transitional Justice: The Tokyo Trial and the Nuremberg Legacy* (London, 2007). See further Boister and Cryer, *Tokyo: A Reappraisal*, ch. 11.

85 Although the 60th anniversary of the trial has led to an upsurge in interest see, e.g. Timothy L. H. McCormack, Gerry J. Simpson and Yuki Tanaka (eds.), *The Tokyo IMT After 60 Years* (The Hague, 2010).

86 'Poll Shows Ignorance of Tokyo Tribunal', *Asahi Shimbun*, 5 March 2006.

87 Futamura, *War Crimes Tribunals and Transitional Justice*; Boister and Cryer, *Tokyo: A Reappraisal*, ch. 11.

business, were known as the 'subsequent proceedings'. These included trials of Nazi doctors and judges, the *Einsatzgruppen* and members of the German High Command. These trials have had a considerable influence on international criminal law.[88] Proceedings in the British zone of Germany were carried out under the Royal Warrant of 1946.[89] There were also proceedings in the French and Soviet zones of Germany. The trials were guided, to varying degrees, by the findings of the Nuremberg IMT.[90]

In the Pacific sphere a large number of trials were undertaken by the Allies, including the UK, US, Australia, China and the Philippines.[91] These were on the basis of various domestic war crimes provisions. In the UK, this was the Royal Warrant. Even though there were literally thousands of such proceedings, the trials are on the whole rather less well known than those in the European sphere of the Second World War.[92] The most famous of the trials is the US prosecution of General Yamashita,[93] which was an early modern use of the principle of command responsibility. Other interesting trials of the era include the proceedings against Admiral Toyoda before a mixed panel of Allied judges.

Further reading

John Appleman, *Military Tribunals and International Crimes* (Indianapolis, 1954).

Neil Boister and Robert Cryer, *The Tokyo International Military Tribunal: A Reappraisal* (Oxford, 2008).

Neil Boister and Robert Cryer (eds.), *Documents on the Tokyo International Military Tribunal: Charter, Indictment and Judgments* (Oxford, 2008).

Arnold Brackman, *The Other Nuremberg: The Story of the Tokyo War Crimes Trial* (New York, 1987).

Hans Ehard, 'The Nuremberg Trial Against the Major War Criminals and International Law' (1949) 43 *AJIL* 223.

Madaoka Futamura, *War Crimes Tribunals and Transitional Justice: The Tokyo Trial and the Nuremberg Legacy* (London, 2007).

George Ginsburgs and Vladimir Kudriavtsev (eds.), *The Nuremberg Trial and International Law* (Dordrecht, 1990).

---

88 See Howard Levie, *Terrorism in War: The Law of War Crimes* (New York, 1992) 72–98; Matthew Lippman, 'The Other Nuremberg, American Prosecutions of Nazi War Criminals in Occupied Germany' (1992) 3 *Indiana International and Comparative Law Review* 1.

89 See Anthony P. V. Rogers, 'War Crimes Trials Under the Royal Warrant, British Practice 1945–1949' (1990) 39 *ICLQ* 780.

90 See Adam Basak, 'The Influence of the Nuremberg Judgment on the Practice of the Allied Courts in Germany' (1977–1978) 9 *Polish Yearbook of International Law* 161.

91 See Levie, *Terrorism*, 155–83; Piccigallo, *The Japanese*; Robert W. Miller, 'War Crimes Trials at Yokohama' (1948–1949) 15 *Brooklyn Law Review* 19.

92 Although some are reported in the Law Reports, Trials of War Criminals series.

93 *US* v. *Yamashita* 327 US 1.

Solis Horwitz, 'The Tokyo Trial' (1950) 645 *International Conciliation* 465.

Hans Kelsen, 'Will the Judgment in the Nuremberg Trial Constitute a Precedent in International Law?' (1947) 1 *International Law Quarterly* 153.

Elizabeth Kopelman, 'Ideology and International Law: The Dissent of the Indian Justice at the Tokyo War Crimes Trial' (1991) 23 *New York University Journal of International Law and Politics* 373.

Otto Kranzbühler, 'Nuremberg: Eighteen Years Afterwards' (1965) 14 *De Paul Law Review* 333.

Matthew Lipmann, 'Nuremberg Forty-Five Years Later' (1991) 7 *Connecticut Journal of International Law* 1.

Guénaël Mettraux, *Perspectives on the Nuremberg Trial* (Oxford, 2008).

Richard H. Minear, *Victor's Justice: The Tokyo War Crimes Trial* (Princeton, 1971).

Radhabinodh Pal, *Crimes in International Relations* (Calcutta, 1955).

Anne-Marie Prevost, 'Race and War Crimes: the 1945 War Crimes Trial of General Tomoyuki Yamashita' (1992) 14 *Human Rights Quarterly* 303.

R. John Pritchard and Sonia M. Zaide, *The Tokyo War Crimes Trial: Transcripts* (New York, 1981).

A. Frank Reel, *The Case of General Yamashita* (Chicago, 1949).

B. V. A. Röling and Antonio Cassese, *The Tokyo Trial and Beyond* (Cambridge, 1992).

Georg Schwarzenberger, 'The Judgment of Nuremberg' (1947) 21 *Tulane Law Review* 329.

Henry Stimson, 'The Nuremberg Trial: Landmark in Law' (1947) 25 *Foreign Affairs* 179.

Telford Taylor, *The Anatomy of the Nuremberg Trial* (London, 1993).

Yuma Totani, *The Tokyo War Crimes Trial: The Pursuit of Justice in the Wake of World War II* (Cambridge, MA, 2008).

Ann Tusa and John Tusa, *The Nuremberg Trial* (London, 1983).

Quincy Wright, 'The Law of the Nuremberg Trial' (1947) 41 *AJIL* 37.

7

The ad hoc International Criminal Tribunals

7.1 Introduction

Until the early 1990s, it seemed unlikely that the progeny of Nuremberg and Tokyo IMTs would appear soon. However, in response to two conflicts in the 1990s (the Yugoslav wars of dissolution and the Rwandan genocide of 1994) the United Nations revived the idea of international criminal tribunals. This chapter will introduce those tribunals, and explain their practice. Although it is too early to come to any final conclusions about the Tribunals, this chapter will also draw out some of the plaudits and criticisms that have attended the operation of the Tribunals so far. This chapter does not, however, attempt to provide a comprehensive analysis of the jurisprudence of the Tribunals, as their output is analysed elsewhere in this book.[1]

7.2 The International Criminal Tribunal for Yugoslavia

7.2.1 The creation of the ICTY

Although some of the roots of the dissolution of Yugoslavia go back to the Second World War if not further, political developments in what was then the Socialist Federal Republic of Yugoslavia in the 1980s led that country to break up through a number of linked armed conflicts starting in 1991.[2] The conflicts were characterized by large-scale violations of international criminal law committed especially against civilians, most notably sexual offences and the practice of 'ethnic cleansing'. Pictures of concentration camps in Bosnia,

---

1 See also generally William Schabas, *The UN International Criminal Tribunals: the former Yugoslavia, Rwanda and Sierra Leone* (Cambridge, 2006). The decisions of the Tribunals are regularly noted and explained in the 'Current Developments in the *ad hoc* Tribunals' section of the *JICJ*. See also Geoffrey Watson, 'The Changing Jurisprudence of the International Criminal Tribunal for the Former Yugoslavia' (2002–2003) 37 *New England Law Review* 871; Payam Akhavan, 'The Crime of Genocide in the ICTR Jurisprudence' (2005) 3 *JICJ* 989.
2 See, e.g. Laura Silber and Alan Little, *The Death of Yugoslavia* (Harmondsworth, 1996).

which evoked memories of the Holocaust, caused public outcry and led to demands that something be done about the situation.

Even before the conflict was formally brought to an end in December 1995, the Security Council had taken action in relation to prosecuting those crimes. The Council approached the Rubicon to prosecution in autumn 1992, with Resolution 780 (1992), which created a Commission to investigate allegations of international crimes in Yugoslavia.[3] The Commission did not obtain significant State support, materially or financially, so its first chairman, Frits Kalshoven, resigned. Under its second chairman, M. Cherif Bassiouni, the Commission obtained financing from private sources and engaged in considerable evidence-gathering in Former Yugoslavia.[4] It reported in 1994.[5]

While the Commission was still at work, the Secretary-General consulted States about the creation of a possible future tribunal as a Security Council organ, at that time an entirely novel concept. In response to a request by the Council in Resolution 808 (1993), the Secretary-General recommended that it create a tribunal by resolution.[6] The possibility of creating the tribunal by treaty was canvassed, but rejected on the basis that it would take too long, and there was no guarantee that all the relevant States (in particular those in what was by then Former Yugoslavia) would ratify it.[7] The Report annexed a draft Statute for the tribunal, modelled in some ways on the Nuremberg IMT's charter, but also creating a cooperation regime which was to be streamlined when compared to inter-State coopera-tion, and mandatory in nature.[8] The Security Council adopted the draft Statute in Resolution 827 (1993),[9] although some States and commentators questioned whether the Security Council had the power to set up such a tribunal.[10] Although there is no real evidence of overt interference by the Council in the operation of the ICTY,[11] the question of the extent to which a political organ such as the Security Council ought to be able to act in this area is a highly controversial one, and one which has also arisen in relation to the ICC.

Resolution 827 (1993) set out the aims of the Security Council in setting up the ICTY, these were that, in the circumstances in Yugoslavia, the Tribunal could 'put an end to such crimes and take effective measures to bring to justice the persons who are responsible for

---

3 6.10.1992.
4 See generally M. Cherif Bassiouni, 'The United Nations Commission of Experts Established Pursuant to Security Council Resolution 780' (1994) 88 *AJIL* 784.
5 Final Report of the Commission of Experts Established Pursuant to Security Council Resolution 780 (1993).
6 Report of the Secretary General Pursuant to Security Council Resolution 808 (1993), para. 20.
7 *Ibid.*
8 See generally Larry D. Johnson, 'Ten Years Later: Reflections on the Drafting' (2004) 2 *JICJ* 368.
9 25.5.1993.
10 S.PV/3217, 20–2. Alfred P. Rubin, 'An International Criminal Tribunal for Former Yugoslavia' (1994) 6 *Pace International Law Review* 7. Most of these doubts were laid to rest after *Tadić* ICTY A.Ch. 2.10.1995.
11 The only possible exception is the completion strategy, see section 7.2.4.

them', and thus 'contribute to the restoration and maintenance of peace'.[12] The Council further asserted that it believed that creating the ICTY would 'contribute to ensuring that such violations are halted and effectively redressed'.[13] Such goals were certainly broad and optimistic, and perhaps overstated the extent to which criminal punishment, alone, can create international peace and security, although the Council only asserted that the ICTY would contribute to, rather than single-handedly create, reconciliation in Former Yugoslavia.

7.2.2   The structure of the ICTY

There are three main organs of the ICTY: the Registry, the Office of the Prosecutor and the Chambers. The Registry is responsible for the administrative management of the Tribunal, including, for example the victims and witnesses programme, transport of accused, their conditions of detention and public affairs. The Office of the Prosecutor is the organ whose responsibility it is to investigate allegations, issue indictments (which have to be confirmed by a judge) and bring matters to trial. The final organ of the ICTY is the Chambers. There are currently three Trial Chambers, each consisting of a presiding judge and two other judges.[14] The Trial Chambers are subject to the appellate control of the Appeals Chamber. This seven-member chamber (which sits in a panel of five) is headed by the President and is the final authority on matters of law in the Tribunal.[15]

7.2.3   The jurisdiction of the ICTY and its relationship to national courts

The ICTY has jurisdiction over war crimes, crimes against humanity and genocide committed after 1 January 1991 on the territory of the Former Yugoslavia.[16] Article 2 grants the Tribunal jurisdiction over grave breaches of the Geneva Conventions (which only apply in international armed conflicts),[17] whilst Article 3 provides the Tribunal with jurisdiction over a non-exhaustive list of violations of the laws or customs of war. The Tribunal decided in 1995 that this provision covered war crimes in both international and non-international

---

12 Security Council Resolution 827 (1993), preamble.
13 *Ibid.* See also Michael Scharf, 'The Tools for Enforcing International Criminal Justice in the New Millennium: Lessons from the Yugoslavia Tribunal' (1999) 49 *DePaul Law Review* 925, 928–33.
14 ICTY Statute, Art. 11.
15 The *ratio decidendi* of its decisions bind the Trial Chambers, see *Aleksovski* ICTY A.Ch. 24.3.2000 para. 112. The Appeals Chamber does not bind itself, but will only depart from its previous jurisprudence if there are 'cogent reasons in the interests of justice' to do so: *ibid.*, para. 107. Trial Chambers do not bind one another: *ibid.*, para. 113.
16 ICTY Statute, Arts. 1, 8.
17 *Tadić* ICTY A.Ch. 2.10.1995 paras. 79–8.

armed conflicts,[18] a decision that paved the way for some of the Tribunal's most innovative jurisprudence.[19] The Tribunal has jurisdiction over genocide and crimes against humanity pursuant to Articles 4 and 5 of its Statute respectively. Aggression is not included in the jurisdiction of the ICTY. The open-ended nature of the temporal jurisdiction of the Tribunal means that it has jurisdiction over the later conflicts in Kosovo and the Former Yugoslav Republic of Macedonia,[20] and over peacekeepers in the area, which was not anticipated by the drafters.

The ICTY also has primacy over national courts.[21] Pursuant to this principle, the Tribunal may require States to defer to it any proceedings they were contemplating or undertaking.[22] The situations when deferral is justified are given in Rule 9 of the Rules of Procedure and Evidence. Those situations are when the conduct is not charged as an international crime, where the proceedings are not fair or impartial, or what is in issue is closely related to, or otherwise involves, significant factual or legal questions which may have implications for investigations or prosecutions before the tribunal.[23] The last is a very broad provision, effectively allowing the ICTY to demand transfer of cases at will. As the Tribunal has begun winding up its work though, it has gone from taking cases from domestic jurisdictions to referring them back.

7.2.4 Milestones in the practice of the ICTY[24]

Beginnings and the Tadić case

It is fair to say that the ICTY began slowly. A skeleton staff, beset with funding and cash-flow problems, had to create an international criminal court effectively from nothing.[25] Staff had to be appointed, premises for the tribunal had to be found, and this before the legal work, including investigations, could even begin. When they began, investigations were hampered by the continuing armed conflicts in Yugoslavia.[26] In the absence of indictments or

18 *Ibid.*, paras. 86–93.
19 See Chapter 12.
20 See Security Council Resolution 1160 (1998), *Multinović et al.* ICTY A.Ch. 8.6.2004. *In re: The Republic of Macedonia* ICTY T.Ch. 4.10.2002.
21 ICTY Statute, Art. 9(1). Göran Sluiter, *International Criminal Adjudication and the Collection of Evidence: Obligations of States* (Antwerp, 2002) 81–8.
22 E.g. In the Matter of a Proposal for a Formal Request for Deferral to the Competence of the Tribunal Addressed to the Republic of Bosnia and Herzegovina in Respect of Radovan Karadžić, Ratko Mladić and Mico Stanišić, IT-95-5-D, T.Ch. 16.5.1995. Compare the relationship between the ICC and national courts: section 8.6.
23 Rule 9(i)–(iii).
24 Detailed statements of the ICTY's practice may be found in the Annual Reports which the ICTY submits to the Security Council.
25 The financial problems arose because of a disagreement between the Security Council and the General Assembly over the appropriate budget from which to fund it. See generally Annual Report of the ICTY 1994, S/1994/1007, paras. 34–6, 143–9.
26 Annual Report of the ICTY 1995, S/1995/728, paras. 4, 194–6.

defendants, there was relatively little for the judges to do other than write and refine the Rules of Procedure and Evidence.[27] The first major breakthrough occurred in April 1995, when Germany deferred its own proceedings against a (low ranking) Bosnian Serb accused of various international crimes, Duško Tadić, and transferred him to the ICTY for trial.[28]

Tadić challenged the ICTY's jurisdiction over him. This led to the seminal Interlocutory Appeal decision of October 1995.[29] Tadić had asserted that the Security Council had no authority to set up a criminal court, that the ICTY's primacy over national courts was unlawful, and that anyway the Tribunal had no jurisdiction over the crimes he was alleged to have committed.[30]

First, Tadić's challenge required the ICTY to decide whether it had the authority to pass on the legality of its own creation, a matter made more sensitive by the fact that the question of judicial review of the actions of the Security Council was an area in which the ICJ had, soon before, feared to tread too heavily.[31] Given this, and the fact that the ICTY is formally a subsidiary body of the Security Council, it was perhaps unsurprising that the Trial Chamber in the *Tadić* jurisdictional case simply denied that it had the authority to rule on the legality of its parent's actions, stating that its powers were limited to passing judgment on crimes in Former Yugoslavia.[32]

The Appeals Chamber, on the contrary, decided that it had the authority to determine the legality of its own creation.[33] It decided this on the basis that it had an inherent power to do so, in order to determine if it could lawfully exercise its primary jurisdiction over criminal cases.[34] The Tribunal's claim that it had incidental jurisdiction over something that it could not exercise primary jurisdiction to decide was bold.[35]

In his Separate Opinion, Judge Sidhwa provided one of the stronger arguments for the Tribunal's decision, noting that unlike the ICJ, the ICTY is a criminal court with mandatory jurisdiction over individuals, and this militated in favour of review.[36] Judge Li, on the other hand, took the view that since there was no express power granted to the ICTY to do so, and

---

27 On the Rules, see Annual Report of the ICTY 1994, paras. 52–97; for frustration with the lack of visible progress see Annual Report of the ICTY 1995, paras. 171–8.

28 *Ibid.*, paras. 179–84.

29 *Tadić* ICTY A.Ch. 2.10.1995.

30 *Ibid.*, para. 8.

31 *Questions of Interpretation and Application of the 1971 Montreal Convention Arising from the Aerial Incident at Lockerbie (Libya v. US, Libya v. UK)* (1992) ICJ Rep 114.

32 *Tadić* ICTY T.Ch. II 10.8.1995 paras. 8, 16.

33 *Tadić* ICTY A.Ch. 2.10.1995 paras. 14–25. See generally José E. Alvarez, 'Nuremberg Revisited: The *Tadić* Case' (1996) 7 *EJIL* 245.

34 *Tadić* ICTY A.Ch. 2.10.1995 para. 20.

35 See Colin Warbrick, 'The International Criminal Tribunal for Yugoslavia: The Decision of the Appeals Chamber on the Interlocutory Appeal on Jurisdiction in the *Tadić* Case' (1996) 45 *ICLQ* 691, 691–2.

36 *Tadić* ICTY A.Ch. 2.10.1995 Separate Opinion of Judge Sidhwa, para. 34. For discussion, see George Aldrich, 'Jurisdiction of the International Criminal Tribunal for the Former Yugoslavia' (1993) 90 *AJIL* 64 at 65; Alvarez, 'Nuremberg Revisited', 251, 255.

it did not have the expertise to determine the appropriateness of the Security Council's action, the review was 'worthless both in fact and in law'.[37]

Judge Li's comments not only relate to the power of the Tribunal, but also to whether the question was a political one which, as a court, the tribunal ought to decline to answer. The majority, on the authority of a number of ICJ decisions, in particular the *Certain Expenses* advisory opinion,[38] responded that the notions of 'political questions and non-justiciable disputes' were an anachronism in international adjudication, and that so long as a question has a legal answer, it may be given.[39] The majority had a point; the ICJ has shown itself willing to deal with the legal sides of disputes which have considerable political dimensions, including the use of force,[40] nuclear weapons[41] and aspects of the Middle East situation,[42] in the face of claims that they were political rather than legal questions.

When reviewing the actions of the Council, the majority in *Tadić* adopted a deferential standard. First, it said that it was clear that the Security Council was entitled to invoke its powers under Chapter VII of the charter, as there was an armed conflict in Yugoslavia at the relevant time.[43] This is correct, but it is not clear that the Council based the determination of a threat to the peace in Resolution 827 on the armed conflict. That resolution, after expressing its grave alarm at violations of humanitarian law, determined that 'this situation' was a threat to peace. Equally, the Council had the right to invoke Chapter VII over such events regardless of circumstances.

Next the Tribunal determined that the Council could set up a court. It based the authority of the Council to do this on Article 41 of the UN Charter. Although Article 41 does not expressly state that the Council can do so, this did not trouble the Appeals Chamber, as the list of measures it contains is not exhaustive.[44] The Tribunal also rejected the idea that the Council could not create a court as it had no judicial functions to pass to such a body. Its reasoning was that the Council did not purport to do such a thing, but to create a court in the exercise of its functions in relation to peace and security, in an analogous manner to the General Assembly's creation of an administrative tribunal, an action which received the sanction of the ICJ.[45] Finally, the majority refused to second-guess the Security Council's

---

37 *Tadić* ICTY A.Ch. 2.10.1995 Separate and Dissenting Opinion of Judge Li, paras. 2–4.

38 *Certain Expenses of the United Nations* (1962) ICJ Reports 151.

39 *Tadić* ICTY A.Ch. 2.10.1995 paras. 24–5.

40 See, e.g. *Case Concerning Military and Paramilitary Activities in and Against Nicaragua (Nicaragua v. USA)* (1986) ICJ Reports 4.

41 *Legality of the Threat or Use of Nuclear Weapons* Advisory Opinion, (1996) ICJ Reports 226.

42 *Legal Consequences of the Construction of a Wall in Palestinian Territory* ICJ List 131, (2004) 43 *ILM* 1009.

43 *Tadić* ICTY A.Ch. 2.10.1995 para. 30. Judge Sidhwa agreed, adding that the appraisal of the evidence leading to the determination was 'based on a proper appraisal of the evidence, and was reasonable and fair and not arbitrary or capricious'. Separate Opinion of Judge Sidhwa, para. 61.

44 *Tadić* ICTY A.Ch. 2.10.1995 paras. 34–5.

45 *Ibid.*, paras. 37–8, referring to *Effect of Awards of Compensation Made by the United Nations Administrative Tribunal* (1954) ICJ Reports 47 at 61.

belief that the establishment of a court could help restore international peace and security as, it said, an *ex post facto* evaluation as to whether or not this belief was correct would be inappropriate.[46] The question was not if that belief was correct, but whether it was held. On these points, the Chamber was right.

Further, the Tribunal also determined that owing to the membership of the Former Yugoslav States in the UN, primacy did not violate the sovereignty of the Former Yugoslav States,[47] or the (non-existent) right of the defendant to be tried before his own domestic courts.[48] On the former point, all the States emerging out of the Yugoslav wars of dissolution either had been accepted as members of the UN by the time of the creation of the ICTY, or claimed to be successor States to the Socialist Federal Republic of Yugoslavia at the time.[49]

The Chamber also dealt with the suggestion that, under human rights law, the ICTY was not 'established by law'. The Appeals Chamber, rather generously, took the view that although human rights treaties were not directly applicable to the Tribunal, the requirement that a tribunal be set up by law was a general principle of law, thus binding on the Tribunal.[50] With some justification, the Chamber asserted that this principle could not be applied in an unadulterated fashion without respect for the specific situation of an international tribunal. Therefore the Chamber asserted that the principle only required at the international level that the Tribunal be set up with sufficient safeguards for fair trial, which the Tribunal was.[51]

Shortly after the decision, at the end of 1995, the Yugoslav wars of dissolution were formally brought to an end by the Dayton Peace Agreement.[52] This agreement included an obligation on all the Former Yugoslav States to cooperate with the ICTY,[53] and provided that international forces in Former Yugoslavia had the authority to arrest those indicted by the ICTY.[54] This power was not used immediately, however, although those forces did provide

---

46 *Tadić* ICTY A.Ch. 2.10.1995 para. 39.

47 *Ibid.*, paras. 55–60.

48 *Ibid.*, paras. 61–4.

49 Although the position on point has since been made more complex by the *sui generis* status of the Federal Republic of Yugoslavia seemingly imputed to it by the ICJ: see *Application for Revision of the Judgment of 11 July 1996 in the Case concerning Application of the Convention on the Prevention and Punishment of the Crime of Genocide (Bosnia and Herzegovina* v. *Yugoslavia), Preliminary Objections (Yugoslavia* v. *Bosnia and Herzegovina)* Judgment of 3.2.2003, ICJ General List 122; and *Case Concerning the Application of the Convention on the Prevention and Punishment of the Crime of Genocide (Croatia* v. *Serbia)* (Preliminary Objections) Decision of 18.11.2008.

50 *Tadić* ICTY A.Ch. 2.10.1995 para. 42.

51 *Ibid.*, para. 46.

52 (1996) 35 *ILM* 75.

53 Article X, Annex 1-A.

54 Article IV(4) Annex IA; see Paula Gaeta, 'Is NATO Authorized or Obliged to Arrest Persons Indicted by the International Criminal Tribunal for former Yugoslavia?' (1998) 9 *EJIL* 174.

security for the prosecutor to engage in on-site investigations.[55] Cooperation from the States of Former Yugoslavia, other than Bosnia-Herzegovina, was still not forthcoming.[56]

The time of trials

By 1996 its judicial workload led the ICTY to ask for the creation of a second Trial Chamber.[57] This prospect was boosted when international forces began to arrest indictees in 1997.[58] The Federal Republic of Yugoslavia remained uncooperative. Croatia transferred one defendant that year.[59] By 1998 the Tribunal had nineteen people in custody, including three who had voluntarily surrendered themselves for trial.[60] Owing to the increased violence in Kosovo, the Security Council requested that the prosecutor look into events there.[61] This led, in May 1999, to the ICTY indicting Slobodan Milošević,[62] for alleged crimes in Kosovo. The prosecutor was assisted in this process by considerable evidence made available to her by western States.[63]

In 1999 the prosecutor was asked by a number of people and groups to investigate NATO States for alleged war crimes during its air campaign in relation to Kosovo. In response the prosecutor set up a committee to engage in a preliminary assessment of the evidence presented and to advise her on whether or not to initiate a full investigation. Even this action caused consternation in some circles.[64] The committee recommended in June 2000 that no full investigation be undertaken.[65] This recommendation was accepted by the prosecutor and caused considerable controversy.[66] Whether or not this decision reflected an unwillingness to investigate NATO officials, and whether or not the conclusions reached in the report are sound, aspects of the report's reasoning are certainly open to challenge.[67]

---

55 Annual Report of the ICTY 1996, S/1996/665, paras. 75–9.

56 *Ibid.*, paras. 167–71.

57 *Ibid.*, para. 72.

58 Annual Report of the ICTY 1997, S/1997/729, para. 190. Darryl Robinson, 'Trials, Tribulations and Triumphs: Major Developments in 1997 at the International Criminal Tribunal for Yugoslavia' (1997) 35 *Canadian Yearbook of International Law* 179.

59 Annual Report of the ICTY 1997, para. 183.

60 Annual Report of the ICTY 1998, S/1998/737, paras. 113–14.

61 Security Council Resolution 1160, Annual Report of the ICTY 1998, para. 118.

62 *Milošević et al.* ICTY Indictment 24.5.1999.

63 Annual Report of the ICTY 1999, S/1999/846, paras. 126, 128.

64 See, e.g. Rachel Kerr, *The International Criminal Tribunal for Former Yugoslavia: An Exercise in Law, Politics and Diplomacy* (Oxford, 2004) 202–3.

65 Final Report to the Prosecutor by the Committee Established to Review the NATO Bombing Campaign Against the Federal Republic of Yugoslavia 8 June 2000, (2000) 38 *ILM* 1257, para. 90.

66 See, in favour of the decision, Kerr, *International Criminal Tribunal*, 199–204. (Strongly against, see Michael Mandel, 'Politics and Human Rights in International Criminal Law: Our Case Against NATO and the Lessons to be Learnt From It' (2001–2002) 25 *Fordham International Law Journal* 95.

67 See Paolo Benvenuti, 'The ICTY Prosecutor and the Review of the NATO Bombing against the Federal Republic of Yugoslavia' (2001) 12 *EJIL* 503; Michael Bothe, 'The Protection of the Civilian Population and NATO Bombing on Yugoslavia: Comments on a Report to the Prosecutor of the ICTY' (2001) 12 *EJIL* 531.

Moving towards completion

Around 2000 the judges of the ICTY concluded that their work could take them until at least 2016 to complete.[68] This was considered to be too long. Therefore the ICTY suggested to the Security Council that there be a 'completion strategy'.[69] This involved a number of steps. The first was the creation of *ad litem* judges, peripatetic judges who would sit for one case.[70] This was achieved when a set of twenty-seven such judges were authorized by Security Council Resolution 1329 (2000).[71] The next step was getting senior lawyers to deal with some pre-trial matters rather than judges.[72] The third step of the plan was to expand the Appeals Chamber, a move that was also accepted in Resolution 1329 (2000).

The visibility and perceived effectiveness of the Tribunal increased considerably in 2001, when the Federal Republic of Yugoslavia began, after considerable economic and political pressure, sporadic cooperation with the Tribunal, most notably with the surrender of ex-President Milošević to the ICTY in June 2001. Just over a month later, the ICTY issued its first conviction for genocide, of General Radislav Krstić, for his role in the Srebrenica massacre.[73] During this period, the prosecutor undertook a number of initiatives to ensure that investigations would be completed by the end of 2004.[74] These involved, inter alia, focusing on high-level offenders, as lower level offenders could be tried at the domestic level.[75] It was hoped that this would permit the Tribunal to complete its trial-level work by 2008, although this was contingent on State cooperation in transferring evidence and indictees.[76]

The possibility of the Tribunal living up to its timetable was assisted by three factors. First, increasing numbers of defendants were willing to plead guilty, in particular, in October 2002, Biljana Plavšić, a wartime president of the Republika Srpska.[77] Second, the Federal Republic of Yugoslavia increased its cooperation with the Tribunal, although the two highest profile fugitives, Radovan Karadžić and Ratko Mladić remained at liberty.[78] Finally, more indictees began to surrender voluntarily to the ICTY.[79] On its side, the ICTY revised Rule of Procedure and Evidence 11*bis*, to permit the ICTY to transfer indictments, and later, cases, after it had considered the appropriateness of doing so, taking

---

68 Annual Report of the ICTY 2000, S/2000/777, para. 336.
69 See generally Dominic Raab, 'Evaluating the ICTY and Its Completion Strategy' (2005) 3 *JICJ* 82.
70 Annual Report of the ICTY 2000, para. 340.
71 30 November 2000. The roles of such judges have gradually expanded.
72 Annual Report of the ICTY 2001, S/2001/865, para. 4.
73 *Krstić* ICTY T.Ch. I 2.8.2001.
74 Annual Report of the ICTY 2002, S/2002/985, para. 7.
75 *Ibid.*, para. 218.
76 *Ibid.*, para. 328.
77 Annual Report of the ICTY 2003, S/2003/829, para. 2. See *Plavšić* ICTY T.Ch. III 23.11.2003.
78 Annual Report of the ICTY 2003, para. 8.
79 *Ibid.*, para. 232.

into account, inter alia, the gravity of the crime, the role of the accused, and the fair trial guarantees that would be accorded to the accused.[80]

A major development occurred in August 2003, when the Security Council explained its approach to the ICTY's completion strategy in Resolution 1503. This suggested that the prosecutor should concentrate on high-level offenders, and the resolution also set out the ICTY's completion timetable. In addition to the prosecutor completing investigations by 2004, the Trial Chambers were required to complete their business by 2008 and appeals were to end by 2010.[81] Scepticism about the ability of the Tribunal to keep to this timetable was not unfounded.[82] Nonetheless, the Security Council adopted Resolution 1534 (2003), which required the Tribunal's judges to check that any new indictment focused on 'the most senior leaders suspected of being most responsible for crimes' in the Tribunal's jurisdiction, a requirement adopted in Amended Rule of Procedure and Evidence 28(A). Some have questioned whether this is consistent with the requirements of prosecutorial independence.[83] Although such critiques are worth taking seriously, it is unlikely that it altered the prosecutor's strategy in a practical way, as she had already been focusing on such offenders for some time.

On the other hand, one of the ICTY's own judges issued a stinging critique of the completion strategy from the viewpoint of the fair-trial rights of the defendants. Judge Hunt asserted that the international community expected trials to be in accordance with fair trial rights, but were unwilling to give the time and money necessary. However, the answer was not to curtail defence rights, since '[t]his Tribunal will not be judged by the number of convictions which it enters, or by the speed with which it concludes the Completion Strategy which the Security Council has endorsed, but by the fairness of its trials. The ... [decisions] ... in which the Completion Strategy has been given priority over the rights of the accused will leave a spreading stain on this Tribunal's reputation.'[84] Whether or not this is agreed with,[85] it is true that the completion strategy has led to a number of procedural innovations, and an increased use of documentary evidence.[86]

---

80 See generally, Michael Bohlander, 'Referring an Indictment from the ICTY and ICTR to Another Court – Rule 11*bis* and the Consequences for the Law of Extradition' (2006) 55 *ICLQ* 219.

81 See Raab, 'Completion Strategy', 85–6.

82 *Ibid.*, at 86, 95.

83 Darryl A. Mundis, 'The Judicial Effects of the "Completion Strategies" on the ad hoc International Criminal Tribunals' (2005) 99 *AJIL* 142; Larry D. Johnson, 'Closing an International Criminal Tribunal While Maintaining International Human Rights Standards and Excluding Impunity' (2005) 99 *AJIL* 158.

84 *Milošević* ICTY, Dissenting Opinion of Judge David Hunt on Admissibility of Evidence In Chief in the Form of Written Statement (Majority Decision Given 30.09.2003), 21.10.2003, paras 21–2.

85 See Fausto Pocar, 'Completion or Continuation Strategy?' (2008) 6 *JICJ* 655, 657–8; 'Discussion' (2008) 6 *JICJ* 681, at 682–7.

86 O-Gon Kwon, 'The Challenge of the International Criminal Trial as Seen from the Bench' (2007) 5 *JICJ* 360.

In 2005, after the prosecutor completed investigations for war crimes,[87] the Tribunal began to refer cases to national jurisdictions, in particular in Bosnia and Croatia, for trial.[88] A transfer to Serbia was made in 2007, although the Tribunal no longer considers any other cases to be appropriate for referral anywhere pursuant to Rule 11*bis*.[89] As of July 2009, the Tribunal had, of the 161 people charged, 36 in custody, 3 on provisional release, and had completed proceedings against 120 accused with 60 convictions and 11 acquittals. It is continuing proceedings against 41 accused (others have had their indictments withdrawn or have died).[90] The death of the most (in)famous of these, Slobodan Milošević, in 2006, just before the end of his lengthy and often controversial trial robbed the Tribunal of the possibility of completing proceedings against one of the main leaders involved in the wars of 1991–1995.[91] There are only two indictees at large at the time of writing, Goran Hadžić (a Croatian General) and Ratko Mladić (the commander of Serb forces that perpetrated the Srebrenića massacre). But these absences, alongside the number of accused currently still undergoing proceedings at the ICTY (39 – including Radovan Karadžić, who was transferred to the Court in July 2008) make it unlikely that the ICTY will close before at least mid 2013.[92] In July 2009 the Security Council extended the mandate of all the judges until 31 December 2010 (or until they complete their caseload, whichever is earlier), with a provision for review of the terms of Appeal Chamber judges to decide upon any further extension in December 2009.[93]

Ironically, given the staffing problems at the outset of the ICTY's history, the impending closure of the ICTY is leading to difficulties again, as people leave for more secure employment elsewhere.[94] Even so, the ICTY is currently working on defining and setting up its 'residual functions', i.e. those functions such as deciding upon early release, supervision of the enforcement of sentences and possible reopening of cases.[95] Its eye is also turning to what

---

87 Annual Report of the ICTY 2005, para. 172.

88 See Bohlander, 'Referring an Indictment'.

89 Report to the Security Council 24 November 2008, S/2008/743, Annex II, para. 43.

90 http://www.icty.org/sections/TheCases/KeyFigures.

91 Gideon Boas, *The Milošević Trial: Lessons for the Conduct of Complex International Criminal Proceedings* (Cambridge, 2007); Maya Steinitz, 'The Milošević Trial – Live! An Iconical Analysis of International Law's Claim to Legitimate Authority' (2005) 3 *JICJ* 310. The leaders of Croatia and Bosnia in the relevant periods, Franjo Tudjman and Alija Izetbegović respectively, died unindicted, if not uninvestigated.

92 Report to the Security Council 18 May 2009, S/2009/252, para. 14, Enclosure IX.

93 Security Council Resolution 1877 (2009). Appeals Chamber Judges' terms are due to expire on 31 December 2010, by virtue of Security Council Resolution 1837 (2009).

94 *Ibid.*, para. 43.

95 *Ibid.*, para. 52. The 12 functions identified by Judge Pocar were '(1) trials of fugitives; (2) review of earlier judgments; (3) referrals of cases to national jurisdictions; (4) supervision of prison sentences, early release, pardon and commutation; (5) contempt or perjury proceedings; (6) prevention of double jeopardy in national courts; (7) witness protection; (8) issues relating to defence counsel and legal aid; (9) claims for compensation; (10) archives; (11) public information, capacity building and outreach; (12) human resources issues' (address at the Meeting of Legal Advisers to Ministries of Foreign Affairs 27 October 2007), available at http://www.un.org/icty/pressreal/2007/pr1194e-annex.htm. See Gabriel Oosthuizen and Robert Schaeffer, 'Complete justice:

it terms its 'legacy', which includes ensuring that large amounts of its judicial and other materials are properly archived and available, creating a compilation of its practices[96] and undertaking capacity building in domestic jurisdictions.[97]

7.2.5   Appraisal of the ICTY

The ICTY itself has set out a number of its achievements.[98] These are, inter alia, that it has promoted accountability rather than impunity, including to leaders, established the facts of the crimes in Former Yugoslavia, brought justice for victims and given them a voice, developed international law and strengthened the rule of law.[99] The Tribunal has, to some extent, fulfilled these goals.

It is true that the creation of the ICTY has contributed to the trend against impunity, not least as its creation and Statute provided a direct precedent for the ICTR, and a slightly less direct one for the ICC.[100] Also the ICTY showed that international prosecutions were possible outside the situation of a complete defeat of one side in a conflict. Equally, at times the Tribunal has struggled to contain the size of trials against high-ranking defendants, and has similarly had difficulty containing the disruptive activities of a number of defendants[101] (although the upcoming Karadžić trial may prove that lessons have been learned).[102] The Tribunal has taken considerable pains to determine what happened in Former Yugoslavia accurately, even if its approach has been criticized.[103] The Tribunal spent considerable time and resources to attempt to bring (corrective) justice to victims, even if its practice has not always been perfect by the exacting standards of victims' rights advocates,[104] nor the experiences of victims appearing before it uniformly positive.[105]

Residual functions and potential residual mechanisms of the ICTY, ICTR and SCSL' (2008) 3 *Hague Justice Journal* 48.

96 Which is available at http://www.icty.org/x/file/About/Reports%20and%20Publications/ICTY_Manual_on_Developed_Practices.pdf.

97 *Ibid.*, para. 53.

98 http://www.icty.org/sid/324.

99 *Ibid.*

100 Ralph Zacklin, 'The Failings of ad hoc International Tribunals' (2004) 2 *JICJ* 541.

101 See, e.g. Göran Sluiter, 'Compromising the Authority of International Criminal Justice: How Vojislav Šešelj Runs His Trial' (2007) 5 *JICJ* 529; Michael P. Scharf, 'Chaos in the Courtroom: Controlling Disruptive Defendants and Contumacious Counsel in War Crimes Trials' (2006–2007) 39 *Case Western Reserve Journal of International Law* 155; Robert Cryer, 'Prosecuting the Leaders: Promises, Politics and Practicalities' (2009) 1 *Göttingen Journal of International Law* 45, at 72–4.

102 Göran Sluiter, 'Karadžić on Trial: Two Procedural Problems' (2008) 6 *JICJ* 617; Marko Milanović, 'The Arrest and Impending Trial of Radovan Karadžić' (2009) 58 *ICLQ* 212; Boas, *The Milošević Trial*.

103 José E. Alvarez, 'Rush to Closure: Lessons of the Tadić Judgment' (1998) 96 *Michigan Law Review* 2031.

104 Marie-Bénédict Dembour and Emily Haslam, 'Silencing Hearings? Victim–Witnesses at War Crimes Trials' (2004) 15 *EJIL* 151.

105 Eric Stover, *The Witnesses* (New York, 2007).

It is difficult, if not impossible, to doubt the ICTY's impact on international law.[106] Although the Tribunal has been accused of being too quick to decide that aspects of the law are customary,[107] and of seeking always to expand its own authority,[108] most of its decisions are well reasoned, and have not been criticized by States.[109] Although it might be queried whether all of the ICTY's decisions on custom have been irreproachable, it is not clear that they have violated the *nullum crimen sine lege* principle.[110] The more recent judgments of the ICTY may be less discursive of larger issues of law than earlier decisions such as *Tadić*; as the major issues were decided in the earlier decisions, there is less scope for iconic case law from the ICTY now.

On the downside, the ICTY has been accused, with varying degrees of accuracy, of various sins against international law and justice.[111] Some accusations, such as that it has been systematically biased towards or against one of the sides in the Yugoslav wars of dissolution, are easily dismissable,[112] even though the necessity of obtaining cooperation from States has probably led to some necessary diplomatic manoeuvring by the prosecutors.[113] Other critiques have included that the Tribunal has been too expensive and bureaucratic,[114] that its trials are characterized by delay,[115] violate the rights of defendants,[116] and are far removed from the populations of Former Yugoslavia.[117] More generally it has been alleged that the Tribunal was created in place of more effective action to prevent crimes in Former Yugoslavia.[118]

---

106 See, e.g. Robert Cryer, 'Of Custom, Treaties, Scholars and the Gavel: The Influence of the International Criminal Tribunals on the ICRC Customary Study' (2006) 11 *Journal of Conflict and Security Law* 239.

107 See Guénaël Mettraux, *International Crimes and the ad hoc Tribunals* (Oxford, 2005) 13–18.

108 See, e.g. Gregory Lombardi, 'Legitimacy and the Expanding Power of the ICTY' (2002–2003) 37 *New England Law Review* 887. A counterexample would be the *Blaškić* decision, see Chapter 20.

109 One exception is *Kupreškić et al.* ICTY T.Ch. II 14.1.2000 paras. 521–36, which rather unconvincingly derived the prohibition of practically all reprisals from contradictory practice and a bold interpretation of the Martens clause. See Christopher Greenwood, 'Belligerent Reprisals in the Jurisprudence of the International Criminal Tribunal for the Former Yugoslavia' in Claus Kreß et al. (eds.), *National and International Prosecution of Crimes Under International Law* (Berlin, 2001) 539. The Tribunal has now, in essence, overturned this decision though, see Chapter 16.9.2.

110 See generally, Mohamed Shahabuddeen, 'Does the Principle of Legality Stand in the Way of Progressive Development of the Law?' (2004) 2 *JICJ* 1007.

111 On the more general questions about criminal prosecution here, see section 2.4.

112 Although see also nn. 66, 67 and corresponding text on the critiques in relation to the NATO/Kosovo Report.

113 Victor Peskin, *International Justice in Rwanda and the Balkans: Virtual Trials and the Struggle for State Cooperation* (Cambridge, 2008); Carla del Ponte, *Madame Prosecutor* (New York, 2009).

114 Zacklin, 'Failings', at 543–4.

115 See, e.g. Patrick L. Robinson, 'Ensuring Fair and Expeditious Trials at the ICTY' (2000) 11 *EJIL* 569.

116 *Ibid.*

117 Laurel E. Fletcher and Harvey Weinstein, 'A World Unto Itself: The Application of International Criminal Justice in former Yugoslavia' in Eric Stover and Harvey Weinstein (eds.), *My Neighbour, My Enemy: Justice and Community in the Aftermath of Mass Atrocity* (Cambridge, 2004) 29.

118 See, e.g. David Forsythe, *Human Rights in International Relations* (Cambridge, 2000) 221.

All of these critiques have some purchase. The ICTY is expensive. Between 1993 and 2009 the official budget of the ICTY has amounted to US$1,585,490,022. It may simply be that international justice is expensive,[119] equally, excessive bureaucracy in the UN contributing to both cost and delay is not unprecedented. Trials have taken a long time, although some delays have been referable to attempts to ensure fair trials for defendants. Nonetheless, some of the decisions of the Tribunal have been controversial in relation to fair trial. Notable in this regard has been the use of anonymous witnesses. Although understandable witness protection issues arise in relation to prosecutions of international crimes, the practice of the Trial Chamber in the *Tadić* case of granting witnesses complete anonymity proved very controversial, in particular owing to the false testimony of one such protected witness, Dragan Opacić.[120]

The question of distance from the relevant populations is a difficult one, but the ICTY did not initially give such matters sufficient consideration in its early practice, which allowed local actors to distort matters,[121] a point the Tribunal has attempted to rectify by setting up various 'outreach' programmes.[122] In defence of the Tribunal, it can be said that the relationship between the media and international justice is not simple, in particular as proceedings are rarely akin to the court dramas many are used to watching and there are other calls on their attention.[123] In addition, the security situation in Former Yugoslavia would not have permitted the ICTY to have sat there, at least until recently. In relation to the final critique mentioned above, that the ICTY was created in place of more effective action to prevent crimes in Former Yugoslavia, it raises an important issue, although it is likely that the best available option was to create a tribunal. If it had not been created, there would not have been any more effective response to the crimes in Former Yugoslavia forthcoming. Equally, a more general issue, that of selectivity, certainly arises whenever an ad hoc tribunal is set up.[124]

7.3   The International Criminal Tribunal for Rwanda

7.3.1   The creation of the ICTR

Fears of selectivity fed into the decision to create the ICTR. Given the creation of the ICTY for a European conflict, when genocide clearly occurred in Africa, it was considered

---

119 David Wipmann, 'The Costs of International Justice' (2006) 100 *AJIL* 861.

120 *Tadić* ICTY T.Ch. II 7.5.1997 paras. 553–4.

121 Mirko Klarin, 'The Impact of the ICTY Trials on Public Opinion in the Former Yugoslavia' (2009) 7 *JICJ* 89.

122 David Tolbert, 'The International Criminal Tribunal for the Former Yugoslavia: Unforeseen Successes and Foreseeable Shortcomings' (2002) 26(2) *Fletcher Forum of World Affairs* 7, 13–14; Gabrielle Kirk McDonald, 'Problems, Obstacles and Achievements of the ICTY' (2004) 2 *JICJ* 558, 569–70.

123 Marlise Simons, 'International Criminal Tribunals and the Media' (2009) 7 *JICJ* 83.

124 Gerry Simpson, 'War Crimes: A Critical Introduction' in Timothy McCormack and Gerry Simpson (eds.), *The Law of War Crimes* (The Hague, 1997) 1 at 8.

necessary and appropriate to create an analogous tribunal for crimes committed there.[125] The UN and its members (who reduced the number of peacekeepers in Rwanda at the start of the genocide in April 1994),[126] treated the creation of a tribunal for Rwanda largely as they treated the ICTY, beginning with condemnation, then setting up a Commission of Experts and, before they reported, deciding to set up an international tribunal.[127]

Unlike the ICTY Statute, the ICTR Statute was drafted by the members of the Security Council, following closely the model of the ICTY Statute. While Rwanda, then a member of the Council, was initially supportive, it did not succeed in including the death penalty, excluding crimes other than genocide from the court's jurisdiction or granting the court jurisdiction before 1994, and therefore voted against the creation of the ICTR.[128] This does not affect the legality of the creation of the Tribunal, which finds its basis, like the ICTY, in Chapter VII of the UN Charter.[129]

7.3.2   The structure of the ICTR

The structure of the ICTR is very similar to that of the ICTY; it too has an Office of the Prosecutor, a Registry, and three Trial Chambers, which have the same functions as their counterparts in The Hague. To ensure a consistent jurisprudence between the ICTY and ICTR, they share a joint Appeals Chamber (based in The Hague).[130] Originally this was staffed only by judges from the ICTY. This gave rise to a feeling that the ICTR was the 'poor cousin' of the ICTY, but was rectified in late 2000 when two ICTR judges were appointed to that Chamber. Originally, the ICTY and ICTR shared a prosecutor. However, the job was split in 2003 and a separate prosecutor for the ICTR was appointed. The ICTR has always had its own president.

7.3.3   The jurisdiction of the ICTR and its relationship to national courts

The ICTR, like the ICTY, has jurisdiction over war crimes, crimes against humanity and genocide,[131] although the definitions of the last two crimes are different from those in the ICTY. In particular the definition of crimes against humanity has an additional requirement of discrimination for all crimes against humanity (Article 3), and the jurisdiction of the ICTR

---

125 Payam Akhavan, 'The International Criminal Tribunal for Rwanda: The Politics and Pragmatics of Punishment' (1996) 90 *AJIL* 501.

126 See Security Council Resolution 912 (1994). More generally see, e.g. Gerard Prunier, *The Rwanda Crisis* (London, 1997).

127 Security Council Resolutions 935 (1994) (Commission) and 955 (1994) (Court).

128 S/PV.3453, 2, 10–12. China abstained on the resolution.

129 The ICTR affirmed the legality of its own creation in *Kanyabashi* ICTR T.Ch. II 18.6.1997. The decision is, however, terse and amounts to little more than a refusal to investigate the legality of Security Council actions.

130 ICTR Statute, Art. 12(2).

131 *Ibid.*, Arts. 2, 3 and 4 respectively.

over war crimes is limited to those in non-international armed conflicts (Article 4). The ICTR's jurisdiction over these crimes is limited to where they occurred in Rwanda, or were committed by Rwandans in neighbouring States, between 1 January and 31 December 1994.[132] The ICTR has primacy over domestic courts, in the same way as the ICTY.[133] Like the ICTY, it has also adopted a Rule 11*bis*, which allows it to refer cases to domestic jurisdictions.

7.3.4 The practice of the ICTR

Teething troubles

The ICTR began at a snail's pace. Its seat, in Arusha, Tanzania, was only decided upon in February 1995.[134] Also, staffing was a problem, recruitment being difficult and slow.[135] Even so, the first indictment was confirmed in November 1995.[136] Early cooperation from some African States was quite quick, and proceedings opened against Georges Rutaganda and Jean-Paul Akayesu on 30 May 1996.[137] Rwanda, however, remained rather lukewarm in its relations with the Tribunal.

Although funding for the Tribunal at the time was inadequate,[138] there were also concerns about the extent to which resources, and the Tribunal as a whole, were being managed.[139] These were brought into the open in a highly critical report of the UN Office of Internal Oversight Services of 6 February 1997.[140] Whilst accepting that sporadic funding for the Tribunal limited its effectiveness,[141] and deciding that the 'evidence adduced did not confirm allegations of corrupt practices or misuse of funds',[142] the Report uncovered 'mismanagement in almost all areas of the Tribunal, and frequent violations of United Nations rules and regulations'.[143] The Registry was singled out for very heavy criticism, in particular, for financial irregularities, employing under-qualified staff, and weak asset management.[144] The Office of the Prosecutor was considered inefficient, and beset by leadership failure by the deputy prosecutor.[145] Of the three organs, only the Chambers

---

132 *Ibid.*, Art. 1.
133 *Ibid.*, Art. 8(1).
134 Security Council Resolution 977 (1995).
135 Annual Report of the ICTR 1996, S/1996/778, para. 12.
136 *Ibid.*, para. 31.
137 *Ibid.*, para. 39.
138 *Ibid.*, para. 77.
139 General Assembly Resolution 52/213 C.
140 *Report of the Secretary-General on the Activities of the Office of Internal Oversight Services*, A/51/789.
141 *Ibid.*, para. 5.
142 *Ibid.*, para. 6.
143 *Ibid.*
144 *Ibid.*, paras. 11–33.
145 *Ibid.*, paras. 55–9.

escaped serious critique.[146] As a result of the report, both the registrar's and the deputy prosecutor's resignations were sought, and obtained.[147] Also, attempts were made to recruit appropriate people to managerial positions and to improve financial discipline.[148]

Moving forwards

The ICTR's fortunes took a turn for the better in May 1998, when Jean Kambanda, the Prime Minister of the government that presided over the genocide, pleaded guilty to genocide. Notwithstanding his guilty plea, which recognized, importantly, that genocide had occurred in Rwanda, he was sentenced to life imprisonment.[149] In spite of continuing technical, logistical and resourcing problems, the Tribunal moved into a phase of increased trial work, which led the Security Council to increase the number of Trial Chambers to three in April 1998.[150] The first full trial ended in September 1998, with the conviction of Akayesu for genocide, in a judgment that not only offered the first express application of the Genocide Convention by an international tribunal, but also determined that sexual offences could form the *actus reus* of genocide.[151]

Trials were moving slowly but forward during 1999, when the relationship between the ICTR and Rwanda collapsed. The reason for this was the decision of the Appeals Chamber that the pre-trial detention of Jean-Bosco Barayagwiza, one of the mass media advocates of the genocide, violated his human rights, and so the Tribunal should use its inherent power to decline jurisdiction over him.[152] Rwanda was outraged, and suspended cooperation with the Tribunal, which owing to the vast majority of evidence and witnesses being located in Rwanda made progress with trials very difficult. The Appeals Chamber quickly revisited its decision on the point and determined that on the basis of further factual submissions by the prosecutor, the Tribunal ought to continue to exercise jurisdiction over him, but he ought to receive a reduction in any sentence he received if he were to be convicted, to take into account his pre-trial predicament.[153] Although relations between the ICTR and Rwanda improved, many thought that politics, more than law, was involved in the decision.[154]

---

146 *Ibid.*, paras. 60–63.
147 Annual Report of the ICTR 1997, S/1997/868, para. 57.
148 *Ibid.*
149 *Kambanda* ICTR T.Ch. I 4.9.1998. Kambanda unsuccessfully appealed; *Kambanda* ICTR A.Ch. 19.10.2000.
150 Security Council Resolution 1165 (1998). See Annual Report of the ICTR 1999, S/1999/943, paras. 5, 126.
151 *Akayesu* ICTR T.Ch. I 2.9.1998; see section 10.3.1.
152 *Barayagwiza* ICTR A.Ch. 3.11.1999.
153 *Barayagwiza*, ICTR A.Ch. 31.3.2000. In the event, he was convicted, and sentenced to thirty-five years' imprisonment, unlike his co-defendants, both of whom were sentenced to life. *Nahimana, Barayagwiza and Ngeze* ICTR T.Ch. I 3.12.2003 paras. 1106–7. His sentence was reduced to thirty-two years on appeal.
154 William A. Schabas, 'Prosecutor v. Barayagwiza' (2000) 94 *AJIL* 563, 565.

Nonetheless, the position of the ICTR was improved in 2001 when, pursuant to Security Council Resolution 1329,[155] *ad litem* judges were appointed to assist in trials. By early 2001, it was thought that the prosecutor would complete her investigative work by 2005.[156] Trial work remained slow, however,[157] and pre-trial detention of suspects remained very long.

The completion strategy

As the ICTR began to think in terms of completion, plans were formulated to pass up to forty cases to national jurisdictions (including Rwanda) rather than have them prosecuted by the ICTR.[158] Thus in July 2002 the ICTR adopted its own Rule 11*bis*, permitting the transfer of cases to national jurisdictions. To assist the ICTR in completing its judicial business (which was still taking a great deal of time) the Security Council adopted Resolution 1431 on 14 August 2002, which set up a pool of eighteen *ad litem* judges.[159] Although the ICTR was assisted by a number of States, relations with Rwanda remained less than friendly.[160]

In August 2003, Security Council Resolution 1503 (2003) set out the Security Council's timetable for completion, which was the same as that for the ICTY. This resolution also split the role of the prosecutor in two, creating separate positions of ICTY and ICTR prosecutor on the stated basis that the job was too large for one person and thus Rwanda was being overlooked.[161] The completion strategy was expanded upon by Resolution 1534, which required both Tribunals to review their caseloads to determine which cases could be tried at the domestic level.[162] The ICTR declared its ability to meet the various deadlines (subject to State cooperation) in 2005.[163] Its ability to do so was, it was hoped, to be assisted by negotiations with Rwanda to facilitate transfer of cases from the ICTR to Kigali.[164] However, although some transfers have occurred (to France),[165] none, to date, has been made to Rwanda. Indeed the ICTR has been critical of the

---

155 5.12.2000.

156 Annual Report of the ICTR 2002, S/2002/733, para. 121.

157 *Ibid.*, paras. 1–6.

158 *Ibid.*, para. 10. The ICTR had, early on in its practice, unsuccessfully attempted such an approach, with respect to Bernard Ntuyuhaga; *Ntuyuhaga*, ICTR T. Ch. I 18.3.1999.

159 See Annual Report of the ICTR 2003, S/2003/707, paras. 7–8; Annual Report of the ICTR 2005, S/2005/534, para. 5.

160 *Ibid.*, para. 63.

161 For the view that this was more to do with del Ponte's stated willingness to begin investigating allegations against the RPF, see Luc Reydams, 'The ICTR Ten Years On: Back to the Nuremberg Paradigm?' (2005) 3 *JICJ* 977 and del Ponte, *Madame Prosecutor*, Chapter 9.

162 26.3.2004.

163 S/2005/336.

164 Annual Report of the ICTR 2005, para. 49.

165 *Buchiybaruta* ICTR T.Ch. 20.11.2007; *Munyeshaka* ICTR T.Ch. 20.11.2007.

possibility of fair trials in Rwanda and of the standards of imprisonment there. This stance has led to consternation in Rwanda, and to other States being wary of extraditing suspects there.[166] This reticence to transfer to Rwanda, alongside the fact that thirteen indictees are still at large, makes it difficult to predict accurately when the ICTR will complete its work. The Tribunal does not believe it will be before 2011 at the earliest.[167] Given that the ICTR began ten new trials in 2009,[168] it is likely to be some time after that. The Security Council has extended the terms of the judges until 31 December 2010 (unless they finish their cases earlier) and will review the extension of the terms of Appeals Chamber judges before 31 December 2009.[169] Like the ICTY, the winding-up of its activities has led to staff leaving the ICTR for permanent employment, whilst it is working on analogous 'legacy' activities.[170]

7.3.5   Appraisal of the ICTR[171]

The Tribunal has come in for a great deal of criticism in the past,[172] but the picture is more mixed than critics would suggest, and the ICTR has been working hard. The ICTR has had notable success in obtaining, and trying, high-level suspects. As of May 2009, the Tribunal had tried forty-four people, thirty-five of whom were convicted and was in the process of trying or about to try thirty-two more.[173] Although it has not obtained all of the ringleaders of the genocide, it has many of them, both civilian and military, and they are being prosecuted or have been convicted.[174] Its successes on this point are perhaps greater than those of the ICTY. Also the early *Akayesu* decision has formed an important authoritative determination that genocide had occurred in Rwanda, a point that some in the mid-1990s denied or tried to minimize.[175] Indeed the ICTR now takes juridical notice of the fact that there was genocide in Rwanda in 1994.[176]

---

166   See, e.g. *Munyakazi* ICTR A.Ch. 8.10.2008; *Brown and others* v. *Government of Rwanda and Secretary of State for the Home Department* [2009] EWCA 770. See also section 5.4.5.
167   Report of the ICTR to the Security Council of 14 May 2009, S/2009/247, para. 55.
168   *Ibid.*, para. 69.
169   Security Council Resolution 1878 (2009).
170   Report of 14 May, S/2009/247, paras. 46, 66–8.
171   For an early (positive) appraisal see Djiena Wembou, 'The ICTR: Its Role in the African Context' (1997) 321 *International Review of the Red Cross* 685.
172   See, e.g. Todd Howland and William Calathes, 'The UN's International Criminal Tribunal: Is it Justice or Jingoism for Rwanda? A Call for Transformation' (1998) 39 *Virginia Journal of International Law* 135.
173   Report of 14 May, S/2009/247, Annex 1.
174   Larissa J. van den Herik, *The Contribution of the Rwanda Tribunal to the Development of International Law* (The Hague, 2005) 263; these include Kambanda and top-ranking military officials such as Théoneste Bagosora, *Bagosora* ICTR T. Ch. I 18.12.2008.
175   See Prunier, *The Rwanda Crisis*, 345.
176   *Karemera, Ngirumpatse and Nzirorera* ICTR A. Ch. 16.6.2006. Some are critical of this, however, see Kevin Jon Heller, 'Prosecutor v Karamera' (2007) 101 *AJIL* 157.

The Tribunal has assisted in the development of international criminal law, perhaps most notably by its treatment of sexual offences,[177] but also in relation to the responsibility of controllers of mass media for incitement to commit genocide.[178] It is nonetheless true that the quality of the legal reasoning contained in judgments of the ICTR is variable.[179]

Trials at the ICTR have taken an extremely long time, and have been subject to manifold delays. These are, in part, because of the difficulties involved in translation of Kinyarwanda into English and French,[180] and the awkward logistics of having the Tribunal based in Arusha, and the Office of the Prosecutor based in Kigali, neither of which are cities with a strong infrastructure.[181] Problems relating to repeated changes of defence counsel by the defendants have also contributed to trials' dilatory nature,[182] but the judges too have not always helped to move things along speedily.[183] Also, attempts to assist victims although laudable,[184] have not always been effective, and treatment of victims by the Tribunal has not always lived up to its aspirations, or basic standards.[185]

One of the major critiques that has been made of the ICTR is its failure to prosecute alleged offences committed by the RPF after the genocide in 2004. The ICTR has undertaken some investigations into the RPF,[186] but referred some allegations back to Rwanda after investigation and the establishment of a *prima facie* case.[187] The necessity of ensuring Rwandan cooperation for prosecutions of *génocidaires* may have been relevant here, although the current prosecutor has said that it is owing to the fact that the allegations are less serious than those against Hutu defendants and because of the completion strategy.[188]

It has been suggested that the ICTR is both geographically and metaphorically too distant from the people of Rwanda, who remain for the most part uninformed about and unaffected by the Tribunal.[189] The Tribunal has created an outreach programme, which includes a

---

177 Kelly Askin, 'Gender Crimes at the ICTR: Positive Developments' (2005) 3 *JICJ* 1007. On other aspects of the ICTR's practice on sexual offences, see Annual Report of the ICTR 2000, S/2000/927, para. 133; Annual Report of the ICTR 2001, S/2001/863, para. 108; Annual Report of the ICTR 2002, S/2002/733, para. 75; Annual Report of the ICTR 2004, S/2004/601, paras. 59–61.

178 *Nahimana, Barayagwiza and Ngeze*, ICTR T.Ch. 3.12.2003, (and on Appeal) ICTR A. Ch. 28.11.2007; although see Dina Temple-Raston, *Justice on the Grass* (New York, 2005).

179 See van den Herik, *The Contribution of the Rwanda Tribunal*, 261.

180 About which the Tribunal has been candid, see, e.g. *Akayesu* T. Ch. I 2.9.1998 para. 145.

181 Eric Møse, 'The Main Achievements of the ICTR' (2005) 3 *JICJ* 920 at 923, 927.

182 Annual Report of the ICTR 2001, para. 14.

183 Alison des Forges and Timothy Longman, 'Legal Responses to the Genocide in Rwanda' in Stover and Weinstein, *My Neighbour, My Enemy*, 53–5.

184 See Møse, 'The Main Achievements', 937; also the Annual Report of the ICTR 1999, S/1999/943, para. 113.

185 Göran Sluiter, 'The ICTR and the Protection of Witnesses' (2005) 3 *JICJ* 962.

186 Report of the ICTR to the Security Council 12 May 2008, S/2008/322, para. 45.

187 Eric Møse, 'The ICTR's Completion Strategy, Challenges and Possible Solutions' (2008) 6 *JICJ* 667 at 674.

188 Peskin, *International Justice in Rwanda*, ch. 8; Vanessa Thalman, 'French Justice's Endeavors to Substitute for the ICTR' (2008) 6 *JICJ* 995 at 1001–2.

189 José E. Alvarez, 'Crimes of Hate/Crimes of State, Lessons from Rwanda' (1999) 24 *Yale Journal of International Law* 365 at 403–18, 459–62.

visitors' centre in Rwanda, radio broadcasts and the creation of a satellite television station,[190] but whether these have proved effective is a matter of controversy.[191] A linked critique is the cost of the ICTR, which has been high (although lower than the cost of the ICTY).[192] Some have suggested that the money spent on the ICTR would have been put to better use supporting Rwandan justice efforts.[193] Whether or not that would have been the case, similar levels of funding would not have materialized if a call had instead gone out for assistance to rebuild the Rwandan justice system.

Further reading

The websites of both Tribunals are very useful. They may be found at www.icty.org and
    www.ictr.org.
Useful symposia on the ICTY can be found at (2004) 2 *JICJ* 353–597 and (2002–2003) 37
    New England Law Review 865–1080. Similarly on the ICTR see (1997) 321
    International Review of the Red Cross 665–732 and (2005) 3 *JICJ* 801–1033.
    The completion strategy is the subject of discussion in a symposium in (2008) 6
    JICJ 655–709.
M. Cherif Bassiouni and Peter Manikas, *The Law of the International Criminal Tribunal for
    Yugoslavia* (Ardsley, 1996).
Gideon Boas, *The Milošević Trial: Lessons for the Conduct of Complex International
    Criminal Proceedings* (Cambridge, 2007).
John Hagan, *Justice in the Hague: Prosecuting War Crimes in the Balkans* (Chicago, 2003).
Pierre Hazan, *Justice in a Time of War: The True Story Behind the International Criminal
    Tribunal for the Former Yugoslavia*, James Snyder (trans.) (College Station, TX,
    2004).
Rachel Kerr, *The International Criminal Tribunal for Former Yugoslavia: An Exercise in
    Law, Politics and Diplomacy* (Oxford, 2004).
André Klip and Göran Sluiter, *Annotated Leading Cases of International Criminal
    Tribunals (1999–)* (Antwerp, 1999).
Virginia Morris and Michael P. Scharf, *An Insider's Guide to the International Criminal
    Tribunal for Former Yugoslavia* (New York, 1995).
Virginia Morris and Michael P. Scharf, *The International Criminal Tribunal for Rwanda*
    (New York, 1998).

---

190 See generally Annual Report of the ICTR 1999, para. 1208; Annual Report of the ICTR 2001, paras. 135ff; Annual Report of the ICTR 2004, para. 55; Annual Report of the ICTR 2005, paras. 61–3.
191 See Timothy Longman et al., 'Connecting Justice to Human Experience: Attitudes Towards Accountability and Reconciliation in Rwanda' in Stover and Weinstein, *My Neighbour, My Enemy*, 206.
192 The ICTR's annual budget for 2008–09 was approximately $270 million, the ICTY's $342 million.
193 Alvarez, 'Crimes of Hate', 461.

John C. O'Brien, 'The International Tribunal for Violations of International Humanitarian Law in the Former Yugoslavia' (1993) 77 *AJIL* 639.

Victor Peskin, *International Justice in Rwanda and the Balkans: Virtual Trials and the Struggle for State Cooperation* (Cambridge, 2008).

Alfred Rubin, 'An International Criminal Tribunal for Former Yugoslavia' (1994) 6 *Pace International Law Review* 7.

William Schabas, *The UN International Criminal Tribunals: the former Yugoslavia, Rwanda and Sierra Leone* (Cambridge, 2006).

L. J. van den Herik, *The Contribution of the Rwanda Tribunal to the Development of International Law* (The Hague, 2005).

8

The International Criminal Court

8.1 Introduction

The creation of a permanent international criminal court with potentially worldwide jurisdiction is one of the most important developments in international criminal law. The Statute
of the International Criminal Court has not only established a new judicial institution to
investigate and try international offences, but has also set out a new code of international
criminal law. This chapter describes the steps leading to the establishment of the ICC, its
principal features, early developments and some of the legal and political responses to the
Court; it also attempts a brief assessment of the Court's first years, while recognizing that its
practice is still at a very early stage.

8.2 The creation of the ICC

In spite of the so-called Nuremberg Promise that the trials after the Second World War
would set a precedent for others,[1] there was no early successor to the Nuremberg and Tokyo
Tribunals to prosecute international crimes at the international level. There had been earlier
proposals for a permanent international criminal court[2] and a proposal was discussed during
the negotiations on the 1948 Genocide Convention, but the Convention as agreed looks only
to the possibility of such a court in the future. Article VI provides that persons charged with
genocide are to be tried by a court in the territory where the act was committed or 'by such
international penal tribunal as may have jurisdiction with respect to those Contracting
Parties which shall have accepted its jurisdiction'.

---

1 See section 6.3.2.
2 The first serious proposal for an international court was probably that made in 1872 by Gustav Moynier, one
of the founders of the International Committee of the Red Cross, who was concerned that national judges would
not be able fairly to judge offences committed in wars in which their countries had been involved: Christopher
Keith Hall, 'The First Proposal for a Permanent International Criminal Court' (1998) 322 *International Review
of the Red Cross* 57.

When it approved the Genocide Convention, the United Nations General Assembly also requested the International Law Commission to study the desirability and possibility of establishing an international judicial organ for the prosecution of, inter alia, the crime of genocide.[3] A draft statute for a permanent court was produced by a special committee appointed in 1950, but the General Assembly postponed the matter until consideration of the definition of aggression and the draft Code of Offences was complete.[4] In turn, progress on the draft Code stalled. The concept of a permanent international criminal court had not received universal support, and during the Cold War allegations of the commission of international crimes were usually regarded as largely propagandistic. Attention was turned to the development of more effective means of inter-State cooperation in the national prosecution of crimes, under treaties providing for extradition or prosecution and for legal assistance from one State to another.

It is ironic that it was a wish by Trinidad and Tobago to secure international prosecutions for drugs offences that finally gave the impetus to the creation of the International Criminal Court: ironic because the court that was finally established does not have any jurisdiction over drugs offences. Trinidad and Tobago proposed in 1989 that the creation of a permanent international criminal court be put back on the agenda of the United Nations; the General Assembly asked the International Law Commission to draft a Statute for such a court, and the Commission responded swiftly, producing a final text[5] in 1994.

The draft statute proposed by the ILC gave the court jurisdiction over more offences than the ICC has now: as well as the four categories in the ICC Statute, there was a list of 'treaty crimes' which included offences under the multilateral terrorism conventions and a UN drugs convention.[6] But in most respects the ILC draft was more protective of States' sovereignty than the eventual ICC Statute. Only States Parties and the Security Council could refer situations to the proposed court; the Prosecutor was not able to initiate investigations on his or her own initiative. In respect of most of the crimes,[7] and in the absence of a referral by the Security Council, the court would have jurisdiction only if *both* the State with custody of the alleged offender and the State on whose territory the alleged crime had been committed had accepted the jurisdiction of the court for the purpose of that crime. This

---

3 GA Res. 260(III)B. This study was to be undertaken by the ILC in parallel with its drafting of the substantive rules of international criminal law.

4 GA Res. 898(IX).

5 *Report of the International Law Commission on the work of its forty-sixth session*, UNGAOR 49th session Suppl. No. 10, A/49/10 (1994); included, without commentary, in M. Cherif Bassiouni, *The Statute of the International Criminal Court: A documentary history* (New York, 1998) 657. The drafting of the draft ILC statute is discussed in James Crawford, 'The Making of the Rome Statute' in Philippe Sands (ed.), *From Nuremberg to the Hague: The Future of International Criminal Justice* (Cambridge, 2003) 109.

6 The full list of treaty crimes comprised grave breaches of the Geneva Conventions and AP 1, and offences under six terrorism instruments, the Apartheid Convention, and the UN Drugs Convention.

7 There was worldwide jurisdiction over genocide, provided that a complaint was lodged by a State which was a party both to the court's Statute and to the Genocide Convention.

was the so-called opt-in provision: States were not required, by becoming parties to the Statute, to accept the jurisdiction of the court for their nationals or for crimes occurring on their territory in respect of any crime except genocide; they were free to opt in for additional specific crimes, or for none at all. The ILC draft also had a provision which precluded the court from taking jurisdiction over a situation which was on the agenda of the Security Council under Chapter VII of the UN Charter, unless the Council agreed. This provision, the precursor to Article 16 of the ICC Statute, would have allowed the Council to prevent court action by putting any matter on its agenda under its peace and security mandate.

The 1994 ILC draft statute was submitted at a fortunate time in international relations: Cold War divisions had thawed, there was enthusiasm for international tribunals, and the international community had embarked on several treaty-based initiatives strengthening human rights and humanitarian law. Scepticism about the prospects for a permanent international criminal court was diminishing. A significant number of States, however, still doubted the wisdom of creating a new court, both on principle and with respect to the specific details of the project. An ad hoc committee was established to examine the issues more closely.[8] A year later there was enough support to set up a Preparatory Committee[9] to prepare a text of a possible draft convention. Working on the basis of the ILC draft Articles, the Preparatory Committee began to negotiate texts, collated proposals for alternatives to many of the ILC Articles and, progressing beyond the ILC text, prepared a complete draft statute with hundreds of different alternative proposals. During the Preparatory Committee meetings, a 'Like-Minded Group' of States supportive of a new court emerged, and agreement was reached to hold a conference in Rome in the summer of 1998 to finalize and conclude the treaty. The draft statute which had emerged from the Preparatory Committee, with its numerous alternative texts, served as the basis for negotiation at the Rome Conference.[10]

8.2.1   The 1998 Rome Conference

In the five weeks allocated to the conference to draft the ICC Statute, there was a cornucopia of controversies, from the highly political, like the role of the Security Council, to detailed aspects of criminal procedure negotiated by criminal lawyers from very diverse legal

---

8 The Ad Hoc Committee on the Establishment of an International Criminal Court, convened by GA Res. 49/53, met for two sessions in 1995 and produced a report (UNGAOR A/50/22) which records the early discussions on the major features of the court.

9 Convened by GA Res. 50/46 and with its mandate reaffirmed in GA Res. 51/207 and 52/160, the Preparatory Committee on the Establishment of an International Criminal Court met for six sessions during the years 1995 to 1998; its reports may be found in UNGAOR A/51/22 and in the conference records at UN Doc. A/CONF.183/13 (Vol. III) 5.

10 UN Doc. A/CONF.183/13 (Vol. III) 5.

systems. Much of the negotiation of specific texts at the conference was carried out in informal committees. The process was slow since each committee worked without voting and by consensus. Compromises were necessary if agreement was to be reached, even where the issues concerned technical but important subjects such as the general principles of criminal law.

Of the various objectives of the negotiators, two of the strongest were the conflicting aims, often reflected within a single government delegation, of ensuring the prosecution of those responsible for the world's worst atrocities but avoiding undue exposure of national leaders to the new Court. The sixty-strong Like-Minded Group was influential both in driving forward the process as a whole and in seeking specific solutions on some aspects of the text. Other groupings of States such as the European Union, the Southern African Development Community, and the Non-Aligned Movement all met at different times during the conference and formulated coordinated positions on various of the provisions of the Convention.[11] Non-governmental organizations were represented in large numbers; although they could not take part directly in the negotiations, they were able to present papers and lobby from the margins. It was largely due to these organizations that the impetus for the establishment of the Court was maintained.

By the last week of the conference most of the technical matters had been settled, but a few major questions remained. The most difficult issues related to the jurisdiction of the new Court and, in particular, how broad the jurisdiction of the Court would be and which States would have to agree before its jurisdiction could be exercised. In the absence of agreement and with two days left before the end of the conference, it fell to the Bureau of the Committee of the Whole and associated delegates, under the Chairman, Philippe Kirsch, to propose a compromise on these controversial issues. This proposal, including in particular the texts of Articles 12 and 124, was put forward with the rest of the negotiated treaty on the penultimate day in an attempt to balance the conflicting positions of different delegations.

While most delegations supported the text, some were not prepared to accept it as it stood and chose to put their own amendments to the vote. The delegation of India asked for a vote on its proposals[12] to include a crime related to the use of weapons of mass destruction and to exclude any role for the Security Council. The United States called for a vote on their amendments[13] to the jurisdiction provision, which would have required the consent of the State of nationality of the suspect, the territorial State and, if the suspect was committing official acts which were acknowledged as such by the State concerned, the consent of that State. Only the intervention of a 'no-action motion' on both sets of amendments avoided the text of the Statute being broken apart; this procedural device was a means of allowing delegations to vote against putting the amendments to the vote, an easier step for many to

---

11 Many States belonging to each of these groups were also members of the Like-Minded Group.

12 A/CONF.183/C.1/L.94 and A/CONF.183/C.1/L.95.

13 A/CONF.183/C.1/L.70 and A/CONF.183/C.1/L.90.

take than voting against the amendments themselves. The final text of the Statute was adopted by a vote of 120 to 7, with 21 abstentions.[14]

Although it is not necessary to revisit in detail the course of the Rome Conference, there are two features of the negotiations which help to explain some aspects of the Statute.

The problem of travaux préparatoires

The Vienna Convention on the Law of Treaties provides that a treaty is to be interpreted in good faith in accordance with the ordinary meaning to be given to the terms of the treaty in their context and in the light of its object and purpose. To confirm this meaning, or if the meaning is ambiguous, obscure or manifestly absurd or unreasonable, supplementary means of interpretation may be used, including the preparatory work of the treaty and the circumstances of its conclusion.[15] One result of the informal process of negotiation at Rome is that there are only limited written records of the conference.[16] Another factor is that some of the provisions result from the negotiations during the Preparatory Committee in New York, rather than during the conference. Except for those few provisions which follow the draft prepared by the International Law Commission, therefore, or the history of which is to be found in the formal conference records, there is a marked absence of the *travaux préparatoires* which are usually to be expected in the drafting of a major treaty. The reasoning behind most of the texts which emerged from New York and from Rome is not to be found in the record of the views of delegates who argued for them or in an examination of the written proposals for amendments. The lack of standard *travaux préparatoires* means that those seeking for help with the meaning of a difficult or controversial provision of the Statute will have to place more reliance than would normally be the case on written commentaries and books about the ICC;[17] if these record the recollections of the negotiators at the conference they are the nearest things to *travaux* that we have, although they cannot always be relied upon to be neutral.

Working methods during the negotiations

As indicated above, individual sections of the text of the draft statute were negotiated by different committees and through different processes, and parts of those sections were sometimes remitted to very informal consultation groups for decision if they proved

---

14 The votes were not officially recorded, but China, Israel and the United States announced that they had been among those who voted against.
15 Arts. 31 and 32 of the ICC Statute, which are generally regarded as reflecting customary international law.
16 For the Official Records see UN Doc. A/CONF.183/13 (Vols. I to III).
17 The two most comprehensive of those written immediately after the conference are R. S. Lee, *The International Criminal Court: The Making of the Rome Statute* (The Hague, 1999) and Triffterer, *Observers' Notes*.

particularly difficult to agree. The methods of work adopted by the conference led to disconnections among some parts of the Statute and to different usages in terminology. Had there been more time, the Drafting Committee would have been able to do the work normally undertaken by such a committee and to draw attention to inconsistencies and ambiguities in the text, rather than simply reconciling some of the linguistic differences.[18] But the pressure of time and the fact that some of the major issues were left until the last two days resulted in difficulties in the text which cannot be explained except by an understanding of how the Statute was negotiated.[19]

8.2.2   Preparations for the Court

The closing session of the Rome Conference adopted both the text of the Statute and a number of resolutions, one of which set up a Preparatory Commission to prepare the subsidiary documents necessary for the establishment of the Court.

Sixty States were required to become parties to the Statute before it came into force. The pace of ratifications was quicker than expected, and the Statute came into force on 1 July 2002, bringing the Court formally into existence. The Assembly of States Parties, created by the Statute to oversee the administration of the Court, then met and adopted the Elements of Crimes, the Rules of Procedure and Evidence and the Agreement on the Privileges and Immunities of the Court,[20] all of which had been negotiated by the Preparatory Commission.

8.3   Structure and composition of the ICC

The judges of the Court are divided into Pre-Trial, Trial and Appeals Chambers; the Presidency, composed of the President and two Vice-Presidents and elected by the judges from among their number, is responsible for the administration of the Court, while the Registry provides the 'non-judicial aspects' of administration.[21] The inclusion of a Pre-Trials Division is a compromise between the common law prosecutorial system and the French system of *juges d'instruction*, providing a contrast with the largely common law character of the pre-trial stage at the ad hoc Tribunals; this mix of two different systems needs further working through in practice to avoid unprofitable tension between the Pre-Trial

---

18 Even the linguistic differences could not all be resolved at the conference, and the final text of the Statute had to undergo a large number of more or less technical corrections after it had been signed by a number of States. The official text – in all languages – is slightly different from the one voted on at the conference.

19 See Shabtai Rosenne, 'Poor drafting and imperfect organisation: flaws to overcome in the Rome Statute' (2000) 41 *Virginia Journal of International Law* 164, which addresses the discrepancy between the wording of Arts. 9 and 21 with regard to the weight to be attached by the Court to the Elements of Crimes.

20 These documents may all be found on the website of the ICC.

21 The composition and administration of the Court are dealt with in Part 4 of the Statute.

Chamber and the Prosecutor's Office in relation to the conduct of investigations.[22] Indeed the lengthy preliminary proceedings in the first cases before the Court show that expected difficulties in establishing a satisfactory institutional relationship have already been encountered.

As with the two Tribunals, the Prosecutor's Office is made an integral part of the Court; care needs to be taken in referring to the 'Court' when only the judicial arm is intended.

In recognition of the importance for the success of the Court in having judges of the highest possible calibre, the Statute sets out detailed provisions for the qualifications of candidates for the judiciary. Article 36(3) requires candidates to have competence in criminal law or in relevant areas of international law. This requirement for professional qualifications is combined with a duty for States selecting the judges to 'take into account' the need for representation of the principal legal systems of the world, equitable geographical representation and, for the first time in criteria for composition of an international tribunal, the need for a fair representation of female and male judges.[23] The complex voting rules used for the first election of the eighteen judges of the Court[24] by the Assembly of States Parties took into account all of these provisions except for the representation of the world's legal systems (an exclusion justified on the basis that this criterion would largely be met if geographical representation were equitable). The Statute envisages the possibility of the Assembly establishing an advisory committee on nominations of judges,[25] but this approach has not been adopted and so far the standard international practice in elections at the United Nations, which can involve votes being traded among States for reasons other than the personal and professional qualities and attributes of the judges, has been followed.

8.4   Crimes within the jurisdiction of the ICC

The Court has jurisdiction over 'the most serious crimes of international concern': genocide, crimes against humanity, war crimes and aggression (Article 5(1)). The Court cannot, however, exercise jurisdiction over the crime of aggression until the Statute has been amended by the addition of a definition of that crime and the inclusion of preconditions for the ICC to take jurisdiction (Article 5(2)). The offences are discussed in Chapters 10 to 13 of this book.

Whereas the Statutes of the two ad hoc Tribunals and the ILC draft statute for the ICC do not provide detailed definitions of crimes, the ICC Statute defines war crimes and crimes against

---

22 The respective roles of these organs in relation to an investigation, together with other aspects of the procedures of the Court, are described in Chapter 17.

23 Art. 36(8) of the ICC Statute.

24 ICC-ASP/1/Res.2. A list of the judges currently on the Court, as well as those chosen in past elections, may be found on the ICC website. As may be seen from close examination of the judges' biographical details not all of them have had experience of the kind required by the Statute.

25 Art. 36(4)(c) of the ICC Statute.

humanity in unprecedented detail; the negotiators cited reasons of certainty and the principle of legality, having in mind also that clear definitions would help to limit unexpected exposure to prosecution. They also wanted to avoid judicial creativity of too broad a nature and Article 22(2) therefore provides that the definitions 'shall be strictly construed and shall not be extended by analogy'. The definitions of crimes do not represent the whole picture. They must be read with the general principles of liability in Part 3 of the Statute (see Chapter 15) and are further elaborated in the Elements of Crimes which are to be used by the Court in the interpretation and application of the provisions on offences (Articles 9 and 21).[26]

The oft-stated aim of the process of definition was to codify existing customary law for the purpose of the new Court and the definitions are therefore by and large conservative. But in crystallizing and clarifying those provisions which had not been previously expressed as written criminal law, the process inevitably moved the law along.[27] There are provisions which arguably go beyond a mere codification of existing law as it stood in 1998,[28] but some of them have since been referred to as customary law in the jurisprudence. The Rome Statute has thus contributed to the development of customary law.[29]

On the other hand there are provisions which are arguably not as extensive as customary law allows.[30] Article 10 attempts to address this point by providing that the Statute does not limit or prejudice existing or developing rules of international law 'for purposes other than this Statute'. This both mitigates the concern that the Statute will in some way freeze the development of customary international law and confirms that so far as the Court is concerned it must apply the provisions in the Statute even if customary law creates wider offences.

The position is perhaps best described by an ICTY Trial Chamber in the *Furundžija* case:

> In many areas the Statute may be regarded as indicative of the legal views, i.e. *opinio juris* of a great number of States. Notwithstanding article 10 of the Statute, the purpose of

---

26 See section 8.5 below.

27 For discussion of the process see Leila Sadat, *The International Criminal Court and the Transformation of International Law* (New York, 2002) 12,261–74; Darryl Robinson, 'Crimes against Humanity: Reflections on State Sovereignty, Legal Precision and the Dictates of the Public Conscience' in Flavia Lattanzi and William Schabas (eds.), *Essays on the Rome Statute of the International Criminal Court* (Il Sirente, 1999), vol. I, 139 at 140–4.

28 For example, the provision on child soldiers; see Herman von Hebel and Darryl Robinson, 'Crimes within the Jurisdiction of the Court' in Lee, *The Making of the Rome Statute*, 117–18.

29 For example, the Special Court for Sierra Leone decided that recruitment of child soldiers was a crime in customary law (*Prosecutor* v. *Norman, Lack of Jurisdiction*, SCSL-2004-14-AR72(E) paras. 30–53); but see Justice Robertson's view that 'until the Rome Treaty itself, the rule against child recruitment was a human rights principle and an obligation upon States, but did not entail individual criminal liability in international law. It did so for the first time when the Treaty was concluded and approved on 17th July 1998.' (Dissenting opinion at para. 38.)

30 For example, the commentary to Rule 156 in Henckaerts & Doswald-Beck, *ICRC Customary Law*, 586 maintains that a list of war crimes not mentioned in the ICC Statute forms part of customary international law. In addition there is no crime regarding the use of biological or chemical weapons in the Statute, not because there were strong views against regarding this as customary law but because there was no agreement for the inclusion of nuclear weapons (see von Hebel and Robinson, 'Crimes within the Jurisdiction', 113–16).

which is to ensure that existing or developing law is not 'limited' or 'prejudiced' by the Statute's provisions, resort may be had *cum grano salis* to these provisions to help elucidate customary international law. Depending on the matter at issue, the Rome Statute may be taken to restate, reflect or clarify customary rules or crystallise them, whereas in some areas it creates new law or modifies existing law. At any event, the Rome Statute by and large may be taken as constituting an authoritative expression of the legal views of a great number of States.[31]

8.4.1   Other crimes

During the negotiations, unsuccessful proposals were made for other crimes to be added to the list.[32] A resolution adopted by the conference at its closing session recommended that the crime of terrorism and drugs crimes be considered at a review conference 'with a view to arriving at an acceptable definition and their inclusion in the list of crimes within the jurisdiction of the Court'. These and any other additional crimes may be added by amendments adopted at a review conference if there is sufficiently wide agreement (Article 123).[33] States Parties, however, do not have to accept the jurisdiction of the Court for any additional crimes in relation to their own nationals or crimes committed on their own territory if they do not wish to do so (Article 121(5)).

8.5   Applicable law

Article 21 requires the Court to apply 'in the first place' the Statute, the Elements of Crimes and its Rules of Procedure and Evidence. As regards the Elements, the wording of Article 9 (Elements 'shall assist' the Court) appears to conflict with a requirement to *apply* them, but the Court has not had difficulty in reconciling these provisions. The Pre-Trial Chamber in the *Al Bashir* Arrest Warrant case has found that 'the Elements of Crimes and the Rules must be applied unless the competent Chamber finds an irreconcilable contradiction between these documents on the one hand, and the Statute on the other hand.' The Chamber found that a fully discretionary power to apply the Elements would be inconsistent with the

---

31 *Furundžija* ICTY T. Ch. II 10.12.1998 para. 227, supported in *Tadić* ICTY A. Ch. 15.7.1999 para. 223 although Judge Shahabuddeen reserved his position on the matter (Separate Opinion of Judge Shahabuddeen, para. 3). See also *Kupreškić* where the Trial Chamber said that 'although the Statute of the ICC may be indicative of the *opinio juris* of many States, Article 7(1)(h) is not consonant with customary international law' (ICTY T. Ch. II 14.1.2000 para. 580); and *Hadžihasanović*, where the Appeals Chamber considered that the fact that the Rome Conference voted for Art. 28, though not legally conclusive of the matter, at least cast doubt on views opposing the law contained in that text, and that the fact that 'the Rome Statute embodied a number of compromises among the States parties that drafted and adopted it hardly undermines its significance. The same is true of most major multilateral conventions.' (ICTY A. Ch. 16.7.2003 para. 53.)
32 Proposals included terrorist offences and drugs offences. See Patrick Robinson, 'The Missing Crimes' in Cassese, *Commentary*, 497.
33 For the first review conference in 2010 see the ICC website.

principle of *nullum crimen sine lege* and on that basis went on to apply a controversial part of the Elements on genocide.[34]

The Court is also required to apply 'in the second place' treaties and principles and rules of international law, and 'failing that' general principles of law, including national laws consistent with the Statute and with internationally recognized norms and standards. The Court has indicated that these other sources of law 'can only be resorted to when the following two conditions are met: (i) there is a lacuna in the written law contained in the Statute, the Elements of Crimes and the Rules; and (ii) such lacuna cannot be filled by the application of the criteria of interpretation provided in articles 31 and 32 of the Vienna Convention on the Law of the Treaties and article 21(3) of the Statute'.[35]

8.6 Complementarity and other grounds of inadmissibility

8.6.1 The complementarity principle

The ICC is a court of last resort. The Court is intended to supplement, not to supplant, national jurisdictions and the preamble to the ICC Statute[36] recognizes that every State has a responsibility to exercise its own criminal jurisdiction over international crimes. The first Article of the Statute describes the Court as being 'complementary' to national criminal jurisdictions. The principle of complementarity is based not only on respect for the primary jurisdiction of States but also on practical considerations of efficiency and effectiveness, since States will generally have the best access to evidence and witnesses and the resources to carry out proceedings. An international court is only one way to enforce international criminal law and it may not in every instance be the best one.[37]

The concept of complementarity originated in the ILC draft but was substantially remodelled during the negotiations. It was crucial for the success of the negotiations that the complementarity principle be settled at an early stage; before they could agree to

---

34 *Situation in Darfur* (*Al Bashir* Arrest Warrant case) ICC PT.Ch. I 4.3.2009 paras. 128–132. But see the Separate and Partially Dissenting Judgment of Judge Usacka, who seemed to prefer the view that the Elements are not binding on the Court; whether or not they are, she considered that the contextual element for genocide was met, so that the element's consistency with the definition of genocide did not have to be decided (paras. 16–20). For discussion of the majority view, see Robert Cryer, 'The Definitions of International Crimes in the Al Bashir Arrest Warrant Decision' (2009) 7 *JICJ* 283 and Claus Kreß, 'The Crime of Genocide and Contextual Elements' (2009) 7 *JICJ* 297. For the background to the wording of the different Statute provisions regarding the Elements, see Herman von Hebel, 'The Making of the Elements of Crimes' in Lee, *Elements and Rules*, 7–8.
35 *Al Bashir*, Arrest Warrant case, para. 44.
36 Para. 6 of the preamble.
37 The advantages of national judicial systems were described in the course of the negotiations on the Statute: Report of the Ad Hoc Committee on the Establishment of an International Criminal Court (GAOR 50th Session Suppl. No 22 (A/50/22)). For discussion of the relative merits of international and national trials see sections 2.3.4 and 2.4.

support the establishment of a new international court, States which were content with their own administration of justice had to be satisfied that the new court would not be able to take over cases which were being dealt with perfectly well at home. The provision which is now Article 17 was therefore substantially agreed before the conference even began.

A case will be inadmissible, and the Court will not be able to exercise its jurisdiction, if a national authority is investigating or prosecuting the case or has already done so, unless the circumstances indicate that the State is nevertheless unwilling or unable to carry out proceedings genuinely. The term 'genuinely' was chosen in preference to other terms, such as 'effectively': the latter could have given the impression that a case would be admissible if the national system was, for example, proceeding more slowly (less effectively) than the ICC would or if the ICC could do a better job.[38] Where national efforts are underway, the case will be admissible only where those efforts cannot be considered genuine.[39] It is for the Court itself to decide whether these conditions are met, not the national authorities.

The Prosecutor has indicated that his policy is to take an approach to complementarity which, rather than competing with States for jurisdiction, will lead to encouragement and facilitation of genuine national proceedings where possible, and a 'consensual division of labour' between national courts and the ICC where appropriate.[40] Where situations are 'self-referred' by a State,[41] however, it is unlikely that there will be competition for jurisdiction. Questions of admissibility have to be considered both before the Prosecutor opens an investigation and before he chooses a case to prosecute. Although Article 17 applies at both stages of the proceedings, the Prosecutor may not have identified specific 'cases' before he opens an investigation, so his assessment of inadmissibility on the ground of complementarity will necessarily have a less specific focus.

8.6.2   National proceedings relating to the 'case'

According to Article 17(1), a case is only inadmissible on the ground of complementarity if 'the case is being investigated or prosecuted' (Article 17(1)(a)) or 'the case has been investigated' (Article 17(1)(b)) by a State with jurisdiction over it. Article 17(1)(c) contemplates the further possibility that both an investigation and trial have been completed, in

---

38 John Holmes, 'Complementarity: National Courts versus the ICC' in Cassese, *Commentary*, 674.

39 At the Rome Conference an alternative approach was suggested by the representative of Mexico who proposed a text which read: 'The court has no jurisdiction where the case in question is being investigated or prosecuted, or has been prosecuted, by a State which has jurisdiction over it.' (Vol. III of the Official Records of the Conference at p. 28.)

40 'Paper on some policy issues before the Office of the Prosecutor', September 2003, on the website of the ICC ('*Policy Paper*'), 5.

41 See section 8.7.4.

which case the principle of *ne bis in idem* governs the situation (see 8.6.7). Where no State has taken any action in relation to the case, none of these criteria for inadmissibility are met, and thus the case is admissible before the ICC.

The requirement of national proceedings in relation to the 'case' raises important questions. First, how broadly is 'case' to be interpreted? In *Lubanga*, for example, the Pre-Trial Chamber held that for a case to be inadmissible it is a condition 'that national proceedings encompass both the person and the conduct which are the subject of the case before the Court'.[42] The Chamber held that the DRC was not acting in relation to the specific charge before the Court (conscription of children) and thus that it was not proceeding in relation to the 'case'; hence the case was admissible before the Court.[43] In *Katanga and Ngudjolo Chui* the Appeal Chamber did not find it necessary to rule on whether the person/conduct test was the correct one. The government of the DRC (the Minister of Justice himself attending the proceedings) stated that the accusations against the defendant were not subject to investigation in the DRC and that the DRC did not have the capacity to conduct the necessary inquiry; there had been five million deaths in the DRC and three million displaced persons. The Trial Chamber dismissed the challenge to admissibility, resting its decision largely on the unequivocal statement of the DRC that it was not investigating the matters covered by the Court's proceedings, while being ready to continue its full cooperation with the Court; its decision was upheld on appeal.[44]

As a general principle, it seems too stringent an interpretation of complementarity for the Court to insist that there be *identical* charges in a national court if a case is to be ruled inadmissible. It remains to be seen whether the ICC will defer where a national case is roughly equivalent to the one of interest to the ICC. An alternative would be for the Court to allow the domestic courts to amend domestic charges in such a case.[45]

Another question that arises is whether *any* State with jurisdiction may bring proceedings and thus oust the jurisdiction of the ICC. Many States take wide or universal jurisdiction over the Statute crimes. The Statute does not prioritize between bases of jurisdiction. It is enough to render a case inadmissible if any State 'with jurisdiction' takes criminal proceedings, whatever the basis for jurisdiction may be.

---

42 *Lubanga Dyilo* ICC PT. Ch. I 10.2.2006 para. 31. See also *Ahmad Harun and Al Kushayb* ICC PT. Ch. I 27.4.2007 paras. 21, 24 (proceedings being taken in Sudan against Al Kushayb but not in relation to the same conduct).

43 *Lubanga Dyilo* ICC PT. Ch. I 10.2.2006 paras. 31–9. Pre-Trial Chambers have made admissibility determinations on their own motion in the course of their decisions to issue arrest warrants under Art. 58(1), but it has since been held by the Appeals Chamber that for the issue of a warrant of arrest, an admissibility assessment is not a requirement and it will be only in appropriate instances that a Pre-Trial Chamber should exercise its discretion to address admissibility at that stage of the proceedings: *Situation in the DRC* ICC A. Ch. 13.7.2006 paras. 42–53.

44 *Katanga and Ngudjolo Chui* ICC T. Ch. I 12.06.2009 para. 95; see also A. Ch. 25.9.2009 paras. 74–9.

45 See Kleffner, '*Complementarity in the Rome Statute*', 201.

8.6.3   Unwillingness to carry out proceedings genuinely

Article 17(1) renders a case inadmissible before the ICC if a State is investigating or prosecuting the case, *unless* the Prosecutor can show that the State is in reality 'unwilling' or 'unable' to carry out the ostensible proceedings genuinely. In determining whether a case is inadmissible by reason of 'unwillingness', the Court must consider whether one of the following factors exists:

> (a) The proceedings were or are being undertaken or the national decision was made for the purpose of shielding the person concerned from criminal responsibility for crimes within the jurisdiction of the court referred to in Article 5;
>
> (b) There has been an unjustified delay in the proceedings which in the circumstances is inconsistent with an intent to bring the person concerned to justice;
>
> (c) The proceedings were not or are not being conducted independently or impartially, and they were or are being conducted in a manner which, in the circumstances, is inconsistent with an intent to bring the person concerned to justice.[46]

The first criterion gives the Court the difficult task of assessing the motives of the national authorities (whether judicial, executive or legislative); the second two more clearly allow inferences to be drawn from objective factors.[47] All the criteria are based on procedural and institutional factors, not the substantive outcome of a case or an investigation. A case will not be admissible by reason only of the closure of the investigation or an acquittal of an apparently guilty accused. In taking its decisions on the complementarity principle, the Court is to have regard to the principles of due process recognized by international law, and may have before it information submitted by a State showing that its courts meet internationally recognized standards for the prosecution of similar conduct.[48]

Arguments have been made that the Court is thus given a general role in monitoring the human rights standards of domestic authorities.[49] The better view is that delay and lack of independence are relevant only in so far as either of them indicates an intention to shield the person concerned from justice.[50] There does not appear to be anything in the Statute to make

46 Art. 17(2).

47 For differing views as to whether the criteria are or are not exhaustive, see Markus Benzing, 'The Complementarity Regime of the International Criminal Court: International Criminal Justice between State Sovereignty and the Fight against Impunity' (2003) 7 *Max Planck Yearbook of United Nations Law* 591 at 606; Holmes, 'Complementarity: National Courts', 675; and Darryl Robinson, 'Serving the Interests of Justice: Amnesties, Truth Commissions and the International Criminal Court' (2003) 14 *EJIL* 481 at 500.

48 Rule 51 of the ICC RPE.

49 See e.g. Federica Gioia, 'State Sovereignty, Jurisdiction and "Modern" International Law: The Principle of Complementarity in the International Criminal Court" (2006) 19 *LJIL* 1095 at 1110–13.

50 For the extent to which the Court may take into account the fairness of the national proceedings, see Enrique Rojo, 'The Role of Fair Trial Considerations in the Complementarity Regime of the International Criminal Court: From "No Peace without Justice" to "No Peace with Victor's Justice"?' (2005) 18 *LJIL* 829; and see Benzing, 'The Complementarity Regime of the International Criminal Court', 606–7.

the Court responsible for the protection of the human rights of the accused in the *national* enforcement of international criminal law; the principle of complementarity addresses the particular aspects of the proceedings which are referred to in Article 17, whereas more general human rights considerations about the conduct of national prosecutions are more properly addressed by human rights treaties and bodies.

8.6.4   Inability to carry out proceedings genuinely

The assessment of inability may be easier than that of unwillingness, since the concept depends upon objective criteria which do not demand that motives be inferred. Article 17(3) reads:

> In order to determine inability in a particular case, the Court shall consider whether, due to a total or substantial collapse or unavailability of its national judicial system, the State is unable to obtain the accused or the necessary evidence and testimony or otherwise unable to carry out its proceedings.

The last three criteria (inability to obtain the accused or the evidence and testimony, or other inability to carry out the proceedings) must result from the collapse or unavailability of the legal system, not from any other factor (such as absence of an extradition agreement resulting in difficulties in obtaining the presence of the accused). Absence of the necessary legislation to enable prosecution of the Statute crimes may give rise to 'inability' in the sense of Article 17(3). But if a person is prosecuted only for 'ordinary' crimes, that should be treated, it has been suggested, as a question of unwillingness, with the requirement that shielding from justice be proved, rather than inability.[51]

8.6.5   Voluntary relinquishment of jurisdiction and uncontested admissibility

If national authorities take no proceedings themselves, the express requirements of Article 17(1) (investigations or prosecutions by a State) cannot be met and the case remains admissible. It is only where those authorities are engaged or have been engaged in apparent exercise of their own jurisdiction that the exceptions of 'unwillingness' or 'inability' may be considered. The alternative view – that the Court must nonetheless establish whether the criteria in Article 17(2) and (3) are met and may not simply accept concessions of admissibility[52] – is not tenable in the light of the wording of Article 17(1), and it has not been accepted by the ICC in its early decisions.[53]

---

51 Benzing, 'The Complementarity Regime of the International Criminal Court', 614–16.

52 See, e.g. Mahnoush Arsanjani and Michael Reisman, 'The Law-in-action of the International Criminal Court' (2005) 99 *AJIL* 385 at 395–7; William Schabas, 'First Prosecutions at the International Criminal Court' (2006) 27 *Human Rights Law Journal* 25 at 32.

53 *Lubanga Dyilo* ICC Decision on the Prosecutor's Application for a Warrant of Arrest PT. Ch. I 10.2.2006 para. 29; *Katanga and Ngudjolo Chui* ICC T.Ch.II 16.6.2009 paras.76–80 and A. Ch. 25.9.2009 paras. 74–9. The Appeal Chamber stated that 'the question of unwillingness or inability of a State having jurisdiction over

If a State refers to the Court a situation on its territory, which its own legal system has the capacity to prosecute, the question is raised as to whether that State may voluntarily relinquish its jurisdiction to the Court. The issue has arisen in the context of the referrals of the situations in northern Uganda, the DRC and the Central African Republic (CAR).[54] The Ugandan authorities declared that they did not intend to conduct proceedings against the persons with the greatest responsibility for the relevant crimes.[55] The DRC authorities stated that they were not pursuing investigations when they made the referral[56] although Thomas Lubanga Dyilo, the ICC's first arrested suspect, was held on charges for other domestic crimes by the DRC before being transferred to the ICC. The statement by the DRC before the Trial Chamber in *Katanga* that they did not intend to investigate the charges against the defendant was treated as decisive of the admissibility proceedings by the Court.[57] Following the referral of the situation in the CAR, the *Cour de Cassation*, the country's highest judicial body, confirmed that 'the national justice system was unable to carry out the complex proceedings necessary to investigate and prosecute the alleged crimes'.[58]

8.6.6   Amnesties and truth and reconciliation commissions

The Statute does not address the relationship between the jurisdiction of the Court and non-judicial approaches to past atrocities, such as amnesties and truth and reconciliation commissions.[59] If a State emerging from a bitter internal conflict decides to grant amnesties, would these amnesties preclude the Court from taking jurisdiction? Should they? The Rome Conference did not consider itself able to deal with the issue explicitly[60] and the issue will therefore be left to the application of the complementary provisions and the powers of the Prosecutor and Chambers.[61]

the case becomes relevant only where, due to ongoing or past investigations or prosecutions in that State, the case appears to be inadmissible'.

54 Payam Akhavan, 'The Lord's Resistance Army Case: Uganda's Submission of the First State Referral to the International Criminal Court' (2005) 99 *AJIL* 403; William Burke-White, 'Complementarity in Practice: the International Criminal Court as part of a system of Multi-level Global Governance in the Democratic Republic of Congo' (2005) 18 *LJIL* 557 at 567–8. See discussion of 'self-referrals' at section 8.7.4.

55 Schabas, 'First Prosecutions', 31. But Uganda is now legislating to allow the trial of international crimes in its own courts, so the situation may change.

56 Letter from President Kabila of 3.3.2004.

57 *Katanga and Ngudjolo Chui* ICC T. Ch. II 16.6.2009 para. 95. See also A. Ch. 25.9.2009.

58 Press release from the Office of the Prosecutor 22.05.2007 (ICC-OTP-20070522-220).

59 Amnesties and truth and reconciliation commissions generally are dealt with in sections 22.2 and 22.3.

60 Questions of amnesties and pardons are addressed at Art. 19 and fn. 47 in the draft statute submitted to the conference (Vol. III, p. 27 of the Official Records; the brief recorded discussion in the Committee of the Whole is at Vol. II, pp. 213–21).

61 See section 22.2.2 and Darryl Robinson, 'Serving the Interests of Justice: Amnesties, Truth Commissions and the International Criminal Court' (2003) 14 *EJIL* 481; Michael Scharf, 'The Amnesty Exception to the Jurisdiction of the International Criminal Court' (1999) 32 *Cornell International Law Journal* 507; Jessica

At first sight, the case of a crime covered by an amnesty would clearly be admissible before the Court in that there would have been no national investigation or prosecution or, if there had been, it would have been 'for the purpose of shielding the person concerned from criminal responsibility'.[62] It has been argued, however, that if amnesties are accompanied by some form of inquiry (as with the South African Truth and Reconciliation Commission), that could constitute an investigation sufficient to render the case inadmissible before the Court.[63] The counterview is that the wording of Article 17(2)(a) and (c) makes clear that the investigation must be for the purpose of bringing the person concerned to justice. It would only be if the term 'justice' could be interpreted so as to include forms of justice alternative to criminal justice that such a case might be inadmissible;[64] in view of the reference to 'national judicial system' in Article 17(3) and the wording of the fourth and sixth preambular paragraphs of the Statute, such an interpretation would seem unlikely.[65]

The Prosecutor may, however, decide, having regard to a particular amnesty, that there would be 'substantial reasons to believe that an investigation would not serve the interests of justice', taking into account 'the gravity of the crime and the interests of victims'.[66] But if a decision not to initiate an investigation is taken solely on the ground that it would be against the interests of justice, the Prosecutor must inform the Pre-Trial Chamber, which may decide to review the decision.[67]

Gavron, 'Amnesties in the Light of Developments in International Law and the Establishment of the International Criminal Court' (2002) 51 *ICLQ* 91; Anja Seibert-Fohr, 'The Relevance of the Rome Statute of the International Criminal Court for Amnesties and Truth Commissions' (2003) 7 *Max Planck Yearbook of United Nations Law* 553.

62 The power to 'overturn' amnesties has been criticized by some as interfering in democratic decision-making: John Bolton, 'The Risks and Weaknesses of the International Criminal Court from America's Perspective' (2000–2001) 41 *Virginia Journal of International Law* 199–200.

63 Seibert-Fohr, 'The Relevance of the Rome Statute', 569; Robinson, 'Serving the Interests of Justice', 500.

64 Carsten Stahn, 'Complementarity, Amnesties and Alternative Forms of Justice: some Interpretative Guidelines for the International Criminal Court' (2005) 3 *JICJ* 695 at 716.

65 See, however, the declaration made on ratification of the Statute by Colombia, which expresses the view of that State that none of the Statute's provisions prevent Colombia from granting amnesties, reprieves or judicial pardons for political crimes if they are in conformity with the Colombian constitution and with international law principles accepted by Colombia (5.8.2002). Since reservations are not permitted by the Statute, that declaration may have to be assessed in accordance with the provisions of the Statute.

66 Art. 53(1)(c) of the ICC Statute; and note that Art. 53(2)(c) relating to the initiation of a prosecution is in similar but not identical terms. See Stahn, 'Complementarity, Amnesties', 718 for the view that Art. 53 does not allow the Prosecutor the scope to weigh interests of national reconciliation against interests of individual accountability, since the concept of interests of justice under that Article is linked to individual and case-related considerations. The Prosecutor himself in his *Policy Paper on the Interests of Justice* has stated that 'the broader matter of international peace and security is not the responsibility of the Prosecutor; it falls within the mandate of other institutions'. (September 2007, at p. 8, available at http://www2.icc-cpi.int/NR/rdonlyres/772C95C9-F54D-4321-BF09-73422BB23528/143640/ICCOTPInterestsOfJustice.pdf.)

67 Art. 53(1) and (3)(b) of the ICC Statute.

8.6.7   Other grounds for inadmissibility

Ne bis in idem

The principle of *ne bis in idem*[68] protects a person from being tried before the ICC for conduct which has already been tried by the Court itself or by other courts in previous proceedings.[69] The exceptions to the principle with regard to proceedings in other courts are in very similar terms to two of the criteria for 'unwillingness' in Article 17(2). A case will be admissible therefore if the purpose of the completed proceedings was to shield the person from criminal responsibility or they were otherwise not independent and were inconsistent with an intent to bring the person to justice.[70] A difficulty arises with regard to the grant of pardons for purely political reasons, akin to the grant of an amnesty. If such a pardon follows apparently genuine proceedings, the case would not appear to be admissible before the Court, unless an inference can be drawn from all the circumstances that the original proceedings in fact came within the exceptions just mentioned.[71]

'Not of sufficient gravity'

A final ground for inadmissibility is that a case 'is not of sufficient gravity to justify further action by the Court'.[72] While all crimes within the Statute are 'grave', Article 17 contemplates an additional threshold of gravity for the selection of situations and cases.

Gravity, like other grounds for inadmissibility, is considered by the Prosecutor at the situation-selection stage as well as at the case-selection stage. The Office of the Prosecutor has stated that it regards factors relevant in assessing gravity as including the scale of the crimes, the nature of the crimes, the manner of their commission and their impact.[73]

So far, all situations in which investigations have been initiated involved hundreds or thousands of the gravest forms of crimes (such as murder or sexual violence). In his letter to senders of communications concerning alleged crimes committed in Iraq in the 2003 conflict, the Prosecutor concluded that in the context of the hundreds and thousands of victims in the other situations he was investigating, '4 to 12 victims of wilful killing and a limited number of victims of inhuman treatment' was not sufficient to initiate an investigation.[74]

---

68 See section 4.7.
69 Arts. 17(1)(c), 20(1) and (3) of the ICC Statute.
70 Art. 20(3).
71 John Holmes, 'The Principle of Complementarity' in Lee, *The Making of the Rome Statute*, 76, 77.
72 Arts. 17(1)(d) and 53(1)(c).
73 OTP, *Report on Prosecutorial Policy*, 14.09.2006, p. 5, available at http://www.icc-cpi.int/NR/rdonlyres/ 699AA4B3-E8C2-4E41-9EFA-EBA503BDBF7F/143694/OTP_ProsecutorialStrategy20060914_English.pdf.
74 OTP response to communications received concerning Iraq, 10.2.2006, available at http://www.icc-cpi.int/ Menus/ICC/Structure+of+the+Court/Office+of+the+Prosecutor/Comm+and+Ref/Iraq/. For criticism of the Prosecutor's approach to the gravity criterion, see William Schabas, 'Prosecutorial Discretion v. Judicial Activism at the International Criminal Court' (2008) 6 *JICJ* 731.

Gravity is also considered in the selection of specific cases within a situation. In the Darfur situation, a case was brought concerning war crimes causing the death of 'only' twelve peacekeepers and severe wounding of eight; the Prosecutor's view that the nature, manner and impact of the crimes were critical factors in assessing gravity was approved by the Pre-Trial Chamber in its confirmation decision.[75]

The meaning of the gravity criterion was examined by the Appeals Chamber in the case of *Ntaganda*. The Pre-Trial Chamber had held that three criteria must be met: first, the conduct concerned must be systematic or large-scale and the social alarm caused to the community should be taken into account; second, the suspect should be one of the most senior leaders in the situation under investigation; third, regard should be had to the role played by him and the role played by the State or organization in the overall commission of crimes. The Appeals Chamber found that none of these tests was in conformity with the Statute: the first because it blurred the distinction between the jurisdictional requirements for war crimes and crimes against humanity, and the 'social alarm' test had no source in the Statute, the second and third because there was nothing in the Statute to restrict the level of perpetrator.[76] The Chamber did not produce its own criteria for gravity.

The Prosecutor's stated policy of bringing charges against those bearing the *greatest responsibility* for the crimes within the ICC's jurisdiction[77] is a sensible one in view of the limitations of resources of an international court, but neither he nor the Appeals Chamber regard it as a *legal* limitation on the power of the Court. Similarly, the gravity of a case should not be assessed only from a quantitative perspective by considering only the number of victims.[78]

8.6.8   Challenges to admissibility

The Statute provides procedures ensuring that all States which could take jurisdiction themselves will hear of the possibility of ICC proceedings at the earliest opportunity. When deciding to initiate an investigation *proprio motu* or after a State Party referral, the Prosecutor is required to notify all States Parties and other States which, 'taking into

---

75 *Situation in Darfur, Sudan (Bahar Idriss Abu Garda)* Decision on the Prosecutor's Application under Article 58 ICC PT. Ch. 8.2.2010, paras. 30–4. The Chamber however declined to confirm the charges.

76 *Situation in the DRC* ICC A. Ch. 13.7.2006 paras. 66–82.

77 *Policy Paper*, 7.

78 *Situation in Darfur (Abu Garda)* ICC PT. Ch. 8.2.2010 para. 31. See also Ignaz Stegmiller, 'The Gravity Threshold under the ICC Statute: Gravity Back and Forth in Lubanga and Ntaganda' (2009) 9 *ICLR* 547, which makes a distinction between 'two gravity facets', one legal and one relative (or discretionary).

account the information available, would normally exercise jurisdiction over the crimes concerned'.[79]

The admissibility of a case may be challenged by an accused or a person subject to an arrest warrant,[80] a State with jurisdiction if it is investigating or prosecuting the case itself, and any other State from which acceptance of jurisdiction is required under Article 12.[81] It is not only States Parties to the Statute which have the right to make a challenge; States which are not parties may also do so (but are not under any obligation of cooperation to comply with requests for information and other such matters).[82] The aim of complementarity is to ensure that some judicial system is dealing with a case; so long as the proceedings are being carried out genuinely it does not matter whether they are in a State Party or not.

8.6.9   The Rome Statute as an incentive to national legislation

One of the results of the principle of complementarity is that States are encouraged to improve standards of investigations and trials in their own domestic systems. While the assertion that States Parties are *obliged* to introduce the Statute offences into their own law[83] puts too much weight on the effect of preambular paragraph 6 of the Statute, States do have an *interest* in incorporating the offences if they wish to allow their own nationals to be investigated in their home country rather than by the ICC.[84] The admissibility criteria may also have the effect of encouraging improvement in procedural standards. Such national legislation should not be seen as an inappropriate avoidance scheme since national and international jurisdictions may thus together provide the means of bringing offenders to justice. The frequently cited statement of the first Prosecutor of the Court, while arguably exaggerated in its aspiration for an absence of cases for the Court, reflects this view:

> The effectiveness of the International Criminal Court should not be measured by the number of cases that reach the Court. On the contrary, the absence of trials by the ICC, as a consequence of the effective functioning of national systems, would be a major success.[85]

---

79 Art. 18(1) of the ICC Statute. The Article also sets out procedures for the deferral of an ICC investigation if relevant national authorities are exercising jurisdiction, subject to appeal by the Prosecutor to the Pre-Trial Chamber. For the negotiating history and the interpretation of the term 'normally exercise jurisdiction', see Hector Olasolo, *The Triggering Procedure of the International Criminal Court* (Leiden, 2005) 72–5.
80 E.g. challenge to admissibility made by Katanga, fn. 57 above.
81 Art. 19(2) of the ICC Statute; see section 17.4.
82 Unless the non-party State has accepted the Court's jurisdiction in accordance with Art. 12(3) or has agreed separately to cooperate.
83 See Kleffner, 'Complementarity in the Rome Statute', ch. VI.
84 See section 4.4.2.
85 *Policy Paper*, 4.

8.7   Initiation of proceedings (the 'trigger mechanisms')

There are three means of bringing a matter before the Court:[86] a referral by a State Party, a referral by the Security Council acting under Chapter VII of the UN Charter, and the institution of an investigation by the Prosecutor acting on his own initiative (Article 13). States and the Security Council may only refer a 'situation' to the Court: it is for the Prosecutor, not for political bodies, to determine the specific cases and suspects warranting investigation.

8.7.1   States Parties

Only States which are parties to the Statute may refer situations to the Court. Those which are not may seek referral by the Security Council if the situation threatens international peace and security, or may pass information to the Prosecutor in the hope that the Prosecutor will begin an investigation on his own motion.

Some of the first parties to the Statute were States on whose territories large-scale atrocities were being committed. Three referrals to the Court have been made by States Parties – Uganda, the Democratic Republic of the Congo (DRC) and the Central African Republic – all related to situations on their own territories.[87]

8.7.2   Security Council

While there was some opposition during the negotiation of the Statute to the role of the Security Council in referring situations to the Court, it was widely recognized that such a role would be both useful and appropriate. The Statute does not 'confer' any such role on the Council; it could not add to the powers which the Council is given by the UN Charter. But the establishment of the ad hoc Tribunals has already illustrated that the Council can have a role in international criminal justice when international peace and security are threatened. When the Council refers situations to the ICC, it is not establishing a new institution as it did with the ICTY and the ICTR; the situation is being referred to the ICC as it stands, with all the powers and responsibilities laid down by the Statute.[88] It is open to the Council to

---

86 For the negotiations at the conference see: on referral by States, Philippe Kirsch and Darryl Robinson, 'Referral by States Parties' in Cassese, *Commentary*, 619; on the Prosecutor's authority, Silvia Fernández de Gurmendi, 'The Role of the International Prosecutor' in Lee, *The Making of the Rome Statute*, 175; Morten Bergsmo and Jelena Pejic, 'Article 15: Prosecutor' in Triffterer, *Observers' Notes*, 581; on referral by the Security Council, Lionel Yee, 'The International Criminal Court and the Security Council: Articles 13(b) and 16' in Lee, *The Making of the Rome Statute*, 143.

87 See section 8.7.4.

88 Agreement on this proposition does not, however, resolve all difficulties: see the different conclusions reached regarding the application of Art. 27 of the Statute to President Al-Bashir, in Dapo Akande, 'The Legal Nature of Security Council Referrals to the ICC and its Impact on Al Bashir's Immunities' (2009) 7 *JICJ* 333 and Paola Gaeta, 'Does President Al Bashir Enjoy Immunity from Arrest?' (2009) 7 *JICJ* 315.

impose additional obligations on States; for example, the obligation to cooperate with the Court, but the Court itself is an independent institution and its powers conferred by treaty cannot be changed by the Council.

The situation in Darfur, Sudan was referred to the ICC by the Security Council under resolution 1593(2005). This was a welcome example of the US allowing, indeed welcoming, the invocation of the Court's jurisdiction, in spite of its then firm objections to the Court; cases are pending as a result of the referral. But the resolution itself presented a number of problems. It required that no funding for the ICC investigations should come from the UN, in spite of Article 115 of the ICC Statute; it had unnecessary and meaningless references to Article 16 and to the bilateral non-surrender agreements of the US;[89] and, in its paragraph 6, it granted troop-contributing States which are not parties to the Statute exclusive jurisdiction over their nationals.[90]

8.7.3   Prosecutor's power to initiate an investigation

The chief point of controversy in the negotiation of the trigger mechanisms related to the power of the Prosecutor to begin investigations *proprio motu* – on his or her own initiative. On the one hand, there were concerns that if a provision to this effect were included in the Statute, the Prosecutor might institute politically motivated investigations and would not be subject to the oversight which national authorities have of their own prosecutors. On the other hand, there were concerns that the Court should not be entirely dependent on the decisions of external actors to trigger its work. Article 15 provides that the Prosecutor may initiate prosecutions without a State Party or Security Council referral, but to do so requires the authorization of the Pre-Trial Chamber. In addition, the procedures for investigation and prosecution which ensure both that the case is a proper one for the Court in terms of evidence and jurisdiction, and that national courts are not genuinely handling the case, have the effect of restricting the Prosecutor's authority, while not infringing on his independence.[91] The complex admissibility requirements in particular, including the requirement that the Prosecutor inform all States with jurisdiction before beginning an investigation,[92] addresses concerns about a hypothetical maverick Prosecutor getting away with pursuing a personal agenda.

The early experience of the Court has underlined the difficulties faced by the Prosecutor in exercising his discretion to choose situations to investigate among all the atrocities in the

---

89 See statement of the US on adoption of the resolution at UN Doc. S/PV.5158, at 4. The representatives of Denmark and Brazil made statements attempting to limit the effect of this reference; *ibid.*, at 6 and 11 respectively.
90 For a comment on the resolution see Robert Cryer, 'Sudan, Resolution 1593 and International Criminal Justice' (2006) 19 LJIL. For further discussion of US actions in opposition to the ICC see section 8.11.3.
91 See Allison Marston Banner, 'Enhancing the Legitimacy and Accountability of Prosecutorial Discretion at the International Criminal Court' (2003) 97 *AJIL* 510.
92 Art. 18.

world. A large number of communications have been transmitted to the Prosecutor from individuals and organizations who have wanted him to begin investigations of crimes coming within the ICC's jurisdiction.[93] In relation to allegations of crimes in Iraq and Venezuela, the Prosecutor decided that the requirements for opening investigations had not been met; his letters about those allegations indicate the procedure that is followed at the pre-investigative stage, when the Prosecutor must consider whether the available information provides a reasonable basis to believe that a crime within the jurisdiction of the Court is committed; if so, he must give consideration to admissibility requirements and to the interests of justice.[94]

While concerns were expressed at the Rome Conference about the possible use to which the *proprio motu* powers of the Prosecutor might be put, he has sought to initiate only one investigation on this basis (Kenya). The first four investigations have followed referrals by States Parties or the Security Council. The decision by the Prosecutor to await or to seek referrals rather than use his *proprio motu* powers reflects his view that explicit demonstrations of support can generate cooperation exceeding the Statute obligations of cooperation, and that strong State support is needed to enable him to carry out his responsibilities.[95]

8.7.4   'Self-referrals'

The first situations to be dealt with by the Court were referred by States in relation to crimes committed on their own territories. While some commentators doubt whether 'self-referral' is contemplated in the Statute,[96] the wording of the Statute suggests otherwise. The Statute simply says that 'a State Party may refer to the Prosecutor a situation', without any limitations.[97] Moreover, the drafting history shows that referrals by 'interested' States, such as territorial States, were specifically foreseen and even preferred.[98] A self-referral can be of benefit to the Court; it may indicate that far from an international investigation being intrusive, it is welcomed and will be supported by full cooperation by the State concerned, including by granting protection to investigators and witnesses. The Prosecutor

---

93 For example, over 300 communications were submitted to the Prosecutor regarding alleged crimes committed during the conflict in Gaza between December 2008 and January 2009.

94 See Prosecutor's letters of 9 February 2006; the letter about alleged crimes in Iraq is available at http://www2.icc-cpi.int/NR/rdonlyres/04D143C8-19FB-466C-AB77-4CDB2FDEBEF7/143682/OTP_letter_to_senders_re_Iraq_9_February_2006.pdf. For criticism of the Prosecutor's approach to these allegations, see Schabas, 'Prosecutorial Discretion'.

95 See Banner, 'Enhancing the Legitimacy', 518.

96 See, e.g. William Schabas, 'First Prosecutions at the International Criminal Court' (2006) 27 *Human Rights Law Journal* 25 at 32.

97 Art. 14(1).

98 Indeed, the debate in the negotiations was whether States Parties who were *not* 'interested States' (territorial, nationality or custodial) should be allowed to make referrals. See, e.g. UN Doc. A/AC.249/1 paras. 162–3; UN Doc. A/CONF.183/2/Add.1, p. 36.

has indeed expressed his intention to 'seek where possible to make this support [from a State] explicit through a referral'.[99]

There are risks, however.[100] A government of a divided country may use a referral to seek the Court's intervention against its own political opponents.[101] The referral by Uganda in 2003 concerned the 'situation concerning the Lord's Resistance Army' and the Prosecutor had to make it clear that this would be interpreted as covering crimes 'within the situation of northern Uganda by whomever committed'.[102]

Self-referrals may also present the risk that States will overburden the Court with cases they could handle themselves. The Prosecutor is not, however, obliged to initiate an investigation when a referral is made, and may decline to take a case on grounds such as lack of gravity, complementarity and the interests of justice.

8.8   Jurisdiction: personal, territorial and temporal

The Court has *potentially* worldwide jurisdiction, but this will be fully realized only after all States become parties to its Statute. In the meantime, Article 12(2) provides:

> [T]he Court may exercise its jurisdiction if one or more of the following States are Parties to this Statute or have accepted the jurisdiction of the Court in accordance with paragraph 3:
>
> (a) The State on the territory of which the conduct in question occurred or, if the crime was committed on board a vessel or aircraft, the State of registration of that vessel or aircraft;
>
> (b) The State of which the person accused of the crime is a national.

Article 12(3) allows a State not party to declare that it accepts the jurisdiction of the Court with respect to the crime in question.

The Court also has jurisdiction where a situation has been referred to the Court by the Security Council under Chapter VII of the UN Charter.[103] In the event of referral by the Council, the Court has jurisdiction even if none of the relevant States is a party to the Statute or gives its consent.[104]

---

99 Annex to the 'Paper on some policy issues before the Office of the Prosecutor': Referrals and Communications, at section D, on ICC website.
100 Claus Kreß, 'Self-Referrals and Waivers of Complementarity: Some Considerations in Law and Policy' (2004) 2 *JICJ* 944; Mahnoush Arsanjani and Michael Reisman, 'The Law-in-action of the International Criminal Court' (2005) 99 *AJIL* 385 at 392.
101 See also William Burke-White, 'Complementarity in Practice: the International Criminal Court as part of a system of Multi-level Global Governance in the Democratic Republic of Congo' (2005) 18 *LJIL* 557 at 567–8.
102 Letter of the Prosecutor of 17 June 2004 attached to the Presidency Decision to assign the situation in Uganda to Pre-Trial Chamber II.
103 This is the Chapter of the Charter under which the Council takes decisions, binding on States, to maintain or restore international peace and security; it was under this Chapter that the Council established the two ad hoc Tribunals.
104 As in the situation in Darfur, Sudan, referred to the Court by Security Council resolution 1593(2005).

The rationale for requiring the consent of the territorial State or the State of nationality is that these are the two most uncontroversial bases for the jurisdiction of States themselves.[105] The consent of one of these States therefore gives a solid basis for the taking of international jurisdiction. But these are not of course the only bases of State jurisdiction; the crimes listed in the Statute are ones over which universal jurisdiction may be taken by States. Why was a narrower jurisdiction agreed upon for the Court? As previously described,[106] the ILC draft Statute, with which the negotiations on the Court began, made large concessions to State sovereignty. For all crimes except genocide[107] the ILC model of a court had jurisdiction only if *both* the State with custody of the suspect *and* the territorial State had accepted the jurisdiction of the court *in respect of that category of crime*. During the negotiations, various different proposals emerged. The most ambitious was a German proposal[108] to give unlimited jurisdiction to the Court: wherever the crime was committed, whether or not in the territory of a State Party and of whatever nationality the suspect, the Court would have jurisdiction. Another alternative was a South Korean proposal[109] to confer jurisdiction on the Court with the acceptance of any one of four States: those with territorial jurisdiction, or active nationality jurisdiction, or passive nationality jurisdiction, or with custody of the suspect. At the other end of the spectrum, the United States argued that the consent of *both* the territorial and the nationality State ought to be required. The South Korean proposal had a great deal of support, but a compromise text was accepted by the conference and is now reflected in Article 12; it gives a more limited jurisdiction to the Court, but one which was thought to entail a greater likelihood of acceptance by the Rome Conference as a whole.[110]

Under the ILC draft statute, ratification of the Statute did not entail in itself acceptance of jurisdiction; a State could choose whether to 'opt in' to any crime (except in respect of genocide, for which there was a form of universal jurisdiction). As it became clear during the course of the negotiations that the list of crimes would include only the 'core crimes', the 'opt-in' regime was seen to be less necessary and, over time, the great majority of the negotiators came to favour 'automatic jurisdiction', meaning that a State upon ratification signified its acceptance of jurisdiction for all core crimes. During the Rome Conference, a third alternative emerged, which would have permitted a State Party to 'opt out' of war crimes and crimes against humanity for renewable periods of ten years. This alternative was not widely accepted but was the origin of Article 124.

---

105 See Chapter 3.

106 See section 8.2.

107 The ICC had jurisdiction over genocide whenever a complaint was brought by a State Party which was also a party to the Genocide Convention; this was a form of universal jurisdiction.

108 The German proposal, with many other proposals on this issue, was contained in the draft text of the Statute submitted to the conference by the Preparatory Committee (A/CONF.183/13 (Vol. III)).

109 A/CONF.183/C.1/L.6.

110 For the history of the negotiations see Sharon Williams and William Schabas, 'Article 12' in Triffterer, *Observers' Notes*, 547; Elizabeth Wilmshurst, 'Jurisdiction of the Court' in Lee, *The Making of the Rome Statute*, 127.

8.8.1   Article 124

The Statute follows the automatic acceptance model, meaning that a State upon ratification accepts jurisdiction over all core crimes, but Article 124 contains an exception which allows a State, upon ratification of the Statute, not to accept the jurisdiction of the ICC over war crimes with regard to its nationals or to crimes committed on its territory for a period of seven years. This provision, which has no justification other than as a concession necessary to secure agreement on the final text of the Statute,[111] could have created a serious obstacle to the exercise of the Court's jurisdiction, but has not proved to be so; of the first 110 States Parties, only two, France and Colombia, took advantage of the opt-out regime and France has now withdrawn its declaration under Article 124.[112] The first Review Conference, held under Article 123 in 2010, has the opportunity to remove the Article from the Statute altogether.

8.8.2   'Ad hoc' acceptance of jurisdiction

An acceptance of the jurisdiction of the Court under Article 12(3) by a State not party to the Statute extends the territorial and personal jurisdiction of the Court. It does not constitute a referral to the Court; indeed States that are not parties may not refer situations to the Court. Following or before the making of the declaration of acceptance, there will therefore need to be either a referral by a State or, more likely, the initiation of an investigation by the Prosecutor under his own powers, before the Court may exercise its jurisdiction.[113] The legal effect of a declaration will simply be to put a non-party State on the same jurisdictional basis as a State Party, but in practice the declaration will indicate to the Prosecutor that the State concerned is willing to have the particular situation dealt with by the Court. There is, however, no obligation on the Prosecutor to begin an investigation.[114] The cooperation obligations of Part 9 of the Statute will apply to the State making the declaration.

It is important to note that the declaration accepting jurisdiction 'with respect to the crime in question' has as a consequence the acceptance of jurisdiction for *all* the crimes relevant to the situation.[115] This avoids the possibility of a non-party State consenting to the Court's jurisdiction with regard to enemy nationals, while shielding its own.

---

111 For criticism of the French attempt at justification of the provision, see Alain Pellet, 'Entry into force and amendment of the Statute' in Cassese, *Commentary*, 145 at 168–9.

112 With effect from 15.6.2008.

113 For the procedures applicable to such a declaration, see Carsten Stahn, Mohamed El Zeidy and Héctor Olásolo, 'The International Criminal Court's Ad Hoc Jurisdiction Revisited' (2005) 99 *AJIL* 421.

114 For example, Côte d'Ivoire accepted the jurisdiction of the ICC in 2003 but the Prosecutor has not, as at October 2009, opened an investigation. On 22.1.2009 the Palestinian National Authority lodged a declaration under Art. 12(3), but the Prosecutor will have to decide whether the PA is 'a State which is not a Party' to the Statute, without which the declaration cannot be accepted.

115 Rule 44(2) of the ICC RPE.

8.8.3 Persons over 18

The Court's jurisdiction is limited to persons over the age of 18 at the time the alleged offence was committed.[116] Turning the question of age into a jurisdictional issue avoids having to choose between different national age limits for criminal responsibility.[117] Prosecuting minors would have required the provision of a special regime and was not a sensible use of the Court's slender resources. This does not of course exclude national jurisdiction over minors for the commission of international crimes.

8.8.4 Temporal jurisdiction

The ICC does not have jurisdiction over offences committed before the entry into force of the Statute on 1 July 2002. States were unwilling to allow the ICC to deal with past practices. If a State becomes a party to the Statute after its entry into force, the Court may exercise jurisdiction only with respect to crimes committed after the Statute has entered into force for that State (Article 11); the State may, however, make a declaration under Article 12(3) to fill this temporal gap. Crimes committed before 1 July 2002 may not be tried by the ICC under any circumstance.[118]

8.9 Deferral of investigation or prosecution: Article 16

Article 16 reads as follows:

> No investigation or prosecution may be commenced or proceeded with under the Statute for a period of 12 months after the Security Council, in a resolution adopted under Chapter VII of the Charter of the United Nations, has requested the Court to that effect; that request may be renewed by the Council under the same conditions.

This Article originates in an even wider restriction on the Court's jurisdiction which was contained in the ILC draft Articles; that provision would have removed jurisdiction over any matter which was being considered by the Security Council unless the Council agreed otherwise. The draft was reversed by the negotiators, who saw it as unacceptably subordinating the ICC to the Security Council.[119] Thus, instead of requiring a positive Council decision (requiring nine positive votes and no veto by a permanent member) to *allow* the

---

116 See Roger Clark and Otto Triffterer, 'Article 26' in Triffterer, *Observers' Notes*, 771.
117 Per Saland, 'International Criminal Law Principles' in Lee, *The Making of the Rome Statute*, 189 at 200–2.
118 Even if the Security Council were minded to refer a situation to the ICC in which the alleged crimes were committed before the entry into force of the Statute, the Court would not be able to exercise its jurisdiction, since it is a creature of the Statute, not of the Security Council, and although the Council's resolutions may override the treaty obligations of States (Art. 103 of the Charter), they cannot change the powers of an independent organization.
119 Morten Bergsmo and Jelena Pejic, 'Article 16' in Triffterer, *Observers' Notes*, 595 at 597–9.

ICC to proceed in such circumstances, Article 16 now requires a positive decision to *defer* a proceeding. The Council has to act under Chapter VII of the Charter, which applies only where there is a 'threat to the peace, breach of the peace or act of aggression'. The Council request for deferral has effect for twelve months and may be renewed.

The intervention in judicial proceedings of a political organ in this way requires some explanation.[120] The purpose was to allow the Council, under its primary responsibility for the maintenance of peace and security, to set aside the demands of justice at a time when it considered the demands of peace to be overriding; if the suspension of legal proceedings against a leader will allow a peace treaty to be concluded, precedence may be given to peace. Any suspension of the proceedings is only temporary.

Assessments of whether the demands of peace processes should occasion the suspension of Court proceedings sometimes differ. Unsuccessful requests have been made to the Council in the perceived interests of peace to suspend proceedings in relation to the situation in northern Uganda and in relation to the arrest warrant against the President of Sudan. The adoption by the Council of resolutions suspending non-existent proceedings in 2002 and 2003, at the behest of the previous US administration, was a surprising and controversial use of Article 16.[121]

8.10   Enforcement of the ICC's decisions

A national court may rely on local police to arrest suspects for the purpose of trial, and on local detention facilities to imprison them on conviction. The ICC has to rely entirely on the international community for these matters. Part 9 of the Statute requires States Parties to cooperate with the Court in providing various forms of assistance such as the taking of evidence and the tracing of assets. Article 89(1) imposes the all-important obligation to surrender any person found within a State's territory when the Court so requests. The limitations on the Court in making such requests where the person concerned enjoys immunity or where there is a relevant international agreement are laid down in Article 98. International organizations may also be requested to provide information or any other form of assistance to the ICC (Article 87(6)). As regards sentences of imprisonment imposed by the Court, there is no obligation on States to provide prison facilities, and sentences will be served in a State selected by the Court from a list of those that have declared their willingness to accept sentenced persons (Article 103).[122]

If a State Party fails to comply with a request to cooperate from the Court, in breach of its obligations under the Statute, the Court may refer the matter to the Assembly of States

---

120 See Franklin Berman, 'The Relationship between the International Criminal Court and the Security Council' in H. von Hebel, J. Lammers and J. Schukking (eds.), *Reflections on the International Criminal Court* (The Hague, 1999).
121 The relevant resolutions are discussed at section 8.11.3.
122 See Chapter 19.

Parties or, in the case of a referral by the Security Council, to the Council.[123] Although the Council has the power to impose mandatory requirements on the defaulting State, the Assembly has no powers of enforcement.

All of the existing investigations by the Prosecutor are being conducted in situations of ongoing violence or actual conflict where security is a problem, presenting considerable challenges to the investigators and witnesses in the field. This will be typical of most situations brought before the ICC. The possibilities of collecting evidence may be limited. Although the commission of atrocities may be common knowledge, information about incidents and command structures may be very difficult to obtain: local governments may be unwilling or unable to provide significant assistance; humanitarian organizations in the field may be reluctant to assist so as not to put at risk their continued presence; international peacekeeping missions may not have a wide enough mandate or may wish to avoid prejudicing their neutrality; other governments may not wish to disclose evidence obtained by their intelligence services or may have their own political interests in the region which conflict with their interests in the enforcement of international criminal justice. Seen against such difficulties as these, the provisions of the Statute enforcing the Court's requests and decisions have been described as 'paltry, at best'.[124]

For discussion of cooperation with the ICC and a comparison with the cooperation requirements of the two Tribunals, see Chapter 20. Chapter 21 deals with the way in which the Court handles the issue of immunities.

8.11   Opposition to the ICC

The ICC has enjoyed strong support from much of the international community, as may be seen from the speed with which the first sixty ratifications were reached. Nonetheless, some opposition to the Court was evident at the time the Statute was adopted and it quickly became clear that the Court in the form that had been agreed would not achieve universal acceptance, at least in the first decade of its existence.[125] The United States was by no means the only State to oppose the creation of the Court.[126] But because it has been the most open and vocal in expressing its opposition and in taking action pursuant to its views, it is largely the early practice of the US that is considered here. During the second term of the

---

123 Art. 87(7) of the ICC Statute.
124 Leila Sadat and Richard Garden, 'The New International Criminal Court: an Uneasy Revolution' (2000) 88 *Georgetown Law Journal* 381 at 389.
125 See generally Dominic McGoldrick, 'Political and Legal Responses to the International Criminal Court' in McGoldrick et al. (eds.), *The Permanent International Criminal Court*, 389.
126 For discussion of the opposition of some other States, see Lu Jianping and Wang Zhixiang, 'China's Attitude towards the ICC' (2005) 3 *JICJ* 608; Bakhtiyar Tuzmukhamedov, 'The ICC and Russian Constitutional Problems' *ibid.*, 621; Usha Ramanathan, 'India and the ICC' *ibid.*, 627; Hirad Abtahi, 'The Islamic Republic of Iran and the ICC' *ibid.*, 635.

Bush administration, relations with the Court thawed somewhat, but with a change of administration in 2009, a more positive attitude to the Court has come about on the part of the US.

The United States, under the Clinton administration, signed the Statute on 31 December 2001, the last day that it was possible to do so. Its signature may be attributed to the fact that the US at that time was not in principle opposed to the creation of a new court to dispense international criminal justice, and hoped to resolve some of its points of difficulty by means of changes to the rules of procedure and other documents. Signature imposed an obligation on the United States under Article 18 of the Vienna Convention of the Law of Treaties: a signatory State may not 'defeat the object and purpose of a treaty prior to its entry into force' unless it has made clear its intention not to become a party to the treaty. With the advent of the Bush administration came fiercer opposition to the ICC and, in order to avoid the obligation under Article 18, the US made clear its intention not to ratify the Statute in a communication to the UN Secretariat on 6 May 2002. Israel followed suit, in respect of its own signature, on 28 August 2002.[127]

8.11.1 Opposition to jurisdiction over nationals of non-party States

The principal objection made against the ICC on legal grounds is that under Article 12 it may take jurisdiction over nationals of a State not a party to the Statute without that State's consent.[128] The claim that this is contrary to international law is made first by reference to the Vienna Convention on the Law of Treaties, Article 34 of which provides: 'A treaty does not create either obligations or rights for a third State without its consent.' However, the Statute clearly does not create obligations for States not parties to it. The fact that a foreign court or tribunal may have jurisdiction over a State's nationals, on grounds such as territorial jurisdiction, is nothing novel, and does not entail any 'obligations'. While it undoubtedly affects a State's *interests* that the Court may have jurisdiction over its nationals, that is not a ground for claiming that the Statute is contrary to international law. It is also asserted in this context that there is nothing in customary international law to justify the delegation of jurisdiction over the nationals of non-party States to an international court. However, international law does not preclude States from acting collectively by delegating to an

---

127 Sudan made a similar communication on 26 August 2008. The various communications are available at http://treaties.un.org/Pages/ViewDetails.aspx?src=TREATY&mtdsg_no=XVIII-10&chapter=18&lang=en.

128 There is an extensive literature on arguments about Article 12; see, e.g. Eve La Haye, 'The Jurisdiction of the International Criminal Court' (1999) XLVI *Netherlands International Law Review* 1; M. Scharf, 'The ICC's Jurisdiction Over the Nationals of Non-Party States: A Critique of the US Position' (2001) 64 *Law and Contemporary Problems* 98; Madeline Morris, 'High Crimes and Misconceptions: The ICC and Non Party States' (2000) 64 *Law and Contemporary Problems* 131; Frederic Megret, 'Epilogue To An Endless Debate: The International Criminal Court's Third Party Jurisdiction And The Looming Revolution Of International Law' (2001) 12 *EJIL* 241; Dapo Akande, 'The Jurisdiction of the International Criminal Court over Nationals of Non-Parties: Legal Basis and Limits' (2003) 1 *JICJ* 618.

international court the jurisdiction which they would be entitled to exercise themselves[129] and there is no requirement for a positive rule of international law allowing States to exercise their jurisdiction collectively in this manner. On the contrary, any suggestion that there is such a rule would be contrary to the principle of territorial jurisdiction and generally retrogressive.

8.11.2 Other arguments against the Statute

There are other provisions of the Statute which have given rise to controversy, although the arguments here are less of law than of legitimacy.[130] Some arguments are based on a general mistrust of the ICC.[131] They include the concern that States with effective legal systems cannot be sure that the Court will not take over the prosecutions of their nationals, because the Statute leaves it to the Court itself to judge whether the national court is 'unable or unwilling' genuinely to deal with a case. On this view, the complementarity principle is not a reliable safeguard since the ICC cannot be trusted to apply it without political bias. A further concern is that the Prosecutor, unlike national prosecutors, is accountable to no outside agency or authority in exercising his power of initiating investigations.

The arguments overlook or downplay the various restraints and limits on the Prosecutor's actions which are provided throughout the Statute system, and formal and informal methods of securing accountability.[132] They also fail to take fully into account the ability of States not parties to the Statute to avoid the exercise of the ICC's jurisdiction by prosecuting Statute crimes themselves; although if such States wish to take advantage of the complementarity principle they will have to ensure that their own legislation gives them jurisdiction over all the crimes concerned.[133] It is to be hoped that general mistrust of the ICC will be reduced if the Court shows that it is able to operate, as it has been created to do, independently and impartially.

---

129 The Nuremberg judgment decided that that trial was justified on the basis that what States could do alone could be done together: '. . . they have done together what any one of them might have done singly; for it is not to be doubted that any nation has the right thus to set up special courts to administer law' (International Military Tribunal (Nuremberg) Judgment and Sentences, reprinted in (1947) 41 *AJIL* 172 at 216).

130 See, e.g. Michael Lohr and William Lietzau, 'One Road Away From Rome: Concerns Regarding the International Criminal Court' (1999) 9 *US Air Force Journal of Legal Studies* 33.

131 John Bolton, 'The Risks and Weaknesses of the International Criminal Court From an American Perspective' (2000–2001) 41 *Virginia Journal of International Law* 186; David Forsythe, 'The United States and International Criminal Justice' (2002) 24 *Human Rights Quarterly* 974.

132 See Banner, 'Enhancing the Legitimacy'. The arguments on informal means of accountability may, however, understate the importance of prosecutorial independence.

133 See Thomas Pittman and Matthew Heaphy, 'Does the United States Really Prosecute its Service Members for War Crimes? Implications for Complementarity before the International Criminal Court' (2008) 21 *LJIL* 165.

8.11.3 Challenges to the ICC

The US opposition to the ICC led them to make various attempts to prevent the possibility of US nationals being tried by the Court. Their action on the international front was supported and partially instigated by domestic legislation. The American Servicemembers' Protection Act prohibits various forms of US cooperation with the ICC, provides for the cessation of military and other aid to States Parties which do not sign a non-surrender agreement with the US, and authorizes the use of 'all means necessary, including military force' to release persons arrested by the ICC.[134]

Security Council resolutions

In the months immediately prior to the entry into force of the ICC Statute, the US looked to the possibility of using a Security Council resolution to exempt US nationals from the Court's jurisdiction. One course of action involved an unexpected use of Article 16 of the Statute. Security Council resolution 1422(2002), pushed through the Council by the US with the threat of refusal to support a peacekeeping operation, requested the ICC to defer any exercise of its jurisdiction for twelve months 'if a case arises involving current or former officials or personnel from a contributing State not a party to the Rome Statute over acts or omissions relating to a United Nations established or authorised operation'. A further resolution asking for suspension for another twelve months was adopted in 2003 (resolution 1487(2003)). The following year, however, support for the US action had dwindled and there was not the necessary majority in the Security Council to adopt another resolution in the series.

The two resolutions have been highly controversial and doubts have been expressed as to their compatibility with the UN Charter as well as their effectiveness under the Rome Statute.[135] Scepticism was expressed in a Security Council meeting open to all UN members[136] as to whether the Council was acting within its powers under Chapter VII of the Charter, since it was not obvious that the decisions of the Council concerned a matter of

---

134 2002 Supplemental Appropriations Act for Further Recovery from and Response to Terrorist Attacks on the United States, as amended; see Sean Murphy, 'Contemporary Practice of the United States' (2002) 96 *AJIL* 975.

135 See, e.g. Aly Mokhtar, 'The fine art of arm-twisting: The US, Resolution 1422 and Security Council deferral power under the Rome Statute' (2002) 3 *International Criminal Law Review* 295; Neha Jain, 'A Separate Law for Peacekeepers; the Clash between the Security Council and the International Criminal Court' (2005) 16 *EJIL* 239; Carsten Stahn, 'The Ambiguities of Security Council Resolution 1422 (2002)' (2003) 14 *EJIL* 85; Dominic McGoldrick, 'Political and Legal Responses to the ICC' in McGoldrick et al. (eds.), *The Permanent International Criminal Court*, 415–22.

136 See statements by representatives of Canada and Jordan at the first Security Council meeting on 10.7.2002 (S/PV.4568).

international peace and security. The Security Council has used its Chapter VII powers too often on purely political grounds, however, for this appeal to the Charter to be, in the final analysis, convincing.[137] Another argument, based on the Rome Statute, maintains that the resolutions would not be effective to oblige the ICC to accede to the Council's requests. The negotiating history of Article 16 indicates that the intention was that the Council would consider, on a case-by-case basis, whether the continuation of ICC proceedings would prejudice the maintenance of international peace and security; a request for the suspension of hypothetical proceedings which might arise at some time in the future would not appear to come within the objective of Article 16 even though it fell within its wording.[138] While there has been a great deal of academic debate about the resolutions, they have had no practical impact on the Court, no case having arisen in the relevant period. It is to be hoped that they are now of historical interest only.

There are other resolutions, however, which remain in force. In a further approach to seeking exemption from the ICC's jurisdiction over its personnel, the US promoted the decision in resolution 1497(2003) that personnel from a State which is not a party to the ICC Statute will be subject to the exclusive jurisdiction of that State for all acts related to the multinational force or United Nations force in Liberia.[139] This was used as a precedent in the resolution referring the situation in Darfur, Sudan, to the ICC.[140] Both of these decisions have the aim of shielding a group of persons from any courts save those of their own States. Unlike the requests under Article 16, the resolutions do not have to be renewed every year; they will stay in force as long as the authorized forces remain in existence.

In purporting to set aside the jurisdiction not only of the ICC but also of national courts, the provisions of these two resolutions attempt to interfere with treaties – the Rome Statute as well as the Geneva Conventions, since the latter require all States to exercise jurisdiction over grave breaches of international humanitarian law wherever they occur. The Charter obligation on States to comply with binding Security Council resolutions and the hierarchy of treaties established by Article 103 of the Charter ensure that the resolutions will be effective to prevent a State from taking jurisdiction over persons covered by their provisions. The ICC, however, is not a Council organ and is not itself bound by Council resolutions; as the Relationship Agreement between the ICC and the UN recognizes, it is an independent institution with international legal personality. The resolutions would not therefore have any

---

137 To the contrary, Karl Doehring, 'Unlawful Resolutions of the Security Council and their Legal Consequences' (1997) 1 *Max Planck Yearbook of United Nations Law* 91.

138 See statement of New Zealand at the Security Council meeting on 10.7.2002 (S/PV.4568).

139 Para. 7 of the resolution. Mexico, France and Germany abstained, asserting that the paragraph not only undermined the ICC but also prevented countries from exercising jurisdiction over persons accused of murdering their citizens (S/PV.4803).

140 Res. 1593(2005), para. 6. Brazil explained that this paragraph was one of the reasons for its abstention from the vote (S/PV.5158).

restrictive effect on the jurisdiction of the ICC;[141] it is debatable whether they would preclude States from surrendering suspects to the Court.

Non-surrender agreements

Under the Bush administration, the US negotiated bilateral agreements with other States, some of them parties to the Statute, others not, which provide that no nationals, current or former officials, or military personnel of either party may be surrendered or transferred by the other State to the ICC for any purpose.[142] The US referred to Article 98(2) of the Rome Statute as the basis for these agreements, maintaining that the ICC will not be able to request a State to surrender a US national to the Court, once that State has entered into such an agreement with the US. The agreements will of course only be effective in preventing the Court from making such a request if they are in truth compatible with the Statute.

Article 98(2) precludes the Court from asking for the surrender of a suspect if that would require the requested State 'to act inconsistently with its obligations under international agreements pursuant to which the consent of a sending State is required to surrender a person of the State to the Court'. The provision was inserted in the Statute to address the problem of conflicting obligations where, for example, a State in which foreign military personnel are stationed has agreed under a status of forces agreement (SOFA) to accord the right to the sending State to exercise criminal jurisdiction over its troops for certain kinds of offences. Without Article 98(2), such an agreement would conflict with the obligation in the ICC Statute to surrender suspects to the Court when so requested. Another example of an agreement covered by the provision is an extradition arrangement under which the rule of specialty would normally require the State receiving a suspect extradited from another State to obtain the consent of that State before dealing with the suspect in any other way than prosecuting him for the offence for which his extradition was requested.

In assessing the compatibility of the US agreements with the Rome Statute, a preliminary question is whether Article 98(2) covers agreements entered into after the entry into force of the Statute. The natural meaning of the words 'obligations under international agreements' supports the view that Article 98(2) is not limited to agreements existing at the time a State becomes a party to the Statute.[143]

---

141 Other (weak) arguments as to the efficacy of para. 6 of res. 1593(2005) in relation to the ICC are that preambular para. 2 has a reference to Art. 16 of the Rome Statute; but this does not turn it into a request to the Court to defer investigations under that Article: it is not worded as a request to the ICC and does not seek temporary deferral. Nor can the resolution be regarded as a referral of a situation *minus* the activities of peace-keepers and other personnel: see Cryer, 'Sudan, Resolution 1593', 17–18; for reasoning to the contrary see David Scheffer, 'Staying the Course With the International Criminal Court' (2001–2) 35 *Cornell International Law Journal* 47 at 90.

142 For the text of one example, that with East Timor, see (2003) 97 *AJIL* 201–2.

143 See Opinion by James Crawford SC, Philippe Sands QC and Ralph Wilde available at http://www.iccnow. org/documents/SandsCrawfordBIA14June03.pdf. For an alternative view see Markus Benzing, 'U.S. Bilateral

As regards wider questions of compatibility with the Rome Statute, the key to the interpretation of Article 98(2) is in the phrase 'sending State'. There is nothing in the provision to prevent the Court requesting the surrender of a person who has not been 'sent' by one State to another State. But the US agreements cover all US nationals. Tourists and businessmen can by no stretch of the imagination be regarded as persons 'sent' by one State to another.[144] The agreements entered into by the US therefore do not fall within the terms of Article 98(2) and would not have the effect of preventing the ICC from requesting surrender.[145] The requested State party will continue to be obliged to cooperate with the ICC by surrendering the person concerned and will have the problem of attempting to reconcile conflicting treaty obligations.

Other challenges to the Court

While the number of African States Parties to the ICC Statute is large,[146] there has been some reluctance from other States in the region to support the Court and criticisms have been made in the African Union that some of the Court's proceedings have interfered with peace processes, in particular the investigations and subsequent arrest warrant issued against the President of Sudan.[147] The African Union adopted a decision on 8 July 2009 which 'expresses its deep concern at the indictment' issued against the President and 'notes with grave concern the unfortunate consequences that the indictment has had on the delicate peace processes underway in the Sudan'.[148] The AU has pressed for the adoption by the Security Council of a resolution requesting the deferral of these proceedings.

Non-Surrender Agreements and Article 98 of the Statute of the International Criminal Court: An Exercise in the Law of Treaties' (2004) 8 *Max Planck Yearbook of United Nations Law* 182 at 219; Hans-Peter Kaul and Claus Kreß, 'Jurisdiction and Cooperation in the Statute of the International Criminal Court: Principles and Compromises' (1999) 2 *YIHL* 143 at 165.

144 The former US administration's attempt to interpret the reference in Art. 98(2) to a 'sending State' in a manner which allows inclusion of all nationals of that State seeks (misplaced) reliance on the use of that term in the Vienna Convention on Consular Relations 1963; see David Scheffer, 'Article 98(2) of the Rome Statute: America's Original Intent' (2005) 3 *JICJ* 333 at 347–50.

145 This is the view generally reflected in the guidelines agreed upon by the EU Council, binding upon all EU Member States; EU Council of Ministers 2459th session, GAER Doc. 12134/02 30.9.2002; reprinted in McGoldrick et al. (eds.), *The Permanent International Criminal Court*, 430–1. On the subject generally see Benzing, 'U.S. Bilateral Non-Surrender Agreements', 182; Herman van der Wilt, 'Bilateral Agreements between the US and States Parties to the Rome Statute' (2005) 18 *LJIL* 93.

146 30 as at September 2009.

147 There has been discussion in the African Union about the proceedings brought in relation to the situation in Darfur and note was taken of this in Security Council res. 1828(2008) (extending the mandate of UNAMID) as follows: 'Taking note of the African Union (AU) communique of the 142nd Peace and Security Council (PSC) Meeting dated 21 July 2008 and having in mind concerns raised by members of the Council regarding potential developments subsequent to the application by the Prosecutor of the International Criminal Court of 14 July 2008, and taking note of their intention to consider these matters further'.

148 Assembly/AU/Dec/3(XIII).

8.12 Appraisal

After a slow start, prosecutions and trials are underway at the Court. There has been a huge number of preliminary proceedings in respect of most of the situations and cases in progress, in the course of which the interrelationship of the Prosecutor and the Chambers, as well as the relationships between the Chambers themselves, are being gradually established. The unique procedures for victims' rights are being developed.[149] The ICC will have to address the problem of dealing more speedily, though fairly, with its case load. The *Lubanga* trial, the first of the new Court, faced particular difficulties regarding the disclosure of evidence and protection of the witnesses at the trial, illustrating the importance of having judges who have had experience of dealing with all the various challenges of a criminal trial.[150]

The dependence of the Court on the international community to ensure cooperation by reluctant States and to implement arrest warrants has led to serious delays where that support is not forthcoming. Warrants of arrest have not been enforced. The ability of President Bashir to travel to other countries without apparent fear of arrest causes concern. The voluntary appearance of one person against whom a summons was issued for offences against peacekeepers in Darfur was a welcome exception to the absence of all others in the Darfur situation, but the charges against him were not confirmed. The future success of the ICC will depend in part on the extent to which States are prepared to 'take ownership'[151] of the Court. They will need to lend it their cooperation and support not only through strict and willing compliance with their obligations to the Court, but also by multilateral measures such as enlarging the mandates of Security Council peacekeeping missions and proactively assisting with evidence by incorporating assistance to the Court into their intelligence-gathering capabilities.

The Court – and the international community – has had to face the challenge posed to international criminal justice generally by the so-called peace and justice dilemma. The jurisdiction of the ICC makes it inevitable that cases will be brought before the Court while conflicts are still ongoing. The statement is often quoted that 'Justice, peace and democracy are not mutually exclusive objectives, but rather mutually reinforcing imperatives',[152] but there have been demands in particular situations that justice should be subordinated either temporarily or indefinitely to the needs of a peace process. In Uganda, the opening of the investigation and the subsequent refusal to withdraw the arrest warrants against the LRA leaders were criticized as impeding the peace process and efforts to persuade members of the

---

149 See Chapter 18.
150 See, on his experience in the ICTY, Judge Iain Bonomy, 'The Reality of Conducting a War Crimes Trial' (2007) 5 *JICJ* 348: 'My constant aim is to ensure that the proceedings before me are conducted fairly. I rely on my years of experience in the conduct of such proceedings …'
151 To use the Prosecutor's phrase; see *Policy Paper*, 6.
152 Report of the Secretary-General on the Rule of Law and Transitional Justice, 23.8.2004 (S/2004/616), introduction.

LRA to defect.[153] The arrest warrant against President Bashir has, as we have seen, given rise to demands that where peace and justice clash, as here allegedly, peace should be put first.[154] The Prosecutor has said that the 'matter of international peace and security is not the responsibility of the Prosecutor; it falls within the mandate of other institutions', but others have argued that he should take account of peace processes within his inherent prosecutorial discretion, and avoid bringing politically destablizing cases for a necessary period.[155] The way in which such dilemmas are handled by both the Prosecutor and the wider international community will provide a further marker for the success or failure of the Court.

The exercise of the Prosecutor's discretion more generally is a further test for the Court. The Prosecutor necessarily has to make choices among situations to investigate and among cases within situations referred to him. His own selections will inevitably be met by criticisms from those who would have selected differently, bringing challenges to the Court's legitimacy. It is also inevitable that the Court, which is one of last resort, will have its cases drawn largely from those regions which cannot rely on their own justice systems to deal with international crimes. But in making choices for his investigations, the Prosecutor should have in mind the finite nature of the Court's resources (leading to a choice of those most responsible for atrocities rather than only lesser warlords), the need to be impartial between government forces and rebels (if both have committed international crimes), and the need to keep scrupulously to his own powers under the Statute (even where the temptation to investigate atrocities of dubious admissibility and jurisdiction is strong).

The difficulties for the ICC are immense. It is premature to attempt a thorough appraisal of its work. This chapter has discussed some of the challenges with which the Court is faced. At the very least, the role played by the ICC will ensure that international crimes do not get ignored or forgotten.

Further reading

The website of the ICC is useful; it may be found on http://www.icc-cpi.int/.

Markus Benzing, 'The Complementarity Regime of the International Criminal Court: International Criminal Justice between State Sovereignty and the Fight against Impunity' (2003) 7 *Max Planck Yearbook of United Nations Law* 591.

---

153 See discussion in Payam Akhavan, 'The Lord's Resistance Army Case: Uganda's Submission of the First State Referral to the International Criminal Court' (2005) 99 *AJIL* 403, 416–21; Manisuli Ssenyonjo, 'Accountability of non-State actors in Uganda for war crimes and human rights violations: between amnesty and the ICC' (2005) 10 *Journal of Conflict and Security Law* 405.

154 Julie Flint and Alex de Waal, 'To put justice before peace spells disaster for Sudan' *Guardian* 6.3.2009, available at http://www.guardian.co.uk/commentisfree/2009/mar/06/sudan-war-crimes. See, to the contrary, Christopher Gosnell, 'The Request for an Arrest Warrant in *Al Bashir*: Idealistic Posturing or Calculated Plan?' (2008) 6 *JICJ* 841.

155 See, e.g. Kenneth Rodman, 'Is Peace in the Interests of Justice? The Case for Broad Prosecutorial Discretion at the International Criminal Court' (2009) 22 *LJIL* 99.

Bruce Broomhall, *International Justice and the International Criminal Court: Between Sovereignty and the Rule of Law* (Oxford, 2003).

Antonio Cassese, Paola Gaeta and John R. W. D. Jones (eds.), *The Rome Statute of the International Criminal Court: A Commentary* (Oxford, 2002).

José Doria, M. Cherif Bassiouni and Hans-Peter Gasser (eds.), *The Legal Regime of the International Criminal Court* (Leiden, 2009).

Philippe Kirsch and John Holmes, 'The Rome Conference of an International Criminal Court: The Negotiating Process' (1999) 93 *American Journal of International Law* 2.

Jann Kleffner, *Complementarity in the Rome Statute and National Criminal Jurisdictions* (Oxford, 2008).

Mark Lattimer and Philippe Sands (eds.), *Justice for Crimes against Humanity* (Oxford, 2003).

Roy Lee (ed.), *The International Criminal Court: the Making of the Rome Statute* (The Hague, 1999).

Dominic McGoldrick, Peter Rowe, Eric Donnelly (eds.), *The Permanent International Criminal Court: Legal and Policy Issues* (Oxford, 2004).

Leila Sadat, *The International Criminal Court and the Transformation of International Law* (New York, 2002).

Philippe Sands (ed.), *From Nuremberg to the Hague: The Future of International Criminal Justice* (Cambridge, 2003) chs. 2 and 4.

Benjamin Schiff, *Building the International Criminal Court* (Cambridge, 2008).

Carsten Stahn and Göran Sluiter (eds.), *The Emerging Practice of the International Criminal Court* (Leiden, 2009).

Otto Triffterer (ed.), *The Rome Statute of the International Criminal Court: Observers' Notes, Article by Article*, 2nd edn (Baden-Baden, 2008).

9

Other Courts with International Elements

9.1 Introduction

The increased concern to combat impunity for international crimes has resulted not only in the creation of international criminal tribunals and courts, but also in other forms of international assistance to the States concerned. There are various reasons for avoiding resort to a new international tribunal. International institutions like the ICTY and the ICTR tend to be large and expensive; calls for similar tribunals have been unsuccessful. Their capacity is limited to a few cases and they have hitherto been located away from the State in question for security or other reasons. In a number of cases, therefore, an alternative has been preferred: the creation of criminal courts with national and international elements.

The models developed for Sierra Leone, Kosovo, East Timor, Cambodia and Bosnia and Herzegovina are described in this chapter. The special courts in Iraq and Serbia are briefly mentioned, as well as one internationalized court (Lebanon) and one domestic court established for a particular trial (the Lockerbie trial). The creation of other such courts has been proposed.[1]

Each of the models is different, as were their political backgrounds and the legal bases for establishing them. In Sierra Leone and Cambodia, the conflicts were a civil war and persecution by a murderous regime respectively, and the courts result from an agreement between the United Nations and the post-conflict government. East Timor and Kosovo, on the other hand, experienced conflicts of self-determination or secession and the courts were created as a direct result of international intervention and installation of an international transitional administration. The court in Bosnia and Herzegovina was also established by an international agency, mandated by a peace agreement. The special court in Iraq, which was

---

1 For example, the report of the Mbeki Panel, established by the AU, recommended a Hybrid Criminal Chamber within the Sudanese justice system. Another proposed initiative was a special war crimes chamber in the Burundi court system (see UN Doc. S/2005/158 of 11.3.2005 paras. 57–66, and SC res. 1606(2005) of 20.6.2005); rejected by the government in favour of a special tribunal, the future establishment of any such institution is uncertain.

originally created by the occupying powers, and that in Serbia, are purely domestic institutions and the international assistance to them is more limited. Common to the courts is that they are all designed to deal with international crimes, exclusively or at least in part; the Lebanese court and the Lockerbie court being exceptions and included only as examples of yet different approaches. This necessarily brief synopsis of these courts ends with an even briefer analysis of their merits.

9.2   Courts established by agreement between the United Nations and a State

9.2.1   Special Court for Sierra Leone

Almost a decade of very violent civil war began in 1991 when a rebel group, the Revolutionary United Front (RUF), entered Sierra Leone from neighbouring Liberia, aiming to overthrow the government. The ensuing stages of the conflict featured all forms of gross human rights violations, but it was particularly characterized by the use of child soldiers and widespread mutilation of civilians by amputation of arms and other limbs. In 2000, the intervention of a British force and a large UN peace-keeping presence, replacing a regional mission, was required before hostilities could be brought to an end.

The Special Court for Sierra Leone (SCSL) was established by treaty between Sierra Leone and the UN. A request from the President of Sierra Leone to the Security Council for the creation of a special court to deal with crimes committed in the civil war, led to a Council resolution[2] requesting the Secretary-General to enter into negotiations with Sierra Leone. An agreement between the Government and the UN Secretary-General, attaching the Statute of the Court, was concluded on 16 January 2002.[3] Thereafter, Sierra Leone adopted implementing legislation[4] and the SCSL began work in July 2002.

The UN Secretary-General has described the SCSL, which follows a model for Cambodia, later abandoned, as 'a treaty-based sui generis court of mixed jurisdiction and composition'.[5] The international judges, who were appointed by the UN Secretary-General, form a majority; a minority was appointed by the Government of Sierra Leone. The UN also appointed the Prosecutor and the Registrar, and Sierra Leone a Deputy Prosecutor.

The SCSL is not a subsidiary organ of the UN Security Council but a separate international institution and, as clarified in the Sierra Leonean implementing legislation, it is not part of the domestic legal system. The Court applies its own Statute and Rules of Procedure

---

2 SC res. 1315(2000) of 14.8.2000.

3 The agreement, and the Statute of the SCSL, are available at the Court's webpage: www.sc-sl.org.

4 The Special Court Agreement (2002) Ratification Act, Suppl. to Sierra Leone Official Gazette Vol. CXXX No. 2 of 7.3.2002 (as amended).

5 Report by the Secretary-General on the Establishment of a Special Court for Sierra Leone, UN Doc. S/2000/915 of 4.10.2000 para. 9 ('Secretary-General's Report').

and Evidence but these make reference to international instruments and some national laws.[6] The Statute provides that the SCSL and national courts of Sierra Leone have concurrent jurisdiction, but the SCSL has primacy.[7]

The mechanism chosen for the creation of the SCSL prompted a number of jurisdictional challenges. The Court established its competence to determine its own jurisdiction and dismissed challenges concerning its creation to the effect that the Sierra Leonean government acted in contravention of the Constitution or the Lomé Peace Agreement[8] when agreeing to the Court, and that the Secretary-General did not have the power to enter into the agreement.[9] The SCSL also established, in a controversial decision, that it is an international court,[10] and that consequently, by reference to the ICJ *Yerodia* case,[11] State immunity does not bar prosecution of a head of State. Another difficult issue was the amnesty granted in the Lomé Peace Agreement, which had the objective of preventing domestic prosecutions and, thus, partially motivated the internationalized solution. The Statute explicitly states that an amnesty does not bar prosecution of international crimes at the SCSL, and this was confirmed by the Court.[12] A peculiarity of this Court, intended to speed up the process, is that jurisdictional challenges are heard by the Appeals Chamber as the first and last instance.[13]

The SCSL has jurisdiction to prosecute persons 'who bear the greatest responsibility for serious violations of international humanitarian law and Sierra Leonean law' committed in the territory of Sierra Leone since 30 November 1996.[14] The reference to 'greatest responsibility' was intended as guidance for a prosecutorial policy rather than a formal limitation of jurisdiction;[15] the objective was that the SCSL should target a limited number of perpetrators and have a short period of operation. Offences by peacekeepers and related personnel are, with some exceptions, left to the jurisdiction of the sending State.[16] A very controversial

---

6 Art. 14 of the SCSL Statute (which refers to the ICTR RPE; these, however, have been substantively amended by the SCSL judges). The Appeals Chamber is also to be guided by the decisions of the ICTY and the ICTR Appeals Chambers: Art. 20.3.

7 SCSL Statute, Art. 8. See also Art. 9 on *ne bis in idem*.

8 Peace Agreement between the Government of Sierra Leone and the Revolutionary United Front of Sierra Leone (RUF), signed on 7.7.1999 after a meeting in Lomé, Togo (Lomé Peace Agreement).

9 *Kallon, Norman and Kamara* SCSL A. Ch. 13.3.2004; *Kallon and Kamara* SCSL A. Ch. 13.3.2004; *Fofana* SCSL A. Ch. 25.5.2004 (UN competence); and *Gbao* SCSL A. Ch. 25.5.2004.

10 *Taylor* SCSL A. Ch. 31.5.2004; see also Chapter 20. For a commentary, see Micaela Frulli, 'The Question of Charles Taylor's Immunity' (2004) 2 *JICJ* 1118.

11 *Case Concerning the Arrest Warrant of 11 April 2000 (Democratic Republic of Congo* v. *Belgium)*, Judgment, 14 February 2002; ICJ Rep 2002. See also Chapter 21.4.2.

12 Art. 10 of the SCSL Statute; *Kallon and Kamara* SCSL A. Ch. 13.3.2004. Cf. Art. IX of the Lomé Peace Agreement.

13 Rule 72 of the SCSL RPE.

14 Art. 1(1) of the SCSL Statute. The date relates to an earlier peace agreement between the Government of Sierra Leone and RUF, signed in Abidjan on 30.11.1996 (Abidjan Peace Agreement).

15 Secretary-General's Report, para. 30; and see *Kallon, Kamara and Kanu*, SCSL A.Ch. 3.3.08 paras. 272–85.

16 Art. 1(2)–(3) of the SCSL Statute.

issue was what to do with the many child soldiers who had committed serious crimes during the civil war; the solution finally chosen was to exclude jurisdiction over children under the age of 15 at the time of the crime and to include special provisions about treatment before and after conviction of juvenile offenders (between 15 and 18 years of age).[17]

Owing to the nature of the conflict, the subject-matter jurisdiction of the SCSL was confined to crimes against humanity and to war crimes committed in a non-international armed conflict.[18] Genocide and war crimes in an international armed conflict were not included. The Court decided, however, that the war crimes within its jurisdiction might be prosecuted regardless of whether the armed conflict was international or non-international in nature.[19] The Court's jurisdiction also covers some specified crimes under Sierra Leonean law.[20]

The definition of crimes against humanity was inspired by, but not identical with, the definition in the ICTR Statute; there is no reference to discriminatory intent as a general requirement for the crime and some of the underlying acts – sexual offences and persecution – have been further developed for the SCSL.[21] As to war crimes, Article 3 of the Statute regarding violations of Article 3 common to the Geneva Conventions and of Additional Protocol II, reproduces almost verbatim the war crimes provisions of the ICTR Statute. In addition, however, the SCSL Statute lists certain other serious violations of international humanitarian law, reflecting only some of the equivalent violations included in the ICC Statute. The inclusion of recruitment of child soldiers in the list was challenged as a breach of the principle of legality, but the Court determined that this was a war crime under customary international law before November 1996.[22]

The Special Court, at the time of writing, is well on its way to being wound up. It has indicted thirteen suspects in all (although two indictments were withdrawn due to the death of the accused). Three joint trials of nine accused were held,[23] and eight persons were convicted on charges of war crimes and crimes against humanity, one having died in custody. One accused remains at large, and arrangements have been made for his trial in another jurisdiction if he is ever captured.[24] The most famous person to be tried was

---

17 *Ibid.*, Arts. 7, 15(5) and 19(1).

18 *Ibid.*, Arts. 2–4.

19 *Fofana* SCSL A. Ch. 25.5.2004 (war crimes).

20 Art. 5 of the SCSL Statute.

21 The elaboration of sexual offences and persecution is clearly influenced by the ICC Statute. The definition also departs from the ICTY Statute in that no nexus to an armed conflict is required. See further Chapter 10.

22 *Norman* SCSL A. Ch. 31.5.2004; cf. Judge Robertson who, in a dissenting opinion, asserted that non-forcible enlistment had first entered international criminal law with the ICC Statute in 1998.

23 The trials were of members of the Civil Defence Force (a force set up by the government), the RUF, and the Armed Forces Revolutionary Council (AFRC). For an account of the establishment of the Court, and the indictments and their background, see Stephen Rapp, 'The Compact Model In International Criminal Justice: The Special Court for Sierra Leone' (2008) 57 *Drake Law Review* 11.

24 Rule 11*bis*, added to the Rules of Procedure and Evidence on 27.5.08.

the former President of Liberia, Charles Taylor, the first former African head of State to stand trial before any court. He was tried on charges of crimes against humanity and war crimes, at the premises of the ICC in The Hague, by special arrangement due to security concerns.[25]

With the end of the Taylor trial, the Court is likely to finish its work in 2011.

9.2.2   Cambodia: Extraordinary Chambers

Another approach was followed to deal with the atrocities committed during the Khmer Rouge rule in Cambodia – then known as Democratic Kampuchea – under Pol Pot, which lasted from 1975 to 1979 when the regime was ousted by invading Vietnamese forces. During these years an estimated 1.7 million people are believed to have died by execution, starvation and forced labour.

The introduction of so-called Extraordinary Chambers in the domestic courts is the culmination of a long process which began by a request from Cambodia to the UN for assistance in bringing Khmer Rouge officials to justice, followed by a UN expert group report recommending the establishment of an ad hoc Tribunal. Cambodia insisted on a domestic solution, however, and negotiations between the Cambodian Government and the UN started in 1999 but broke down in 2002; the UN Secretary-General withdrew from the process concluding that the Cambodian court, as then envisaged, would not guarantee the required independence, impartiality and objectivity, and that Cambodia refused to accept that UN assistance would be governed by a UN-Cambodian agreement.

Nevertheless, later in 2002 the UN General Assembly adopted a resolution[26] requesting the Secretary-General to resume negotiations towards establishing domestic Chambers, with a model based on the criticized Cambodian law. An agreement between the UN and Cambodia was adopted by the General Assembly in May 2003,[27] and ratified by the Cambodian National Assembly in October 2004, an international agreement which is subject to the law of treaties and cannot be circumvented by Cambodian legislation.[28]

Unlike the SCSL, the Extraordinary Chambers in the Courts of Cambodia (ECCC) form part of the domestic system of Cambodia and apply municipal law. The Pre-Trial Chamber has, however, concluded that the ECCC has distinctive features and is an entirely 'independent entity within the Cambodian court structure'.[29] The Chambers are to try 'senior leaders

---

25 See SC Res. 1688 (2006) of 16.6.2006.

26 GA Res. 57/228A of 18.12.2002.

27 GA Res. 57/228B of 13.5.2003 (to which the UN-Cambodia Agreement is attached).

28 Arts. 2 and 31 of the UN-Cambodia Agreement. The agreement is implemented by Cambodian national legislation under which the ECCC operate: the Law on the Establishment of Extraordinary Chambers in the Courts of Cambodia for the Prosecution of Crimes Committed During the Period of Democratic Kampuchea, NS/RKM/1004/006 (2004).

29 *Prosecutor* v. *Kaing Guek Eav ('Duch')*, ECCC PT Ch. 3.12.2007 paras. 17–20.

of Democratic Kampuchea and those most responsible for the crimes and serious violations of Cambodian penal law, international humanitarian law and custom, and international conventions recognized by Cambodia'; the offences include genocide under the 1948 Genocide Convention, crimes against humanity as defined in the ICC Statute, grave breaches of the Geneva Conventions, and certain other crimes under Cambodian law.[30] War crimes in non-international armed conflicts are not covered: Cambodia was not party to the Additional Protocols before 1980 and there were doubts as to the customary status of these crimes in the 1970s when the crimes were committed.[31] The temporal jurisdiction is exclusively retroactive and limited to crimes committed between 17 April 1975 and 6 January 1979. Of course, the death of Pol Pot means that the one person probably most responsible will never stand trial.

The mixed composition of the ECCC and the prosecution was a matter of dispute during the negotiations with the UN. The Cambodian side insisted on supremacy and, therefore, the national judges are in the majority both in the Trial Chamber and in the Supreme Court Chamber. For balance a qualified majority is required for any decision,[32] a difficult solution which could result in deadlock and, arguably, an acquittal even if all the international judges vote for a conviction. Due to the civil law origin of the Cambodian criminal procedures, investigative judges are responsible for the investigations; one international and one local judge operate together with disagreements being resolved by a Pre-Trial Chamber, again with local judges in the majority.[33] A similar scheme applies to the two co-prosecutors.[34] All the judges and prosecutors are appointed by the Cambodian Supreme Council of Magistracy, although the international officials are nominated by the UN Secretary-General. Internal rules may help to remove some of the potential for blocks in the system, but the arrangements have resulted in concerns being expressed about the independence, impartiality and efficiency of the ECCC and their future activities.[35]

With the trial of Duch,[36] the ECCC began their first proceedings and there are four other persons in detention who have been charged with crimes against humanity and war crimes. One of these is former Foreign Minister Ieng Sary, who was accorded a royal pardon and amnesty following his conviction *in absentia* for genocide after the fall of the Khmer

---

30 Arts. 1 and 9 of the UN-Cambodia Agreement.

31 Report of the Group of Experts for Cambodia Established Pursuant to General Assembly Resolution 52/135, UN Doc. A/53/850, paras. 72–5.

32 *Ibid.*, Arts. 3 and 4.

33 *Ibid.*, Arts. 5 and 7.

34 *Ibid.*, Art. 6 and Rule 71 of the Internal Rules.

35 See, e.g. Sarah Williams, 'The Cambodian Extraordinary Chambers: A Dangerous Precedent for International Justice?' (2004) 53 *ICLQ* 227. See also Goran Sluiter, 'Due Process and Criminal Procedure in the Cambodian Extraordinary Chambers' (2006) 4 *JICJ* 314.

36 Case 001: Kaing Guek Eav otherwise known as Duch. Duch, convicted of crimes against humanity, war crimes and the national law offences of murder and torture, directed the site called S21, the headquarters of the Secret Police special branch under the Khmer Rouge. Duch has been in a Cambodian prison since 1999.

Rouge in 1979. The agreement with the UN includes a commitment by the Cambodian Government not to request amnesties or pardon and leaves the Chambers to decide the scope of previously granted pardons.[37] The co-investigating judges have held that the amnesty and pardon granted to Ieng Sary did not cover the offences subject to the jurisdiction of the ECCC and is therefore no bar to the proceedings against him.[38]

The co-prosecutors were divided as to whether these five persons were to be the only ones to be tried by the ECCC and their disagreement went to the Pre-Trial Chamber. The Chamber was unable to reach the required 'super-majority'[39] and the resulting situation is that new investigations can be opened.

9.2.3   Special Tribunal for Lebanon

Upon the killing of Lebanon's former Prime Minister, Rafiq Hariri on 14 February 2005, the Security Council established a Commission to assist the Lebanese authorities in their investigation of the assassination, including the links to neighbouring Syria.[40] Lebanon requested the creation of an international tribunal, and the Secretary-General was asked by the Security Council to negotiate an agreement with the Government of Lebanon on a 'tribunal of an international character'.[41] After negotiations with Lebanon and the members of the Security Council, the Secretary-General presented a draft agreement and Statute for a tribunal, which were accepted by the Security Council.[42] The Government of Lebanon signed the agreement but because of constitutional difficulties the agreement could not come into force in accordance with its terms; the Security Council therefore brought its provisions into force, at the request of the Lebanese Prime Minister, by means of a Chapter VII resolution.[43]

Like the Special Court for Sierra Leone, the Tribunal is treaty-based and is not a subsidiary organ of the UN (although its provisions were brought into force by Security Council resolution). It does not form part of the Lebanese court system. It sits in The Hague and has a majority of international judges, including an international pre-trial judge, an international chief prosecutor and a Lebanese deputy prosecutor, a registry and a defence office. It is established for a specific trial or trials with jurisdiction covering those

---

37 Art. 11 of the UN-Cambodia Agreement.
38 Provisional Detention Order, ECCC 14.11.2007.
39 *Considerations of the Pre-Trial Chamber regarding the Disagreement between the Co-Prosecutors Pursuant to Internal Rule 71*, ECCC PTC 18.8.2009.
40 SC res.1595(2005) established the UN International Independent Investigation Commission (UNIIC). SC Res. 1636(2005) and 1644(2005) required Syria to cooperate with UNIIC.
41 SC res. 1664 (2006) of 29.3.2006.
42 See the Report of the Secretary-General on the establishment of a special tribunal for Lebanon, UN Doc. S/2006/893 of 15.11.2006, and Letter dated 21 November 2006 from the President of the Security Council addressed to the Secretary-General, UN Doc. S/2006/911 of 24.11.2006.
43 SC res. 1757(2007). The five members of the Council who abstained on the vote on the resolution criticized the use of a Chapter VII resolution to bypass national constitutional procedures.

responsible for the attack on Hariri and other related crimes of a similar nature and gravity committed within a limited time period.[44] The Tribunal applies Lebanese law, with some modifications such as the inapplicability of the death penalty; crimes within its jurisdiction are crimes under Lebanese criminal law relating to terrorism and 'offences against life and personal integrity, illicit associations and failure to report crimes and offences'.[45] It does not have jurisdiction over any international crime.[46] The Tribunal has primacy over national courts in Lebanon.

The agreement establishing the Tribunal came into force on 10 June 2007, and after a period of transition from UNIIC to the Office of the Prosecutor, the Prosecutor continued the investigations begun by the Commission. Rules of Procedure and Evidence have been drafted. Shortly after the beginning of the Tribunal's work in March 2009, the pre-trial judge requested the Lebanese court to defer to the Tribunal's competence, and to refer to the Prosecutor the results of any investigation and the court's records on the *Hariri* case.[47] The pre-trial judge then ordered the release of four Lebanese generals with ties to Syrian security services, who had spent nearly four years in Lebanese custody on suspicion of involvement in the 2005 assassinations; the Prosecutor had not asked for their continued custody since there was insufficient evidence to hold them.[48]

9.3   Courts established by the United Nations or other international administration

9.3.1   *Kosovo and East Timor: Special Panels*

Both Kosovo and East Timor (Timor-Leste) suffered violence during struggles for independence. In Kosovo, the revocation of autonomy and a government policy aimed at changing the ethnic composition of the province led to a Kosovar Albanian insurgency and brutal counter-measures by Serbian forces, including ethnic cleansing. In response, a NATO-led bombing campaign was launched against the Federal Republic of Yugoslavia in March–June 1999. As for East Timor, this former Portuguese colony was forcibly annexed by Indonesia in 1975. A referendum in 1999, in which a majority of the East Timorese voted

---

44 In addition to the attack of 14 February 2005, the Tribunal has jurisdiction over other attacks in Lebanon between 1.10.2004 and 12.12.2005 if it finds that they are connected with, and are of similar nature and gravity to, the February attack, and the UN and the Lebanese Government can decide to fix a date later than 12.12.2005 to extend jurisdiction to other 'connected' crimes, subject to the approval of the Security Council.

45 Statute, Art. 2(a). The Statute is set out in Security Council Resolution 1757(2007).

46 The inclusion of crimes against humanity, to be defined in the Statute, was considered but later rejected due to insufficient support within the Security Council; see the Report, UN Doc. S/2006/893, paras. 23–5.

47 Order directing the Lebanese judicial authority seized with the case of the attack against Prime Minister Rafiq Hariri and others to defer to the Special Tribunal for Lebanon, 27.3.2009.

48 Order regarding the detention of persons detained in Lebanon in connection with the case of the attack against Prime Minister Rafiq Hariri and others, 29 April 2009, CH/PTJ/2009/06.

for independence, was accompanied by widespread violence by pro-Indonesian militias, which ended only when UN-authorized forces intervened.

Following Security Council resolutions in 1999, the UN temporarily assumed the sovereign activities of the previous authorities in East Timor and Kosovo. The UN Mission in Kosovo (UNMIK)[49] was empowered to exercise all executive and legislative authority in that territory, including the administration of justice. The UN Transitional Administration in East Timor (UNTAET)[50] had similar powers. The essentially State-building mandates to establish law and order, and a credible and fair justice system, included powers to repeal and rewrite laws and to administer courts, develop legal policy, draft legislation, assess the quality of justice and address allegations of human rights violations. Questions have been raised as to the legal authority for taking such far-reaching measures and criticisms have been made about the democratic deficiency of the UN administrations.[51]

Both territories suffered the destruction of infrastructure, a shortage of qualified lawyers, a compelling security situation and a history of ethnic discrimination. But since the creation of the special courts had different aims, the institutional solutions differed. In Kosovo, where the ICTY also has jurisdiction,[52] the main purpose was to support more peaceful relations between different groups in society and to address a broader range of crimes, while the East Timor scheme was intended mainly to prosecute international crimes.

In Kosovo, the plan was initially to establish a transitional court with a mixed composition of international and national judges, and concurrent but primary jurisdiction with other domestic courts – a Kosovo War and Ethnic Crimes Court (KWECC).[53] But this initiative was both politically sensitive and costly. It was abandoned in favour of a less ambitious scheme with international judges and prosecutors embedded in the ordinary courts of Kosovo, balancing the conflicting interests of local ownership and neutralization of ethnic bias. Since the appointment of new domestic judges and prosecutors did not quell discriminatory practices, international judges and prosecutors were introduced,[54] initially in one troubled district (Mitrovice/Mitrovica) and subsequently in all municipal courts and in the Supreme Court. UNMIK also assumed the power to assign an international prosecutor, an international investigative judge, or a court panel with a majority of international judges – so-called 'Regulation 64 Panels' – to a particular case, when this was considered necessary 'to ensure

---

49 Established by SC res. 1244(1999) of 10.6.1999.
50 Established by SC res. 1272(1999) of 25.10.1999.
51 See, e.g. M. Brand, 'Institution Building and Human Rights Protection in Kosovo in the Light of UNMIK Legislation' (2001) *70 Nordic Journal of International Law* 461; David Marshall and Shelley Inglis, 'The Disempowerment of Human Rights-Based Justice in the United Nations Mission in Kosovo' (2003) 16 *Harvard Human Rights Journal* 95; Carsten Stahn, 'Justice under Transitional Administration: Contours and Critique of a Paradigm' (2005) 27 *Houston Journal of International Law* 311.
52 This jurisdiction was exercised in *Milutinović et al.* ICTY T. Ch. III 6.5.2003.
53 Proposed by a Technical Advisory Commission on Judiciary and Prosecution Service (UNMIK Reg. 1999/5 of 7.9.1999), composed of both international and national experts.
54 UNMIK Reg. 2000/6 of 15.2.2000 and Reg. 2000/34 of 29.5.2000 (available at www.unmikonline.org).

the independence and impartiality of the judiciary or the proper administration of justice'.[55] The powers of the international prosecutors were extended and 'Regulation 64 Panels' tried a large number of major or high-profile cases, including war crimes trials against Kosovar Serbs. On review, internationalized panels of the Supreme Court also overturned questionable convictions by lower courts. But while the international presence improved the appearance of objectivity, the legal quality of their work was criticized and there were other problems relating to detention, defence representation, witness protection, and sentencing.[56]

The 'Regulation 64 Panels' were domestic courts and applied municipal law. UNMIK initially decided that pre-existing domestic law should apply which, with respect to international crimes, primarily meant the Yugoslav Federal Criminal Code.[57] Additionally, international human rights law was expressly incorporated into the domestic system. Thereafter, however, UNMIK increasingly introduced new legislation, including a Provisional Criminal Code of Kosovo[58] and a Provisional Criminal Procedure Code of Kosovo.[59] The criminal code included modern definitions of genocide, crimes against humanity, war crimes, general principles of criminal law and provisions on jurisdiction over crimes committed outside the territory of Kosovo.

The controversial declaration of independence by the Kosovo Assembly in February 2008 led to a replacement of some of the functions of UNMIK by an EU presence, 'EULEX'.[60] The Kosovo Assembly has substituted the 'Regulation 64 Panels' with a law under which EULEX judges and prosecutors operate, either separately or in mixed composition, within the national system.[61] In particular, EULEX judges have competence concerning cases investigated and prosecuted by the Special Prosecution Office of the Republic of Kosovo,[62] which deals with all war crimes and terrorism cases; EULEX prosecutors also have authority to investigate and prosecute such cases.[63]

In East Timor, a proposal to set up an international criminal tribunal[64] was rejected in favour of focusing on the domestic legal system. UNTAET began with the creation of a new court system consisting of six district courts and a Court of Appeal, all with jurisdiction in

---

55 UNMIK Reg. 2000/64 on Assignment of International Judges/Prosecutors and/or Change of Venue, of 15.12.2000 (the time limit for its application was extended).

56 See, e.g. in reports by the OSCE Mission in Kosovo, Legal System Monitoring Section; available at www.osce.org/kosovo.

57 UNMIK Reg. 1999/1 of 10.6.1999, Reg. 1999/24 of 12.12.1999 and Reg. 2000/59 of 27.10.2000.

58 UNMIK Reg. 2003/25 of 6.7.2003 (entering into force 6.4.2004).

59 UNMIK Reg. 2003/26 of 6.7.2003.

60 The European Union Rule of Law Mission in Kosovo.

61 Law No. 03/L-053 on the Jurisdiction, Case Selection and Case Allocation of EULEX Judges and Prosecutors in Kosovo, adopted on 13 March 2008.

62 Law No. 03/L-052 on the Special Prosecution Office of the Republic of Kosovo, adopted on 13 March 2008.

63 Law No. 03/L-053 arts. 3.1 and 8.1; and Law No. 03/L-052.

64 Report of the International Commission of Inquiry on East Timor to the Secretary General, UN Doc. A/54/726, S/2002/59 (2000) at 153.

both criminal and civil cases.[65] This was soon followed by the establishment of 'Serious Crimes Panels' of the District Court in Dili (the capital) and the Court of Appeal, similar to the abandoned model for Kosovo, with exclusive jurisdiction over certain serious criminal offences and with a mixed composition of East Timorese and international judges.[66] On each panel, the international judges were in the majority. UNTAET also established a national prosecution service for the prosecution of crimes before the 'Serious Crimes Chambers', with both local and international prosecutors.[67]

The jurisdiction of the 'Serious Crimes Panels' covered genocide, crimes against humanity and war crimes, as well as certain domestic crimes (murder, sexual offences and torture), the international crimes being defined in the UNTAET Regulation together with provisions on general principles of criminal law and penalties.[68] The jurisdiction covered crimes in East Timor, or elsewhere if committed against an East Timorese citizen, during a limited time period (1 January–25 October 1999).[69]

The 'Serious Crimes Panels' did not apply only UNTAET Regulations but also domestic law and, where appropriate, applicable treaties and recognized principles and norms of international law.[70] A provisional Code of Criminal Procedures was adopted to apply alongside the Indonesian criminal code.[71] Adding to the complexity, the Court of Appeal ruled that Indonesian law could not be applied as domestic law, since the Indonesian occupation of East Timor was illegal, applying instead the law of the old colonial power, Portugal;[72] this turned prior practice on its head and created legal uncertainty. Initially most of the cases were pursued as violations of domestic law, such as murder, and not as international crimes, but subsequently there were a number of convictions for crimes against humanity, many of them based on guilty pleas. Difficult issues have arisen, but have not always been sufficiently addressed, concerning the characterization of the conflict for the purpose of war crimes, the prerequisites for crimes against humanity, and the legal import of duress and superior orders.[73]

---

65 UNTAET Reg. 2000/11 of 6.3.2000 (later amended).

66 UNTAET Reg. 2000/15 of 5.7.2000.

67 UNTAET Reg. 2000/16 of 5.7.2000. A legal aid service, including public defenders, was also created; UNTAET Reg. 2001/24 of 5.9.2001.

68 UNTAET Reg. 2000/15 of 5.7.2000, ss. 4–6 (and torture, s. 7) and ss. 10–21.

69 *Ibid.*, s. 2(3).

70 *Ibid.*, s. 3.

71 UNTAET Reg. 2000/30 of 25.9.2000 (subsequently amended).

72 *Armando Dos Santos*, Court of Appeals, East Timor 15.7.2003; for a critical view see, e.g. Sylvia de Bertodano, 'Current Developments in Internationalized Courts: East Timor – Justice Denied' (2004) 2 *JICJ* 910.

73 See, e.g. Suzannah Linton, 'Prosecuting Atrocities at the District Court of Dili' (2001) 2 *Melbourne Journal of International Law* 414; Suzannah Linton and Caitlin Reiger, 'The Evolving Jurisprudence and Practice of East Timor's Special Panels for Serious Crimes on Admission of Guilt, Duress and Superior Orders' (2001) 4 *YIHL* 1; Claus Kreß, 'The 1999 Crisis in East Timor and the Threshold of the Law on War Crimes' (2002) 13 *Criminal Law Forum* 409; Kai Ambos and Steffen Wirth, 'The Current Law of Crimes Against Humanity: An Analysis of UNTAET Regulation 15/2000' (2002) 13 *CLF* 1; Guy Cumes, 'Murder as a Crime against Humanity in International Law: Choice of Law and Prosecution of Murder in East Timor' (2003) 11 *European Journal of Crime, Criminal Law and Criminal Justice* 40.

On 20 May 2002, after general and presidential elections, the UN handed over its authority to the new democratic institutions of East Timor. UNTAET was replaced by another UN mission, which did not have governmental powers but continued to provide the 'Serious Crimes Panels' with practical support. The UNTAET Regulations continued to apply provisionally and the 'Serious Crimes Panels' functioned under the authority of the new East Timorese Constitution. Gradually the Regulations were replaced and in May 2005 the 'Serious Crimes Panels' suspended operations indefinitely. The international judges and prosecutors left and ordinary courts now handle cases involving international crimes.

In both situations, these domestic institutions depended upon the respective home States to secure international cooperation, requiring accession to international agreements as well as adoption of domestic legislation. Where the administration was essentially carried out by the UN, the question has been raised concerning to what extent the UN missions are competent to fulfil such tasks and, if competent, whom they represent. In practice, lack of cooperation hindered efforts to prosecute. This was particularly pronounced in East Timor since Indonesia refused to cooperate, in spite of a bilateral agreement, and instead pursued some proceedings before a much criticized ad hoc tribunal in Jakarta.[74]

9.3.2   Bosnia and Herzegovina: the War Crimes Chamber

During the demise of the Former Yugoslavia, tens of thousands of people died and perhaps a million people were displaced in Bosnia and Herzegovina. With the 1995 Dayton Peace Agreement, a complex political structure and two 'entities' were created, the Federation of Bosnia and Herzegovina, and Republika Sprska. The Office of the High Representative (OHR) oversees the civilian aspects of the Agreement on behalf of the international community. The 'State Court' has jurisdiction over both entities and within that court a War Crimes Chamber has been established as a domestic institution with international components.[75] The Chamber, which began its work in March 2005, stems from a joint initiative of the ICTY and the OHR. Individual States provided the initial funding, with responsibility now being transferred to the national budget.

As well as being part of the reform of the national justice system by the High Representative, the Chamber also forms an essential element of the ICTY completion strategy,[76] being a domestic court to which the ICTY can refer cases against lower-level

---

74 See, e.g. Suzannah Linton, 'Unravelling the First Three Trials at Indonesia's Ad Hoc Court for Human Rights Violations in East Timor' (2004) 17 *LJIL* 303. East Timor and Indonesia did, however, establish a joint Commission of Truth and Friendship to report on violence in 1999; see Commission of Truth and Friendship's Final Report on the 1999 Atrocities in East Timor.
75 See, e.g. Bogdan Ivanišević, *The War Crimes Chamber in Bosnia and Herzegovina: From Hybrid to Domestic Court* (2008), International Center for Transitional Justice, available at http://www.ictj.org/images/content/1/0/1088.pdf.
76 See, for example, the Completion Strategy Report of ICTY of 14.5.09 (S/2009/589).

perpetrators in accordance with rule 11*bis* of the ICTY RPE.[77] This rule allows the referral of an indictment against an accused, regardless of whether he is in the ICTY's custody or not, to any State which has jurisdiction and which is willing and adequately prepared to accept such a case. The ICTY will consider the gravity of the crime and the level of responsibility of the perpetrator; it must also be satisfied that the accused would receive a fair trial and that the death penalty would not be imposed. Some cases have been referred, and the accused transferred, to Bosnia and Herzegovina from the ICTY.[78]

With the conclusion of the work of the ICTY, the Chamber's work will consist entirely of cases which have been been initiated locally. The Chamber operates under national law, including new criminal and criminal procedure codes introduced by the OHR,[79] and deals with the most serious war-related crimes in Bosnia. But it does not have exclusive or superior jurisdiction over war crimes, which are also prosecuted in the district or cantonal courts. The criminal code applied by the Chamber defines, inter alia, genocide, crimes against humanity and war crimes, regulates general criminal law principles such as command responsibility and provides for far-reaching criminal jurisdiction. Apart from the international involvement in the establishment of the institution and the adoption of applicable law, the Chamber has international judges at both trial and appeals levels. The Office of the Prosecutor of the State Court has a Special Department for War Crimes with both international and local prosecutors and other staff, and an organization to accept ICTY referrals. International defence counsel are also provided for. International legal cooperation is crucial though often difficult. Bosnia has adhered to certain European cooperation treaties, but cooperation with neighbouring States can be difficult, particularly having regard to constitutional bans on extraditing nationals.

The intention from the outset was to terminate the Chamber's international features relatively quickly. Initially the international judges and prosecutors were appointed by the OHR but since July 2006 they have been appointed locally in accordance with national procedures. Until 2008 each of the five trial panels and the appellate panel included two international members and one national member but the balance of composition has now been reversed, with national judges in a majority. The international prosecutors and judges are gradually being phased out and their continuation is now in doubt. Adoption of a national war crimes prosecution strategy will assist in tackling the huge domestic caseload still remaining.[80]

---

77 See Michael Bohlander, 'Referring an indictment from the ICTY and ICTR to another court – Rule 11*bis* and the consequences for the law of extradition' (2006) 55 *ICLQ* 219 (also noting that the Tribunals under this scheme may issue an arrest warrant and direct States to surrender the accused to another State).

78 See, e.g. *Janković and Stanković* ICTY A. Ch. 1.9.2005.

79 Criminal Code of Bosnia and Herzegovina, Official Gazette No. 37/03, and Criminal Procedure Code of Bosnia and Herzegovina, Official Gazette No. 36/03, both of 24.1.2003 (with amendments).

80 See paras. 29–38 of the Thirty-fifth report of the High Representative for Bosnia and Herzegovina to the UN Secretary-General (S/2009/206).

9.4   Courts established by a State with international support

9.4.1   *Iraq: the Iraqi High Tribunal*

During Saddam Hussein's authoritarian regime, lasting for over thirty-five years, individuals and ethnic communities were violently suppressed and wars were fought against neighbouring Iran and Kuwait. In the wake of his expulsion from power by coalition forces, a specialized court for genocide, crimes against humanity and war crimes was created in Iraq, primarily to deal with crimes of the old regime. The international aspects are distinctly different, and limited, compared with the courts previously mentioned.

The court began as the Iraqi Special Tribunal, which was established by the Iraqi Interim Governing Council (IGC) on 10 December 2003. Three days later Saddam Hussein was captured. This was not a tribunal established by the Security Council, by a UN administration, by treaty, or directly by occupying powers like the post-Second World War Tribunals. Instead, the body representing the occupying powers, the Coalition Provisional Authority (CPA), authorized the IGC, itself appointed by the CPA, to establish the Special Tribunal with a Statute which had been drawn up with considerable international input.[81]

Concerns were raised about the legal basis for the Tribunal and its legitimacy.[82] These were put to rest by a new law, adopted by the Iraqi Transitional National Assembly in 2005,[83] which provides a new Statute for the Tribunal, now called the Iraqi High Tribunal. The Tribunal is integrated into the domestic legal system. It has jurisdiction over certain crimes committed in Iraq or elsewhere between 16 July 1968 (the Ba'athist *coup d'état*) and 1 May 2003 (the 'end of major combat operations') by Iraqi nationals or residents; members of the coalition are thus excluded, as are juridical persons.[84] The subject-matter jurisdiction covers genocide, crimes against humanity and war crimes, all defined almost exactly as in the ICC Statute but not previously included in Iraqi law,[85] and some crimes under domestic law relating to abuse of power.[86] Interestingly, one of the domestic crimes, 'the pursuit of policies that may lead to the threat of war or use of the armed forces of Iraq against an Arab country', could apply as a kind of crime of aggression, though not of course in relation to the

---

81 Coalition Provisional Authority Order Number 48 of 10.12.2003 (to which the Iraqi Special Tribunal Statute was attached).

82 See, e.g. Ilias Bantekas, 'The Iraqi Special Tribunal for Crimes against Humanity' (2004) 54 *ICLQ* 237, and Cherif Bassiouni, 'Post-Conflict Justice in Iraq: An Appraisal of the Iraq Special Tribunal' (2005) 38 *Cornell International Law Journal* 327.

83 The Law on the Iraqi High Tribunal was signed by the Iraqi President on 11.10.2005. See Charles Garraway, 'The Statute of the Iraqi Special Tribunal' in Susan Breau and Agnieszka Jachec-Neale (eds.), *Testing the Boundaries of International Humanitarian Law* (London, 2006) 155–89.

84 Art. 1 of the Statute.

85 See, e.g. Yuval Shany, 'Does One Size Fit All?' (2004) 2 *JICJ* 338.

86 Arts. 11–14 of the Statute.

2003 intervention in Iraq itself.[87] The Tribunal has concurrent jurisdiction with, but also primacy over, all other Iraqi courts, and it may under certain circumstances try someone who has already been tried by another Iraqi court.[88] The judges and prosecutors of the Iraqi High Tribunal are all Iraqi nationals; the Statute allows the appointment of non-Iraqi judges, appointed by a national authority, but only if one of the parties in the case is a State.[89] Nonetheless, international advisers, observers, and defence co-counsel may work in the Tribunal,[90] and many did so, particularly in the early days. Coalition members also provided substantial support with regard to funding, training, security and personnel. However, the Tribunal's power to impose the death penalty had the consequence that many States and international human rights groups were not willing to support it or cooperate with it.[91] The first trial before the Tribunal was of Saddam Hussein and other former top-ranking officials; Saddam Hussein was sentenced to death for crimes against humanity and later hanged. The Tribunal continues its work, its trials being subjected to a certain amount of international criticism for lack of judicial independence and weak guarantees of fair trial.[92] However understandable the wish to try national criminals in a national court, the Tribunal illustrates the difficulties of a domestic court within a post-conflict situation, dealing, without previous experience, with vast and complex international crimes.

9.4.2 Serbia: the War Crimes Chamber

The War Crimes Chamber of the Belgrade District Court in Serbia is another example of a specialized court for international crimes that was created with international assistance, primarily the OSCE, but which is entirely national in nature.[93] The Chamber and a specialized Prosecutor's Office for War Crimes were both established in 2003.

---

87 See Claus Kreß, 'The Iraqi Special Tribunal and the Crime of Aggression' (2004) 2 *JICJ* 347. See Chapter 13.

88 Arts. 29–30 of the Statute.

89 *Ibid.*, Arts. 4(3) and 28.

90 *Ibid.*, Arts. 7(2)-(3), 8(10), 9(7)-(8) and 18(3).

91 See, e.g. Tom Parker, 'Prosecuting Saddam: The Coalition Provisional Authority and the Evolution of the Iraqi Special Tribunal' (2005) 38 *Cornell International Law Journal* 899.

92 For discussion of some of the trials, see e.g. Miranda Sissons and Ari Bassin, 'Was the Dujail Trial Fair?' (2007) 5 *JICJ* 272; Cherif Bassiouni and Michael Hanna, 'Ceding the High Ground: the Iraqi High Criminal Court Statute and the Trial of Saddam Hussein' (2006–2007) 39 *Case Western Reserve Journal of International Law* 21; Michael Newton, 'Implementing International Law: A Qualified Defense of the Al Dujail Trial' (2006) 9 *Yearbook of International Humanitarian Law* 117; Nehal Bhuta, 'Fatal Errors: The Trial and Appeal Judgments in the Dujail Case' (2008) 6 *JICJ* 39; Jennifer Trahan, 'A Critical Guide to the Iraqi High Tribunal's Anfal Judgment: Genocide against the Kurds' (2009) 30 *Michigan Journal of International Law* 305. For a wider discussion of the Hussein trial and its background, see Michael Newton and Michael Scharf, *Enemy of the State* (New York, 2008).

93 Law on Organization and Competence of Government Authorities in War Crimes Proceedings, Official Gazette of the Republic of Serbia No. 67/2003. See Mark Ellis, 'Coming to Terms with Its Past: Serbia's New Court for the Prosecution of War Crimes' (2004) 22 *Berkeley Journal of International Law* 165; International

Jurisdiction extends to crimes committed anywhere in the former Socialist Federal Republic of Yugoslavia, regardless of the citizenship of the perpetrator or victims. The ICTY has referred some cases to the Chamber, including crimes in Vukovar (Croatia) and Zvornik (Bosnia and Herzegovina), primarily in cases where no ICTY indictment was issued but, more recently, a post-indictment referral was made by the ICTY under rule 11*bis* of the ICTY RPE.[94]

9.5   Lockerbie: an ad hoc solution for a particular incident

Yet another solution, although not for dealing with international crimes, was chosen for the prosecution of two Libyan nationals accused of the 1988 bombing of Pan Am flight 103 over Lockerbie in Scotland. The surrender of the accused from Libya, in return for the suspension of sanctions imposed by the Security Council against Libya under Chapter VII of the UN Charter,[95] was secured only by coming to a special arrangement for the criminal proceedings. The court, prosecution and applicable law were all Scottish, but the court sat in a neutral venue in the Netherlands rather than in Scotland.

The compromise was worked out by the UN, Libya, the United States and the United Kingdom. Scottish law had to be amended to allow the Scottish High Court of Justiciary to sit abroad without a jury;[96] an agreement also had to be concluded between the United Kingdom and the Netherlands following the adoption of a Security Council resolution under Chapter VII of the Charter.[97] The indictment was confined to charges of murder. Criminal jurisdiction was based on territoriality. On 31 January 2001 the High Court convicted one and acquitted one of the accused,[98] a verdict that was upheld on appeal on 14 March 2002.[99] This is not an example of an international court or of international crimes, but an ad hoc arrangement relating to a domestic trial brokered at the international level.[100]

Center for Transitional Justice, *Against the Current – War Crimes Prosecutions in Serbia (2007)*, author, available at http://www.ictj.org/images/content/7/8/780.pdf.

94 See *Vladimir Kovačević* ICTY Referral Bench 17.11.2006.

95 SC res. 731(1992) of 21.1.1992, res. 748(1992) of 31.3.1992, res. 883(1993) of 11.11.1993, and res. 1192 (1998) of 27.8.1998. See Chapter 14.

96 High Court of Justiciary (Proceedings in the Netherlands) (United Nations) Order 1998.

97 Agreement of 18.9.1998, reprinted in (1999) 38 *ILM* 926, following the adoption of SC res. 1192(1998).

98 *Her Majesty's Advocate* v. *Al Megrahi* (High Ct. Justiciary at Camp Zeist).

99 *Al Megrahi* v. *HM Advocate* 2002 SCCR 509; the case was then referred back to the appeal court in Edinburgh by the Scottish Criminal Cases Review Commission. Al Megrahi served part of his sentence but did not proceed with the appeal; he was released on compassionate grounds in 2009 since he was suffering from a terminal illness.

100 For a critique of the arrangements see Donna Arzt, 'The Lockerbie "Extradition By Analogy" Agreement: "Exceptional Measure" or Template for Transnational Criminal Justice?' (2002) 18 *American University International Law Review* 163.

9.6   Relationship with the ICC

An interesting question is how these internationalized or hybrid courts relate to the ICC. In many of the examples mentioned in this chapter there is no jurisdictional conflict between the court and the ICC; even where the territorial, personal and subject-matter jurisdictions overlap, the non-retroactive jurisdiction of the ICC prevents it from dealing with many past crimes. But some of the internationalized courts, for example those in East Timor and Kosovo, have not been confined to dealing with past crimes and other internationalized courts may be established in the future.

Since most of the courts, so far, form part of the domestic system, the scheme of Article 17 of the ICC Statute (the complementarity principle) will apply to them and if the ICC has jurisdiction it will be only complementary.[101] An arrangement like the Special Court for Sierra Leone, which was not established within a domestic court system, gives rise to different considerations – although it may be that the ICC would apply the principle of complementarity by analogy. It is to be expected that there would be opposition if the establishment of similar courts under UN auspices were proposed in the future with jurisdiction coinciding with that of the ICC.[102]

9.7   Appraisal

The use of these arrangements, rather than international courts, does not of course indicate that there is a hierarchy of atrocities, with one level meriting less effort and expenditure from the international community. Indeed, the crimes prosecuted in most of the courts discussed in this chapter are among the worst ever recorded in human history. The Cambodia Chambers, for example, are having to address, in however limited a way, responsibility for the 'killing fields of Cambodia'. And the atrocities dealt with by the Sierra Leone Special Court were such that the Court could not recall 'any other conflict in the history of warfare in which innocent civilians were subjected to such savage and inhumane treatment'.[103]

The models for the internationalized courts discussed in this chapter have their disadvantages compared with tribunals established by a Security Council resolution under Chapter

---

101 See Chapter 8. See also, e.g. Markus Benzing and Morten Bergsmo, 'Some Tentative Remarks on the Relationship between Internationalized Criminal Jurisdictions and the International Criminal Court' in Romano et al., *Internationalized Criminal Courts*, 407–16, and Carsten Stahn, 'The Geometry of Transitional Justice: Choices of Institutional Design' (2005) 18 *LJIL* 425 at 462–5.

102 See also the opposition to different alternatives discussed for Darfur prior to the SC referral to the ICC, e.g. Robert Cryer, 'Sudan, Resolution 1593, and International Criminal Justice' (2006) 19 *LJIL* 195. Suggestions have been made, however, for regional courts with international criminal jurisdiction, e.g. for the new African Human and People's Rights Court.

103 *Brima, Kamara and Kanu* SCSL T. Ch. II 19.7.07 Sentencing Judgement, at paras. 34 and 35. The AFRC defendants were found responsible 'for some of the most heinous, brutal and atrocious crimes ever recorded in human history'.

VII of the UN Charter. A problem common to almost all of them is the shortage of financial and other resources. Their resources consist chiefly of voluntary contributions by States, in money, personnel and equipment.[104] Indeed, cost-related considerations played a major role when decisions were taken to opt for the various hybrid models instead of international criminal tribunals. Funding difficulties may have a detrimental impact not only on the effectiveness and efficiency of the tribunal concerned, but also on the rights of the accused to a fair trial; the independence and impartiality of the institution may even be questioned, as was (unsuccessfully) argued before the Special Court for Sierra Leone.[105] Having to rely on voluntary funding by States, rather than on UN-assessed contributions, has led to a precarious existence for some institutions, with court staff having to spend a great deal of time fundraising. At various periods of their existence, the SCSL and the ECCC have both come near to having their work terminated for lack of funding.

A further potential problem is that courts which are largely domestic may suffer from the influence of their national systems, political or otherwise, where the judiciary and the legal system are not strong. This is particularly so in those cases where the international element is less powerful than the national one, as with the ECCC, or almost non-existent, as with the Iraq High Tribunal.

These courts may suffer from the disadvantage of difficulties in securing cooperation from other States. Because the Security Council has not created them by Chapter VII resolution, there is no legal requirement for other States to proffer cooperation;[106] the court or State concerned has to seek the putting in place of voluntary arrangements with regional States or rely on existing agreements. This has led to difficulties for the SCSL and the Bosnia War Crimes Chamber, and has the potential to block the work of the Lebanon tribunal.

Nevertheless, there are advantages. The creation of these courts is expected to have positive influences on the relevant domestic legal system.[107] Unlike the ICTY and the ICTR (and perhaps the ICC),[108] most courts sit in the country in question and, with the exception of Sierra Leone and Lebanon, operate within existing or newly created domestic judicial structures. Some form part of the restoration of the domestic system, and all of them are intended to assist in building local capacity, enhancing respect for the rule of law and providing independent, impartial and fair criminal proceedings for past crimes as well as an example for the future. Outreach programmes are established to assist with these goals, and

---

104 See, e.g. Thordis Ingadottir, 'The Financing of Internationalized Criminal Courts and Tribunals' in Romano et al. (eds.), *Internationalized Criminal Courts*, 271–89.

105 *Norman* SCSL A. Ch. 13.3.2004.

106 Chapter VII resolutions were necessary in the course of the establishment of both the Lebanon Tribunal and the Lockerbie court and these resolutions required cooperation of certain States.

107 See, e.g. Laura Dickinson, 'The Promise of Hybrid Courts' (2003) 97 *EJIL* 295.

108 See Arts. 3 and 62 of the ICC Statute (the ICC may sit elsewhere than at its seat in The Hague). Rule 4 of the ICTY RPE and of the ICTR RPE respectively also allows those Tribunals to exercise their functions away from the seat, but this has rarely happened in practice.

the domestic impact will depend on how dedicated are these efforts of engagement with the local communities.[109] The courts are also contributing to case law on international criminal law: the SCSL has added significantly to jurisprudence on the war crime of conscripting or enlisting children under the age of fifteen years into the armed forces and on the crime against humanity of forced marriage.[110] The courts discussed in this chapter, each of which has been chosen to suit a particular situation, add to the network of arrangements to combat impunity; their success will be judged by the results.

Further reading

The following websites are useful:

SLSCL: http://www.sc-sl.org/

ECCC: http://www.eccc.gov.kh/english/ http://www.cambodiatribunal.org/

Special Tribunal for Lebanon: http://www.stl-tsl.org/

Bosnia War Crimes Chamber: http://www.sudbih.gov.ba/?jezik=e

Serbia: Office of the War Crimes Prosecutor: http://www.tuzilastvorz.org.rs/html_trz/ index_eng.htm

EULEX in Kosovo: www.eulex-kosovo.eu/training/?id=13

Kai Ambos and Mohamed Othman (eds.), *New Approaches in International Criminal Justice: Kosovo, East Timor, Sierra Leone and Cambodia* (Freiburg i. Br, 2003).

Hervé Ascensio, Elisabeth Lambert-Abdelgawad and Jean-Marc Sorel (eds.), *Les jurisdictions pénales internationalisées (Cambodge, Kosovo, Sierra Leone, Timor Leste)* (Paris, 2006).

M. Cherif Bassiouni (ed.), *Post-Conflict Justice* (New York, 2002).

Stuart Beresford and A. S. Müller, 'The Special Court for Sierra Leone: An Initial Comment' (2001) 14 *LJIL* 635.

Marcus Brand, 'Institution-Building and Human Rights Protection in Kosovo in the Light of UNMIK Legislation' (2001) 70 *Nordic Journal of International Law* 461.

William W. Burke-White, 'The Domestic Influence of International Criminal Tribunals: The International Criminal Tribunal for the Former Yugoslavia and the Creation of the State Court of Bosnia & Herzegovina' (2008) 46 *Columbia Journal of Transnational Law* 279.

Robert Cryer, 'A "Special Court" for Sierra Leone' (2001) 50 *ICLQ* 435.

Helen Horsington, 'The Cambodian Khmer Rouge Tribunal: The Promise of a Hybrid Tribunal' (2004) 5 *Melbourne Journal of International Law* 462.

---

109 For the necessity of good outreach programmes, particularly in relation to the ECCC, see Norman Pentelovitch, 'Seeing Justice Done: the Importance of Prioritizing Outreach Efforts at International Criminal Tribunals' (2008) 39 *Georgetown Journal of International Law* 445.

110 See, e.g. on forced marriage, *Brima, Kamara and Kanu* SCSL A.Ch. 22.2.08 para. 195; on recruitment of child soldiers, *Norman* SCSL A. Ch. 31.5.2004.

Suzannah Linton, 'Cambodia, East Timor and Sierra Leone: Experiments in International Justice' (2001) 12 *CLF* 414.

Daryl Mundis, 'New Mechanisms for the Enforcement of International Humanitarian Law' (2001) 95 *AJIL* 934.

Cesare Romano, André Nollkaemper and Jann Kleffner (eds.), *Internationalized Criminal Courts – Sierra Leone, East Timor, Kosovo, and Cambodia* (Oxford, 2004).

Hansjörg Strohmeyer, 'Collapse and Reconstruction of a Judicial System: The United Nations Missions in Kosovo and East Timor' (2001) 95 *AJIL* 46.

Sarah Williams, *Hybrid and Internationalised Criminal Tribunals* (Oxford, forthcoming 2010).

PART D

Substantive Law of International Crimes

10

Genocide

10.1 Introduction

10.1.1 Overview

Genocide, as General Assembly Resolution 96(1) declared, 'is a denial of the right of existence of entire human groups, as homicide is the denial of the right to live of individual human beings'. It is a crime simultaneously directed against individual victims, the group to which they belong, and human diversity.

The legal concept of genocide is narrowly circumscribed, the term 'genocide' being reserved in law for a particular subset of atrocities which are committed with the intent to destroy groups, even if colloquially the word is used for any large-scale killings. Most of the crimes committed by the Pol Pot regime in Cambodia in 1975–78, for example, are atrocities which do not readily fit within the narrow definition, however dreadful the suffering they caused.[1] A decision that a particular atrocity is not 'genocide' does not of course remove the moral or legal guilt for conduct that falls within the definition of other international crimes. Many acts which do not constitute genocide will constitute crimes against humanity.

The form of intent that is a necessary element of the crime, that of intending to destroy a group, marks it out from all other international crimes. This explains why genocide is regarded as having a particular seriousness, and has been referred to as the 'crime of crimes'.[2] The

---

[1] Steven Ratner and Jason Abrams, *Accountability for Human Rights Atrocities in International Law*, 3rd edn (Oxford, 2009) chs. 12–14, although see John Quigley, *The Genocide Convention: An International Law Analysis* (Aldershot, 2006) 27–31; Beth Van Schaack, 'The Crime of Political Genocide: Repairing the Genocide Convention's Blind Spot' (1997) 106 *Yale Law Journal* 2259.

[2] *Kambanda* ICTR T. Ch. 4.9.1998 para. 16. But note the statement of the International Commission of Inquiry on Darfur: genocide 'is not necessarily the most serious international crime. *Depending upon the circumstances, such international offences as crimes against humanity or large scale war crimes may be no less serious and heinous than genocide.*' (UN Doc. S/2005/60 para. 522; emphasis added). The fact that genocide is sometimes said to stand at the apex of international criminality can lead to unhelpful debates about whether or not an atrocity is genocide or 'merely' a crime against humanity. This has led some to advocate the use of the term

seriousness of the crime is underlined by the fact that its prohibition has attained the status of a *ius cogens* norm[3] and an *erga omnes* obligation on States (owed to the international community as a whole).[4]

When the conduct constituting the offence is attributable to a State, genocide, like other international crimes, is not only a crime of individual responsibility: it also engages State responsibility. In the *Bosnian Genocide* case, Bosnia took proceedings in the ICJ alleging breaches of the Genocide Convention[5] by Serbia in attempting to destroy protected groups, in particular the Muslim population. The Court confirmed that the Convention not only imposes on States a duty to prevent and punish genocide but also an obligation to refrain from genocide.[6] This is not to introduce a concept of State crime or State criminal responsibility; the obligation is one of State responsibility under general international law.[7]

The standard definition of genocide is contained in Article II of the Genocide Convention, which is adopted verbatim in the Statutes of the ad hoc Tribunals and of the ICC. It is:

> any of the following acts committed with the intent to destroy, in whole or in part, a national, ethnical, racial or religious group, as such:
>
> (a) Killing members of the group;
> (b) Causing serious bodily or mental harm to members of the group;
> (c) Deliberately inflicting on the group conditions of life calculated to bring about its physical destruction in whole or in part;
> (d) Imposing measures intended to prevent births within the group;
> (e) Forcibly transferring children of the group to another group.

Almost every word of this definition has raised difficulties of interpretation. It is the purpose of this chapter to explain some of these controversies, and the way in which academics and courts have attempted to deal with them.

'atrocity crimes' instead; see David Scheffer, 'Genocide and Atrocity Crimes' (2006) 1 *Genocide Studies and Prevention* 229.

3 *Case concerning Armed Activities on the Territory of the Congo (DRC v. Rwanda)* Jurisdiction of the Court and Admissibility of the Application, ICJ Judgment of 3 February 2006, para. 64.

4 *Reservations to the Convention on the Prevention and Punishment of the Crime of Genocide* Advisory Opinion (1951) ICJ Rep 15 at 23.

5 The Convention on the Prevention and Punishment of the Crime of Genocide, adopted by the General Assembly on 9 December 1948.

6 *Case concerning the Application of the Convention on the Prevention and Punishment of the Crime of Genocide (Bosnia and Herzegovina v. Serbia and Montenegro)* ICJ 26 February 2007 (*Bosnian Genocide* case) paras. 162–6. The Court also held that Art. III obliges States to refrain from engaging in conspiracy, incitement, attempt and complicity in genocide (para. 167). For comment on the case see Claus Kreß, 'The International Court of Justice and the Elements of the Crime of Genocide' (2007) 18 *EJIL* 619; Richard Goldstone and Rebecca Hamilton, '*Bosnia v. Serbia*: Lessons from the Encounter of the International Court of Justice with the International Criminal Tribunal for former Yugoslavia' (2008) 21 *LJIL* 95.

7 *Bosnian Genocide* case, para. 170.

10.1.2 Historical development

The identification of genocide as an international crime came as a response to the Holocaust. Massacres with the purpose of exterminating national or ethnic minorities were not a twentieth-century novelty, but the term 'genocide' was not coined until 1944 by Raphael Lemkin, a Polish lawyer.[8] The indictment of the defendants at Nuremberg stated that they had conducted 'deliberate and systematic genocide, viz., the extermination of racial and national groups, against the civilian population of certain occupied territories in order to destroy particular races and classes of people, and national, racial or religious groups, particularly Jews, Poles, and Gypsies'.[9] But genocide as such was not a crime within the jurisdiction of the Nuremberg Tribunal, and the term was not mentioned in its judgment. As the ICTR said many years later: 'The crimes prosecuted by the Nuremberg Tribunal, namely the holocaust of the Jews or the "Final Solution", were very much constitutive of genocide, but they could not be defined as such because the crime of genocide was not defined until later.'[10]

All of the crimes prosecuted by the Nuremberg Tribunal and its immediate successors were defined as having a connection with war. It was because of this restriction that it was necessary to recognize the crime of genocide as a separate international crime. This was done in General Assembly Resolution 96(1) of 11 December 1946. Two years later, the Genocide Convention was concluded, having been drafted largely by the Sixth Committee of the UN General Assembly; it came into force on 12 January 1951. In the same year, the ICJ declared that the prohibitions contained in the Convention constituted customary international law.[11]

Although Article VI refers to the possibility of an international court being available to try cases of genocide, it was not until the establishment of the ad hoc Tribunals in 1993 and 1994 that this became a reality. The first conviction for genocide by an international court was recorded on 2 September 1998 by the ICTR, of Jean-Paul Akayesu, a Rwandan mayor. Two days after that, Jean Kambanda, the former Prime Minister of Rwanda was sentenced to life imprisonment after pleading guilty to genocide, conspiracy, incitement and complicity in genocide, as well as crimes against humanity.

---

8 Raphael Lemkin, *Axis Rule in Occupied Europe: Laws of Occupation, Analysis of Government, Proposals for Redress* (Washington, 1944) 79.

9 *The Trial of German Major War Criminals* (London, 1946), part I, 22; Indictment presented to the International Military Tribunal, Cmd 6696, 14. For the development of the concept of genocide in the cases brought under Control Council Law No. 10, see Matthew Lippman, 'The Convention on the Prevention and Punishment of the Crime of Genocide: Fifty Years Later' (1998) 15 *Arizona Journal of International and Comparative Law* 415.

10 *Kambanda* ICTR T. Ch. I 4.9.1998 para. 16.

11 *Reservations to the Convention on the Prevention and Punishment of the Crime of Genocide* Advisory Opinion (1951) ICJ Rep 15 at 23.

10.1.3 Relationship to crimes against humanity

Genocide has obvious similarities to crimes against humanity. As mentioned in section 10.1.2, the Nuremberg defendants were charged with war crimes and crimes against humanity for what would now be prosecuted as genocide. The Genocide Convention makes clear in Article I that genocide can be committed in time of peace as in war and now that there is no longer a nexus between crimes against humanity and conflict[12] it is even clearer that genocide can be, indeed typically is, a form of crimes against humanity.[13]

The chief difference between the two categories of crimes is the intent to destroy the whole or part of a group that is a necessary element of genocide. And the interests protected by the law against genocide are narrower than for crimes against humanity. The law against genocide protects the rights of certain groups to survival, and thus human diversity,[14] but the similar crime against humanity – persecution 'against any identifiable group or collectivity on political, racial, national, ethnic, cultural, religious, gender ... or other grounds that are universally recognised as impermissible under international law ...' – protects groups from discrimination rather than elimination. Thus, 'when persecution escalates to the extreme form of wilful and deliberate acts designed to destroy a group or part of a group, it can be held that such persecution amounts to genocide'.[15]

Unlike crimes against humanity, genocide does not explicitly include any objective requirement of scale. The threshold for a crime against humanity is its connection to a widespread or systematic attack directed against a civilian population, and for a war crime, its commission during an armed conflict. The required elements for the latter two crimes therefore include an objectively existing situation of scale and gravity in which civilians are at risk. In contrast, the gravity of genocide is primarily marked not by an objective circumstantial element but by the subjective *mens rea*, the intent to destroy a national, ethnic, racial or religious group as such.

10.1.4 The nature of genocide

The significance of the genocidal intent in the definition of the crime raises important questions about the nature of genocide and its status as the 'crime of crimes'. Can it be 'genocide' where an isolated individual acts with a fervent, albeit unrealistic, intent to destroy a group? During the negotiation of the ICC Elements of Crimes, for example, the US delegation pointed out that an isolated hate crime, if committed with the requisite intent,

---

12 See section 11.2.1.
13 *Kayishema* ICTR T. Ch. 21.5.1999 para. 89.
14 'Those who devise and implement genocide seek to deprive humanity of the manifold richness its nationalities, races, ethnicities and religions provide.' *Krštić* ICTY A. Ch. 19.4.2004 para. 36.
15 *Kupreskić et al.* ICTY T. Ch. II 14.1.2000 para. 636.

would satisfy the description in the Genocide Convention, and yet it would seem absurd to label a single murder by an isolated individual as a 'genocide'.[16]

Further, does there need to be a collective plan to commit genocide before the crime is committed? In *Jelisić*, an ICTY Trial Chamber stated that killings committed by a single perpetrator are enough 'to establish the material element of the crime of genocide and it is a priori possible to conceive that the accused harboured the plan to exterminate an entire group without this intent having been supported by any organisation in which other individuals participated'. The Chamber 'did not discount the possibility of a lone individual seeking to destroy a group as such'.[17] Such a view is not supported consistently in the case law, or in the academic writing.[18] William Schabas, for example, described the possibility as 'little more than a sophomoric *hypothèse d'école*'.[19] Others go further, taking the view that the very nature of genocide requires a structural element.[20]

To include in the scope of genocide an isolated crime, committed in the absence of any attack or genocidal context, even if legally possible, risks overly expanding the concept of genocide, and effacing the profound stigma and mobilizing power of the term. As the ICTY prosecution has warned:

> in the interests of international justice, genocide should not be diluted or belittled by too broad an interpretation. Indeed, it should be reserved only for acts of exceptional gravity and magnitude which shock the conscience of humankind and which, therefore, justify the appellation of genocide as the 'ultimate crime'.[21]

It is ordinarily assumed therefore that several protagonists are involved in the crime of genocide.[22] Although it is not a formal element of the crime that there be a genocidal plan,[23] the Tribunals have noted that it would be difficult to commit genocide without one.[24] The only realistic exception may be where others were committing crimes against humanity – without genocidal intent – but a single perpetrator had the intent to eliminate a group while

---

16 Valerie Oosterveld, 'Context of Genocide' in Roy Lee et al. (eds.), *The International Criminal Court: Elements of Crimes and Rules of Procedure and Evidence* (Ardsley, NY, 2001) 44 at 45.

17 *Jelisić* ICTY T. Ch. 19.12.1999 para. 400.

18 Even in *Jelisić* the Trial Chamber went on to say, at para. 78: '... the Trial Chamber will have to verify that there was both an intentional attack against a group and an intention on the part of the accused to participate in or carry out this attack'. And see *Kayishema* ICTR T. Ch. II 21.5.1999 paras. 94, 276. On both sides of the academic debate, see William Schabas, 'The *Jelisić* Case and the *Mens Rea* of the Crime of Genocide' (2001) 14 *LJIL* 125; Otto Triffterer, 'Genocide, Its Particular Intent to Destroy in Whole or in Part the Group as Such' (2001) 14 *LJIL* 399; J. Quigley: *The Genocide Convention: An International Law Analysis* (Aldershot, 2006) 164–70.

19 William Schabas, 'Darfur and the "Odious Scourge": The Commission of Inquiry's Findings on Genocide' (2005) 18 *LJIL* 871 at 877.

20 Hans Vest, 'A Structure-Based Concept of Genocidal Intent' (2007) 5 *JICJ* 781.

21 *Karadžić and Mladić* ICTY T. Ch. (transcript of hearing) 27.6.1996 at 15–16.

22 *Krstić* ICTY T. Ch. I 2.8.2001 para. 549.

23 *Jelisić* ICTY A. Ch. 19.7.2001 para. 48.

24 *Kayishema* ICTR T. Ch. II 21.5.1999 para. 94; *Jelisić* ICTY T. Ch. 19.12.1999 para. 101.

committing the same atrocities. In such a situation, the surrounding crimes against humanity would already provide the pattern of mass atrocities, so it might be conceivable for an individual with the necessary intent to carry out acts that could be described as 'genocide'.

But if genocide generally has a collective nature, and is to be limited to serious situations, how is this reflected in the elements of the offence when a court is assessing the guilt or innocence of one individual accused? There are two ways the issue may be addressed: in the material elements of the crime or in the mental element.[25]

The first approach is that taken by the Elements of Crimes adopted for the ICC, which add a 'contextual element' to the *actus reus*, requiring that the conduct for which the defendant is on trial takes place in the context of 'a manifest pattern of similar conduct' or is of itself able to destroy the group or part of it. This contextual element rules out most situations of isolated crimes by requiring either a broader pattern of crimes or a concrete threat to the group. It is discussed in more detail at section 10.3.2.

The alternative approach, proposed in the context of the intent requirement, is that there must be an organized and widespread plan to exterminate a group and the perpetrator must act with knowledge that the commission of the individual act would, or would be likely to, further the implementation of the plan.[26] This approach is discussed at section 10.4.4.

10.2   The protected groups

Not all groups of people are protected by the Genocide Convention. The Convention lists only national, ethnic, racial and religious groups, and the list is a closed one. During the negotiation of the Convention attempts were made to include others, such as social and political groups, but these failed.[27] Ever since the conclusion of the Convention there have been criticisms of its narrow focus and proposals have been made to expand it, but these have all been similarly unsuccessful.[28] It has also been suggested that other groups come within the scope of genocide by virtue of customary international law[29] or that the existing terms should be expansively interpreted so as to include other groups within the definition. The highest-profile example of this was by the ICTR Trial Chamber sitting in the *Akayesu* case. On the basis of a (mis)reading of the *travaux préparatoires* the Chamber determined that the drafters of the Convention intended to protect any stable and permanent group,

---

25 Schabas, 'The *Jelisić* Case', 133–8.
26 See John R. W. D. Jones, 'Whose Intent is it Anyway?' in Lal Chand Vohrah et al. (eds.), *Man's Inhumanity to Man: Essays in Honour of Antonio Cassese* (The Hague, 2003) 467.
27 UN GAOR, 3rd session, 6th Committee, p. 664; see Schabas, *Genocide*, 153–71.
28 For attempts made during the ICC negotiations, see *Report of the Ad Hoc Committee on the Establishment of an International Criminal Court*, UN GAOR 50th Sess., Supp. No. 22, A/50/22 (1995) paras. 60–1 and *Report of the Preparatory Committee on the Establishment of an International Criminal Court*, vol. I, UN GAOR, 51st Sess., Supp. No. 22, A/51/22 (1996) paras. 59–60.
29 Beth Van Schaack, 'The Crime of Political Genocide: Repairing the Genocide Convention's Blind Spot' (1997) 106 *Yale Law Journal* 2259.

rather than simply the groups specifically mentioned.[30] While stability and permanence were certainly used as criteria by some delegates in the Sixth Committee to argue for or against the inclusion of a particular group in the drafting of the Convention, there is no evidence at all that that was adopted as an open-ended description of protected groups. All the evidence is that the enumerated list of groups was intended to be exhaustive.

The view that *any* 'stable and permanent group' is included within the Convention's protected groups was, however, followed by the Commission of Inquiry established at the request of the Security Council to investigate violations of international humanitarian law and human rights in Darfur.[31] The Commission found indeed that this expansive interpretation has 'become part and parcel of international customary law'.[32] But the Commission's finding in this regard, which indicates that the Convention list of groups is not exhaustive, is not supported by case law other than *Akayesu* nor by State practice and *opinio juris*, and cannot be seen as reflective of current law. No other Trial Chamber of the two ad hoc Tribunals has followed the *Akayesu* approach, and the Appeals Chamber has consistently, albeit quietly, kept to the view that the four groups are the exclusive focus of the Genocide Convention.[33] The ICC, in its early practice, has adopted the same view.[34]

There are national jurisdictions that have adopted wider formulations of the protected groups in their domestic law.[35] At the domestic level, States are entitled to use broader definitions but other States are not required to accept those definitions.[36] It has been rightly said that it is precisely because of the rigours of the definition, and because of its focus on crimes aimed at the eradication of particular groups, that genocide is especially stigmatized.[37]

---

30 *Akayesu* ICTR T. Ch. I 2.9.1998 para. 516. For critique see Schabas, *Genocide*, 151–3. In support see Diane Marie Amann, 'International decisions: Prosecutor v Akayesu' (1999) 93 *AJIL* 195.

31 Res. 1564 (2004) of 18.9.2004. The Commission ('the Darfur Commission') was established by the UN Secretary-General 'to investigate reports of violations of international humanitarian law and human rights law in Darfur by all parties, to determine also whether or not acts of genocide have occurred, and to identify the perpetrators of such violations with a view to ensuring that those responsible are held accountable'.

32 *Report of the International Commission of Inquiry on violations of international humanitarian law and human rights law in Darfur* UN Doc.S/2005/60 para. 501.

33 *Krštić* ICTY A. Ch. 19.4.2004 paras. 6–8; see Guglielmo Verdirame, 'The Genocide Definition in the Jurisprudence of the *ad hoc* Tribunals' (2000) 49 *ICLQ* 579 at 588–92.

34 *Situation in Darfur (Al Bashir* arrest warrant case) ICC PT Ch. I 4.3.2009 paras. 134–7.

35 For example, see the Spanish *Pinochet* case, noted at (1999) 93 *AJIL* 690, especially p. 693. A further example is the Ethiopian law which defines as genocide acts designed to eliminate 'political groups' and 'population transfer or dispersion'; see Firew Kebede Tiba; 'The *Mengistu* Genocide Trial in Ethiopia' (2007) 5 *JICJ* 513 at 518.

36 Genocide charges against General Pinochet were not considered in the extradition process in the UK, on the basis that they relied on an interpretation of genocide broader than that in international law; see David Turns, 'Pinochet's Fallout: Jurisdiction and Immunity for Criminal Violations of International Law' (2000) 20 *Legal Studies* 566 at 567–8.

37 Schabas, *Genocide*, 10.

10.2.1 *National, ethnical, racial and religious groups*

Given that these four groups are the exclusive beneficiaries of the protection of the Genocide Convention, it is unfortunate that there is no internationally recognized definition of any of the terms it uses. It is difficult to attribute a distinct meaning to each, since they overlap considerably.[38] The ICTR has attempted to give each one a meaning. In past judgments it has described a national group as a 'collection of people who are perceived to share a legal bond based on common citizenship, coupled with reciprocity of rights and duties';[39] what it describes as the 'conventional definition' of racial group 'is based on the hereditary physical traits often identified with a geographical region, irrespective of linguistic, cultural, national or religious factors';[40] an ethnic group it described as 'a group whose members share a common language or culture';[41] and 'a religious group includes denomination or mode of worship or a group sharing common beliefs'.[42]

But to attempt to give each term its own definition risks missing the wood for the trees. The ICTR Trial Chamber in *Akayesu* ran into difficulties in assessing whether the Tutsi were a protected group in the context of the widespread massacres in Rwanda.[43] Having defined an ethnic group as sharing a common language or culture, the evidence before the Chamber made it clear that it was not thus that the Tutsi were distinguished from the Hutu. The Chamber had to rely on the fact that Rwandans were required to carry identification cards indicating the ethnicity of the bearer as Hutu, Tutsi or Twa and that the Tutsi constituted a group referred to as 'ethnic' in official classifications. It was only by virtue of its determination that any 'stable and permanent' group was covered by the Convention, and therefore by the ICTR Statute, that the Chamber was able to find that the Tutsi were a protected group.[44] As mentioned above, the decision on this point is not legally defensible. That would not, however, change the outcome in this case, as the Tutsi would be considered an ethnic group on the correct interpretation of the Convention.

The better approach, followed by the *Krstić* Trial Chamber, is to recognize that the list is exhaustive but to accept that the four groups were not given distinct and different meanings in the Convention:

> European instruments on human rights use the term 'national minorities', while universal instruments more commonly make reference to 'ethnic, religious or linguistic minorities'; the two expressions appear to embrace the same goals. In a study conducted for the

---

38 For a powerful argument in *favour* of identifying separate meanings see Claus Kreß, 'The Crime of Genocide under International Law' (2006) 6 *International Criminal Law Review* 461.

39 *Akayesu* ICTR T. Ch. I 2.9.1998 para. 511.

40 *Ibid.*, para. 513.

41 *Ibid.*, paras. 512–15 and see *Kayishema* ICTR T. Ch. II 21.5.1999 para. 98.

42 *Ibid.*

43 For critique of the Chamber's reasoning, see Payam Akhavan, 'The Crime of Genocide in the ICTR Jurisprudence' (2005) 3 *JICJ* 989.

44 *Akayesu* ICTR T. Ch. I 2.9.1998 para. 702.

Sub-Commission on Prevention of Discrimination and Protection of Minorities in 1979, F. Capotorti commented that 'the Sub-Commission on Prevention of Discrimination and Protection of Minorities decided, in 1950, to replace the word "racial" by the word "ethnic" in all references to minority groups described by their ethnic origin'. The International Convention on the Elimination of All Forms of Racial Discrimination defines racial discrimination as 'any distinction, exclusion, restriction or preference based on race, colour, descent, or national or ethnic origin'. The preparatory work on the Genocide Convention also reflects that the term 'ethnical' was added at a later stage in order to better define the type of groups protected by the Convention and ensure that the term 'national' would not be understood as encompassing purely political groups.

The preparatory work of the Convention shows that setting out such a list was designed more to describe a single phenomenon, roughly corresponding to what was recognised, before the second world war, as 'national minorities', rather than to refer to several distinct prototypes of human groups. To attempt to differentiate each of the named groups on the basis of scientifically objective criteria would thus be inconsistent with the object and purpose of the Convention.[45]

The groups also 'help to define each other, operating much as four corner posts that delimit an area within which a myriad of groups covered by the Convention find protection'.[46] This 'four corners' approach avoids the difficulties of fitting a group such as the Tutsis precisely into one of the listed categories, but ensures that it comes within the area of protection that was intended by the negotiators, while also respecting the negotiators' intent that the list be a closed one.

10.2.2 Identification of the group and its members

As is clear from the wording of the different parts of the *actus reus* of the offence, the acts must be directed at members of the group. However, determination of the groups and their members is not a simple matter; it is certainly more difficult than the drafters of the Convention, working against the presuppositions (and perhaps prejudices) of their era, thought. There are genuine difficulties in deciding if a person is a member of the group, and the complex question of who ought to be able to make that determination arises.[47] A subjective approach has its attractions: that is, the criterion for the identification of members of the group is that a perpetrator considers the victims to be members of a group he or she is targeting. The most significant factor in a particular case may be that the perpetrators have

---

45 *Krštić* ICTY T. Ch. I 2.8.2001 paras. 555–6 (footnotes not included); the Chamber followed the approach in Schabas, *Genocide*, 128–32; and see *Rutaganda* ICTR T. Ch. 19.12.1999 para. 56. See also *Fourth Report on the Draft Code of Offences against the Peace and Security of Mankind*, by Doudou Thiam, Special Rapporteur, UN Doc. A/CN.4/398 para. 56.
46 Schabas, *Genocide*, 129.
47 In the human rights context, see the decision of the Human Rights Committee in *Lovelace* v. *Canada* Human Rights Committee (22/47).

the specific intent to destroy a group identified by themselves. As was said in the *Bagilishema* case:

> A group may not have precisely defined boundaries and there may be occasions when it is difficult to give a definitive answer as to whether or not a victim was a member of a protected group. Moreover, the perpetrators of genocide may characterize the targeted group in ways that do not fully correspond to conceptions of the group shared generally, or by other segments of society. In such a case, the Chamber is of the opinion that, on the evidence, if a victim was perceived by a perpetrator as belonging to a protected group, the victim should be considered by the Chamber as a member of the protected group, for the purposes of genocide.[48]

It is by no means clear that groups intended to be protected by the Genocide Convention always have an objective existence in the manner which the drafters thought. Groups are often social constructs, rather than scientific facts. This problem was discussed by the Darfur Commission, owing to the fact that, although the US had described the crimes committed in Darfur as 'genocide',[49] on close analysis the question of group existence in Darfur was complicated. The Commission found that the Fur, Massalit and Zaghawa groups did not appear to make up ethnic groups distinct from those to which their attackers belonged. They had the same religion, and the same language, though the 'Africans' spoke their own dialect in addition to Arabic, while the 'Arabs' spoke only Arabic. Years of inter-marriage and coexistence had blurred the distinction between the groups. The sedentary or nomadic character of the groups appeared to constitute one of the main distinctions between them.[50] The Commission relied upon a partially subjective concept of groups in deciding that the victim groups nevertheless came within the scope of the crime of genocide. Victims and perpetrators had 'come to perceive themselves as either "African" or "Arab"'. A 'self-perception of two distinct groups' had emerged.[51] When the same question came before the ICC Pre-Trial Chamber in the *Al Bashir* arrest warrant case, the majority found that each of the three groups had 'its own language, its own tribal customs and its own traditional links to its lands' and was therefore a distinct ethnic group. The majority did not consider it necessary to explore the subjective or objective approach to the definition of groups.[52] Interestingly, Judge Ušaka, in dissent, argued that the three groups ought to be taken together as, in the Darfurian context, the ethnic faultline was considered to fall along the grounds of 'Arab' and 'African', the latter encompassing all three groups.[53]

---

48 *Bagilishema* ICTR T. Ch. I 7.6.2001 para. 65.
49 House Concurrent Resolution 467, Senate Concurrent Resolution 133, 22.7.2004.
50 Report, UN Doc. S/2005/60 para. 508.
51 *Ibid.*, paras. 510–1.
52 *Al Bashir* arrest warrant case ICC PT Ch. I 4.3.2009 para. 137 and fn. 152. Judge Ušacka adopted the mixed objective/subjective approach that the ICTY and ICTR now use; Partially Dissenting Opinion of Judge Ušacka, para. 23.
53 *Ibid.*, paras. 24–6.

Reliance on a purely subjective approach is uncomfortable, but it may be that with racism there is not always an objective basis: perceptions may be based on imagined distinctions rather than genuine ones.[54] While the Tribunals have in some cases appeared to use an entirely subjective approach,[55] the better view is that the group must have some form of objective existence in the first place; otherwise the Convention could be used to protect entirely fictitious national, ethnic, racial or religious groups. It now seems settled that the identification of members of the group cannot be *solely* subjective. To overcome the problems of purely objective and purely subjective approaches, the Tribunals have adopted an approach that blends the two, but with sensitivity to the fact that the idea of a separate group may not have a basis in objective fact, but can be a set of reified beliefs about difference. Thus, whether a group is a protected one should be 'assessed on a case-by-case basis by reference to the *objective* particulars of a given social or historical context, and by the *subjective* perceptions of the perpetrators'.[56]

In addition, it is now well established that, notwithstanding some case law to the contrary,[57] a group cannot be defined 'negatively', i.e. by identifying persons not sharing the group characteristics of the perpetrators, for example, 'non-Serbs'.[58] It is also the case that where a person has a mixed identity, if he or she is targeted on the basis of membership of the protected group, the person so targeting them may be guilty of genocide. Thus in the *Ndindabahizi* case, the ICTR accepted that a half-Belgian, half-Rwandan man, who was targeted as a Tutsi in the Rwandan genocide, was a Tutsi for the purpose of convicting the defendant of genocide.[59]

10.3 Material elements

10.3.1 The prohibited acts

Not every act committed with the intention to destroy, in whole or in part, a protected group will lead to a conviction for genocide. Only those which are mentioned in Article II of the Genocide Convention may form the *actus reus* of genocide. Although all of the underlying crimes are defined by reference to victims in the plural, the ICC elements state that even one victim suffices, if the relevant act is committed with the necessary intent. This is a

---

54 See Schabas, 'Darfur and the "Odious Scourge"', 879.
55 *Kayishema* ICTR T. Ch. II 21.5.1999 para. 98; *Jelisić* ICTY T. Ch. 14.12.1999 paras. 69–72.
56 *Semanza* ICTR T. Ch. 15.5. 2003 para. 317.
57 *Jelisić* ICTY T. Ch. 14.12.1999 paras. 70, 71; and see Judge Shahabudeen's powerful dissent in *Stakić* ICTY A. Ch. 22.3.2006 paras. 8–18.
58 *Stakić* ICTY T. Ch. II 31.7.2003 para. 512; A. Ch. 22.3.2006 paras. 19–28. See also *Bosnian Genocide* case paras. 193–4.
59 *Ndindabahizi*, ICTR T. Ch. 15.7.2004 paras. 467–9. The conviction was overturned on appeal, on factual rather than legal grounds. *Ndindabahizi*, ICTR A. Ch. 16.1.2007 para. 117.

controversial conclusion in relation to subparagraph (c) of Article II, which refers to inflicting conditions of life on the 'group'.

Killing

Article II(a) covers what is the paradigmatic conduct that amounts to genocide: killing members of the group. However, there are certain interpretative problems which have had to be resolved. The English term 'killing' (which the ICC Elements of Crimes state is interchangeable with 'caused death') is neutral as to whether the killing is intentional, or whether reckless (or perhaps even negligent) causing of death suffices. The term used in the French version of the Genocide Convention, '*meurtre*', is more precise. In *Kayishema*, the Appeal Chamber confirmed the Trial Chamber's view that there is virtually no difference between the terms in the English and French versions *in the context* of genocidal intent.[60] The act must be intentional but not necessarily premeditated.[61] Owing to the operation of Article 30 of the Rome Statute, genocidal killings must be intentional in proceedings before the ICC. If there is doubt about the intention to kill, rather than the intention to cause serious harm, it is of course possible to charge the defendant pursuant to Article II(b) of the Convention for the conduct that led to the death.

Causing serious bodily or mental harm to members of the group

In spite of the popular understanding of genocide as being confined to conduct causing death, the drafters of the Genocide Convention were not so limited in their understanding of the crime. Article II(b) of the Convention also criminalizes the causing of serious bodily or mental harm to victims. In the *Eichmann* case, the District Court of Jerusalem said that serious bodily and mental harm could be caused 'by the enslavement, starvation, deportation and persecution of people ... and by their detention in ghettos, transit camps and concentration camps in conditions which were designed to cause their degradation, deprivation of their rights as human beings and to suppress them and cause them inhumane suffering and torture'.[62] The ICTR in the *Akayesu* case broke new ground in deciding that acts of sexual violence and rape can constitute genocide; sexual violence was found to be an integral part of the process of destruction in the Rwanda genocide.[63] The ICC Elements follow this approach.[64]

---

60 *Kayishema* ICTR A. Ch.1.6.2001 para. 151; for a critique see David Nersessian, 'The Contours of Genocidal Intent: Troubling Jurisprudence from the International Criminal Tribunals' (2002) 37 *Texas International Law Journal* 231.

61 See, e.g. *Stakić* ICTY T. Ch. II 31.7.2003 para. 515.

62 *A-G of Israel* v. *Eichmann* (1968) 36 ILR 5 (DC) 340.

63 *Akayesu* ICTR T. Ch. I 2.9.1998 para. 731.

64 ICC EOC, Art. 6(b), n. 3.

Owing to its concerns about the possible breadth of the *mental* harm aspect of genocide, the US entered an 'understanding' to the Convention on ratifying, which stated that the term 'means permanent impairment of mental faculties through drugs, torture or similar techniques'. Serious mental harm does mean more than minor or temporary impairment of mental faculties,[65] but neither mental nor physical harm need be permanent or irremediable.[66] Obviously, as the term 'serious' is one which involves a value judgment, there will be differing views on what treatment is included. In *Kayishema*, it was held that decisions on what is meant by serious bodily or mental harm should be made on a case-by-case basis.[67]

Deliberately inflicting on the group conditions of life calculated to bring about its physical destruction in whole or in part

This category of prohibited acts comprises methods of destruction whereby the perpetrator does not immediately kill the members of the group, but which seek to bring about their physical destruction in the end.[68] The ICC Elements of Crimes interpret the term 'conditions of life' as including but 'not necessarily restricted to, deliberate deprivation of resources indispensable for survival, such as food or medical services, or systematic expulsion from homes'.[69] Unlike the two previous categories, this is not a result-based form of the crime[70] but it requires that the conditions are 'calculated' to achieve the result.[71]

The question of the forced migration of people, commonly known by the ugly neologism 'ethnic cleansing', has been addressed under this subparagraph of Article II. This practice, when committed by the Serbs to eliminate the Muslim presence in large parts of Bosnia-Herzogovina, was regarded by ad hoc Judge Lauterpacht in the ICJ provisional measures ruling of 13 September 1993 as constituting genocide,[72] though his view was not shared by the majority. As seen above, the ICC elements give 'systematic expulsion from homes' as one of the illustrations of this category of prohibited act.

---

65 *Semanza* ICTR T. Ch. 15.5.2003 para. 321.

66 *Akayesu* ICTR T. Ch. I 2.9.1998 para. 502. The *Kayishema* Trial Chamber gave perhaps a narrower interpretation as 'harm that seriously injures the health, causes disfigurement or causes any serious injury to the external, internal organs or senses'; *Kayishema* ICTR T. Ch. II 21.5.1999 para. 109.

67 *Ibid.*, para. 110. Examples of mental harm were given in *Blagovejić* T. Ch. I 17.1.2005 para. 647.

68 *Akayesu* ICTR T. Ch. I 2.9.1998 para. 505.

69 ICC EOC, Art. 6(c), n. 4.

70 See, e.g. *Stakić* ICTY T. Ch. II 31.7.2003 para. 517.

71 As pointed out in Kreß, 'The Crime of Genocide', 481–3, 'calculated' and 'physical destruction' are difficult concepts.

72 *Application of the Convention on the Prevention and Punishment of the Crime of Genocide (Bosnia and Herzegovina v. Yugoslavia (Serbia and Montenegro))* [1993] ICJ Rep. 325 at 431–2. Ethnic cleansing was also considered genocide by the ICTY in the decision confirming the second indictment in *Karadžić and Mladić*; review of the Indictments pursuant to Rule 61 of the Rules of Procedure and Evidence ICTY T. Ch. I 11.7.1996 para. 94.

But ethnic cleansing does not necessarily constitute genocide. In the case of *Eichmann* the District Court of Jerusalem found that, before 1941, Nazi persecution of the Jews was aimed at persuading them to leave Germany. Only later did the policy develop into one for their destruction. Since the court doubted that there was a specific intent to exterminate before 1941, Eichmann was acquitted of genocide for acts before that date.[73]

Eichmann is authority for the proposition that if and in so far as the objective of a forced migration is 'only' to remove a group or part of it from a territory, it differs from that of genocide. In *Brđanin*, for example, the Trial Chamber found a 'consistent, coherent and criminal strategy of cleansing the Bosnian Krajina' but determined that the crimes had been committed with 'the sole purpose of driving people away'.[74] There was no evidence that they had been committed with the intent required for genocide.[75] The fact of forced migration alone is not enough for a court to deduce the special intent of destruction of the group.

The matter was usefully summed up by the ICJ in the *Bosnian Genocide* case:

> Neither the intent, as a matter of policy, to render an area 'ethnically homogeneous', nor the operations that may be carried out to implement such policy, can *as such* be designated as genocide: the intent that characterizes genocide is 'to destroy, in whole or in part' a particular group, and deportation or displacement of the members of a group, even if effected by force, is not necessarily equivalent to destruction of that group, nor is such destruction an automatic consequence of the displacement. This is not to say that acts described as 'ethnic cleansing' may never constitute genocide, if they are such as to be characterized as, for example, 'deliberately inflicting on the group conditions of life calculated to bring about its physical destruction in whole or in part', contrary to Article II, paragraph *(c)*, of the Convention, provided such action is carried out with the necessary specific intent *(dolus specialis)*, that is to say with a view to the destruction of the group, as distinct from its removal from the region … [W]hether a particular operation described as 'ethnic cleansing' amounts to genocide depends on the presence or absence of acts listed in Article II of the Genocide Convention, and of the intent to destroy the group as such. In fact, in the context of the Convention, the term 'ethnic cleansing' has no legal significance of its own. That said, it is clear that acts of 'ethnic cleansing' may occur in parallel to acts prohibited by Article II of the Convention, and may be significant as indicative of the presence of a specific intent *(dolus specialis)* inspiring those acts.[76]

Imposing measures intended to prevent births within the group

This provision (Article II(d) of the Genocide Convention) was inspired by the Nazis' practice of forced sterilization before and during the Second World War. Examples of

---

73 *A-G of Israel* v. *Eichmann* (1968) 36 ILR 5 (DC). See Schabas, *Genocide*, 233–4.
74 *Brđanin* ICTY T. Ch. II 1.9.2004 para. 118.
75 *Ibid.*, para. 989. See also *Stakić* ICTY T. Ch. II 31.7.2003 paras. 519, 557; *Stakić* ICTY A. Ch. 22.3.2006 paras. 46–8.
76 *Bosnian Genocide* case ICJ Rep. para. 190.

these measures given by the ICTR Trial Chamber in *Akayesu* are sexual mutilation, sterilization, forced birth control, separation of the sexes and prohibition of marriages.[77] The Trial Chamber added:

> In patriarchal societies, where membership of a group is determined by the identity of the father, an example of a measure intended to prevent births within a group is the case where, during rape, a woman of the said group is deliberately impregnated by a man of another group, with the intent to have her give birth to a child who will consequently not belong to its mother's group. Furthermore, the Chamber notes that measures intended to prevent births within the group may be physical, but can also be mental. For instance, rape can be a measure intended to prevent births when the person raped subsequently refuses to procreate, in the same way that members can be led, through threats or trauma, not to procreate.[78]

While this may stray into the separate crime of forced impregnation, it is not too broad, given that both genocidal intent, and the intent to prevent births within the group must also be proved.

Forcibly transferring children of the group to another group

This is a form of genocide which has received little judicial consideration.[79] Probably the most authoritative interpretative source on the point is to be found in the ICC Elements of Crimes, defining children as being those below 18 and noting that '[t]he term "forcibly" is not restricted to physical force, but may include threat of force or coercion, such as that caused by fear of violence, duress, detention, psychological oppression or abuse of power, against such person or persons or another person, or by taking advantage of a coercive environment'.

The provision (Article II(e)) was included in the Genocide Convention as a compromise for the exclusion of cultural genocide. In 1997, the Australian Human Rights and Equal Opportunities Commission controversially decided that the forcible transfer of Aboriginal children to non-indigenous institutions and families constituted genocide.[80] The wording of the Commission's findings indicated, however, that it was 'cultural genocide' that was in mind, since the objective of the transfers was to assimilate the children into non-Aboriginal

---

77 *Akayesu* ICTR T. Ch. I 2.9.1998 para. 507.

78 *Ibid.*, paras. 507–8.

79 Although see *Akayesu* ICTR T. Ch. I 2.9.1998 para. 509. In the *Bosnian Genocide* case, Bosnia claimed that forced pregnancy constituted this form of genocide since rape was used as a means of affecting the demographic balance; children born as a result of the forced pregnancies would not be considered to be part of the protected group and the intent of the perpetrators was to transfer the unborn children to the group of Bosnian Serbs. The ICJ found that the evidence did not establish any form of policy of forced pregnancy, 'nor that there was any aim to transfer children of the protected group to another group within the meaning of Article II *(e)* of the Convention'; paras. 362–7.

80 Cited in Schabas, *Genocide*, 205.

society. Cultural genocide is not within the scope of the Convention,[81] nor in customary law,[82] although forcibly transferring children can be close to such a concept.

10.3.2 The 'contextual element'

The ICC Elements have an additional material element, which was introduced to avoid the problem that isolated hate crimes could fall within the Convention definition, diluting the seriousness of the term 'genocide'.[83] In relation to each prohibited act the element requires that:

> [t]he conduct took place in the context of a manifest pattern of similar conduct directed against that group or was conduct that could itself effect such destruction.[84]

The first branch of this element reflects the more likely situation, where the individual accused is acting within a broader context in which others are also committing acts of genocide against the targeted group.[85] The adjective 'manifest', included at the insistence of the US, means that the pattern must be a clear one and not one of a few isolated crimes occurring over a period of years.[86] The second branch applies where the conduct in question 'could itself effect such destruction'. Although by far the less likely, this could occur where a group is particularly small or where the accused has access to powerful means of destruction (such as the use of a nuclear or biological weapon) with genocidal intent. In such a case there is no need for a pattern of similar conduct, since the accused is in a position to pose a real threat to a protected group. The provision would be relevant for prosecutions of ringleaders and instigators. It would also capture those who had the means to destroy a group but for whatever reason managed to cause only a single death or a few deaths, such that there would be no objective 'pattern'.[87]

The contextual element does not exclude entirely the possibility of a 'lone *génocidaire*', since it requires similar *conduct* not similar *intent*;[88] the second clause of the element also envisages a single perpetrator with the means to destroy the group or part of it. It does however require either a pattern of crimes, or a concrete danger to a group, thereby ruling out isolated hate crimes.

---

81 See section 10.4.1.

82 *Krstić* ICTY T. Ch. I 2.8.2001 para. 580, *Krstić* ICTY A. Ch. 19.4.2004 para. 25.

83 See section 10.1.4.

84 See Valerie Oosterveld and Charles Garraway, 'The Elements of Genocide' in Roy Lee et al. (eds.), *The International Criminal Court: Elements of Crimes and Rules of Procedure and Evidence* (New York, 2001) 41 at 44, 45.

85 Or, if the other perpetrators do not have the genocidal intent, they may be committing crimes against humanity rather than genocide, while still in a 'manifest pattern of similar conduct'.

86 Oosterveld and Garraway, 'The Elements of Genocide', 47.

87 Wiebke Ruckert and Georg Witschel, 'Genocide and Crimes Against Humanity in the Elements of Crimes' in H. Fischer, C. Kreß and S. R. Lüder (eds.), *International and National Prosecution of Crimes under International Law* (Berlin, 2000) 66.

88 Oosterveld, 'Context of Genocide', 47–8.

The Elements of Crime are equivocal on the mental element attaching to this element:

> Notwithstanding the normal requirement for a mental element provided for in article 30, and recognizing that knowledge of the circumstances will usually be addressed in proving genocidal intent, the appropriate requirement, if any, for a mental element regarding this circumstance will need to be decided by the Court on a case-by-case basis.[89]

The 'contextual element' was not drawn directly from Tribunal jurisprudence; it was based very loosely on two passages in the *Akayesu* trial judgment.[90] The Trial Chamber in *Krštić* adopted the element,[91] but the ICTY Appeals Chamber was hostile to the Trial Chamber's view:

> The Trial Chamber relied on the definition of genocide in the Elements of Crimes adopted by the ICC. This definition, stated the Trial Chamber, 'indicates clearly that genocide requires that "the conduct took place in the context of a manifest pattern of similar conduct."' The Trial Chamber's reliance on the definition of genocide given in the ICC's Elements of Crimes is inapposite ... the requirement that the prohibited conduct be part of a widespread or systematic attack does not appear in the Genocide Convention and was not mandated by customary international law. Because the definition adopted by the Elements of Crimes did not reflect customary law as it existed at the time Krštić committed his crimes, it cannot be used to support the Trial Chamber's conclusion.[92]

After *Krštić* the Tribunals will not be accepting the contextual element within their own jurisprudence.

In the ICC, on the other hand, a majority in a Pre-Trial Chamber has taken the view that the contextual provision in the Elements is not inconsistent with the ICC Statute (which includes the Genocide Convention definition) and it has therefore applied it.[93] The Chamber took the view that the contextual element was 'fully consistent with the traditional consideration of the crime of genocide as the "crime of crimes"'.[94] Indeed, if genocide is to be seen as a particularly serious crime, some threshold of objective 'scale and gravity'[95] must be maintained and the ICC Elements provision offers a formulation which has been accepted and adopted by consensus by the international community.

---

89 Para. 3 of introduction to EOC for Art. 6.
90 *Akayesu* ICTR T. Ch. I 2.9.1998 paras. 520 and 523.
91 *Krštić* ICTY T. Ch. I 2.8.2001 para. 682.
92 *Krštić* ICTY A. Ch. 19.4.04 para. 224.
93 *Al Bashir* arrest warrant case ICC PT Ch. I 4.3.2009 paras. 117–33. But the majority's conclusion that the contextual element means that 'the relevant conduct presents a concrete threat to the existence of the targeted group' imposes a requirement not included in the element; see Separate and Partly Dissenting Opinion of Judge Anita Ušacka, para. 19, fn. 26. See also Claus Kreß, 'The Crime of Genocide and Contextual Elements: A Comment on the ICC Pre-Trial Chamber's Decision in the Al Bashir Case' (2009) *JICJ* 1, and Robert Cryer, 'The Definitions of International Crimes in *Al Bashir* Arrest Warrant Decision' (2009) 7 *JICJ* 283.
94 *Al Bashir* arrest warrant case, para. 133.
95 *Krštić* ICTY T. Ch. I 2.8.2001 para. 549.

10.4 Mental elements

The mental elements of genocide comprise both the requisite intention to commit the underlying prohibited act (such as killing) and the intent special to genocide. It is the special intent 'to destroy in whole or in part [a protected group] as such' that distinguishes genocide from other crimes.[96] But the meaning to be attributed to this intent requirement is a matter of some difficulty. There are four aspects to be considered, and they are interconnected. Does every perpetrator have to have a specific intent to destroy or is it sufficient, either for all, or at least for non-leaders, that they have knowledge of a collective plan and foresee that their conduct will further it? What is the meaning of 'as such': is motive relevant? What is the 'whole' or 'part' of a group? What is the meaning of 'destroy' for the purpose of the special intent? These four issues will be considered in reverse order.

10.4.1 'to destroy'

There must be an intent to destroy. The destruction specified here is physical or biological, although the means of causing the destruction of the group may be by acts short of causing the death of individuals.[97] Other forms of destruction, for example, the social assimilation of a group into another, or attacks on cultural characteristics which give a group its own identity, do not constitute genocide if they are not related to physical or biological destruction. While the preamble to GA Resolution 96(1) stated that genocide 'results in great losses to humanity in the form of cultural and other contributions represented by these human groups', this did not suggest that cultural loss, in the absence of physical destruction, can amount to genocide. The *travaux préparatoires* of the Convention indicate that the inclusion of cultural genocide was hotly debated and eventually rejected.[98]

Some national jurisdictions have extended the meaning of genocide to cover other forms of destruction within their own law.[99] But, as the Trial Chamber in *Krštić* (which was quoted approvingly on appeal) put it:

> despite recent developments, customary international law limits the definition of genocide to those acts seeking the physical or biological destruction of all or part of the group. An enterprise attacking only the cultural or sociological characteristics of a human group in order to annihilate these elements which give to that group its own identity distinct from the rest of the community would not fall under the definition of genocide.[100]

---

96 *Kambanda* ICTR T. Ch. I 4.9.1998 para. 16; *Kayishema* ICTR T. Ch. II 21.5.1999 para. 91.
97 *Ibid.*, para. 95.
98 Summarized in Schabas, *Genocide*, 207–14.
99 See, e.g. the decision of the German Federal Constitutional Court 2 BvR 290/99, 12.12.2000 para. III (4)(a)(aa).
100 *Krštić* ICTY T. Ch. I 2.8.2001 para. 580; *Krštić* ICTY A. Ch. 19.4.2004 para. 25.

The Trial Chamber in the later case of *Blagojević* appears to have departed from this in finding that 'the forcible transfer of individuals could lead to the material destruction of the group, since the group ceases to exist as a group, or at least as the group was'. It emphasized 'that its reasoning and conclusion are not an argument for cultural genocide, but rather an attempt to clarify the meaning of physical and biological destruction'[101] but this looks like an attempt to square the circle. In the *Bosnian Genocide* case, the ICJ confirmed that genocide was limited to physical or biological destruction of a group.[102]

10.4.2 'in whole or in part'

There must be an intent to destroy the protected group in whole or in part. This aspect of the intention[103] is one which has caused considerable controversy. This is because the ambit of the protections granted by the prohibition of genocide is quite heavily dependent on how broadly or narrowly the relevant group is conceptualized. The first issue is a geographical one. To take an example from a clear case of genocide – Rwanda – the Hutu *génocidaires* did not appear to want to destroy all Tutsis everywhere, but only in Rwanda.[104] The relevant group could be conceived of as Tutsis everywhere, in which case Rwandan Tutsis were protected only as a 'part' of that group. Or it could be thought that the relevant group was the Rwandan Tutsis. This difference matters as, in the latter instance, an intention to destroy all the Tutsis in part of Rwanda could fulfil this aspect of the mental element of genocide. In the former, it could not. According to the ICJ, 'it is widely accepted that genocide may be found to have been committed where the intent is to destroy the group within a geographically limited area'.[105]

A further issue is the meaning of 'part' of a group. The case law of the Tribunals has established that it is not genocide if the intention is to target a part which is less than 'substantial'[106] and this has been confirmed by the ICJ:

> ... the intent must be to destroy at least a substantial part of the particular group. That is demanded by the very nature of the crime of genocide: since the object and purpose of the Convention as a whole is to prevent the intentional destruction of groups, the part targeted must be significant enough to have an impact on the group as a whole.[107]

---

101 *Blagojević and Jokić* ICTY T. Ch. 17.1.2005 para. 666.
102 *Bosnian Genocide* case ICJ para. 344.
103 It is worth emphasizing that this part of the offence is a part of the mental element, not the material elements of genocide – it is not necessary to establish whether all or part of a group was actually destroyed to prove genocide.
104 *Krstić* ICTY A. Ch. 19.4.2004 para. 13.
105 *Bosnian Genocide* case ICJ para. 199.
106 *Kayishema* ICTR T. Ch. II 21.5.1999 para. 96; *Bagilishema* ICTR T. Ch. I 7.6.2001 para. 64; *Semanza* ICTR T. Ch. 15.5.2003 para. 316.
107 *Bosnian Genocide* case ICJ para.198.

The findings in *Krštić* illustrate the difficulties of determining both the whole and the substantial part of the group for the purpose of assessing whether the special intent is present. The Trial Chamber determined that the Bosnian Muslims constituted the protected group and 'the Bosnian Muslims of Srebrenica or the Bosnian Muslims of Eastern Bosnia constitute a part of the protected group'.[108] This finding was affirmed by the Appeal Chamber, which also pointed out that, in determining what a 'substantial' part was, the prominence of the targeted individuals within the group as well as the number targeted (in absolute and in relative terms) could also be relevant; hence, both qualitative and quantitative criteria should be considered. 'If a specific part of the group is emblematic of the overall group, or is essential to its survival, that may support a finding that the part qualifies as substantial.'[109] Here the fate of the Srebenica Muslims was emblematic of that of all Bosnian Muslims.

The decision has been criticized as having set too low a threshold for the scale of genocide.[110] The killings were of 7,000–8,000 men, and it therefore appeared that the people targeted formed a part of a part of a group. However, the Chamber also took into account the fact that women and children were transferred from the area, to argue that the 'part' of the group was the Bosnian Muslims of Srebrenica. The prosecution had urged the ICTY to take the view that the Bosnian Muslims of Srebrenica were the relevant whole group.[111] If the Chamber had accepted this, it would have made proving genocide considerably simpler for the prosecution, as the Bosnian Muslim men of military age could have been seen as a substantial part of the group. This would, however, have diluted the concept of genocide considerably.

10.4.3 'as such'

There must be an intent to destroy the group, or part of it, 'as such'. During the negotiation of the Convention there were those who wanted to include motive as a necessary element of genocide. Others did not. The compromise which allowed agreement to be reached was to exclude any explicit reference to motive, but to include the words 'as such'.[112] While these

---

108 *Krštić* ICTY T. Ch. I 2.8.2001 para. 560.
109 *Krštić* ICTY A. Ch. 19.4.2004 para. 12.
110 William Schabas, 'Was Genocide Committed in Bosnia and Herzegovina? First Judgments of the International Criminal Tribunal for the Former Yugoslavia' (2002) 25 *Fordham International Law Journal* 23 at 45–7: 'categorising [the atrocities] as "genocide" seems to distort the definition unreasonably'. And see Katherine Southwick, 'Srebrenica As Genocide? The Krštić Decision And The Language Of The Unspeakable' (2005) 8 *Yale Human Rights and Development Law Journal* 188 at 206–11.
111 *Krštić* ICTY T. Ch. I 2.8.2001 para. 545.
112 The negotiations are well summarized in A. Greenawalt, 'Rethinking Genocidal Intent: The case for a Knowledge-Based Interpretation' (1999) 99 *Columbia Law Review* 2259 at 2274–9 and Schabas, *Genocide*, 294–306.

words are therefore relied upon by some as evidence for the need for motive[113] the *travaux préparatoires* disclose that that was not the meaning that all the negotiators attached to the words.

The motive for which a crime is committed, as opposed to the intention with which it is committed, is ordinarily irrelevant to guilt in criminal law. But the discriminatory nature of genocide seems to require a motive: the victims are singled out not by reason of their individual identity but *because* of their membership of a national, ethnic, racial or religious group.[114] It is not surprising therefore that decisions by the ad hoc Tribunals have sometimes used the language of motive, referring to the need for the accused to 'seek' or 'aim at' the destruction of the group.[115] If it is possible to untangle the sometimes apparently conflicting case law of the Tribunals, it can be said that the Tribunals do distinguish between motive and genocidal intent[116] – personal motivation (such as a wish to profit financially from the genocide) for the perpetrator's participation in the crime is not relevant – but having a discriminatory purpose for the crime is intrinsic to the special intent.[117] Further, in cases where a set of facts and their consequences may have different explanations it may be that a consideration of motive may be relevant in assessing intent, even though it will not itself be decisive.[118]

10.4.4 Intent

It is worth noting that, unlike the crime of aggression, genocide is not a crime that may be committed only by those who lead and plan the campaign of destruction. The rank and file may also be principal perpetrators of genocide, provided they have the requisite intent.[119] The special intent required for genocide necessitates each individual perpetrator, whether leader or foot soldier, having the intention to destroy the group or part of it when committing any of the prohibited acts.[120] It differs from the 'normal' intent in criminal law, as exemplified in Article 30 of the ICC Statute. That Article provides that in relation to conduct, the individual must mean to engage in the conduct, and in relation to a consequence, the individual must mean to cause that consequence 'or is aware that it will occur in

113 See the discussion in Quigley, *The Genocide Convention*, 120–6.

114 *Niyitegeka* ICTR A. Ch. 9.7.2004 para. 53; *Musema* ICTR A. Ch. 16.11.2001 para. 165.

115 See, e.g. *Jelisić* ICTY A. Ch. 5.7.2001 para. 46; *Rutaganda* ICTR A. Ch. 26.5.2003 para. 524.

116 *Krštić* ICTY T. Ch. I 2.8.2001 para. 561; and see *Tadić* ICTY A. Ch. 15.7.1999 paras. 269, 270.

117 *Krštić* ICTY T. Ch. I 2.8.2001 para. 545; *Krštić* ICTY A. Ch. 19.4.2004 para. 45; *Kayishema and Ruzindana* ICTR A. Ch. 1.6.2001 para. 161; *Stakić* ICTY A. Ch. 22.3.2006 para. 45; *Jelisić* ICTY A. Ch. 5.7.2001 para. 49.

118 See criticism of the *Krštić* case on the ground that the Trial Chamber did not take any account of motive, in Southwick, 'Srebrenica as Genocide?'.

119 *Kayishema* ICTR A. Ch. 1.6.2001 para. 170.

120 See, e.g. *Akayesu* ICTR T. Ch. I 2.9.1998 para. 498; *Kayishema* ICTR T. Ch. II 21.5.1999 para. 91; *Musema* ICTR T. Ch. I 27.1.2000 para.164.

the ordinary course of events'. That is a less stringent requirement than what is now regarded as constituting the special intent for genocide and, subject to what is said below, the intent requirement of Article 30 will therefore not be applicable in the ICC to genocide cases (but will apply to some other forms of liability in relation to genocide).[121]

In time of conflict, where the intention is to defeat the opposing side, it may be difficult to assess whether mass killings are with a genocidal intent or with the intent of winning the war. The findings of the ICTY in the *Krstić* case and of the Commission of Inquiry on Darfur provide a useful illustration. The defence in *Krstić* argued that the purpose of the killings in Srebenica was not to destroy the group as such; it was to remove a military threat and this was evidenced by the fact that men of military age had been targeted. The Trial Chamber held, however, as affirmed by the Appeals Chamber, that the killings did constitute genocide. Its reasoning, which was upheld on appeal,[122] deserves setting out in detail:

> the Bosnian Serb forces could not have failed to know, by the time they decided to kill all the men, that this selective destruction of the group would have a lasting impact upon the entire group. Their death precluded any effective attempt by the Bosnian Muslims to recapture the territory. Furthermore, the Bosnian Serb forces had to be aware of the catastrophic impact that the disappearance of two or three generations of men would have on the survival of a traditionally patriarchal society . . . The Bosnian Serb forces knew by the time they decided to kill all of the military aged men, that the combination of those killings with the forcible transfer of the women, children and elderly would inevitably result in the physical disappearance of the Bosnian Muslim population at Srebrenica. Intent by the Bosnian Serb forces to target the Bosnian Muslims of Srebrenica as a group is further evidenced by their destroying homes of Bosnian Muslims in Srebrenica and Potocari and the principal mosque in Srebrenica soon after the attack. Finally, there is a strong indication of the intent to destroy the group as such in the concealment of the bodies in mass graves, which were later dug up, the bodies mutilated and reburied in other mass graves . . . By killing all the military aged men, the Bosnian Serb forces effectively destroyed the community of the Bosnian Muslims in Srebrenica and eliminated all likelihood that it could ever re-establish itself on that territory.[123]

On the other hand, General Krstić himself, the Appeals Chamber decided, did not have a genocidal intent:

> His own particular intent was directed to a forcible displacement. Some other members of the VRS Main Staff harboured the same intent to carry out forcible displacement, but viewed this displacement as a step in the accomplishment of their genocidal objective . . . [A]ll that the evidence can establish is that Krstić was aware of the intent to commit genocide on the part of some members of the VRS Main Staff, and with that knowledge, he did nothing to prevent the use of Drina Corps personnel and resources to facilitate those killings. This knowledge on his part alone cannot support an inference of genocidal intent.

---

121 See section 15.4.
122 *Krstić* ICTY A. Ch. 19.4.2004 paras. 24–38.
123 *Krstić* ICTY T. Ch. I 2.8.2001 paras. 595–7.

Genocide is one of the worst crimes known to humankind, and its gravity is reflected in the stringent requirement of specific intent. Convictions for genocide can be entered only where that intent has been unequivocally established. There was a demonstrable failure by the Trial Chamber to supply adequate proof that Radislav Krštić possessed the genocidal intent. Krštić, therefore, is not guilty of genocide as a principal perpetrator.[124]

In the same direction, the Darfur Commission decided that the policy of attacking, killing and forcibly displacing members of some tribes in Darfur did not show the special intent of genocide, but rather the intent 'to drive the victims from their homes, primarily for purposes of counter-insurgency warfare'.[125] The material elements of genocide – the killing and other prohibited acts, and the existence of a protected group – were present, but not the special intent and the Commission therefore found that the Government of Sudan had not pursued a policy of genocide.[126] The Commission's finding is not of course binding on the ICC. The Prosecutor made an application to the Pre-Trial Chamber in 2009 for an arrest warrant against President Al Bashir, alleging genocide among other crimes. The Chamber refused to grant a warrant in respect of genocide, while allowing it for war crimes and crimes against humanity. The counts of genocide were excluded because 'the existence of reasonable grounds to believe that the GoS acted with a *dolus specialis/* specific intent to destroy in whole or in part the Fur, Masalit and Zaghawa groups is not the only reasonable conclusion that can be drawn' from the facts described by the Prosecutor. That finding has been overturned on appeal.[127]

Proof of special intent

Direct evidence of genocidal intent may not be available. In the absence of such, the Tribunals have been prepared to deduce intent from circumstantial evidence including the actions and words of the perpetrator. In *Seromba*, for example, the defendant, a priest, had approved the decision to destroy a church to kill those inside it, had shown the bulldozer driver the weakest side of the church and directed him to destroy it. The Appeals Chamber found that Seromba 'knew that there were approximately 1,500 Tutsis in the church and that the destruction of the church would necessarily cause their death'. In the context of Seromba's previous actions and statements with regard to the Tutsis, the Chamber found that he had the requisite specific intent (and had directly participated in acts of genocide); the

---

124 *Krštić* ICTY A. Ch. 19.4.2004 paras. 133, 134. See also *Stakić* ICTY A. Ch. 22.3.2006 para. 47: no genocidal intent existed when the defendant's 'intention was only to displace the Bosnian Muslim population and not to destroy it'.
125 Report, UN Doc. S/2005/60 para. 518.
126 For a useful comment on the Commission's report see Schabas, 'Darfur and the "Odious Scourge"'; see also Kreß, 'The Crime of Genocide'.
127 *Al Bashir* arrest warrant case ICC PT Ch. I 4.3.2009 para. 205 and A.Ch. 3.2.2010 paras. 20–42.

Chamber replaced Seromba's conviction of aiding and abetting genocide with that of perpetration of genocide.[128]

Less reasonably, the ICTR has also stated that intent may be deduced from the behaviour of *others*; it may be deduced, the *Akayesu* Trial Chamber said, from:

> the general context of the perpetration of other culpable acts systematically directed against that same group, whether these acts were committed by the same offender or by others. Other factors, such as the scale of atrocities committed, their general nature, in a region or a country, or furthermore, the fact of deliberately and systematically targeting victims on account of their membership of a particular group, while excluding the members of other groups, can enable the Chamber to infer the genocidal intent of a particular act.[129]

This was somewhat tempered by the Appeals Chamber in *Stakić*, which noted that the Trial Chamber in that case 'considered whether the apparent intentions of others ... could provide indirect evidence of the Appellant's own intentions when he agreed with those others to undertake criminal plans'.[130] As the Appeals Chamber also noted, all the evidence (such as the type of attacks, discriminatory animus, the use of derogatory slurs, attacks on religious sites and 'targeting of ... leaders for death or slander')[131] must be taken together when determining intent since, looking at each piece individually rather than cumulatively, as the Trial Chamber did, 'obscured the proper inquiry'.[132] In spite of this error, however, the Appeals Chamber did not consider that the prosecution had shown that the Trial Chamber had such evidence before it that it was obliged to find genocidal intent.[133]

Intent; not knowledge

The interpretation of the special intent element given above has been criticized. It is said that simple foot soldiers will normally follow orders without necessarily having an intent to destroy a whole group[134] and that it would not be realistic to look for an intent from one individual to destroy the group through his own conduct. In relation to an accused who participated in a genocidal campaign, courts may therefore face the difficult choice between acquittal for lack of evidence of the special intent as normally defined and 'squeezing

---

128 *Seromba* ICTR A. Ch. 12.3.2008 paras. 177–82. The Chamber in this case also adopted a wide definition of 'perpetration'; see section 15.2.
129 *Akayesu* ICTR T. Ch. I 2.9.1998 para. 523.
130 *Stakić* ICTY A. Ch. 22.3.2006 para. 40.
131 Ibid., para. 53.
132 Ibid., para. 55.
133 Ibid., para. 56.
134 Harmen van der Wilt, 'Complicity in Genocide and International v. Domestic Jurisdiction' (2006) 4 *JICJ* 242.

ambiguous fact patterns into the specific intent paradigm'.[135] Courts will be tempted to ease the requirements of evidence by drawing wide deductions from the facts, as indicated above, thus establishing the special intent 'by the evidentiary backdoor'.[136] These difficulties have led commentators to propose alternative formulations of the intent necessary for genocide. In particular Greenawalt has suggested:

> In cases where a perpetrator is otherwise liable for a genocidal act, the requirement of genocidal intent should be satisfied if the perpetrator acted in furtherance of a campaign targeting members of a protected group and knew that the goal or manifest effect of the campaign was the destruction of the group in whole or in part.[137]

This so-called knowledge-based approach, as distinct from the conventional purpose-based approach, is closer to that described in Article 30 of the ICC Statute. Commentators argue that the current purpose-based approach goes beyond what is envisaged in the Genocide Convention.[138] They distinguish between the collective intent manifested in the overall genocidal plan or campaign, and the individual intent which, in their view, should involve only knowledge of the plan by the individual perpetrator together with foresight or recklessness as to the occurrence of the planned destruction.[139]

As indicated above[140] such an approach would be one way of reflecting the nature of genocide as a collective crime. It was illustrated in *Kayishema* where the Trial Chamber first found that there was a genocidal plan and went on to say:

> The killers had the common intent to exterminate the ethnic group and Kayishema was instrumental in the realisation of that intent.[141]

In *Krstić*, however, the Appeals Chamber, while noting that the intent to destroy must be discernible in the joint participation of the crime itself, held that individual participators must each have the necessary intent.[142] This insistence on the special intent for each individual perpetrator remains the standard required for the crime of genocide by the case law and may be seen as correctly reflecting the need to reserve genocide convictions only for those who have the highest degree of criminal intent. In practice, however, the approach of the Tribunals to modes of liability which do not require a special intent, such as aiding and abetting and joint criminal enterprise, has led to a blurring of the

---

135 Alexander Greenawalt, 'Rethinking Genocidal Intent: The Case for a Knowledge-Based Interpretation' (1999) 99 *Columbia Law Review* 2265 at 2281.
136 Claus Kreß, 'The Darfur Report and Genocidal Intent' (2005) 3 *JICJ* 565 at 572.
137 Greenawalt, 'Rethinking Genocidal Intent', 2288; and see Alicia Gil Gil, *Derecho penal internacional. Especial consideratión del delito de genocidio* (Madrid, 1999); Kreß, 'The Darfur Report', 577.
138 Otto Triffterer, 'Genocide, Its Particular Intent to Destroy in Whole or in Part the Group as Such' (2001) 14 *LJIL* 399; Jones, 'Whose Intent?', 478.
139 See Jones, 'Whose Intent?'; Kreß, 'The Darfur Report', 576–7.
140 See section 10.1.4.
141 *Kayishema* ICTR T. Ch. II 21.5.1999 paras. 533, 535.
142 *Krstić* ICTY A. Ch. 19.4.2004 para. 549.

lines.[143] General Krštić himself was acquitted of genocide, as lacking the specific intent to destroy, but he was convicted of aiding and abetting acts of genocide. Prosecutors who are not sure of being able to prove the special intent are likely to charge such lesser modes of liability rather than genocide as a principal perpetrator.

10.5   Other modes of participation

The 'other acts' of participation in genocide listed in Article III of the Convention – conspiracy, 'direct and public incitement', attempt and complicity – are expressly incorporated in the Statutes of the ad hoc Tribunals. The ICC, on the other hand, relies on the general principles of law in Part 3 of its Statute, which apply to all of the crimes within the jurisdiction of the Court, for all these forms of liability. The exception is incitement to genocide, for which specific provision was made in Article 25(3)(e) of the ICC Statute. For the ICC, the omission of conspiracy, due to hesitations of civil law countries, has left a gap, although the Statute provision on contribution to a common purpose may largely fill it. Further discussion of these other acts and of command responsibility in relation to genocide may be found in Chapter 15.

Further reading

Hirad Abtahi and Philippa Webb, *The Genocide Convention: The Travaux Préparatoires*, 2 vols. (The Hague, 2008).
Antonio Cassese, 'Genocide' in A. Cassese, P. Gaeta and J. R. W. D. Jones (eds.), *The Rome Statute of the International Criminal Court* (Oxford, 2002) 335.
Alexander Greenawalt, 'Rethinking Genocidal Intent: The Case for a Knowledge-Based Interpretation' (1999) 99 *Columbia Law Review* 2259.
Nina Jørgensen, 'The Definition of Genocide: Joining the Dots in the Light of Recent Practice' (2001) 1 *International Criminal Law Review* 285.
Claus Kreß, 'The Crime of Genocide under International Law' (2006) 6 *International Criminal Law Review* 461.
Laurence J. Le Blanc, 'The Intent to Destroy Groups in the Genocide Convention: The Proposed US Understanding' (1984) 78 *AJIL* 369.
Raphael Lemkin, *Axis Rule in Occupied Europe: Laws of Occupation, Analysis of Government, Proposals for Redress* (Washington, 1944).
Raphael Lemkin, 'Genocide as a Crime Under International Law' (1947) 41 *AJIL* 145.
Matthew Lippman, 'The Convention On The Prevention And Punishment Of The Crime Of Genocide: Fifty Years Later' (1998) 15 *Arizona Journal of International and Comparative Law* 415.

---

143 See section 15.4.

Guénaël Mettraux, *International Crimes and the ad Hoc Tribunals* (Oxford, 2005) ch. 6.

John Quigley, *The Genocide Convention: An International Law Analysis* (Aldershot, 2006).

William Schabas, *Genocide in International Law*, 2nd edn (Cambridge, 2009) (Schabas, *Genocide*).

Malcolm Shaw, 'Genocide in International Law' in Yoram Dinstein (ed.), *International Law at a Time of Perplexity* (Dordrecht, 1989) 797.

Dinah Shelton (ed.), *The Encyclopaedia of Genocide and Crimes Against Humanity* (Farmington Mills, 2005), vols. I–III.

11

Crimes Against Humanity

11.1 Introduction

11.1.1 Overview

Crimes against humanity are as old as humanity itself.[1] However, it is only in the last seven decades that the international legal prohibition on crimes against humanity has emerged, and it is only in the last fifteen years that the precise contours of the crime have been clarified.

Whereas genocide and war crimes have been codified in conventions with widely accepted definitions, crimes against humanity have appeared in a series of instruments with somewhat inconsistent definitions. The law of crimes against humanity was initially created to fill certain gaps in the law of war crimes, but many parameters were left undefined. The recent increase in the application of international criminal law has produced a fruitful interplay between international instruments, jurisprudence and commentaries, leading to a more coherent picture of the scope and definition of crimes against humanity today.

A crime against humanity involves the commission of certain inhumane acts, such as murder, torture, rape, sexual slavery, persecution and other inhumane acts, in a certain *context*: they must be part of a widespread or systematic attack directed against a civilian population. It is this context that elevates crimes that might otherwise fall exclusively under national jurisdiction to crimes of concern to the international community as a whole. An individual may be liable for crimes against humanity if he or she commits one or more inhumane acts within that broader context. It is not required that the individual be a ringleader or architect of the broader campaign.

11.1.2 Historical development

The most significant early reference to 'crimes against humanity' as a legal concept was a joint declaration by France, Great Britain and Russia in 1915. Responding to the massacre of

---

1 Jean Graven, 'Les Crimes Contre l'Humanité' (1950) 76 *Hague Recueil* 427 at 433.

Armenians by Turkey, the joint declaration denounced 'crimes against humanity and civilization' and warned of personal accountability.[2] After the First World War, an international war crimes commission recommended the creation of an international tribunal to try not only war crimes but also 'violations of the laws of humanity'. However, the US representative objected to the references to the laws of humanity on the grounds that these were not yet precise enough for criminal law, and the concept was not pursued at that time.[3]

In the wake of the events of the Second World War, the drafters of the Nuremberg Charter were confronted with the question of how to respond to the Holocaust and the massive crimes committed by the Nazi regime. The classic definition of war crimes did not include crimes committed by a government against its own citizens. The drafters therefore included 'crimes against humanity', defined in Article 6(c) as:

> murder, extermination, enslavement, deportation and other inhumane acts committed against any civilian population, before or during the war, or persecutions on political, racial or religious grounds in execution of or in connection with any crime within the jurisdiction of the Tribunal, whether or not in violation of the law of the country where perpetrated.

Three major features may be noted. First, the reference to 'any' civilian population meant that even crimes committed against a country's own population were included. This was a major advancement, given that at that time, prior to the advent of the human rights movement, international law generally regulated conduct *between* States and said little about a government's treatment of its own citizens. Second, the requirement of connection to war crimes or the crime of aggression meant in effect that crimes against humanity could occur only with some 'nexus' to armed conflict.[4] Third, the reference to 'population' was understood to create some requirement of scale, but the precise threshold was specified neither in the Charter nor in the Nuremberg Judgment.[5]

It remains controversial whether the Nuremberg Charter created new law, or whether it recognized an existing crime.[6] Among those concluding that it was a new crime, many argued that the principle of non-retroactivity had to give way to the overriding need for

---

2 For more information on these historical developments, see United Nations War Crimes Commission, *History of the United Nations War Crimes Commission and the Development of the Laws of War* (London, 1948); Roger Clark, 'Crimes Against Humanity' in G. Ginsburgs and V. N. Kudriavstsev (eds.), *The Nuremberg Trials and International Law* (Dordrecht/Boston/London, 1990); Egon Schwelb, 'Crimes Against Humanity' (1946) 23 *BYBIL* 178.

3 War Crimes Commission, *History*.

4 The text as originally adopted contained a semi-colon following the word 'war', which would give rise to the interpretation that the connection requirement applied only to persecution. This was promptly amended by the Berlin Protocol of 6 October 1945, which replaced the semi-colon with a comma, thereby supporting the interpretation that the connection requirement applied to all crimes against humanity. See Clark, 'Crimes', 190–2.

5 War Crimes Commission, *History*, 192–3.

6 See, e.g. M. Cherif Bassiouni, *Crimes Against Humanity in International Criminal Law*, 2nd edn (The Hague, 1999) 123–76.

accountability for large-scale murder and atrocities recognized as criminal by all nations.[7] Perhaps because of this uncertainty in the status of crimes against humanity, the Nuremberg Judgment tended to blur discussion of crimes against humanity and war crimes and provided very little guidance on the particular elements of the crime.[8]

The Tokyo Charter included a similar definition with some modifications.[9] The Allied Control Council, creating law for occupied Germany, adopted Law No. 10 with a similar definition, except that it added rape, imprisonment and torture to the list of inhuman acts, and did not require a connection to war crimes or aggression.

The concept of crimes against humanity was promptly endorsed by the UN General Assembly,[10] but in the decades that followed there was only a limited body of national cases[11] as well as a few treaties and instruments recognizing enforced disappearance and apartheid as crimes against humanity.[12] The International Law Commission also developed several drafts of an international code of crimes.

A major advance occurred when the Security Council created the ICTY and ICTR in response to mass crimes in the Former Yugoslavia and in Rwanda. The Statute of each Tribunal contained a list of acts based on the Allied Control Council Law No. 10 list. The ICTY Statute (Article 5) defined the contextual threshold as 'when committed in armed conflict, whether international or internal in character, and directed against any civilian population'. The Tribunal itself, referring to the Report to the Secretary-General and other authorities, interpreted this threshold as requiring a 'widespread or systematic attack'.[13] The ICTR Statute (Article 3) defined the context as 'when committed as part of a widespread or

---

7 Hans Kelsen, 'Will the Judgment in the Nuremberg Trial Constitute a Precedent in International Law?' (1947) 1 *International Law Quarterly* 153 esp. at 165; see also E. Schwelb, 'Crimes' Against Humanity' (1946) 23 *BYBIL* 178; and see treatment of the question in *R* v. *Finta* [1994] 1 SCR 701; *Polyukhovic* [1991] HCA 32; (1991) 172 CLR 501 at 661–2, HCA; *Eichmann* 36 ILR 277 at 283, SC.

8 Nuremberg Judgment, reproduced (1947) 41 *AJIL* 172 esp. at 248–9.

9 Tokyo Charter, Art. 5(c), included the same definition with the omission of racial and religious persecution, on the grounds that such crimes had not occurred in that theatre of conflict. The term 'any civilian population' was also deleted, on which basis the prosecution argued that all killing during an aggressive war was murder. Such arguments were rejected at Nuremberg and Tokyo, as they would undermine the distinction between the law governing *justification for* armed conflict and the law governing *conduct during* armed conflict. See Chapter 12.

10 UNGA Res. 95(I), UN Doc A/64/Add.1 (1946).

11 Including cases in France, the Netherlands, Israel, Canada and Australia, as discussed at section 11.2.2. See also Joseph Rikhof, 'Crimes Against Humanity, Customary International Law and the International Tribunals for Bosnia and Rwanda' (1995) 6 *National Journal of Constitutional Law* 231; Matthew Lippman, 'Crimes Against Humanity' (1997) 17 *Boston College Third World Law Journal* 171; Leila Sadat Wexler, 'The Interpretation of the Nuremberg Principles by the French Court of Cassation: From Touvier to Barbie and Back Again' (1994) 32 *Columbia Journal of Transnational Law* 289.

12 Examples include the Convention on the Non-Applicability of Statutory Limitations to War Crimes and Crimes Against Humanity 1968, the Apartheid Convention 1973, the Inter-American Convention on Enforced Disappearance 1994, and the UN Declaration on Enforced Disappearance 1992.

13 *Tadić* ICTY T. Ch. II 7.5.1997 para. 644; *Tadić* ICTY A. Ch. 15.7.1999 para. 248.

systematic attack against any civilian population on national, political, ethnic, racial or religious grounds'. Thus, the definitions are similar, except that the ICTY Statute requires armed conflict and the ICTR Statute requires discriminatory grounds.

The ICC Statute contains the same list of acts but adds forced transfer of population, sexual slavery, enforced prostitution, forced pregnancy, enforced sterilization, sexual violence, enforced disappearance and the crime of apartheid.[14] The ICC Statute rejects both the armed conflict requirement and the requirement of discriminatory grounds. The contextual threshold in Article 7 of the ICC Statute is 'when committed as part of a widespread or systematic attack directed against any civilian population'. The ICC Statute includes supplementary definitions in Article 7(2), some of which have been generally welcomed as helpful clarifications, whereas others have been controversial, as will be discussed further in this chapter.

Additional sources on the definition of crimes against humanity may now be found in national and international jurisprudence, the ICC Elements of Crimes, and instruments of other tribunals (Sierra Leone, Iraq). Each of these includes a comparable list of acts as well as the now-standard requirement of widespread or systematic attack directed against any civilian population.

11.1.3 Relationship to other crimes

War crimes and crimes against humanity can and do frequently overlap. For example, a mass killing of civilians during an armed conflict could constitute both types of crimes. There are, however, significant differences. First, unlike war crimes, crimes against humanity may occur even in the absence of armed conflict. Second, crimes against humanity require a context of widespread or systematic commission, whereas war crimes do not; a single isolated incident can constitute a war crime. Third, war crimes law was originally based on reciprocal promises between parties to conflict, and hence primarily focuses on protecting 'enemy' nationals or persons affiliated with the other party to the conflict. The law of crimes against humanity protects victims regardless of their nationality or affiliation. Fourth, war crimes law regulates conduct even on the battlefield and against military objectives,[15] whereas the law of crimes against humanity concerns actions directed primarily against civilian populations.[16]

Thus, the 'international dimension' of war crimes arises from the armed conflict, and the 'international dimension' of crimes against humanity arises from the attack on a civilian population. Cumulatively, the two bodies of law, working together, penalize atrocities committed during armed conflict or committed on a widespread or systematic basis.

---

14 See Art. 7 ICC Statute.
15 See Chapter 12.
16 See section 11.2.3.

Isolated crimes occurring in the absence of armed conflict continue to be governed by national criminal law. War crimes law is sometimes useful to interpret the law of crimes against humanity, so that the two bodies of law function coherently.[17]

Genocide was initially regarded as a particularly odious form of crime against humanity,[18] in that it was a crime against humanity committed with the intent to destroy, in whole or in part, a national, ethnical, racial or religious group as such. Over time, however, the definitions of the two crimes have evolved and pose differing requirements. Therefore it is no longer useful to describe genocide as a subset of crimes against humanity. Nonetheless, almost any conceivable example of genocide would also satisfy the requirements of crimes against humanity.[19]

11.2 Common elements (the contextual threshold)

As already noted, a crime against humanity entails the commission of a listed inhumane act, in a certain context: a widespread or systematic attack directed against a civilian population.

11.2.1 Aspects not required

No nexus to armed conflict

The Nuremberg and Tokyo Charters both required a connection to war crimes or to aggression, in effect requiring some nexus to armed conflict.[20] On the other hand, Allied Control Council Law No. 10 did not include such a requirement. Subsequent case law of military tribunals split over whether such a nexus must be read in to the definition, or was not required. For example, the *Flick* and *Weizsäcker* cases imported the requirement from the Nuremberg Charter, whereas the *Ohlendorf* and *Altstötter* decisions concluded that it was unnecessary.[21]

Subsequent international conventions[22] indicated that a nexus to armed conflict was not required. However, the ICTY Statute, adopted in 1993 by the Security Council, restricted crimes against humanity to those 'committed in armed conflict, whether international or internal in character' (Article 5). The Security Council promptly reversed this position in

---

17 See section 11.2.3 and see also Payam Akhavan, 'Reconciling Crimes Against Humanity with the Laws of War' 6 *JICJ* (2008) 21.

18 UN War Crimes Commission, *History*, 196–7.

19 See section 10.1.3.

20 See, e.g. Bassiouni, *Crimes*, 60–9.

21 *United States* v. *Ohlendorf et al.* 4 TWC 411; *United States* v. *Altstötter et al.* (the 'Justice Trial') VI LRTWC 1; *United States* v. *Flick* IX LRTWC 1; *United States* v. *Weizsäcker*, (the 'Ministries Trial') 14 TWC 1.

22 Including the Genocide Convention, the Convention on the Non-Applicability of Statutory Limitations to War Crimes and Crimes Against Humanity 1968, the Apartheid Convention 1973 and the Inter-American Convention on Enforced Disappearance 1994.

1994, when it adopted the ICTR Statute without such a requirement (Article 3). Finally, after extensive debates at the 1998 Rome Conference, agreement was reached on a definition of crimes against humanity rejecting any such requirement (Article 7).[23]

Today, it seems well settled that a nexus to armed conflict is not required. The majority of instruments and precedents oppose such a requirement. The limitation in the Nuremberg Charter is generally seen as a jurisdictional limitation only,[24] and the ICTY Statute definition appears to be the anomaly. Indeed, the jurisprudence of the ICTY itself concludes that the requirement is a deviation from customary law.[25] This view is also supported by national case law, international bodies of experts, and the writings of commentators.[26] No requirement of armed conflict has appeared in subsequent definitions of crimes against humanity.

No requirement of discriminatory animus

The ICTR Statute, Article 3, requires that crimes against humanity be committed on 'national, ethnic, racial or religious grounds'. Such a requirement was supported by a few cases in France, but did not appear in most precedents.[27]

Although an early ICTY trial decision reluctantly adopted the 'discriminatory grounds' requirement for the purposes of consistency, it explicitly noted that it was not supported in previous authorities, and the ICTY Appeals Chamber subsequently ruled that discrimination is not a requirement.[28] The ICC Statute, adopted in 1998, rejected a discrimination requirement. It appears reasonably well settled today that discriminatory animus is not a requirement, and it has not been included in subsequent instruments (Sierra Leone, Iraq). The ICTR Appeals Chamber has held that the restriction in the ICTR Statute relates only to the Tribunal, and also that the requirement relates to the attack as a whole; thus discriminatory intent of the perpetrator is not required.[29]

Thus, it would appear that discriminatory grounds are not required in customary law, except for the specific crime of persecution, discussed in section 11.3.9.

---

23 Darryl Robinson, 'Defining Crimes Against Humanity at the Rome Conference' (1999) 93 *AJIL* 43.

24 War Crimes Commission, *History*, 192–3; see also Clark, 'Crimes', 196; Diane Orentlicher, 'Settling Accounts: The Duty to Prosecute Human Rights Violations of a Prior Regime' (1991) 100 *Yale Law Journal* 2537 at 2588–90.

25 *Tadić* ICTY T. Ch. II 7.5.1997 para. 627; *Tadić* ICTY A. Ch. 15.7.1999 paras. 282–8.

26 *Eichmann* (1968) 36 ILR 5 at 49, DC; *Barbie* (1990) 78 ILR 124 at 136, Cour de Cassation; ILC Report 1996, UN Doc A/51/10 (1996) p. 96; Orentlicher, 'Settling Accounts' 2588–90; Theodor Meron, 'International Criminalization of Internal Atrocities' (1995) 89 *AJIL* 554; Beth van Schack, 'The Definition of Crimes Against Humanity: Resolving the Incoherence' (1999) 37 *Columbia Journal of Transnational Law* 787.

27 Some French cases, including *Barbie* (1990) 78 ILR 124, Cour de Cassation and *Touvier* 100 ILR 338, Cour d'Appel, suggested that a policy of discrimination is required.

28 *Tadić* ICTY T. Ch. II 7.5.1997 para. 652; *Tadić* ICTY A. Ch. 15.7.1999 paras. 282–305.

29 *Akayesu* ICTR A. Ch. I 1.6.2001 paras. 461–9.

11.2.2 Widespread or systematic attack

Widespread or systematic

The concept of 'widespread or systematic attack directed against any civilian population' emerged in the 1990s as the accepted formulation for the contextual threshold, thus contributing to clarity and consistency in this area of law. Nonetheless, some aspects of the definition of these terms remain to be resolved.

The widespread or systematic test is disjunctive;[30] a prosecutor need only satisfy one or the other threshold. As discussed below, however, in addition to 'widespread or systematic', there must also be an 'attack', and some authorities indicate that an 'attack directed against a civilian population' necessarily entails at least some modest degree of scale and organization.[31] This would mean that, while the rigorous thresholds of 'widespread' or 'systematic' are disjunctive, the 'attack' requires at least some minimal aspect of each.

The term 'widespread' has been defined in various ways, and generally connotes the 'large-scale nature of the attack and the number of victims'.[32] No numerical limit has been set; the issue must be decided on the facts. While 'widespread' typically refers to the cumulative effect of numerous inhumane acts, it could also be satisfied by a singular massive act of extraordinary magnitude.[33]

The term 'systematic' has also been defined in various ways. Early decisions set high thresholds: in *Akayesu*, it was defined as (1) thoroughly organized, (2) following a regular pattern, (3) on the basis of a common policy and (4) involving substantial public or private resources.[34] In *Blaškić*, it was defined as requiring (1) a plan or objective, (2) large-scale or continuous commission of linked crimes, (3) significant resources, and (4) implication of high-level authorities.[35] It is understandable to pose a significant threshold, especially given that non-widespread crimes should not lightly be labelled as a crime against humanity, but these definitions may set the bar too high.[36] Other cases refer more simply to 'pattern or methodical plan', 'organized nature of the acts' or 'organized pattern of conduct'.[37] The most recent cases seem to be settling on 'the organized nature of the acts of violence and the

---

30 The French version of the ICTR Statute referred to the requirements conjunctively (*généralisée et systématique*), but this was held to be a simple error: *Akayesu* ICTR T. Ch. I 2.9.1998 para. 579.

31 See Art. 7(2)(a) ICC Statute, and see *Haradinaj* ICTY T. Ch. I 3.4.2008 para. 122.

32 *Tadić* ICTY T. Ch. II 7.5.1997 para. 206, *Kunarac* ICTY T. Ch. II 22.2.2001 para. 428; *Nahimana*, ICTR A. Ch. 28.11.2007 para. 920; *Situation in Darfur* (*Al Bashir* arrest warrant case) ICC PTC-I, 4.3.2009 para. 81.

33 *Kordić* ICTY T. Ch. 26.2.2001 para. 176; *Blaškić* ICTY T. Ch. I 3.3.2000 para. 206; ILC Draft Code, pp. 94–5.

34 *Akayesu* ICTR T. Ch. I 2.9.1998 para. 580.

35 *Blaškić* ICTY T. Ch. 3.3.2000 para. 203.

36 See also Kai Ambos and Steffen Wirth, 'The Current Law of Crimes Against Humanity: An Analysis of UNTAET Regulation 15/2000' (2002) 13 *Criminal Law Forum* 1 at 18–20.

37 *Tadić* ICTY T Ch. II 7.5.1997 para. 648; *Kunarac* ICTY T. Ch. II 22.2.2001 para. 429; *Ntakirutimana* ICTR T. Ch. I 21.2.2003 para. 804.

improbability of their random occurrence'.[38] Consistent with the ordinary meaning of the term, it may be that the hallmark of 'systematic' is the high degree of organization, and that features such as patterns, continuous commission, use of resources, planning, and political objectives are important factors.

Attack

The term 'attack' is not used in the same sense as in the law of war crimes. An 'attack' need not involve the use of armed force, and can encompass mistreatment of the civilian population.[39] It refers to the broader course of conduct, involving prohibited acts, of which the acts of the accused form part.[40]

The ICC Statute and Tribunal jurisprudence indicate there must at least be multiple acts or multiple victims in order to warrant the label 'attack directed against a civilian population'.[41] These acts may be all of the same type or of different types, for example murder, rape and deportation.[42] This requirement of 'multiple acts' does not mean that 'widespread' is a requirement in all cases. Both terms measure scale, but 'multiple' is a low threshold and 'widespread' is a high threshold.

'Attack directed' and the controversy concerning the policy element

Crime, even on a 'widespread' basis – for example, a crime wave, or anarchy following a natural disaster – does not by itself constitute a crime against humanity. The random acts of individuals are not sufficient; some thread of connection between acts is needed so that they can accurately be described collectively as an *attack directed* against a civilian population. Some authorities seek to make this proposition explicit by indicating that there must be an underlying governmental or organizational policy that directs, instigates or encourages the crimes. Other authorities reject any requirement of plan or policy. It is therefore controversial whether the policy element is a necessary component of crimes against humanity.

---

38 See, e.g. *Nahimana*, ICTR A. Ch. 28.11.2007 para. 920; *Al Bashir* arrest warrant case ICC PTC-I, 4.4.2009 para. 81. As will be suggested below, improbability of random occurrence arguably should not only be an aspect of the disjunctive 'systematic' test, it should already be inherent in the concept of an 'attack'; otherwise widespread but random crime would constitute a crime against humanity.

39 ICC Elements, Crimes Against Humanity Introduction para. 3; *Kunarac* ICTY A. Ch. 12.6.2002 para. 86; *Akayesu* ICTR T. Ch. I 2.9.1998 para. 581.

40 Art. 7(2)(a) of the ICC Statute; *Tadić* ICTY T. Ch. 7.5.1997 para. 644; *Akayesu* ICTR T. Ch. I 2.9.1998 para. 205.

41 Art. 7(2)(a) of the ICC Statute; *Kunarac* ICTY T Ch. II 22.2.2001 para. 415; *Krnojelac* ICTY T. Ch. II 15.3.2002 para. 54.

42 *Kayishema* ICTR T. Ch. II 21.5.1999 para. 122.

The divide in the authorities

National jurisprudence on crimes against humanity following the Second World War frequently indicated that governmental policy is a requirement.[43] In the 1990s, the very same authorities that established the 'widespread or systematic' test also coupled this with a requirement of policy or of direction, instigation or encouragement by a State or organization.[44] Early Tribunal cases tended to follow this approach.[45]

At the Rome Conference, there was strong opposition to an unqualified disjunctive 'widespread or systematic' test, on the grounds that it would incorrectly include widespread but unconnected crimes, such as a crime wave. It was argued in response that the customary law concept of an 'attack' excluded random crimes. Agreement was reached on the disjunctive 'widespread or systematic' test, provided that the definition of 'attack' included this clarification. Article 7(2)(a) therefore defines 'attack' and includes the policy element, which was based on the authorities at the time. 'Policy' was understood as a low threshold which could be inferred from the manner in which the acts occur.[46] The definition followed more recent authorities indicating that the policy need not be that of a government, but could also be that of an organization.

Strong concerns were already growing about the policy element, both in Tribunal jurisprudence and the ICC negotiations. The major concerns were that it imposed a novel burden, that it would be difficult to prove, and that it contradicted the disjunctive test.[47] Tribunal cases began to split, with some supporting, then some declining to take a position,

---

43 Examples include: the Justice Trial VI LRTWC 1; *Brandt* (the 'Doctors' Trial') IV LRTWC 91 (US Military Tribunal); *Barbie* 78 ILR 124, Court of Cassation, 6 December 1983 (France); *Menten* 75 ILR 362–3 (Netherlands); *R* v. *Finta* [1994] 1 SCR 701 at 814 (Canada); *Polyukhovic* 172 CLR 501 (Australia); *Pinochet (No. 3)* [1999] 2 All ER 97 (United Kingdom) (Lord Hope, Lord Millet; but see *contra* Lord Browne-Wilkinson).

44 Commission of Experts (Former Yugoslavia), *Final Report of the Commission of Experts Established Pursuant to Security Council Resolution 780* (1992), UN Doc. S/1994/674 at 23; Commission of Experts (Rwanda), *Final Report of the Commission of Experts Established Pursuant to Security Council Resolution 935* (1994), UN Doc. G/SO 214 at para. 135; ILC, Report on the work of its forty-eighth session (ILC draft Code), UN Doc A/51/10 at 93 and 95–6; and see Final Report on Systematic Rape, Sexual Slavery and Slavery-like Practices During Armed Conflict, UN Doc. E/CN.4/Sub.2/1992/13 (1998).

45 *Tadić* ICTY T. Ch. II 7.5.1997 para. 644; *Bagilishema* ICTR T. Ch. I 7.6.2001 para. 78.

46 *Tadić* ICTY T. Ch. II 7.5.1997 paras. 653–5; Robinson, 'Defining Crimes Against Humanity', 50–1; Timothy H. L. McCormack, 'Crimes Against Humanity' in Dominic McGoldrick, Peter Rowe and Eric Donnelly (eds.), *The Permanent International Criminal Court: Legal and Policy Issues* (Oxford, 2004) 186–9.

47 See Margaret McAuliffe de Guzman, 'The Road From Rome: The Developing Law of Crimes Against Humanity' (2000) 22 *Human Rights Quarterly* 335; Phyllis Hwang, 'Defining Crimes Against Humanity in the Rome Statute of the International Criminal Court' (1998) 22 *Fordham International Law Journal* 457. In relation to the latter concern, it may be noted that, in the same manner that 'multiple' was a lower threshold than 'widespread', 'policy' was understood as a lower threshold than 'systematic'. Thus the disjunctive test is not necessarily contradicted.

and then some expressing doubt.[48] Finally, in *Kunarac*, the ICTY Appeals Chamber held, rather succinctly, that 'nothing in the Statute or in customary international law ... required proof of the existence of a plan or policy to commit these crimes'.[49] Whereas decisions on other issues of customary law have tended to involve an extensive review of precedents, the Appeals Chamber resolved this major controversy with reasoning appearing only in a single footnote, and declining to address (or acknowledge) most of the contrary authorities.

Thus, the main indicators of customary law are now divided. On one hand, the ICC Statute indicates that policy is required. The Statute was adopted by a great number of States purporting to codify existing customary law, and hence it is a strong indicator of customary law. A similar requirement appears in much national jurisprudence, and in legislation based on the ICC Statute definitions, which will also shape State practice. On the other hand, Tribunal jurisprudence, which also purports to reflect customary law, and which is also a strong indicator, rejects the policy element. Moreover, Article 10 of the ICC Statute indicates that its definitions 'shall not be interpreted as limiting or prejudicing in any way existing or developing rules of international law for purposes other than this Statute'.

Interpretation of the authorities

In order for international criminal law to become a clear and credible edifice of law, it is desirable to resolve such issues in a consistent and coherent manner. It may be possible to read the authorities in light of the agreed properties of crimes against humanity, so as to reduce the apparent inconsistency of international criminal law. Much of the controversy over the policy element may result from differing understandings of what the element *means*.[50] Some commentators reject the policy element, but agree that random criminality of individuals does not amount to an 'attack'.[51] To other commentators, that is precisely what the policy element means:[52] indeed, the necessary logical corollary of excluding isolated individual acts is to require some instigation or encouragement by something *other than* individuals, namely a State or organization. Some scholars argue that the

---

48 *Kupreškić* ICTY T. Ch. II 14.1.2000 paras. 554–5; *Kunarac* ICTY T. Ch. II 22.2.2001 para. 432; *Kordić* ICTY T. Ch. 26.2.2001 paras. 181–2; *Krnojelac* ICTY T. Ch. II 15.3.2002 para. 58.

49 *Kunarac* ICTY A. Ch. 12.6.2002 para. 98. The reasoning of the Chamber appears strikingly similar to that in Guénaël Mettraux, 'Crimes Against Humanity in the Jurisprudence of the International Criminal Tribunals for the Former Yugoslavia and Rwanda' (2002) 43 *Harvard International Law Journal* 237 at 270–82.

50 See, e.g. Mettraux, 'Crimes', 275, rejecting some authorities as precedent for a policy element because all they meant is to exclude isolated crimes. See also Hwang, 'Defining Crimes', 502–3, fearing that 'policy' might be misinterpreted as more stringent than 'systematic'.

51 Mettraux, 'Crimes', 254, 273 and 275.

52 See, e.g. Yoram Dinstein, 'Crimes Against Humanity After *Tadić*' (2000) 13 *LJIL* 273 at 389; Simon Chesterman, 'An Altogether Different Order: Defining the Elements of Crimes Against Humanity' (2000) *Duke Journal of Comparative & Inernationational Law* 283 at 316.

collective character reflected in the policy element is the fundamental essence of crimes against humanity; they are 'politics gone cancerous'.[53]

For those jurisdictions that apply a policy element, the policy element must be interpreted in accordance with the previous jurisprudence as a modest threshold that excludes random action.[54] First, as noted in jurisprudence, a 'policy' need not be formally adopted, nor expressly declared, nor even stated clearly and precisely.[55] Thus, it must be given an ordinary meaning such as 'a course of action adopted as advantageous or expedient',[56] rather than any connation of a formal and official strategy. Second, the element may be satisfied by inference from the manner in which the acts occur;[57] it is sufficient to show the improbability of random occurrence. Third, it is not required to show *action* by a State or organization; case law indicates that the requirement is satisfied by 'explicit or implicit approval or endorsement' or that the conduct is 'clearly encouraged' or 'clearly fits within' a general policy.[58] Thus, inaction designed to encourage the crimes would also suffice.[59]

For those jurisdictions that have rejected the term 'policy', it is essential not to lose sight of the principle that unconnected random acts cannot constitute an 'attack'.[60] Tribunal jurisprudence may partially achieve this result in its requirement to examine whether a 'population' was 'targeted' or was a 'primary object', all of which imply some direction from some source.[61] Recent Tribunal jurisprudence mentions the element of 'improbability of random occurrence', but only as part of the definition of 'systematic'.[62] The element of improbability of random occurrence must, however, be inherent in all 'attacks'; otherwise crime waves become included.[63] In the absence of such clarification, a literal and mechanistic application of Tribunal definitions would encompass widespread but random crimes

---

53 See, e.g. David Luban, 'A Theory of Crimes Against Humanity' (2004) 29 *Yale Law Journal* 85 at 90; see also Ambos and Wirth, 'The Current Law', 26–34; William Schabas, 'State Policy as an Element of International Crimes' (2008) 98 *Journal of Criminal Law & Criminology* 953.

54 McAuliffe de Guzman, 'Road From Rome', 374.

55 *Tadić* ICTY T. Ch. II 7.5.1997 para. 653; *Blaškić* ICTY T. Ch. I 3.3.2000 paras. 204–5.

56 *Oxford English Dictionary*, 2nd edn (Oxford, 1989), vol. XII, 27 provides this as the 'chief living sense'.

57 *Tadić* ICTY T. Ch. II 7.5.1997 para. 653; *Blaškić* ICTY T. Ch. I 3.3.2000 para. 204.

58 *Kupreškić* ICTY T. Ch. II 14.1.2000 paras. 554–5.

59 Commission of Experts (former Yugoslavia), *Final Report*, 23. The ICC Elements, footnote 6, reach this result but in a particularly tortured manner, twice emphasizing a need for action, before acknowledging, in a restrictive manner, the possibility of passive encouragement. The ICC Elements also add that inaction alone is not enough to infer a policy; this cannot be interpreted as repudiating the preceding sentence. Rather, it acknowledges that there may be other reasons for inaction (lack of knowledge of crimes, lack of ability), and hence policy should not be inferred without considering alternative explanations.

60 *Kunarac* ICTY T. Ch. II 22.2.2001 para. 422.

61 See, e.g. *Kunarac* ICTY A. Ch. 12.6.2002 paras. 90–2. In *Haradinaj* ICTY T. Ch. I 3.4.2008, a Chamber found that a 'relative small number of incidents', lacking scale or frequency, and without significant evidence of structure, organization or targeting, did not amount to an attack directed against a civilian population.

62 *Kunarac* ICTY T. Ch. II 22.2.2001 para. 429; *Krnojelac* ICTY T. Ch. II 15.3.2002 para. 57.

63 Ambos and Wirth, 'The Current Law', 30–1.

of individuals, which reflects either a failure to describe the crime accurately, or else a loss of the basic conceptual foundation for crimes against humanity.[64]

11.2.3 'Any civilian population'

The word '*any*' highlights the central innovation and *raison d'être* of crimes against humanity. The law of crimes against humanity not only protects enemy nationals, it also covers, for example, crimes by a State against its own subjects.[65] The nationality or affiliation of the victim is irrelevant.

The term '*civilian*' connotes crimes directed against non-combatants rather than combatants, while the term '*population*' indicates that 'a larger body of victims is visualized', and that 'single or isolated acts against individuals' fall outside the scope of the concept.[66] The reference to population implies 'crimes of a collective nature' but does not require that the entire population be targeted.[67]

Antonio Cassese has put forward a significant argument that in customary international law the crime is not restricted to 'civilian' populations, relying on certain Second World War cases that identify crimes against military personnel as crimes against humanity.[68] It is certainly important to scrutinize limitations to determine whether they are arbitrary or rational, and whether they are indeed supported by customary law. However, the major precedents – including the seminal Nuremberg Charter as well as the ICTY, ICTR, ICC and SCSL Statutes and the great majority of case law – not only refer to 'civilian population' but regard it as a defining feature of crimes against humanity. Moreover, current international law clearly *permits* widespread and systematic attacks directed against military targets, in accordance with humanitarian law, even if it involves killing and injury.

There remains an open and important question as to the extent to which the law of crimes against humanity may protect military personnel outside combat situations. Is it possible to address persecution of military personnel without rejecting the 'time-honoured'[69] hallmark requirement of 'civilian population'? Many strands of the jurisprudence would suggest a positive answer. First, the population need only be '*predominantly* civilian in nature'; the 'presence of certain non-civilians in their midst does not change the character of the population'.[70] Second, several early Trial Chamber decisions interpreted the term 'civilian' to include all those no longer taking part in hostilities at the time the crimes were committed.

---

64 See, e.g. David Luban, 'A Theory of Crimes Against Humanity' (2004) 29 *Yale Law Journal* 85; Ambos and Wirth, 'The Current Law', 30–1; Bassiouni, *Crimes*, 245–7; Geoffrey Robertson, *Crimes Against Humanity: The Struggle for Global Justice* (London, 1999) 311 and 314.

65 War Crimes Commission, *History*, 193.

66 *Ibid.*

67 *Tadić* ICTY T. Ch. II 7.5.1997 para. 644; *Kunarac* ICTY T. Ch. II 22.2.2001 para. 425.

68 A. Cassese, 'Crimes Against Humanity' in Cassese, *Commentary*, 375.

69 Dinstein, 'Crimes Against Humanity After Tadić' (2000) 13 *LJIL* 273 at 381–2.

70 *Tadić* ICTY T. Ch. II 7.5.1997 para. 638; see also *Kordić* ICTY T. Ch. 26.2.2001 para. 180.

This includes former combatants who had been decommissioned, as well as combatants placed *hors de combat* ('out of the fight') by being wounded or detained.[71]

Examining these cases, it is possible to form a hypothesis that the 'civilian' reference serves a rational purpose, which is simply to *exclude military actions against legitimate military objectives in accordance with international humanitarian law*. This would provide a coherent underlying rationale for the requirement: given that the laws of war are a special regime in which killing, wounding and destruction can be allowed, attacks on military targets are more appropriately assessed under that law.[72]

Several doctrinal developments are consistent with this theory. In addition to the above mentioned developments to protect all non-combatants, the Tribunals' approach to determining an 'attack against a civilian population' distinguishes lawful attacks on military targets from other attacks. Tribunal jurisprudence requires that the civilian population be the 'primary object' of the attack,[73] thereby excluding attacks that appear to be directed primarily at military targets, with the result that such activities are assessed under the more appropriate *lex specialis* of the laws of war. Moreover, Tribunal jurisprudence expressly considers compliance with the laws of war as an indicator of whether there was an attack against a civilian population.[74] Thus, lawful military action would be excluded, whereas actions targeting civilians would be covered.[75] Patterns of indiscriminate or clearly excessive attacks would indicate that the attacks were in reality directed against a civilian population.

However, recent ICTY cases complicate this picture. In *Martić*, the Appeals Chamber clarified its interpretation that 'civilian' has the same meaning as in Article 50 of Additional Protocol I (AP I), and hence does not include persons *hors de combat* (such as prisoners of war).[76] The Chamber affirmed that persons *hors de combat* could be victims of crimes against humanity, but only where the broader attack was directed at civilians in the narrower sense.[77] The unfortunate effect of this interpretation is that large-scale extermination or torture directed entirely against prisoners of war would not constitute crimes against humanity.

---

71 *Akayesu* ICTR T. Ch. 2.9.1998 para. 582; *Tadić* ICTY T. Ch. II 7.5.1997 para. 643; *Kordić* ICTY T. Ch. 26.2.2001 para. 180. Note that a current member of an armed force or organization remains a combatant even in moments when he or she is not armed or in combat, and thus may be lawfully attacked by an enemy party to the conflict. See, e.g. *Blaškić* ICTY A. Ch. 29.7.2004 para. 114.

72 See, e.g. Ambos and Wirth, 'The Current Law', 22–6, and on a related theme, see Akhavan, 'Reconciling'.

73 *Kunarac* ICTY A. Ch. 12.6.2002 para. 91.

74 *Ibid*. See also Mettraux, 'Crimes', 245–50.

75 See also *Fofana*, SCSL A. Ch. 28.5.2008 paras. 300–8; note that the emphasis is on the intentional *targeting* of civilians. This means that legitimate attacks on military targets are excluded, but intentionally indiscriminate or disproportionate attacks may be included: Chile Eboe-Osuji, 'Crimes Against Humanity: Directing Attacks Against a Civilian Population' (2008) 2 *African Journal Legal Studies* 118.

76 *Martić*, ICTY A. Ch. 8.10.2008 paras. 296–302.

77 *Ibid*., paras. 301–14. See also *Mrkšić* ICTY A. Ch. 5.5.2009 paras. 29–33.

Reliance on AP I was not the only available interpretation; 'civilian' could very plausibly have been interpreted as 'non-combatant', as was the prior trend in the authorities.[78] First, 'attack against a civilian population' is already given a different meaning in crimes against humanity than it receives in war crimes, since it does not require actual force but can refer to a series of non-violent acts amounting to inhumane acts.[79] Second, the definition of 'civilian' in AP I arises in a detailed legislative regime that already grants protection to POWs, whereas the 'civilian' reference in crimes against humanity arose decades earlier, and likely harked to a simpler bifurcation between those taking part in hostilities and those who are not. Third, the Appeals Chamber relied on the principle of distinction,[80] but for the purposes of principle of distinction, a deliberate targeting of prisoners of war is also prohibited. As the language is open to more than one interpretation, it may be hoped that other jurisdictions will consider the function of the 'civilian' reference, the consequences of different interpretations, and consistency with past cases, before following the same path.[81]

11.2.4 The link between the accused and the attack

The rigorous requirements relating to the attack must be distinguished from the requirements relating to the accused. With respect to the individual accused, what is required is that the accused committed a prohibited act, that the act objectively falls within the broader attack, and that the accused was aware of this broader context.[82]

Only the attack, not the acts of the individual accused, must be widespread or systematic.[83] A single act by the accused may constitute a crime against humanity if it forms part of the attack.[84] The act of the accused may also in itself *constitute* the attack, if it is of great magnitude, for example, the use of a biological weapon against a civilian population.[85]

---

78 *Akayesu* ICTR T. Ch. 2.9.1998 para. 582; *Tadić* ICTY T. Ch. II 7.5.1997 para. 643; *Kordić* ICTY T. Ch. 26.2.2001 para. 180. See also Ambos and Wirth, 'The Current Law', 22–6.

79 See, e.g. *Nahimana* ICTR A. Ch. 28.11.2007 para. 918.

80 *Martić* ICTY A. Ch. 8.10.2008 note 806.

81 The position of the ICC is as yet unknown. In its decision on the *Al Bashir* arrest warrant case, a Pre-Trial chamber noted that killing of combatants is excluded from crimes against humanity: *Al Bashir* arrest warrant case ICC PTC-I, 4.3.2009. This proposition, which is clearly correct, is compatible with both the approach of the ICTY and the approach suggested above.

82 *Tadić* ICTY A. Ch. 15.7.1999 para. 271. To determine if an act is 'part of' an attack, one may consider its characterstics, aims, nature or consequence: *Semanza* ICTR T. Ch. 15.5.2003 para. 326. A crime may be committed several months after, or several kilometres away from, the main attack, and still, if sufficiently connected, be part of the attack: *Krnojelac* ICTY T. Ch. II 15.3.2002 para. 127.

83 *Kunarac* ICTY A. Ch. 12.6.2002 para. 96; *Blaškić* ICTY A. Ch. 29.7.2004 para. 101.

84 *Kunarac* ICTY A. Ch. 12.6.2002 para. 96; *Blaškić* ICTY A. Ch. 29.7.2004 para. 101.

85 *Blaškić* ICTY T. Ch. I 3.3.2000 para. 206.

The accused need not be an architect of the attack, need not be involved in the formation of any policy, and need not be affiliated with any State or organization nor even share in the ideological goals of the attack.[86]

The acts of the accused need not be of the same type as other acts committed during the attack. For example, if a group launches a killing campaign, and a person commits sexual violence in the execution of that campaign, the person is guilty of the crime against humanity of sexual violence. It is irrelevant whether the State or organization encouraged sexual violence, since the necessary contextual element is already satisfied because of the attack based on killing.[87]

11.2.5 Mental element

In addition to the requisite mental elements for the particular offences, the accused must also be aware of the 'broader context in which his actions occur', namely the attack directed against a civilian population.[88] It is the context of a widespread or systematic attack against a civilian population that makes an act a crime against humanity, and hence knowledge of this context is necessary in order to make one culpable for a crime against humanity as opposed to an ordinary crime or a war crime.[89]

Tribunal cases indicate that awareness, wilful blindness, or knowingly taking the risk that one's act is part of an attack, will suffice.[90] It is less clear if the ICC will take a similar approach, because of the different wording of Article 30 of the ICC Statute (mental element), but the ICC Elements of Crimes suggest that the mental element required for 'contextual elements' is lower.[91] It is not required that the perpetrator had detailed knowledge of the attack or its characteristics.[92] In most conceivable circumstances, the existence of a widespread or systematic attack would be notorious and knowledge could not credibly be denied. Thus, knowledge may be inferred from the relevant facts and circumstances.[93]

---

86 See the denunciation cases at section 11.2.5.

87 Art. 7(2)(a) of the ICC Statute.

88 *Tadić* ICTY A. Ch. 15.7.1999 para. 248; *Kupreškić* ICTY T. Ch. II 14.1.2000 para. 134.

89 *Tadić* ICTY T. Ch. II 7.5.1997 para. 656; *Kupreškić* ICTY T. Ch. II 14.1.2000 para. 138; *Semanza* ICTR T. Ch. 15.5.2003 para. 332; and see also *R* v. *Finta* [1994] 1 SCR 701 at 819: 'the mental element of a crime against humanity must involve an awareness of the facts or circumstances which would bring the acts within the definition of a crime against humanity'.

90 *Tadić* ICTY T. Ch. II 7.5.1997 para. 657; *Kunarac* ICTY A. Ch. 12.6.2002 para. 102; *Blaškić* ICTY T. Ch. I 3.3.2000 para. 251; *Krnojelac* ICTY T. Ch. II 15.3.2002 para. 59; see also *R* v. *Finta* [1994] 1 SCR 701 at 819.

91 See, e.g. Maria Kelt and Herman von Hebel, 'General Principles of Criminal Law and the Elements of Crimes' in Lee, *Elements and Rules*, 34–5.

92 ICC Elements, Crimes Against Humanity Introduction, para. 2, states that it is not required that the perpetrator 'had knowledge of all characteristics of the attack or the precise details of the plan or policy of the State or organization'; see also *Blaškić* ICTY T. Ch. I 3.3.2000 para. 251; *Kunarac* ICTY A. Ch. 12.6.2002 para. 102.

93 ICC Elements, General Introduction, para. 3.

The perpetrator need not share in the purpose or goals of the overall attack.[94] The mental requirement relates to knowledge of the context, not motive.[95] After the Second World War, several cases dealt with instances where individuals had denounced others to the Nazi regime, for personal opportunistic reasons. Such persons were held liable for crimes against humanity, because even though they acted out of personal motives, their actions were objectively part of the persecutory system, and they acted with knowledge of the system and the likely consequences.[96]

11.3 Prohibited acts

11.3.1 The list of prohibited acts

The definition of crime against humanity includes certain prohibited acts when committed in the necessary context (widespread or systematic attack). The list of prohibited acts has gradually evolved over the decades.

The first list, appearing in the Nuremberg Charter, comprised murder, extermination, enslavement, deportation, persecution and other inhumane acts. Shortly thereafter, Control Council Law No. 10 added rape, imprisonment and torture. The ICTY and ICTR Statutes follow the same expanded list.

In 1998, the ICC Statute added sexual slavery, enforced prostitution, forced pregnancy, other sexual violence, enforced disappearance and apartheid. At first glance, this may seem to be an expansion on existing customary law. However, the list of prohibited acts in the previous precedents ended with the residual clause 'or other inhumane acts'. If sexual slavery and these other acts are inhumane acts, the Article 7 simply codified explicitly what was already contained implicitly in the residual clause. The view that these acts were already inhumane acts is supported by the following considerations. First, each of these acts was already recognized as an inhumane act or crime against humanity in previous international instruments. Second, the agreed objective of States at the Rome Conference was to reflect, not to expand, existing customary law, and thus Article 7 reflects a simultaneous statement of *opinio juris* by 120 States. Third, their status has been supported in subsequent jurisprudence and instruments.[97]

For each of the following crimes, where no specific observations are made about the mental element, the normal mental element applies: the relevant conduct must be committed

---

94 *Kunarac* ICTY A. Ch. II 22.2.2001 para. 103.
95 *Tadić* ICTY A. Ch. 15.7.1999 paras. 271–2, overturning a suggestion to the contrary by the Trial Chamber.
96 See cases discussed in *Tadić* ICTY A. Ch. 15.7.1999 paras. 255–69.
97 See, e.g. *Kvočka* ICTY T. Ch. I 2.11.2001 para. 208, and *Kupreškić* ICTY T. Ch. II 14.1.2000 para. 566, recognizing enforced disappearance, sexual violence, forced prostitution, and forced transfer of populations. Article 2 of the SCSL Statute recognizes the sexual violence offences, and the Iraq Special Tribunal Statute includes each of the ICC Statute crimes other than apartheid and enforced sterilization.

intentionally and with knowledge of the relevant circumstances.[98] With respect to legal requirements (for example 'unlawful') or other normative requirements (for example 'inhumane', 'severe'), it is not required that the perpetrator personally considered the conduct inhumane or severe; it is sufficient that the perpetrator was aware of the underlying facts.[99]

11.3.2 Murder

The crime of murder is well known to all legal systems and is an archetypal form of crime against humanity. There is general conformity between Tribunal jurisprudence and the ICC Elements that murder refers to unlawfully and intentionally causing the death of a human being.[100]

Tribunal jurisprudence, consistent with jurisprudence in many national systems, indicates that the mental element is satisfied if the perpetrator intends to kill, or intends to inflict grievous bodily harm likely to cause death and is reckless as to whether death ensues.[101] It is unclear whether the ICC will be able to adopt the same approach, in light of the different wording of Article 30 of the ICC Statute (mental element), although it may be possible to interpret the statute consistently with previous authorities.[102]

The conduct element of murder (crime against humanity) and wilful killing (war crime) is the same; the difference is the contextual element. The distinction between murder and extermination is discussed in section 11.3.3.

11.3.3 Extermination

The issue of how to define extermination is inextricably linked to the question of how to distinguish it from the crime against humanity of murder. Both involve killing, but 'extermination' connotes killing on a large scale. Is extermination distinct from murder on the basis that the perpetrator must carry out killing on a large scale, or is there another way to distinguish between the two? Rather than requiring that the accused personally carried out or directed large-scale killing, both Tribunal jurisprudence and the ICC Elements indicate that extermination involves killing by the accused *within a context* of mass killing.[103]

---

98 See, e.g. Art. 30 of the ICC Statute.

99 See, e.g. Art. 32(2) of the ICC Statute; ICC Elements, General Introduction, para. 4.

100 ICC Elements, Art. 7(1)(a); *Akayesu* ICTR T. Ch. I 2.9.1998 para. 589; *Jelisić* ICTY T. Ch. 14.12.1999 para. 35; *Kupreškić* ICTY T. Ch. II 14.1.2000 paras. 560–1.

101 See, e.g. *Čelebići* ICTY T. Ch. II 16.11.1998 para. 439; *Akayesu* ICTR T. Ch. I 2.9.1998 para. 589; *Kordić* ICTY T. Ch. 26.2.2001 para. 236.

102 C. K. Hall, 'Article 7' in Triffterer, *Observers' Notes*, 188–9.

103 ICC Elements, Art. 7(1)(b); *Kayishema* ICTR T. Ch. 21.5.1999 para. 147.

Thus, the first and major difference between murder and extermination is that extermination requires a surrounding circumstance of mass killing.[104] The perpetrator need not carry out the mass killing personally; he only needs to know of the context of mass killing.

A second difference is that extermination expressly includes indirect means of causing death. This distinction was recognized as early as the 1948 UN War Crimes Commission, which included 'implication in the policy of extermination without any direct connection with actual acts of murder'.[105] Tribunal jurisprudence also includes indirect means of causing death,[106] as does the ICC Statute. Article 7(2)(b) of the ICC Statute expressly includes 'inflicting conditions of life . . . calculated to bring about the destruction of part of a population', a phrase adapted from the Genocide Convention.[107]

A third issue is whether the crime of extermination requires that the accused personally be responsible for a substantial number of deaths. While some cases have held that 'responsibility for one or for a limited number of killings is insufficient',[108] the ICTY Appeals Chamber indicates that a single killing is sufficient provided that the accused is aware of the necessary context of mass killing.[109] The ICC Elements of Crimes also follow the latter interpretation.[110]

There are also significant overlaps between extermination and the crime of genocide. Indeed, the concepts of killing or inflicting conditions of life calculated to bring about the destruction of part of a population are common to both extermination and genocide. The major difference between the two crimes is the requisite special intent for the crime of genocide (the intent to destroy a group as such). Moreover, genocide can only be committed where there is an intent to target one of four types of groups (national, ethnical, racial or religious).[111]

11.3.4 Enslavement

The accepted definition of enslavement is 'exercising the powers attaching to the right of ownership' over one or more persons. This definition is drawn from the 1926 Slavery Convention and the 1956 Supplementary Slavery Convention, and has been adopted in the ICC Statute (Article 7(2)(c)) and in Tribunal jurisprudence.[112]

Enslavement may take various forms. It includes the traditional concept of 'chattel slavery', that is to say the treatment of persons as chattels, as in the slave trade. It also includes other

---

104 Whereas a crime against humanity of murder can occur on the basis of a single killing, committed in the context of a widespread or systematic attack based on other crimes.
105 UN War Crimes Commission, *History*, 194.
106 *Rutaganda* ICTR T. Ch. 6.12.1999 para. 81; *Kayishema* ICTR T. Ch. 21.5.1999 para. 146.
107 Art. 2(c) of the Genocide Convention 1948.
108 *Vasiljević* ICTY T. Ch. I 29.11.2002 para. 228.
109 *Stakić* ICTY A. Ch. 22.3.2006 paras. 260–1; see also *Kayishema* ICTR T. Ch. 21.5.1999 para. 147.
110 ICC Elements, Art. 7(1)(b), element 1.
111 See Chapter 10.
112 1926 Slavery Convention, Art. 1; 1956 Supplementary Slavery Convention; *Kunarac* ICTY T. Ch. II 22.2.2001 para. 539; *Krnojelac* ICTY T. Ch. II 15.3.2002 para. 353.

practices, which are not limited to these 'transactional' or 'chattel slavery' examples, but which also involve exercising powers attaching to the right of ownership.[113]

First, with respect to 'chattel slavery', the Slavery Convention definition of 'slave trade' refers to the capture, acquisition, sale, exchange, transport or disposal of persons with intent to reduce them to slavery or to sell or exchange them.[114] The ICC Elements of Crimes also list, as examples, such transactions as 'purchasing, selling, lending or bartering'.

Second, the ICC Statute explicitly mentions the example of trafficking in persons, in particular, women and children (Article 7(2)(c)).[115]

Third, as noted in the ICC Elements of Crimes, enslavement also includes 'reducing a person to a servile status' as defined in the 1956 Supplementary Slavery Convention. This includes practices of debt bondage, serfdom, forced marriage and child exploitation, as defined in that Convention.[116]

Fourth, forced labour can also constitute enslavement.[117] In determining whether labour is 'forced' as prohibited under customary law, regard may be had to instruments such as the 1949 Geneva Convention III (Articles 49–57), the ICCPR (Article 8(3)(c)) and the 1930 Forced or Compulsory Labour Convention. In general, these instruments prohibit forced or compulsory labour, with various recognized exceptions, such as military and national service, normal civic obligations, hard labour as lawful punishment for crime, and certain forms of labour for prisoners of war.[118] In *Krnojelac*, the Appeals Chamber held that severely overcrowded conditions, deplorable sanitation, insufficient food, locked doors, frequent beatings, psychological abuse, and brutal living conditions rendered it impossible for detainees to consent to work and that their labour was indeed forced.[119]

Fifth, other activities may also amount to enslavement. The ICTY Appeals Chamber in the *Kunarac* decision indicated that relevant factors include 'control of someone's movement, control of physical environment, psychological control, measures taken to prevent or deter escape, force, threat of force or coercion, duration, assertion of exclusivity, subjection to cruel treatment and abuse, control of sexuality and forced labour'.[120] A specific form of enslavement, namely sexual slavery, is discussed in section 11.3.8.

In *Kunarac*,[121] the victims were kept in an abandoned house for approximately six months, where they were raped and sexually assaulted whenever the soldiers returned to the house. The Chamber found that they were constantly and continuously raped, forced to

---

113 Valerie Oosterveld, 'Sexual Slavery and the International Criminal Court: Advancing International Criminal Law' (2003) 25 *Michigan Journal of International Law* 605 at 643.
114 1926 Slavery Convention, Art. 1(2).
115 See also Tom Obokata, 'Trafficking of Human Beings as a Crime Against Humanity' (2005) 54 *ICLQ* 445.
116 ICC Elements, footnote 11; 1956 Supplementary Slavery Convention, Art. 1.
117 ICC Elements, footnote 11.
118 See, e.g. Geneva Convention III 1949, Arts. 49–57; Art. 8(3) of the ICCPR.
119 *Krnojelac* ICTY T. Ch. II 15.3.2002 paras. 193–5.
120 *Kunarac* ICTY A. Ch. 12.6.2002 para. 119.
121 *Kunarac* ICTY T. Ch. II 22.2.2001 paras. 732–42.

do household chores and obey all demands. Although at some point they were given the keys to the house, they had nowhere to go or to hide and hence:

> no realistic option whatsoever to flee the house ... or to escape their assailants. They were subjected to other mistreatments, such as Kunarac inviting a soldier into the house so that he could rape [the victim] for 100 Deutschmark if he so wished ... The two women were treated as ... personal property ...

The two men responsible were found guilty of enslavement.

11.3.5 Deportation or forcible transfer

Deportation and forcible transfer of population are frequently-seen examples of crimes against humanity, particularly in contexts of 'ethnic cleansing'. The terms refer to forced displacement of persons by expulsion or other coercive acts from the area in which they are lawfully present, without grounds permitted under international law.[122]

'Deportation' is generally regarded as referring to displacement across a border, whereas 'forcible transfer' is generally regarded as referring to internal displacement.[123] ICTY jurisprudence follows this distinction. In the *Stakić* case the Appeals Chamber confirmed that 'deportation' must be across a border, usually a *de jure* border, or in some circumstances a *de facto* border, but in any event crossing of 'constantly changing frontlines' would not suffice.[124]

Deportation or transfer must be *forced* in order to be a crime against humanity.[125] This does not require actual physical force, but may also include the threat of force or coercion, psychological oppression, or other means of rendering displacement involuntary.[126] Thus, if a group flees of its own genuine volition, for example to escape a conflict zone, that would not be forced displacement.[127] On the other hand, if a group flees to escape deliberate violence and persecution, they would not be exercising a genuine choice.[128]

The forced displacement must also be *unlawful* under international law. Most or all States carry out legitimate acts of deportation on a frequent basis. Deportation of aliens not

---

122 Art. 7(2)(d) ICC Statute; *Stakić* ICTY A. Ch. 22.3.2006 para. 278.

123 ILC draft Code, 1996, p. 100.

124 *Stakić* ICTY A. Ch. 22.3.2006 para. 300. The Appeals Chamber therefore allowed the appeal from an anomalous Trial Chamber decision which had held that 'deportation' could be internal. The Appeals Chamber did not clarify the circumstances in which crossing a *de facto* border would suffice. For other cases see *Krstić* ICTY T. Ch. I 2.8.2001 para. 521; *Krnojelac* ICTY T. Ch. II 15.3.2002 para. 474; *Kupreškić* ICTY T. Ch. II 14.1.2000 para. 566.

125 ICC Statute, Art. 7(2)(d); *Krštić* ICTY T. Ch. I 2.8.2001 para. 528; *Krnojelac* ICTY T. Ch. II 15.3.2002 para. 475.

126 ICC Elements, Art. 7(1)(d); *Stakić* ICTY A. Ch. 22.3.2006 para. 281; *Krnojelac* ICTY T. Ch. II 15.3.2002 para. 475; *Kunarac* ICTY T. Ch. II 22.2.2001 para. 129.

127 Jean Pictet, *Commentary on Geneva Convention IV* (ICRC, Geneva, 1960) 279; Akhavan, 'Reconciling', 34–5.

128 *Krštić* ICTY T. Ch. I 2.8.2001 para. 530.

lawfully present in the territory is an established practice of States.[129] International humanitarian law, for example, allows transfers when the security of the population or imperative
military reasons so demand; such transfers must meet certain stringent conditions and
humanitarian safeguards.[130]

11.3.6 Imprisonment

Although imprisonment did not appear in the Nuremberg or Tokyo Charters, it was listed in
Allied Control Council Law No. 10 and subsequent definitions. The term 'imprisonment' is
broadly construed, capturing not only detention in prison-like conditions but other serious
forms of confinement and detention. Out of an abundance of caution, the ICC Statute added
'or other severe deprivation of physical liberty' to ensure that a narrow definition was not
applied, and that situations such as house arrest were included.[131] It remains to be determined precisely how restrictive or how long a confinement must be in order to constitute
imprisonment or severe deprivation of physical liberty.

Imprisonment must be arbitrary to constitute a crime against humanity. After all, there are
many contexts in which persons may be lawfully detained, including following lawful
arrest, conviction following trial, lawful deportation or extradition procedures, quarantine,
and, during armed conflict, assigned residence, internment on security grounds and internment of prisoners of war.[132] Tribunal jurisprudence refers to imprisonment without due
process of law.[133] Article 7(1)(e) of the ICC Statute refers to deprivation 'in violation of
fundamental rules of international law'.

The requirement that the imprisonment be 'arbitrary' (and similarly, in violation of
'fundamental rules') does not mean that a minor procedural defect would expose the authorities involved to international prosecution; significant failings are required. For this reason, the
ICC Elements refer to the 'gravity of the conduct' being such as to violate fundamental rules of
international law.[134] Tribunal jurisprudence states that deprivation will be arbitrary and
unlawful 'if no legal basis can be called upon to justify the initial deprivation of liberty'.[135]
Even where the initial detention was justified, imprisonment will become arbitrary if the legal
basis ceases to apply and the person remains imprisoned.[136]

---

129 The question whether an individual was 'lawfully' present would probably be assessed under international
as well as national law. For example, a government could not circumvent the definition of this crime through an
arbitrary legislative act declaring members of a group not lawfully present.
130 Art. 49 of the Geneva Convention IV 1949; Art. 87 of the AP I.
131 Hall, 'Article 7', 202.
132 Arts. 5, 42 and 43 of the Geneva Convention IV 1949; Arts. 21–32 of the Geneva Convention III 1949.
133 *Kordić* ICTY T. Ch. 26.2.2001 para. 302; *Krnojelac* ICTY T. Ch. II 15.3.2002 para. 113.
134 ICC Elements, Art. 7(1)(e), element 2.
135 *Krnojelac* ICTY T. Ch. II 15.3.2002 para. 114.
136 For example, if the procedural safeguards of Art. 43 of the Geneva Convention IV 1949 for internment of
civilians are disregarded: *Kordić* ICTY T. Ch. 26.2.2001 para. 286; *Čelebići* ICTY T. Ch. II 16.11.1998 para. 579.

While caution must always be used when relying on human rights standards in a criminal law context,[137] the three categories suggested by the UN Working Group on Arbitrary Detention seem to capture the forms of this crime admirably: (1) absence of any legal basis for the deprivation of liberty, (2) deprivation of liberty resulting from exercise of specified rights and freedoms (that is to say political prisoners), and (3) 'when the total or partial non-observance of the international human rights norms relating to the right to a fair trial . . . is of such gravity as to give the deprivation of imprisonment an arbitrary character'.[138]

The material elements of arbitrary imprisonment are comparable to the material elements for unlawful confinement (war crime); the difference between the two is the contextual element (armed conflict or widespread or systematic attack).

11.3.7 Torture

The crime of torture appeared in Allied Control Council Law No. 10 and subsequent definitions of crimes against humanity. The prohibition against torture is well established in numerous conventions and instruments, including the Universal Declaration of Human Rights, the International Covenant on Civil and Political Rights, the European Convention on Human Rights, the American Convention on Human Rights, the African Charter of Human and Peoples' Rights, the Convention Against Torture, the Inter-American Convention to Prevent and Punish Torture, and the Geneva Conventions and the Additional Protocols thereto. It is well recognized as a norm of customary law and amounts to *jus cogens*.[139]

Much of the definition in the 1984 Convention Against Torture (CAT) is also accepted as the core definition for torture as a crime against humanity or war crime: the intentional infliction of severe pain or suffering, whether physical or mental, upon a person.[140] There are, however, several open questions.

The first open question is that of official capacity. The CAT definition requires that the pain or suffering be 'inflicted by or at the instigation of or with the consent or acquiescence of a public official or other person acting in an official capacity'.[141] Early Tribunal cases adopted the requirement of official instigation or acquiescence.[142] However, in *Kunarac*, the Trial Chamber departed from this approach, noting structural differences between international criminal law and human rights law.[143] Human rights law focuses on the State because

---

137 See section 1.4.1.

138 Report of the UN Working Group on Arbitrary Detention, UN Doc. E/CN.4/1998/44 para. 8.

139 *Čelebići* ICTY T. Ch. II 16.11.1998 para. 454. For discussion of the crime of torture under the Convention Against Torture, see section 14.3.

140 Art. 1 of the CAT.

141 *Ibid.*

142 *Akayesu* ICTR T. Ch. I 2.9.1998 para. 594; *Furundžija* ICTY T. Ch. II 10.12.1998 para. 162.

143 *Kunarac* ICTY T. Ch. II 22.2.2001 paras. 387–91.

it regulates State treatment of human beings. International criminal law holds individuals accountable for crimes, and applies to everyone whether or not affiliated with a State. Similarly, the ICC Statute and the ICC Elements do not require a linkage between the act of torture and a public official.[144] Thus, torture by rebel groups, paramilitaries and others is included.

The second is the 'purpose' element. The CAT definition requires a specific purpose, such as 'obtaining from him or a third person information or a confession, punishing him for an act he or a third person has committed or is suspected of having committed, or intimidating or coercing him or a third person, or for any reason based on discrimination of any kind'.[145] It is not yet settled whether the customary law crime against humanity of torture requires the act to be committed with a specific purpose.

Many authorities, including the CAT and related international instruments, as well as Tribunal jurisprudence, regard the purpose element as a defining feature of torture.[146] On this approach, the presence of prohibited purpose distinguishes torture from inhuman treatment.[147] The purpose need not be the sole or predominant purpose, but must be part of the motivation.[148] The list is illustrative and some cases suggest the addition of 'humiliation' as a prohibited purpose.[149]

In other authorities, such as jurisprudence of the European Court of Human Rights, the difference between torture and lesser violations, such as inhuman treatment, is *severity*: the special stigma of torture requires infliction of 'very serious and cruel suffering'.[150] Article 7 of the ICC Statute followed this approach, and did not include a purpose element.

Further adding to the uncertainty, the ICC Elements of Crimes adopted the 'purpose' requirement with respect to the war crime of torture but not with respect to the crime against humanity of torture.[151] Thus, it would seem that the divergent treatment in the Elements must either be given a principled explanation or else regarded as an anomaly.

---

144 Art. 7(2)(e) of the ICC Statute; but see Art. 7(2)(a) which appears to require some sort of linkage between a State or organization and the attack as a whole, albeit not the particular crimes of the accused.

145 Art. 7(2)(e) of the ICC Statute.

146 *Akayesu* ICTR T. Ch. I 2.9.1998 paras. 593–5; *Čelebići* ICTY T. Ch. II 16.11.1998 para. 459; *Furundžija* ICTY T. Ch. II 10.12.1998 para. 161; *Krnojelac* ICTY T. Ch. II 15.3.2002 para. 180.

147 *Čelebići* ICTY T. Ch. II 16.11.1998 para. 469; *Krštić* ICTY T. Ch. I 2.8.2001 para. 516.

148 *Kunarac* ICTY A. Ch. 12.06.2002 para. 155; *Kvočka* ICTY T. Ch. I 2.11.2001 para. 153; *Čelebići* ICTY T. Ch. II 16.11.1998 para. 470.

149 *Furundžija* ICTY T. Ch. II 10.12.1998 para. 162, but see *Krnojelac* ICTY T. Ch. II 15.3.2002 para. 186, doubting the customary law status of this extension.

150 *Ireland* v. *United Kingdom*, 18 January 1978, Series A 25, (1978) ECHR 1 para. 167; *Selmouni* v. *France*, 28 July 1999, ECHR Appl. No. 25803/94 (1999) 29 EHRR 403 para. 105; *Aydin* v. *Turkey* (1998) 25 EHRR 251 para. 82.

151 Delegates followed Tribunal precedents with respect to war crimes, but they did not do so for crimes against humanity, out of fidelity to the decision taken at the Rome Conference not to require such an element for the crime against humanity of torture. Footnote 14 of the ICC Elements therefore specifies that no purpose element is required.

Third, the ICC Statute, while dropping any requirements of purpose or link to an official, adds a requirement that the victim be in the 'custody or control' of the perpetrator. The requirement should not be onerous to prove since, as a practical matter, torture entails such custody or control. Various explanations have been offered for this addition, including establishing a link of power or control given the deletion of a link to a public official, or excluding the use of force against military objectives during armed conflict.[152]

It should also be noted that most definitions of torture, including the CAT and the ICC Statute, expressly exclude 'pain or suffering arising only from, inherent in or incidental to, lawful sanctions'. 'Lawful' in this context would appear to mean lawful in accordance with national law, provided, however, that the national law is not in violation of international law.[153]

Tribunal jurisprudence and regional human rights bodies have recognized that rape can constitute a form of torture.[154] Rape causes severe pain and suffering, both physical and psychological. In *Furundžija*, the accused was convicted of torture for acts during an interrogation, including sexual threats, rapes and forced nudity, inflicted on the victim for purposes of intimidation, humiliation and extracting confession.[155]

11.3.8 Rape and other forms of sexual violence

The crime of rape appeared in Allied Control Council Law No. 10 and subsequent instruments, including the ICTY and ICTR Statutes. The 1996 draft Code of Crimes prepared by the International Law Commission proposed that the definition be updated by adding enforced prostitution and other forms of sexual abuse.[156] The ICC Statute took up the idea of modernizing the definition, by including 'rape, sexual slavery, forced pregnancy, enforced sterilization, or any other form of sexual violence of comparable gravity' (Article 7(1)(g)).[157] The inclusion was seen not as an expansion but rather as an acknowledgement that these acts, which have persisted in history, including during the violence in the Former

---

152 Darryl Robinson, 'Elements of Crimes Against Humanity' in Lee, *Elements and Rules* 90; Hall, 'Article 7', 253.

153 Report of the UN Special Rapporteur on Torture, UN Doc. E/CN.4/1988/17, para. 42.

154 *Akayesu* ICTR T. Ch. I 2.9.1998 para. 597; *Kunarac* ICTY A. Ch. 12.6.2002 para. 150; *Semanza* ICTR T. Ch. 15.5.2003 para. 482; *Čelebići* ICTY T. Ch. II 16.11.1998 para. 495; *Fernando and Racquel Meiji* v. *Peru*, Annual Report of the Inter-American Commission on Human Rights, Report No. 5/96, Case No. 10 970, 1 March 1996; *Aydin* v. *Turkey* (1998) 25 EHRR 251, para. 86.

155 *Furundžija* ICTY T. Ch. II 10.12.1998 para. 267.

156 Report of the International Law Commission on the work of its forty-eighth session, 1996, UN GAOR 51st Sess, Supp. No. 10 (A/51/10) at 102–3.

157 See, e.g. Vienna Declaration, World Conference on Human Rights, UN Doc. A/CONF.157/24 (1993) Part I, para. 28 and Part II, para. 38: Beijing Declaration and Platform for Action, Fourth World Conference on Women, 15 September 1995, A/CONF.177/20 (1995) and A/CONF.177/20/Add.1 (1995), Chapter II, paras. 114–15*bis*.

Yugoslavia and Rwanda, are inhumane acts falling within the definition of crimes against humanity.[158]

The same definitions apply both in crimes against humanity and in war crimes, so the relevant issues for both war crimes and crimes against humanity will be discussed here.

Rape

The crime of rape has two components. The first is a physical invasion of a sexual nature. The second component is, according to some authorities, the presence of coercive circumstances, or according to other authorities, the absence of consent.

The first component, the conduct element, was described in *Akayesu*, the first case defining the crime against humanity of rape. The ICTR Trial Chamber held that rape 'is a form of aggression and ... cannot be captured in a mechanical description of objects and body parts', which led it to the definition 'a physical invasion of a sexual nature, committed on a person in circumstances which are coercive'.[159] A slight rift emerged in Tribunal jurisprudence, however, when a subsequent decision of an ICTY Trial Chamber (*Furundžija*) concluded that greater clarity was needed, and defined the physical element (rather mechanically) as: the sexual penetration, however slight, of (*a*) the vagina or anus of the victim by the penis of the perpetrator or any other object, or (*b*) the mouth of the victim by the penis of the perpetrator.[160] This definition was subsequently endorsed by the Appeals Chamber in *Kunarac*.[161]

The ICC Elements of Crimes falls in between the two definitions:

> The perpetrator invaded the body of a person by conduct resulting in penetration, however slight, of any part of the body of the victim or of the perpetrator with a sexual organ, or of the anal or genital opening of the victim with any object or any other part of the body.[162]

This definition is closer to the later Tribunal jurisprudence, in that it is comparably specific, yet it is slightly broader and gender neutral.

The second component is less settled; some sources focus on coercive circumstances and some focus on absence of consent. Early Tribunal jurisprudence required coercive circumstances, that is to say coercion or force or threat of force against the victim or a third person.[163] This approach was followed in the ICC Elements of Crimes, albeit significantly expanded:

> The invasion was committed by force, or by threat of force or coercion, such as that caused by fear of violence, duress, detention, psychological oppression or abuse of power,

---

158 For a more detailed overview of the advances and difficulties, see Kelly Askin, 'Prosecuting Wartime Rape and Other Gender-Related Crimes under International Law: Extraordinary Advances, Enduring Obstacles' (2003) 21 *Berkeley Journal International Law* 288.

159 *Akayesu* ICTR T. Ch. I 2.9.1998 paras. 597–8.

160 *Furundžija* ICTY T. Ch. II 10.12.1998 para. 185.

161 *Kunarac* ICTY T. Ch. II 22.2.2001 para. 127.

162 ICC Elements, Art. 7(1)(g)–1, element 1.

163 *Akayesu* ICTR T. Ch. I 2.9.1998 para. 598; *Furundžija* ICTY T. Ch. II 10.12.1998 para. 185.

against such person or another person, or by taking advantage of a coercive environment, or the invasion was committed against a person incapable of giving genuine consent.[164]

This definition was an advance on previous definitions focused on coercive circumstances, as it more thoroughly encompasses the possible circumstances.

More recently, Tribunal jurisprudence has moved away from cataloguing coercive circumstances and has adopted a simpler element, known in most or all legal systems: the lack of consent of the victim. In *Kunarac*, the Trial Chamber analysed various legal systems and concluded that the correct element was lack of consent of the victim. This was the true common denominator and reflected the basic principle of penalizing violations of sexual autonomy.[165] The Appeals Chamber confirmed this approach, and held that force or threat of force may be relevant, in providing clear evidence of non-consent, but force is not an element per se of rape.[166]

Strong arguments can be made that the new line of cases better reflects national legal systems and indeed the underlying principle of sexual autonomy,[167] and that the newer interpretation is also more compatible with the ICC Rules of Procedure and Evidence.[168] If so, this may be an instance where, although the Elements should be given due weight as a consensus instrument, the ICC judges may find that the Elements do not reflect the correct reading of the Statute.

In a plausible counter-argument, Catharine MacKinnon argues that the 'coercion' approach is preferable to the 'nonconsent' approach.[169] She argues that in circumstances of 'mass sexual coercion', an inquiry into consent is decontextualized and unreal.[170] War crimes and crimes against humanity of sexual violence are almost invariably committed in coercive circumstances where consent or reasonable belief in consent is simply not a credible possibility. Where such circumstances are shown, inquiry into consent should not be necessary.[171]

---

164 ICC Elements, Art. 7(1)(g)–1, element 2.

165 *Kunarac* ICTY T. Ch. II 22.2.2001 paras. 440–60.

166 *Kunarac* ICTY A. Ch. 12.6.2002 para. 129.

167 Kristen Boon, 'Rape and Forced Pregnancy under the ICC Statute: Human Dignity, Autonomy and Consent' (2001) 32 *Columbia Human Rights Law Review* 625.

168 The ICC RPE contain rules on evidence of consent in cases of sexual violence, and yet the current elements do not refer to consent as a significant factor.

169 Catharine MacKinnon, 'Defining Rape Internationally: A Comment on *Akayesu*' (2005/6) 44 *Columbia Journal International Law* 940.

170 *Ibid.*, at 950.

171 See section 16.9.1, text of footnote 129, which discusses consent as a defence and concludes that 'In most cases relating to international crimes it is difficult to think of situations in which consent would be a genuine issue.' Suggestions have at times been made to go further, to legally exclude entirely the relevance of consent in any context of armed conflict. If such an approach were adopted, and consent were deemed irrelevant, then even consensual relations between longstanding sexual partners would become 'war crimes'. One might argue that 'prosecutorial discretion' is the solution to such problems, but the fact of liability in such circumstances indicates that the suggested rule is too broad. It therefore seems more appropriate to restrict consent defences to those circumstances where there is no air of reality to such a claim.

On either approach, it is desirable to adopt procedural and evidentiary rules to limit how the issue of consent may be raised, in order to prevent harassment of witnesses and spurious lines of questioning; see section 17.10.

Sexual slavery

Sexual slavery is a particularly serious form of enslavement.[172] The first element of sexual slavery is therefore identical to enslavement.[173] The additional requirement is that the perpetrator caused the victim to engage in one or more acts of a sexual nature.[174] Particularly egregious examples include the 'comfort stations' maintained by the Japanese in the Second World War and the 'rape camps' in the Former Yugoslavia.[175] The examples of enslavement from the Tribunal cases discussed above,[176] would clearly qualify as sexual slavery.

Sexual slavery includes many acts that in the past would have been categorized as 'enforced prostitution'.[177] The latter concept is, however, problematic in that it obscures the violence involved, it is rooted in chastity and family honour, and it degrades the victim; thus 'sexual slavery' is generally preferred as properly reflecting the nature and seriousness of the crime.[178] Sexual slavery may also overlap with 'forced marriage', discussed in section 11.3.12.

Enforced prostitution

Enforced prostitution is prohibited in the Geneva Convention IV 1949, but as an example of an attack upon a woman's honour; in Additional Protocol I it is prohibited as an outrage upon personal dignity.[179] The ICC Statute lists it as a crime against humanity and war crime in its own right, removing the outdated linkage to 'honour'.

The ICC Elements of Crimes refer to (1) causing one or more persons to engage in one or more acts of a sexual nature, (2) by force or by threat of force (or under the coercive

---

172 Special Rapporteur, *Final Report on Systematic Rape, Sexual Slavery and Slavery-Like Practices During Armed Conflict*, UN Doc. E/CN.4/Sub.2/1998/13, 22 June 1998, para. 30.
173 ICC Elements, Art. 7(1)(g)–2, element 1.
174 ICC Elements, Art. 7(1)(g)–2, element 2.
175 *Final Report on Systematic Rape*, para. 30.
176 See section 11.3.4.
177 *Final Report on Systematic Rape*, para. 31.
178 Oosterveld, 'Sexual Slavery'; Kelly D. Askin, 'Women and International Humanitarian Law' in Kelly D. Askin and Dorean M. Koening (eds.), *Women and International Human Rights Law* (1999), vol. I, 48; Rhonda Copelon, 'Surfacing Gender: Re-Engraving Crimes Against Women in Humanitarian Law' (1994) 5 *Hastings Law Journal* 243.
179 Art. 27 of GC IV 1949: 'Women shall be especially protected against any attack on their honour, in particular against rape, enforced prostitution, or any form of indecent assault.'

circumstances as noted above in the discussion of rape).[180] In addition, pursuant to a US proposal, it is required that (3) 'the perpetrator or another person obtained or expected to obtain pecuniary or other advantage in exchange for or in connection with the acts of a sexual nature'.[181] There were considerable misgivings among some delegations concerning the paucity of precedent for this element. In the end, however, it was adopted, in order to create some distinction from sexual slavery and in light of the ordinary meaning of the term 'prostitution'. In the absence of such anticipated advantage, the relevant conduct could still be prosecuted as sexual slavery or sexual violence.

Forced pregnancy

The inclusion of 'forced pregnancy' was the subject of intense debate in the negotiation of the ICC Statute.[182] It had previously been recognized in instruments such as the Vienna Declaration and Programme of Action and the Beijing Declaration and Platform for Action.[183] The inclusion recognized a particular harm inflicted on women, including during the conflicts in the Former Yugoslavia, where captors indicated that they tried to impregnate women and hold them until it was too late to obtain an abortion.[184]

However, some delegations were concerned that the concept would be used to criminalize national systems that did not provide a right to abortion, which would conflict with their religious convictions and their constitutional provisions. It was agreed that discussion of the right to abortion will continue in a human rights context[185] but was not part of the crimes against humanity debate. Agreement was reached on the following definition: (1) unlawful confinement (2) of a woman forcibly made pregnant (3) with the intent of affecting the ethnic composition of a population or carrying out other grave violations of international law.[186] The reference to grave violations of international law includes, for example, biological experiments. For greater clarity, Article 7(2)(f) states that '[t]his definition shall not in any way be interpreted as affecting national laws relating to pregnancy'.

Enforced sterilization

The ICC Statute is the first treaty expressly recognizing enforced sterilization as a crime against humanity and war crime. The conduct has, however, been prosecuted before, in the

---

180 ICC Elements, Art. 7(1)(g)–3, element 1.
181 ICC Elements, Art. 7(1)(g)–3, element 2.
182 Cate Steains, 'Gender Issues' in Lee, *The Making of the Rome Statute*, 363–9.
183 Vienna Declaration, World Conference on Human Rights, UN Doc. A/CONF.157/24 (1993) Part II, para. 38; Beijing Declaration and Platform for Action, Fourth World Conference on Women, 15 September 1995, A/CONF.177/20 (1995) and A/CONF.177/20/Add.1 (1995) Chapter II, para. 115.
184 Commission of Experts (Former Yugoslavia), *Report*, paras. 248–50.
185 On the difference between human rights and crimes against humanity, see section 1.4.1.
186 Art. 7(2)(f) of the ICC Statute.

context of unlawful medical experiments such as were seen in the Second World War.[187] The ICC Elements of Crimes is the first instrument to define this particular crime. The elements are that (1) the perpetrator deprived one or more persons of biological reproductive capacity and (2) that the conduct was neither justified by the medical or hospital treatment of the persons concerned nor carried out with their genuine consent.[188] This definition is not restricted to medical operations, but could also include an intentional use of chemicals for this effect.[189] The concept of 'genuine consent' excludes consent obtained by deception.[190]

Enforced sterilization can also satisfy the conduct requirements of genocide (Article 6(e) of the ICC Statute) and can amount to genocide where genocidal intent is present.

Other sexual violence

The ICC Statute also includes 'other sexual violence of comparable gravity'. The ICC Elements document elaborates the following elements: (1) the perpetrator committed an act of a sexual nature against one or more persons *or* caused one or more persons to engage in an act of a sexual nature, (2) by force or threat of force or coercion[191] and (3) the gravity of the conduct was comparable to the other offences in Article 7(1)(g).[192]

The first element covers both acts against the victim as well as forcing the victim to perform sexual acts. It is not restricted to cases of assault, and therefore can include examples of forced nudity.[193] The second element, coercive circumstances, is discussed above in the context of rape. The third element creates a threshold of seriousness, so that the acts warrant being described as crimes against humanity.[194]

The UN Special Rapporteur on systematic rape, sexual slavery and slavery-like practices observed that sexual violence includes:

> any violence, physical or psychological, carried out by sexual means or targeting sexuality. Sexual violence covers both physical and psychological attacks directed at a person's sexual characteristics, such as forcing a person to strip naked in public, mutilating a person's genitals or slicing off a woman's breasts. Sexual violence also characterizes situations in which two victims are forced to perform sexual acts on one another or to harm one another in a sexual manner.[195]

---

187 *Brandt* (The Doctors' Trial) IV LRTWC 91.
188 ICC Elements, Art. 7(1)(g)–5, elements 1 and 2.
189 Eve La Haye, 'Sexual Violence' in Lee, *Elements and Rules*, 195. The ICC Elements exclude 'birth control measures with a non-permanent effect'.
190 ICC Elements, footnote 55.
191 With the same list of coercive circumstances discussed above in the context of rape.
192 ICC Elements, Art. 7(1)(g)–6, elements 1 and 2.
193 Eve La Haye, 'Sexual Violence', 198; *Final Report on Systematic Rape*, paras. 21–2.
194 In the context of war crimes, the requirement refers to gravity comparable to a grave breach (or Common Article 3 in the case of internal armed conflicts) of the Geneva Conventions.
195 *Final Report on Systematic Rape*, paras. 21–2.

11.3.9 Persecution

Persecution involves the intentional and severe deprivation of fundamental rights, against an identifiable group or collectivity on prohibited discriminatory grounds. In addition, the ICC Statute requires that persecution be committed in connection with another crime or at least one inhumane act.

Severe deprivation of fundamental rights

Until recently, the crime of persecution was not well defined, and the need for adequate precision was highlighted both in Tribunal jurisprudence and in the drafting of the ICC Statute.[196] The test developed in Tribunal jurisprudence requires (1) a gross or blatant denial, (2) on discriminatory grounds, (3) of a fundamental right, laid down in international customary or treaty law, (4) reaching the same level of gravity as other crimes against humanity.[197] Although there is some different terminology, this is generally compatible with the ICC definition, which refers to intentional and severe deprivation of fundamental rights, on specified discriminatory grounds.

The emergent definition, with the notions of fundamental rights, severe deprivation, and discriminatory grounds, provides the needed precision for criminal law. Nonetheless, the test necessarily remains somewhat open with respect to the particular *acts* that may constitute persecution, as it is impossible to anticipate all future examples. Tribunal jurisprudence has noted that:

> neither international treaty law nor case law provides a comprehensive list of illegal acts encompassed by the charge of persecution, and persecution as such is not known in the world's major criminal justice systems. [Thus] the crime of persecution needs careful and sensitive development in light of the principle of *nullum crimen sine lege*.[198]

Gravity or severity

Tribunal jurisprudence indicates that persecution requires a gravity comparable to other crimes against humanity;[199] in the ICC definition this requirement may be subsumed in the requirements of 'severe' deprivation and the requirement of 'connection' to other acts.

---

196 *Kupreškić* ICTY T. Ch. II 14.1.2000 para. 618: 'However, this Trial Chamber holds the view that in order for persecution to amount to a crime against humanity it is not enough to define a core assortment of acts and to leave peripheral acts in a state of uncertainty. There must be clearly defined limits on the types of acts which qualify as persecution. Although the realm of human rights is dynamic and expansive, not every denial of a human right may constitute a crime against humanity.'
197 See, e.g. *Kupreškić* ICTY T. Ch. II 14.1.2000 para. 621.
198 *Kordić* ICTY T. Ch. 26.2.2001 para. 694.
199 See, e.g. *Kupreškić* ICTY T. Ch. II 14.1.2000 paras. 619 and 621; *Kvočka* ICTY T. Ch. I 2.11.2001 para. 185; *Ruggiu* ICTR T. Ch. 1.6.2000 para. 21.

Discriminatory grounds

The fundamental feature of persecution is that it be committed on discriminatory grounds. The ICTY and ICTR Statutes refer to persecution on political, racial or religious grounds.[200] The ICC Statute contains an updated and more inclusive list of prohibited grounds: political, racial, national, ethnic, cultural, religious, or gender.[201] In addition, the ICC list is cautiously open-ended in referring to 'other grounds that are universally recognized as impermissible under international law'.[202] The standard of 'universal' means that the threshold to read in additional grounds is a high one, but a high standard was considered necessary in order to satisfy the principle of legality.

Connection to other acts

The ICC Statute requires that persecution be committed in connection with (*a*) any crime within the jurisdiction of the Court or (*b*) any other act listed in Article 7(1). This require-ment was included because of the concern of several States about the possible elasticity of the concept of persecution. The fear was that any practices of discrimination, more suitably addressed by human rights bodies, would be labelled as 'persecution', giving rise to international prosecutions. The connection requirement was inserted to ensure at least a context of more recognized forms of criminality. Although the original proposal was to require a link to another crime within the jurisdiction of the Court, this was widened to include a link to any other act referred to in Article 7(1).

The customary law status of this requirement is open to doubt. Such a requirement is not applied in Tribunal jurisprudence; in *Kupreškić*, an ICTY Trial Chamber found that 'although the Statute of the ICC may be indicative of the *opinio juris* of many States, Article 7(1)(h) is not consonant with customary international law'.[203] In any event, the requirement should not pose a significant obstacle for legitimate prosecutions of persecu-tion, since it is satisfied by a linkage to even *one* other recognized act (a killing or other inhumane act), which one would expect to find in a situation warranting international prosecution. In so far as such an element exists, it is purely an objective element to ensure the seriousness of the situation, and does not require any mental element.[204]

---

200 Art. 5(h) of the ICTY Statute; Art. 3(h) of the ICTR Statute.
201 Art. 7(1)(h) of the ICC Statute.
202 *Ibid.*
203 *Kupreškić* T. Ch. II 14.1.2000 para. 580. Antonio Cassese argues persuasively that the requirement is inconsistent with the elimination of the general nexus requirement in the Nuremberg Charter and therefore is a restriction on customary law: Cassese, 'Crimes Against Humanity', 376.
204 ICC Elements, footnote 22.

Civilian population?

There is also a question whether persecution, unlike other crimes against humanity, need not be directed against a civilian population. On the one hand, the Nuremberg definition dealt separately with persecution, such that it was not linked to civilian population, and post-war cases have dealt with persecution of military personnel.[205] On the other hand, the Nuremberg approach may be overtaken by current practice, since all modern instruments unify the prohibited acts under a single chapeau, a move that was welcomed as rationalizing the structure and eliminating the 'awkward bifurcation'.[206] Concerns about protective coverage for military personnel may be addressed if a broad interpretation of 'civilian population' is adopted, as discussed in section 11.2.3.[207]

Mental element

In addition to the normal mental element relating to the conduct and the broader context, persecution requires a particular intent to target a person or group on prohibited grounds of discrimination.[208] Tribunal jurisprudence indicates that a particular *intent* to discriminate is required, not simply a *knowledge* that one is acting in a discriminatory way.[209] With respect to the requirement in the ICC Statute of a 'connection' to other crimes or prohibited acts, this requirement is purely objective and no mental element is required.[210]

Relationship to other crimes

Persecution and genocide each require a particular discriminatory intent. In the case of genocide, however, the intent is more specific; it must be an intent to destroy a group as such, and the target must be a national, ethnical, racial or religious group. Genocide can only be based on the listed acts (see, for example Article 6 of the ICC Statute) whereas the conduct potentially amounting to persecution is broader. Acts amounting to other crimes against humanity can constitute persecution if the additional aggravating element of discriminatory intent is present.

---

205 Antonio Cassese, *International Criminal Law*, 2nd edn (Oxford, 2008) 117, 121.

206 Steven Ratner and Jason Abrams, *Accountability for Human Rights Atrocities in International Law* (Oxford, 2001) 59.

207 If the provision excludes only battlefield action against legitimate military objectives then there would be no gap in coverage. Protection would apply in all circumstances where military personnel could feasibly be victims of persecution – during peacetime, in their civilian lives, when captured or rendered *hors de combat*.

208 ICC Elements, Art. 7(1)(h), element 3; *Kordić* ICTY T. Ch. 26.2.2001 para. 212.

209 *Krnojelac* ICTY T. Ch. II 15.3.2002 para. 435; *Kordić* ICTY T. Ch. 26.2.2001 para. 212.

210 ICC Elements, footnote 22.

Examples of persecutory acts

Persecutory acts include the prohibited acts already listed in the definition of crimes against humanity, when committed with discriminatory intent.[211] Examples that have been prosecuted include murder, extermination, imprisonment, deportation, transfer of populations, torture, enslavement and beatings (inhumane acts).[212] In addition, they can include other conduct that severely deprives political, civil, economic or social rights. Examples include the passing of discriminatory laws, restriction of movement and seclusion in ghettos, the exclusion of members of an ethnic or religious group from aspects of social, political and economic life, including exclusion from professions, business, educational institutions, public service and inter-marriage.[213] It also includes overt violence such as burning of homes and terrorization.[214] The ICTR Appeals Chamber has held that, while hate speech alone does not constitute persecution, hate speech and calls to violence, contributing to acts of violence, and in a broader context of persecution, can be of comparable gravity to other crimes and hence constitute acts of persecution.[215]

Attacks on property can constitute persecution. This includes 'systematic destruction of monuments or buildings representative of a particular social, religious, cultural or other group',[216] and destruction of homes and means of livelihood.[217] The *Tadić* decision noted doubts whether attacks on purely industrial property would suffice, but economic measures with personal effects, including deprivation of livelihood, would suffice.[218] The *Blaškić* decision affirmed that persecution includes 'targeting property, so long as the victimized persons were specially selected on grounds linked to their belonging to a particular community'.[219] This may be seen in destruction of private dwellings, businesses, symbolic buildings, looting and plunder of businesses and private property, boycott of businesses and shops, and forcing the group out of economic life.[220]

11.3.10 Enforced disappearance

The ICC Statute expressly includes enforced disappearance as a crime against humanity. Enforced disappearance was recognized previously as an international crime and indeed as a crime against humanity. It was exemplified in the 'Night and Fog Decree' issued by the

---

211 *Kupreškić* ICTY T. Ch. II 14.1.2000 paras. 593–607.
212 *Tadić* ICTY T. Ch. II 7.5.1997 paras. 704–10; *Kupreškić* ICTY T. Ch. II 14.1.2000 para. 594.
213 *Ibid.*, paras. 608–15.
214 *Krstić* ICTY T. Ch. I 2.8.2001 para. 537.
215 *Nahimana* ICTR A. Ch. 28.11.2007 paras. 986–8.
216 ILC Report, 1991, p. 268.
217 *Kordić* ICTY T. Ch. 26.2.2001 para. 205.
218 *Tadić* ICTY T. Ch. II 7.5.1997 para. 707.
219 *Blaškić* ICTY T. Ch. I 3.3.2000 para. 233.
220 *Ibid.*, paras. 220–33.

Nazis, to execute people and to provide no information to the families as to their whereabouts or fate.[221] It was also a prevalent feature under military regimes in Latin America in the 1980s, and is still practised today in various regimes around the world. Enforced disappearance is expressly recognized as a crime against humanity in the 1992 UN Declaration on the Protection of All Persons from Enforced Disappearance, the 1994 Inter-American Convention on the Forced Disappearance of Persons and, more recently, in the 2005 International Convention on the Protection of All Persons from Enforced Disappearance.[222]

The definition in the ICC Statute is based on the UN Declaration and the Inter-American Convention,[223] and refers to the 'arrest, detention or abduction of persons by, or with the authorization, support or acquiescence of, a State or political organization, followed by a refusal to acknowledge that deprivation of freedom or to give information on the fate or whereabouts of those persons, with the intention of removing them from the protection of law for a prolonged period of time'.[224]

A welcome development in the negotiation of the ICC Elements was the realization that there are various ways in which an *individual* may be liable for this crime. Previous definitions described the whole system of enforced disappearance, but it is unlikely that a single individual would be involved in the arrest, detention or abduction phase, as well as the refusal to acknowledge the deprivation or to provide information. Enforced disappearance typically involves many actors. Therefore, the ICC Elements recognize that the crime may be committed (*a*) by arresting, detaining or abducting a person, with knowledge that a refusal to acknowledge or give information would be likely to follow in the ordinary course of events, or (*b*) by refusing to acknowledge the deprivation of freedom or to provide information on the fate or whereabouts, with knowledge that such deprivation may well have occurred.[225]

Previous instruments required commission, authorization, support or acquiescence from the State. The ICC Statute expanded this to refer as well to 'political organizations', consistent with the fundamental proposition that crimes against humanity may be committed by non-State actors.

Those arresting, detaining or abducting a person must know that a refusal to acknowledge or give information would be likely to follow in the ordinary course of events. Those refusing to acknowledge the deprivation of freedom or to provide information on the fate or whereabouts must know that such deprivation may well have occurred. In addition, the

---

221 *Nuremberg Judgment*, reproduced (1947) 41 AJIL 172 at 230.
222 Preamble paras. 4, 5 and 6 of the respective instruments.
223 Preamble para. 3 of the UN Declaration and Art. 2 of the Inter-American Convention.
224 Art. 7(2)(i) of the ICC Statute.
225 Georg Witschel and Wiebke Rückert, 'Crime Against Humanity of Enforced Disappearance of Persons' in Lee, *Elements and Rules*, 98–103.

crime of enforced disappearance requires a particular intention, to remove a person from the protection of the law.

Enforced disappearance may involve other crimes such as killing, torture or arbitrary imprisonment. The essence of the crime, however, is that the friends and families of the direct victims do not know whether the persons concerned are alive or dead. It is this uncertainty that is the hallmark of enforced disappearance, and indeed the friends and families of the direct victims are also the special victims of this crime.

11.3.11 Apartheid

The ICC Statute includes the crime of apartheid as a crime against humanity. Apartheid was recognized as a crime against humanity in instruments such as the 1968 Convention on the Non-Applicability of Statutory Limitations to War Crimes and Crimes Against Humanity and the 1973 Apartheid Convention.[226]

The definition was adjusted in order to refer not only to the situation which had prevailed in South Africa, but also any similar situations in the future. The ICC Statute, Article 7(2)(h), defines it as 'inhumane acts of a character similar to those referred to in paragraph 1, committed in the context of an institutionalized racial regime of systematic oppression and domination by one racial group over any other racial group and committed with the intention of maintaining that regime'.

The definition of crimes against humanity always included a residual clause encompassing other inhumane acts of a similar character. Thus, by requiring in the crime of apartheid definition that the inhumane acts be 'of a character similar to those referred to in paragraph 1', the drafters ensured that they did not exceed existing law. What the ICC Statute provides is simply an express recognition of the crime of apartheid where inhumane acts are committed in the context of an institutionalized racial regime of systematic oppression and domination.

Most or all of the acts listed in the Apartheid Convention are captured by the ICC definition. The requirement of 'similar character' naturally covers acts of *identical* character,[227] and hence the examples in the Apartheid Convention of murder, torture, arbitrary imprisonment and persecution are clearly included. In addition, inflicting conditions calculated to cause physical destruction of a group; legislative measures to prevent a racial group from participation in political, social, economic and cultural life; legislative measures to divide the population through ghettos, prohibiting mixed marriage, and expropriating property; and forced labour, appear to be of character similar to 'persecution' and 'other inhumane acts' and therefore would be covered. The significant difference between the two definitions is that the ICC Statute specifies that the crime must be committed 'in the context

---

226 Art. 1(b) of the Convention on Statutory Limitations, quoted in Apartheid Convention, Preamble, para. 5.
227 A point clarified in the ICC Elements, Art. 7(1)(j), element 2.

of an institutionalized regime of systematic oppression and domination by one racial group over any other racial group or groups'. To constitute the crime of apartheid, the conduct must be committed with the particular intent of maintaining the regime.

11.3.12 Other inhumane acts

All definitions of crimes against humanity close with the general residual clause 'or other inhumane acts'. A residual clause remains necessary because:

> [h]owever much care were taken in establishing all the various forms of infliction, one would never be able to catch up with the imagination of future torturers who wished to satisfy their bestial instincts; and the more specific and complete a list tries to be, the more restrictive it becomes.[228]

Jurists have, however, been aware that any such residual clause must be infused with adequate precision to satisfy the criminal law principle of legality. The ICC Statute provides the necessary threshold by requiring that the inhumane acts (1) be of a similar character to other prohibited acts and (2) that they cause great suffering or serious injury to body or to mental or physical health.[229] Tribunal jurisprudence provides the threshold by requiring 'similar gravity and seriousness' to other prohibited acts.[230]

The accused must carry out the conduct intentionally. It is not required that the accused considered his or her actions 'inhumane', it is sufficient that the accused was aware of the factual circumstances that established the character of the act.[231] The accused must intend to inflict serious bodily or mental harm.[232]

Tribunals have held the conduct element of 'inhumane acts' to be synonymous with the conduct element of the war crime of 'cruel treatment'.[233]

The Tribunal Statutes, unlike the ICC Statute, do not expressly include forced disappearance, sexual violence, forced prostitution, forced transfer of populations in their list of prohibited acts, and hence Tribunal jurisprudence has found that each of these are encompassed in the Tribunal Statutes under 'other inhumane acts'.[234] Other acts that have been characterized as inhumane acts include mutilation, severe bodily harm, beatings, serious physical and mental injury, inhumane or degrading treatment falling short of the definition of torture, imposing inhumane conditions in concentration camps, forced nudity and forced

---

228 *Blaškić* ICTY T. Ch. I 3.3.2000 para. 237, referring to Jean Pictet, *Commentary on Geneva Convention IV* (Geneva, 1960) 54.
229 Art. 7(1)(k) of the ICC Statute.
230 See, e.g. *Kayishema* ICTR A. Ch. 1.6.2001 para. 583.
231 ICC Elements, Art. 7(1)(k), element 3; *Čelebići* ICTY T. Ch. II 16.11.1998 para. 543.
232 ICC Elements, Art. 7(1)(k); *Blaškić* ICTY T. Ch. I 3.3.2000 para. 243.
233 *Jelisić* ICTY T. Ch. 14.12.1999 para. 52. The ICC Elements use different terms for the two crimes, so it remains to be seen whether the ICC will adopt the same approach.
234 *Kvočka* ICTY T. Ch. I 2.11.2001 para. 208; *Kupreškić* ICTY T. Ch. II 14.1.2000 para. 566.

marriage.[235] More recently, Sierra Leone Special Court has recognized 'forced marriage' as an 'inhumane act', and defined it as 'forced conjugal association with another person resulting in great suffering, or serious physical or mental injury on the part of the victim'.[236]

Further reading

Kai Ambos and Steffen Wirth, 'The Current Law of Crimes Against Humanity: An Analysis of UNTAET Regulation 15/2000' (2002) 13 *Criminal Law Forum* 1.

M. Cherif Bassiouni, *Crimes Against Humanity in International Criminal Law*, 2nd edn (The Hague, 1999).

Machteld Boot, *Genocide, Crimes Against Humanity and War Crimes* (Oxford, 2002).

Machteld Boot, Rodney Dixon and Christopher K. Hall, 'Article 7' in Triffterer, *Observers' Notes*.

Antonio Cassese, 'Crimes Against Humanity' in Cassese, *Commentary*.

Simon Chesterman, 'An Altogether Different Order: Defining the Elements of Crimes Against Humanity' (2000) *Duke Journal of Comparative and International Law* 283.

Roger Clark, 'Crimes Against Humanity' in G. Ginsburgs and V. N. Kudriavstsev (eds.), *The Nuremberg Trials and International Law* (Dordrecht/Boston/London, 1990).

Phyllis Hwang, 'Defining Crimes Against Humanity in the Rome Statute of the International Criminal Court' (1998) 22 *Fordham International Law Journal* 457.

David Luban, 'A Theory of Crimes Against Humanity' (2004) 29 *Yale Law Journal* 85.

Timothy McCormack, 'Crimes Against Humanity' in Dominic McGoldrick, Peter Rowe and Eric Donnelly (eds.), *The Permanent International Criminal Court: Legal and Policy Issues* (Oxford, 2004).

Joseph Rikhof, 'Crimes Against Humanity, Customary International Law and the International Tribunals for Bosnia and Rwanda' (1995) 6 *National Journal of Constitutional Law* 231.

Darryl Robinson, Georg Witschel and Wiebke Rückert, 'Elements of Crimes Against Humanity' in Lee, *Elements and Rules*.

Beth van Schack, 'The Definition of Crimes Against Humanity: Resolving the Incoherence' (1999) 37 *Columbia Journal of Transnational Law* 787.

Egon Schwelb, 'Crimes Against Humanity' (1946) 23 *BYBIL* 178.

---

[235] *Akayesu* ICTR T. Ch. I 2.9.1998 paras. 685–97; *Tadić* ICTY T. Ch. II 7.5.1997 para. 730; *Blaškić* ICTY T. Ch. I 3.3.2000 para. 239; *Kvočka* ICTY T. Ch. I 2.11.2001 para. 209; *Čelebići* ICTY T. Ch. II 16.11.1998 paras. 554–8.

[236] *Brina* SCSL A. Ch. 22.2.2008 para. 195. For discussion of this gender-based crime, see Valerie Oosterveld, 'International Decisions: Prosecutor v. Brima; Prosecutor v. Fofana' (2009) 103 *AJIL* 103.

12

War Crimes

12.1 Introduction

12.1.1 Overview

A war crime is a serious violation of the laws and customs applicable in armed conflict (also known as international humanitarian law) which gives rise to individual criminal responsibility under international law. Because the law of war crimes is based on international humanitarian law, section 12.1 will explain the relevant underlying principles of international humanitarian law, and then the development of war crimes law. Section 12.2 will review issues common to all war crimes, namely the existence of armed conflict, the nexus between the conduct and the armed conflict, and the role of the perpetrator and victim. Section 12.3 will survey the specific offences constituting war crimes.

Unlike crimes against humanity, war crimes have no requirement of widespread or systematic commission. A single isolated act can constitute a war crime. For war crimes law, it is the situation of armed conflict that justifies international concern.

12.1.2 A brief history of humanitarian law

Laws and customs regulating warfare may be traced back to ancient times. While such norms have varied between civilizations and centuries, and were often shockingly lax by modern standards, it is significant that diverse cultures around the globe have recorded agreements, religious edicts and military instructions laying out ground rules for military conflict. In recent centuries, military codes – such as the Lieber Code promulgated during the American Civil War – have refined and developed these customs.[1]

---

1 See, e.g. Leslie Green, *The Contemporary Law of Armed Conflict* (Manchester, 2000) 20–53; Christopher Greenwood, 'Historical Development and Legal Basis' in Dieter Fleck, *Handbook of International Humanitarian Law*, 2nd edn (Oxford, 2008) 1–44; M. Sassoli and A. Bouvier, *How Does Law Protect in War? Cases, Documents and Teaching Materials on Contemporary Practice in International Humanitarian Law* (Geneva, 1999) 97–104.

Codification and progressive development at the international level was spurred in part by the efforts of one individual. In 1859, Henri Dunant, a businessman from Geneva, witnessed the aftermath of the Battle of Solferino, and was shocked by the horrors of wounded soldiers left to die on the battlefield. He published a poignant and evocative account of the carnage, urging measures to reduce such unnecessary suffering.[2] This appeal led promptly to the creation of the International Committee of the Red Cross in 1863 and the adoption of the first Geneva Convention for the Amelioration of the Condition of the Wounded in Armies in the Field in 1864.

Since then, there have been many treaties developing international humanitarian law (IHL). These are sometimes divided into 'Geneva law', which primarily focuses on protecting civilians and others who are not active combatants (such as the wounded, sick, shipwrecked and prisoners of war), and 'Hague law', which regulates specific means and methods of warfare, with a view to reducing unnecessary destruction and suffering. Among the most significant in the latter category are the 1907 Hague Regulations, which recognized that 'the right of belligerents to adopt means of injuring the enemy is not unlimited', and laid down many provisions on the means and methods of warfare that are now recognized as customary law.

The four Geneva Conventions of 1949, adopted in response to the inhumanities of the Second World War, considerably added to and updated previous Geneva Conventions. The 1949 Conventions deal with sick and wounded in the field ('GC I'), the wounded, sick and shipwrecked at sea ('GC II'), prisoners of war ('GC III') and civilians ('GC IV'). In 1977, these rules were again updated by two Additional Protocols, the first concerning international armed conflicts ('AP I') and the second, non-international (hereafter, for the sake of brevity, 'internal') armed conflicts ('AP II'). AP I combines elements of 'Hague law' and 'Geneva law', making this traditional distinction less relevant.

Other significant treaty developments have strengthened the protection of cultural property,[3] the prohibition or regulation of certain weapons (such as biological and chemical weapons and anti-personnel mines),[4] and the prohibition on the use of child soldiers.[5] One

---

2 Henri Dunant, *Un Souvenir de Solférino* (Geneva, 1862).

3 1954 Hague Convention for the Protection of Cultural Property in the Event of an Armed Conflict, 14 May 1954, and two protocols thereto, the 1954 First Hague Protocol, 24 May 1954, and the 1999 Second Hague Protocol, 29 March 1999.

4 Convention on the Prohibition of the Development, Production and Stockpiling of Bacteriological (Biological) and Toxin Weapons and on their Destruction, 10 April 1972; Convention on Prohibitions or Restrictions on the Use of Certain Conventional Weapons which may be Deemed to be Excessively Injurious or to have Indiscriminate Effects, 10 October 1980; four protocols thereto including Convention on the Prohibition of the Development, Production, Stockpiling and Use of Chemical Weapons and on their Destruction, 13 January 1993; Convention on the Prohibition of the Use, Stockpiling, Production and Transfer of Anti-Personnel Mines and on their Destruction, 18 September 1997.

5 Optional Protocol to the Convention on the Rights of the Child on the involvement of children in armed conflict. Adopted and opened for signature, ratification and accession by General Assembly Resolution A/RES/54/263 of 25 May 2000.

of the most significant developments in recent decades is the gradual expansion of the principles applicable in international armed conflicts to internal armed conflicts, which will be discussed in this chapter.

The provisions of the 1907 Hague Regulations as well as much of the 1949 Geneva Conventions have come to be recognized as customary law; hence they apply regardless of whether parties to the conflicts have ratified those conventions.[6] Some, but not all, provisions of the Additional Protocols have obtained recognition as customary law.[7]

12.1.3 Key principles of humanitarian law

The resulting principles may be summarized in different ways, but key elements include:

- non-combatants are to be spared from various forms of harm; this category includes not only civilians but also former combatants, such as prisoners of war and fighters rendered *hors de combat* because they are wounded, sick, shipwrecked or have surrendered;
- combatants must distinguish between military objectives and the civilian population, and attack only military objectives (the principle of distinction);
- in attacking military objectives, combatants must take measures to avoid or minimize collateral civilian damage and refrain from attacks that would cause excessive civilian damage (the principle of proportionality);
- there are restrictions on the means and methods of war, to reduce unnecessary suffering and to maintain respect for humanitarian principles.

IHL is triggered by the outbreak of armed conflict and seeks to regulate the conduct of such conflict. The goal of abolishing armed conflict altogether is left to other legal and political domains.[8]

Indeed, a fundamental principle of IHL is the complete separation of the *ius ad bellum* (the law regarding resort to armed conflict) and the *ius in bello* (the law governing conduct during the armed conflict). In previous centuries, some scholars had suggested that the party fighting a 'just' war should benefit from more permissive IHL provisions.[9] The obvious difficulty with this proposition is that both sides claim to be fighting with just cause, leading to confusion and obfuscation as to the applicable rules. Moreover, the victims of armed conflict still need protection regardless of the purpose of the conflict. In order to advance the

---

6 Theodor Meron, *Human Rights and Humanitarian Norms as Customary Law* (Oxford, 1999) 41–62.

7 See, e.g. *Hamdan* v. *Rumsfeld* 126 S Ct 2749 (2006) (re Art. 75 API); *Strugar* ICTY A. Ch. 22.11.2002 para. 9 (re Arts. 51 and 52 AP I); Meron, *Customary Law*, 62–78.

8 See, e.g. Preamble, Arts. 1 and 2 of the Hague Regulations: 'Seeing that while seeking means to preserve peace and prevent armed conflicts between nations, it is likewise necessary to bear in mind the case where the appeal to arms has been brought about by events which their care was unable to avert; Animated by the desire to serve, even in this extreme case, the interests of humanity and the ever progressive needs of civilization . . . '

9 See, e.g. Hugo Grotius, *De Jure Belli ac Pacis* (1625); Peter Haggenmacher, *Grotius et la doctrine de la guerre juste* (Paris, 1983) 597–612.

fundamental humanitarian aims of IHL, it is now a clearly established principle that IHL applies equally and uniformly, irrespective of the origins of or reasons for the conflict.[10] *Ius ad bellum* considerations have no bearing on the interpretation or application of IHL in a conflict, and hence it cannot be argued, for example, that a war was unjustified and therefore that all killings of combatants were war crimes or that all attacks were disproportionate.[11] The question whether the decision to resort to force was legal or illegal is addressed under other law such as the UN Charter (and some day, perhaps, the crime of aggression).[12]

12.1.4 The challenge of regulating warfare

The effort to regulate the exceptional situation of armed conflict is rife with difficulty. Indeed, war in many ways seems to be the antithesis of law, leading to the mistaken saying that *silent enim leges inter arma* (law is silent in war). Normal rules – including the fundamental legal and moral prohibitions on killing and destruction – are to some extent displaced in armed conflict, and combatants cannot be punished for lawful acts of war. Nonetheless, the outbreak of armed conflict does not create a legal vacuum. The law that grants a right to engage in conduct that would normally be criminal also imposes limits on such conduct. Militaries are still subject to discipline, and compliance with IHL norms is required. But enforcement of international norms, which can be challenging in the best of circumstances, is all the more difficult in the context of a deadly struggle among armed groups.[13] International criminal justice is one means of deterring violations and educating people that some basic laws apply in all circumstances.

Permeating the development and interpretation of IHL and war crimes law is the tension between military and humanitarian considerations. Combatants may put too great a weight on military imperatives at the expense of humanitarian considerations. Conversely, those fortunate enough not to have been involved in conflict may discount or neglect military considerations when making assertions about IHL and war crimes law. Either oversight would lead to an emaciated appreciation of the law.

When appraising war crimes law, it is important to consider the chaotic situations faced in armed conflict and the requirements of military strategy and tactics. Destruction and death will occur even in lawfully conducted conflict. Mistakes may occur, with tragic consequences, without necessarily amounting to war crimes.

---

10 See, e.g. Preamble, para. 5 of AP I: 'provisions … must be fully applied in all circumstances … without any adverse distinctions based on the nature or origin of the conflict or on the causes espoused by or attributed to the parties to the conflict'; and see Sassoli and Bouvier, *How Does Law Protect*, 83–8, 681–2; *US* v. *List* (the 'Hostages Case') VIII LRTWC at 59; François Bugnion, 'Guerre juste, guerre d'agression et droit international humanitaire' (2002) 84 *Revue International de la Croix-Rouge* 523. See, however, discussion of Art. 1(4) AP I in section 12.2.2.

11 See, e.g. Sassoli and Bouvier, *How Does Law Protect*, 665; *Altstötter* (the 'Justice Trial') VI LRTWC 1 at 52.

12 See Chapter 13.

13 Hersch Lauterpacht, 'The Problem of the Revision of the Law of War' (1952) 29 *BYIL* 360, 382.

While IHL involves a balancing of military and humanitarian considerations, it is also clear that the weight assigned to these considerations has been shifting over the years in a progressive direction. This process has been aptly referred to as 'the humanization of humanitarian law'.[14] Many factors have contributed to this process, including the increasing emphasis in international law and international relations on protecting human beings as opposed to an exclusive focus on State interests. The result has been stricter rules of conduct, protecting more classes of victims and applying in more circumstances, including during internal armed conflicts.

In addition, while egregious violations remain common in many conflicts, the practice among many States has been to place greater and greater weight on humanitarian considerations. The phenomena of mass media, democratization and globalization mean that images of civilian suffering are more readily available (although censorship and propaganda remain ubiquitous). In addition, technological advances have raised expectations about precision attacks.[15] Those who plan operations know that incidents causing significant civilian casualties can erode support from domestic populations, coalition partners and the international community. Anecdotal evidence also indicates that awareness of international criminal justice institutions is inducing greater compliance among military leaders. Conversely, the difficulties of 'asymmetric' warfare against non-State actors with no regard for humanitarian law have at times led some governments to seek to deny or restrict the application of IHL, creating new points of tension.[16]

12.1.5 The relationship between war crimes and IHL

War crimes law criminalizes a narrower subset of IHL.[17] The major question is which of the rules of IHL constitutes a criminal offence when violated.

Some treaties, such as the Geneva Conventions, expressly criminalize violations of identified fundamental provisions.[18] War crimes may also be found in customary law even in the absence of a treaty provision criminalizing the norm. For example, the Nuremberg Tribunal held that key provisions of the 1907 Hague Regulations reflected customary law and that violations amounted to crimes, even though the Hague Regulations did not expressly criminalize such violations.[19]

---

14 Theodor Meron, 'The Humanization of Humanitarian Law' (2000) 94 *AJIL* 239.

15 Michael N. Schmitt, 'Precision Attack and International Humanitarian Law' (2005) 87 *International Review of the Red Cross* 445.

16 Toni Pfanner, 'Asymmetric Warfare from the Perspective of Humanitarian Law and Humanitarian Action' (2005) 87 IRRC 149; Luisa Vierucci, 'Prisoners of War or Protected Persons *qua* Unlawful Combatants? The Judicial Safeguards to which Guantanamo Bay Detainees are Entitled' (2003) 1 *JICJ* 284.

17 M. Bothe, 'War Crimes' in Cassese, *Commentary*, 387–8.

18 See section 12.1.6.

19 *Nuremberg Judgment* (1947) 41 *AJIL* at 218 and 248–9; *United States* v. *von Leeb* XII LRTWC 1 at 61–2 and 86–92.

In the seminal *Tadić* decision on jurisdiction, the Appeals Chamber interpreted the ICTY Statute provision on 'violations of the laws or customs of war', giving guidance on how to identify the content of war crimes law. The decision confirmed that not every IHL violation amounts to a war crime.[20] Such a conclusion is clearly correct, since IHL includes a great many technical regulations that would be inappropriate for criminalization.[21] For example, GC III requires that prisoners of war have a canteen where they may purchase foodstuffs, soap and tobacco at local market prices, and that they be given a specific monthly advance of pay depending on rank;[22] an unavailability of tobacco, or providing goods slightly above market rates, or providing slightly less pay would be a breach of IHL, but is not really appropriately considered a war crime.

The Appeals Chamber in *Tadić* set the following requirements for war crimes within the jurisdiction of the Tribunal: (1) the violation must infringe a rule of IHL, (2) that rule must be found in customary law or applicable treaty law, (3) the violation must be 'serious', in that the rule protects important values and the breach involves grave consequences for the victim, and (4) the violation must entail individual criminal responsibility.[23]

This test has been applied in subsequent Tribunal cases.[24] Questions have been raised as to whether the fourth requirement is in reality redundant, since the evidence presented of criminalization has typically been sparse, and it may simply be that all serious violations are criminalized.[25] It has also been argued though, that simply applying the adjective 'serious' is question-begging and is not operational as a distinguishing criterion;[26] hence more may be needed to elaborate upon the requirement. In an article presaging the *Tadić* decision, Theodor Meron referred to factors such as whether the norm is directed to individuals, whether it is unequivocal in character, the gravity of the act and the interests of the international community.[27] In any event, the approach of recognizing serious violations of IHL as war crimes largely inspired the selection of crimes in the ICC Statute.[28]

---

20 *Tadić* ICTY A. Ch. 2.10.1995 para. 94.

21 See, e.g. Henckaerts and Doswald-Beck, *ICRC Customary Law*, 568; and Hersch Lauterpacht, 'The Law of Nations and the Punishment of War Crimes' (1944) 21 *BYBIL* 58 at 78–9.

22 Arts. 28 and 60 GC III.

23 *Tadić* ICTY A. Ch. 2.10.1995 para. 94.

24 See, e.g. *Galić* ICTY T. Ch. 5.12.2003 paras. 13–32; *Galić* ICTY A. Ch. 30.11.2006 paras. 86–98, applying the test to find a war crime of committing acts of violence with the primary purpose of spreading terror among the civilian population. See also Chapter 14 and see Robert Cryer, '*Prosecutor* v. *Galić* and the War Crime of Terror Bombing' (2005–2006) 2 *Israel Defence Forces Law Review* 73.

25 *Ibid.*, 91–5.

26 Georges Abi-Saab, 'The Concept of War Crimes' in Sienho Yee and Wang Tieya (eds.), *International Law and the Post-Cold War World: Essays in Memory of Li Haopei* (London, Routledge) 112.

27 Theodor Meron, 'International Criminalization of Internal Atrocities' (1995) 89 *AJIL* 554 at 562.

28 Herman von Hebel and Darryl Robinson, 'Crimes Within the Jurisdiction of the Court' in Lee, *The Making of the Rome Statute*, 103–5.

Since war crimes are serious violations of IHL, it is often necessary to refer to the relevant principles of IHL to interpret international criminal law in this area.[29] This is why the chapeau of Article 8(2)(a) of the ICC Statute refers to the provisions of the relevant Geneva Conventions, and the chapeau of Article 8(2)(b) refers to 'the established framework of international law'. Some uncertainties have been expressed as to the interpretation of the latter provision,[30] but it is simply a *renvoi* to the relevant rules of IHL to aid in the interpretation of the various provisions.[31]

IHL and war crimes law have similar aims but somewhat different scopes and consequences. IHL is addressed to governments and other parties to a conflict; it sets out standards expected in armed conflict, and violations can culminate in compensation or other satisfaction. War crimes law is addressed to individuals, and sets out offences amounting to the most serious crimes of concern to the international community as a whole, and can culminate in imprisonment as a war criminal. For these reasons, similar provisions may warrant a more restrictive interpretation in the context of war crimes law, consistent with the narrower focus of war crimes law on the most serious violations as well as general principles of criminal law (strict construction). For example, IHL requires that, before any sentencing of protected persons, a party must provide a fair trial affording all indispensable judicial guarantees.[32] A minor breach of even one such right would fall below this standard and violate IHL, requiring an appropriate remedy. However, it would be incorrect to say that as a consequence all involved in conducting the trial should thereby be branded as war criminals. For the purpose of war crimes law, it is necessary to look at the cumulative effect of shortcomings to see whether there was a deprivation of fair trial amounting to a war crime.[33]

12.1.6 A brief history of the law of war crimes

War crimes law deals with the *criminal responsibility of individuals* for serious violations of international humanitarian law. National laws have long provided for prosecution of war crimes.[34] For example, the Lieber Code recognized criminal liability of individuals for

---

29 Peter Rowe, 'War Crimes' in Dominic McGoldrick, Peter Rowe and Eric Donnelly (eds), *The Permanent International Criminal Court: Legal and Policy Issues* (Oxford, 2004) 217–19.

30 Antonio Cassese, 'The Statute of the International Criminal Court: Some Preliminary Reflections' (1999) 10 *EJIL* 149, 150–2 expresses concern that it may require proof of customary law status, while preferring an interpretation that it reflects the drafters' view that the crimes are already customary law. See also Machteld Boot, *Genocide, Crimes Against Humanity and War Crimes* (Oxford, 2002) 564–6.

31 This understanding is now confirmed in ICC Elements, Introduction to War Crimes, para. 2, and dovetails with Art. 21(1)(b) ICC Statute. The ICC Elements also make clear that this encompasses the law of armed conflict at sea where relevant.

32 Common Article 3 to the Geneva Conventions.

33 ICC Elements, footnote 59; Knut Dörman, 'Article 8' in Triffterer, *Observers' Notes* at 316.

34 Timothy L. H. McCormack, 'From Sun Tzu to the Sixth Committee: The Evolution of an International Criminal Law Regime' in Timothy L. H. McCormack and Gerry. J. Simpson (eds.), *The Law of War Crimes* (The Hague, 1997); Leslie Green, *The Contemporary Law of Armed Conflict* (Manchester, 2000) 286–90.

violations of its strictures, and similar provisions are in military manuals of many countries.[35] Following some prominent historical examples of war crimes prosecutions,[36] and after abortive efforts to conduct international trials at the end of the First World War,[37] the Nuremberg Charter gave form to the international law of war crimes. Article 6(b) of the Charter included:

> War crimes: namely, violations of the laws or customs of war. Such violations shall include, but not be limited to, murder, ill-treatment or deportation to slave labour or for any purpose of civilian population of or in occupied territory, murder or ill-treatment of prisoners of war or persons on the seas, killing of hostages, plunder of public or private property, wanton destruction of cities, towns or villages, or devastation not justified by military necessity ...

Within the scope of 'war crimes' the Nuremberg Tribunal included key provisions of the Hague Regulations, which it held gave rise to individual criminal responsibility under customary law.[38]

The four Geneva Conventions of 1949 included 'grave breach' provisions, expressly recognizing certain violations as crimes subject to universal jurisdiction.[39] These provisions have come to be regarded as reflective of customary international law.[40] Additional Protocol I to those Conventions ('AP I'), adopted in 1977, introduced additional 'grave breaches', although not all of these have attained recognition as customary law.[41]

The ICTY Statute included grave breaches of the Geneva Conventions (Article 2 of the ICTY Statute) as well as violations of other laws or customs of war, featuring an open-ended list with five examples.[42] The ICTR Statute, designed to deal with an internal armed conflict, included serious violations of common Article 3 and Additional Protocol II of 1977 ('AP II'), featuring an open-ended list with eight examples.[43]

The ICC Statute, adopted a few years later in 1998, contains the longest and most comprehensive list of war crimes of any of the tribunal statutes. Unlike previous lists, the

---

35 Instructions for the Government Armies of the United States in the Field, General Orders No. 100, 24 April 1863.

36 For example, the 1474 trial of Peter von Hagenbach for crimes during the occupation of Breisach.

37 See Chapter 6.

38 Nuremberg Judgment, reproduced (1947) 41 *AJIL* 172 at 218; *von Leeb* XII LRTWC 1 at 86–92.

39 Art. 49 GC I, Art. 51 GC II, Art. 130 GC III, Art. 147 GC IV. See Chapter 3 for a discussion of whether these provisions confer universal jurisdiction strictly so called.

40 See Art. 2 ICTY Statute, Art. 8(2)(a) ICC Statute, and ICJ, *Advisory Opinion on Legality of the Threat or Use of Nuclear Weapons* (1996) ICJ Rep 226, 257 (8 July 1996) at paras. 79 and 82.

41 Art. 85 AP I. But see the study of customary law undertaken under ICRC auspices: Henckaerts & Doswald-Beck, *ICRC Customary Law*.

42 Art. 3 ICTY Statute. The list included use of poisonous weapons or weapons calculated to cause unnecessary suffering; wanton destruction; attack of undefended places; seizure or destruction of historic monuments, works of art, or institutions dedicated to certain purposes; and plunder.

43 Art. 4 ICTR Statute. The list included murder, cruel treatment, torture, mutilation, collective punishments, hostage taking, terrorism, and outrages on dignity which includes rape, enforced prostitution and indecent assault, pillage and passing sentences without proper trial.

list in Article 8 is exhaustive. Some States, such as the United States, which had been quite content to impose an open-ended list upon others (Nuremberg, ICTY, ICTR) had a notable change of heart when confronted with a permanent court that could potentially apply to their own forces.[44] There may also have been a concern to avoid the initiatives of judge-made law within the ad hoc Tribunals.[45] In any event, despite the seeming double standards, an exhaustive list is certainly more consistent with criminal law principles, particularly the principle *nullum crimen sine lege*.

The ICC Statute contains an extensive list of fifty offences, including grave breaches of the Geneva Conventions, serious violations of common Article 3 and other serious violations drawn from various sources. Since the goal of the drafters was to reflect customary law rather than to create new law, many provisions from previous instruments were excluded because of a lack of consensus on their customary law status. The ICC list, while lengthy, does not include all war crimes recognized in customary law; an example often cited is the prohibition on the use of chemical or biological weapons.[46] As expressly noted in Article 10 of the ICC Statute, the absence of a provision in the ICC Statute list does not affect its status as existing or developing international law.

The SCSL Statute and the Iraq Special Tribunal Statute have included some of the key provisions in the ICC list. Article 14 of the Iraq Special Tribunal Statute copies the ICC Statute definitions, providing another instance of State practice confirming those definitions. The SCSL Statute includes violations of common Article 3 and a short list of other serious violations, reflecting certain crimes from the ICC Statute, namely attacks directed against civilians, attacks on humanitarian aid workers and child conscription.[47]

In addition to the extensive list of war crimes in the ICC Statute, other war crimes may be identified in customary law and treaty law. As mentioned above, the ICC Statute is not a complete codification of all crimes in customary law, and hence other provisions may be identified applying the *Tadić* test, described in section 12.1.5. Moreover, war crimes may be established under treaty law – for example, among parties to AP I, the entire set of grave breaches in that Protocol is applicable as a matter of treaty law, regardless of whether they are also customary law.

12.1.7 War crimes in internal armed conflicts

Traditionally, neither IHL nor war crimes law applied in non-international armed conflicts. Before the advent of human rights law, States were regarded as entitled to deal with their own citizens more or less as they pleased, including in situations of rebellion and insurrection. This was an 'internal affair', in which other States should have no say. States sought

---

44 See Robert Cryer, *Prosecuting International Crimes* (Cambridge, 2005) 263–9.
45 See William Schabas, *Introduction to the International Criminal Court* (Cambridge, 2001) 54.
46 See section 12.3.7.
47 Arts. 3 and 4 SCSL Statute.

to preserve latitude in putting down rebels, and they did not wish to bestow any possible recognition on rebel groups. Exceptionally, States involved in intense internal conflicts occasionally recognized a situation of 'belligerency', in which case IHL was applied to the conflict.[48]

During the negotiation of the four Geneva Conventions of 1949, several delegations pressed for recognition of rules in internal conflicts, a proposal strongly opposed by others.[49] After intense discussions, agreement was reached to include in each Convention a common Article – Article 3 – laying out some very basic norms recognized to apply even in internal armed conflicts. Even this very modest provision was an achievement.

Regulation of internal armed conflict was expanded significantly in AP II of 1977. Again, the negotiation was difficult, with many States opposing regulation. Agreement was reached on a short list of provisions, expanding upon and developing those rules in common Article 3 but still falling far short of that applicable to international armed conflict.[50]

Significantly, common Article 3 and AP II contained no grave breaches provisions, leading many to the conclusion that violations of those provisions were not criminalized. As of 1990, it was widely accepted that the law of war crimes did not apply in internal armed conflict.[51]

By the 1990s, the gap in coverage had become increasingly problematic, and several factors converged to precipitate a necessary legal evolution. First, internal conflicts had increased in magnitude and duration, causing vastly more civilian deaths than in previous centuries.[52] Second, internal conflicts had become more prevalent than international conflicts,[53] making change necessary if war crimes law was to have relevance for victims of conflict. Third, the increasing interdependence of States meant that internal conflicts had greater consequences for surrounding regions, increasing the urgency of regulating the conflicts. Fourth, the increased prioritization of human rights and human security meant that States were more willing to insist on extending protection even in contexts previously considered an 'internal affair'.[54]

---

48 See, e.g. Eric David, *Principes de Droit des Conflits Armés*, 2nd edn (Brussels, 1999) 124–7; Lindsay Moir, *The Law of Internal Armed Conflict* (Cambridge, 2002) at 3–21.

49 Jean Pictet, *Commentary to I Geneva Convention* (Geneva, 1952) 38–48.

50 Howard S. Levie, *The Law of Non-International Armed Conflict* (Dordrecht, 1987) 27–90; Michael Bothe, *New Rules for Victims of Armed Conflict* (The Hague, 1982) 605–8; Yves Sandoz et al., *Commentary on the Additional Protocols of 8 June 1977* (Geneva, 1987) 1336.

51 '[A]ccording to humanitarian law as it stands today, the notion of war crimes is limited to situations of international armed conflict': ICRC DDM/JUR442 b, 25 March 1993, para. 4 (cited in the Separate Opinion of Judge Li, *Tadić* ICTY A. Ch. 2.10.1995 para. 7); Denise Plattner, 'The Penal Repression of Violation of International Humanitarian Law' (1990) 30 *International Review of the Red Cross* 409.

52 UN Development Programme, *Human Development Report* 2005 (UNDP, 2005) 153–61.

53 Human Security Centre, *Human Security Report* 2005 (Oxford, 2005) 22–5.

54 *Tadić* ICTY A. Ch. 2.10.1995 paras. 94–6; and see discussion in, e.g. Theodor Meron, 'International Criminalization of Internal Atrocities' (1995) 89 *AJIL* 554; Darryl Robinson and Herman von Hebel, 'War Crimes in Internal Conflicts: Article 8 of the ICC Statute' (1999) 2 *YIHL* 193.

The UN Security Council took the first major step forward when it adopted the ICTR Statute. Because the conflict in Rwanda was internal, the Council was confronted with the question of war crimes in internal conflict. The Council included in the Statute serious violations of common Article 3 and core provisions of AP II, thus expressly recognizing a criminalization of these prohibitions.

The *Tadić* decision on jurisdiction by the ICTY Appeals Chamber had a considerable impact on the development of the law in this area.[55] The decision reviewed State practice, resolutions of the League of Nations, General Assembly, Security Council and European Union, ICJ decisions, military codes of conduct, and agreements and understandings, and concluded that the traditional stark dichotomy between international and internal conflicts was becoming blurred, and that some war crimes provisions were now applicable in internal armed conflicts. The Chamber held that there had not been a wholesale trans-position or a complete convergence, but rather that *'only a number of rules* and principles … have gradually been extended to apply to internal conflicts'.[56] Moreover, 'this extension has not taken place in the form of a full and mechanical transplant of those rules to internal conflicts; rather, *the general essence* of those rules, and not the detailed regulation they may contain, has become applicable to internal conflicts'.[57] To determine whether a norm also applies in internal armed conflict, one must consider: whether there is clear and unequivocal recognition of the norm, state practice indicating an intention to criminalize the norm, the gravity of the acts, and the interest of the international community in their prohibition.[58]

The decision was seen as groundbreaking at the time,[59] but it was rapidly digested by the international community. The approach was followed soon afterward by the ICTR,[60] and more significantly, it received a remarkable level of State acceptance during the negotiation of the ICC Statute.[61] Although a determined minority in Rome strongly opposed the inclusion of war crimes in internal conflicts, a clear majority was equally strongly committed to their inclusion. Opposition gave way to acceptance of common Article 3 and a limited list of other fundamental provisions in the Statute. Significantly, the approach taken by the

---

55 *Tadić* ICTY A. Ch. 2.10.1995.

56 *Ibid.*, para. 126.

57 *Ibid.*

58 *Ibid.*, paras. 128 and 129.

59 See, e.g. Christopher Greenwood, 'International Humanitarian Law and the *Tadić* Case' (1996) 7 *EJIL* 265; George Aldrich, 'Jurisdiction of the International Criminal Tribunal for the Former Yugoslavia' (1996) 90 *AJIL* 64; Geoffrey Watson, 'The Humanitarian Law of the Yugoslavia War Crimes Tribunal: Jurisdiction in *Prosecutor* v. *Tadić*' (1996) 36 *Virginia Journal of International Law* 687.

60 *Kanyabashi* ICTR T. Ch. II 18.6.1997 para. 8.

61 In effect, the theory of partial convergence of the law of international and internal armed conflicts was put to the international community: Claus Kreß, 'War Crimes Committed in Non-International Armed Conflict and the Emerging System of International Criminal Justice' (2001) 30 *Israel Yearbook on Human Rights* 1 at 5; Moir, *Law of Internal Conflict*, 160–7.

Rome Conference largely followed that of *Tadić*: identifying fundamental prohibitions and transposing them to internal conflicts.[62]

In the result, roughly half of the provisions from international conflicts were transplanted to internal conflicts in the ICC Statute. For other provisions, there was not consensus that they were so fundamental that customary law at that point recognized them in internal conflicts. While the recognition of half of the provisions was a remarkable achievement in 1998, there is good reason to believe that the list of war crimes in Article 8(2)(e) falls short of the list that the *Tadić* test would permit. For example, the prohibition of starvation as a means of warfare, the use of chemical weapons, attacking civilian objects, and launching disproportionate attacks, are all fundamental provisions with long recognition in the laws and customs of war, and hence merit recognition in internal conflicts.[63] Indeed, the incompleteness of the list in Article 8(2)(b)(e) produces a number of strange consequences.[64] As noted in section 12.1.6, Article 10 affirms that nothing in the ICC Statute limits or prejudices the development of other international law.

It has been suggested that the ICC Statute is 'retrograde' in that it did not abolish completely the international–internal distinction.[65] However, while the trend certainly favours continued convergence, State practice and *opinio juris* do not currently support the view that the two regimes have become identical. Indeed, even the high-water mark of the *Tadić* decision did not assert that there had been a full and mechanical transplant of rules from international conflicts to their internal counterparts, but rather that the essence of some of the most important rules was applicable. Moreover, some provisions from international armed conflict simply would not make sense in internal conflict, particularly provisions concerning occupied territory, prisoners of war, and transfer of the civilian population into occupied territory.

The law does, however, continue to progress.[66] Given the convergence already recognized, it would already be useful in any future catalogues of war crimes to consolidate those provisions that are common to both internal and international conflicts. The bifurcated structure in current statutes can create unnecessary complications, because it requires a determination of the character of an armed conflict in order to know which provisions to charge (for example Article 8(2)(b) or 8(2)(e)), even where the provisions are similar or identical. It may be necessary to collect evidence and litigate on complex issues, such as the role of third States,[67] when ultimately this has no bearing on the role and liability of the

---

62 Robinson and von Hebel, 'War Crimes', 197–200.

63 Kreß, 'War Crimes', 37, 39.

64 *Ibid*.

65 Antonio Cassese, 'The Statute of the International Criminal Court: Some Preliminary Reflections' (1999) 10 *EJIL* 149, 150.

66 See, e.g. the study of customary law undertaken under ICRC auspices: Henckaerts and Doswald-Beck, *ICRC Customary Law*.

67 See section 12.2.2.

perpetrator. Indeed, this problem has already arisen in the first case to be tried by the ICC, where the Prosecutor and the Pre-Trial Chambers took different views on the character of the armed conflict, an issue irrelevant to the criminal wrongdoing, yet necessary to determine whether charges should fall under Article 8(2)(b) or (e).[68]

The ICTY has partially sidestepped such problems by relying heavily on common Article 3 and other provisions applicable in internal conflicts.[69] In any future catalogue of war crimes it would be more efficient to establish one list of crimes applicable in both international and internal conflicts, and a short list of those crimes applicable only in international conflict.[70] Such a list would not entail any change in customary law, but simply a clearer presentation of the existing legal situation.

12.2 Common issues

12.2.1 Armed conflict

The essential element for any war crime is the nexus with armed conflict. It is the insecure and volatile situation of armed conflict that warrants international interest and gives rise to international jurisdiction over the crime. Whereas early IHL depended on a declaration of a state of war, this was problematic in that parties to conflict might raise formalistic arguments denying a state of war.[71] Current IHL and war crimes law therefore focus on the objective existence of armed conflict, even if one or both of the parties deny the state of war.[72]

In the case of internal conflict, a certain threshold of intensity and organization must be met, in order to distinguish armed conflict from mere internal disturbances and riots, as is discussed below.[73] In the case of State-to-State conflict, most authorities indicate that *any* resort to force involving military forces amounts to armed conflict.[74]

The concept of armed conflict includes not only the application of force between armed forces, but also an invasion that meets no resistance,[75] aerial bombing, or an unauthorized border crossing by armed forces.

---

68 *Lubanga Dyilo*, ICC PTC-I, 29.1.2007 paras. 200–37.

69 S. Boelaert-Suominen, 'The Yugoslavia Tribunal and the Common Core of Humanitarian Law Applicable to all Armed Conflicts' (2000) 13 *LJIL* 619.

70 As a model, see the German Code of Crimes Against International Law, reproduced in, e.g. Gerhard Werle, *Principles of International Criminal Law* (The Hague, 2005) 428–33.

71 Pictet, *Commentary to I Geneva Convention*, 32–3.

72 See, e.g. Art. 2 common to the Geneva Conventions of 1949.

73 See section 12.2.3.

74 Tribunal jurisprudence requires 'protracted' violence for internal conflict but not for State-to-State conflict: *Tadić* ICTY A. Ch. 2.10.1995 para. 70. According to the ICRC commentary on the Geneva Conventions, the concept of armed conflict includes 'any difference arising between two States and leading to the intervention of members of the armed forces': Pictet, *Commentary to I Geneva Convention*, 20; and see discussion in Claus Kreß, 'The 1999 Crisis in East Timor and the Threshold of the Law of War Crimes' (2002) 13 *CLF* 409 at 412–13.

75 Art. 2 GC I.

The state of armed conflict does not end with each particular ceasefire; rather, it continues until the 'general close of military operations'.[76] According to Tribunal jurisprudence, the state of armed conflict extends 'until a general conclusion of peace is reached, or in the case of internal armed conflict, until a peaceful settlement is achieved'.[77] The state of conflict may also be ended by a decisive close of military operations even without an agreement.[78] The state of armed conflict also applies during occupation, that is to say when territory is placed under the authority of a hostile army.[79]

12.2.2 Distinguishing between international and internal conflicts

The paradigmatic situation of international armed conflict is the resort to force between the military forces of States. Complex issues arise outside this paradigm, with respect to wars of national liberation, UN enforcement operations and foreign intervention through proxy forces.[80]

Wars of national liberation

According to Article 1(4) of AP I, the concept of international armed conflict also includes conflicts in which 'peoples are fighting against colonial domination and alien occupation and against racist régimes in the exercise of their right of self-determination'. This definition applies, as a matter of treaty law, to any prosecutions based on the grave breaches regime of AP I.[81]

The more difficult question is whether this expansion of the concept of international armed conflict also applies in the general law of war crimes.[82] On the one hand, if the question is answered in the negative, parties to AP I would be simultaneously subject to two regimes: an international conflict regime under AP I and an internal conflict regime under (for example) the ICC Statute, which would seem an undesirable result. On the other hand, if the question is answered in the affirmative, the AP I definition might be applied in conflicts where the parties had not ratified AP I, which would also seem undesirable.

---

76 Art. 6 GC IV.

77 *Tadić* ICTY A. Ch. 2.10.1995 para. 70. In addition, '[u]ntil that moment, international humanitarian law continues to apply in the whole territory of the warring States or, in the case of internal conflicts, the whole territory under control of a party, whether or not actual combat takes place there'.

78 Art. 6 GC IV; Christopher Greenwood, 'The Scope of Application of Humanitarian Law' in Fleck, *Handbook*, 72; see also UN Security Council Resolution 95 (1951), finding an interdiction by Egypt to be contrary to an armistice agreement (even without a general peace treaty).

79 See, e.g. Art. 52 Hague Regulations; Art. 6 GC IV; ICC Elements, footnote 34; *Naletilić* ICTY T. Ch. I 31.3.2003 paras. 214–17.

80 The complexities of these distinctions have further strengthened calls for a single body of IHL applicable in all conflicts: James Stewart, 'Toward a Single Definition of Armed Conflict in International Humanitarian Law: A Critique of Internationalized Armed Conflict' (2003) 85 *IRRC* 313.

81 Art. 85 AP I.

82 See, e.g. discussion in Andreas Zimmerman, 'Article 8' in Triffterer, *Observers' Notes*, 479–80.

The answer to the question seems to hinge on whether the AP I definition can be regarded as customary law.[83] The scant State practice makes it prudent to avoid any hasty pronouncements on that provision's customary status. Moreover, different fact patterns may make it easier or harder to characterize a conflict as international. A conflict involving a people with a clear national identity resisting colonial domination can be more readily seen as 'international'. On the other hand, a conflict involving local oppressed groups fighting against a racist regime, without foreign intervention, may well be a worthy cause but it would seem counterfactual to describe it as 'international'.[84]

UN forces

Another interesting question is the legal effect of intervention by UN enforcement operations. The first question is whether IHL applies at all to such forces; after all, the UN is an international organization and hence not party per se to the Geneva Conventions and other IHL treaties. It is now recognized that the law of armed conflict applies to the operations of UN forces;[85] the UN has accepted and declared that the fundamental principles and rules of IHL apply to UN forces.[86] Participants in a conflict cannot be exempted from basic principles of IHL because they are fighting in a just cause (maintenance of international peace and security); victims of conflict are entitled to protection of IHL in all conflicts. Experience shows, regrettably, that even peacekeeping forces may be involved in IHL violations and war crimes.

The remaining question is whether the intervention of UN forces – whether operations under the UN flag or simply approved by the UN – can render a previously internal conflict an international one. The law on this point does not appear to be settled. To regard UN forces as being 'parties to a conflict' may seem inimical to the role of the UN, and one could argue that an otherwise internal conflict remains internal.[87] However, this may be blurring the issue of the justness of the cause with the issue of whether forces are in fact engaged in armed conflict. When enforcement actions involve a significant application of force, the objective fact remains that foreign forces are thereby engaged in conflict. The practice on this question is ambiguous.[88]

---

83 The ICC might be able to avoid the problem by insisting that it applies only the terms of Articles 8(2)(d) and (f), which do not include 'national liberation' as a factor. The fact that Article 8 repeatedly refers to the 'established framework of international law' may, however, drive the Court back into an analysis of customary international law.

84 On the fundamental separation between 'just cause' doctrine and IHL, see section 12.1.3.

85 Ray Murphy, 'United Nations Military Operations and International Humanitarian Law: What Rules Apply to Peacekeepers?'(2003) 14 *CLF* 153.

86 Secretary-General's Bulletin: Observance by United Nations Forces of International Humanitarian Law, 6 August 1999, UN Doc. ST/SGB/1999/13.

87 See, e.g. Dietrich Schindler, 'The Different Types of Armed Conflicts According to the Geneva Conventions and Protcols' (1979) 163 *Hague Recueil* 121 at 151.

88 Christopher Greenwood, 'International Humanitarian Law and United Nations Military Operations' (1998) 3 *Yearbook of International Humanitarian Law* 3.

Proxy forces

Finally, a seemingly internal conflict may be rendered international where it is found that local armed groups are in fact acting on behalf of an external State. For example, in the *Tadić* case, the determination of whether the grave breaches provision applied depended on whether the conflict was international, which in turn depended on whether acts of certain forces (the VRS) were attributable to the Federal Republic of Yugoslavia. The Federal Republic of Yugoslavia (FRY) had purported to withdraw its forces (the JNA) from Bosnia, but left behind the VRS, composed of former JNA soldiers of Bosnian origin, with the same officers, the same weapons, the same equipment, the same suppliers and the same objectives, with funding still coming from the FRY.

The majority of the Trial Chamber referred to the International Court of Justice *Nicaragua* decision, which had adopted a stringent 'effective control' test to determine whether acts of an armed band could be attributed to a State.[89] The majority in the Trial Chamber found that while the FRY had the capacity to direct operations, there was no evidence of specific orders or that the FRY had actually directed operations.[90] The decision was criticized in a powerful dissent and in commentary for not reflecting the reality of the situation.[91]

The Appeals Chamber clarified that for individuals, or for groups not militarily organized, instructions or *ex post facto* endorsement or approval from a third State may be required; however, with respect to armed groups, the Chamber replaced the test of 'effective control' by that of 'overall control'.[92] Under the 'overall control' test, it is not necessary to produce evidence of specific orders or instructions relating to particular military actions.[93] It is sufficient to establish 'overall control going beyond the mere financing and equipping of such forces and involving also participation in the planning and supervision of military operations'.[94]

12.2.3 Distinguishing internal conflict from riots and disturbances

Section 12.2.2 discussed the line between international and internal armed conflict. There is also a lower threshold, dividing situations of sufficient intensity to be called 'armed

---

89 *Case Concerning Military and Paramilitary Activities in and Against Nicaragua (Nicaragua* v. *USA)* (Merits) [1986] ICJ Rep 14 para. 115.

90 *Tadić* ICTY T. Ch. II 7.5.1997 paras. 588–607.

91 McDonald, Dissent in *Tadić* ICTY T. Ch. II 7.5.1997; see, e.g. Theodor Meron, 'Classification of Armed Conflict in the Former Yugoslavia: *Nicaragua's* Fallout' (1998) 92 *AJIL* 236.

92 *Tadić* ICTY A. Ch. 15.7.1999 para. 137.

93 *Ibid.*, para. 145.

94 *Ibid.* In a subsequent case, the ICJ disapproved of the ICTY Appeals Chamber's purported distinguishing of *Nicaragua* and its pronouncements on general international law. The ICJ conceded, without deciding, that 'overall control' may be an appropriate test for determining the character of armed conflict in international criminal law, but it is not an appropriate test for determining the responsibility of States under general international law: *Case Concerning the Application of the Convention on the Prevention and Punishment of Genocide (Bosnia and Herzegovina* v. *Serbia and Montenegro)* ICJ General List No. 91, paras. 402–7.

conflict' from lesser situations of riots and disturbances which are insufficient to activate IHL and the law of war crimes. It is sometimes difficult to determine the point at which mere civil strife crosses the threshold to amount to internal armed conflict.

Further complicating this task is the fact that different authorities appear to suggest slightly different thresholds, leading to the prospect of different thresholds for different purposes. Common Article 3 says nothing about the threshold defining armed conflict, whereas AP II poses a very high threshold, so that it applies only to armed conflicts:

> which take place in the territory of a High Contracting Party between its armed forces and dissident armed forces or other organized groups which, under responsible command, exercise such control over a part of its territory as to enable them to carry out sustained and concerted military operations and to implement this protocol.[95]

The question arises whether the customary law of war crimes also involves different thresholds for different crimes (for example common Article 3 and AP II crimes). Tribunal jurisprudence does not indicate different thresholds for different crimes in internal conflict. While there are many different ways to interpret the differing authorities,[96] we suggest that general war crimes law applies a single threshold for all crimes in internal armed conflict. This conclusion is based on four straightforward propositions.

The first proposition is that 'armed conflict' entails a certain intensity of fighting and level of organization of the parties. The widely accepted test articulated by the ICTY Appeals Chamber in the *Tadić* case states that 'armed conflict exists whenever there is a resort to armed force between States or *protracted armed violence* between governmental authorities and *organized armed groups* or between such groups within a State'.[97] This test has been interpreted as involving two criteria: intensity of the conflict and organization of the parties.[98] This standard was also applied by the ICTR in *Akayesu*.[99]

---

95 Art. 1(1) AP II. Green, *Contemporary Law*, 67 regards the test as 'so high that it would exclude most revolutions and rebellions'.

96 For a more detailed study, see Bahia Tahzib-Lie and Olivia Swaak-Goldman, 'Determining the Threshold for the Application of International Humanitarian Law' in L. Lijnzaad et al. (eds.), *Making the Voice of Humanity Heard* (Netherlands, 2004).

97 *Tadić* ICTY A. Ch. 2.10.1995 para. 70 (emphasis added).

98 *Tadić* ICTY T. Ch. II 7.5.1997 para. 562. For other examples applying the test, see *Boskoski*, ICTY T. Ch. 10.7.2008 paras. 175–205; *Haradinaj* ICTY T. Ch. 3.4.2008 paras. 37–60. *Haradinaj* mentioned factors such as the existence of a command structure, disciplinary mechanisms, headquarters, control of territory, access to weapons, military training, ability to plan and carry out military operations, and ability to speak with one voice and negotiate and conclude agreements such as cease-fire or peace accords. The Inter-American Commission appears to have applied a rather lower threshold for the 'protracted' nature of the conflict. An attack by forty-two persons on military barracks, resulting in a military response to retake the barracks, lasting around thirty hours and resulting in the deaths of twenty-nine attackers and several State agents, was found sufficient to constitute an armed conflict: *La Tablada*, IACHR Report No. 55/97, Case No. 11.137, Argentina; OEA/L/V/II.97, Doc. 38, 20 Oct. 1997.

99 *Akayesu* ICTR T. Ch. I 2.9.1998 paras. 619–20. The *Akayesu* decision also noted with approval a series of factors suggested in the ICRC commentary to the Additional Protocols, including: whether the government was

The second proposition is that the statement in AP II and in Article 8(2)(d) and (f) of the ICC Statute that 'situations of internal disturbances and tensions, such as riots, isolated and sporadic acts of violence and other acts of a similar nature' do not constitute armed conflicts, is also implicit in the concept of armed conflict. Indeed, the statement is simply the corollary of the requirements of intensity and organization.[100]

The third proposition is that the additional restrictions appearing in AP II have not been absorbed into the general law of war crimes. For example, AP II requires that one party to the conflict be a government, whereas Tribunal jurisprudence and the ICC Statute recognize armed conflict entirely between armed groups.[101] In addition, control of territory was rejected as a requirement in Tribunal jurisprudence and the ICC Statute, although it has been recognized as an important *indicative factor* as to the existence of an armed conflict.[102] Thus, these restrictions may continue to limit the applicability of AP II as a matter of treaty law, but they do not affect the interpretation of the concept of 'armed conflict' for other purposes, including the customary law of war crimes.[103]

The fourth proposition is that the thresholds in the ICC Statute can be interpreted consistently with Tribunal jurisprudence. Indeed Tribunal and ICC cases have referenced each other.[104] While the requirement of 'protracted' violence appears only in Article 8(2)(f) (other serious violations),[105] the requirement is inherent in the concept of armed conflict and hence applicable to all war crimes in internal conflict.[106] Thus, it should not be interpreted as creating different thresholds for different crimes, but as a clarification to facilitate acceptance of the controversial Article 8(2)(e).[107] Moreover, while Article 8(2)(f) refers to 'protracted armed *conflict*' rather than 'armed *violence*', this appears to have been a straightforward drafting error, since the intent was to incorporate the threshold from

---

obliged to have recourse to the regular military forces; recognition by the government of a state of belligerency; and inclusion of the situation on the agenda of the Security Council or General Assembly.

100 A conclusion confirmed in *Tadić* ICTY T. Ch. II 7.5.1997 para. 562 and *Akayesu* ICTR T. Ch. I 2.9.1998 para. 620.

101 Art. 8(2)(f) ICC Statute; *Tadić* ICTY A. Ch. 2.10.1995 para. 70.

102 Art. 8(2)(f) ICC Statute; *Akayesu* ICTR T. Ch. I 2.9.1998 paras. 619–20. An ICC Pre-Trial Chamber referred to control of territory as a 'key' factor (*Situation in Darfur* (*Al Bashir* arrest warrant case) ICC PTC I, 4.3.2009 para. 60) which is an unfortunate wording insofar as it may suggest the factor is almost indispensable, given that it was expressly rejected by the ICC Statute drafters. See, e.g. Robert Cryer, 'International Crimes in the Al Bashir Arrest Warrant Decision' (2009) 7 *JICJ* 283 at 285–6. The *Lubanga Dyilo* PTC confirmed that territorial control is not a requirement: *Lubanga Dyilo*, ICC PTC I, 29.1.2007 para. 233.

103 As discussed in cases such as *Tadić* ICTY A. Ch. 2.10.1995 para. 70; *Akayesu* ICTR T. Ch. I 2.9.1998 paras. 619–20; *Lubanga Dyilo*, ICC PTC I, 29.1.2007 para. 233.

104 *Limaj* ICTY T. Ch. II 30.11.2005 paras. 83–174, made reference to the ICC Statute and found that it was consistent with the *Tadić* test. And, for example, *Lubanga Dyilo*, ICC PTC I, 29.1.2007 paras. 208, 210, 233 and *Al Bashir* arrest warrant case ICC PTC I, 4.3.2009 para. 59 adopt ICTY jurisprudence.

105 Art. 8(2)(f): 'Paragraph 2(e) applies ... to armed conflicts that take place in the territory of a State when there is protracted armed conflict between governmental authorities and organized groups or between such groups.'

106 *Tadić* ICTY A. Ch. 2.10.1995 para. 70.

107 Kreß, 'War Crimes', 15–17; Meron, 'Humanization', 260.

Tadić, not to exclude a class of armed conflicts.[108] The French version of the Statute supports the view that the intent was to refer to the established concept of 'protracted violence' and not to create a new standard. Indeed, ICC jurisprudence has interpreted 'protracted' in the same manner as Tribunal jurisprudence.[109]

If these four propositions are correct, as current jurisprudence indicates, then both Tribunals and the ICC posit a single, consistent threshold for war crimes in internal armed conflicts.[110]

12.2.4 Nexus between conduct and conflict

In order to constitute a war crime, conduct must be linked to an armed conflict. For example, the ICC Elements of Crimes require that the conduct be committed 'in the context of and associated with' an armed conflict.[111]

The term 'in the context of' refers to the temporal and geographic context in a broad sense: the conduct occurred during an armed conflict and on a territory in which there is an armed conflict.[112] This requirement is very general, since a state of armed conflict is recognized throughout the territory, beyond the time and place of the hostilities.[113] There is no need for military activities at the time and place of the crime; crimes can be temporally and geographically remote from the actual fighting.[114]

The term 'associated with' refers to the specific nexus between the conduct of the perpetrator and the conflict, and matches the ICTY requirement that the conduct be 'closely related to' the conflict.[115] Not all criminal activity on a territory experiencing armed conflict amounts to a war crime. For example, if a person kills a neighbour purely out of jealousy or because of a private dispute over land, and this happens to occur during an armed conflict, that is not a war crime.[116]

In the *Kunarac* judgment, the ICTY Appeals Chamber provided a helpful elaboration of this test, focusing on whether the existence of conflict played a substantial part in

108 Kreß, 'War Crimes', 15–17. See also Sandesh Sivakumaran, 'Identifying an Armed Conflict not of an International Character' in Stahn and Sluiter, *Emerging Practice*, 363.
109 *Lubanga Dyilo*, ICC PTC I, 29.1.2007 para. 234; *Al Bashir* arrest warrant case ICC PTC I, 4.3.2009 para. 60.
110 In a similar vein, see International Committee of the Red Cross, Opinion Paper, 'How is the Term "Armed Conflict" Defined in International Law', March 2008, available at www.icrc.org.
111 See, e.g. ICC Elements Art. 8(2)(a)–1. The test was referenced by the ICTR in *Kayishema* ICTR T. Ch. II 21.5.1999 para. 187, although the Chamber ultimately declined to articulate a legal test: *ibid.*, para. 188.
112 Knut Dörmann, Eve La Haye and Herman von Hebel, 'War Crimes' in Lee, *Elements and Rules*, 120–1.
113 *Tadić* ICTY A. Ch. 2.10.1995 para. 70.
114 *Kunarac* ICTY A. Ch. 12.6.2002 para. 57.
115 *Tadić* ICTY A. Ch. 2.10.1995 para. 70. While some nexus is needed, the crime need not be committed during combat, nor need it be part of a policy or practice or in the interests of a party to the conflict: *Tadić* ICTY T. Ch. II 7.5.1997 paras. 572–3.
116 Knut Dörmann, *Elements of War Crimes under the Rome Statute of the International Criminal Court* (Cambridge, 2003) 19–20.

the perpetrator's *ability* to commit a crime, his *decision* to commit it, the *manner* in which it was committed or the *purpose* for which it was committed.[117] Hence, it is sufficient that the perpetrator acted in furtherance of or under the guise of the armed conflict.[118] In assessing these questions, one may take into account, inter alia, the following factors: the status of perpetrator (e.g. combatant); the status of the victim (e.g. non-combatant, combatant of opposing party); whether the act serves a goal of a military campaign; and whether it was committed in the context of the perpetrator's official duties.[119]

12.2.5 The perpetrator

The law of war crimes does not govern only members of armed forces or groups and their leaders. The fact that a perpetrator is a member of an armed force does help to establish the nexus to armed conflict, but it is not a requirement.[120] The conduct of civilians can be a war crime even if it is not imputable to a party to the conflict, provided that the nexus requirement is met.[121]

A more difficult question is whether the perpetrator must have some awareness of the armed conflict. Early Tribunal jurisprudence did not inquire into knowledge of the conflict,[122] which suggests either that the judges saw the existence of the conflict as a purely jurisdictional matter or that they saw the knowledge as obvious. In *Kordić* and subsequent cases, the ICTY Appeals Chamber indicated that the knowledge of the accused of the fact of armed conflict is indeed required, as the conflict is an element of the crime.[123]

Similarly, the ICC Elements of Crimes[124] indicate that a person cannot be convicted as a war criminal unless he or she has the necessary awareness of the factual circumstances that make the conduct a war crime. The final element for each war crime requires that the perpetrator was 'aware of factual circumstances that established the existence of an armed conflict'.[125] The knowledge requirement in the Elements is clarified or attenuated in three

---

117 See *Kunarac* ICTY A. Ch. 12.6.2002 para. 58.

118 *Ibid.*

119 *Kunarac* ICTY A. Ch. 12.6.2002 para. 59; *Rutaganda* ICTR A. Ch. 26.5.2003 para. 569.

120 *Akayesu* ICTR A. Ch. 1.6.2001 paras. 444–5.

121 See, e.g. *Essen Lynching Trial* I LRTWC 88; *Tesch* (The Zyklon B Case) I LRTWC 93.

122 *Tadić* ICTY T. Ch. II 7.5.1997 para. 572.

123 *Kordić* ICTY A. Ch. 17.12.2004 para. 311; *Naletilić* ICTY A. Ch. 3.5.2006 paras. 116–20. In both cases, the Appeals Chamber required knowledge of 'the *factual* circumstances, *e.g.* that a foreign state was involved in the armed conflict' (emphasis in original). This test is more onerous than that in the ICC Elements, where knowledge of the international character of the conflict is not required: ICC Elements, Introduction to War Crimes, para. 3.

124 Dörmann, La Haye and von Hebel, 'War Crimes' in Lee, *Elements and Rules*, 121–3. Some national jurisprudence reaches the same conclusion, see, e.g. the Supreme Court of Canada decision of *R* v. *Finta* [1994] 1 SCR 701 at 820.

125 See, e.g. ICC Elements Art. 8(2)(a)(i), element 5.

ways. First, the Introduction to War Crimes clarifies that no *legal* evaluation by the perpetrator is required; it is sufficient that the accused be aware of the facts.[126] Second, the Introduction clarifies that there is no requirement of awareness of the factual circumstances establishing the *character* of the conflict as international or internal.[127] Third, and most remarkably, the Introduction states that:

> There is only a requirement for the awareness of the factual circumstances that established the existence of an armed conflict that is implicit in the terms 'took place in the context of and was associated with'.

The result is not a model of legislative clarity, but it appears to require only sufficient factual awareness so that the crime may be said objectively to meet the 'associated with' or 'closely related' test.[128] The judges are left ample room to clarify based on relevant facts. In any event, the issue seems to be of theoretical interest rather than practical importance, since it is difficult to conceive of situations where a perpetrator's conduct could satisfy the nexus to conflict, while the perpetrator was somehow unaware of the armed conflict going on around him or her.

12.2.6 The victim or object of the crime

The definitions of many war crimes include certain criteria with respect to the victim (or object) of the crime. For example, for grave breaches of the Geneva Conventions, the crime must affect 'protected persons or objects'.[129] Protected persons include civilians, prisoners of war and combatants who are no longer able to fight because they are sick, wounded or shipwrecked.[130] Similarly, common Article 3 protects 'persons no longer taking active part in hostilities, including members of armed forces who have laid down their arms and those placed *hors de combat* by sickness, wounds, detention or other cause'. These restrictions are necessary because some acts, such as wilful killing, are not a crime when committed against a combatant.

Other war crimes specify a particular victim or object of the crime (for example civilian population, civilian objects, persons involved in humanitarian assistance, undefended towns, etc.).[131] Some war crimes regulate battlefield conduct, to reduce unnecessary suffering of combatants, and hence even combatants are protected as victims of the crime.[132]

---

126 ICC Elements, Introduction to War Crimes, para. 3.
127 *Ibid.*
128 See section 12.2.4.
129 See, e.g. Art. 147 GC IV, Art. 8(2)(a) ICC Statute, Art. 2 ICTY Statute.
130 See, e.g. Arts. 12 and 13 GC I, Arts. 12 and 13 GC II, Art. 4 GC III, Art. 4 GC IV.
131 Art. 8(2)(b)(i)–(v) ICC Statute.
132 See, e.g. Art. 8(2)(b)(vi), (vii), (xi), (xii), (xvii)–(xx).

Because IHL originally developed as a series of reciprocal promises between parties to a conflict, most of IHL regulates conduct towards those affiliated with the 'enemy'.[133] For this reason, many war crimes require that the victim be 'in the hands of'[134] or 'in the power of'[135] an adverse party.[136] Some of the most important protections for civilians arise in GC IV, which protects persons 'who find themselves, in case of a conflict or occupation, in the hands of a Party to the conflict or Occupying Power of which they are not nationals'.[137] This provision was drafted bearing in mind a classic State-to-State international armed conflict.

However, recent history has shown that conflicts can be far more complex. The armed conflict in Bosnia was international in character, due to the involvement of neighbouring States, yet it was also predominantly an ethnic conflict. Persons were frequently detained by, and abused by, persons of another ethnic group, that is to say a different party to the conflict, yet they were all of the same nationality. Applying the Geneva Conventions literally, the victims would not be entitled to protection, because all concerned held the same passport, even though they were in fact hostile forces.

In the *Tadić* decision, the ICTY Appeals Chamber held that the crucial test is allegiance, and that ethnicity rather than nationality may become the ground of allegiance.[138] Thus, the Chamber chose to look at the substance of the relations rather than formalities.[139]

12.2.7 The 'jurisdictional' threshold in the ICC Statute

Article 8(1) of the ICC Statute provides that the ICC 'shall have jurisdiction in respect of war crimes in particular when committed as part of a plan or policy or as part of a large-scale commission of such crimes'. It must be emphasized that this is not an element of a war crime; unlike crimes against humanity, even a single isolated act can constitute a war crime. Article 8(1) is rather an indicator to the ICC as to how it ought to exercise its jurisdiction; namely to focus its resources not on isolated war crimes but on the most serious situations. The term 'large-scale' is either synomymous with, or less demanding than, the 'widespread' element of crimes against humanity, and 'plan or policy' is less demanding than

---

133 There are exceptions; for example, Art. 75 AP I protects *all* persons in the hands of a party to conflict; and see section 12.3.8 concerning child soldiers. As the emphasis has shifted to the duty of any party toward victims of conflict, the role of reciprocity is diminishing in IHL, although it is still significant: see René Provost, *International Human Rights and Humanitarian Law* (Cambridge, 2002) 121–238.
134 Art. 4 GC IV.
135 See, e.g. Art. 4 GC III; ICC Elements Art. 8(2)(b)(x)–1, element 4.
136 It has been suggested that the requirement of 'in the hands of' or 'in the power of' is also needed to distinguish Geneva-type provisions from provisions regulating methods and means of combat. For example, it might be anticipated that an aerial bombing of a military target will cause a civilian death, but this is not a 'wilful killing' since the civilian is not 'in the hands' of the attacking party. On this view a comparable requirement should be imported into internal conflicts: Kreß, 'War Crimes'.
137 Art. 4 GC IV.
138 *Tadić* ICTY A. Ch. 2.10.1995 para. 166.
139 *Ibid.*, para. 168.

'systematic', corresponding instead to the lower threshold in Article 7(2)(a).[140] The words 'in particular' indicate that this is a guide rather than a requirement.[141] Thus the ICC may still act with respect to isolated war crimes which are of sufficient gravity to warrant action, such as crimes with a particularly grave impact.

12.3 Specific offences

12.3.1 The lists of war crimes in the Statutes of the Tribunals and the ICC

Section 12.3 examines the specific offences constituting war crimes. This examination will start with some observations on the lists of war crimes in the relevant instruments.

The ICTY Statute lists grave breaches of the Geneva Conventions (Article 2), and other violations of the laws and customs of war, drawing on other customary law sources (Article 3).[142] The ICTR Statute lists only serious violations of common Article 3 and AP I (Article 4). The ICC Statute follows the same approach of listing by source, and is the most elaborate. It features four lists: grave breaches of the Geneva Conventions (Article 8(2)(a)), other serious violations of the laws and customs applicable in international armed conflict (Article 8(2)(b)), serious violations of common Article 3 (Article 8(2)(c)), and other serious violations of the laws and customs applicable in non-international armed conflict (Article 8 (2)(e)). The 'other serious violations' lists in Article 8(2)(b) and (e) are drawn from various sources that were accepted as customary law, including provisions from Geneva law,[143] Hague law and other sources.

Because of the desire to adhere to customary law, and to reach agreement, the drafters of the ICC Statute relied on provisions from well-accepted instruments. Even when there was overlap, provisions were often included to avoid missing any customary norms. The drafters also declined to attempt to consolidate overlapping provisions, as this would have been seen as legislating. As a result of this reliance on various sources, there is considerable duplication. Furthermore, the order of the provisions in Article 8(2)(b) and (e) largely reflects the original instruments and the order of proposals, and the dynamics of reaching agreement did not allow for technical review and thematic resequencing. The list has been described as 'unwieldy',[144]

---

140 Chapter 11. The Appeals Chamber in *Ntaganda*, ICC A. Ch. 13.7.2006 para. 70 also notes that Art. 8(1) does not refer to 'systematic'.

141 Art. 8(1) was discussed by the Appeals Chamber in *Ntaganda*, ICC A. Ch. 13.7.2006 paras. 70–71 and by the ICC Office of the Prosecutor, Response to Communications Concerning the Situation in Iraq, 10 February 2006, available at www.icc-cpi.int/organs/otp/otp_com.html.

142 Report of the Secretary-General Pursuant to Paragraph 2 of Security Council Resolution 808 (1993), Presented 3 May 1993, UN Doc. S/25704.

143 Including some grave breaches from AP I and some other provisions of the Geneva Conventions not listed as grave breaches.

144 M. Cherif Bassiouni, 'Negotiating the Treaty of Rome on the Establishment of an International Criminal Court' (1999) 32 *Cornell International Law Journal* 462.

a 'hodgepodge',[145] lacking 'a clear and analytically convincing structure',[146] and not readily comprehensible to commanders.[147]

While there are many possible ways to group and order the specific war crimes, this chapter will present them in the following order, regardless of the original source of the norm. First, we examine provisions protecting non-combatants (section 12.3.2) and then two provisions governing attacks by combatants: the principle of distinction (section 12.3.3) and proportionality (section 12.3.4). We will then examine prohibitions relating to property (section 12.3.5), which reflect some of the overlaps in these principles (protecting rights of non-combatants and the principles of distinction and proportionality). This will be followed by an explanation of provisions regulating the means (section 12.3.6) and methods (section 12.3.7) of warfare. Finally, there are two significant war crimes provisions that do not fall neatly into the above categories, as they protect other interests (section 12.3.8).

12.3.2 Crimes against non-combatants

Violence and mistreatment

At the heart of war crimes law is a series of prohibitions of violence against and mistreatment of non-combatants (including civilians, prisoners of war and wounded or sick former combatants). These prohibitions are derived from the basic principle that non-combatants must be treated humanely. While these provisions are legally and conceptually straightforward, they are frequently violated in armed conflict, sometimes as practice or policy and sometimes as acts of individual soldiers. Deliberate and blatant violations of these provisions make up the majority of war crimes charges that have been brought in national and international jurisdictions.

The war crime of murdering or wilfully killing protected persons is well recognized in international and internal armed conflict.[148] Killing of *combatants* is of course permitted in lawfully conducted operations; moreover, civilians may also die as a consequence of military actions against military objectives, and such deaths must be assessed using the more specific tools of the prohibition on disproportionate collateral damage. While the international armed conflict provisions refer to 'wilful killing' and the internal armed

---

145 Bothe, 'War Crimes' in Cassese, *Commentary*, 396.
146 Kreß, 'War Crimes', 29.
147 While recognizing that sticking to traditional text made Art. 8 acceptable, Sunga notes that it would have been desirable to consolidate the provisions and build coherence, rather than following *lex lata* so literally, and that the result makes the list less comprehensible to commanders, thereby hindering compliance among even the most cooperative: Lyal Sunga, 'The Crimes Within the Jurisdiction of the International Criminal Court' (1998) 6/4 *European Journal of Crime, Criminal Law and Criminal Justice* 377 at 393–4.
148 Art. 8(2)(a)(i), 8(2)(c)(i) ICC Statute; Art. 2(a) ICTY Statute; Art. 4(a) ICTR Statute; Art. 147 GC IV; common Article 3 to the GCs.

conflict provisions refer to 'murder', the basic elements of the crime are the same, and correspond to those for the crime against humanity of murder, as already discussed.[149]

Torture, inhuman treatment, mutilation, and biological, medical or scientific experiments are also prohibited in any armed conflict.[150] Different instruments present the crimes with different structures, but the basic prohibitions are the same.[151]

The elements of torture and inhuman treatment have been discussed, in relation to crimes against humanity. However, unlike in the context of crimes against humanity,[152] the war crime of torture has a purpose requirement – that the perpetrator inflicted pain or suffering 'for such purposes as obtaining information or a confession, punishment, intimidation or coercion or for any reason based on discrimination of any kind'.[153] In the absence of such a purpose, the conduct could still amount to inhuman treatment.

Various forms of experimentation are prohibited in different instruments.[154] The prohibitions contain comparable requirements of endangering the physical or mental health or integrity of persons, not being justified by medical reasons (the treatment of the person) and not being carried out in the person's interest.[155]

The war crime of wilfully causing great suffering or serious injury to body or health arises from the GC grave breach provisions.[156] It can include actions deliberately causing long-lasting and serious harm without satisfying the elements of torture.[157]

The war crime of committing outrages upon personal dignity, in particular humiliating and degrading treatment, is drawn from common Article 3 and the Additional Protocols,[158] and therefore applies in any armed conflict. The prohibition is broader than the previously mentioned prohibitions, in that it also covers acts which, without directly causing harm to the integrity and physical and mental well-being of persons, are aimed at humiliating and ridiculing them, or forcing them to perform degrading acts.[159] The conduct

---

149 See Chapter 11.

150 Art. 8(2)(a)(ii), 8(2)(b)(x), 8(2)(c)(i), 8(2)(e)(xi) ICC Statute; Art. 2(b) ICTY Statute, reflecting the grave breach provisions (e.g. Art. 147 GC IV), common Article 3, and Art. 11 AP I.

151 Compare ICC Statute Art. 8(2)(a)(ii) (grave breach), 8(2)(b)(x) (AP I), 8(2)(c)(i) (common Article 3), 8(2)(e)(xi) (AP I).

152 See Chapter 11.

153 See ICC Elements Art. 8(2)(a)(ii)–1, element 2; *Delalić* ICTY T. Ch. II 16.11.1998 para. 459; and *Kunarac* ICTY T. Ch. II 22.2.2001 para. 485.

154 Biological experiments appear in the GC grave breach provisions and medical or scientific experiments appear in AP I.

155 See, e.g. ICC Elements Art. 8(2)(a)(ii)–3 and 8(2)(b)(x)–2.

156 See, e.g. Art. 8(2)(a)(iii) ICC Statute; Art. 2(c) ICTY Statute; Art. 147 GC IV. Under the ICC Statute, the provision applies only in international armed conflict.

157 *Delalić* ICTY T. Ch. II 16.11.1998 paras. 508–11; *Akayesu* ICTR T. Ch. I 2.9.1998 para. 502; *Blaškić* ICTY T. Ch. I 3.3.2000 para. 156; *Kordić* ICTY T. Ch. 26.2.2001 para. 245.

158 Common Article 3 to the GCs; Art. 95 GC IV; Arts. 75(2)(b) and 85(4)(c) AP I; Art. 4(2)(e) AP II; Art. 8(2)(b)(xxi), Art. 8(2)(c)(ii) ICC Statute.

159 J. Pictet et al., *Commentary to Additional Protocol I* (Geneva, 1987) 873; *Aleksovski* ICTY T. Ch. 25.6.1999 para. 56; *Kunarac* ICTY T. Ch. II 22.2.2001 paras. 501–4.

must meet a certain objective level of seriousness to be considered an outrage upon personal dignity. Indignities against corpses can fall within the prohibition, as can deliberately debasing prisoners by forcing them to violate religious requirements.[160]

The most important development in this area is the recognition that various forms of sexual violence amount to war crimes. Until recently, international law has done a poor job of dealing with the sexual abuses routinely committed against women.[161] In most military cultures in the past, and in some military cultures today, licence to rape was seen as a reward for troops, an expected occurrence after the taking of a city or village, and a means of terrorizing and demoralizing the enemy.[162] In such a climate, sexual violence has been pervasive in armed conflicts.[163] While IHL has criminalized rape for centuries, this was not always explicit, and it was rarely prosecuted. IHL treaties, negotiated by men, tended to reflect the perspectives and concerns of men, and thus did not explicitly recognize sexual violence as a form of war crime.[164] Article 27 of GC IV stipulated that women should be protected against rape, but did not make rape a grave breach. Sexual violence was mentioned again in the Additional Protocols I and II, but not as a crime.[165] Moreover, it was listed as an example of 'outrages upon personal dignity', which treated rape as an attack on 'honour', trivializing the nature of the violation.

The ICTY Statute did not list rape as a war crime (although it was listed as a crime against humanity). This lacuna triggered the efforts to establish that rape could fall within the definition of grave breaches, such as 'torture' or 'inhuman treatment'.[166] It also reinforced the need to establish that rape is a war crime per se.[167] The ICTR Statute was an improvement, in that its war crimes provision expressly included rape, enforced prostitution and other forms of sexual violence.[168] However, mirroring the language of Additional Protocol II, these were included as 'outrages upon personal dignity', thus maintaining the patriarchal perspective of rape as an assault on family honour. The ICC Statute took the further step, explicitly

---

160 See, e.g. ICC Elements, footnote 49.

161 Elizabeth Odio-Benito, 'Sexual Violence as a War Crime' in Pablo Antonio Fernández-Sánchez, *The New Challenges of Humanitarian Law in Armed Conflict* (The Hague, 2005).

162 See, e.g. Kelly Askin, *War Crimes Against Women: Prosecution in International Tribunals* (The Hague, 1997) esp. at 12–42.

163 See, e.g. Susan Brownmiller, *Against Our Will: Men, Women and Rape* (New York, 1975); Christine Chinkin, 'Rape and Sexual Abuse of Women in International Law' (1994) 5 *EJIL* 1.

164 Some military codes did recognize sexual violence as a punishable war crime; for example, the Lieber Code provided the death penalty for rape.

165 Art. 4(2)(e) AP II, referring to rape, enforced prostitution and indecent assault; Art. 75(2)(b) AP I, referring to enforced prostitution and indecent assault.

166 Patricia Viseur Sellers and Kaoru Okuizumi, 'International Prosecution of Sexual Assaults' (1997) 7 *Transnational Legal and Contemporary Problems* 45; see *Akayesu* ICTR T. Ch. I 2.9.1998 para. 731 (rape and sexual violence can constitute the actus reus of other crimes); *Delalić* ICTY T. Ch. II 16.11.1998 paras. 475–96 (rape can constitute torture where the elements of torture are satisfied).

167 Theodor Meron, 'Rape as a Crime under International Humanitarian Law' (1993) 87 *AJIL* 424.

168 Art. 4(e) ICTR Statute.

recognizing rape, sexual slavery, enforced prostitution, forced pregnancy, enforced sterilization and other sexual violence as war crimes.[169] The ICC Statute also confirms that sexual violence can amount to grave breaches of the Geneva Conventions.[170] For the elements of these offences, see the discussion in Chapter 11.

Further compounding the historical lack of legal recognition of crimes of sexual violence, an additional problem was that prosecutors shied away from bringing charges of sexual violence even when applicable law did recognize the crime. For example, in the Nuremberg proceedings, where there was ample evidence of widespread use of rape as a weapon of war, the French prosecutor simply submitted a dossier and asked forgiveness 'if I avoid citing the atrocious details' – even though many atrocious details were scrutinized thoroughly in relation to other charges.[171] As a result there were no convictions for sexual violence in Nuremberg proceedings. The record of the Tokyo Tribunal was somewhat better, as there were war crimes convictions of leaders for rapes and sexual violence, including in relation to the 'Rape of Nanking', in which Japanese soldiers raped approximately 20,000 women and children.[172] The sexual slavery of women as 'comfort women' by the Japanese military was, however, largely overlooked.[173] In response to these experiences, many NGOs, academics and lawyers have successfully engaged with the ICTY and ICTR to ensure that crimes of sexual violence are diligently investigated and prosecuted.[174] These efforts have culminated in rules of procedure sensitive to victims, gender advisers on staff, and several landmark decisions. In the same spirit, the ICC Statute has a number of provisions to ensure the effective investigation and prosecution of such crimes, while preserving the safety, dignity and privacy of victims and witnesses.[175]

Other legal interests of protected persons

In addition to prohibiting violence against and mistreatment of protected persons, war crimes law also protects other rights of persons. For example, several provisions protect

---

169 Art. 8(2)(b)(xxii) ICC Statute.
170 *Ibid.*
171 Gabrielle Kirk McDonald, 'Crimes of Sexual Violence: The Experience of the International Criminal Tribunal' (2000) 39 *Columbia Journal Transnational Law* 1 at 10.
172 *Ibid.*
173 *Ibid.* The crime was mentioned only at Judgment of the Tokyo IMT, 49 617.
174 Christine Chinkin, 'Women: The Forgotten Victims of Armed Conflict' in Helen Durham and Timothy L. H. McCormack, *The Changing Face of Conflict and the Efficacy of International Humanitarian Law* (The Hague, 1999).
175 Arts. 36(8)(b) (judges with expertise in violence against women and children), 42(6) (advisers on sexual and gender violence and violence against children), 44(2) (staff with such expertise), 54(1)(b) (prosecutor to respect interests of victims and witnesses and take into account sexual violence, gender violence and violence against children), 68 (protection of victims and witnesses and participation in proceedings). See, e.g. Valerie Oosterveld, 'The Making of a Gender-Sensitive International Criminal Court' (1999) 1 *International Law FORUM du droit international* 38.

liberty and mobility rights. In international conflicts, the unlawful deportation, transfer or confinement of civilians is a grave breach.[176] In internal conflicts, there is a more modest prohibition on displacement of the civilian population for reasons unrelated to the conflict.[177] Since IHL permits the transfer and/or confinement of civilians under certain conditions, it is necessary to refer to IHL to determine whether a particular act is unlawful.[178]

The taking of hostages is a war crime in international or internal conflicts.[179] Tribunal jurisprudence requires an unlawful deprivation of freedom perpetrated in order to obtain a concession or to gain an advantage,[180] and the ICC Elements contain a comparable but more detailed definition drawing on the Hostages Convention 1979.[181]

Unjustified delay in the repatriation of prisoners of war and civilians is identified as a grave breach in AP I,[182] which therefore applies as a matter of treaty law for parties to that protocol. The provision was not included in the ICC Statute, due to lack of agreement on the customary law status of the provision. This lack of agreement at the Rome Conference is not conclusive as to the customary status of the provision for jurisdictions other than the ICC.[183]

Other provisions protect the legal rights of persons. Punishment of protected persons without a regular trial is a grave breach (international conflict) and a serious violation of common Article 3 (internal conflict).[184] In international conflict, it is also a war crime to declare abolished, suspended or inadmissible the rights and actions of nationals of a hostile party.[185]

Two closely related provisions, one from Geneva law, the other from Hague law, protect persons from being compelled to fight against their own side during international conflicts. It is a grave breach to compel a prisoner of war or civilian to serve in the forces of a hostile power,[186] and it is also a war crime to compel persons to participate in operations of war against their own country.[187] The two provisions overlap but have some different scope of

---

176 See Art. 8(2)(a)(vii) ICC Statute; Art. 2(g) ICTY; Art. 147 GC IV. Significantly, this provision appears only in GC IV, allowing the conclusion that only civilians may be victims of this offence.

177 See Art. 8(2)(e)(viii) ICC Statute; Art. 17(1) AP II.

178 See, e.g. Arts. 41–3, 68, 78 and 79–141 GC IV.

179 See, e.g. Art. 8(2)(a)(viii) and 8(2)(c)(iii) ICC Statute; Arts. 34(4) and 147 GC IV; Art. 75(2)(c) AP I; Art. 4(2)(c) AP II. See also *Altstötter* (the Justice Trial) VI LRTWC 1.

180 *Blaškić* ICTY T. Ch. I 3.3.2000 para. 158.

181 Article 8(2)(a)(viii) ICC Elements: The perpetrator intended to compel a State, an international organization, a natural or legal person or a group of persons to act or refrain from acting as an explicit or implicit condition for the safety or the release of [the detained persons].

182 Art. 85(4)(b) AP I.

183 Art. 10 ICC Statute.

184 Art. 8(2)(a)(vi) and 8(2)(c)(iv) ICC Statute; Art. 2(f) ICTY Statute; Art. 3(g) ICTR Statute; Art. 130 GC III; Art. 147 GC IV; common Art. 3(1)(d). See *Hamdan* v. *Rumsfeld*, 126 S Ct 2749 (2006), finding that military tribunals established by the Administration, allowing the exclusion of the accused from his own trial, did not meet the common Art. 3 standard.

185 Art. 8(2)(b)(xiv) ICC Statute; Art. 23(h) Hague Regulations. On the ambiguous drafting of the Hague Regulations, see Michael Cottier, 'Article 8' in Triffterer, *Observers' Notes*, 232–5.

186 Art. 8(2)(a)(v) ICC Statute; Art. 130 GC III; Art. 147 GC IV.

187 Art. 8(2)(b)(xv) ICC Statute; Art. 23(h) Hague Regulations.

application; one focuses on conscription into forces (fighting against any party) and the other focuses on the forced breach of loyalty in fighting one's own country (whether or not as part of military forces).[188]

Slavery and forced labour, while not listed as war crimes in the ICC Statute, have been recognized as war crimes in Tribunal jurisprudence.[189] It is necessary to make reference to IHL, which permits parties to require prisoners of war to carry out work under certain conditions, to determine the ambit of these prohibitions.[190]

12.3.3 Attacks on prohibited targets (principle of distinction)

With respect to the conduct of military operations, perhaps the most fundamental principle is the principle of distinction: belligerents are required to distinguish between military objectives and the population and objects, and to 'direct their operations only against military objectives'.[191] As already explained in section 12.1.3, this is a cardinal principle of IHL.[192]

The relevant IHL instruments provide guidance on the differences between civilians, civilian population and objects, and military objectives. In case of doubt whether a person is a civilian, that person shall be considered to be a civilian.[193] With respect to 'civilian population', '[t]he presence within the civilian population of individuals who do not come within the definition of civilians does not deprive the population of its civilian character'.[194] The population must be of a 'predominantly civilian nature'.[195] Civilian objects are 'all objects which are not military objectives'.[196]

Military objectives include combatants, whether on or off duty, as well as objects:

> which by their nature, location, purpose or use make an effective contribution to military action and whose total or partial destruction, capture or neutralization, in the circumstances ruling at the time, offers a definite military advantage.[197]

---

188 The ICC Elements combine both aspects in the elements of Art. 8(2)(a)(v).

189 *Krnojelac* ICTY T. Ch. II 15.3.2002 paras. 350–60; *Naletilić* ICTY T. Ch. 31.3.2003 paras. 250–61.

190 See Arts. 49–57 GC III on authorized work and working conditions.

191 Art. 48 AP I; see also Art. 51 AP I and Art. 13 AP II. For a discussion on the law of targeting, see Michael N. Schmitt, 'Fault Lines in the Law of Attack' in Susan C. Breau and Agnieszka Jachec-Neale (eds.), *Testing the Boundaries of International Humanitarian Law* (London, 2006) 277–92.

192 *Advisory Opinion on Legality of the Threat or Use of Nuclear Weapons* (1996) 1 ICJ Rep 226, 257 (8 July 1996) para. 78.

193 Art. 50(1) AP I.

194 Art. 50(3) AP I.

195 *Tadić* ICTY T. Ch. II 7.5.1997 para. 638; *Blaškić* ICTY T. Ch. I 3.3.2000 para. 214; *Strugar* ICTY T. Ch. II 31.1.2005 para. 282.

196 Art. 50(3) AP I; also *Blaškić* ICTY T. Ch. I 3.3.2000 para. 180; *Kordić* ICTY T. Ch. 26.2.2001 para. 53; *Strugar* ICTY T. Ch. II 31.1.2005 para. 282.

197 This definition, found in Art. 52(2) AP I, is widely accepted as reflecting customary law. For further discussion of this two-part test, see, e.g. Yoram Dinstein, *Legitimate Military Objectives Under The Current Jus In Bello*, in Andru E. Wall (ed.), 'Legal and Ethical Lessons of NATO's Kosovo Campaign' (2002) 78 *US Naval*

The war crimes of directing attacks against civilians or the civilian population,[198] or against civilian objects,[199] are the most elementary and straightforward expression of these principles.[200]

The other 'prohibited target' provisions are simply examples of this prohibition, focusing on certain specially protected objects or interests. These include: attacking or bombarding undefended towns, villages, dwellings or buildings which are not military objectives;[201] intentionally directing attacks against buildings dedicated to 'religion, education, art, science or charitable purposes, historic monuments, hospitals and places where the sick and wounded are collected, provided they are not military objectives';[202] and directing attacks against buildings, transport and personnel using the distinctive emblems of the Geneva Conventions.[203] The first two examples are early illustrations recognized in Hague law and reproduced in the ICTY, ICTR and ICC Statutes. The third arises from the Geneva Conventions, which have particular provisions emphasizing the protection to be accorded to these distinctive emblems, so that personnel of these organizations may carry out their work of ameliorating the suffering of victims of warfare.[204]

The ICC Statute also specifically prohibits attacks on personnel, installations and vehicles involved in a humanitarian assistance mission or peacekeeping mission in accordance with the UN Charter.[205] This provision may, at first glance, appear to extend beyond existing customary law; however, since it only protects those 'entitled to the protection given to civilians' it is evident that it is simply a specific illustration of the undisputed prohibition on attacking civilians.[206] The inclusion of this provision was inspired by the same considerations that led to the 1994 Convention on Safety of UN and Associated Personnel[207] and specifically addresses attacks on those who risk their lives to bring humanitarian aid. Such

---

War College International Law Studies; Pictet et al., *Commentary to AP I*, notes 2014–18, pp. 635–7. The definition can still give rise to disagreement as to its application; see for example the controversial analysis of attacks on TV stations in the ICTY Final Report to the Prosecutor by the Committee Established to Review the NATO Bombing, 13 June 2000, available at www.icty.org/sid/10052.

198 Art. 8(2)(b)(i) and 8(2)(e)(i) ICC Statute; Art. 51(2) AP I; Art. 13(2) AP II.

199 Art. 8(2)(b)(ii) ICC Statute; Art. 62(1) AP I.

200 In internal armed conflicts, the ICC Statute recognizes the prohibition on attacking civilians but not civilian objects; thus attacks on civilian objects are covered only if they are specially protected objects (buildings dedicated to certain purposes, or objects under the Geneva Conventions symbols or a humanitarian mission).

201 Art. 8(2)(b)(v) ICC Statute; Art. 3(c) ICTY; Art. 25 Hague Regulations; Art. 59(1) AP I.

202 Art. 8(2)(b)(ix) and 8(2)(e)(iv) ICC Statute; Arts. 27 and 56 Hague Regulations; and see 1954 Hague Convention on Cultural Property and 1999 Second Hague Protocol.

203 Art. 8(2)(b)(xxiv) and 8(2)(e)(ii) ICC Statute.

204 Arts. 38–44 GC I; Arts. 41–45 GC II.

205 Art. 8(2)(b)(iii) and 8(2)(e)(iii) ICC Statute; see also Art. 4(b) SCSL Statute.

206 The restriction to those with civilian status means that peacekeepers engaged in military operations under Chapter VII are not protected. This is a necessary outcome consistent with general principles of IHL; otherwise for one side of the conflict, killing combatants would be a crime.

207 2051 UNTS (1999) 391.

attacks may cause the failure of or withdrawal of humanitarian missions, with grave repercussions for the affected population.

Two other prohibitions flow from the principle of sparing the civilian population. First, it is prohibited to use the starvation of civilians as a method of war, including wilfully impeding relief supplies.[208] Second, under Tribunal jurisprudence, it is a war crime to commit acts of violence primarily intended to spread terror among the civilian population.[209]

12.3.4 Attacks inflicting excessive civilian damage

The principle of proportionality

The companion to the principle of distinction is the principle of proportionality: even where an attack is directed against a military objective, the anticipated incidental civilian damage must not be disproportionate to the anticipated military advantage.[210] This principle is well established as customary law.[211]

No other principle of IHL illustrates so clearly the tension between military and humanitarian considerations. The various prohibitions on mistreatment of civilians are important but they are legally and conceptually straightforward, whereas the prohibition on disproportionate attacks poses problems of interpretation even for – indeed, *particularly* for – military forces striving to comply fully with IHL. Even with precision weapons and sophisticated intelligence, military strikes often result in significant civilian casualties, injuries and property damage. As the prohibition on disproportionate attacks brings to the fore many complex and sensitive questions, this chapter will examine it in some detail.

The prohibition is criminalized in Article 85(3)(b) of AP I and in Article 8(2)(b)(iv) of the ICC Statute. Article 8(2)(b)(iv) criminalizes:

> Intentionally launching an attack in the knowledge that such attack will cause incidental loss of life or injury to civilians or damage to civilian objects or widespread, long-term and severe damage to the natural environment which would be clearly[212] excessive in relation to the concrete and direct overall military advantage anticipated.

---

208 Art. 8(2)(b)(xxv) ICC Statute; Art. 54 AP I; see also, on the general duty not to impede relief, Arts. 10, 23, 59–63 and 108–11 GC IV and Arts. 70–1 AP I. Under the ICC Statute the provision is recognized only in international conflicts, although it would appear to meet the *Tadić* test; see also Art. 14 AP I.

209 *Galić* ICTY T. Ch. 5.12.2003 paras. 87–138; *Galić* ICTY A. Ch. 30.11.2006 paras. 87–104. See Art. 51(2) AP I and Art. 13(2) AP II: 'Acts or threats of violence the primary purpose of which is to spread terror among the civilian population are prohibited.'; Robert Cryer, 'War Crime of Terror Bombing', 73. For further discussion of the crime of terrorism, see Chapter 14.

210 Art. 51(5)(b) AP I.

211 Henckaerts & Doswald-Beck, *ICRC Customary Law*, 46–50; *Kupreškić* ICTY T. Ch. II 14.1.2000 paras. 522–6; Schmitt, 'Fault Lines', 292.

212 The AP I standard is 'excessive' whereas the ICC Statute standard is 'clearly excessive'. On the one hand, the adjective seems to raise the standard required under AP I. On the other hand, the difference may not be

The application of this test therefore requires an assessment of:

(a) the anticipated civilian damage or injury;

(b) the anticipated military advantage; and

(c) whether (a) was excessive in relation to (b).

Article 8(2)(b)(iv) requires the launching of such an attack, with the requisite knowledge, but does not appear to require that any particular *result* occur;[213] whereas the Geneva Conventions and Tribunal jurisprudence require that the attack actually results in harm.[214] The ICC Statute lists this provision only in the context of international conflicts; however, the prohibition relates to one of the most fundamental principles of IHL and hence would appear to meet the *Tadić* test for customary law war crimes in internal armed conflicts.[215]

First side of the equation: harm to civilians, civilian objects and the environment

The terms 'civilian', 'civilian population' and 'civilian object' are discussed in section 12.3.3.

Article 8(2)(b)(iv) of the ICC Statute differs from Article 85(3)(b) of AP I in that it also includes damage to the environment in the assessment. The terminology is drawn from Article 35(3) of AP I, which prohibits attacks causing 'widespread, long-term and severe damage to the natural environment'.[216] The ICC Statute has been criticized on the grounds that it is more restrictive than Article 35(3) of AP I, since the damage must satisfy not only the 'widespread, long-term and severe' requirement but also the disproportionality test.[217] This overlooks, however, that the prohibition in Article 35(3), while absolute, was not criminalized in AP I, and it is unclear if the prohibition can be criminalized to the extent that

significant in practice since prosecution would not be viable or appropriate except in clear cases, see below in this section.

213 The chapeau of Art. 85(3) AP I requires that the attack must have caused death or serious injury to body or health; this requirement could arguably be incorporated by virtue of the chapeau of Art. 8(2) ('within the established framework of international law'). However, during the negotiation of the Elements of Crimes, the decision was reached not to include a result requirement. Daniel Frank, 'Article 8(2)(b)(i)' in Lee, *Elements and Rules*, 141.

214 *Kordić* ICTY A. Ch. 17.12.2004 paras. 55–68. An attack that would have been excessive based on the available information, but which unexpectedly caused no harm, could, however, still be prosecuted as an attempt.

215 The *Tadić* decision refers specifically to proportionality in relation to internal armed conflicts: *Tadić* ICTY A. Ch. 2.10.1995 para. 111. See also *Kupreškić* ICTY T. Ch. II 14.1.2000 paras. 521 et seq.

216 On these terms, see ILC, GAOR, 46th Sess, Supp. No. 10 (A/46/10) 276 and Dörmann, *Elements of War Crimes under the Rome Statute*, 175. More generally see Jay E. Austin and Carl E. Bruch, *The Environmental Consequences of War* (Cambridge, 2000); Karen Hulme, *War Torn Environment: Interpreting the Legal Threshold* (The Hague, 2004).

217 Cassese describes the environmental provision as 'a huge leap backwards': Antonio Cassese, *International Criminal Law*, 2nd edn (Oxford, 2008) 96.

it goes further than the prohibition of wanton devastation or disproportionate attacks. The ICC Statute recognizes individual criminal liability, but in connection with the well-established principle of proportionality. The inclusion of environmental considerations in the proportionality assessment is consistent with other authorities.[218] The dual threshold in Article 8(2)(b)(iv) does, however, mean that environmental damage will only be considered in the criminal law context where it is both widespread, long-term and severe *and* disproportionate to the military advantage.

Second side of the equation: military advantage

Military objectives include combatants, whether they are on or off duty, unless and until they have surrendered, are sick or wounded, or have ceased to take part in hostilities.[219] Objects may also be military objectives, as defined above.[220] Article 8(2)(b)(iv) also requires an assessment of the 'concrete and direct overall military advantage anticipated'.[221] The obvious tension between these modifiers ('concrete and direct', 'overall') is addressed in footnote 36 of the Elements of Crimes:

> The expression 'concrete and direct overall military advantage' refers to a military advantage that is foreseeable by the perpetrator at the relevant time. Such advantage may or may not be temporally or geographically related to the object of the attack.[222]

One example of an anticipated advantage that is specific and foreseeable, yet not temporally or geographically linked to the target, could be a feint. For example, in the Second World War, the Allies attacked military targets in the Pas de Calais, but the greater intended contribution was to deceive Germany into believing that the amphibious assault would take place in the Pas de Calais rather than at Normandy.[223]

Comparing the two sides of the equation: the proportionality test

It is comparatively simple to state the proportionality test in the abstract, yet it is profoundly difficult to assess compliance with it in practice, given that: (1) assessing the anticipated civilian damage is a difficult task, requiring a prediction of consequences based on variables

---

218 *Advisory Opinion on Legality of the Threat or Use of Nuclear Weapons Case* (1996) 1 ICJ Rep 226 (8 July 1996) para. 30; ICTY Final Report to the Prosecutor by the Committee Established to Review the NATO Bombing, para. 15.

219 Arts. 43, 48, 51(3) AP I.

220 See section 12.3.3.

221 On 'concrete and direct', see Jean Pictet, *Commentary on the Additional Protocols* (ICRC, Geneva, 1987) para. 2209. On 'overall' see statements of understanding of Belgium, Canada, Germany, Italy, Netherlands, New Zealand, Switzerland and the United Kingdom available in A. Roberts and R. Guelff (eds.), *Documents of the Laws of War*, 3rd edn (Oxford, 2000) 499–512.

222 ICC Elements, footnote 36. The footnote was the subject of intense negotiations.

223 Dörmann, *Elements of War Crimes under the Rome Statute*, 171.

and probabilities, relying on available information under circumstances of urgency; (2) assessing the anticipated military advantage involves the same problems of variables and uncertainties, taking into account the broader military strategy and possible future ramifications of the action; and (3) comparing the two is even more challenging, given that they are entirely unlike properties with no common unit of measurement.[224]

Because of these difficulties, it is generally recognized that decision makers must be allowed a 'considerable margin of appreciation'.[225] During the negotiation of the Rome Statute, many States were concerned about the inclusion of Article 8(2)(b)(iv), on the grounds that the officials and judges of the ICC would not be likely to have military experience and hence would apply an incorrectly onerous standard, and that the Court would be reviewing decisions *ex post facto* with the benefit of hindsight, failing to take into account the 'fog of war' (incomplete information, urgency, confusion, limited time for critical decisions).[226]

To address these concerns, and to reflect the concept of a margin of appreciation, the term 'clearly' was inserted, so that the ICC will act only with respect to cases that are 'clearly excessive'.[227] This may well be seen as an unwarranted restriction on the standard in AP I, a view bolstered by the fact that Tribunal jurisprudence has not as of this point endorsed the 'clearly excessive' standard.[228] Alternatively, it may be seen as an appropriate clarification given that the Statute deals not with the basic ground rules for parties to conflict, but rather with the criminalization of individual behaviour.[229] Some commentators, including the ICRC study on customary law and the ICTY report on NATO bombing, have concluded that inclusion of the word 'clearly' does not entail a significant new hurdle, since prosecution would in any event be viable only in cases where the proportionality requirement was clearly breached.[230]

Some authorities indicate that proportionality must be assessed from the point of view of a 'reasonable military commander'[231] or 'a reasonably well-informed person in the

---

224 Michael Bothe, 'War Crimes' in Cassese, *Commentary*, 398; see also ICTY Final Report, para. 48; W. J. Fenrick, 'Targeting and Proportionality During the NATO Bombing Campaign against Yugoslavia' (2001) 12 *EJIL* 489 at 499; Schmitt, 'Fault Lines', 292–8.

225 Stefan Oeter, 'Methods and Means of Combat' in Fleck, *Handbook*, 205; see also Fenrick, 'Targeting and Proportionality', 499.

226 The provision has therefore been highlighted as creating undue exposure. See, e.g. David Scheffer, 'Statement in the 6th Committee of the General Assembly', 21 October 1998, US Mission to the UN, Press Release No. 179; Cassandra Jeu, 'A Successful Permanent International Criminal Court – Isn't It Pretty To Think So?' (2004) 26 *Houston Journal of International Law* 411.

227 von Hebel and Robinson, 'Crimes Within the Jurisdiction', 111.

228 Cryer, *Prosecuting*, 277–9.

229 D. Pfirter, 'Article 8(2)(b)(iv)' in Lee, *Elements and Rules*, 148.

230 Henckaerts & Doswald-Beck, *ICRC Customary Law*, 576–7; ICTY Final Report on NATO Bombing para. 21; Roberta Arnold, 'Article 8' in Triffterer, *Observer's Notes* at 341.

231 ICTY, 'Final Report to the Prosecutor by the Committee Established to Review the NATO Bombing Campaign Against the Federal Republic of Yugoslavia', 13 June 2000, para. 50. See comments on this standard circumstances of the actual perpetrator, making reasonable use of the information available to him'.[232] However, even such points of reference do not provide measurable ratios of military advantage and civilian damage that would be considered disproportionate.[233] A review of State practice, even among States with traditions of IHL compliance and political incentive to minimize collateral damage, suggests that significant numbers of casualties can be inflicted in pursuit of military advantages without falling foul of the prohibition. Further clarity, through State practice or jurisprudence, would help give valuable content to the prohibition. To assess compliance, it may also be useful to examine the actual *conduct* of the parties: were target selections reviewed; were decision makers advised by military lawyers; were efforts taken to reduce incidental damage; were precautionary measures taken; and were precision weapons used when targets required?[234] Despite the present difficulties in measuring compliance with this provision, it does allow a criminal law response to the more glaringly disproportionate attacks.[235]

The mental element

A critical element is the knowledge of the perpetrator at the time of launching the attack.[236] The Elements of Crimes clarify that the information available to the perpetrator at the time is central.[237] This is consistent with general principles of criminal law[238] and with State practice.[239]

in Paolo Benvenuti, 'The ICTY Prosecutor and the Preview of the NATO Bombing Campaign against the Federal Republic of Yugoslavia' (2001) 12 *EJIL* 503 at 517 and Michael Bothe, 'The Protection of the Civilian Population and NATO Bombing on Yugoslavia: Comments on a Report to the Prosecutor of the ICTY' (2001) 12 *EJIL* 531 at 535.

232 *Galić* ICTY T. Ch. 5.12.2003 para. 8.

233 One of the few relevant cases is *Galić*, where shells were fired in the midst of a football tournament. The Trial Chamber noted the presence of some soldiers at the game, but found that an attack on a crowd of approximately 200 people, including numerous children, was excessive in relation to military advantage anticipated: *Galić* ICTY T. Ch. 5.12.2003 para. 387.

234 The ICC OTP appears to have taken such considerations into account in its analysis of allegations against States Parties operating in Iraq: 'OTP Response to communications received concerning Iraq', 9.2.2006, pp. 6–7, available at www.icc-cpi.int, under 'Structure of the Court', 'Office of the Prosecutor', 'Communications and Referrals', 'Iraq'.

235 See, e.g. *Galić* ICTY T. Ch. 5.12.2003 para. 387; ICTY Final Report on NATO Bombing para. 21. The Report of the International Commission of Inquiry on Darfur, 25 January 2005 at para. 260 observes that the principle of proportionality 'remains a largely subjective standard' but it 'nevertheless plays an important role, first of all it must be applied in good faith, and secondly because its application may involve the prohibition of at least the most glaringly disproportionate injuries to civilians'.

236 ICC Elements, Art. 8(2)(b)(iv) para. 3.

237 ICC Elements, footnote 37, second sentence.

238 Art. 30 (mental element) and Art. 32 (mistake of fact) of the ICC Statute.

239 See, e.g. declarations by Algeria, Australia, Belgium, Canada, Egypt, Germany, Ireland, the Netherlands, New Zealand, Spain and the UK that what is relevant is 'the information available to them at the relevant time'.

It is clear that a perpetrator must have awareness of the extent of the anticipated harm and military advantage. The more difficult issue is whether the perpetrator must also consider the former clearly excessive in relation to the latter, or whether that determination is to be made by the ICC on an objective basis.[240] Footnote 37 of the ICC Elements indicates that this crime requires that the perpetrator personally completes a particular value judgment.[241] As the ICC Elements reflect a consensus statement by the international community as to the content of the crimes, their provisions should not lightly be disregarded. Nonetheless, this particular footnote was included at the last minute of the negotiations, without discussion in the working group, and there are grave reasons to doubt its compatibility with general principles and hence the ICC Statute,[242] since it seems to make the 'perpetrator, in a way, the judge in his own cause'.[243] Other commentators have suggested that the provision should be interpreted as reflecting the need for a margin of appreciation, but not as insulating reckless or incredible assessments.[244]

12.3.5 War crimes against property

Several war crimes provisions address crimes involving property, namely the destruction, appropriation, seizure and pillage of property.[245] These provisions flow from different instruments, and protect slightly different interests, but in practice they overlap considerably. The ICC Statute includes destruction, appropriation, seizure and pillage in international conflict, but in internal conflict it includes only the long-established prohibition on pillage.

The grave breach regime includes 'extensive destruction and appropriation of property, not justified by military necessity and carried out unlawfully and wantonly'.[246] The Hague Regulations prohibit 'destroying or seizing the enemy's property unless such destruction or seizure be imperatively demanded by the necessities of war'.[247] These two provisions are similar in scope, although they arise from different interests. The Geneva provisions protect property from the vantage point of upholding the rights of protected persons (including their property), whereas the Hague provisions protect property from the vantage point of the proper conduct of hostilities – military force should be applied for military aims and with minimal impact on the civilian population and objects. The Hague law provision simply

---

240 Pfirter, 'Article 8(2)(b)(iv)', 151.
241 ICC Elements, footnote 37. This is a departure from the principle in the General Introduction, para. 4, that value judgments of the perpetrator are not relevant; it is sufficient that a perpetrator is aware of the relevant facts.
242 Art. 9 ICC Statute requires that ICC Elements be consistent with the ICC Statute.
243 Bothe, 'War Crimes' in Cassese, *Commentary*, 400.
244 Pfirter, 'War Crimes' in Lee, *Elements and Rules*, 151; see also Dörmann, *Elements of War Crimes under the Rome Statute*, 165.
245 See, e.g. Art. 8(2)(a)(iv), 8(2)(b)(xiii), 8(2)(e)(xii), 8(2)(b)(xvi) and 8(2)(e)(v) ICC Statute.
246 See, e.g. Art. 8(2)(a)(iv) ICC Statute; Art. 2(d) ICTY Statute.
247 See, e.g. Art. 8(2)(b)(xiii) ICC Statute; Art 23(g) Hague Regulations 1907.

requires an assessment of military necessity, whereas the Geneva law provision contains additional elements of 'excessive' and 'wanton'. The ICC Statute includes both provisions, since the Hague provision is more inclusive and hence more useful, whereas excluding the Geneva provision would have meant an incomplete list of grave breaches of the Geneva Conventions.

In addition, *pillage* of property is also a war crime.[248] Pillage is distinct from appropriation or seizure because it refers to taking for private or personal use[249] as opposed to taking for military purposes. It is more akin to the domestic crime of theft. This is why for appropriation or seizure, one must consider excessiveness and military necessity, whereas for pillage there is no 'balancing' test, since the property is not taken for military reasons. Tribunal jurisprudence indicates that to be criminalized, pillage must be serious; hence for example, the theft of a single loaf of broad would not be considered a war crime.[250]

The result is a set of overlapping provisions. The *destruction* of property may be examined under the above-mentioned Article 8(2)(a)(iv) or 8(2)(b)(xii), which require a review of military necessity, or under the generic provision on disproportionate attacks (Article 8(2)(b)(iv)) or, where an attack is deliberately directed against civilian property without any military purpose, it can be assessed simply as an attack on a prohibited target (for example Article 8(2)(b)(ii)). Where property is *appropriated or seized* for military purposes, then it must be assessed under Article 8(2)(a)(iv) or 8(2)(b)(xiii). Where property is taken for personal or private use, it is pillage, which is a war crime (Article 8(2)(b)(xvi)).

12.3.6 Prohibited means of warfare (weapons)

Each of the foregoing provisions was aimed primarily at sparing *non-combatants* and their property as far as possible from the effects of war. War crimes law also contains provisions that regulate the methods and means of conducting hostilities. These provisions are distinct in that *combatants* are also beneficiaries of the protections granted.

This section examines prohibited means of warfare, that is to say, prohibited weapons.[251] The prohibition on certain weapons flows from two rationales. One is to protect civilians: some weapons are *inherently indiscriminate* – that is to say they cannot be used in a manner distinguishing civilian and military. The other is to protect combatants: some weapons are of a nature to cause superfluous injury or *unnecessary suffering*.[252]

---

248 Art. 8(2)(b)(xvi), 8(2)(e)(v) ICC Statute; Art. 4(f) ICTR Statute; Art. 3(e) ICTY Statute (plunder being synonymous with pillage); Art. 28 Hague Regulations; Art. 33 GC IV.

249 ICC Elements Art. 8(2)(b)(xvi), element 2.

250 *Tadić* ICTY A. Ch. 2.10.1995 para. 94.

251 Art. 8(2)(b)(xvi)–(xix) ICC Statute; Art. 3(a) ICTY Statute.

252 Note here the underlying peculiarity of IHL and war crimes law. It is accepted that one may kill combatants, and that combat operations may inflict great suffering on combatants, so the rather modest objective is to reduce *superfluous* injury or *unnecessary* suffering. In regulating weapons, States therefore examine the

Although the ICC Statute contains war crimes provisions on prohibited weapons only in the context of international conflicts, there is ample support for the recognition of such war crimes in internal conflict as well.[253]

Weapons which have been banned from the battlefield on the grounds of unnecessary suffering include poison and poisoned weapons;[254] asphyxiating or poisonous gases and analogous liquids, materials or devices;[255] and 'dum dum' bullets (bullets which expand or flatten easily upon impact).[256]

Equally prohibited under the customary law of war crimes are chemical weapons and biological and toxic weapons.[257] However, even though the customary law status of these crimes was not disputed at the Rome Conference, these crimes were excluded from the ICC Statute due to a standoff with respect to nuclear weapons. At the Conference, some delegations, most notably India, insisted on the inclusion of nuclear weapons in the list of prohibited weapons.[258] However, nuclear weapons could not be included because there was no agreement that such weapons were prohibited per se under customary law. Indeed, the International Court of Justice had specifically found that nuclear weapons are not prohibited per se.[259] A large number of delegations then insisted that it was unfair to exclude nuclear weapons – 'the rich man's weapons of mass destruction' – but to include biological and chemical weapons – 'the poor man's weapons of mass destruction'.[260] When no breakthrough could be found for this impasse, the drafters deferred the whole issue: no such weapons were included in Article 8 but a placeholder was inserted, inviting review of the question once the Statute is open for amendment at a future review conference.[261]

---

military efficacy of a particular weapon as well as its consequences to determine if it inflicts *unnecessary* suffering, which can be a rather fine question.

253 See, e.g. *Tadić* ICTY A. Ch. 2.10.1995 paras. 119–24 (specifically finding weapons prohibitions applicable in internal conflicts).

254 Art. 8(2)(b)(xvii) ICC Statute; Art. 23(a) Hague Regulations.

255 Art. 8(2)(b)(xviii) ICC Statute; Geneva Chemical Weapons Protocol, 17 June 1925.

256 Art. 8(2)(b)(xix) ICC Statute; Declaration on the Use of Bullets Which Expand or Flatten Easily in the Human Body, 29 July 1899.

257 See, e.g. Henckaerts & Doswald-Beck, *ICRC Customary Law*, 1607–1770; Bacteriological and Toxin Weapons Convention 1972; Chemical Weapons Convention 1993.

258 Explanation Of Vote By Mr. Dilip Lahiri, Head Of Delegation Of India, On The Adoption Of The Statute Of The International Court, 17 July 1998, *United Nations Diplomatic Conference of Plenipotentiaries on the Establishment of an International Criminal Court Rome, 15 June–17 July 1998, Official Records*, vol. II, 122.

259 *Advisory Opinion on Legality of the Threat or Use of Nuclear Weapons* (1996) 1 ICJ Rep 226 (8 July 1996) paras. 52 and 74.

260 Michael Cottier, 'Article 8' in Triffterer, *Observers' Notes*, 412; von Hebel and Robinson, 'Crimes Within the Jurisdiction', 113–16; for detailed discussion of the history and its implications see Roger S. Clark, 'The Rome Statute of the International Criminal Court and Weapons of a Nature to Cause Superfluous Injury or Unnecessary Suffering, or which are Inherently Indiscriminate' in John Carey, William V. Dunlap and P. John Pritchard (eds.), *International Humanitarian Law: Challenges* (Ardsley NY, 2003).

261 Arts. 8(2)(b)(xx), 121 and 123 ICC Statute.

While chemical,[262] biological and nuclear weapons are not prohibited per se in the ICC Statute, their use can still constitute a war crime if they are employed in a manner contravening other provisions (such as Article 8(2)(b)(i) or (iv)). Indeed, the ICJ has noted that in most imaginable circumstances the use of nuclear weapons would be likely to fall foul of one of the existing prohibitions.[263]

Other weapons are frequently mentioned as candidates for a comprehensive prohibition. Perhaps the closest to achieving a status as a war crime is the use of anti-personnel mines (APMs). APMs cannot distinguish between combatants and civilians, and remain long after conflict, causing a great toll of suffering for civilians. APMs are the subject of a widely ratified convention[264] and therefore the use of such weapons may be on its way to becoming a customary law war crime. Before concluding that the use of APMs is a war crime in customary law, one would have to consider the large number of States that have not accepted the norm, and the contrary State practice among major military powers.

Strong concerns are often raised about the use of cluster bombs[265] and depleted uranium projectiles,[266] but again caution must be shown before one declares that there is a customary law prohibition on their use, let alone a criminalization of their use.[267] A ban on many forms of cluster munitions has come a significant step closer with the recent adoption of a Convention on Cluster Munitions.[268]

12.3.7 Prohibited methods of warfare

In addition to the prohibition on certain *means* of warfare (weapons), war crimes law also prohibits certain *methods* of warfare. Many of these provisions find their origin in traditions

---

262 Some chemical weapons would fall within the definition of Art. 8(2)(b)(xviii) and hence would be prohibited under the ICC Statute.

263 *Advisory Opinion on Legality of the Threat or Use of Nuclear Weapons* (1996) 1 ICJ Rep 226 (8 July 1996), held that the use of nuclear weapons would be illegal if they were used in contravention of specific rules, such as the principle of proportionality. The ICJ indicated that in most conceivable circumstances, the use of nuclear weapons would contravene a rule of IHL (para. 95), but it did not rule out the possibility of a legal use (para. 97).

264 1997 Ottawa Convention on the Prohibition of the Use, Stockpiling, Production and Transfer of Anti-Personnel Mines and on their Destruction, 2056 UNTS 241.

265 Cluster bombs drop numerous bomblets and hence are valued by the military for attacking soft targets over a certain area (e.g. vehicles). However, because of their area effect, they can cause significant incidental damage. In addition, some bomblets fail to detonate on impact, remaining behind as a continuing hazard to civilians.

266 Depleted uranium projectiles are particularly dense and hence are effective in penetrating armour. However, there are concerns about radioactive dust created upon impact as well as the effects of spent projectiles remaining in the soil.

267 See ICTY Final Report on NATO Bombing paras. 26 and 27. Similarly, the ICC OTP in its Iraq analysis held that the use of cluster munitions was not per se a war crime under the Rome Statute, but it examined whether such weapons were used in a manner satisfying the definition of other war crimes, such as attacks on civilians or excessive attacks. OTP Iraq response, p. 5.

268 Convention on Cluster Munitions, Dublin, 30 May 2008. The Convention will enter into force six months after thirty States become parties to it.

of chivalry, namely codes of fair conduct to be respected even among combatants. Such rules are based not only on notions of honour and humanity, but also on preventing deliberate abuse of the rules of IHL to obtain advantage over the enemy, since this would rapidly undermine compliance with IHL.

It is a war crime to kill or wound a combatant who has surrendered or is otherwise *hors de combat* ('out of the fight'),[269] a prohibition which is drawn from the Hague Regulations and AP I.[270] The provision ensures there is no gap in protection between the moment of becoming *hors de combat* and the moment of being taken into custody as a prisoner of war.[271] Compliance with this norm not only shows respect for IHL and the humanity of the surrendering combatant, but also helps to encourage surrender rather than fights to the death.

The war crime of 'declaring that no quarter will be given' refers to orders or announcements that no prisoners will be taken or that there will be no survivors.[272] Such orders violate the duty to spare persons who are *hors de combat* or who are civilians. It is a crime whether the declaration is made publicly, that is to say to threaten the enemy, or as a private order, namely to conduct hostilities on the basis that there be no survivors.[273]

The war crime of 'killing or wounding treacherously a combatant adversary' is drawn from the Hague Regulations.[274] This antiquated language raises the question, what is killing 'treacherously' during combat, when enemy forces are making all efforts to deceive and kill each other? The answer is found in the concept of 'perfidy', that is to say 'inviting the confidence of an adversary to lead him to believe that he is entitled to, or obliged to accord protection' under the rules of IHL, with intent to betray that confidence.[275] Thus, it is not deception per se that makes an act perfidious. Deception and ruses are a sound aspect of military strategy and tactics. Ruses – such as the use of camouflage, decoys, mock operations and misinformation – mislead the adversary but do not invite confidence of the adversary with respect to the protection of IHL.[276]

Perfidy, however, involves a false promise to bestow protection, or an invitation to accord protection with an intent to betray that confidence. Examples of perfidy include feigning an intent to negotiate under a flag of truce, feigning an intent to surrender, feigning incapacitation by wounds or sickness, feigning civilian or non-combatant status, and feigning protected status by use of signs or emblems of the United Nations, neutral States, or the recognized emblems of the Geneva Conventions.[277] Thus, to pretend to surrender in order to attack the enemy off-guard is a war crime, as is promising to take persons prisoner in order to

---

269 Art. 8(2)(b)(vi) ICC Statute, as clarified in the ICC Elements.
270 Art. 23(c) Hague Regulations; Arts. 41 and 42 AP I.
271 Pictet et al., *Commentary to Additional Protocol I*, 481–2.
272 Art. 8(2)(b)(xii) and (e)(x) ICC Statute; Art. 23(d) Hague Regulations; see also Art. 40 AP I.
273 ICC Elements Art. 8(2)(b)(xii); Art. 40 AP I.
274 Art. 8(2)(b)(xi) and (e)(ix) ICC Statute; Art. 23(b) Hague Regulations; see also Art. 37 AP I.
275 ICC Elements Art. 8(2)(b)(xi) elements 1 and 2; Art. 37 AP I.
276 Art. 37(2) AP I.
277 Arts. 23(c), 23(f), 24, 33, 34, 35, 40 and 41 Hague Regulations; Arts. 37, 38, 39, 85(3)(f) AP I.

massacre them once they relinquish their weapons. Perfidy not only breaches a code of honour, it also undermines compliance with IHL, as adversaries learn that compliance with IHL will be used against them, with grave consequences for efforts to reduce suffering in war.

The war crime of 'making improper use of a flag of truce, of the flag or of the military insignia and uniform of the enemy or of the United Nations, as well as of the distinctive emblems of the Geneva Conventions, resulting in death or serious personal injury' also addresses the problem of perfidy.[278] Whereas 'treacherous killing' focuses on the *result* (wounding or killing by any perfidious means), the 'improper use' offences focus on a particular *means* – using particular symbols, emblems or uniforms. For example, the laws of war require combatants not to attack or disrupt those working under the emblem of the ICRC, so that they can, inter alia, help to deliver relief supplies and check on detainees.[279] The protective force of these symbols would be greatly eroded if combatants were to use those symbols to conceal military operations, leading the adversary to distrust such symbols or to respect them at their own peril. On permissible and impermissible uses of such symbols, flags, emblems and uniforms, one must refer to relevant IHL rules. The regimes may be open to interpretation,[280] giving rise to questions about when it is fair to hold persons criminally accountable for misuse, and indeed the ICC Elements suggest a certain hesitation on the part of the drafters to hold persons criminally accountable when the relevant regime on the use of certain symbols and emblems may be unclear.[281]

Finally, it is a war crime to use 'human shields', that is to say, to utilize 'the presence of a civilian or other protected person to render certain points, areas or military forces immune from military operations'.[282] The Geneva Conventions do not expressly criminalize this conduct, but it was recognized as criminal in the ICC Statute on the grounds that it satisfies the *Tadić* test for identifying war crimes, due to its seriousness. It has been recognized as a war crime in Tribunal jurisprudence.[283] The use of human shields improperly abuses the adversary's respect for IHL, including the principle of proportionality, to frustrate attacks on

---

278 Art. 8(2)(b)(vii) ICC Statute; Art 23(f) Hague Regulations, adding also UN insignia in accordance with Arts. 37 and 38 AP I.

279 See, e.g. Art. 8(2)(b)(iii) and (xxiv).

280 See, e.g. Art. 39(2) AP I: enemy uniforms may not be worn while engaged in attack, but might be used in other circumstances, such as espionage.

281 ICC Elements, footnotes 39, 40 and 41 requiring knowledge (or constructive knowledge) of the prohibited nature of the use, and actual knowledge of the prohibited nature of the use with respect to UN flags because of the variable and regulatory nature of the prohibition. While mistake of law is not a defence under the ICC Statute, the Statute does permit some scope where a mistake as to another body of law negates the mental element for a crime: see Art. 32(2) ICC Statute and Chapter 15. See also C. H. B. Garraway, 'War Crimes' in Lee, *Elements and Rules* at 157–9. Bothe suggests that a solution is to focus on perfidy and perfidious intent: Bothe, 'War Crimes' in Cassese, *Commentary*, 404–5.

282 Art. 8(2)(b)(xxiii) ICC Statute, drawing from Art. 23(1) GC III, Art. 28 GC IV 28 and Arts. 51(7) and 58 AP I.

283 See, e.g. *Blaškić* ICTY T. Ch. I 3.3.2000 paras. 742–3.

legitimate targets. The prohibition covers both bringing civilians to the military targets and bringing military targets to civilians.[284] The fact that an adversary is illegally using human shields does not relieve the attacking force from the duty not to launch attacks causing excessive incidental harm.[285]

The ICC Statute recognizes each of the above crimes in international armed conflict, whereas in internal armed conflict it recognizes treacherous killing and declaring no quarter but not killing a combatant *hors de combat*,[286] improper use of flags and symbols, and use of human shields.

12.3.8　War crime provisions protecting other values

Finally, there are two war crimes provisions that do not originate in classic concerns of reciprocal protection of persons and property affiliated with the 'other side', and may be characterized as protecting interests and values other than those listed above.

Transfer of population into occupied territory

It is a war crime for an Occupying Power to transfer parts of its own civilian population into the territory it occupies.[287] This provision protects an interest or value distinct from the other 'transfer' crimes because it is not aimed at protecting enemy civilians who have fallen under a party's power; it refers to transfer of a party's own nationals, and does not require that the transfer be forcible. The purpose of this provision is to ensure respect for the temporary nature of occupation, and to prevent an Occupying Power from changing the demographic composition of a territory in order to make the occupation permanent.

The inclusion of this provision was controversial during the Rome Conference, with Israel voicing strong opposition.[288] It is undoubtedly true that some of the Arab delegations insisting on inclusion of the provision were seeking to highlight activities by Israel in its occupied territories. However, the majority of delegations at the Conference agreed to its inclusion because the *legal* basis for the provision was well established: the provision was based on Article 85(4)(a) of AP I, which in turn was based on Article 49 of GC IV.

---

284 Art. 51(7) AP I.
285 Art. 51(8) AP I.
286 Although killing a combatant *hors de combat* would most likely be captured anyway under Art. 8(2)(c)(i).
287 Art. 8(2)(b)(viii) ICC Statute; Art. 85(4)(a) AP I; Art 49 GC IV. The second variation of this war crime, transferring 'all or parts of the population of the occupied territory within or outside this territory' is more akin to the other transfer-related war crimes, since it protects the original population, although this provision is also intended to prevent ethnic cleansing.
288 Statement by the Head of the Delegation of Israel Judge Eli Nathan, 17 July 1998, *Rome Conference Official Report*, vol. II, 122.

A particular point of controversy related to the departure from the wording of the Geneva Convention provision by the insertion of 'directly or indirectly' in Article 8, with some arguing it was inherent in the definition and others arguing that it expanded the definition. This controversy was put to rest when a footnote was added to the Elements of Crimes, clarifying that the term 'transfer' is to be interpreted in accordance with existing IHL,[289] enabling the ICC Elements to be adopted by consensus.

Child soldiers

A comparatively recent addition to the corpus of war crimes law is the use of child soldiers, namely 'conscripting or enlisting children under the age of fifteen years into armed forces or groups or using them to participate actively in hostilities'.[290]

The proliferation of inexpensive and light weapons, which can be carried and wielded by children, has led to a great increase in the use of child soldiers, who are seen as cheap, malleable and expendable. Of ongoing or recently-ended conflicts, eighty per cent include fighters under the age of fifteen. Child soldiers are often used for the most dangerous missions and for tasks such as detecting land mines.[291] The use of child soldiers was included in the first indictments of the SCSL and is the subject of the *Lubanga* case, the first trial before the ICC.

This provision serves a distinct interest and value, because it is not aimed solely at protecting enemy civilians who have fallen under a party's power; its primary purpose is to protect all children. The prohibition on the use of child soldiers is a norm of both IHL and human rights law.[292]

The recognition of this crime was initially somewhat controversial during the negotiations of the ICC Statute, because it had not previously been recognized expressly as a criminalized prohibition. However, agreement was reached to include it in the ICC Statute because it was a well-established prohibition (appearing in Article 77(2) of AP I, Article 4(3)(c) of AP II and Article 38(3) of the Convention on the Rights of the Child) and it was a serious

---

289 ICC Elements footnote 44; Michael Cottier, 'Article 8' in Triffterer, *Observers' Notes*, 369; von Hebel 'War Crimes', 158–62.

290 Art. 8(2)(e)(vii), 8(2)(b)(xxvi) ICC Statute; Art 4(c) SCSL Statute. Art. 8(2)(b)(xxvi) contains an additional restriction, so that it applies only to recruitment into 'national' armed forces, which may appear to exclude armed groups. Such a restriction is not found in any other instruments and seems rather inconsonant with general principles of humanitarian law, and there is therefore reason to doubt its applicability for other jurisdictions: Art. 10 ICC Statute.

291 P. W. Singer, *Children at War* (New York, 2005); *Report of the Special Representative of the Secretary-General for Children and Armed Conflict*, UN Doc. A/60/335, 7 September 2005; *Children and Armed Conflict, Report of the Secretary-General*, UN Doc. A/59/695 – S/20005/72, 9 February 2005; Human Security Centre, *Human Security Report 2005* (Oxford, 2005); Coalition to Stop the Use of Child Soldiers, *Child Soldiers Global Report 2008*, available www.childsoldiersglobalreport.org.

292 Art. 4(3)(c) AP II and Art. 38(3) of the Convention on the Rights of the Child 1989.

violation protecting important values and warranting criminalization. The crime was also recognized in Article 4(c) of the SCSL Statute. In a split decision, the Special Court for Sierra Leone held that the provision was already customary international law prior to the adoption of the ICC Statute in 1998; that is to say that the ICC Statute codified an existing customary norm rather than forming a new one.[293]

The term 'conscripting' refers to forcible recruitment, whereas 'enlisting' encompasses 'voluntary' recruitment,[294] to the extent that decisions of children under fifteen, usually living in circumstances of poverty, hardship and armed conflict, may even be described as 'voluntary'. 'Enlisting' includes 'any conduct accepting the child as part of the militia'.[295] Using children to 'participate actively in hostilities' includes combat as well as scouting, spying, sabotage, the use of children as decoys and requiring them to guard military objectives.[296]

The ICC Elements apply a modified mental element for this crime, namely that the perpetrator 'knew or should have known' that the persons were under the age of fifteen years. The first judicial treatment by the ICC interpreted the provision, plausibly, as covering situations where the perpetrator failed to know the age because of a failure to exercise due diligence in the circumstances.[297] Some commentators have expressed concern that 'should have known' is an inappropriate standard in criminal law.[298] However, criminal law routinely imposes duties on individuals, and a failure to carry out the duty can satisfy the requisite elements, including mental elements.[299] In crimes designed to protect children, it is not uncommon to impose a duty to take reasonable steps to ascertain age.[300] It is entirely plausible that parties to a conflict have a positive duty to verify the age of children before recruiting them or using them in hostilities.[301]

---

293 *Norman* SCSL A. Ch. 31.5.2004. See also the dissent of Judge Robertson.
294 *Lubanga Dyilo* ICC PTC-I, 29.1.2007 paras. 246–7; *Fofana* SCSL A. Ch. 28.5.2008 para. 140.
295 *Ibid.*, para. 144.
296 *Lubanga Dyilo* ICC PTC-I, 29.1.2007 paras. 260–3.
297 *Ibid.*, para. 358.
298 Bothe, 'War Crimes' in Cassese, *Commentary*, 117–18. Some commentators also query whether the Elements can provide for a modified mental element. Article 30 provides a default mental element 'unless otherwise provided'. The question is whether the Elements can so 'provide'. The view endorsed in *Lubanga Dyilo* (para. 359), and by the Assembly of States Parties (Elements of Crimes, General Introduction, para. 2) is that the Elements can 'provide otherwise'; see also Donald Piragoff and Darryl Robinson, 'Article 30' in Triffterer, *Observers' Notes*, 856; Roger Clark, 'The Mental Element in International Criminal Law: The Rome Statute of the International Criminal Court and the Elements of Offences' (2001) 12 *Criminal Law Forum* 291.
299 See, e.g. the principle of command responsibility, which also imposes duties of inquiry and hence a 'should have known' standard: Art. 28 ICC Statute.
300 As an example, see Canada's Criminal Code, RSC 1985, C-46, ss. 150(4), (5) and (6), providing, in the context of sexual assault, that it is no defence that the accused believed that a person was over 16 unless the accused 'took all reasonable steps to ascertain the age' of the person.
301 Garraway, 'War Crimes', 207.

In 2000 an Optional Protocol to the Convention on the Rights of the Child was adopted, raising the minimum ages for conscription and for participation in hostilities to eighteen.[302] However, the *criminal* prohibition continues to deal with those who use child soldiers under fifteen years of age, since the new limits are treaty law and have not developed into customary law, let alone customary criminal law.

Further reading

Roberta Arnold et al., 'Article 8' in Triffterer, *Observers' Notes* 275–504.

Kelly Askin, *War Crimes Against Women: Prosecution in International Tribunals* (The Hague, 1997).

Machteld Boot, *Genocide, Crimes Against Humanity and War Crimes* (Oxford, 2002).

Michael Bothe, 'War Crimes' in Cassese, *Commentary*.

Knut Dörmann, *Elements of War Crimes under the Rome Statute of the International Criminal Court* (Cambridge, 2003).

Knut Dörmann, Daniel Frank et al., 'War Crimes' in Lee, *Elements and Rules* 109–218.

Dieter Fleck, *Handbook of International Humanitarian Law*, 2nd edn (Oxford, 2008).

Leslie Green, *The Contemporary Law of Armed Conflict* (Manchester, 2000).

Jean-Marie Henckaerts and Louise Doswald-Beck, *Customary International Humanitarian Law* (Cambridge, 2000).

Howard M. Hense (ed.), *The Law of Armed Conflict: Constraints on the Contemporary Use of Military Force* (Aldershot, 2005).

Claus Kreß, 'War Crimes Committed in Non-International Armed Conflict and the Emerging System of International Criminal Justice' (2001) 30 *Israel Yearbook on Human Rights* 1.

Timothy L. H. McCormack and Gerry J. Simpson (eds.), *The Law of War Crimes* (The Hague, 1997).

Theodor Meron, *War Crimes Law Comes of Age* (Oxford, 1998).

Theodor Meron, 'The Humanization of Humanitarian Law' (2000) 94 *AJIL* 239.

Lindsay Moir, *The Law of Internal Armed Conflict* (Cambridge, 2002).

Adam Roberts and Richard Guelff, *Documents of the Laws of War*, 3rd edn (Oxford, 2000).

Anthony Rogers, *Law on the Battlefield*, 2nd edn (Manchester, 2004).

Marco Sassoli and Antoine A. Bouvier, *How Does Law Protect in War?* (Geneva, 1999) 97–104.

UK Ministry of Defence, *Manual of the Law of Armed Conflict* (Oxford, 2005).

---

302 Optional Protocol to the Convention on the Rights of the Child on the Involvement of Children in Armed Conflict, adopted and opened for signature, ratification and accession by General Assembly Resolution A/RES/54/263 of 25 May 2000. The age for voluntary recruitment may be set at any age above fifteen, but specified conditions are to be followed.

13

Aggression

13.1 Introduction

13.1.1 Overview

Aggression is widely regarded as a crime under customary international law, although at present there is no universally agreed definition and no international court or tribunal which can try offenders. It is formally within the jurisdiction of the ICC but the Court cannot exercise its jurisdiction unless and until the parties to the ICC Statute have agreed both a definition of the crime and the conditions under which the Court may exercise its jurisdiction.[1]

This is a crime which differs from all others within the scope of this book in being inextricably connected with an unlawful act of a State: the crime of aggression comprises the participation by a State's leaders and policy-makers in certain aggressive acts by a State. To understand the crime, therefore, it is necessary to understand the rules of international law about the responsibility of States for the unlawful use of force; these are discussed briefly at section 13.2.2, where we consider the elements of the crime.

13.1.2 Historical development

Leaving aside historical curiosities,[2] the first international trial for aggression, under the name of 'crimes against peace', was before the Nuremberg International Military Tribunal following the Second World War.[3] There was an attempt at a trial after the First World War: the 1919 Treaty of Versailles provided for the establishment of a special tribunal to try Kaiser Wilhelm. The intention was to try him not for 'aggression', but for 'a supreme

---

1 Art. 5(2) ICC Statute. By the time the second edition of this volume is printed, the Review Conference for the ICC may have reached the agreement necessary to activate ICC jurisdiction.
2 E.g. the trial of Conradin von Hohenstaufen in 1268 for waging aggressive war.
3 See further section 6.3.

offence against international morality and the sanctity of treaties',[4] a provision that was explained as having 'not a juridical character as regards its substance, but only in its form. The ex-Emperor is arraigned as a matter of high international policy ...'.[5] The Kaiser, however, took refuge in the Netherlands and was never put on trial.

During the Second World War, the discussions in the United Nations War Commission and elsewhere which preceded the drafting of the London Charter setting up the Nuremberg IMT showed that it was by no means a widely held view that there existed a crime of aggression under international law as it then stood.[6] Nevertheless, agreement was reached on Article 6(a) of the Charter, which gave the Nuremberg IMT jurisdiction over 'crimes against peace', defined as the 'planning, preparation, initiation, or waging of a war of aggression, or a war in violation of international treaties, agreements, or assurances, or participation in a common plan or conspiracy for the accomplishment of any of the foregoing'. The equivalent provisions in the Charter for the Tokyo IMT and in Control Council Law No. 10 were very similar.[7]

The Nuremberg IMT had to deal with the objection of the accused that the Charter created new law and that the Tribunal applied law *ex post facto*. It dismissed this claim by ruling that ever since the 1928 Kellogg-Briand Pact,[8] aggressive war had been a crime under international law:

> In the opinion of the Tribunal, the solemn renunciation of war as an instrument of national policy necessarily involves the proposition that such a war is illegal in international law; and that those who plan and wage such a war, with its inevitable and terrible consequences, are committing a crime in so doing.[9]

This reasoning was followed in the judgment of the Tokyo Tribunal, although Judges Röling, Bernard and Pal in their dissenting judgments disagreed with it.[10] Indeed the

---

4 Art. 227. See section 6.2.

5 *Reply of the Allied and Associated Powers to the Observations of the German Delegation and the Conditions of Peace* (HMSO Misc. No. 4, 1919).

6 See Ian Brownlie, *International Law and the Use of Force by States* (Oxford, 1963) 159–66; William Schabas, 'The Unfinished Work of Defining Aggression: How Many Times must the Cannonballs Fly, Before they are Forever Banned?' in D. McGoldrick, P. Rowe and E. Donnelly (eds.), *The Permanent International Criminal Court* (Oxford and Oregon, 2004) 124.

7 The Charter for the Tokyo IMT defined crimes against peace as 'the planning, preparation, initiation, or waging of a declared or undeclared war of aggression, or a war in violation of international law, treaties, agreements or assurances ...'; Control Council Law No. 10 Art. II(a) began: 'Initiation of invasions of other countries and wars of aggression in violation of international laws and treaties, including but not limited to planning ...' (as in the London Charter).

8 The General Treaty for the Renunciation of War, 27.8.1928.

9 International Military Tribunal (Nuremberg) Judgment and Sentences, reprinted in (1947) 41 *AJIL* 172 (hereafter 'Judgment') at 218.

10 Judgment of the Tokyo IMT 48,437–9. Judge Röling did, however, agree that the occupiers were entitled to prosecute for the initiation of wars on the basis that they threatened their security. See section 6.4.2.

1928 Pact had not intended to give rise to individual criminal responsibility.[11] But whatever the merits of the decisions by the two Tribunals as to the status of the crime after the Second World War, it is widely accepted that there is now a crime of aggression under customary international law.[12]

Following the judgment of the Nuremberg Tribunal, the recently formed United Nations was quick to endorse the law as laid down in the judgment. General Assembly Resolution 95(I) of 11 December 1946 affirmed 'the principles of international law' recognized by the London Charter and the Judgment, and the next year the GA directed the new International Law Commission to formulate those principles and to prepare a code of offences against the peace and security of mankind.[13] Thereafter progress stalled. The ILC's draft principles, which described aggression in the same way as the London Charter, were neither accepted nor rejected by the General Assembly.[14] In 1950 the ILC was requested to elaborate a definition of aggression[15] but did not succeed in reaching agreement, the Special Rapporteur indeed deciding that aggression 'by its very essence, is not susceptible of definition'.[16] Although the ILC included a provision on aggression in its 1954 draft code of crimes, the GA decided that the code raised problems 'closely related to that of the definition of aggression' and postponed further consideration until the special committee, established by the GA in 1952 to consider the definition of aggression, had reported.[17]

After protracted intergovernmental negotiations,[18] made difficult by the tensions of the Cold War in which they were conducted, a 'definition of aggression' was finally adopted in 1974 by GA Resolution 3314.[19] The definition begins with a broad definition of aggression

---

11 See further section 6.3.2.

12 See Brownlie, *International Law and the Use of Force*, 185–94; Yoram Dinstein, *War, Aggression and Self-Defence*, 4th edn (Cambridge, 2005) 121. That was not, however, the universal view in 1950 when the Nuremberg principles were discussed in the Sixth Committee of the GA (UNGAOR 5th Session, 6th Committee, 231st meeting); and see Christian Tomuschat, 'Crimes against the Peace and Security of Mankind and the Recalcitrant Third State' (1995) 24 *Israel Yearbook on Human Rights* 41 at 53. In the UK case of *R* v. *Jones* [2006] UKHL 16 the House of Lords unanimously found, contrary to the view of the Court of Appeal, that aggression was a crime under customary international law.

13 Res. 177(II) of 21.11.1947.

14 See Res. 488(V) of 12.12.1950.

15 Res. 378B(V) of 17.11.1950. See further Ahmed Rifaat, *International Aggression* (Stockholm, 1979).

16 UN doc. A/CN.4/44 at 69.

17 Res. 897(IX) of 4.12.1954. The definition of aggression in the draft code read in part: 'Any act of aggression, including the employment by the authorities of a State of armed force against another State for any purpose other than national or collective self-defence or in pursuance of a decision or recommendation of a competent organ of the United Nations'; threats were also included.

18 The special committee established in 1952 was to draft 'definitions of aggression or draft statements of the notion of aggression' (Res. 688 (VII)). Neither this committee nor two subsequent ones (created by Res. 895 (IX) and Res. 118(XII)) reached agreement on a definition. It required the establishment of a fourth special committee (Res. 2330 (XXII)) and sixteen more years before a definition of aggression was finally adopted.

19 GA Res. 3314(XXIX) of 14.12.1974. The definition is contained in the Annex to the Resolution.

and then lists specific examples.[20] It is clear that the resolution does not as such provide a customary law definition for the individual crime of aggression.[21] Article 5.2 provides:

> A war of aggression is a crime against international peace. Aggression gives rise to international responsibility.

This distinguishes between a war of aggression, participation in which engages individual criminal responsibility, and acts of aggression, engaging the responsibility of States.[22] The Friendly Relations Declaration has a similar provision.[23] After a revival of its earlier mandate,[24] the ILC adopted a draft Code of Crimes against the Peace and Security of Mankind in 1996, Article 16 of which reads as follows:

> An individual who, as leader or organiser, actively participates in or orders the planning, preparation, initiation or waging of aggression committed by a State shall be responsible for a crime of aggression.[25]

The provision begs the question of what aggression is. The ILC noted in its commentary that the issue was 'beyond the scope of the present Code', but stated that individual responsibility for the crime was incurred only if the conduct of the State was 'a sufficiently serious violation of the prohibition' in Article 2(4) of the UN Charter. The Commission also noted that the Charter and Judgment of the Nuremberg Tribunal were the main sources of authority with regard to individual criminal responsibility.[26] The Code was not adopted by governments, their attention being absorbed by the negotiations on the crimes within the jurisdiction of the ICC.

20 See section 13.2.3.
21 As the ILC noted in its commentary on its 1994 draft statute for an international criminal court, the resolution 'deals with aggression by States, not with the crimes of individuals, and is designed as a guide for the Security Council, not as a definition for judicial use. But, given the provisions of Article 2(4) of the Charter of the United Nations, that resolution offers some guidance'. The view that the resolution does provide a customary law definition was expressed during the course of the ICC negotiations by some State representatives, see, e.g. Mohammed Gomaa, 'The Definition of the Crime of Aggression and the ICC Jurisdiction over that Crime' in Mauro Politi and Giuseppe Nesi (eds.), *The International Criminal Court and the Crime of Aggression* (Aldershot, 2004) 56.
22 For the negotiating history on this point, see Bengt Broms, 'The Definition of Aggression' (1977) 154 *Hague Recueil* 299; Benjamin Ferencz, *Defining International Aggression* (New York, 1975), vol. II, 45; Rifaat, *International Aggression*, 275, 276.
23 Declaration on Principles of International Law concerning Friendly Relations and Cooperation among States in accordance with the Charter of the United Nations (Res. 2625(XXV) of 24.10.1970, Annex, para.1) states inter alia: 'A war of aggression constitutes a crime against the peace, for which there is responsibility under international law.'
24 GA Res. 36/106 of 10.12.1981, by which the ILC was invited to resume its work on the draft code of offences against the peace and security of mankind.
25 *Yearbook of the International Law Commission 1996*, vol. II, Part Two, 42.
26 *Ibid.*

The International Criminal Court negotiations

The international negotiations to establish the ICC began on the basis of the draft statute proposed by the ILC in 1994.[27] This provided that the crime of aggression (undefined) would be within the jurisdiction of the court but that no complaint of 'or directly related to' an act of aggression could be brought before the court unless the Security Council had first determined that a State had committed that act.[28] The provision was controversial from the start. Opinion was very much divided on three issues: whether the crime of aggression should be included in the Statute at all, how it should be defined, and how and whether the role of the Security Council should be reflected in the statute.[29]

As regards the definition, one school of thought favoured using the list of acts of aggression in GA Resolution 3314. This met with arguments that the list was illustrative only, thus conflicting with the *nullum crimen* principle[30] if it was used to define a crime, and that the purpose of the resolution was to provide guidance for the Security Council in its determinations of aggression by States[31] and not to provide a definition for the purpose of individual responsibility. Another approach to an ICC definition was to specify that participation in *any* unlawful use of force by a State under the UN Charter was criminal. A third category of proposals started from the proposition that only participation in a war of aggression reflected customary law. To deal with the fact that 'war' is now uncommon, suggestions were made to define aggression as the unlawful use of force but adding a threshold of manifest illegality, or an unlawful purpose such as military occupation or annexation.

Proposals reflecting these approaches were transmitted to the Rome Conference,[32] but there was again failure to reach agreement on the definition and on a role for the Security Council.[33] Article 5(2) of the ICC Statute was inserted at a very late stage of the conference; it reflects the impossibility of reaching agreement on the details but also the firm insistence of the majority at the conference that the crime somehow be included in the Statute. It reads:

> The Court shall exercise jurisdiction over the crime of aggression once a provision is adopted in accordance with Articles 121 and 123 defining the crime and setting out the conditions under which the Court shall exercise jurisdiction with respect to this crime.

---

27 See section 8.2.

28 Art. 23(2). For discussion of the role of the Security Council see section 13.4.2.

29 For the early discussions, see Report of the Ad Hoc Committee on the Establishment of an International Criminal Court GAOR 50th Session Supplement No. 22 (A/50/22) paras. 63–71; Report of the Preparatory Committee on the Establishment of an International Criminal Court Vol. I GAOR 51st Session Supplement No. 22 (A/51/22).

30 See section 1.5.1.

31 Para. 4 of the Resolution.

32 They are to be found in the Report of the Prepcom on the Establishment of an International Criminal Court UN Doc. A/CONF.183/2, included in the Official Records of the Conference (A/CONF.183/13(Vol. III)) at 14–15.

33 For a brief description of the negotiations at Rome, see Herman von Hebel and Darryl Robinson, 'Crimes within the Jurisdiction of the Court' in Lee, *The Making of the Rome Statute*, 79 at 81–5.

Such a provision shall be consistent with the relevant provisions of the Charter of the United Nations.

Accordingly, the ICC is not able to try any case of aggression unless and until the States Parties to the Statute reach agreement on these further provisions. Subsequent negotiations, first in the Preparatory Commission established by the Rome Conference to prepare for the entry into force of the Statute,[34] and then in the Special Working Group on the Crime of Aggression[35] have made progress in identifying and clarifying the issues. The papers put forward by the Chairman of the Special Working Group in 2009 (the 'draft ICC definition', and the 'draft Elements'[36]) form a basis for decisions to be reached at the 2010 Review Conference. At the time of writing, it is not clear whether there will be agreement on the definition and conditions for ICC jurisdiction – or not.

13.1.3 Relationship to other crimes

Aggression differs markedly from genocide, crimes against humanity and war crimes in that, unlike those crimes, it concerns the *ius ad bellum* (the law governing recourse to conflict), and therefore raises questions of international law regarding State responsibility for aggressive acts.[37]

Aggression provides an *occasion* for the commission of the other crimes. War on a major scale causes great suffering and almost inevitably involves the commission of atrocities. In the view of the Nuremberg Tribunal, '[t]o initiate a war of aggression ... is not only an international crime; it is the supreme international crime differing only from other war crimes in that it contains within itself the accumulated evil of the whole'.[38] Genocide has now been described as the 'crime of crimes',[39] but there cannot be any need to engage in an abstract competition for the dreadful title of the worst international crime.

---

34 Res. F of the Rome Conference required the Prepcom to prepare definition, elements and conditions for the exercise of the court's jurisdiction for submission to the Assembly of States Parties ('ASP') at a Review Conference 'with a view to arriving at an acceptable provision on the crime of aggression for inclusion' in the statute. For a summary of the negotiations in the Prepcom, see Silvia Fernandez de Gurmendi, 'The Working Group on Aggression at the Preparatory Commission for the International Criminal Court' (2002) 25 *Fordham International Law Journal* 589; and see Roger Clark, 'Rethinking Aggression as a Crime and Formulating its Elements: the Final Work-Product of the Preparatory Commission for the International Criminal Court' (2002) 15 *LJIL* 859.

35 This working group, established by ICC-ASP/1/Res.1 of 9 September 2002, was open to States on an equal footing, not simply to States Parties to the ICC Statute. It has been holding meetings both during the Assembly of States Parties sessions and intersessionally.

36 Res. ICC-ASP/8/Res.6, Annex II.

37 See further Yoram Dinstein, 'The Distinction between War Crimes and Crimes against Peace' (1995) 24 *Israel Yearbook on Human Rights* 1.

38 Judgment 186 (reprinted in (1947) 41 *AJIL* 172).

39 *Kambanda* ICTR T. Ch. I 4.9.1998 para. 16.

A further distinction from the other crimes is that while genocide, crimes against humanity and war crimes may be, indeed typically are, committed by members of the armed forces of a State or a State-like entity, aggression can *only* be committed on behalf of a State and as part of a State plan or policy. Expansion of the crime to acts by non-State entities has not been widely supported.[40] Further, unlike other international crimes, aggression is a leadership crime and is only committed by persons in policy-making positions in a State.[41]

Unlike the other crimes within the jurisdiction of the ICC, the crime of aggression is not included in the Elements of Crimes for the ICC. Until the ICC Statute and the Elements of Crimes are amended to include the crime of aggression, any discussion of its elements will be guided by the case law of the post-Second World War tribunals and the draft ICC definition and draft Elements of the crime.

13.2   Material elements

The collective act of aggression by a State is the point of reference for the act of the individual perpetrator. The crime is committed (i) by perpetrators in leadership positions in a State (ii) who have participated (iii) in the collective act of the State. Each of these aspects of the material elements of the crime of aggression are described below.

13.2.1 Perpetrators

Aggression is a 'leadership crime': it is committed only by leaders and high-level policy-makers. While the reference in the London Charter to the 'waging' of a war of aggression seems to imply that *all* persons carrying out the State's acts of aggression are individually responsible, from the general down to the foot soldier, that is not how the Charter was interpreted in practice.[42] The point is well illustrated by *Von Leeb and others* (the High Command case), tried before an American Military Tribunal constituted under Control Council Law No. 10.[43] The fourteen accused were all in positions of high military authority: thirteen generals and one admiral. But, one defendant having committed suicide, all the others were acquitted of the charge of crimes against peace on the ground that 'the criminality which attaches to the waging of an aggressive war should be confined to those who participate in it at

---

40 There is an African treaty, the 2006 Protocol on Non-Aggression and Mutual Defence in the Great Lakes Region, which defines aggression as including acts by non-State actors, and requires States to criminalize acts of aggression as so defined. But this extension of the definition of the crime to persons representing non-State actors has not been followed in the negotiations for the ICC Statute and does not reflect customary international law.

41 See section 13.2.1.

42 See G. Brand, 'The War Crimes Trials and the Laws of War' (1949) 26 *BYIL* 414 at 419. For a useful compilation of relevant sections of the post-Second World War case law, see the UN Secretariat paper, 'Historical review of developments relating to aggression' PCNICC/2002/WGCA/L.1.

43 XII LRTWC 1.

the policy level'.[44] In spite of their senior military positions, the defendants were not at the required policy level and they were not criminalized by not having refused to implement the aggressive plans. Accordingly, in countries where the military are largely kept out of the political decisions on the initiation of force, it will less often be the military who are responsible for the crime of aggression than their political superiors. The exact threshold of criminal responsibility is not clear and there may not have been complete consistency in the findings of the Nuremberg IMT and in the subsequent proceedings.[45] But somewhere 'between the Dictator and Supreme Commander of the military forces of the nation and the common soldier is the boundary between the criminal and the excusable participation in the waging of an aggressive war by an individual engaged in it'.[46]

The relevant levels of policy-making are not necessarily confined to government or the military. Some of the accused in the proceedings subsequent to Nuremberg were industrialists, not part of the government but closely associated with it. In *Krauch and others* (the IG Farben case)[47] the accused were, however, acquitted on the ground that, like Albert Speer, one of the Nuremberg IMT defendants, their efforts 'were in aid of the war effort in the same way that other productive enterprises aid in the waging of war'.[48] Their responsibility was below that of planning and leading.

The draft ICC definition and draft Elements specify that a person be 'in a position effectively to exercise control over or to direct the political or military action' of the State which committed the act of aggression. While this phrase adequately encompasses the leaders of the government and of the military, it retreats from the earlier case law, which included other persons with power to shape and influence policy.[49]

The crime of aggression constitutes participation in a collective act by a State against another State. There is no evidence in customary law and no tendency in the ICC negotiations to extend the crime to acts committed by individual mercenaries not sponsored by a State, even though the devastation caused by such acts may be comparable to inter-State military intervention.

13.2.2 Planning, preparation, initiation or waging

The nexus between the State's act of aggression, however defined, and the act of the individual leader or other high-level policy-maker was described in Article 6 of the

---

44 *Ibid.*, 67. The conspiracy charges were dismissed as raising no different issues; eleven of the accused were convicted of war crimes and crimes against humanity.
45 Brownlie, *International Law and the Use of Force*, 205.
46 XII LRTWC 67.
47 X LRTWC 1; see also *Krupp and others* X LRTWC 69.
48 Judgment (1947) 41 *AJIL* 321.
49 See Kevin Heller, 'Retreat from Nuremberg: The Leadership Requirement in the Crime of Aggression' (2007)18 *EJIL* 477.

Nuremberg Charter as the 'planning, preparation, initiation or waging' of an aggressive war and 'participation in a common plan or conspiracy' for the foregoing. Participation in the formulation of aggressive plans, largely of course dependent on Hitler's decisions, was one of the most typical bases for criminal responsibility in the Nuremberg IMT and subsequent proceedings. It is difficult to distinguish planning from preparation in the jurisprudence. Preparation had to be closely linked with planning; preparation for some vague future programme of aggression was not sufficient.[50]

The ICC draft definition uses the terms 'planning, preparation, initiation or execution'. Conspiracy is not included. As interpreted by the Nuremberg IMT, conspiracy differed little from planning and preparation;[51] the charge of conspiracy was in effect superfluous, and led to criticism of the Tribunal.[52] Charges of conspiracy were more important to the Tokyo IMT, which relied on the concept of inchoate conspiracy; its rulings have also come in for extensive criticism.[53]

Participation in *threats* to use military force does not come within the crime of aggression. The collective act must have been completed in order to found criminal responsibility. The threat of aggression was not included in the Charters of the Nuremberg or Tokyo IMTs, nor in Control Council Law No. 10. The unopposed invasions of Austria and Czechoslovakia, following the successful threat of aggressive force, were treated as evidence of the aggressive conspiracy but were not charged as crimes against peace before the Nuremberg IMT. They were, however, charged in indictments under Control Council Law No. 10 (which included 'invasions' within the jurisdiction of the tribunals constituted under it).[54]

13.2.3 Act of aggression

The underlying collective act is the act of a State committed against another State. There are two questions: (i) how is the collective act described for the purpose of individual criminal responsibility, and (ii) what are the rules of international law regarding the collective act, as so described?

As regards the description of the crime under customary international law, there has been little State practice since the aftermath of the Second World War and only a minority of

---

50 Judgment (1947) 41 *AJIL* 172 at 222.
51 Quincy Wright, (1947) 41 *AJIL* 38 at 68.
52 See Brownlie, *International Law and the Use of Force*, 201.
53 See comment and authorities cited in Neil Boister and Robert Cryer, *The Tokyo International Military Tribunal: A Reappraisal* (Oxford, 2008) ch. 8.
54 E.g. in the case of *United States of America* v. *Ernst von Weizsäcker et al.* (the Ministries case) the tribunal held: 'The fact that the aggressor was here able to so overawe the invaded countries does not detract in the slightest from the enormity of the aggression, in reality perpetrated. The invader here employed an act of war.' (Judgment, 11–13 April 1949 (*Trials of War Criminals before the Nuremberg Military Tribunals*) United States Government Printing Office vol. XIV at 330.)

States have adopted national legislation criminalizing aggression.[55] Customary international law, therefore, probably remains as in the jurisprudence of Nuremberg, supplemented by the subsequent proceedings under Control Council Law No. 10 and by the Tokyo IMT. This means that under customary law it is only aggressive *war* that founds individual criminal responsibility.[56] Declared war is now uncommon, however, and the term is not employed in the legal regimes of the UN Charter and the Geneva Conventions; a definition of the crime of aggression which relied on the existence of a 'war' for its material element would revive old arguments about the meaning of the word. But it is possible to give the term content even when it has lost its currency in international relations,[57] and a definition which sought to reflect customary law would have to do this. In particular, not every unlawful use of force by a State comes within the concept of aggression, only large-scale and serious instances. Such a limitation is of the nature of aggression, and should not simply be a jurisdictional threshold for a court.

As discussed above,[58] the negotiations for the purpose of the ICC Statute considered a number of different options for defining the collective act, including some proposals which tried to capture the meaning of war. The current draft ICC definition, however, defines the act of aggression as 'the use of armed force by a State against the sovereignty, territorial integrity or political independence of another State, or in any other manner inconsistent with the Charter of the United Nations'.[59] This reflects the wording of Article 1 of the Definition in GA resolution 3314, which is itself similar to Article 2(4) of the Charter;[60] it thus incorporates the general rules of international law regarding *all* unlawful uses of force by States. Such a formulation will require the ICC to rule on whether the collective act of the State is in breach of international law; the Court will need to consider any defences under

---

55 Germany is one that has (although it is a narrow definition, limited to preparation, and linked to German participation; s. 80 of the German Criminal Code). The statute of the Supreme Iraqi Criminal Tribunal, Art. 14(c), which refers to violations of stipulated Iraqi law, includes '[t]he abuse of position and the pursuit of policies that may lead to the threat of war or the use of the armed forces of Iraq against an Arab country, in accordance with Article 1 of Law Number 7 of 1958, as amended'. So far as the UK is concerned, it is clear that even though the crime is one under international law, it is not part of domestic law (*R* v. *Jones* [2006] UKHL 16).

56 T. Bruha, *Die Definition der Aggression* (Berlin, 1980) 126; Dinstein, *War, Aggression*, 125–6, noting that the extension in the 1996 ILC draft Code to 'acts of aggression "short of war" represents a striking departure from the law as perceived in the London Charter and in the consensus Definition of Aggression'; Gerhard Werle, *Principles of International Criminal Law* (The Hague, 2005) 391, 394; Claus Kreß, 'The German Chief Federal Prosecutor's Decision not to Investigate the Alleged Crime of Preparing Aggression against Iraq' (2004) 2 *JICJ* 245 at 249. See to the contrary Richard Griffiths, 'International Law, the Crime of Aggression and the Ius Ad Bellum' (2002) 2 *International Criminal Law Review* 301 at 303–4.

57 See, e.g. Dinstein, *War, Aggression*, 151–2.

58 Section 13.1.2.

59 The draft also lists the acts listed in the 1974 General Assembly Definition, and it limits the crime to participation in ' . . . an act of aggression which, by its character, gravity and scale, constitutes a manifest violation of the Charter of the United Nations'.

60 For the differences between Art. 1 of the Definition and Article 2(4) of the Charter see Dinstein, *War, Aggression*, 127, 128.

international law which are available to the State (for example, self-defence in accordance with Article 51 of the UN Charter) in reaching its decision.[61]

Although the rules on State responsibility for the use of force form a different regime from that of international criminal law, they must be addressed – for both the customary law crime of aggression and the draft ICC definition of the crime – since violation of them by a State, with or without qualification, is a constituent part of the offence. We give a brief overview below. We then consider further the ICC definition of the collective act.

I. International law regarding the use of force by a State[62]

Article 2(4) of the Charter of the United Nations reads as follows:

> All Members shall refrain in their international relations from the threat or use of force against the territorial integrity or political independence of any State, or in any other manner inconsistent with the purposes of the United Nations.

The Charter put in place a new structure for international peace and security, requiring the settlement of disputes by peaceful means and introducing a collective system for States to act through the UN to suppress aggression and other breaches of international peace. While the collective system has developed in a different direction from that envisaged by the drafters, the prohibition on the use of force remains as set out in Article 2(4). This is the fundamental legal principle governing the use of force and it reflects customary international law.[63]

Although the provision is at the heart of the rules of international law on the use of force, its interpretation and application are not easy. In particular, there are differences of view as to the exceptions to the prohibition. The only exceptions universally admitted are, first, individual or collective self-defence and, second, force authorized by the Security Council acting under Chapter VII of the Charter. There is controversy over whether there is also an exception for humanitarian intervention.

Self-defence

The relevant provision of the Charter is Article 51, which provides in part:

> Nothing in the present Charter shall impair the inherent right of individual or collective self-defence if an armed attack occurs against a Member of the United Nations, until the

---

61 These international law defences are not expressly included in the ICC Statute, but will have to be ruled on within the Court's decision as to whether the use of force in question was contrary to international law.
62 What follows is an extremely brief discussion of a difficult area of public international law. For useful summaries of the law, see Humphrey Waldock, 'The Regulation of the Use of Force by Individual States in International Law' (1952) 81 (II) *Hague Recueil* 455; Malcolm Shaw, *International Law*, 6th edn (Cambridge, 2008) ch. 20; see further Brownlie, *International Law and the Use of Force*; Dinstein, *War, Aggression*; and Christine Gray, *International Law and the Use of Force*, 3rd edn (Oxford, 2008) chs. 2, 4, 6.
63 *Case concerning Military and Paramilitary Activities in and against Nicaragua (Nicaragua v. USA)* (1986) ICJ Rep 14, paras. 188–90.

Security Council has taken measures necessary to maintain international peace and security . . .

The Charter does not elaborate on the conditions for a lawful use of force in self-defence, but international law requires that self-defence is lawful only if it is *necessary* to use force, and only if that force is *proportionate*, that is, it is not excessive in relation to the need to avert or respond to the attack.[64] A classic formulation of the applicable rules is that of US Secretary of State Webster in the 1837 Caroline incident.[65] In an exchange of correspondence with the British he stated that, for action to be lawful, there must be a 'necessity of self-defence, instant, overwhelming, leaving no choice of means, and no moment for deliberation' and that the action must not be 'unreasonable or excessive; since the act justified by the necessity of self-defence, must be limited by that necessity, and kept clearly within it'.

Commentators differ as to whether force may be used in anticipatory self-defence, that is, against an attack that is threatened and not ongoing. On one view, the right to self-defence applies only once an armed attack has begun.[66] The contrary view, that States have a right to act in order to avert the threat of an imminent attack, is supported not least by the practical argument that it is unrealistic in all cases to await an actual attack; this consideration applies particularly to attacks from nuclear weapons.[67] The ICJ has left open the issue of the lawfulness of a response to the threat of an imminent armed attack.[68] However, the claim to 'pre-emptive self-defence' to prevent the emergence of a security threat is widely rejected as impermissible under international law.[69] Further controversial questions about the right to self-defence are whether force may be used to rescue a State's nationals in a State which is unable or unwilling to protect them,[70] and whether the 'armed attack' must cross some threshold of intensity before self-defence is justified.[71]

---

64 The requirement of necessity and proportionality has been confirmed by the ICJ; see, e.g. *Case concerning Armed Activities on the Territory of the Congo (DRC* v. *Uganda)* (2005) ICJ Rep, para. 147.

65 The incident concerned the destruction over the Niagara Falls of a steamer thought to be supplying Canadian rebels against the British. See Robert Jennings, 'The Caroline and Macleod Cases' (1938) 32 *AJIL* 86.

66 See Brownlie, *International Law and the Use of Force*, 275–8; B. Simma et al. (eds.), *The Charter of the United Nations: A Commentary*, 2nd edn (Oxford, 2002) 803; Dinstein, *War, Aggression*, 182–7 (but giving a wide interpretation of what constitutes the start of the attack justifying self-defence).

67 See, e.g. Waldock, 'The Regulation of the Use of Force', 495–505; Derek Bowett, *Self-Defence in International Law* (Manchester, 1958) 184–93; Christopher Greenwood, 'International Law and the United States' Air Operation against Libya' (1987) 89 West Virginia Law Review 933 at 942.

68 *Case concerning Military and Paramilitary Activities in and against Nicaragua (Nicaragua* v. *USA)* (1986) ICJ Rep 14, para. 194). See also *Case concerning Armed Activities on the Territory of the Congo (DRC* v. *Uganda)* (2005) ICJ Rep, para. 143.

69 The claim is made in the 2002 'National Security Strategy of the United States' (2002) 41 *ILM* 1478; see Christopher Greenwood, 'International Law and the Pre-emptive Use of Force: Afghanistan, Al-Quaida and Iraq' (2003) 4 *San Diego International Law Journal* 7; for a contrary view see Ruth Wedgwood, 'The Fall of Saddam Hussein: Security Council Mandates and Preemptive Self-Defense' (2003) 97 *AJIL* 576, at 582–5.

70 See Gray, *International Law and the Use of Force*, 156–60; Dinstein, *War, Aggression*, 231–4.

71 See *Case concerning Military and Paramilitary Activities in and against Nicaragua (Nicaragua* v. *USA)* (1986) ICJ Rep 14, paras. 191 and 195 and *Oil Platforms (Islamic Republic of Iran* v. *USA)* (2003) ICJ Rep,

One of the frequent questions of modern times is whether there is a right of self-defence against non-State organizations operating from another State;[72] for example, whether military force may lawfully be used by a threatened State against terrorist groups who are in the territory of another State. Commentators differ as to whether, if force may be used against such groups, it is lawful if the State from which they are operating is not complicit with or tolerating the actions of those groups; developing State practice seems to support the view that States have the right of self-defence against terrorist groups in other States where the 'harbouring' States are unable or unwilling to deal with the threat themselves, but this is by no means settled law.[73]

Authorization under Chapter VII

The Security Council, acting under Chapter VII of the UN Charter, may authorize the use of force, either by UN peacekeeping or peace-enforcement missions ('blue helmets') or by coalitions of forces of States. Such authorizations provide undoubted exceptions to the prohibition on the use of force set out in Article 2(4). Even here there may be controversy. For example, the legal justification put forward by the United Kingdom and the United States for the military intervention in 2003 in Iraq was that their military action had been authorized by the Security Council; the argument, which is widely accepted as having little substance, interpreted Resolution 1441(2002) as reviving the authorization (given in Resolution 678 (1991)) to use military action to counter Iraq's invasion of Kuwait in 1990, without the need for any further decision by the Council.[74]

Humanitarian intervention

This term is given to military action taken for humanitarian purposes but without Security Council authorization and without the agreement of the State concerned. On its face such

paras. 51, 63–4 and 72; for critique of this point, see Oscar Schachter, 'In Defense of International Rules on the Use of Force' (1986) 53 *University of Chicago Law Review* 113.

72 For arguments in favour of the right to self-defence in such circumstances, see Christopher Greenwood, 'International Law and the "War on Terrorism"' (2002) 78 *International Affairs* 301; Michael Byers, 'Terrorism, the Use of Force and International Law after 11 September' (2002) 51 *ICLQ* 401; for arguments against, see Antonio Cassese, 'Terrorism is also Disrupting some Crucial Legal Categories in International Law' (2001) 12 *EJIL* 993; Eric Myjer and Nigel White, 'The Twin Towers Attack: an Unlimited Right to Self-Defence?' (2002) 7 *Journal of Conflict and Security Law* 5; J. Kammerhofer, 'Armed Activities Case and Non-state Actors in Self-defence Law' (2007) 20 *LJIL* 89. See also *Advisory Opinion on the Legal Consequences of the Construction of a Wall in the Occupied Palestinian Territory* (2004) ICJ Rep 36, para. 139, and *Case concerning Armed Activities on the Territory of the Congo (DRC v. Uganda)* (2005) ICJ Rep, paras. 146, 147; the majority decisions in both cases have been criticized for disregarding the possibility of self-defence against non-State actors, see, e.g. Separate Opinions, in the former case by Judge Higgins, paras. 33–6, in the latter by Judge Kooijmans, paras. 26–30 and Judge Simma, paras. 7–12; and see Sean Murphy, 'Self-Defence and the Israeli Wall Advisory Opinion: an *Ipse Dixit*' (2005) 99 *AJIL* 62.

73 For a useful overview of State practice, see Christian Tams, 'The Use of Force against Terrorists' (2009) 20 *EJIL* 1.

74 On these and other arguments for and against the legality of the intervention, see papers in 'Agora: Future Implications of the Iraq Conflict' (2003) 97 *AJIL*, 553–642; Sean Murphy, 'Assessing the Legality of Invading Iraq' (2004) 92 *Georgetown Law Journal* 173.

action breaches the prohibition on the use of force set out in Article 2(4), but commentators differ as to whether interventions such as that in 1991 in northern Iraq, and in 1999 by NATO in Kosovo, are nevertheless lawful. The conservative, and perhaps the better, view is that humanitarian intervention is contrary to international law; a few doubtful examples of humanitarian practice cannot constitute a new rule of customary international law. Other commentators state either that there is an emerging norm of customary law allowing the implementation of the responsibility to protect, or that such intervention is already lawful under existing international law; these views rely on arguments about the interpretation of Article 2(4), and as to the continued existence of a customary law right which has not been displaced by the Charter.[75] Military interventions with benign purposes remain a difficulty in defining the crime of aggression: whether lawful or unlawful, such actions have not been committed with an aggressive purpose.[76]

II. ICC definition

As we have seen above, the draft ICC definition describes an 'act of aggression' – the collective act by the State – as 'the use of armed force by a State against the sovereignty, territorial integrity or political independence of another State, or in any other manner inconsistent with the Charter of the United Nations.' It also lists the acts set out in General Assembly Resolution 3314 (XXIX) of 1974 and provides that any of these acts, 'in accordance with' that Resolution, qualifies as an act of aggression. The list of acts includes invasion, bombardment and annexation of another State's territory, attack on another State's armed forces, and sending armed groups which commit aggressive acts against another State.

A number of points are worth noting. First, the draft ICC definition adopts a major part of the 1974 Definition although the latter did not deal with individual criminal responsibility and it is doubtful that, as regards the law on State responsibility, it reflects customary law in its entirety.[77]

---

75 All of these views are discussed in J. L. Hozgrefe and Robert Keohane (eds.), *Humanitarian Intervention* (Cambridge, 2003); see also Bruno Simma, 'NATO, the UN and the Use of Force: Legal Aspects' (1999) 10 *EJIL* 1; Nico Krisch, 'Unilateral Enforcement of the Collective Will: Kosovo, Iraq, and the Security Council' (1999) 3 *Max Planck United Nations Yearbook* 59; Adam Roberts, 'The So-called "Right" of Humanitarian Intervention' (2000) 3 *YIHL* 3; International Development Research Centre, *The Responsibility to Protect: Report of the International Commission on Intervention and State Sovereignty* (Ottawa, 2001); Danish Institute of International Affairs, *Humanitarian Intervention: Legal and Political Aspects* (Copenhagen, 1999); Gray, *International Law and the Use of Force*, 33–53.

76 For the view that humanitarian intervention is included within the draft definition of aggression, see Kriangsak Kittichaisaree, 'The NATO Military Action and the Potential Impact of the International Criminal Court' (2000) 4 *Singapore Journal of International & Comparative Law* 498 at 506, 507.

77 As we have seen above (section 13.1.2), the 1974 definition made clear that it did not deal with individual criminal responsibility. As regards State responsibility, the ICJ has held that one paragraph of the definition, para. 3(g), which relates to the sending of armed groups into another State, does reflect customary law (*Case*

Second, the draft ICC definition reflects the substance of the 1974 definition without recognizing the conditions and qualifications of that text. The 1974 definition was adopted to provide guidance to the Security Council in the Council's determination of the existence of acts of aggression under Article 39 of the Charter,[78] and it states that the Security Council may conclude that in specific circumstances a listed act does not constitute aggression,[79] for example if 'the acts concerned or their consequences are not of sufficient gravity' (Article 2). The 1974 definition states that it does not enlarge or diminish the scope of the Charter (Article 6). Perhaps, however, the reference in the ICC definition to the list of acts qualifying as aggression 'in accordance with' the 1974 Resolution can be interpreted to mean that any relevant conditions and qualifications of that Resolution are incorporated.

Third, the draft ICC definition does not in terms limit the acts it lists to instances of major, serious or large-scale use of force. On its face the list would include border skirmishes and infringements of maritime limits or air space. While a case before the ICC is inadmissible if it 'is not of sufficient gravity to justify further action by the Court' (Article 17), this threshold leaves a great deal of discretion to the Court: an infringement of maritime limits may be considered grave by the territorial State, but it should not be regarded as aggression.[80]

Finally, there is the problem that, as we have seen, many modern-day military interventions are given different legal analyses in different parts of the world. The draft definition does not attempt to resolve the controversial areas of international law on the use of force, and indeed it would not have been possible to reach agreement had such an attempt been made.

The draft definition does, however, include a threshold. It defines the crime of aggression as participation (in the manner and by the persons discussed above[81]) in ' ... an act of aggression which, by its character, gravity and scale, constitutes a manifest violation of the Charter of the United Nations'. From the reference to 'scale' it may be thought that the phrase qualifying aggression is intended to exclude from the jurisdiction of the Court such small-scale violations as minor border incursions, but the use of the word 'manifest' is a strange one in this context, since there may be a border incident which is manifestly in violation of the Charter, although of a minor nature. The intention was probably to exclude grey areas of international law on the use of force and such controversial uses of force as

concerning Military and Paramilitary Activities in and against Nicaragua (Nicaragua v. *USA)* (1986) ICJ Rep 14 at para. 195); see also *Case concerning Armed Activities on the Territory of the Congo (DRC* v. *Uganda)* (2005) ICJ Rep at para. 146; but Judge Kooijmans in the latter case stated that the resolution, 'as important as it may be from a legal point of view, does not in all its terms reflect customary law' (para. 63, Separate Opinion).
78 See e.g. paragraph 4 of Res. 3314.
79 Arts. 2 and 4. See further on the negotiation of the definition, Rifaat, *International Aggression*, ch. 15; Julius Stone, 'Hopes and Loopholes in the 1974 Definition of Aggression' (1977) 71 *AJIL* 224; Benjamin Ferencz, *Defining International Aggression* (New York, 1975), vol. II.
80 See, e.g. Theodor Meron, 'Defining Aggression for the International Criminal Court' (2001) 25 *Suffolk Transnational Law Review* 1 at 4; Antonio Cassese, 'On some Problematic Aspects of the Crime of Aggression' (2007) 20 *LJIL* 841 at 845.
81 See sections 3.2.1 and 3.2.2.

humanitarian intervention, self-defence against terrorist groups in other States, and anticipatory self-defence.[82] A great deal is demanded of the term 'manifest violation'. The law lacks the necessary certainty if State leaders cannot predict in advance whether they will be vulnerable to prosecution or not depending upon whether the ICC eventually concludes that the law is sufficiently controversial for the violation not to be 'manifest'. The draft Elements make clear that the violation must be 'manifest' to the Court, not simply to the State concerned.

Other ways have been suggested for excluding from a definition of aggression instances of illegal use of force which should not come within the Court's jurisdiction. It has been suggested that a necessary part of the crime of aggression is the aggressive aim or intention of the leader or the central leadership,[83] of which the individual perpetrator must be aware. To include this as a material or mental element would help to avoid classifying as the crime of aggression participation in military intervention carried out for humanitarian objectives, for example. One of the German proposals put forward in the ICC negotiations followed this approach; it referred to the unlawful use of force carried out 'with the object or result of establishing a military occupation of, or annexing' the foreign territory.[84] The choice of those purposes would, however, exclude acts which might be regarded as properly coming within the criminal category;[85] aggressive wars to extract economic or political advantages of some kind are not inconceivable. As the draft ICC definition stands, no aggressive purpose is included.

13.3   Mental elements

The post-Second World War case law indicates that there must be an intent to participate in the aggressive act. If the perpetrator had knowledge of the collective intent to initiate and wage aggressive war but continued to participate, the requirement was satisfied. Two examples from the Nuremberg trial will suffice. Schacht was at some relevant periods President of the Reichsbank and a central figure in Germany's rearmament programme. 'But', said the Tribunal, 'rearmament of itself is not criminal under the Charter. To be a crime against peace under Article 6 of the Charter it must be shown that Schacht carried out this rearmament as part of the Nazi plans to wage aggressive wars.'[86] He was acquitted since

---

[82] See Claus Kreß, 'The Crime of Aggression before the First Review of the ICC Statute' (2007) 20 *LJIL* 851. International criminal law is 'ill-equipped to decide major controversies about the content of existing legal rules' (at 851). See also discussion at Kreß, 'The German Prosecutor's Decision', 259.

[83] This is variously described as a special intent required for participants in aggression, or as a material element of the crime: Stefan Glaser, '*Quelques remarques sur la définition de l'agression en droit international pénal*' in S. Hohenleitner et al. (eds.), *Festschrift für Theodor Rittler* (Aalen, 1957) 383; Brownlie, *International Law and the Use of Force*, 213; Werle, *Principles*, 395; Kreß, 'The German Prosecutor's Decision', 256; Cassese, 'On some Problematic Aspects', 848.

[84] PCNICC/1999/DP.13.

[85] Clark, 'Rethinking Aggression as a Crime', 878.

[86] Judgment (1947) 41 *AJIL* 172 at 300.

it could not be inferred from the evidence that he knew of the plans for aggressive war. Bormann rose to a position of great power and was finally of great influence over Hitler. But the evidence did not show that he knew of the plans; he did not attend the crucial planning meetings; he was acquitted of the crimes against peace charged against him.[87]

If the crime is prosecuted before the ICC, the intent requirement will be different. The draft Elements for the ICC include two mental elements, 4 and 6. Element 4 requires that the perpetrator is aware of the factual circumstances establishing the inconsistency of the use of armed force by the State with the Charter of the United Nations. Element 6 requires that the perpetrator is aware of the factual circumstances establishing the manifest violation of the Charter of the United Nations. Neither of these requires it to be proved that the perpetrator knew of the illegality, or made a legal evaluation of the act's inconsistency with the Charter or its 'manifest' nature. Provided, therefore, that the perpetrator intended to lead his country into a conflict and knew of the circumstances surrounding the conflict, it is not necessary that he knew that the conflict was unlawful. Presumably the defence of mistake of law may in certain circumstances be available.

13.4   Prosecution of aggression in the ICC

13.4.1 Jurisdiction of the ICC

In contrast with the other crimes triable by the ICC, jurisdiction over the crime of aggression will be exercised by the Court only in respect of States Parties which have accepted the amendment incorporating a definition and the necessary conditions.[88] Article 121(5) provides in effect an opt-in system for jurisdiction over aggression, an arrangement rejected as a general mechanism for the Statute during the early negotiations on the establishment of the ICC.[89] Accordingly, for a State Party which has not accepted the relevant amendment, the Court will not be able to try the crime of aggression if committed by its nationals or on its territory.[90] The wording of the Statute does not appear to allow States not party to the Statute any equivalent right to object to an amendment on aggression (or on any other additional crime). This difference in treatment has been criticized[91] but the position is not dissimilar

---

87 *Ibid.*, 329.

88 Art. 121(5).

89 See section 8.2.

90 Art. 121(5), second sentence. See Giorgio Gaja, 'The Long Journey towards Repressing Aggression' in Cassese, *Commentary*, 427 at 439; Danesh Sarooshi, 'The Statute of the ICC' (1999) 48 *ICLQ* 387 at 401. A different interpretation of the provision has been put forward in the ICC negotiations, according to which an addition of the definition of aggression to the Statute would not be an 'amendment', since already foreseen by the Statute, and thus would not come within Art. 121(5).

91 Ruth Wedgwood in 'The International Criminal Court: an American View' (1999) 10 *EJIL* 93 at 104 refers to it as an 'asymmetric immunity for treaty Parties'.

from that of non-party States under the Statute generally, and is not inconsistent with the law of treaties or the traditional principles of jurisdiction.

13.4.2 Conditions for the exercise of the ICC's jurisdiction

The crime of aggression presupposes that an act has been committed by a State. When the ILC included aggression in its draft Statute, it considered that there was a problem with the ICC's trying individuals in the absence of a finding of aggression against the State concerned.[92] The ILC proposed that, in view of the Security Council's responsibilities under the UN Charter, the way to resolve the problem was to require that, before the ICC could exercise its jurisdiction, there had to be a prior determination by the Security Council that a State had committed the act of aggression which was the subject of the proceedings.[93] The legal effect of any such determination would be for the ICC itself to decide.

As we have seen,[94] this provision was not included in the ICC Statute. There is, however, a requirement in Article 5(2) that the conditions for the exercise of the ICC's jurisdiction must be 'consistent with the relevant provisions of the Charter of the United Nations'. This has been interpreted by some as requiring a determination by the Council, prior to ICC prosecution, that the State concerned has committed aggression.[95] Such a condition would solve the problem that holding individuals responsible for a crime of participation in a State's act condemns the State itself. It has been argued that under Chapter VII of the UN Charter it is the Council alone which has exclusive power to determine the existence of an act of aggression by a State. Provision for a prior Security Council determination regarding a State's responsibility would reflect this logic.[96]

This view is contentious.[97] It is clear that the Council does not have *exclusive* responsibility with regard to threats to international peace and security. Its responsibility is exclusive only for the purpose of its powers under Chapter VII which include deciding upon economic sanctions and other responses to breaches of the peace. The General Assembly has the power to take decisions provided that the Council is not dealing with the matter, and has

---

92 James Crawford, 'The ILC's draft Statute for an International Criminal Tribunal' (1994) 88 *AJIL* 134 at 147.
93 Art. 23(2) ILC draft Statute. See Crawford, 'The ILC's draft Statute'; and James Crawford, 'The ILC adopts a Statute for an International Criminal Court' (1995) 89 *AJIL* 404 at 411.
94 In section 13.1.2.
95 This was the understanding of the UK, as indicated in its statement made on adoption of the statute on 17.7.1998 (A/CONF.183/13 (Vol. II) at p. 124); see also Zimmerman in Triffterer, *Observers' Notes*, 140, 144, who states that Art. 5(2) and the Charter require prior determination, or referral to the ICC, by a relevant UN organ; see also Fife, 'Criminalizing Individuals', 67.
96 See Allegra Carpenter, 'The International Criminal Court and the Crime of Aggression' (1995) 64 *NJIL* 223 at 234; Irina Müller-Schieke, 'Defining the Crime of Aggression under the Statute of the International Criminal Court' (2001) 14 *LJIL* 409 at 423.
97 See, e.g. Gaja, 'The Long Journey', 433; Claus Kreß, 'Versailles-Nuremberg-The Hague: Germany and the International Criminal Law' (2006) 40 *The International Lawyer* 15 at 38 and n. 133.

adopted a number of resolutions in which it refers to aggressive acts by States.[98] It is undeniable that the ICJ may adjudicate upon questions of aggression:

> The Council has functions of a political nature assigned to it, whereas the Court exercises purely judicial functions. Both organs can therefore perform their separate but complementary functions with respect to the same events.[99]

There are also arguments of a practical and political nature. On the one hand, to require the Court to act only after the Council's determination would give the Permanent Members of the Council an effective veto over prosecutions relating to themselves and their allies. The Court ought to be allowed to act without Council interference.[100] The Council has in fact very rarely made a determination of aggression,[101] and if this inaction continued there would be a risk that the Court would be blocked from ever considering a case of aggression. On the other hand, it is pointed out that if the ICC, in the absence of a Security Council determination, had to decide that an act of aggression had taken place, it would require the Court to decide highly political questions of public international law.[102] There is a risk that investigations undertaken by the ICC for an act of aggression without a prior Council authorization might bring about an escalation of the situation.[103] Further, if the ICC were to make its own assessment, without the prior determination of the Council, as to the justification of military action in self-defence or other lawful reasons, it might infringe on the responsibilities of the Council with regard to the actions of the State concerned.

Proposals have been made for alternative institutional mechanisms to determine responsibility by a State before an individual can be tried by the ICC. These seek to avoid the Council blocking a case through inertia.[104] In particular, it has been proposed that if the Council fails to act, the UN General Assembly, or the ICJ under its advisory jurisdiction, may be asked for a prior determination. While a reference to the ICJ would have some logic if a legal decision is required, the use of the ICJ's advisory jurisdiction for such a purpose presents difficulties, in that the nature of the case would essentially be contentious, while the ruling would (presumably) be binding on the ICC, unlike the determinations of a political

---

98 Arts. 11(2) and 12 of the UN Charter. See GA resolutions listed in 'Historical review' PCNICC/2002/WGCA/L.1 at paras. 405–29.

99 *Case Concerning Military and Paramilitary Activities in and against Nicaragua (Nicaragua* v. *US)* (1984) ICJ Rep 392, para. 95.

100 Antonio Cassese, 'The Statute of the International Criminal Court: Some Preliminary Reflections' (1999) 10 *EJIL* 144 at 147.

101 Although in relation to several situations the Council has described certain conduct as acts of aggression: see 'Historical review' PCNICC/2002/WGCA/L.1 at paras. 381–404.

102 Meron, 'Defining Aggression', 1.

103 Andreas Zimmerman, 'The Creation of a Permanent International Criminal Court' (1998) 2 *Max Planck Yearbook of International Law* 169 at 203.

104 See proposals at e.g. UN Doc. PCNICC/2001/WGCA/DP.1, now largely reflected in the options in Article 15*bis* in ICC-ASP/8/Res.6, Annex II.

organ. Further, there would be no possibility for the individual accused to appear before the ICJ and bring evidence.

The problem is a difficult one. Because of the inextricable connection between State act and individual responsibility, a determination that a State is responsible for an aggressive act of a certain magnitude would seem to render much of the upper leadership of that State individually responsible under criminal law, subject of course to the degree of their personal involvement. If that determination were to be made by the Security Council, which inevitably takes decisions for political reasons,[105] the ICC would have to be able to do more than simply decide upon the participation and intent of a particular accused. It would have to reach its own conclusions on any international law defences available to the accused with regard to the act of the State concerned, as did the Nuremberg Tribunal with regard to the self-defence arguments by the defendants concerning the invasion of Norway by Germany.[106] The principles of fair trial would be infringed if a decision by a political organ could itself effectively constitute part of the judgment against the accused. But if the ICC were able to take its own decision on the acts of a State, that could result in a finding which differed from a Security Council determination, in that the former might decide that there had been no aggression where the latter had decided that there was.[107] That may, however, be a necessary price to pay for compliance with the requirements of fair trial.

It may be asked whether there is any reason why there should first be the interposition of a ruling of another body, if the ICC itself will have to judge the legality of the act of the State. While the legal reasons for the proposal that the Security Council should make a prior determination may be weak, there are other reasons, considered in the following section, why it may be wise to have an external filter or trigger to ensure the necessary support of the international community before resorting to a judicial process which might have an effect on the maintenance of international peace and security. Such a mechanism need not require a determination on aggression to be made; there could be a requirement, for example, that no case of aggression be tried without a referral of the situation to the Court by the Security Council.

13.4.3 Implications of the prosecution of aggression before the ICC

The political and practical implications of the prosecution of the crime of aggression which result from the connection between individual and State responsibility help to explain past difficulties in reaching agreement on a definition of aggression and on the conditions for the exercise of the ICC's jurisdiction.

---

105 As described in, for example, Judge Schwebel's dissenting opinion in *Case Concerning Military and Paramilitary Activities in and against Nicaragua (Nicaragua v. US)* (1986) ICJ Rep 14, para. 60.
106 Judgment (1947) 41 *AJIL* 172 at 203–7.
107 But if the ICC could act only with a prior Council determination of aggression, it would not be able to find aggression if the Council had not.

The legal principles of the *ius ad bellum* give rise to significantly more controversy than the *ius in bello*. Illustrations of situations which would call for difficult determinations of the legality of military intervention need be sought no further back in time than the conflict in Afghanistan in 2001, the intervention in Iraq in 2003 by the US, the UK and others, and the action by Israel in Lebanon in 2006. Judicial decisions which involve determinations of State conduct will be likely to have repercussions for the maintenance of international peace and security. The problems relating to jurisdiction by the ICC over a State which is not a State Party will be exacerbated if the ICC is to decide whether such a State has committed an act of aggression.

There will be difficulties for the ICC itself, difficulties of a kind which may sometimes arise in respect of the other crimes within the Court's jurisdiction but which will be particularly severe in relation to aggression. The constitution and procedures of the ICC are designed for the determination of individual, not State, responsibility.[108] Investigations of the crime will involve questions of the greatest sensitivity for a State's defence and national security. Except where the documents of a defeated State are available to the international community, as with Germany and Japan in the Second World War – when the Tribunals had a glut of the defeated governments' most secret papers[109] – there will be severe difficulties of access to evidence.

Issues such as these have evoked a cautious attitude towards what is, in effect, the invocation of criminal law to regulate the use of force by States. To turn the ICC into a forum for litigating disputes between States risks harm both to the Court and to the maintenance of international peace and security.[110] The Court is not best placed to settle controversies about the content of international law on the use of force which have dogged the international community for decades. Doubts have been expressed about the inclusion of aggression in the ICC Statute at all,[111] and about whether its inclusion will be more than pure symbolism.[112] When the crime is to be tried by the Court, care will have to be taken to ensure that the Court and the international criminal justice project as a whole are not harmed.

---

108 For example, complementarity is a fundamental part of the ICC's structure, but it will be the rare case of aggression that can be tried in national courts. Another important aspect of the ICC Statute is the attention given to the needs of victims of crimes; for example they are accorded rights of participation in trials and rights of protection and reparation. Whereas the victims of the other crimes within the jurisdiction of the Court are individuals, the victim of an act of aggression is in reality a State. (See James Boeving, 'Aggression, International Law, and the ICC: an Argument for the Withdrawal of Aggression from the Rome Statute' (2005) 43 *Columbia Journal of Transnational Law* 557 at 583–8.)

109 In Japan, however, many of the relevant papers had been burnt.

110 Rolf Fife, 'Criminalizing Individuals for Acts of Aggression committed by States' in Morten Bergsmo (ed.), *Human Rights and Criminal Justice for the Downtrodden* (Leiden/Boston, 2003) 53, 70–3.

111 See, e.g. Antonio Cassese, 'The Statute of the ICC: Some Preliminary Reflections' (1999) 10 *EJIL* 144 at 146; a suggestion to delete aggression from the statute is made in Matthias Schuster, 'The Rome Statute of an International Criminal Court and the Crime of Aggression: A Gordian Knot in Search of a Sword' (2003) 14 *CLF* 1.

112 Schabas, 'The Unfinished Work', 141.

Further reading

The website of the ICC may be consulted with regard to the current negotiations on the definition of aggression in the ASP special working group: www.icc-cpi.int.

Cherif Bassiouni and Benjamin Ferencz, 'The Crime against Peace' in Cherif Bassiouni (ed.), *International Criminal Law*, 2nd edn (New York, 1999), vol. I, 313.

Neil Boister and Robert Cryer, *The Tokyo International Military Tribunal: A Reappraisal* (Oxford, 2008).

Ian Brownlie, *International Law and the Use of Force by States* (Oxford, 1963).

Yoram Dinstein, *War, Aggression and Self-Defence*, 4th edn (Cambridge, 2005).

Rolf Einar Fife, 'Criminalizing Individuals for Acts of Aggression committed by States' in Morten Bergsmo (ed.), *Human Rights and Criminal Justice for the Downtrodden* (Leiden/Boston, 2003) 53.

Michael Glennon, 'The Blank-Prose Crime of Aggression' (2010) 35 *Yale Journal of International Law*.

Christine Gray, *International Law and the Use of Force*, 3rd edn (Oxford, 2008) chs. 2, 4, 6.

Ahmed Rifaat, *International Aggression* (Stockholm, 1979).

Matthias Schuster, 'The Rome Statute of an International Criminal Court and the Crime of Aggression: A Gordian Knot in Search of a Sword' (2003) 14 *CLF* 1.

14

Transnational Crimes, Terrorism and Torture

14.1 Introduction

14.1.1 Overview

To focus only on the 'core crimes' and their prosecution would be to ignore a substantial area of criminal law with international implications; there are other crimes of international concern which have a huge impact on people throughout the world and on global economic development.[1] Crimes which are the subject of international suppression Conventions but for which there is as yet no international criminal jurisdiction, are the focus of this chapter. They are here termed 'transnational crimes'.[2] Like the core crimes, these are crimes which have actual or potential transboundary effect or which are intra-State but which offend a fundamental value of the international community.[3]

The prevention and punishment of transnational crimes requires cooperation among governments and among law enforcement agencies. A growing number of agreements are being concluded to provide for this in relation to such crimes as drugs trafficking,[4] piracy,[5] slavery,[6] terrorism offences,[7] torture,[8] apartheid,[9] enforced disappearances,[10] transnational

---

1 In Res. 56/120 the UN General Assembly expressed deep concern over 'the impact of transnational organized crime on the political, social and economic stability and development of societies'. UN Doc. A/RES/56/120 (2002).

2 There is no real conceptual basis for this term; it is, however, now in common use.

3 Neil Boister, 'Transnational Criminal Law?' (2003) 14 *EJIL* 953 at 967–77.

4 UN Convention against Illicit Trafficking in Narcotic Drugs and Psychotropic Substances 1988.

5 Arts. 100–5, UN Law of the Sea Convention 1982. Although serious incidents of piracy have led to suggestions that the crime be placed within the jurisdiction of the ICC or some other international court, assistance with national prosecutions would appear to be the better way forward.

6 Among the more recent agreements on slavery are the 1926 Slavery Convention; the UN Supplementary Convention on the Abolition of Slavery, the Slave Trade and Institutions and Practices Similar to Slavery 1956; the UN Convention on the Law of the Sea 1982, Art. 99.

7 See section 14.2.

8 See section 14.3.

9 International Convention on the Suppression and Punishment of the Crime of Apartheid 1973.

10 International Convention for the Protection of all Persons from Enforced Disappearance 2006.

organized crime including people trafficking, smuggling migrants and illegal arms trafficking,[11] and corruption.[12] Some of these are also covered by customary international law or are international crimes when committed in certain circumstances (for example as crimes against humanity). They include those which were listed as 'treaty crimes' in the ILC draft of the ICC Statute, but which were excluded from the Rome Statute in the course of the negotiations.[13] Particular transnational crimes may in the future come to be dealt with as international crimes within the jurisdiction of an international court,[14] if States believe that the values they conflict with are sufficiently important to the international community and that international prosecution is an effective way of dealing with them. This may of course occur with terrorism and the International Criminal Court.

While each transnational crime deserves a chapter to itself, for reasons of space only two categories, terrorism and torture, will be covered in this chapter, at sections 14.2 and 14.3 respectively; both of them, when committed in certain circumstances, may also constitute an international crime within the jurisdiction of the international courts and tribunals.

14.1.2 International suppression Conventions

The prosecution of transnational crimes is undertaken by domestic legal systems, rather than by international courts and tribunals. To facilitate effective domestic prosecution, as well as to cooperate in the suppression of the crimes, States have concluded international agreements providing for the possibility of cooperation among States which otherwise might have few law enforcement concerns in common.[15] The typical agreement requires States to create criminal offences of the relevant conduct in their domestic law, to take the necessary jurisdiction for the purpose of prosecution, and to provide penalties which take into account the gravity of the offences. States are also required either to extradite an offender or to consider the case for prosecution (*aut dedere aut judicare*), and to provide each other with mutual legal assistance for the purpose of prosecution or extradition.[16] All of these features are to be seen in the agreements on terrorism discussed in section 14.2.2.

---

11 UN Convention against Transnational Organized Crime 2000; Protocol to Prevent, Suppress and Punish Trafficking in Persons, Especially Women and Children, supplementing that Convention; Protocol against the Smuggling of Migrants by Land, Air and Sea, supplementing that Convention; Protocol against the Illicit Manufacturing of and Trafficking in Firearms, Their Parts and Components and Ammunition, supplementing that Convention.

12 UN Convention against Corruption 2003.

13 See section 8.2.

14 Of course terrorism already comes within the jurisdiction of one internationalized court, the Lebanon Tribunal; see Chapter 9.

15 See Ethan A. Nadelmann, 'Global prohibition regimes: the evolution of norms in international society' (1990) 44 *International Organisation* 479 at 481.

16 For discussion of *aut dedere aut judicare* obligations see Chapter 4; for extradition and mutual legal assistance, see Chapter 5.

The jurisdiction which States are required to take differs from one agreement to another but in each case there is a close link between the suspect and the State concerned. Most agreements require States to take jurisdiction based on territory and nationality. Some provide other options on grounds such as the nationality of the victim. For example, in the 1997 Convention for the Suppression of Terrorist Bombings each State is *required* to take jurisdiction where the offence is committed in its territory, on its ships or aircraft, or by its nationals; it is *permitted* to take jurisdiction when the offence is committed against a national or against a State or government facility, by a stateless person, or in an attempt to compel the State to action or inaction, or when committed on an aircraft operated by the State.[17] The agreements also require States to take jurisdiction so that they can prosecute if they do not extradite a suspect on their territory, wherever the crime was committed. This is a 'last resort universal jurisdiction'[18] *as between States Parties*, which is dependent on the presence of the suspect. In effect, the States Parties delegate authority to the other parties to exercise jurisdiction on their behalf.[19]

Because these agreements require that the crimes be prosecuted under domestic law, they do not themselves prescribe in detail the material and mental elements of the offences, although States often adopt the definitions they contain *verbatim* rather than further elaborate upon their definitions.[20] As a unified system of enforcement they are weak.[21] An additional criticism is that they largely rely on domestic legal systems to provide the necessary procedural rights for the accused during investigation and prosecution, and this leaves scope for human rights violations in those States which do not have adequate fair trial and other such protections. In their concern with law and order States Parties to the agreements have neglected human rights requirements, in contrast with the way in which such requirements have been incorporated into the procedure of the International Criminal Court.[22]

14.2 Terrorism

14.2.1 Introduction

The phenomenon of terrorism presents a number of difficulties of legal categorization. The problem of *defining* terrorism is not unique to lawyers: 'one man's terrorist is the other

---

17 Art. 6(1) and (2).

18 See, e.g. Art. 6(4) of the International Convention for the Suppression of Terrorist Bombings (the Terrorist Bombing Convention). See Roger Clark, 'Offences of International Concern: Multilateral Treaty Practice in the Forty Years since Nuremberg' (1988) 57 *NJIL* 49 at 58.

19 See further section 3.3.2.

20 See Clark, 'Offences of International Concern', 72 for further discussion. States often simply include verbatim the treaty definition into their domestic law.

21 See Boister, 'Transnational Criminal Law?'.

22 See Neil Boister, 'Human Rights Protections in the Suppression Conventions' (2002) 2 *Human Rights Law Review* 199.

man's freedom fighter' describes a difficulty common to all who ponder on the concept. But the lawyer has also to consider whether the legal category of terrorism is useful or necessary in law.[23] Terrorism may be regarded as simply the commission of 'ordinary', though serious, criminal acts with a particular purpose. Some States, including the UK, do not have a specific offence of 'terrorism' in domestic law and use the ordinary criminal law to prosecute serious offences of terrorist violence.[24] Some would argue that the categorization of terrorism is positively dangerous, in that it may encourage counter-measures that disregard human rights.

A further difficulty is whether terrorism is properly or adequately addressed solely by the criminal law or whether it is necessary – and justifiable – to use armed force against the terrorists. The attacks in the US on 11 September 2001 were regarded by the US and the UK as constituting an 'armed attack' within the meaning of Article 51 of the UN Charter, thus giving rise to the right to use military force in self-defence against Al-Qaeda and the Taliban in Afghanistan.[25] Appeals to the Taliban to hand over the persons responsible for the attacks had not met with success, so that measures of criminal law enforcement were seemingly not available. In the context of what was termed the 'war on terror' by the Bush administration, the use of armed force was accompanied by the detention of many persons the treatment of whom was widely regarded as failing to meet the standards of international humanitarian law and human rights. The lawfulness of the use of force and military detention to counter terrorism is beyond the scope of this chapter.[26] But some of the responses to terrorism have led one commentator to conclude that it is 'perhaps the ultimate paradox of the "war on

---

23 'We have cause to regret that a legal concept of "terrorism" was ever inflicted upon us. The term … serves no operative legal purpose': R. R. Baxter, 'A Sceptical Look at the Concept of Terrorism' (1973/4) 7 *Akron Law Review* 380. 'Terrorism is a term without legal significance … The term is at once a shorthand to allude to a variety of problems with some common elements and a method of indicating community condemnation for the conduct concerned': Rosalyn Higgins, in discussing early attempts at a definition of terrorism in R. Higgins and M. Flory (eds.), *Terrorism and International Law* (London, 1997) 28.

24 However, a whole raft of offences under UK legislation depend upon a definition of terrorism, which is set out in the Terrorism Act 2000, s. 1, as amended by the Terrorism Act 2006: terrorism means 'the use or threat of action where' 'the use or threat is designed to influence the government or an intergovernmental organisation or to intimidate the public or a section of the public, and' it is made 'for the purpose of advancing a political, religious or ideological cause' and involves 'serious violence against a person or serious danger to property, or endangers a person's life, or creates a serious risk to public health or safety, or is designed seriously to interfere with or disrupt an electronic system'. The offences include crimes associated with membership or support for a proscribed organization, funding and financing terrorist activities, and ancillary offences such as weapons training for terrorist purposes.

25 See letters sent to the President of the Security Council by the US and the UK (S/2001/946 and 947). For a contrary view, see Myra Williamson, *The Legality of the Use of Force Against Afghanistan in 2001* (Ashgate, 2009).

26 For some of the extensive literature, see Christine Gray, *International Law and the Use of Force*, 3rd edn (Oxford, 2008) ch. 6; Juttee Brunee and Stephen Toope, 'The Use of Force after Iraq' (2004) 53 *ICLQ* 785; Gilbert Guillaume, 'Terrorism and International Law' (2004) 53 *ICLQ* 537; Sean Murphy, 'Terrorism and the Concept of "Armed Attack" in Article 51 of the U.N. Charter' (2002) 43 *Harvard International Law Journal* 41.

terror" that the horrendous acts of lawlessness witnessed on 11 September 2001 have been relied upon to justify repeated violations and further disregard for the international rule of law'.[27]

The fight against terrorism is now multi-faceted[28] and includes measures imposed by the UN Security Council, including financial sanctions. But the primary paradigm to address terrorism remains criminal law, and terrorist acts, in one form or another, constitute criminal offences. There remains the difficulty, for national and international systems alike, of classifying and defining who is a terrorist and who is not, for the purposes of criminal law. The question of definition is discussed at section 14.2.3.

Terrorist acts can be prosecuted in an international court at present only if they amount to war crimes or crimes against humanity. It is true that one internationalized court, the Lebanon Tribunal has jurisdiction over terrorist acts (see Chapter 9), but these are crimes under Lebanese, not international, law. Following the restricted usage this book gives to the term 'international crime', this chapter discusses terrorism within the category of 'transnational' rather than international crimes and discusses international cooperation with the purpose of securing prosecution in *national* courts. Brief consideration is, however, given at section 14.2.5 to the circumstances in which terrorism may also constitute an international crime which can be prosecuted by international jurisdictions. It should be noted that at least one commentator maintains that terrorism is already a crime under customary international law and that there is already a customary law definition of terrorism,[29] but this is a decidedly controversial view.

14.2.2 Development of international cooperation against terrorism

One of the earliest attempts at agreeing on an international prohibition of terrorism was the 1937 Convention for the Prevention and Punishment of Terrorism, which was negotiated within the League of Nations following the assassination of King Alexander I of Yugoslavia in 1934. The Convention defined acts of terrorism as 'criminal acts directed against a State and intended or calculated to create a state of terror in the minds of particular persons, or a group of persons or the general public' and listed acts to be criminalized by States Parties, including those causing death, serious injury or loss of liberty to heads of State and public

---

27 Helen Duffy, *The 'War on Terror' and the Framework of International Law* (Cambridge, 2005) 445.

28 See John P. Grant, 'Beyond the Montreal Convention' (2004) 36 *Case Western Reserve Journal of International Law* 453 at 472. In the United Kingdom, the term 'the war on terror' was not used in the literal sense of an armed conflict; see the response of the Parliamentary Under-Secretary of State, Foreign and Commonwealth Office (Baroness Amos): 'The term "the war against terrorism" has been used to describe the whole campaign against terrorism, including military, political, financial, legislative and law enforcement measures.' (Hansard 22 Nov 2001: Col.WA153.)

29 Antonio Cassese in, e.g. 'Terrorism as an international crime' in Andrea Bianchi (ed.), *Enforcing International Law Norms against Terrorism* (Hart, 2004) 213; and in 'The Multifaceted Criminal Notion of Terrorism in International Law' (2006) 4 *JICJ* 1.

officials, damage to public property of another State, and risk to the lives of members of the public. The Convention never received sufficient ratifications to enter into force.[30] The United Nations took on the task of defining and prohibiting terrorism when the General Assembly set up a committee on terrorism in 1972, but although the committee met until 1979 it failed to reach agreement. There was disagreement as to whether acts committed by national liberation movements for causes such as decolonization should be excluded from any definition of terrorism, and there were related arguments that there should be no international ban on terrorist activities unless at the same time the causes of terrorism were understood and resolved.

Global counter-terrorism agreements

The impossibility of securing international agreement on an unqualified condemnation of terrorism led to the adoption of a 'thematic' approach to cooperation to prevent and criminalize terrorist acts. International agreements were negotiated on specific areas of terrorist activity, each separately defined. There are eleven of these agreements, each of them negotiated to deal with specific kinds of terrorist threats prevalent at the time the agreements were concluded.[31] Two of the earliest conventions, for example, the Hague and Montreal Conventions, deal with safety of civil aviation, following instances of terrorist

---

30 League of Nations Doc.C.546(1).M.383(1).1937. V. For an interesting review of its negotiation, see Ben Saul, 'The Legal Response of the League of Nations to Terrorism' (2006) 4 *JICJ* 78.

31 There are at present thirteen agreements altogether, but two of them, as explained below, do not follow the same model of State cooperation. The eleven agreements are: the 1970 Convention for the Suppression of Unlawful Seizure of Aircraft (the Hague Convention); the 1971 Convention for the Suppression of Unlawful Acts against the Safety of Civil Aviation (the Montreal Convention) and its 1988 Protocol for the Suppression of Unlawful Acts of Violence at Airports Serving International Civil Aviation; the 1973 Convention on the Prevention and Punishment of Crimes Against Internationally Protected Persons, including Diplomatic Agents; the 1979 International Convention against the Taking of Hostages; the 1980 Convention on the Physical Protection of Nuclear Material; the 1988 Convention on the Suppression of Unlawful Acts Against the Safety of Maritime Navigation (the SUA Convention) and its 1988 Protocol for the Suppression of Unlawful Acts against the Safety of Fixed Platforms located on the Continental Shelf; the 1997 International Convention for the Suppression of Terrorist Bombings (the Terrorist Bombing Convention); the 1999 International Convention for the Suppression of the Financing of Terrorism (the Terrorist Financing Convention); and the 2005 International Convention for the Suppression of Acts of Nuclear Terrorism (the Nuclear Terrorism Convention). Within the list of global terrorism agreements are often included the 1963 Convention on Offences and Certain Other Acts Committed on Board Aircraft (the Tokyo Convention) and the 1991 Convention on the Marking of Plastic Explosives for the Purpose of Detection but these two differ from the others: the objective of the Tokyo Convention is primarily to assign powers and jurisdiction to different States and persons in relation to activities on board aircraft, while the Plastic Explosives Convention provides for the marking of explosives and the prevention of possession and transfer of unmarked explosives. The UN Convention on the Safety of United Nations and Associated Personnel 1994 (annexed to GA Resolution 49/59) is sometimes added to the list; although not drafted primarily as an instrument against terrorism, it follows the same model as the terrorism agreements.

hijacking and other offences against air travel at the time.[32] The impetus for the drafting of the 1988 SUA Convention, on the other hand, was the hijacking in 1985 of the *Achille Lauro*, an Italian cruise ship, and the accompanying murder of an elderly disabled US citizen of Jewish origin.

With the conclusion of the Terrorist Bombing Convention in 1997, most kinds of 'terrorist' conduct had been covered in one or other of these agreements. For better or worse, however, a proposal was then introduced to negotiate a 'comprehensive' convention to address explicitly all forms of terrorism; as such it would of course require a definition of terrorism.[33] The hope of finally agreeing upon a definition of terrorism for the purpose of such a convention received some impetus from a GA Resolution of 1994,[34] adopted by consensus, which annexed a Declaration on Terrorism containing the following provision:

> Criminal acts intended or calculated to provoke a state of terror in the general public, a group of persons or particular persons for political purposes are in any circumstances unjustifiable, whatever the considerations of a political, philosophical, ideological, racial, ethnic, religious or other nature which may be invoked to justify them.

The Resolution, unlike previous ones, had no preambular reference to acts committed by a national liberation movement; it made quite clear that terrorism was condemned whatever the motivation and by whomever it was committed. Unfortunately, the hope that a similarly unqualified definition could be agreed was not fulfilled, and the negotiation of the Convention has been stalled for years.[35]

The eleven terrorism agreements have as their purpose the effective *national* prosecution of acts of terrorism, and thus their better prevention. They share the main features of the model already described,[36] incorporating the principle *aut dedere aut judicare* and imposing obligations on States Parties to give assistance in criminal and extradition proceedings. In their provisions on extradition, the three most recent agreements, unlike the early ones, specify that the offence in question may not be regarded as a political offence for the purpose of extradition or mutual legal assistance.[37] Since the most typical of terrorist offences is one committed for a political purpose, this removes the loophole by which terrorists could escape extradition and confirms that terrorism cannot be justified, whatever the purpose.

---

32 See Christopher Joyner and Robert Friedlander, 'International Civil Aviation' in M. Cherif Bassiouni (ed.), *International Criminal Law*, 2nd edn (New York, 1999), vol. I, 837.

33 The proposal was made by India in 1996, UN Doc.A/C.6/51/6.

34 Declaration on Measures to Eliminate International Terrorism (1994), annexed to UNGA Res. 49/60 of 9.12.1994.

35 For a study of the negotiations see Tal Becker, *Terrorism and the State* (Oxford, 2006) 84–118. For the text of the draft convention, see UN Doc. A/59/894 and for more recent discussions upon it see the report at GAOR Sixtieth Session Supplement No. 37(A/60/37).

36 At section 14.1.2.

37 Art. 11, Terrorist Bombing Convention, Art. 14, Terrorist Financing Convention and Art. 15, Nuclear Terrorism Convention. See Chapter 5.

Regional counter-terrorism agreements

There are a number of international counter-terrorism agreements which have been concluded within the fora of regional organizations.[38] Like the global conventions, these agreements are generally focused on methods of international cooperation with the aim of national prosecution. Another regional initiative is the European Union's Framework Decision on Combating Terrorism, adopted on 13 June 2002 in implementation of Security Council Resolution 1373(2001).[39] The Council Decision requires that a list of acts must be deemed to be terrorist offences; directing and participating in the activities of a terrorist group is also to be punishable. The differing formulations in these regional instruments illustrate the problem of defining terrorism.

Security Council Resolutions

After the occurrence of specific instances of terrorism the Security Council determined that suppression of international terrorism was essential for the maintenance of international peace and security and took decisions requiring the surrender to justice of persons accused of terrorist acts. On 21 December 1988, Pan American Flight 103, bound from London to New York, exploded over Lockerbie, Scotland. The blast killed all 259 people on board and eleven people on the ground. The suspects identified in the Scottish investigation that followed were believed to be State agents and the governments requiring the suspects to be brought to justice did not proceed under the Montreal Convention on the ground that the Convention, with its focus on national proceedings, did not cover State-sponsored terrorism.[40] The Security Council required Libya to surrender the suspects and imposed sanctions when the request was not acceded to.[41] Examples of similar Council resolutions are those requiring Sudan to hand over the persons accused of attempting to assassinate the President of Egypt,[42] and requiring the Taliban to transfer Osama bin Laden to countries which had indicted him.[43]

---

38 Arab Convention on the Suppression of Terrorism 1998 (the Arab Convention); Convention of the Organization of the Islamic Conference on Combating International Terrorism 1999; European Convention on the Suppression of Terrorism 1977; Organization of American States: Convention to Prevent and Punish Acts of Terrorism Taking the Form of Crimes against Persons and Related Extortion that are of International Significance 1971; OAU Convention on the Prevention and Combating of Terrorism 1999; South Asian Association for Regional Co-operation: Regional Convention on Suppression of Terrorism 1987; Treaty on Cooperation among the States Members of the Commonwealth of Independent States in Combating Terrorism 1999 (the CIS Convention); European Convention on the Prevention of Terrorism 2005.
39 2002/475/JHA, OJ L164/3, 22.6.2002, as amended by Decision 2008/919/JHA, OJ L330/21, 9.12.2008.
40 See Higgins in Higgins and Flory, *Terrorism and International Law*, 23.
41 Security Council resolutions 731(1992) and 748(1992). For the end of the story, see section 9.5, and Michael Plachta, 'The Lockerbie Case: The Role of the Security Council in Enforcing the Principle Aut Dedere Aut Judicare' (2001) 12 *EJIL* 125.
42 Following their flight to Sudan; res. 1044(1966) and 1054(1966).
43 SC res. 1267(1999) and 1333(2000).

The Security Council has also determined that international terrorism more generally is a threat to international peace and security. Resolution 1368(2001), adopted the day after 11 September 2001, stated that the terrorist attacks in Washington and New York were, 'like any act of international terrorism ... a threat to international peace and security'. The Council went further in resolution 1373(2001), adopted under Chapter VII of the Charter, and imposed extensive obligations on States in relation to the suppression of terrorist acts generally and the financing of terrorism in particular. That resolution covers some of the same ground as the global terrorism Conventions, notably the Terrorist Financing Convention. The resolution decides, inter alia, that all States must ensure that any person who participates in financing, planning, preparing for, perpetrating or supporting terrorist acts is brought to justice and States must establish such acts as serious criminal offences in their law with appropriately serious penalties (paragraph 2(e)). But although it imposes binding obligations and establishes the Counter-Terrorism Committee to monitor their implementation, the Resolution contains no definition of terrorism.

Resolution 1373(2001) has been criticized as Security Council 'legislation' in a field which is the preserve of intergovernmental agreement.[44] The obvious advantage of Council action of this kind is its ability to impose immediate obligations on States, with no need for lengthy negotiations in a wider forum and no need to wait for ratifications before the obligations take effect. But the point is justly made that the Council has gone beyond its previously recognized Charter powers and has trespassed on ground previously covered by the General Assembly and agreements negotiated there. Nevertheless, the resolution has been accepted in practice, albeit grudgingly, and is a significant part of the international counter-terrorism effort.

14.2.3 The definition of terrorism

As yet, no definition of terrorism has been agreed for the purpose of a global prohibition of terrorist acts in a legally binding instrument. None of the eleven global agreements defines terrorism except the Terrorist Financing Convention, and that is only for a secondary purpose.[45] Many of the agreements do not even mention the word terrorism, thus exemplifying the view that it is possible to deal with terrorism without creating specific 'terrorist' offences. There are, however, definitions of a kind. Each of the regional counter-terrorism

---

[44] For discussion of the issue see Matthew Happold, 'Security Council Resolution 1373 and the Constitution of the United Nations' (2003) 16 *LJIL* 593; Paul Szasz, 'The Security Council Starts Legislating' (2002) 96 *AJIL* 901; Stefan Talmon, 'The Security Council as World Legislature' (2005) 99 *AJIL* 175.

[45] Art. 2 of the Convention refers to the offence of financing acts of terrorism, which are defined as acts covered by the terrorism Conventions and 'any other act intended to cause death or serious bodily injury to a civilian, or to any other person not taking an active part in the hostilities in a situation of armed conflict, when the purpose of such act, by its nature or context, is to intimidate a population, or to compel a Government or an international organization to do or to abstain from doing any act'.

agreements has a definition of terrorism for the purpose of the agreement; while some merely list the offences covered by the global Conventions with or without other serious offences,[46] others create their own generic definitions.[47] Security Council resolution 1566 (2004) has a description of terrorism (said not to be a 'definition'[48]); it covers only acts included in the global Conventions, but specifies that they are committed with 'the purpose to provoke a state of terror ... intimidate a population or compel a government or an international organization to do or to abstain from doing any act'. The difficulties of reaching agreement on a definition for the purpose of a global prohibition of terrorist acts relate largely to two connected questions: are there causes which justify acts otherwise classed as terrorism, which should therefore be excluded; and should 'State terrorism' be included?

The difficulties of negotiating a definition raise the question whether the effort is worthwhile. Each of the underlying acts which go to make up a terrorist offence are already criminalized. It might make more sense for the focus in the UN to revert to the range of acts that all States regard as impermissible in all circumstances.[49] However, a definition of some kind is needed if there is to be a comprehensive international prohibition on terrorism and a requirement for multilateral cooperation including extradition; a definition is also needed if terrorism is to be added to the jurisdiction of the International Criminal Court. Further, existing instruments imposing obligations in relation to counter-terrorism, for example resolution 1373(2001), need a definition to ensure uniform implementation and effective monitoring. But even if a solution is reached for the purpose of a comprehensive Convention, the drafting compromises that will very likely be needed for the Convention are unlikely to result in a definition suitable for all purposes. And the tendency exhibited in the negotiations on the Convention to seek a broad definition may lead to 'ordinary' criminals being included within the definition and thus being subjected to the full range of domestic and international counter-terrorism measures.

Human rights considerations are important in drafting definitions of terrorism, whether national or international. Terrorist offences are likely to carry higher penalties than other offences, national systems may have more invasive means of investigation for terrorist offences, the political offence exception in extradition agreements may be disapplied and applications for asylum may be refused. If the criminal acts included in a definition of terrorism are not of a very serious nature, and if the purposes for which those acts are

---

46 See, e.g. the European Convention on the Suppression of Terrorism 1977 and the European Convention on the Prevention of Terrorism 2005.

47 See, e.g. the Arab Convention on the Suppression of Terrorism 1998.

48 See, in particular, remarks of the representative of Brazil on the adoption of the resolution (UN Doc.S/PV 3053).

49 G. Levitt, 'Is "Terrorism" worth defining?' (1986) 13 *Ohio Northern University Law Review* 97; John Murphy, 'Defining International Terrorism: a Way out of the Quagmire' (1989) 19 *Israel Yearbook on Human Rights* 13.

committed are defined too broadly, there is a danger that the serious consequences of being a terrorist suspect in national law will be applied to conduct which is 'merely' criminal, and political opponents or even petty criminals may be treated as terrorists. Minor damage to property committed in the course of a political demonstration, for example, ought not to attract the stigma and legal consequences of being classed as terrorism.[50] Further, wide and ambiguous definitions of terrorism offend the principle of fair labelling, and leave undue discretion to State authorities, risking abuse by them. Human rights considerations have motivated the 'UN Special Rapporteur on the promotion and protection of human rights and fundamental freedoms while countering terrorism' to suggest that a definition of terrorism be limited to acts causing death or serious bodily injury or the taking of hostages, provided that these acts are within the scope of the global agreements and are committed with the intention of provoking a state of terror, intimidating a population, or compelling a government or international organization to action or inaction.[51] This limited formulation is attractive in removing the problems caused by international or national definitions that are too wide in scope but it may be unlikely to attract international support.

The elements of a 'transnational' crime of terrorism can be discussed by comparing the descriptions of terrorism in the different multilateral instruments.[52] But, like the suppression Conventions for other transnational crimes, the eleven agreements do not make detailed provision for the material and mental elements of the crimes they cover, leaving these to the domestic law of the States Parties. The same is true of the regional agreements. Leaving aside the early terrorism Conventions, the practice indicates that there are generally two or more tiers to the terrorism definitions used by States in national and international instruments: first, the underlying act, which is generally a criminal offence in itself; and second, the purpose of coercion of a State or international organization, and/or the purpose of causing alarm among the population. There is sometimes added a requirement of political or ideological motive and, in relation to international terrorism, a transnational character to the underlying act (which should not be limited in its effects to one country). While there is particular controversy about the authors of terrorism – whether freedom fighters and State agents are excluded – the practice diverges in relation to *all* aspects of the definition.[53]

---

50 The South African legislation usefully excepts from the definition of terrorism certain kinds of acts committed in pursuance of protests or industrial action if they are not intended to cause particular kinds of harm: Protection of Constitutional Democracy Against Terrorist and Related Activities Act 2004, s. 1(3).
51 Report of 28 December 2005 (E/CN.4/2006/98).
52 For a more thorough discussion of the elements of the eleven global agreements, see Reuven Young, 'Defining Terrorism: The Evolution of Terrorism as a Legal Concept in International Law and its Influence on Definitions in Domestic Legislation' (2006) 29 *Boston College International and Comparative Law Review* 23.
53 See discussion in Robert Kolb, 'The Exercise of Criminal Jurisdiction over International Terrorists' in Bianchi, *Enforcing International Law Norms*, 227. But see Cassese, 'Terrorism as an international crime' and 'The Multifaceted Criminal Notion', for the view that the practice shows a consistent approach and that it is therefore a misconception to allege that there is no generally agreed definition of terrorism.

Material elements

The *actus reus* of the crime of terrorism is the underlying act. With the exception of the Terrorist Financing Convention, the eleven global terrorism agreements require or imply that the underlying act must be an offence in itself.[54] The regional agreements mostly do the same, either by listing the offences covered by the global agreements, or within their own generic definitions. Some of the latter, however, are broad and ambiguous. The 1999 Convention of the OAU (now the African Union), for example, includes: 'any act which is a violation of the criminal laws of a State Party and which … may cause damage to public or private property, natural resources, environmental or cultural heritage …'.[55] This appears to cover relatively minor criminal conduct. The underlying act of a terrorist offence should be a *serious* offence, if it is to capture what is generally regarded as terrorism. The draft comprehensive Convention lists the underlying acts of: causing death or serious personal injury, serious damage to property including public transport or the environment, or (lesser) damage to property or systems which results in major economic loss.[56]

There is divergent practice with regard to the description of those who commit terrorism. In spite of the unqualified condemnation of terrorism in the 1994 General Assembly declaration,[57] the Arab, OIC and AU Conventions, concluded subsequent to that declaration, include an exception for acts committed by peoples struggling against foreign occupation or for national liberation in accordance with the principles of international law.[58] It is not clear whether the reference to international law in these instruments is only to *ius ad bellum* (as the wording in at least the first two mentioned agreements would indicate) or also to international humanitarian law (as is sometimes claimed).[59] If the latter is a permissible interpretation of these agreements, those committing terrorist acts would be excluded from the exemption since terrorism is prohibited by international humanitarian law.

---

54 See, e.g. Art. 2(1) of the Terrorist Bombing Convention 1997 which lists acts committed 'unlawfully and intentionally'. The Terrorist Financing Convention 2000 prohibits the provision or collection of funds (the underlying act) with the intention that the funds should be used for terrorist acts (see fn. 45). In the definition of terrorism in the UK Terrorism Act 2000, the underlying acts are not specified as offences, see fn. 24.

55 Art. 1(3). The Arab Convention 1998 and the OIC Convention 1991 have similarly wide formulations: Art. 1(2) of the former and Art. 1(2) of the latter.

56 See fn. 35. For a critique of individual elements of the draft Convention's elements, see Alexandra Orlova and James Moore, ' "Umbrellas" or "Building Blocks"?: Defining International Terrorism and Transnational Organized Crime in International Law' (2005) 27 *Houston Journal of International Law* 267 at 271–6.

57 See section 14.2.2.

58 Art. 3(1), OAU Convention; preamble and Art. 2(a), Arab Convention; Art. 2, OIC Convention.

59 See Mahmoud Hmoud, 'The Organization of the Islamic Conference' in Nesi, *International Cooperation in Counter-Terrorism*, 166; see also Michael de Feo, 'The Political Offence Concept in Regional and International Conventions relating to Terrorism' in *ibid.*, 116–19. It is interesting to note that the South African legislation implementing the AU agreement adopts this interpretation, referring 'especially' to international humanitarian law: Protection of Constitutional Democracy Against Terrorist and Related Activities Act 2004.

It ought to be acknowledged by all that the targeting of civilians, however just the cause of the conflict, is unacceptable. Attempts have therefore been made to solve the problem of definition by specifying that only civilians are the targets of terrorism (as in Article 2(1)(b) of the Terrorist Financing Convention[60]). As a complete solution this is defective. What after all is the definition of 'civilian' in peacetime? And it does not address the question of how to deal with insurgents of various kinds, as either combatants or common criminals[61] – but admittedly this is a very difficult issue.

Linked to the question of national liberation movements is that of 'State terrorism'. The long-standing Western position in the UN has been that wrongful acts by States, whether properly termed State terrorism or not, are more appropriately regulated by the ordinary rules of State responsibility rather than under criminal law.[62] This was also the view of the former UN Secretary-General in his report 'In Larger Freedom';[63] it is also reflected in Article 19(2) of the Terrorist Bombing Convention, for example. The opposing point of view that terrorism is prohibited 'by whomever committed',[64] including State actors, is being put forward in the negotiations on the comprehensive Convention.[65]

Mental elements

The aspect distinguishing terrorism from other crimes is the purpose with which the under-lying acts are committed. Like genocide, terrorism in its most typical form is a compound offence and needs both the *mens rea* appropriate to the underlying offence, and a special intent for terrorism itself (which, departing from the normal practice of distinguishing between purpose and intention under criminal law, often uses the terms interchangeably). There are two kinds of victims of terrorism: both the targets of the underlying offence and the 'real' targets, those in whom terror has been induced.

Most of the eleven terrorism agreements mentioned in section 14.2.2, in avoiding a definition of terrorism, also avoid specifying an intent or purpose for which the criminal

---

60 The Supreme Court of Canada has stated that this definition 'catches the essence of what the world understands by terrorism' (*Suresh* v. *Canada* [2002] SCC 1 at para. 98). And see para. 164 of the Report of the Secretary-General's High-level Panel on Threats, Challenges and Change (UN Doc. A/59/565).

61 See Jan Klabbers, 'Rebel with a Cause? Terrorists and Humanitarian Law' (2003) 14 *EJIL* 299.

62 See, e.g. the statement of the UK representative in the Security Council of 18 January 2002: 'None of these seminal texts [the global terrorism agreements] refer to State terrorism, which is not an international legal concept. We must be careful not to get caught up in the rhetoric of political conflict. If States abuse their power, they should be judged against the international conventions and other instruments dealing with . . . humanitarian law.' (UN Doc.S/PV.4453 (2002) paras. 24–5).

63 'It is time to set aside debates on so-called "State terrorism". The use of force by States is already thoroughly regulated under international law.' (UN Doc.A/59/2005 para. 91).

64 1994 UNGA Res. 49/60.

65 And it was also the view of Oscar Schachter, 'The Lawful Use of Force by a State against Terrorists in another Country' (1989) 19 *Israel Yearbook on Human Rights* 209 at 210.

acts are committed.[66] For them there is no special intent. This approach made possible the conclusion of these agreements, but it does have the disadvantage that they therefore implicitly include acts committed for merely personal or commercial reasons, and thus miss the unique feature of terrorism. Other terrorism agreements differ in their descriptions of the special intent. Spreading terror[67] would seem the most obvious purpose, but it is wide and may be difficult to prove. The draft comprehensive Convention uses the same formulation as the Terrorist Financing Convention, specifying a purpose or intention of intimidating a population or persuading a government to act.[68] Some instruments go wider. The EU Framework Decision includes the 'aim' of 'seriously destabilising or destroying the fundamental political, constitutional, economic or social structures of a country or an international organisation' (which would mean that a protest against the WTO, for example, would constitute terrorism if it caused damage); the OAU Convention includes the intention to 'create general insurrection in a State'.[69]

Intent must be distinguished from motive. While some national definitions include a motive with which the terrorist act is committed,[70] most international formulations, including the draft comprehensive Convention, do not. Motive cannot be a justification of terrorist action, and if the purpose or intention is specified, it is perhaps unnecessary to limit the offence still further by requiring the action to have a political, religious or other motive.

14.2.4 Prosecution and other national measures

The multilateral Conventions, like other suppression Conventions, focus on international cooperation and include *aut dedere aut judicare* obligations. The goal is national prosecution. Information about how many prosecutions or extraditions have taken place on the basis of the Conventions is hard to secure. In one notorious case of aviation terrorism, the Lockerbie bombing, the prosecution was on the basis of ordinary murder charges, not charges under the Montreal Convention. Post 11 September 2001, many countries have adopted new measures in the light of the perceived new terrorist threat.

One of the major challenges of dealing with terrorist offences is to strike a balance between, on the one hand, the protection of the community from acts of terrorism and, on the other hand, the maintenance of the rights of all citizens, including suspected terrorists. Some national legislation imposing criminal sanctions for offences connected with terrorism

---

66 The exception is the Hostages Convention, Art. 1 (since the imposition of conditions of release is an intrinsic part of the offence of hostage-taking); and see Art. 2, Terrorist Financing Convention; see also the rather odd references to terrorist acts committed for certain purposes in Art. 5, Terrorist Bombing Convention and Art. 6, Nuclear Terrorism Convention.

67 The definition in the CIS Convention includes terrorizing the population as one of the purposes for which terrorist acts are committed. See also Art. 51(2), AP 1.

68 See fn. 45.

69 OAU Convention on the Preventing and Combating of Terrorism 1999.

70 See, e.g. the UK definition at fn. 24, and the South African at fn. 50.

has been widely criticized on human rights grounds.[71] Some rights cannot be balanced against any other interest; chief among these is protection from torture. As is indicated below,[72] there is an absolute prohibition on torture by a State's officials, and on the transfer of an individual to a country where there are substantial grounds for believing that he would be in danger of being tortured.

National prosecutions for terrorism-related offences can meet with a number of problems. They may have to grapple with the difficulties of definition, particularly if national law incorporates international law.[73] Another major difficulty arises from the nature of the evidence on which the charges may be based. In the UK, for example, there has been a reluctance or inability to prosecute suspected terrorists where the evidence comes from intercepted material or is otherwise intelligence-based. Other means of detaining terrorist suspects have been devised, not all of which have been found by the courts to be compatible with human rights law.[74] A further problem may arise from the perceived difficulties of preparing criminal charges in sufficient time to satisfy procedural and human rights obligations regarding the early bringing of suspects before a judge. In the UK this has led to successive attempts to extend periods of pre-charge detention, which again have to be analysed against human rights obligations.

In the US, there is wide-ranging legislation regarding the prevention and prosecution of domestic and international terrorism. But there has been ambivalence about whether to detain suspected terrorists indefinitely as enemy combatants in the 'war against terror' or to prosecute them.[75] And US cooperation with other countries' attempts to mount prosecutions

---

71 See Helen Duffy, *The War on Terror and the Framework of International Law* (Cambridge, 2005) ch. 7; Kalliopi Koufa, 'The UN, Human Rights and Counter-terrorism' in Nesi, *International Cooperation in Counter-Terrorism*, 45. For a discussion of the impact which post-September 11 counter-terrorist legislation has had on human rights in a few common law jurisdictions, see Ben Golder and George Williams, 'Balancing National Security and Human Rights: Assessing the Legal Response of Common Law Nations to the Threat of Terrorism' (2006) 8 *Journal of Comparative Policy Analysis* 43.

72 Section 14.3.1.

73 For a discussion of an illustrative case in Italy's Supreme Court of Cassation, see Lucia Aleni, 'Distinguishing Terrorism from Wars of National Liberation in the Light of International Law' (2008) 6 *JICJ* 525.

74 The UK made a derogation to the ECHR and then adopted legislation allowing the detention, pending deportation, of persons suspected of being international terrorists; the House of Lords ruled in *A(FC)* v. *Secretary of State for the Home Department* (16 Dec. 2004 [2004] UKHL 56) that the legislation was incompatible with human rights obligations. Since the detainees could not be deported to countries where there was a real risk of torture, new legislation was adopted giving the power to make control orders in relation to them; the individuals were not always allowed access to the information which justified the control order against them. In *Secretary of State for the Home Department* v. *AF(FC) and another* (10 June 2009 [2009] UKHL 28) the House of Lords held that where a person subject to a control order was not given sufficient information about the allegations against him he was deprived of the right to a fair trial.

75 For the position under the Bush administration, see Steven Less, 'Country Report on the USA' in Christian Walter et al. (eds.), *Terrorism as a Challenge for National and International Law: Security versus Liberty?* (Berlin, 2004) 633.

has not always been helpful.[76] With the gradual closure of the Guantanamo Bay camps, however, the criminal law model is gaining in importance. Under the Military Commissions Act of 2006 'alien unlawful enemy combatants' engaged in hostilities against the United States can be tried for violations of the laws of war and other offences triable by military commission. These other offences include the crime of terrorism and material support for terrorism; although directed to the prosecution of persons classified as combatants, their definitions are more similar to crimes triable under domestic law than to the international war crime of terror.

Both the UN General Assembly and the Security Council have stressed that, in taking counter-terrorism measures, States should comply with international human rights law.[77] Some of the global terrorism Conventions require expressly that the terrorist suspect be treated fairly in proceedings against him, and provide that there is no obligation to extradite where a State has substantial grounds for believing that the extradition request has been made for the purpose of punishing on the basis of race, religion, or political opinion.[78] But for the most part the agreements leave to national systems the responsibility of protecting the rights of the accused, a responsibility which must be exercised in accordance with international human rights obligations.

14.2.5 Terrorism as an international crime

While there is no international court or tribunal which has jurisdiction over a crime of terrorism as such,[79] a terrorist act may be an international crime within the meaning used in this book if it falls within one of the established categories of crimes against humanity or war crimes. The organized use of terror was considered as both a war crime and a crime against humanity by the Nuremberg Tribunal.[80]

The offences covered by the terrorism Conventions were included in the list of treaty crimes in the ILC draft for the new international criminal court and there was some support during the negotiations for including terrorism within the jurisdiction of the ICC. But this was not done, on the grounds that the existing network of treaties providing for national prosecutions was regarded as adequate and that it would not in any event have been possible to negotiate an agreed definition when the General Assembly had failed to do so. Resolution F of the ICC Final Act recommended that a review conference consider crimes of terrorism

---

76 For example, the US refusal to give access to one detainee led to difficulties in the German prosecutions of el-Motassadeq and Mzoudi.

77 See, e.g. GA Res.51/210 of 17.12.1996, para. 3; Security Council res.1456(2003), para. 6 of the Annex.

78 See, e.g. Arts. 12 and 16, Nuclear Terrorism Convention 2005.

79 But terrorism does come within the jurisdiction of the Lebanon Tribunal, an internationalized court; see Chapter 9.

80 'Nuremberg IMT: Judgment and Sentence' reprinted in (1947) 41 *AJIL* 172 at e.g. 229, 231, 289, 319.

'with a view to arriving at an acceptable definition and their inclusion in the list of crimes within the jurisdiction of the court'.[81]

Terrorism as a war crime

Acts of terrorism are prohibited by international humanitarian law and may constitute war crimes. Article 51(2) of AP I provides:

> The civilian population as such, as well as individual civilians, shall not be the object of attack. Acts or threats of violence the primary purpose of which is to spread terror among the civilian population are prohibited. [82]

This prohibition and its criminalization are part of customary international law.[83] While acts of terrorism are included specifically in the list of violations of common Article 3 in the Statutes of the ICTR and of the Sierra Leone Special Court,[84] the ICTY has no such explicit wording in its Statute. But the Tribunal has held that it has jurisdiction by virtue of the general wording of Article 3 of its Statute (violation of the laws and customs of war).[85] Terrorism is not within the list of war crimes in Article 8 of the ICC Statute and the ICC therefore does not have jurisdiction in respect of it; in the ICC, attacks on civilians committed with the specific intent to terrorize will be a factor in sentencing only.

In the first case involving terrorism before an international court, the ICTY convicted General Galić on the war crimes charge of 'acts of violence the primary purpose of which is to spread terror among the civilian population', based upon command responsibility for a protracted campaign of shelling and sniping in civilian areas of Sarajevo.[86] Evidence was given that civilians were attacked while attending funerals, while in ambulances and buses, while gardening and while shopping in markets; the main thoroughfare of Sarajevo became known as 'Sniper Alley'. The Tribunal found that the campaign was intended to terrorize the civilian population; it had no discernible military significance.

The Trial Chamber first had to show that the war crime of terror was within its jurisdiction as being a 'violation of the laws and customs of war' and prohibited and criminalized at the time of the commission of the alleged offence. For reasons relating to the perceived need to consider only 'serious' violations of treaty law as war crimes (equating to grave breaches), it specifically left to one side the question whether it had jurisdiction over acts of violence which did not cause death or injury, thus apparently coming up with a hybrid crime drawing

---

81 The first review conference will be held at least seven years after the entry into force of the ICC Statute.

82 Art. 51(2) of AP 1; Art. 33(1) of GC IV; Arts. 4(2)(d) and 13(2) of AP 2.

83 *Galić* ICTY A. Ch. 30.11.2006 paras. 87–98. Judge Shahabudeen in his separate opinion noted that the Appeals Chamber was not suggesting, in this finding, that a comprehensive definition of terror was known to customary international law; only the 'core concept'.

84 Art. 4(d) of the ICTR Statute and Art. 3(d) of the SCSL Statute.

85 In *Galić* ICTY T. Ch. 5.12.2003.

86 *Ibid.*

on both parts of Article 51(2) of AP I.[87] The Appeals Chamber has explained this reticence to deal with threats and acts not causing death or injury by stating that that question was not before the Trial Chamber.[88] The SCSL has found that it is indeed unnecessary to prove actual death or injury in order to constitute this war crime.[89]

The war crime does not consist in *causing* terror: it is to be expected that *all* acts of war will result in general fear in the country concerned. In *Galić*, the Appeals Chamber confirmed that actual terrorization of a civilian population is not an element of the crime.[90] As regards the mental element, the Trial Chamber required the prosecution 'to prove not only that the accused accepted the likelihood that terror would result from the illegal acts – or, in other words, that he was aware of the possibility that terror would result – but that that was the result which he specifically intended. The crime of terror is a specific-intent crime.' The spreading of terror does not have to be the only purpose of the acts,[91] but it does have to be the *primary* purpose. In the *AFRC* case, the SCSL held that the use of child soldiers, abduction and forced labour were committed primarily for military purposes, and thus did not constitute the war crime of terrorism, while the brutal amputations of the hands or arms of civilians were committed primarily to spread terror.[92]

In sum, the international case law shows that there are three elements in the war crime of acts of terrorism: (i) acts or threats of violence; (ii) the accused wilfully made the civilian population or individual civilians not taking direct part in hostilities the objects of those acts or threats of violence; and (iii) the acts or threats were carried out with the specific intent of spreading terror among the civilian population.

Terrorism as a crime against humanity

Terrorist acts are not listed as crimes against humanity in the Statutes of the ad hoc Tribunals or the ICC. It is, however, clear that if the acts fall within the list of constituent crimes and if their commission is widespread or systematic (and, in the case of the ICC, are 'against any civilian population'), they will fall within the definition of crimes against humanity in all of the Statutes; they are not excluded from the definition merely because they are also committed with the intention of terrorizing the population and with a particular political or other ideological purpose. In the ICTY case of *Galić*, the accused was charged with and

---

87 Robert Cryer, '*Prosecutor v. Galić* and the War Crime of Terror Bombing' (2005–2006) 2 *Israel Defence Force Law Review* 73.
88 *Galić* ICTY A. Ch. 30.11.2006 para. 100.
89 *Fofana and Kondewa* SCSL 28.5.2008 A. Ch. paras. 350–2.
90 *Galić* ICTY A. Ch. 30.11.2006 para. 104.
91 *Ibid.*
92 The case against members of the Armed Forces Revolutionary Council: *Brima, Kamara, Kanu* SCSL 20.6.2007 paras. 1447–64; upheld on appeal.

convicted of crimes against humanity of murder and inhumane acts on the basis of the same facts as the war crime of terror.[93]

After 11 September 2001, statements were made by public figures condemning the terrorist acts in New York and Washington as crimes against humanity.[94] There were obvious difficulties with any suggestion that the crimes should therefore be tried by the ICC: the State primarily concerned was opposed to such an idea and the principle of complementarity would have stood in the way even if there was otherwise jurisdiction. But the acts may well have been within the subject-matter jurisdiction of the ICC.[95]

14.3 Torture

14.3.1 Introduction

> There can be few issues on which international legal opinion is more clear than on the condemnation of torture. Offenders have been recognised as the 'common enemies of mankind'.[96]

There is a clear and absolute prohibition of torture in international law.[97] The prohibition applies even in times of national emergencies or wars, and there are no exceptions or justifications.[98] The prohibition amounts to *ius cogens* and States incur international responsibility if their officials commit torture.[99] States have not taken the step of classifying torture as an international crime as that term is used in this book:[100] it is not punishable *as such* by any international court or tribunal, although under certain conditions it may constitute a crime against humanity or a war crime. Even though there may be no inter-State element to the

---

93 *Galić* ICTY T. Ch. 5.12.2003. See also *Krstić* ICTY T. Ch. I 2.8.2001 paras. 607, 653.

94 Antonio Cassese, 'Terrorism Is Also Disrupting Some Crucial Legal Categories of International Law' (2001) 12 *EJIL* 993 at 994; see also Antonio Frédéric Mégret, 'Justice in Times of Violence' (2003) 14 *EJIL* 327 at 332–4.

95 See Roberta Arnold, 'Terrorism as a Crime against Humanity under the ICC Statute' in Nesi, *International Cooperation in Counter-Terrorism*, 121; see to the contrary William Schabas, 'Is Terrorism a Crime against Humanity?' (2002) 8 *International Peacekeeping: The Yearbook of International Peace Operations* 255.

96 Lord Bingham in the House of Lords case of *A (FC) and others (FC) (Appellants)* v. *Secretary of State for the Home Department (Respondent)* [2005] UKHL 71 at para. 33.

97 For a list of international instruments prohibiting torture, see section 11.3.7.

98 Art. 2(2), 1984 UN Convention Against Torture: 'No exceptional circumstances whatsoever, whether a state of war or a threat of war, internal political instability or other public emergency, may be invoked as a justification for torture.' The classic argument that torture is sometimes justifiable may be found in Alan M. Dershowitz, *Why Terrorism Works: Understanding the Threat, Responding to the Challenge* (New Haven, CT, 2002). For discussion of whether there are legal exceptions in relation to the crime of torture, see Paola Gaeta, 'May necessity be available as a defence against torture in the interrogation of suspected terrorists?' (2004) 2 *JICJ* 762.

99 *Furundžija* ICTY T. Ch. II 10.12.1998 para.153.

100 In some classifications torture is an international crime; the House of Lords in *Pinochet No. 3* regarded it as such (*R* v. *Bow Street Metropolitan Stipendiary Magistrate ex parte Pinochet Ugarte (No. 3)* [1999] 2 All ER 97 at 198, 249, 260, 288) though their Lordships' remarks are not always easy to follow.

commission of the crime, States have concluded a suppression convention, the Convention against Torture and other Cruel, Inhuman and Degrading Treatment or Punishment 1984.[101]

14.3.2 UN Convention against Torture

The Convention was concluded to 'make more effective' the already existing prohibition under international law.[102] It follows the same pattern as the model discussed above.[103] It requires States Parties to criminalize the offence of torture in their domestic law, including attempts and complicity as well as participation (Article 4).[104] The Committee against Torture, established by the Convention, has confirmed that States must define torture as a separate offence in their criminal law, but they do not have to reproduce the Convention definition verbatim; they may adopt a wider definition.

Material elements

As defined in the Convention – and for the purpose of the Convention – the crime has two objective elements. First, it comprises 'any act by which severe pain or suffering, physical or mental', is inflicted on a person; and second, it is committed 'by or at the instigation of or with the consent or acquiescence of a public official or other person acting in an official capacity'. The second element is not present in some other formulations. The Inter-American Convention to Prevent and Punish Torture 1985 provides a wider definition, which does not specify a purpose, nor a level of pain and suffering; indeed it does not have an element of pain or suffering at all if the act is intended 'to obliterate the personality of the victim or to diminish his physical or mental capacities'.[105] Early commentators have stated that Article 1(1) 'gives a *description* of torture for the purpose of understanding and implementing the *Convention* rather than a legal definition for direct application in criminal law and criminal procedure'.[106] The ICTY has pronounced the definition as reflecting customary international law, but only for the purpose of State obligations under the Convention, not as regards the meaning of the crime more generally.[107]

---

101 Boister, 'Transnational Criminal Law?', 967.
102 Preamble to the Convention.
103 See section 14.1.2.
104 See N. Rodley and M. Pollard, 'Criminalisation of Torture: State Obligations under the United Nations Convention against Torture and other Cruel, Inhuman and Degrading Treatment or Punishment' (2006) 2 *European Human Rights Law Review* 115 at n. 17.
105 Arts. 1(2), 2 and 3.
106 J. H. Burgers and H. Danelius, *The United Nations Convention against Torture: A Handbook on the Convention against Torture and other Cruel, Inhuman or Degrading Treatment or Punishment* (Leiden, 1988) 122.
107 *Kunarac et al.* ICTY A. Ch. 12.6.2002 paras. 146, 147 (and the other cases there cited); and *Kvočka et al.* ICTY A. Ch. 28.2.2005 para. 284.

The Convention definition refers to acts but not to omissions. Does that exclude from the definition omissions such as failure to provide a prisoner with food or water? Such an interpretation would be contrary to common sense, if all the other elements of intention, purpose and connection with a public official are present.[108]

The assessment of whether particular ill-treatment is of a degree to amount to the crime of torture can be a difficult one since the severity threshold qualifies the pain and suffering of the victim, not the treatment itself. Legal memoranda written for the US Administration in 2002 and 2003, which provided an excessively restrictive interpretation of the obligations of the US under the Convention, and the treatment of detainees during the so-called 'war on terror', occasioned a great deal of debate about what kind of treatment constitutes torture.[109] The memorandum of August 2002 from the Office of the Legal Counsel in the US Department of Justice,[110] which was later withdrawn, was written to interpret a US statute enacted to implement the Convention. In describing what pain amounted to torture it stated that 'it must be equivalent in intensity to that which accompanies serious physical injury, such as organ failure, impairment of bodily function, or even death'. The defence in the *Brđanin* case before the ICTY on appeal claimed that the international definition of torture was as interpeted in this memorandum. The Court had no hesitation in dismissing this argument. 'No matter how powerful or influential a country is, its practice does not automatically become customary international law.'[111]

There is particular difficulty in assessing when ill-treatment is to be distinguished from 'cruel, inhuman or degrading treatment or punishment', as that term is used in Article 16 and, of course, in human rights provisions such as Article 3 of the European Convention on Human Rights. Practice under the UN human rights conventions and regional agreements such as the European Convention on Human Rights may be used in the context of criminal law;[112] the case law of the ad hoc Tribunals in relation to war crimes and crimes against humanity is also relevant in assessing the level of pain and suffering which amounts to torture.

---

108 Burgers and Danelius, *The United Nations Convention*, 118, and *Delalić et al.* ICTY T. Ch. II 16.11.1998 para. 468.

109 The memoranda are set out in Karen Greeenberg and Joshua Dretel, *The Torture Papers: The Road to Abu Ghraib* (Cambridge, 2005). See Mary Ellen O'Connell, 'Affirming the Ban on Harsh Interrogation' (2005) 66 *Ohio State Law Journal* 1231; Marcy Strauss, 'The Lessons of Abu Ghraib' *ibid.*, 1269; Seth Kreimer, '"Torture Lite," "Full bodied" Torture, and the Insulation of Legal Conscience' (2005) 1 *Journal of National Security Law and Policy* 187. The Executive Order issued by President Obama on 22.1.2009 prohibits reliance, in conducting interrogations, upon any DOJ memorandum interpreting the Torture Convention issued between 11.9.2001 and 20.1.2009.

110 'The Bybee/Yoo memorandum': memorandum from the Office of the Legal Counsel, Department of Justice, to Alberto R. Gonzales, Re: Standards of Conduct for Interrogation under 18 USC 2340-2340A (1 August 2002).

111 *Brđanin* ICTY A. Ch. 20.2.2001 para. 247.

112 *Furundžija* ICTY A. Ch. II 10.12.1998 para. 159, though see the warning in *Kunarac* ICTY T. Ch. 22.2.2001 para. 471 not to transpose too easily concepts developed in a different legal context.

It is not useful to attempt a catalogue of conduct amounting to torture,[113] but the following points are indicative of some current trends in the case law. The five interrogation techniques in use by the British security forces in the 1970s, namely 'wall standing, hooding, subjection to noise, deprivation of sleep and deprivation of food and drink', were held by the European Court of Human Rights in 1978 to be inhuman treatment, not torture,[114] but there are indications by the ECtHR that this kind of treatment may now be regarded as torture.[115] Some acts establish per se the suffering of those upon whom they were inflicted, so that the level of pain or suffering need not be proved. Sexual violence 'necessarily gives rise to severe pain or suffering, whether physical or mental';[116] 'rape involves the infliction of suffering at a requisite level of severity to place it in the category of torture';[117] solitary confinement may be torture 'to the extent that the confinement of the victim can be shown to pursue one of the prohibited purposes of torture and to have caused the victim severe pain or suffering';[118] 'waterboarding' has been widely acknowledged to constitute torture.[119] There is no absolute threshold level of pain or suffering.[120]

Pain or suffering arising only from lawful punishment, or incidental to it, is excluded from the definition of torture.[121] In recognition of the wide loophole this leaves in the Convention, there was an attempt in the negotiations to specify that the punishment must be limited 'to the extent consistent with' the UN Standard Minimum Rules for the Treatment of Prisoners. This was rejected on the grounds that the Rules are not legally binding, and apply only to prisoners.[122] Article 1(2) makes clear that by excluding from its definition of torture various means of punishment, the Convention does not legitimize any act which would be contrary to some other provision of international law.

The Convention definition of torture is limited to acts committed by 'a public official or other person acting in an official capacity'.[123] That limitation is not included in the definition of torture as a crime against humanity, nor, as now confirmed by the ICTY, in the requirements for war crimes.[124]

---

113 N. Rodley, *The Treatment of Prisoners under International Law*, 2nd edn (Oxford, 1999) reviews the authorities at ch. 3, 'What constitutes torture and other ill-treatment?'; and see *Delalić et al.* ICTY T. Ch. II 16.11.98 paras. 461–9.

114 *Ireland* v. *United Kingdom*, Series A No. 25, 5310/71 [1978] ECHR 1.

115 *Selmouni* v. *France* [1999] ECHR 66; and see Nigel Rodley, 'The Definition(s) of Torture in International Law' (2002) 55 *Current Legal Problems* 467 at 476–7.

116 *Kunarac et al.* ICTY A. Ch. 12.6.2002 para. 150.

117 *Delalić et al.* ICTY T. Ch. II 16.11.1998 para. 489.

118 *Krnojelac* ICTY T. Ch. II 15.3.2002 para. 183.

119 E.g. by US Att. Gen. Holder in his confirmation hearing in January 2009.

120 *Kunarac et al.* ICTY A. Ch. 12.6.2002 para. 149.

121 Art. 1 of the UN Convention against Torture.

122 Burgers and Danelius, *The United Nations Convention*, 46–7 and 121–2.

123 For discussion of the meaning of this term, see Sandesh Sivakumaran, 'Torture in International Human Rights and International Humanitarian Law: The Actor and the Ad Hoc Tribunals' (2005) 18 *LJIL* 541.

124 See sections 11.3.7 and 12.3.2.

Mental elements

The pain or suffering must be 'intentionally' inflicted. A further necessary element of the crime as defined in the Convention is that it is committed against a person 'for such purposes as obtaining from him or a third person information or a confession, punishing him for an act he or a third person has committed or is suspected of having committed, or intimidating him or a third person, or for any reason based on discrimination of any kind' (Article 1(1)). The list is narrow. While it is not exhaustive, the wording demands that other purposes must be of the same kind as those in the list. If the act is committed for essentially private purposes, out of sheer sadism, it would appear not to be covered, although it might be expected that a court interpreting the words would strive to bring any such act within the ambit of the definition.[125] States implementing the Convention in domestic law are not obliged to confine the offence to acts committed only with the listed purposes; the United Kingdom for example has not included any requirement of purpose.[126]

14.3.3 Prosecution and other national measures

The Convention incorporates the *aut dedere aut judicare* principle (Article 7), requiring States to take a wide jurisdiction to prosecute and to extradite anywhere in the world if they do not prosecute.[127] There is generally recognized to be a basis under customary international law for universal jurisdiction in respect of acts of torture.[128] If a decision is taken not to prosecute suspected complicity in torture, the reason for the decision is relevant to the question whether it is in breach of the Convention.[129] The Convention includes other provisions specific to torture; for example, States may not use information obtained by torture in proceedings (Article 15).[130] States must afford effective remedies and adequate reparation to the victims (Article 14). They may not deport, extradite or otherwise transfer a

---

125 Burgers and Danelius maintain that the common element in the list is the existence of a State interest or policy, but that even where the purpose is sadistic there is usually an aspect of punishment or intimidation to bring it within the list: Burgers and Danelius, *The United Nations Convention*, 119.

126 See the Criminal Justice Act 1988, s. 134.

127 Some commentators suggest that the Convention requires States to take universal jurisdiction to allow them to prosecute an act of torture, regardless of whether the State where the act was committed, or the State of nationality of the victim or suspect, is a State party or not: Rodley and Pollard, 'Criminalisation of Torture', 131. This approach would conflict with the ordinary principles of treaty interpretation.

128 See section 3.5.1.

129 For example, if the decision not to prosecute interrogators and officers who carried out or authorized the enhanced interrogation techniques at Guantanamo Bay was taken on grounds that convictions were not likely, that would not have been contrary to the Convention; if taken on other grounds it almost certainly would.

130 For the application of this provision in UK law, see Lord Bingham in the House of Lords case of *A (FC) and others (FC) (Appellants)* v. *Secretary of State for the Home Department (Respondent)* [2004] UKHL 56.

person to a country where there are substantial grounds for believing that he would be in danger of being tortured (Article 3).[131]

14.3.4 Torture as an international crime

Like terrorism, torture is within the jurisdiction of the ad hoc Tribunals and the ICC if committed under certain conditions. It is included expressly within the categories of crimes against humanity and war crimes in all of the relevant Statutes. Although the 'core' part of the Convention definition (the intentional infliction of severe pain or suffering) is also a constituent element of torture as a crime against humanity and as a war crime, there are differences in the other elements. The list of prohibited purposes is extended – and omitted altogether for the prosecution of crimes against humanity before the ICC – and perpetrators are not limited to persons acting in an official capacity. Of course, the other conditions for the commission of war crimes and crimes against humanity must be met; they are discussed in sections 11.3.7 and 12.3.2 above.

Further reading

Transnational crimes

M. Cherif Bassiouni (ed.), *International Criminal Law*, 3rd edn (New York, 2008), vol. I.
M. Cherif Bassiouni, 'Enslavement' in *ibid.*, 535.
Roger Clark, 'Offences of International Concern: Multilateral Treaty Practice in the Forty Years since Nuremberg' (1988) 57 *NJIL* 49.
Alexandra Orlova and James Moore, '"Umbrellas" or "Building Blocks"?: Defining International Terrorism and Transnational Organized Crime in International Law' (2005) 27 *Houston Journal of International Law* 267.

Terrorism

Andrea Bianchi (ed.), *Enforcing International Law Norms against Terrorism* (Hart, 2004).
Helen Duffy, *The 'War on Terror' and the Framework of International Law* (Cambridge, 2005).
John Dugard, 'International Terrorism and the Just War' (1977) 12 *Stanford Journal of International Studies* 21.
Rosalyn Higgins and Maurice Flory (eds.), *Terrorism and International Law* (London, 1997).

---

131 See also case law on the interpretation of Art. 3 of the European Convention on Human Rights, which makes clear that it is not possible to balance other rights and interests against the protection of a person from being deported to a country where he will be subjected to torture or ill-treatment (e.g. *Saadi* v. *Italy*, 37201/06 28.2.2008).

Christopher Joyner, 'Suppression of Terrorism on the High Seas: the 1988 IMO Convention on the Safety of Maritime Navigation' (1989) 19 *Israel Journal on Human Rights* 343.

Giuseppe Nesi (ed.), *International Cooperation in Counter-Terrorism* (Aldershot, 2006).

Eric Rosand, 'Security Council Resolution 1373, the Counter-Terrorism Committee, and the Fight Against Terrorism' (2003) 97 *AJIL* 333.

Robert Rosenstock, 'International Convention against the Taking of Hostages: Another International Community Step against Terrorism' (1980) 9 *Denver Journal of International Law and Policy* 169.

Nicolas Rostov, 'Before and After: The Changed UN Response to Terrorism Since September 11th' (2002) 35 *Cornell International Law Journal* 475.

Ben Saul, *Defining Terrorism in International Law* (Oxford, 2006).

Sami Shubber, 'The International Convention Against the Taking of Hostages' (1981) 52 *BYIL* 205.

Surya P. Subedi, 'The UN Response to International Terrorism in the Aftermath of the Terrorist Attacks in America and the Problem of the Definition of Terrorism in International Law' (2002) 4 *International Law FORUM du droit international* 159.

Christian Walter et al. (eds.), *Terrorism as a Challenge for National and International Law: Security versus Liberty?* (Berlin, 2004).

Samuel M. Witten, 'The International Convention for the Suppression of Terrorist Bombings' (1998) 92 *AJIL* 774.

Michael Wood, 'The Convention on the Prevention and Punishment of Crimes against Internationally Protected Persons, including Diplomatic Agents' (1974) 23 *ICLQ* 791.

Torture

Ahcene Boulesbaa, *The UN Convention on Torture and the Prospects for Enforcement* (The Hague, 1999).

J. Herman Burgers and Hans Danelius, *The United Nations Convention against Torture: A Handbook on the Convention against Torture and Other Cruel, Inhuman or Degrading Treatment or Punishment* (Leiden, 1988).

Nigel Rodley, *The Treatment of Prisoners under International Law*, 3rd edn (Oxford, 2009).

Nigel Rodley and Matt Pollard, 'Criminalisation of Torture: State Obligations under the United Nations Convention against Torture and other Cruel, Inhuman and Degrading Treatment or Punishment' (2006) 2 *European Human Rights Law Review* 115.

Lene Wendland, *A Handbook on State Obligations under the UN Convention against Torture* (Geneva, 2002).

Principles and Procedures of International Prosecutions

15

General Principles of Liability

15.1 Introduction

The substantive definitions of crimes (on which, see Chapters 10–13) provide only a part of the picture of criminal liability. The general principles of liability apply across the various different offences and provide for the doctrines by which a person may commit, participate in, or otherwise be found responsible for those crimes. They include forms of liability such as aiding and abetting, which are familiar to all domestic criminal lawyers, as well as principles like command responsibility, which are specific to international criminal law. It is important to note at the outset that the various forms of liability not only have different conduct elements, but also different mental elements, and the extent to which principles of accomplice liability have been used in some cases to avoid high *mens rea* requirements for primary commission of international crimes has been controversial. Unlike in domestic law, where the traditional image of a criminal is the primary perpetrator such as the person who pulls the trigger, in international criminal law, the paradigmatic offender is often the person who orders, masterminds, or takes part in a plan at a high level.[1] As a result, principles of liability play a comparatively large role in international criminal law.[2]

This chapter will discuss the principles of liability from two points of view, the ambit of liability recognized in customary and conventional international law,[3] alongside the appropriateness of those principles from the point of view of foundational principles of criminal

---

[1] Such persons are often referred to as 'those bearing greatest responsibility' for international crimes (see, e.g. Statute of the Special Court for Sierra Leone, Art. 1) or 'the most senior leaders suspected of being most responsible for' international crimes (Security Council Resolution 1534 (2004)).

[2] See William Schabas, 'Enforcing Individual Criminal Responsibility in International Criminal Law: Prosecuting the Accomplices' (2001) 843 *International Review of the Red Cross* 439. Equally, as we will see, some forms of liability in international criminal law allow people who would traditionally be seen as accomplices to be viewed as principal perpetrators. See also Héctor Olásolo, *The Criminal Responsibility of Senior Political and Military Leaders as Principals to International Crimes* (Oxford, 2009) ch. 1.

[3] As was mentioned in section 8.4, the ICC Statute ought not be taken straightforwardly as determinative of customary international criminal law.

law.[4] It must be noted at the outset though, that the principles of liability are not watertight compartments, and there are overlaps between them. Where they overlap, the ICTY has suggested that 'the Trial Chamber has a discretion to choose which is the most appropriate head of responsibility under which to attach criminal responsibility to the accused'.[5] When exercising such discretion, Trial Chambers have 'entered a conviction under the head of responsibility which better characterises the criminal conduct of the accused'.[6] It also ought to be noted at the outset that the Genocide Convention adopts slightly different principles on aspects of liability for genocide.

15.2 Perpetration/commission

The concept of commission (which in all likelihood is synonymous with 'perpetration')[7] is, unsurprisingly, well established in international criminal law. For example, in the *Jaluit Atoll* case in 1945, three Japanese soldiers were convicted of personally shooting prisoners of war.[8] Article 7(1) of the ICTY Statute (to which Article 6(1) of the ICTR Statute and Article 6(1) of the SCSL Statute conform in all material respects) makes this clear, imposing liability, inter alia, on any 'person … [who] … committed' an international crime. This description is, however, deceptively simple, as it begs the question of precisely who can be considered to have 'committed' a crime. As the ICTY has said, this primarily refers to 'the physical perpetration of a crime by the offender himself, or the culpable omission of an act that was mandated by a rule of criminal law'.[9]

This is not the only form that commission can take; there are other forms of commission that exist in treaty and custom. For example, there is joint criminal enterprise,[10] and the joint Appeals Chamber (of the ICTY and ICTR) in *Seromba* took a broad approach to 'commission', rejecting, for genocide, the idea that it was limited to the physical commission of crimes: '"direct and physical perpetration" need not mean physical killing, other acts can constitute direct participation in the *actus reus* of the crime'.[11] Unfortunately, the Appeals

---

4 See further on this point, Robert Cryer, 'General Principles of Liability in International Criminal Law' in Dominic McGoldrick, Peter Rowe and Eric Donnelly (eds.), *The International Criminal Court: Legal and Policy Issues* (Oxford, 2004) 233.

5 *Krnojelac* ICTY T. Ch. II 15.3.2002 para. 173.

6 *Stakić* ICTY T. Ch. II 31.7.2003 para. 463. See also Chapter 19 concerning indictments.

7 The two will be used interchangeably here. The ICTY considers liability pursuant to joint criminal enterprise to be a form of commission, but this is controversial.

8 *US* v. *Masuda and others* (The Jaluit Atoll Case) I LRTWC 71.

9 *Tadić* ICTY A. Ch. 15.7.1999 (hereinafter *Tadić* 1999 Appeal) para. 188. See similarly, *Kvočka et al.* ICTY T. I Ch. 2.11.2001 para. 251.

10 On which see section 15.3.

11 *Seromba* ICTR A. Ch. 12.3.2008 para. 161. See Flavia Zorzi Giustiniani, 'Stretching the Boundaries of Commission Liability' (2008) 6 *JICJ* 783; as noted at 787–8, a majority of the Appeals Chamber also thought that this would apply to the crime against humanity of extermination. The ICTR in *Gacumbitsi* ICTR A. Ch. 7.7.2006 para. 60 asserted, however, that 'In the context of genocide, however, direct and physical

Chamber did not provide a detailed explanation of what else would amount to 'commission' beyond stating that Seromba's actions (which largely amounted to agreeing, as a priest, to the use of bulldozers to destroy a church in which about 1,500 Tutsis had hidden) were 'as much an integral part of the genocide as were the killings which [they] enabled'. Nor did the Chamber give detailed proof of the customary law nature of this form of commission.[12]

Article 25(3)(a) of the ICC Statute defines perpetration in a more detailed fashion, criminalizing a person who 'Commits such a crime whether as an individual, jointly with another or through another person, regardless of whether that other person is criminally responsible.' This formulation raises some of the important issues relating to the concept of perpetration. The first issue is whether or not perpetration can occur by omission. In customary law this is certainly the case, so long as the charge relates to a failure to live up to a duty to act, and omission has a 'concrete influence' on the crime.[13] Although, owing to the fact that an Article criminalizing omissions was dropped at Rome,[14] some doubt that perpetration by omission is recognized in the ICC Statute,[15] the better view is that liability for omissions was not categorically excluded by the drafters. The ICC Elements of Crimes deliberately avoid the term 'acts' in favour of 'conduct', on the grounds that the latter term includes acts or omissions.[16]

The next issue is the concept of what is described as perpetration 'jointly with another' in Article 25(3)(a). In the narrow sense the provision raises no difficulty, in that when two or more people both work together in a final act to bring a result about, it is often artificial to separate off the respective contributions as being primary and secondary. If two people beat someone to death together, there is no real sense in separating off the person who dealt the particular blow that caused death from the other person, who did not deliver the fatal blow only by chance. The controversy about this, however, is about precisely when someone can be considered to have committed a crime 'jointly' with another, rather than having, for example, aided or abetted it. As will be seen, the ICC has also used this aspect of Article 25 (3)(a) to identify a broader form of 'co-perpetration', which includes acting through other people.[17]

---

perpetration need not mean physical killing; other acts can constitute direct perpetration in the *actus reus* of the crime.' See also the Separate Opinion of Judge Schomberg, paras. 2–4

12 *Seromba* ICTR A. Ch. 12.3.2008 para. 161, citing *Gacumbitsi* ICTR A. Ch. 7.7.2006. See Giustiniani, 'Stretching the Boundaries', 796–9.

13 *Orić* ICTY A. Ch. 3.7.2008 para. 94. For a list of positive obligations in humanitarian law, see Yves Sandoz, Christoph Swiniarski and Bruno Zimmermann (eds.), *Commentary on the Additional Protocols of 8 June 1977 to the Geneva Conventions of 8 August 1949* (Geneva, 1987) 1009. One example of a conviction for an omission is *Delalić et al.* ICTY T. Ch. II 16.11.1998 paras. 1092–6, 1101–5.

14 Per Saland, 'International Criminal Law Principles' in Lee, *Making of the Rome Statute*, 212.

15 See, e.g. Kai Ambos, 'Article 25' in Triffterer, *Observers' Notes* 475, 492; Kerstin Weltz, *Die Unterlassungshaftung im Völkerstrafrecht* (Freiburg im Breisgau, 2004) 320ff.

16 See, e.g. Maria Kelt and Hermann von Hebel, 'The Making of the Elements of Crimes' in Lee, *Elements and Rules*, 14.

17 *Katanga and Ngudjolo* ICC PT. Ch. I 30.9.2008 paras. 490–4.

Article 25(3)(a) also, correctly, recognizes the concept of 'innocent agency' by which a person commits a crime through an unwitting person, who cannot be considered to have any culpable part in the crime, for example because they were incapable of understanding the nature of their acts, or because they were an inadvertent participant. Someone who persuades children under the age of criminal responsibility to commit crimes, or one who does something similar with respect to those who are mentally incompetent would be considered the primary perpetrator. In that situation, there is no question of those legally incompetent people having exercised any form of choice, the concept which underlies criminal responsibility at the most basic level.[18]

Article 25(3)(a) enters more controversial waters, however, by recognizing the possibility of perpetration through a guilty agent separate from joint perpetration. This appears to be close to the concept in German law of the '*Hintermann*' (roughly, 'background man') perpetrator, where the mastermind of an operation who controls the will of those who directly commit the offence is taken to be a direct perpetrator rather than an accomplice.[19] As a Pre-Trial Chamber of the ICC has said:

> The concept of co-perpetration is originally rooted in the idea that when the sum of the coordinated individual contributions of a plurality of persons results in the realisation of all the objective elements of a crime, any person making a contribution can be held vicariously responsible for the contributions of all the others and, as a result, can be considered as a principal to the whole crime.[20]

This expansion of the concept of perpetration is necessary in legal systems where accomplices may only be given a lower sentence than is available for principal perpetrators. As this is not the case in international criminal law it may be questionable whether it was necessary to include this form of liability as a form of commission,[21] especially as it might be thought to downgrade the gravity of the acts committed by those closest to the crime.[22] Nonetheless, the principle has significant defenders,[23] and it does reflect some of the organizational dynamics that characterize the mass commission typical in many instances of international crimes.[24]

---

18 See, e.g. A. P. Simester and G. R. Sullivan, *Criminal Law: Theory and Doctrine*, 3rd edn (Oxford, 2007) 197.

19 See, e.g. Claus Kreß, 'Claus Roxin's Lehre von der Organisationsherrschaft und das Völkerstrafrecht' (2006) *Golddammers Archiv für Strafrecht* 304. For support in the ICTR see *Gacumbitsi* ICTR A. Ch. 7.7.2006 (hereinafter *Gacumbitsi* Appeal), separate Opinion of Judge Schomberg, paras. 14–23, but see Separate Opinon of Judge Shahabuddeen, paras. 42–52 and Partially Dissenting Opinion of Judge Güney, paras. 2–9.

20 *Lubanga Dyilo* ICC PT Ch. I 29.1.2007 para. 326.

21 See *Krnojelac* ICTY T. Ch. II 15.3.2002 paras. 74–5.

22 Some of the problems this caused for the prosecution in the Frankfurt Auschwitz trial are discussed in Devin Pendas, *The Frankfurt Auschwitz Trial 1963–1965: Genocide, History and the Limits of Law* (Cambridge, 2006).

23 Albin Eser, 'Individual Criminal Responsibility' in Cassese, *Commentary* 793–5; Mark Osiel, 'The Banality of Good: Aligning Incentives Against Mass Atrocity' (2005) 105 *Columbia Law Review* 1751, 1831–7. See also *Gacumbitsi* Appeal, Separate Opinion of Judge Schomberg, paras. 16–21.

24 *Katanga and Ngudjolo* ICC PT. Ch.I 30.9.2008 paras. 501–3.

There has been an attempt by at least one Trial Chamber in the ICTY to introduce a form of 'co-perpetratorship',[25] one which took a broad approach to what amounts to commission into the law of the ad hoc Tribunals. In the *Stakić* case the Trial Chamber found that there was a form of liability that consisted of:

> An explicit agreement or silent consent to reach a common goal by coordinated cooperation and joint control over the criminal conduct ... These can be described as shared acts which when brought together achieve the shared goal based on the same degree of control over the execution of the common acts.[26]

Its support for this came from doctrine and national analogies, rather than direct sources of international law. The Appeals Chamber in that case determined that there was no such concept of co-perpetratorship, stating that '[t]his mode of liability, as defined and applied by the Trial Chamber, does not have support in customary international law or in the settled jurisprudence of this Tribunal'.[27] The Appeals Chamber preferred to see such a form of co-perpetratorship as being a form of joint criminal enterprise liability.[28] The Trial Chamber itself admitted that it was 'aware that the end result of its definition of co-perpetration approaches that of the aforementioned joint criminal enterprise and even overlaps in part'.[29]

In spite of the doubts about the customary status of co-perpetration (including co-perpetration through another without regard to that person's criminal responsibility), it has played a large part in the early practice of the ICC, and it is the principle of liability that has been invoked in relation to the President of Sudan, Omar Al Bashir.[30] The Pre-Trial Chamber in *Lubanga* set the tone for discussion in the ICC, by determining that co-perpetration in the Rome Statute is based on the suspect's joint control of the crime, in that 'although none of the participants have overall control over the offence because they all depend on each other for its commission, they all share control because each of them could frustrate commission of the crime by not carrying out their task'.[31] This form of commission has two objective aspects, and three subjective ones.

---

25 Care must be taken when reading judgments on this point, as sometimes such a term is used to mean joint perpetration or the liability of a person participating in a joint criminal enterprise. See, for the former, e.g. *Furundžija* ICTY T. Ch. II 10.12.1998 para. 252; for the latter, see e.g. *Vasiljević* ICTY A. Ch. 25.2.2004 (hereinafter *Vasiljević* Appeal) para. 102; *Kvočka et al.* ICTY A. Ch. 28.2.2005 (hereinafter *Kvočka* Appeal) para. 90.

26 *Stakić* ICTY T. Ch. II 31.7.2003 para. 440.

27 *Stakić* ICTY A. Ch. 22.3.2006 (hereinafter *Stakić* Appeal) para. 62. See also *Multinović et al.* ICTY T. Ch. III 22.3.2006.

28 *Stakić* Appeal paras. 62–3.

29 *Stakić* ICTY T. Ch. II 31.7.2003 para. 441.

30 See Florian Jessberger and Julia Geneuss, 'On the Application of the Theory of Indirect Perpetration in *Al Bashir*: German Doctrine at the Hague?' (2008) 6 *JICJ* 853; Harmen van der Wilt, 'The Continuous Quest for Proper Modes of Criminal Responsibility' (2009) 7 *JICJ* 307.

31 *Lubanga Dyilo* ICC PT. Ch. I 29.1.2007 (hereinafter *Lubanga Dyilo*) para. 342.

The objective aspects are the existence of an explicit or implicit agreement or common plan between the co-perpetrators, and a coordinated essential contribution by the suspect which was essential for the commission of the objective elements of the crime.[32] The plan may be inferred from later concerted action,[33] and it does not need to be for a criminal purpose:

> It suffices: (i) that the co-perpetrators have agreed (a) to start the implementation of the common plan to achieve a non-criminal goal, and (b) to only commit the crime if certain conditions are met, or (ii) that the co-perpetrators are aware (a) of the risk that implementing the common plan (which is specifically directed at the achievement of a non-criminal goal) will result in the commission of the crime and (b) accept such an outcome.[34]

Turning to the conduct by the co-perpetrator, it must be essential to the commission of the objective elements of the crime, in that he or she could frustrate the commission of the crime by not undertaking his or her part, although the conduct does not need to occur at the 'execution' stages of the plan; it may be before.[35]

The ICC has also held that this contribution can be made through control of an organization.[36] In such circumstances, the organization must be hierarchically organized, with sufficient subordinates that if the orders are not carried out by one subordinate, another will do so, nearly automatically[37] and:

> it is critical that the chief, or the leader, exercises authority and control over the apparatus and that his authority and control are manifest in subordinates' compliance with his orders. His means for exercising control may include his capacity to hire, train, impose discipline, and provide resources to his subordinates.[38]

In other words, '[t]he leader must use his control over the apparatus to execute crimes, which means that the leader, as the perpetrator behind the perpetrator, mobilises his authority and power within the organisation to secure compliance with his orders'.[39] There are obvious links between this type of liability and liability for ordering offences under Articles 25(3)(b) and 25(3)(d) and joint criminal enterprise in the ad hoc Tribunals.

The subjective elements of co-perpetration are that (1) the suspect fulfils the subjective elements of the relevant offence (i.e. the war crime, crime against humanity or genocide),

---

32 *Ibid.*, paras. 343–8.

33 *Ibid.*, para. 345.

34 *Ibid.*, para. 344.

35 *Ibid.*, paras. 347–8. In *Katanga and Ngudjolo* ICC PT. Ch. I 30.9.2008 para. 526, a Pre-Trial Chamber has held that 'Designing the attack, supplying weapons and ammunitions, exercising the power to move the previously recruited and trained troops to the fields; and/or coordinating and monitoring the activities of those troops, may constitute contributions that must be considered essential regardless of when are they exercised (before or during the execution stage of the crime).'

36 *Katanga and Ngudjolo* ICC PT. Ch. I 30.9.2008 paras. 500–10.

37 *Ibid.*, paras. 515–7.

38 *Ibid.*, para. 513.

39 *Ibid.*, para. 514.

(2) the co-perpetrators must be mutually aware and accept that implementing the common plan may (or, more likely, 'will') result in the realization of the objective elements of the crime,[40] and (3) the suspect is aware of the circumstances that enable him or her jointly to control the crime.[41] With respect to the second condition, 'co-perpetration of a crime requires that both suspects: (a) are mutually aware that implementing their common plan will result in the realisation of the objective elements of the crime; (b) undertake such activities with the specific intent to bring about the objective elements of the crime, or are aware that the realisation of the objective elements will be a consequence of their acts in the ordinary course of events'.[42]

In addition, where co-perpetration is through another person (i.e 'indirect co-perpetration'), the co-perpetrators must be aware of their ability to exercise control over the crime by that other person, i.e. 'the suspects must be aware of the character of their organisations, their authority within the organisation, and the factual circumstances enabling near automatic compliance with their orders'.[43] The last element requires knowledge that their role is essential and that they could frustrate the commission of the objective elements of the crime by not playing their part.[44] Overall, although there are links to joint criminal enterprise, so long as the ICC sticks, inter alia, to requiring intention for co-perpetration, (i.e. foresight that crimes 'will' occur), it probably balances quite well the countervailing requirements of representing the dynamics of the commission of international crimes and maintaining a strong link to individual culpability.

15.3 Joint criminal enterprise[45]

The Nuremberg and Tokyo IMTs both provided that those who participated in a 'common plan or conspiracy to commit any of the foregoing crimes are responsible for all acts performed by any person in execution of such a plan'.[46] The form of liability contained in these provisions, which both tribunals determined only applied to crimes against peace,[47] is

---

40 In *Lubanga Dyilo* the Pre-Trial Chamber (I) held that 'may' suffice. In *Bemba Gombo* ICC PT. Ch. II 15.6.2009, (hereinafter *Bemba Gombo*) paras. 352–69 a different Pre-Trial Chamber expressly disagreed that anything lower than virtual certainty sufficed and used 'will'.
41 *Lubanga Dyilo*, paras. 349–67.
42 *Katanga and Ngudjolo* ICC PT Ch. I 30.9.2008 para. 533.
43 *Ibid.*, para. 534.
44 *Lubanga Dyilo*, para. 367.
45 For a useful overview, see Elies van Sliedregt, *The Criminal Responsibility of Individuals for Violations of International Humanitarian Law* (The Hague, 2003) 94–110. See also the symposium and anthology in (2007) 5 *JICJ* 67–244.
46 Nuremberg IMT Statute, Art. 6, Tokyo IMT Statute, Art. 5(c).
47 'Nuremberg IMT: Judgment and Sentences' (1947) 41 *AJIL* 172, 221–2; Tokyo IMT Judgment, 48,449, Judges Bernard and Jaranilla dissented on this: Dissenting Opinion of the Member from France, at 5–7; Concurring Opinion of the Member from the Philippines, 1–7.

often called conspiracy.[48] The use of 'conspiracy' in this regard is misleading as it is apt to cause confusion between this type of liability and the separate (common law) offence of conspiracy, which is an agreement to commit an offence, and does not require that any further action is taken in pursuance of that agreement.[49] In international criminal law this inchoate crime only exists in relation to genocide.[50] The Nuremberg and Tokyo IMTs, whilst both using the term conspiracy, were dealing with the situation where the plans were put into effect. Whilst the Nuremberg IMT interpreted the principle quite narrowly,[51] the Tokyo IMT took a very broad approach to it, and was criticized for doing so.[52]

Article 7(1) of the ICTY Statute, Article 6(1) of the ICTR Statute and Article 6(1) of the SCSL Statute do not contain any express provision on this form of liability. Nor do they contain analogous wording to that in Article 25(3)(a) of the Rome Statute about how commission may occur.[53] Nonetheless, the ICTY has developed a detailed jurisprudence on what it terms 'joint criminal enterprise' (or common purpose) liability. The leading judgment on the point was the *Tadić* 1999 Appeal. *Tadić* had been acquitted at trial level of involvement in the killing of five civilians in the village of Jaskici in June 1992 by the armed group he was a member of, as there was no evidence he was involved directly in the killing himself.

The Appeals Chamber overturned this acquittal, and set out its understanding of commission by virtue of participation in a joint criminal enterprise. The Chamber began by looking at Article 7(1) of the ICTY Statute. It decided, on the basis of a teleological interpretation, that as the intention was to cover all those responsible for international crimes in the Former Yugoslavia, Article 7(1) 'does not exclude those modes of participating in the commission of crimes which occur where several persons having a common purpose embark on criminal activity that is then carried out either jointly or by some members of this plurality of persons'.[54] It supported this finding by pointing to the nature of many international crimes, in particular that they are committed jointly by large numbers of people.[55] Since the *actus reus* and *mens rea* were not set out in the ICTY Statute, the Appeals Chamber looked to customary law, primarily as evidenced in case law.

---

48 Including by the Tribunals themselves.

49 *Multinović et al.* ICTY A. Ch. 21.5. 2003 (hereinafter *Odjanić*) para. 23.

50 1948 Genocide Convention, Art. 3(d). See William Schabas, *Genocide in International Law*, 2nd edn (Cambridge, 2008) ch. 6.

51 Nuremberg IMT Judgment (1947) 41 *AJIL* 222.

52 Ian Brownlie, *International Law and the Use of Force by States* (Oxford, 1962) 203; John Piccigallo, *The Japanese on Trial* (Austin, TX, 1979) 21; Neil Boister and Robert Cryer, *The Tokyo International Military Tribunal: A Reappraisal* (Oxford, 2008), ch. 8.

53 See, for discussion, Harmen van der Wilt, 'Joint Criminal Enterprise: Possibilities and Limits' (2007) 5 *JICJ* 91, 102–8.

54 *Tadić* 1999 Appeal paras. 189–90. Another case has, controversially, determined that Art. 7(1) is not exhaustive: *Odjanić* para. 20. Still, the Appeals Chamber in *Stakić* appeared to frown on new doctrines being introduced into the tribunal's jurisprudence: *Stakić* Appeal para. 59.

55 *Tadić* 1999 Appeal para. 191.

15.3.1. Actus reus

Having reviewed post-Second World War proceedings,[56] such as the Almelo Case[57] and the Essen Lynching Trial,[58] the Appeals Chamber in *Tadić* determined that there was a customary basis for such liability in three classes of cases, 'co-perpetration, where all participants in the common design possess the same criminal intent to commit a crime (and one or more of them actually perpetrate the crime, with intent) . . . so-called "concentration camp" cases', and 'type three' joint criminal enterprise, where crimes are committed by members of the group, outside its common purpose, but as a foreseeable incident of it.[59] It further determined that all three types shared a common *actus reus*, namely that there was:

    i. A plurality of persons.
    ii. The existence of a common plan, design or purpose which amounts to or involves the commission of a crime provided for in the Statute.
    iii. Participation of the accused in the common design involving the perpetration of one of the crimes provided for in the Statute.[60]

The Appeals Chamber in *Tadić* elaborated on these criteria. For example, the plurality 'need not be organised in a military, political or administrative structure . . .'.[61] 'There is no necessity for this plan, design or purpose to have been previously arranged or formulated. The common plan or purpose may materialise extemporaneously and be inferred from the fact that a plurality of persons acts in unison to put into effect a joint criminal enterprise.'[62] Participation in the common design 'need not involve commission of a specific crime under one of those provisions . . . but may take the form of assistance in, or contribution to, the execution of the common plan or purpose'.[63]

Later cases have also contributed to understanding of the *actus reus*. It is clear, for example, that membership in the group per se is not enough to ground liability on this basis.[64] There has to be some form of action by the defendant to contribute to the implementation of the plan.[65] Equally, both direct and indirect participation suffice.[66] There is no requirement that the contribution made by the defendant is a 'necessary or

---

56 Not all of which, it must be noted, firmly based their forms of liability in international law.
57 *Otto Sandrock* I LRTWC 35.
58 *Erich Heyer* I LRTWC 88.
59 *Tadić* 1999 Appeal para. 220. See also *Gacumbitsi* Appeal, Separate Opinion of Judge Shahabuddeen, para. 40.
60 *Tadić* 1999 Appeal para. 227.
61 *Ibid.*
62 *Ibid.*
63 *Ibid.* See also *Krajišnik*, ICTY A. Ch. 17.3.2009 (hereinafter *Krajišnik* Appeal) para. 695.
64 *Odjanić* para. 26. *Brđanin and Talić* ICTY T. Ch. 1.9.2004 (hereinafter *Brđanin*) para. 263.
65 *Brđanin* para. 263.
66 *Ibid.*

substantial'one,[67] but a later Appeals Chamber decision has said that it needs to be 'significant'.[68] The ICTY originally had inconsistent jurisprudence on whether or not those who physically commit the relevant crimes need to be parties to the joint criminal enterprise for other participants in that enterprise to be found guilty through this principle,[69] but the matter was settled by the Appeals Chamber in the *Brđanin* case. There, the Appeals Chamber took the view that the direct perpetrators 'on the ground' do not have to be a part of the enterprise, so long as the crimes can be imputed to one member of the enterprise, who is acting pursuant to the common plan when he or she uses those direct perpetrators to commit crimes.[70] Furthermore:

> Factors indicative of such a link include evidence that the JCE [joint criminal enterprise] member explicitly or implicitly requested the non-JCE member to commit such a crime or instigated, ordered, encouraged, or otherwise availed himself of the non-JCE member to commit the crime. However, it is not determinative whether the non-JCE member shared the *mens rea* of the JCE member or that he knew of the existence of the JCE . . . [71]

There is sense in the ICTY's position, in that for genocide, if not for all international crimes, the usual, if not inevitable, collective nature of the crimes means that it would be practically impossible to prove the *mens rea* of all of the direct perpetrators when trying high level participants.[72] In asserting this position though, the ICTY has opened itself up to criticism on the ground that it is stretching liability beyond the appropriate bounds of culpability.[73]

If the common plan or purpose fundamentally alters, then this is a new plan or purpose, not simply a continuation/mutation of the old one,[74] and a person is only responsible for crimes which relate to the plan or purpose he or she subscribed to;[75] if they agree to the expansion they can be responsible for the new crimes. In this circumstance too 'it is not necessary to show that the JCE members *explicitly* agreed to the expansion of criminal

---

67 *Kvočka* Appeal para. 97.

68 *Brđanin and Talić* ICTY A. Ch. 3.4.2007 (hereinafter *Brđanin* Appeal) para. 430. The exact difference between 'substantial' and 'significant' is not entirely clear, but has been repeated; see *Krajišnik* Appeal para. 215.

69 See *Krstić* ICTY T. Ch. I 2.8.2001 para. 612; *contra Brđanin* para. 344; *Limaj* ICTY T. Ch. II 30.11.2005 n. 2264; and *Rwamakuba* ICTR A. Ch. 22.10.2004 para. 24. See also *Odjanić* paras. 18–24, the Separate Opinion of Judge Bonomy is clear that liability may lie in such a situation. At para. 13 he asserts that 'there is certainly no binding decision of the Appeals Chamber that would prevent the Trial Chamber from finding an accused guilty on that basis'.

70 *Brđanin* Appeal paras. 410–14, but see the Dissent of Judge Shahabudeen, paras. 4–20. Nor does there have to be an agreement with the direct perpetrator for them to commit the crime, *ibid.*, 418–9.

71 *Krajišnik* Appeal para. 226.

72 In *ibid.*, para. 156 the Appeals Chamber noted that not all members have to be named; reference by group may be enough in some circumstances, but the 'rank and file consist[ing] of local politicians, military and police commanders, paramilitary leaders, and others' was too vague.

73 E.g. Harmen van der Wilt, 'Joint Criminal Enterprise: Possibilities and Limits' (2007) 5 *JICJ* 91.

74 *Blagojević and Jokić* ICTY T. Ch. 17.1.2005 para. 700.

75 *Krajišnik* ICTY T. Ch. 27.9.2006 para. 1903. See also *ibid.*, para. 701, although if the later plan or purpose is broader, he or she may still be liable for those crimes that fall within the narrower aspect agreed to, *ibid.*, n. 2157.

means; this agreement may materialise extemporaneously and be inferred from circumstantial evidence'.[76]

15.3.2 Mens rea

Although the conduct element of all of the forms of joint criminal enterprise liability is the same, the distinction between them comes in via the mental element. The Appeals Chamber in *Tadić* is the standard reference on the point:

> ... the *mens rea* element differs according to the category of common design under consideration. With regard to the first category, what is required is the intent to perpetrate a certain crime (this being the shared intent on the part of all co-perpetrators). With regard to the second category (which ... is really a variant of the first),[77] personal knowledge of the system of ill-treatment is required (whether proved by express testimony or a matter of reasonable inference from the accused's position of authority), as well as the intent to further this common concerted system of ill-treatment. With regard to the third category, what is required is the *intention* to participate in and further the criminal activity or the criminal purpose of a group and to contribute to the joint criminal enterprise or in any event to the commission of a crime by the group. In addition, responsibility for a crime other than the one agreed upon in the common plan arises only if, under the circumstances of the case, (i) it was *foreseeable* that such a crime might be perpetrated by one or other members of the group and (ii) the accused *willingly took that risk*.[78]

As ought to be clear, the first category of joint criminal enterprise is close to the concept of joint perpetration: the various participants share the intention to commit the crime that occurs. This is possibly slightly diluted in the second type, where knowledge of the system of ill-treatment suffices rather than the intent to commit the specific crime (if knowledge and intention are entirely separable concepts).[79] The broadest form of liability comes in 'type three' joint criminal responsibility, where the foreseeability of a crime is said to be the test.

It might be thought that by using the term 'foreseeable' rather than 'foreseen' in relation to 'type three' joint criminal enterprise, the Appeals Chamber was imposing a negligence standard. That would be inaccurate, as the second aspect of the test – that the accused 'willingly took that risk' – clearly shows that the test is whether the person was subjectively reckless (or, in civil law terms, had *dolus eventualis*) in relation to such a crime.[80] It is also important to note that any inference must take into account what the particular person knew: 'What is natural and foreseeable to one person participating in a systemic joint criminal

---

76 *Krajišnik* Appeal para. 163.
77 Although see *Kvočka* Appeal para. 86; Steven Powles, 'Joint Criminal Enterprise: Criminal Liability by Prosecutorial Ingenuity and Judicial Creativity?' (2004) 2 *JICJ* 606, 609–10.
78 *Tadić* 1999 Appeal para. 228.
79 Although in both instances the Appeals Chamber has said the participants must share the physical perpetrator's *mens rea*: *Krnojelac* ICTY A. Ch. 17.9.2003 para. 83.
80 See *Tadić* 1999 Appeal para. 220; *Stakić* Appeal paras. 99–103.

enterprise, might not be natural and foreseeable to another, depending on the information available to them.'[81] If this is shown, however, 'a person may be found responsible for such acts, even if it is not proved that he or she knew they had occurred'.[82]

15.3.3 The nature of joint criminal enterprise liability

The Appeals Chamber in *Odjanić*, somewhat controversially, determined that joint criminal enterprise liability is a form of 'committing', in the language of Article 7(1).[83] Even if the other two forms can be considered a form of primary liability,[84] which is also not beyond controversy, it might be questioned whether type three liability could really be seen as a form of 'commission'.[85]

The nature of joint criminal enterprise liability is important. For example, if joint criminal enterprise is considered a primary form of liability, participants in the enterprise can be aided and abetted by those outside it.[86] If it is a form of secondary liability, then they could not. Also, from the point of view of the principle of fair labelling, the omnibus nature of treating joint criminal enterprise liability as 'committing', runs together rather different levels of culpability, not expressing a distinction between those who are in essence joint perpetrators, but with a simple division of labour, from those who are far closer to aiders and abettors than primary perpetrators. This is particularly the case if '[r]egardless of the role each played in its commission, all of the participants in the enterprise are guilty of the same crime'.[87] The Appeals Chamber has admitted that this may be disquieting, but claimed that such matters can be dealt with satisfactorily in sentencing.[88]

Perhaps unsurprisingly, this form of liability has proved very controversial. The Appeals Chamber's induction of joint criminal enterprise liability from the Second World War cases has been criticized on the basis that the cases do not support the conclusions they reached.[89]

---

81 *Kvočka* Appeal para. 86.
82 *Milošević* ICTY T. Ch. III 16.6. 2004 para. 150.
83 *Odjanić* para. 20; *Kvočka* Appeal paras. 79–80.
84 Aspects of joint criminal enterprise can perhaps appropriately be seen as forms of commission, given the often large-scale perpetration of international crimes; see e.g. Jens Ohlin, 'Three Conceptual Problems with the Doctrine of Joint Criminal Enterprise' (2007) 5 *JICJ* 69 at 70, 72–4.
85 See also Ohlin, 'Three Conceptual Problems' 85–8.
86 *Vasiljević* Appeal para. 102.
87 *Blagojević and Jokić* ICTY T. Ch. 17.1.2005 para. 702, referring, inter alia, to *Vasiljević* Appeal para. 111. See also Ohlin, 'Three Conceptual Problems', 76–7; and Kai Ambos, 'Joint Criminal Enterprise and Command Responsibility' (2007) 5 *JICJ* 159 at 167–76. For a defence see Antonio Cassese, 'The Proper Limits of Criminal Liability Under the Doctrine of Joint Criminal Enterprise' (2007) 5 *JICJ* 109 at 114–5.
88 *Brđanin* Appeal para. 432.
89 See, e.g. Alison Marston Danner and Jenny S. Martinez, 'Guilty Associations: Joint Criminal Enterprise, Command Responsibility and the Development of International Criminal Law' (2005) 93 *California Law Review* 75, 110–17; Powles, 'Joint Criminal Enterprise', 614–17; Ohlin, 'Three Conceptual Problems', 75–6; Olásolo, *Criminal Responsibility*, ch. 2.

Indeed, this was specifically raised by other defendants before the Appeals Chamber, claiming that imposition of liability on this basis is inappropriate and violates the *nullum crimen sine lege* principle.[90] The Appeals Chamber has been unimpressed, and repeatedly reaffirmed its earlier holdings.[91]

From the point of view of fairness to the defendant, the vague, 'elastic' nature of the doctrine has led to claims that it is overbroad, thus reliant on prosecutorial discretion rather than law to keep it in check.[92] This is particularly the case where large scale enterprises are charged.[93] Fears have also been expressed about the extent to which it encourages prosecutors to bring indictments that assert joint enterprises in a very general manner, making preparation difficult for the defence.[94] Turning to the *mens rea*, a person can be convicted of specific intent crimes such as genocide even if that person did not have the relevant *mens rea* for that offence, but the crimes were a natural and foreseen incident of the enterprise he or she was involved in on the basis of joint criminal enterprise.[95] This has led to criticisms of joint criminal enterprise liability, as allowing the prosecution to circumvent the proper *mens rea* requirements for such serious crimes.[96] The principle remains, however, popular with the ICTY Prosecutor,[97] and does go some way to describing the joint nature of many international crimes and explaining the culpability of some participants not otherwise easily brought under the ambit of criminality, in spite of their blameworthiness.[98]

The formulation of the principle in the ICC Statute may go some way to mitigate some of the problems identified above. Article 25(3)(d) provides for the responsibility of a person who:

> In any other way contributes to the commission or attempted commission of such a crime by a group of persons acting with a common purpose. Such contribution shall be intentional and shall either

---

90 *Odjanić.*

91 *Ibid.*, paras. 29, 40–3. *Martić* ICTY A. Ch. 8.10.2008 paras. 80–1; *Krajišnik* Appeal paras. 652–72.

92 Osiel, 'The Banality of Good', 1799–802; Danner and Martinez, 'Guilty Associations', 135–46; Mohamed Elawa Badar, 'Just Convict Everyone! – Joint Perpetration from Tadić to Stakić and Back Again' (2006) 6 *International Criminal Law Review* 302. Equally, see Katrina Gustafson, 'The Requirement of an "Express Agreement" for Joint Criminal Enterprise Liability: A Critique of Brđanin' (2007) 5 JICJ 134; Cassese, 'Proper Limits', 116–23; and *Brđanin* Appeal paras. 426–32.

93 Which they may be, *Brđanin* Appeal paras. 420–5.

94 Guénaël Mettraux, *International Crimes and the ad Hoc Tribunals* (Oxford, 2005) 293; Osiel, 'The Banality of Good', 1803. Although the ICTY does not think this problematic; see *Limaj* ICTY A. Ch. 27.9.2007 para. 104.

95 *Rwamakuba* ICTR A. Ch. 22.10.2004 paras. 30–1.

96 Mettraux, *International Crimes*, 265; Osiel, 'The Banality of Good', 1796. For a defence see Elies van Sliedregt, 'Joint Criminal Enterprise as a Pathway to Convicting Individuals for Genocide' (2007) 5 JICJ 184.

97 See, e.g. Nicola Piacente, 'Importance of the Joint Criminal Enterprise Doctrine for ICTY Prosecutorial Policy' (2004) 2 JICJ 446.

98 Mettraux, *International Crimes*, 292; Osiel, 'The Banality of Good', 1786–90, but see 1802; Danner and Martinez, 'Guilty Associations', 132–4.

i. Be made with the aim of furthering the criminal activity or criminal purpose of the group, where such activity or purpose involves the commission of a crime within the jurisdiction of the Court; or

ii. Be made in the knowledge of the intention of the group to commit the crime.

The Article is by no means easy to interpret, and the drafting is the outcome more of compromise than craftsmanship.[99] The wording draws upon the 1997 International Convention for the Suppression of Terrorist Bombings.[100] It appears to create liability similar to that which the ICTY has approached as type one and possibly type two joint criminal enterprise. Although it sets a low level of participation ('in any other way contributes'), the requirement of a group with a purpose that is at least known to the defendant limits the ambit of liability. Although the question may depend on the distinction between the use of indefinite and definite article in (i) and (ii) ('a' in the former, 'the' in the latter), Article 25(3)(d) does not appear to recognize at least the outer limits of type three joint criminal enterprise.[101]

15.4 Aiding and abetting

Liability for aiding and abetting (or 'encouraging') international crimes is not new. A notable example of a prosecution for aiding a war crime was the Zyklon B Case,[102] in which two German industrialists were convicted of supplying poison gas to the SS for use in concentration camp killings. The existence of liability for aiding and abetting is uncontroversial; it is recognized, for example in Article 7(1) of the ICTY Statute, Article 6(1) of the ICTR Statute and Article 6(1) of the SCSL Statute, all of which criminalize 'a person ... who aided and abetted in the planning, preparation or execution' of an international crime. There have been, and remain, greater controversies about its precise ambit than its existence.[103] There are also overlaps between this form of liability and joint criminal enterprise,[104] although the ICTY has said that, where people have participated in a joint criminal

---

99 See, e.g. Cryer, 'General Principles', 251.

100 General Assembly Res. A/RES/52/164 (1997), Art. 2(3)(c).

101 Although see further, Ohlin, 'Three Conceptual Problems' 78–9, 89–91.

102 *Tesch and others* I LRTWC 93.

103 There is also a question as to whether complicity in genocide, criminalized in Art. 3(e) of the Genocide Convention, is different from this form of liability; the Appeals Chamber in *Krstić* ICTY A. Ch. 19.4.2004 (hereinafter *Krstić* Appeal) paras. 138–44, hinted that the two differ. Since then the case has been read by the Appeals Chamber as establishing that 'the prohibited act of complicity in genocide, which is included in the Genocide Convention and in Article 2 of the Statute, encompasses aiding and abetting'. *Ntakirutimana and Ntakirutimana* ICTR A. Ch. 13.12.2004 paras. 371 and 500, however, leaves the door open for 'other forms of complicity' than aiding and abetting. See though *Blagojević and Jokić* ICTY T. Ch. 17.1.2005 para. 679. See Chile Eboe-Osuji, '"Complicity in Genocide" versus "Aiding and Abetting Genocide"' (2005) 3 *JICJ* 56; Payam Akhavan, 'The Crime of Genocide in the ICTR Jurisprudence' (2005) 3 *JICJ* 989.

104 The similarities and differences are discussed in *Tadić* 1999 Appeal para. 229 and *Kvočka* Appeal para. 90: the main differences are that an aider or abettor does not need to know of any common plan, but his or her assistance must be substantial, but see below in this section on this criterion. An aider or abettor is only enterprise, to convict them 'only as an aider and abettor might understate the degree of their criminal responsibility',[105] and thus 'aiding and abetting is a form of responsibility which generally warrants lower sentences than responsibility as a co-perpetrator'.[106] The use of the term generally in this context is important, there is no *a priori* reason why an aider or abettor cannot be as responsible as a perpetrator. The views of the ICTY here also need to be understood against the background of its broad interpretation of what perpetration entails, namely as including participation in a joint criminal enterprise.[107]

The law on aiding and abetting in the ad hoc Tribunals is largely explained by the *Tadić* Appeal Judgment of 1999. This set out the requirements as follows: 'The aider and abettor carries out acts specifically directed to assist, encourage or lend moral support to the perpetration of a certain specific crime ... and this support has a substantial effect upon the perpetration of the crime ... the requisite mental element is knowledge that the acts performed by the aider and abettor <u>assist</u> the commission of a specific crime by the principal'.[108]

There are a number of things worth noting about this definition. To begin with, the acts which assist must have a direct and 'substantial' effect on the commission of the crime. However, this should not be taken as setting a high standard: the Yugoslav Tribunal has seen it more as meaning any assistance which is more than *de minimis*.[109] It has accepted, amongst other things, that standing near victims whilst armed to prevent them escaping amounts to aiding,[110] as does providing weapons to a principal,[111] or taking principals to the scene of a crime and pointing at people to be killed.[112] Allowing resources for which a person is responsible to be used for crimes may also suffice.[113] Amongst other things,

---

responsible for crimes known about (again, see below in this section), whereas foresight by the defendant suffices for liability for crimes committed pursuant to a joint criminal enterprise.

105 *Tadić* 1999 Appeal para. 192.

106 *Vasiljević* Appeal para. 182; *Orić* ICTY T. Ch. II 30.6.2006 para. 281. See also *Tadić* 1999 Appeal para. 191.

107 See *Orić* ICTY T. Ch. II 30.6.2006 para. 282.

108 *Tadić* 1999 Appeal para. 229. *Orić* ICTY T. Ch. II 30.6.2006 para. 288 took the view that 'the intention must contain a cognitive element of knowledge and a volitional element of acceptance, whereby the aider and abettor may be considered as accepting the criminal result of his conduct if he is aware that in consequence of his contribution, the commission is more likely than not'. The Trial Chamber in *Halilović* T. Ch. 16.11.2005 para. 286 asserts that 'recent judgments also demand some sort of acceptance of the final result'. There is no express requirement in *Blaškić* ICTY A. Ch. 29.7.2004 (hereinafter *Blaškić* Appeal) para. 46, but in relation to ordering, the Appeals Chamber said that ordering 'with the awareness of the substantial likelihood that a crime will be committed ... has to be regarded as accepting that crime', *ibid.*, para. 42.

109 See, e.g. Kai Ambos, 'Article 25' in Triffterer, *Observers' Notes*, 481.

110 *Vasiljević* Appeal para. 134. Judge Shahabuddeen in that case considered this to suffice for co-perpetratorship through joint criminal enterprise liability: see Partially Dissenting Opinion of Judge Shahabuddeen, para. 40.

111 *Ntakirutimana and Ntakirutimana* ICTR A. Ch. 13.12.2004 para. 530.

112 *Ibid.*, para. 532.

113 *Krštić* Appeal para. 137.

although presence per se does not amount to encouragement,[114] presence of a superior at the scene of an offence may suffice for liability for abetment by tacit approval.[115] Omissions may suffice for aiding or abetting, provided that there is a legal obligation on the defendant to prevent the crime and the ability to intervene.[116] Although there is no necessity that the principal offender know of the assistance for liability for aiding to arise,[117] it would be essentially impossible to abet someone without their being aware of the abetting behaviour. Moreover, 'the lending of practical assistance, encouragement, or moral support may occur before, during, or after the crime or underlying offence occurs'.[118]

As to the *mens rea*, all that is required is that the aider and abettor knows that his or her conduct assists a specific crime. It is not necessary that his or her purpose is to assist. There is, however, the question of how much knowledge about a crime is necessary. Does, for example, the aider or abettor have to know who or what is going to be attacked or in what way? The Appeals Chamber in *Tadić* asserted that 'awareness ... of the essential elements of the crime committed by the principal would suffice'.[119] When a person knows that more than one crime might be committed, the ICTY has said that:

> it is not necessary that the aider and abettor should know the precise crime that was intended and which in the event was committed. If he is aware that one of a number of crimes will probably be committed, and one of those crimes is in fact committed, he has intended to facilitate the commission of that crime, and is guilty as an aider and abettor.[120]

Some have criticized a knowledge-based version of *mens rea* in relation to the crime of genocide, on the basis that it dilutes the special intent that characterizes that offence.[121] These critiques have force. Still, the Tribunals have had no compunction in convicting people of aiding and abetting genocide on the basis of knowledge of the genocidal intentions of others.[122]

The definition of aiding and abetting in the ICC Statute is slightly different from that used by the ICTY and ICTR, the ICC Statute criminalizing anyone who '[f]or the purpose of facilitating the commission of such a crime, aids, abets, or otherwise assists in its

---

114 *Orić* ICTY T. Ch. II 30.6.2006 para. 283.

115 *Aleksovski* ICTY A. Ch. 24.3.2000 paras. 36–7, *Brđanin* Appeal para. 273. Whether or not the obligation has to be imposed by the criminal law is an open question, *Mrksić and Šljivančnin* ICTY A. Ch. 5.5.2009 paras. 148–52.

116 *Orić* ICTY T. Ch. II 30.6.2006 para. 283; *Multinović* ICTY T. Ch. 26.2.2009 para. 90.

117 *Tadić* 1999 Appeal para. 229.

118 *Multinović* ICTY T. Ch. 26.2.2009 para. 91. –

119 *Tadić* 1999 Appeal para. 164. See also *Orić* ICTY T. Ch. II 30.6.2006 para. 288.

120 *Furundžija* ICTY T. Ch. II 10.12.1998 para. 246. Approved in *Blaškić* Appeal para. 50.

121 Mettraux, *International Crimes*, 286–7. Larissa van den Herik and Elies van Sliedregt, 'Ten Years Later, the Rwanda Tribunal still Faces Legal Complexities: Some Comments on the Vagueness of the Indictment. Complicity in Genocide, and the Nexus Requirement for War Crimes' (2004) 17 *LJIL* 544–51; for a prosecution of complicity in a Netherlands court, see H. G. van der Wilt, 'Genocide, Complicity in Genocide and International v. Domestic Jurisdiction' (2006) 4 *JICJ* 239.

122 *Krštić* Appeal para. 140.

commission or its attempted commission, including providing the means for its commission'.[123] The main differences are that there is no express requirement that the assistance or encouragement make a substantial contribution to the crime, although this change is probably not of much great practical importance.[124] More important is the *mens rea*, which is that the accomplice's conduct was 'for the purpose' of assisting. This is a higher requirement than the 'knowledge' required by the ICTY and ICTR, and one which will involve some difficult determinations of motive.[125] It will certainly make prosecuting those who sell arms or other war *matériel* which is used for international crimes difficult to prosecute.[126] Even if an arms dealer knew weapons that he sold to a country were destined to be used for the commission of international crimes, liability would not arise if the sole purpose for selling them was making profit. It will cause further problems for prosecuting acts which, on their face, are neutral or professional acts such as providing chemicals that may be used for an innocent purpose or to make chemical weapons. Equally, a broad approach to what amounts to participation in a joint criminal enterprise liability could undermine this high threshold in some circumstances.

15.5 Ordering, instigating, soliciting, inducing and inciting

15.5.1 Ordering

As many international crimes are committed by a large number of people acting together, it is frequently the case that such crimes are committed at the behest of a superior authority. If defendants in war crimes trials are to be believed, almost every crime is committed pursuant to orders. It has never really been questioned that those ordering international crimes are responsible for them. The reason given by those supporting a defence of superior orders in the early nineteenth century was that liability was more appropriately placed on the person who gave the order than the person who carried it out.[127] However, even though reliance on the defence of superior orders was barred in the Nuremberg IMT, that tribunal had no compunction in imposing liability for giving orders.[128] Although some see those giving orders to commit international crimes as perpetrators acting through innocent or guilty agents,[129] the ICC Statute and the statutes of the ICTY, ICTR and SCSL all treat it as a

---

123 ICC Statute, Art. 25(3)(c).

124 There is also some question as to whether, unlike the ICTY in the *Tadić* 1999 Appeal para. 481, Art. 25 includes assistance after the fact: see van Sliedregt, *Criminal Responsibility*, 111–13.

125 See Cryer, 'General Principles', 248.

126 For a (slightly) more sanguine view, see William A. Schabas, 'Enforcing International Humanitarian Law: Catching the Accomplices' (2001) 842 *International Review of the Red Cross* 439.

127 See, e.g. Lassa Oppenheim, *International Law* (London, 1906), vol. II, 264–5.

128 See, e.g. Nuremberg IMT Judgment (1947) 41 *AJIL* 274 (Göring), 282 (Keitel), 284 (Kaltenbrunner), 289–90 (Frank), 292 (Frick), 312 (Saukel), 315 (Jodl), 320 (Seyss-Inquart), 325 (von Neurath), 329 (Bormann).

129 Ambos, 'Article 25', 480, 491.

separate form of liability.[130] The core aspect of the crime of ordering, as interpreted by the ICTY and ICTR, is that a 'person in a position of authority uses it to convince another to commit an offence'.[131]

This requires three things, a superior/subordinate relationship, the transmission of an order, and the relevant mental element. In relation to the first of these, it is not necessary that the relationship be a legal one, the point is whether there is factually, 'some position of authority on the part of the accused that would compel another to commit a crime in following the accused's order'.[132] The transmission of an order can be established by circumstantial evidence.[133] An example of this would be when there are a remarkable number of similar actions over a disparate area in a short time. A court does not need a paper copy of an order or a tape of it to convict on this basis. A person does not have to be the author of an order to become liable for ordering in international criminal law, passing it down the chain of command can be enough.[134] Similarly, nor does a person who issues an order have to pass it directly to the person who commits the crime, it may go through a number of intermediaries' hands first.[135] This form of liability cannot attach to a pure omission,[136] and the order must substantially contribute to the commission of the crime (but need not be a *sine qua non*).[137]

The mental element of ordering has been set out by the ICTY as being 'the awareness of the substantial likelihood that a crime will be committed in the execution of that order … Ordering with such awareness has to be regarded as accepting that crime.'[138] That said, it is not necessary that an order is illegal on its face for a person to become liable for giving it.[139] This is consonant with the point that a mistake of law that does not affect *mens rea* is not exculpatory, and a mistake about whether certain conduct is criminal does not per se affect *mens rea*.[140] The *mens rea* of the person who issued (or passed on) the order is determinative of what particular crime he or she is responsible for ordering, not the *mens rea* of the person who carries it out.[141]

---

130 ICC Statute, Art. 25(3)(b); ICTY Statute, Art. 7(1); ICTR Statute, Art. 6(1); SCSL Statute, Art. 6(1).
131 *Akayesu* ICTR T. Ch. I 2.9.1998 para. 483; *Blaškić* ICTY T. Ch. I 3.3.2000 para. 601.
132 *Semanza* ICTR A. Ch. 20.5.2005 para. 361. See also *Kordić and Čerkez* ICTY T. Ch. 26.2.2001 para. 388; ICTY A. Ch. 17.12.2004 (hereinafter *Kordić and Čerkez* Appeal) para. 28. The Appeals Chamber in *Gacumbitsi* Appeal para. 182, noted that this is not the same as the requirement in command responsibility of effective control, as it 'requires merely authority to order, a more subjective criterion depends on the circumstances and the perceptions of the listener'.
133 *Blaškić* ICTY T. Ch. I 3.3.2000 para. 281.
134 Nuremberg IMT Judgment (1947) 41 *AJIL* 282; *Kupreškić* ICTY T. Ch. II 14.1.2000 para. 862.
135 *Blaškić* ICTY T. Ch. I 3.3.2000 para. 282.
136 *Galić* ICTY A. Ch. 30.11.2006 para. 176.
137 E.g. *Multinović* ICTY T. Ch. 26.2.2009 para. 88.
138 *Blaškić* Appeal para. 42.
139 *Blaškić* ICTY T. Ch. I 3.3.2000 para. 282.
140 See Chapter 16.
141 *Blaškić* ICTY T. Ch. I 3.3.2000 para. 282.

Article 25(3)(b) of the ICC Statute appears to see ordering as a form of secondary liability, as it provides for responsibility only when the ordered crime 'occurs or is attempted'. The ICTY and ICTR have also conceptualized ordering in this way.[142] It is questionable whether this was necessary or appropriate. Post-Second World War cases such as *von Falkenhorst* imposed liability for issuing orders which were not implemented.[143] There are those who claim that ordering offences should be seen as a form of perpetration by means.[144] Conceptualizing ordering in such a manner would have the advantage of allowing the issuance of orders which were not acted upon to be considered attempts.[145] However, there are specific wrongs involved in ordering which are also not quite captured by such a manner of conceptualization, which may be a form of responsibility all of its own,[146] and difficult problems of demarcation between the two may arise.[147]

15.5.2 Instigating, soliciting, inducing and inciting[148]

Instigation, which the ICTY has described as 'prompting',[149] and the ICTR as 'urging or encouraging'[150] another to commit a crime, seems to be largely the same as soliciting or inducing in Article 25(3)(b) of the ICC Statute.[151] As the Trial Chamber in *Blaškić* put it '[t]he essence of instigating is that the accused causes another person to commit a crime. Although it must be proved that the instigation was a clear contributing factor to the commission of the crime, it need not be a *conditio sine qua non*.'[152] The Chamber also clarified that '[i]nstigation can take many different forms; it can be express or implied, and entail both acts and omissions'.[153] The instigation must have been a substantially contributing factor (but need not be the only cause) of the physical element of the crime.[154] In other words:

---

142 *Ibid.*, paras. 281–2; *Kordić and Čerkez* ICTY T. Ch. 26.2.2001 para. 388; *Akayesu* ICTR T. Ch. I 2.9.1998 para. 483.

143 XI LRTWC 18.

144 Eser, 'Individual Criminal Responsibility', 797; van Sliedregt, *Criminal Responsibility*, 78.

145 And, lest we forget, there is an obligation on subordinates to disobey, at the least, manifestly unlawful orders, see ICC Statute, Art. 33.

146 See Cryer, 'General Principles', 242–7.

147 Kreß, 'Claus Roxin's'.

148 As Mettraux, *International Crimes*, 281, notes, there is considerable overlap here between instigation and abetting.

149 *Blaškić* ICTY T. Ch. I 3.3.2000 para. 280.

150 *Bagilishema* ICTR A. Ch. 2.7.2002 (hereinafter *Bagilishema* Appeal) para. 30.

151 See, e.g. Gerhard Werle, *Principles of International Criminal Law* (The Hague, 2005) 125.

152 *Blaškić* ICTY T. Ch. I 3.3.2000 para. 270; *Orić* ICTY T. Ch. II 30.6.2006 para. 274; *Kordić and Čerkez* Appeal para. 27.

153 *Blaškić* para. 270.

154 *Gacumbitsi* Appeal para. 129; *Kordić and Čerkez* Appeal para. 27.

[i]t requires some kind of influencing the principal perpetrator ... [but] does not necessarily presuppose that the original idea or plan to commit the crime was generated by the instigator. Even if the principal perpetrator was already pondering on committing a crime, the final determination can still be brought about by persuasion or strong encouragement of the instigator. However, if the principal perpetrator ... has definitely decided to commit the crime, further encouragement or moral support may merely, though still, qualify as aiding and abetting.[155]

Turning to the mental element, rather like for ordering, the ICTY has said that 'a person who instigates another person to commit an act or omission with the awareness of the substantial likelihood that a crime will be committed in the execution of that instigation, has the requisite *mens rea* for establishing responsibility ... [for] ... instigating. Instigating with such awareness has to be regarded as accepting that crime.'[156] Some cases have seen the giving of orders which are not carried out as a form of incitement/ instigation.[157]

Direct and public incitement to genocide is specifically criminalized, in essentially the same terms, by Article 3(c) of the Genocide Convention,[158] Article 4(3)(c) of the ICTY Statute, Article 2(3)(c) of the ICTR Statute, and Article 25(3)(e) of the ICC Statute. Unlike the other crimes of encouragement discussed here, for liability to accrue for incitement to commit genocide, it is not necessary to prove that anyone even attempted to commit genocide. Incitement to genocide is an inchoate crime,[159] although sometimes the ICTR has prosecuted defendants under this heading for conduct that has led to the commission of genocide.[160]

The main case in the area is the ICTR's *Media* case.[161] Drawing, inter alia, on the Nuremberg IMT's verdicts on Julius Streicher and Hans Frizsche, the Trial Chamber in that case decided that, in determining liability, the purpose and context of any communication is important.[162] The result was approved by the Appeals Chamber, who also noted that the effect the incitement has on an audience is a relevant factor.[163]

---

155 *Orić* ICTY T. Ch. II 30.6.2006 para. 271. It is questionable whether the implicit assertion that aiding or abetting is per se less serious than incitement ('merely') is appropriate.
156 *Kordić and Čerkez* Appeal para. 32. See similarly, *Orić* ICTY T. Ch. II 30.6.2006 para. 279, which also asserts that the instigator must accept the intentional commission of the relevant crime. *Quaere* whether this is necessary for crimes for which a lesser mental element is required or consistent with *Kordić and Čerkez* Appeal.
157 *Meyer* (Abbaye Ardenne Case) IV LRTWC 97, 98.
158 1948 Convention on the Prevention and Punishment of the Crime of Genocide.
159 *Nahimana, Barayagwiza and Ngeze* ICTR A. Ch. 28.11.2007 (hereinafter 'Media Appeal') para. 678; *Akayesu* ICTR T. Ch. I 2.9.1998 para. 562; *Mugesera* v. *Canada* 2005 2 SCR 100, paras. 84–5.
160 See, e.g. *Akayesu* ICTR T. Ch. I 2.9.1998 paras. 672–5. Such conduct might be better considered abetment or instigation; however, see e.g. *Kalimanzira* ICTR T. Ch. III 22.6.2009 paras. 512–3.
161 *Nahimana, Barayagwiza and Ngeze* ICTR T. Ch. 3.12.2003 (hereinafter *Media*).
162 *Ibid.*, paras. 1000–10.
163 *Media* Appeal paras. 698–700.

On the basis of the earlier *Akayesu* case, the Trial Chamber in the *Media* case determined that the crime required 'a call for criminal action to a number of individuals in a public place or to members of the general public at large by such means as the mass media, for example, radio or television'.[164] So far, determining what is public has not been too difficult, most prosecutions being based on speeches to large groups of people or the mass media. It has been held that:

> Incitement is 'public' when conducted through speeches, shouting or threats uttered in public places or at public gatherings, or through the sale or dissemination, offer for sale or display of written material or printed matter in public places or at public gatherings, or through the public display of placards or posters, or through any other means of audio-visual communication.[165]

As the last part of the quote implies, the internet and e-mail may raise interesting questions regarding the 'public' requirement.

Interpreting what is direct is not simple. As the Trial Chamber in *Akayesu* said, 'the direct element of incitement should be viewed in the light of its cultural and linguistic content. Indeed, a particular speech may be perceived as "direct" in one country, and not so in another, depending on the audience. The Chamber further recalls that incitement may be direct, and nonetheless implicit ... '.[166] The Appeals Chamber largely agreed, noting that simple 'hate speech' may not be enough; the incitement must be to commit genocide, although that call need not be express, so long as it is direct.[167] Particularly difficult issues of culture, context and interpretation arise here, especially when prosecutions are occurring outside the *locus delicti*.[168]

On the authority of the *Akayesu* case the Trial Chamber in the *Media* case held that the *mens rea* was the:

> intent to directly prompt or provoke another to commit genocide. It implies a desire on the part of the perpetrator to create by his actions a particular state of mind necessary to commit such a crime in the minds of the person(s) he is so engaging. That is to say that the person who is inciting to commit genocide must have himself the specific intent to commit genocide, namely, to destroy, in whole or in part, a national, ethnical, racial or religious group, as such.[169]

---

164 *Media* para. 1011.
165 *Kalimanzira* ICTR T. Ch. III 22.6.2009 para. 515.
166 *Akayesu* ICTR T. Ch. I 2.9.1998 para. 557; see also *Kalimanzira* ICTR T. Ch. III 22.6.2009 para. 514.
167 *Media* Appeal paras. 693, 703. The ICTR has held that songs may suffice, *Bikindi* ICTR T. Ch. 2.12.2008 para. 389.
168 See, e.g *Media* Appeal paras. 704–15. William Schabas, 'Mugesera v. Minister of Citizenship and Immigration' (1999) 93 *AJIL* 529.
169 *Media* para. 1012.

15.6   Planning, preparation, attempt and conspiracy

15.6.1   Planning and preparing

Planning or preparing a war of aggression was criminalized in Article 6(a) of the Nuremberg IMT Statute and Article 5(a) of the Tokyo IMT Statute. Both also contained a clause that read 'leaders, organisers, instigators and accomplices participating in the formulation of a common plan ... to commit any of the foregoing crimes are responsible for all acts performed by any person in execution of such a plan'. Both tribunals read this as being limited to crimes against peace, however.

Such crimes are usually considered at the national level to amount to inchoate (incomplete) crimes, that are punishable without proof that the crime itself was completed. Article 7(1) of the ICTY Statute, as well as Article 6(1) of the ICTR Statute and Article 6(1) of the SCSL Statute all criminalize those who 'aided and abetted in the planning, preparation or execution' of an international crime. As aiding and abetting is a secondary form of liability, which requires a primary crime to be committed or attempted to attach to, these documents imply that planning is a primary offence, which in turn implies that planning and preparation are in themselves enough, and do not require that the crimes planned or prepared actually occurred.

For planning,[170] however, the ICTY Appeals Chamber has held differently, stating that '[t]he *actus reus* of "planning" requires that one or more persons design the criminal conduct constituting one or more statutory crimes that are later perpetrated'.[171] A number of trial chamber decisions to the same effect, in particular from the ICTR, have been criticized as misunderstanding the nature of 'planning'.[172] Either way, the *mens rea* has been said to be fulfilled by 'a person who plans an act or omission with the awareness of the substantial likelihood that a crime will be committed in the execution of that plan ... Planning with such awareness has to be regarded as accepting that crime.'[173] The ICC Statute does not have any provision similar to Article 7(1) of the ICTY Statute in relation to planning or preparing.

15.6.2   Attempt

The statutes of all the international criminal tribunals prior to the ICC Statute are silent on attempt liability other than for genocide.[174] The ICTY prosecutor has shown an unwillingness to prosecute attempts to commit international crimes, preferring to conceptualize

---

170   There is no modern jurisprudence on 'preparing' as a separate crime.
171   *Kordić and Čerkez* Appeal para. 26.
172   Mettraux, *International Crimes*, 279–80.
173   *Kordić and Čerkez* Appeal para. 31. The Trial Chamber in *Brđanin* took a narrower view at para. 357.
174   Art. 4(d) ICTY Statute; Art. 2(d) ICTR Statute.

them under other headings of liability (for example 'violence to life and person' or 'inhumane acts' rather than attempted murder).[175] However, there is sufficient evidence from the post-Second World War era to show such a form of liability exists in custom.[176]

The ICC Statute expressly criminalizes attempts to commit international crimes in Article 25(3)(f): a person is liable who:

> Attempts to commit such a crime by taking action that commences its execution by means of a substantial step, but the crime does not occur because of circumstances independent of the person's intentions. However a person who abandons the effort to commit the crime or otherwise prevents the completion of the crime shall not be liable if that person completely and voluntarily gave up the criminal purpose.

This in many ways makes up for the absence of a provision on planning or preparation, although if those types of liability are in fact inchoate crimes, Article 25(3)(f) may be narrower than them.[177] The formulation at Rome was a compromise, making it difficult to interpret precisely when a person has 'commence[d] its execution by a substantial step'.[178] As can be seen, the ICC Statute recognizes that if an attempt is abandoned, or a person prevents the crime, they will not be liable for attempt. However, if they abandon their role in the crime, and it is completed by others, it is possible that liability for aiding and abetting or participating in a joint criminal enterprise might still arise.

15.6.3 Conspiracy

Conspiracy, in the sense of the inchoate crime of agreeing to commit a crime, which does not have to be proved to occur, was applied by the Nuremberg and Tokyo Tribunals to crimes against peace, not war crimes or crimes against humanity.[179] The reason for that limitation was that there was considerable disagreement between the judges on whether or not such a principle existed in international law.[180] This also led the tribunal to take a sensibly narrow view of conspiracy, stating that '[t]he conspiracy must be clearly outlined in its criminal purpose. It must not be too far removed from the time of decision and of action.'[181] The Tokyo IMT, although also limiting its decision to conspiracies to commit crimes against peace, took a very broad interpretation of the concept of conspiracy.[182] Under current

---

175 See *Vasiljević* ICTY T. Ch. I 29.11.2002. See Antonio Cassese, 'Black Letter Lawyering vs Constructive Interpretation: The Vasiljević Case' (2004) 2 *JICJ* 265, 266–71, *contra* Mettraux, *International Crimes*, 293–5.
176 Cassese, 'Black Letter Lawyering'. See also Commentary, XV LRTWC at 89.
177 See Cryer, 'General Principles', 253.
178 Eser, 'Individual Criminal Responsibility', 811–13; Ambos, 'Article 25', 488–9.
179 'Nuremberg IMT: Judgment' (1947) 41 *AJIL* 172, 224.
180 See Telford Taylor, *The Anatomy of the Nuremberg Trials* (London, 1993) 36, 50.
181 'Nuremberg IMT: Judgment' (1947) 41 *AJIL* 172, 222. It must also be noted that the tribunal was dealing with conspiracies which had manifested themselves in later crimes, so was not, strictly speaking, dealing with inchoate conspiracies.
182 See section 6.4.3.

international law, conspiracy does not exist as a form of liability for war crimes or crimes against humanity.[183] Conspiracy to commit genocide, however, is a separate charge. It is included in Article 3(b) of the Genocide Convention, and it is clear that the type of conspiracy included is of the inchoate type.[184] The same crime is included in Article 4(3)(b) of the ICTY Statute and Article 2(3)(b) of the ICTR Statute. It is not, however, present in the ICC Statute. According to the ICTR, conspiracy to commit genocide is '[a]n agreement between two or more persons to commit the crime of genocide'.[185] It has also determined, rightly, that 'With respect to the *mens rea* of the crime of conspiracy to commit genocide, the Chamber notes that it rests on the concerted intent to commit genocide, that is to destroy, in whole or in part, a national, ethnic, racial or religious group, as such. Thus . . . the requisite intent for the crime of conspiracy to commit genocide is, *ipso facto*, the intent required for the crime of genocide, that is the *dolus specialis* of genocide.'[186]

15.7 Mental elements

It is an important aspect of criminal law that a person must have some form of culpability for his or her conduct. This is usually shown through his or her state of mind when he or she acted (or failed to act). There are various forms of mental element that apply to international crimes, from intention, through recklessness to (arguably) negligence.[187] Different offences, and different forms of liability require different forms of *mens rea*. Hence, for the most part, they are thus dealt with when dealing with the specific offence or principle of liability.

There is little in the general parts of the statutes of the ICTY, ICTR and SCSL that deals with *mens rea*. Thus it has had to be dealt with at the level of case law.[188] Perhaps the broadest statement that has been made was that by the Trial chamber in *Blaškić* that, in relation to grave breaches, 'the *mens rea* . . . includes both guilty intent and recklessness which may be likened to serious criminal negligence'.[189] This is too broad. Criminal negligence is only possibly at issue in relation to superior responsibility,[190] and in this

---

183 *Hamdan* v. *Rumsfeld*, 126 S Ct 2749 (2006), 2777–85. The Supreme Court in this case was clear that it was discussing conspiracies that are offences on their own, not forms of participation in completed crimes, see 2785, n. 40.

184 Schabas, *Genocide*, 260. *Kajelijeli* ICTR T. Ch. II 1.12.2003 para. 788; *Musema* ICTR T. Ch. I 27.1.2000 para. 187.

185 *Musema* ICTR T. Ch. I 27.1.2000 para. 189; *Kajelijeli* ICTR T. Ch. II 1.12.2003 para. 787.

186 *Musema* ICTR T. Ch. I 27.1.2000 para. 192.

187 Or in analogous, but not identical civil law terms, *dolus directus, dolus eventualis* and *culpa*.

188 See William Schabas, *The UN International Criminal Tribunals: The former Yugoslavia, Rwanda and Sierra Leone* (Cambridge, 2006) 292–3.

189 *Blaškić* ICTY T. Ch. I 3.3.2000 para. 152; see also *Kayishema and Ruzindana* ICTR T. Ch. II 21.5.1999 para. 146.

190 The Secretary-General described superior responsibility as 'imputed responsibility or criminal negligence': Report of the Secretary-General Pursuant to Paragraph 2 of Security Council Resolution 808(1993), UN Doc. S/25704, para. 56.

regard, the ICTR Appeals Chamber has said (controversially) that '[r]eferences to "negligence" in the context of superior responsibility are likely to lead to confusion of thought'.[191]

Outside the crime of genocide, which has a very specific *mens rea*, the ICTY and ICTR have been surprisingly reticent in setting out the ingredients of intent. Discussions in the case law are also sometimes confused by the use of the term 'intent' not as a term of art, but to refer to *mens rea* generally.[192] The Appeals chamber in *Čelebići* asserted that an 'intentional act or omission ... is an act which, judged objectively, is deliberate and not accidental',[193] but this is decidedly unclear, as there are considerable differences between that which is 'deliberate' and that which is 'not accidental'. Intention has been used to mean only deliberate acts,[194] but the case law on point is inconclusive, not least because as the Tribunals have tended to accept that recklessness suffices for many crimes, they have not drawn the boundaries between intention and recklessness clearly.[195]

When discussing its concept of recklessness (or perhaps *mens rea* in general) the Appeals Chamber in *Blaškić* set down what, although framed in the context of ordering crimes, might be the general standard for recklessness (or *mens rea*) in the ICTY:

> a person who orders an act or omission with the awareness of the substantial likelihood that a crime will be committed in the execution of that order, has the requisite *mens rea* for establishing liability under Article 7(1) pursuant to ordering. Ordering with such awareness has to be regarded as accepting that crime.[196]

It has been argued that the default standard for *mens rea* in the tribunals appears to be recklessness.[197] Whether or not this is correct, the ICC Statute takes a different track, setting intention as the default mental element to be applied. Article 30 of the ICC Statute reads:

1. Unless otherwise provided, a person shall be criminally responsible and liable for punishment for a crime within the jurisdiction of the Court only if the material elements are committed with intent and knowledge.
2. For the purposes of this article, a person has intent where:
   (a) In relation to conduct, that person means to engage in the conduct;
   (b) In relation to a consequence, that person means to cause that consequence or is aware that it will occur in the ordinary course of events.

---

191 *Bagilishema* Appeal para. 35. But see *Orić* ICTY T. Ch. II 30.6.2006 para. 324.
192 *Blaškić* ICTY T. Ch. I 3.3.2000 para. 474. The confusion probably arises out of the difference between the meaning of 'intention' in civil and common law countries. In the former it is a synonym for *mens rea*, in common law countries, it is a specific type of *mens rea*.
193 *Čelebići* ICTY A. Ch. 20.2.2001 para. 426.
194 *Aleksovski* ICTY T. 25.6.1999 para. 56.
195 Although it is clear that neither concept requires motive: see van Sliedregt, *Criminal Responsibility*, 48–9.
196 *Blaškić* Appeal para. 42.
197 Werle, *Principles*, 104–5, although see 113–6. See also van Sliedregt, *Criminal Responsibility*, 48–50.

3. For the purposes of this Article, 'knowledge' means awareness that a circumstance exists or a consequence will occur in the ordinary course of events. 'Know' and 'knowingly' shall be construed accordingly.

Article 30 applies absent specific provision elsewhere.[198] The drafters of the ICC Statute appeared to exclude any lesser mental element, unless the statute (or the elements of crimes) expressly provided for one (such as in Article 28). States Parties at Rome appeared to minimize the chance that the ICC could go outside the Statute and Elements of Crimes to determine, for example, that customary international law set a lower standard than the Statute or the Elements of Crimes. It has been suggested that it could,[199] but this seems unlikely.[200] The early practice of the ICC has been to accept lower *mens rea* standards set out in the Elements of Crimes, but not to look outside the Statute or Elements.[201]

Article 30 sets the mental-element bar high. By requiring intention, in the clear subjectivist sense, the ICC Statute adopts, as a default, a highly culpable form of mental element for all elements of the offence. This may have a specific effect in relation to the offences for which customary international law and many domestic systems differ as to *mens rea* from the provision in the ICC Statute and the ICC Elements of Crimes. An example is in relation to Article 8(2)(b)(i), attacking of civilians requires a higher *mens rea* (intention) than that required by customary international law, for which recklessness suffices.[202] One pre-Trial Chamber has attempted to use the jurisprudence of the ad hoc Tribunals to read subjective recklessness (*dolus eventualis*) into Article 30.[203] Ultimately the wording of Article 30 and the history of its drafting cannot support that interpretation, as a different Pre-Trial Chamber accepted in the *Bemba Gombo* confirmation of charges decision.[204] As that Chamber opined:

> the words 'will occur' ... [in Article 30] ... read together with the phrase 'in the ordinary course of events', clearly indicate that the required standard of occurrence is close to certainty. In this regard, the Chamber defines this standard as 'virtual certainty' or

---

198 As will be seen, precisely where is not necessarily clear, see also Roger Clark, 'The Mental Element in International Criminal Law: The ICC Statute of the International Criminal Court and the Elements of Offences' (2002) 12 *CLF* 291, 321. On Art. 30's default position see also ICC Elements of Crimes, general introduction, para. 2.

199 Knut Dörmann, 'War Crimes in the Elements of Crimes' in Horst Fischer, Claus Kreß and Sascha Lüder (eds.), *International and National Prosecution of Crimes Under International Law: Current Developments* (Berlin, 2001) 95, 98.

200 Maria Kelt and Hermann von Hebel, 'General Principles of Criminal Law and Elements of Crimes' in Lee, *Elements and Rules*, 29–30; Werle, *Principles*, 113–6.

201 E.g. *Lubanga Dyilo* paras. 356–9; *Bemba Gombo* paras. 136, 353.

202 See William Fenrick, 'A First Attempt to Adjudicate Conduct of Hostilities Offences: Comments on Aspects of the ICTY Trial Decision in the Prosecutor v. Tihomir Blaškić' (2000) 13 *LJIL* 931, 936–43.

203 *Lubanga Dyilo* paras. 350–5.

204 *Bemba Gombo* paras. 352–69.

'practical certainty', namely that the consequence will follow, barring an unforeseen or unexpected intervention that prevent its occurrence.[205]

The requirement that the defendant is 'aware ... in relation to a consequence that it will occur in the ordinary course of events' seems to leave a lacuna. Awareness that something will occur in the ordinary course of events implies that a belief that this is the case must be borne out for a person to fall under Article 30. At the very least, by the time the consequence has manifested itself, there seems to be no necessary reason for this. The culpability of the state of mind is essentially the same.[206]

15.8 Command/superior responsibility[207]

Command responsibility[208] is an inculpatory doctrine specific to international criminal law, which does not have a concomitant general principle of liability at the domestic level.[209] It is a broad form of liability, which is justified by the privileges, honours and responsibilities that command entails.[210] Command responsibility as a whole has a lengthy history, going back roughly 2,500 years to the China of Sun Tzu.[211] The responsibility of a commander extends far beyond criminal liability, and disciplinary or administrative action can be pursued even if there is no criminal liability.[212] Discussion here, however, is specifically on the criminal responsibility of a commander for offences committed by his or her subordinates. An early and clear example of such liability, which is remarkably similar to modern command responsibility, may be found in the French Code instituted by Charles VII of Orleans in 1439, which stated:

> The King orders that each captain or lieutenant be held responsible for the abuses, ills and offences committed by members of his company, and that as soon as he receives any complaint concerning any such misdeed or abuse, he bring the offender to justice so that the said offender be punished in a manner commensurate with his offence, according to these ordinances. If he fails to do so or covers up the misdeed or delays taking action, or if, because of his negligence or otherwise, the offender escapes and thus evades punishment, the captain shall be deemed responsible for the offence as if

---

205 *Ibid.*, para. 362.
206 David Ormerod, *Smith and Hogan: Criminal Law*, 12th edn (Oxford, 2008) 99.
207 See generally, Guénaël Mettraux, *The Law of Command Responsibility* (Oxford, 2009); and van Sliedregt, *Criminal Responsibility*, chs. 3–5.
208 The terms 'command responsibility' and 'superior responsibility' are functionally synonymous, although the former is sometimes taken as limited to military personnel. It need not be.
209 Although there are some analogues in limited areas of domestic criminal law.
210 See, e.g. *Hadžihasanović, Alagić and Kubura* ICTY A. Ch. 16.7.2003 (hereinafter *Hadžihasanović* Appeal) para. 14. See also Cryer, 'General Principles', 260–1.
211 See W. Hays Parks, 'Command Responsibility for War Crimes' (1973) 62 *Military Law Review* 1, 1–20.
212 *Bagilishema* ICTR A. Ch. 2.7.2002 para. 36.

he had committed it himself and be punished in the same way as the offender would have been.[213]

The foundation of the modern law of command responsibility may be found in the Report of the Commission of Inquiry on the Responsibility of the Authors of the War in 1919, which opined that superiors could be held responsible for crimes of their subordinates where they knew of them but did not intervene.[214] The first major modern case on the principle, though, was the *Yamashita* case.[215] The case has proved controversial and many of its factual findings, and the fairness of the trial, have been subject to considerable critique.[216] The Nuremberg IMT did not deal with command responsibility in this sense in any real way. The Tokyo IMT, however, took a very broad interpretation of the principle, which at times appeared to shade into joint criminal enterprise liability.[217] Command responsibility was included in military manuals after the Second World War,[218] but made its first clear appearance in a treaty in 1977, in Articles 86 and 87 of Additional Protocol I.

In a provision that is similar to, but not quite the same as the provisions of Additional Protocol I, Article 7(3)[219] of the ICTY Statute reads:

> The fact that [crimes were] committed by a subordinate does not relieve his superior of criminal responsibility if he knew or had reason to know that the subordinate was about to commit such acts or had done so and the superior failed to take the necessary and reasonable measures to prevent such acts or to punish the perpetrators thereof.[220]

Article 28 of the ICC Statute is more detailed, reading:

> In addition to other grounds of criminal responsibility under this Statute for crimes within the jurisdiction of the Court:

---

213 Theodor Meron, *Henry's Laws and Shakespeare's Wars* (Oxford, 1993) 149, n. 40.

214 'Report of the Commission on the Responsibility of the Authors of the War' (1920) 14 *AJIL* 95, 121.

215 *US* v. *Yamashita* (1945) 327 US 1.

216 See, e.g. M. Cherif Bassiouni, *Crimes Against Humanity in International Criminal Law*, 2nd edn (The Hague, 1999) 427–31; Anne-Marie Prevost, 'Race and War Crimes: the 1945 War Crimes Trial of General Tomoyuki Yamashita' (1992) 14 *Human Rights Quarterly* 303, 318–19; Richard Lael, *The Yamashita Precedent: War Crimes and Command Responsibility* (Wilmington, 1982), Mettraux, *Law of Command*, 5ff.

217 Tokyo IMT Judgment, 48,442–7. This engendered dissents from Judges Bernard (12–18), Röling (Dissenting Opinion of the Member from the Netherlands at 54–61) and Pal (Dissenting Opinion of the Member from India at 1027–225). See Neil Boister and Robert Cryer, *The Tokyo International Military Tribunal: A Reappraisal* (Oxford, 2008) 205–36.

218 US Department of the Army Field Manual, The Law of Land Warfare, 1956 (FM 27–10) (as revised) para. 501. See also the 1958 British Manual, The Law of War on Land, being Part III of the Manual of Military Law (London, 1958) para. 631.

219 Which has been taken as applying both to international and non-international armed conflicts as a matter of customary international law: *Hadžihasanović* Appeal paras. 10–31.

220 Arts. 6(1) of the ICTR Statute and 6(1) of the SCSL Statute are essentially the same. The latter, post-dating the ICC Statute, may be a rejection of aspects of the ICC Statute's definition of the concept.

(a) A military commander or person effectively acting as a military commander shall be criminally responsible for crimes within the jurisdiction of the Court committed by forces under his or her effective command and control, or effective authority and control as the case may be, as a result of his or her failure to exercise control properly over such forces, where:

  (i) That military commander or person either knew or, owing to the circumstances at the time, should have known that the forces were committing or about to commit such crimes; and

  (ii) That military commander or person failed to take all necessary and reasonable measures within his or her power to prevent or repress their commission or to submit the matter to the competent authorities for investigation and prosecution.

(b) With respect to superior and subordinate relationships not described in paragraph (a), a superior shall be criminally responsible for crimes within the jurisdiction of the Court committed by subordinates under his or her effective authority and control, as a result of his or her failure to exercise control properly over such subordinates, where:

  (i) The superior either knew, or consciously disregarded information which clearly indicated, that the subordinates were committing or about to commit such crimes;

  (ii) The crimes concerned activities that were within the effective responsibility and control of the superior; and

  (iii) The superior failed to take all necessary and reasonable measures within his or her power to prevent or repress their commission or to submit the matter to the competent authorities for investigation and prosecution.

The Trial Chamber in *Čelebići* helpfully elaborated the requirements of command responsibility under customary law;[221] first, a superior/subordinate relationship; second, the 'mental element' and third, a failure to take reasonable measures to prevent or punish violations of international criminal law.[222] This trio has been adopted by the UN tribunals since and is a helpful list of the requirements.[223] To that, the ICC Statute has added another requirement: causation.[224]

---

221 The taxonomy, though, finds a basis in Judge Röling's Opinion in the Tokyo IMT, 59–61.

222 *Delalić, Mučić, Delić and Landžo* ICTY T. Ch. II 16.11.1998 para. 344; *Blaškić* ICTY T. Ch. I 3.3.2000 para. 294; *Orić* ICTY T. Ch. II 30.6.2006 para. 294 added that crimes were committed by those other than the superior. This is true, but does not really add to the specifics of the principle of liability. The Chamber added it only as it had been challenged by the defence, *Orić ibid.*, para. 295. The Chamber asserted that all forms of participation in Art. 7(1) of the ICTY Statute sufficed to fulfil this criterion, paras. 295–306, 328. This is probably correct, as long as it is remembered that the mental element for superior responsibility must still be fulfilled, Werle, *Principles*, 136–7.

223 See, e.g. *Aleksovski* ICTY T. 25.6.1999 paras. 69–71; *Kayishema and Ruzindana* ICTR T. Ch. II 21.5.1999 para. 209; *Blaškić* ICTY T. Ch. I 3.3.2000 para. 294.

224 Werle, *Principles*, 136–7.

15.8.1 Superior/subordinate relationship

Where there are the clear formal chains of command that characterize modern well-disciplined armies, this criterion may appear simple to apply. However, modern conflicts are not always fought on this basis and by such forces. Therefore, and understandably, the Appeals Chamber in *Čelebići* based itself on a test of 'effective control', defined as 'a material ability to prevent or punish criminal conduct'.[225] Substantial influence is not enough;[226] the ICC agrees with this.[227] It is required that 'the accused has to be, by virtue of his position, senior in some sort of formal or informal hierarchy to the perpetrator'.[228] The *de jure* position of the superior is not determinative of this, it is largely factual ability to prevent and punish that counts.[229] Equally, a *de jure* position may be evidence of effective control.[230] Issuance of orders may also be good evidence, but if they are not obeyed, this will count the other way.[231] Other factors which are probative in this regard include the capacity to alter command structures and promote or remove people, and the ability to require people to engage or withdraw from hostilities.[232] The issue must be decided on a case-by-case basis,[233] and it ought to be noted that even the fact that it is necessary to use force to enforce authority does not automatically mean that a person does not have effective control over subordinates.[234]

---

225 *Delalić, Mučić, Delić and Landžo* ICTY A. Ch. 20.2.2001 (hereinafter *Čelebići* Appeal) para. 256. See generally Mettraux, *Law of Command*, ch. 9.
226 *Ibid.*, para. 266.
227 *Bemba Gombo* paras. 414–6.
228 *Halilović* ICTY A. Ch. 16.10.2007 para. 59. Otherwise, as the Chamber said, police officers could be considered superiors to all in their jurisdiction owing to their ability to prevent and set punishment in motion, see also para. 210. There may be an exception for occupation commanders, who do not have to have this type of relationship, see Mettraux, *Command Responsibility*, 153.
229 *Čelebići* Appeal paras. 186–98; *Halilović* ICTY A. Ch. 16.10.2007 (hereinafter *Halilović* Appeal) para. 59; *Kajelijeli* Appeal ICTR A. Ch. 23.5.2005 para. 85. See also, e.g. *US* v. *List et al.* (The Hostages Case) VIII LRTWC 89; Tokyo IMT Judgment, at 48, 820.
230 *Čelebići* Appeal para. 197; *Hadžihasanović* ICTY A. Ch. 22.4.2008 (hereinafter *Hadžihasanović* 2008 Appeal) para. 21. There is no presumption, however, that *de jure* positions give rise to effective control, *Orić* ICTY A. Ch. 3.7.2008 (hereinafter *Orić* Appeal) paras. 91–2.
231 *Blaškić* Appeal paras. 69 and 399. See also *Strugar* ICTY A. Ch. 17.6.2008 (hereinafter *Strugar* Appeal) para. 254; *Halilović* Appeal para. 207. As noted by Mettraux, *Command Responsibility*, at 176–8, the nature and type of order is relevant, as is whether the person signing the order is, in essence, just passing it on for his or her superiors. Orders to the person may be relevant evidence of their material abilities, but this depends on the interpretation of the order: *Halilović* Appeal para. 193.
232 *Bemba Gombo* para. 417. See also Mettraux, *Command Responsibility*, 164–70.
233 This is not always simple, see e.g. *Orić* Appeal, paras. 28ff. In addition, a failure to initiate investigations, for example, may be because there is no ability to do so, or because a person has failed to take the necessary and reasonable steps international criminal law requires, see *Halilović* Appeal paras. 175–80, 182.
234 *Hadžihasanović* 2008 Appeal para. 228.

It is clear that superior responsibility also attaches to civilian superiors.[235] The standard of control is again 'effective control', 'in the sense that he exercised a degree of control over ... [subordinates] ... which is similar to the degree of control of military commanders'.[236] Also, as Article 28(b)(ii) of the ICC Statute shows, the crimes must fall within the area of responsibility of a civilian commander. The ICTY has on occasion been criticized for taking a narrow approach to effective control, against a background of fluid levels of control and multiple lines of command.[237]

The ICTY Appeals Chamber, in its split 3:2 decision in the *Hadžihasanović* Appeal, determined that for superior responsibility to arise the crimes must be committed whilst the superior had effective control over the offenders.[238] This has particular relevance to failure to punish liability. The case has generated considerable debate.[239] The dissenting judges in particular were very critical of the majority, and asserted that the decision was wrong in law.[240] One judge also asserted that it left a lacuna in protection.[241] In relation to this last point it is relevant that the primary authors of the crimes are still responsible for them. The controversy has continued in the ICTY, with Trial Chambers expressly or implicitly criticizing the majority finding as a matter of law.[242] In the *Orić* Appeal, the Prosecutor asked the Appeals Chamber to revisit the matter. In spite of a bare majority of the judges taking the view that *Hadžihasanović* was wrong, the decision was left undisturbed, as it did not affect the outcome of the case, and Judge Shahabuddeen (a dissenter in the earlier case) preferred to wait for a larger majority to overturn it.[243] This leaves the customary law on point uncertain.[244] The ICC Statute, by requiring that offences occur as 'a result of ... [a superior's] ... failure to exercise control properly over such forces' leads to the same result as the majority decision in

---

235 *Bagilishema* Appeal para. 52; *Orić* ICTY T. Ch. II 30.6.2006 para. 308. This is also provided for expressly in Art. 28(b) of the ICC Statute. See also Tokyo IMT Judgment, 48,442–7; *US* v. *Karl Brandt et al.* (The Doctors' Trial) IV LRTWC 91–3.

236 *Bagilishema* Appeal para. 52, overturning the Trial Chamber on point. As the Appeals Chamber noted *ibid.*, the way authority is exercised may not be the same.

237 Osiel, 'The Banality of Good', 1774–9. The ICTY has admitted the fluidity of such situations: *Orić* ICTY T. Ch. II 30.6.2006 paras. 309–10.

238 *Hadžihasanović* Appeal paras. 37–56.

239 See Mettraux, *International Crimes*, 301, *contra* Christopher Greenwood, 'Command Responsibility and the *Hadžihasanović* Decision' (2004) 2 *JICJ* 598. One ICTY Trial Chamber has seemingly doubted it: *Orić* ICTY T. Ch. II 30.6.2006 para. 335.

240 *Hadžihasanović* Appeal, Partially Dissenting Opinion of Judge Shahabuddeen, paras. 1–40, Separate and Partially Dissenting Opinion of Judge Hunt, paras. 6–34. Part of the disagreement related to the way in which the nature of superior responsibility is seen, see section 15.8.5.

241 *Hadžihasanović* Appeal, Judge Hunt, para. 22.

242 *Orić* ICTY T. Ch. II 30.6.2006 para. 335; *Hadžihasanović* ICTY T. Ch. 15.3.2006 para. 199.

243 *Orić* Appeal, paras. 166–8, Declaration of Judge Shahabuddeen, paras. 2–15.

244 Mettraux, *Command Responsibility*, 192.

Hadžihasanović,[245] but the customary nature or otherwise of this provision was divisive in that case.[246]

15.8.2 *Mental element*

The mental element of command responsibility is one of its most controversial aspects.[247] This is in part because of the broad ambit of this type of liability, which accrues often by omission. The discord is not helped by the opaque nature of the finding in the seminal *Yamashita* case, and the fair trial issues that still cast a pall over that proceeding. The fact that the various documents dealing with the matter use different terminology does not help. The ICTY has been at great pains to explain that superior responsibility is not a form of strict liability.[248] The leading authority in the ICTY determined that:

> [A superior] . . . may possess the *mens rea* for command responsibility where: (1) he had actual knowledge, established through direct or circumstantial evidence, that his subordinates were committing or about to commit crimes . . . or (2) where he had in his possession information of a nature, which at the least, would put him on notice of the risk of such offences by indicating the need for additional investigation in order to ascertain whether such crimes were committed or were about to be committed by his subordinates.[249]

It is accepted that actual knowledge can be determined by a direct proof, or with reference to circumstantial evidence.[250] Relevant circumstantial evidence for this purpose includes 'the number, type and scope of illegal acts, time during which the illegal acts occurred, number and types of troops and logistics involved, geographical location, whether the occurrence of the acts is widespread, tactical tempo of operations, *modus operandi* of similar illegal acts, officers and staff involved, and location of the commander at the time'.[251] What the superior knew or had reason to know must be crimes, and the type of crimes committed (or that 'might'[252] be about to be committed) by their subordinates; it is not sufficient that they are

---

245 *Bemba Gombo* para. 424.

246 *Hadžihasanović* Appeal para. 53, Judge Shahabuddeen, para. 38, Judge Hunt paras. 29–33.

247 See generally Mettraux, *Command Responsibility*, ch. 10.

248 *Čelebići* Appeal paras. 226 and 239.

249 *Ibid.*, paras. 223 and 241. 'Commission' in this regard includes the various forms of liability, *Blagojević and Jokić* ICTY A. Ch. 9.5.2007 para. 280, but a finding on the liability of a subordinate on some form of responsibility seems necessary, *Orić* Appeal, paras 47–8.

250 *Blaškić* ICTY T. Ch. I 3.3.2000 para. 307; *Orić* ICTY T. Ch. II 30.6.2006 para. 319–20; *Halilović* ICTY T. Ch. 16.11.2005 para. 66.

251 *Čelebići* Appeal para. 238; *Limaj* ICTY T. Ch. II 30.11.2005 para. 524; *Halilović* ICTY T. Ch. 16.11.2005 para. 66. Prior crimes may be, although are not necessarily, sufficiently alarming to infer that a person had 'reason to know' of later offences, *Hadžihasanović* 2008 Appeal para. 261. See also the list in Mettraux, *Command Responsibility*, 214–5.

252 *Strugar* Appeal para. 304.

aware of some general form of criminality.[253] Such information can be relevant for proof that the superior had reason to know of offences;[254] they do not need to know the precise identities of the perpetrators.[255]

The Trial Chamber in the *Blaškić* case, in an opinion which canvassed some jurisprudence not discussed in the *Čelebići* Appeal, took a broader approach to the 'had reason to know standard' than the latter decision, and came to the conclusion that:

> if a commander has exercised due diligence in the fulfilment of his duties yet lacks knowledge that crimes are about to be or have been committed, such lack of knowledge cannot be held against him. However, taking into account his particular position of command and the circumstances prevailing at the time, such ignorance cannot be a defence where the absence of knowledge is the result of negligence in the discharge of his duties: this commander had reason to know within the meaning of the Statute.[256]

Despite considerable academic support,[257] this standard has not prevailed in the ICTY,[258] and any talk of negligence has been disavowed by the Appeals Chamber.[259] The *Čelebići* standard has become the accepted one in the ad hoc Tribunals for both military and civilian superiors.[260]

The ICC Statute, however, sets a different standard for military and non-military superiors, the standard for the former being that the superior 'knew or, owing to the circumstances at the time, should have known that the forces were committing or about to commit such crimes'. For civilians, it is that the civilian superior 'knew, or consciously disregarded information which clearly indicated, that the subordinates were committing or about to commit such crimes'. Commentators have questioned whether this distinction is

---

253 *Krnojelac* ICTY A. Ch. 17.9.2003 para. 155; *Orić* Appeal paras. 169–74; and Mettraux, *Command Responsibility*, 200–2.

254 *Strugar* Appeal para. 301.

255 *Blagojević and Jokić* ICTY A. Ch. 9.5.2007 para. 287. Their existence must be proved, however, *Orić* Appeal para. 35.

256 *Blaškić* ICTY T. Ch. I 3.3.2000 para. 332.

257 Monica Feria Tinta, 'Commanders on Trial: The Blaškić Case and the Doctrine of Command Responsibility Under International Law' (2000) 47 *Netherlands International Law Review* 293, 314–22; Yoram Dinstein, *The Conduct of Hostilities Under the Law of International Armed Conflict* (Cambridge, 2004) 24; Robert Kolb, 'The Jurisprudence of the Yugoslav and Rwandan Criminal Tribunals on Their Jurisdiction and on International Crimes' (2000) 69 *BYBIL* 259, 301. Support is not universal though, see Bing Bing Jia, 'The Doctrine of Command Responsibility: Current Problems' (2000) 3 *YIHL* 131, 155–60.

258 *Blaškić* Appeal paras. 58–64.

259 *Bagilishema* Appeal paras. 34–5; *Blaškić* Appeal para. 63; *Halilović* ICTY T. Ch. 16.11.2005 para. 71.

260 *Bagilishema* Appeal paras. 26–37. The ICTR had, on occasion, applied the ICC Statute standard: *Kayishema and Ruzindana* ICTR T. Ch. II 21.5.1999 paras. 227–8, and had been criticized for it. See Alexander Zahar, 'Command Responsibility of Civilian Superiors for Genocide' (2001) 14 *LJIL* 591.

consistent with customary law,[261] and the ICTR Appeals Chamber has at least implicitly rejected the ICC Statute *mens rea* for civilian superiors.[262]

It has been argued that the Statutes of the ad hoc Tribunals and the ICC Statute are broadly consistent on the mental element for military superiors.[263] However, the ICC has adopted a broad approach regarding the *mens rea* for military commanders in the Rome Statute, asserting that 'should have known' is a negligence standard,[264] and that failure to seek out information could lead to liability.[265] In doing so the Pre-Trial Chamber expressly departed from the standards set elsewhere:

> The Chamber is mindful of the fact that the 'had reason to know' criterion embodied in the statutes of the ICTR, ICTY and SCSL sets a different standard to the 'should have known' standard under article 28 (a) of the Statute. However, despite such a difference, which the Chamber does not deem necessary to address in the present decision, the criteria or indicia developed by the ad hoc tribunals to meet the standard of 'had reason to know' may also be useful when applying the 'should have known' requirement.[266]

In relation to civilians, however, the ICC Statute clearly sets a higher *mens rea* standard than exists for military superiors and civilian superiors in customary law.[267]

15.8.3 Failure to take measures

The final link in the chain of liability under customary law is the failure or refusal to take 'necessary and reasonable measures' to prevent or punish the offences the superior knew or culpably ought to have known of. It is important to emphasize in this regard that liability may accrue to a superior for a failure to prevent or a failure to punish those crimes. The two types of liability are separate.[268] There is no necessity that a person knew or should have known of the offences before they occurred for failure to punish liability to arise. Similarly, if a superior knew or should have known of impending offences before they occurred, it is no defence to a charge of failing to take adequate measures to suppress them that he chose to

---

261 See Greg Vetter, 'Command Responsibility of Non-Military Superiors in the International Criminal Court (ICC)' (2000) 25 *Yale Journal of International Law* 89; van Sliedregt, *Criminal Responsibility*, 191–2; Robert Cryer, *Prosecuting International Crimes: Selectivity and the International Criminal Law Regime* (Cambridge, 2005) 321–3.

262 *Bagilishema* Appeal paras. 26–37.

263 See Charles Garraway, 'Command Responsibility: Victor's Justice or Just Deserts?' in Richard Burchill, Nigel White and Justin Morris (eds.), *International Conflict and Security Law: Essays in Memory of Hilaire McCoubrey* (Cambridge, 2005) 68, 82–3.

264 *Bemba Gombo* para. 429.

265 *Ibid.*, paras. 432–3.

266 *Ibid.*, para. 434.

267 Mettraux, *Command Responsibility*, 194–6.

268 *Hadžihasanović* Appeal, Judge Shahabuddeen, paras. 35–6. See also *Blaškić* Appeal paras. 78–85; *Halilović* ICTY T. Ch. 16.11.2005 para. 94; *Orić* ICTY T. Ch. II 30.6.2006 paras. 325–6.

allow them to occur, then punished the perpetrators.[269] As has been said, 'a superior's failure to prevent the commission of the crime by a subordinate, where he had the ability to do so, cannot simply be remedied by subsequently punishing the subordinate for the crime'.[270]

The measures which can be expected were explained by the ICTY Appeals Chamber in *Blaškić* as being those that:

> can be taken within the competence of a commander as evidenced by the degree of effective control he wielded over his subordinates ... What constitutes such measures is not a matter of substantive law but of evidence.[271]

Thus, the measures that can be expected to be taken depend on the precise nature of the control exercised by the superior. As the ICC Statute identifies, this can mean acts intended to prevent or punish where that is possible, and/or, where appropriate, submitting the matter to the appropriate prosecutorial organs.[272] What measures may be expected of a superior relates to what power the superior has, and this requires a contextual analysis.

An ICTY Trial Chamber in the *Orić* case gave some guidance on the yardsticks to be used for failure to prevent: (1) the measures 'depend on the degree of effective control over the conduct of subordinates at the time a superior is expected to act'; (2) measures must be taken to prevent planning of preparation of crimes, not simply their execution; (3) 'the more grievous and/or imminent the potential crimes of subordinates appear to be, the more attentive and quicker the superior is expected to react'; and (4) a superior is not 'obliged to do the impossible'.[273] Relevant actions are issuing special orders to prevent international crimes and ensuring their implementation, where there is information about the possible commission of crimes, investigating their possible commission, protesting and criticizing actions, initiating disciplinary measures and reporting to, and insisting on action from, higher authorities.[274] Turning a 'blind eye' to international crimes is clearly unreasonable in this respect.[275] Basing itself on ICTY jurisprudence, a Pre-Trial Chamber in the ICC has taken the view that the relevant measures include:

---

269 *Blaškić* ICTY T. Ch. I 3.3.2000 para. 336, *Strugar* ICTY T. Ch. II 31.1.2005 para. 373, *Halilović* ICTY T. Ch. 16.11.2005 para. 72. See also *Bemba Gombo* para. 436.

270 *Orić* ICTY T. Ch. II 30.6.2006 para. 326. In addition, to fail to take measures may be considered tacit acceptance of the crime: see *Halilović* ICTY T. Ch. 16.11.2005 para. 95.

271 *Blaškić* Appeal para. 72.

272 The ICTY has agreed, *Halilović* Appeal para. 182. Formal legal competence to take the necessary measures to prevent or repress the crime is not required: see *Čelebići* ICTY T. Ch. II 16.11.1998 para. 395; cf ILC 1996 Draft Code of Crimes 38–9.

273 *Orić* ICTY T. Ch. II 30.6.2006 para. 329.

274 *Ibid.*, para. 331. See also *Halilović* ICTY T. Ch. 16.11.2005 para. 74.

275 *Orić* ICTY T. Ch. II 30.6.2006 para. 331. The Chamber also mentions failing to give instructions not to commit international crimes owing to absences not mandated by 'other overriding obligations.' The Trial Chamber in *Halilović* adds 'failure to secure reports that military actions have been carried out in accordance with international law' and notes that '[t]he Tokyo Trial held that a superior's duty may not be discharged by the issuance of routine orders and that more active steps may be required' ICTY T. Ch. 16.11.2005 para. 89.

> (i) to ensure that superior's forces are adequately trained in international humanitarian law; (ii) to secure reports that military actions were carried out in accordance with international law; (iii) to issue orders aiming at bringing the relevant practices into accord with the rules of war; (iv) to take disciplinary measures to prevent the commission of atrocities by the troops under the superior's command.[276]

In relation to the duty to punish, the *Orić* Trial Chamber noted that:

> the duty to punish commences only if, and when, the commission of a crime by a subordinate can be reasonably suspected. Under these conditions, the superior has to order or execute appropriate sanctions or, if not yet able to do so, he or she must at least conduct an investigation and establish the facts in order to ensure that offenders under his or her effective control are brought to justice. The superior need not conduct the investigation or dispense the punishment in person, but he or she must at least ensure that the matter is investigated and transmit a report to the competent authorities for further investigation or sanction ... Since the duty to punish aims at preventing future crimes of subordinates, a superior's responsibility may also arise from his or her failure to create or sustain, amongst the persons under his or her control, an environment of discipline and respect for the law.[277]

There are certain circumstances in which the possibility that the duty to punish may be fulfilled by the use of disciplinary sanctions rather than criminal prosecutions 'cannot be excluded',[278] but for international crimes, these will be rare.[279]

15.8.4 Causation

The question of causation is an awkward one in relation to superior responsibility. This is, to a large extent, because superior responsibility is a form of liability for omission, to which causation is difficult, but not impossible, to apply.[280] This has caused considerable confusion as failure to prevent and failure to punish liability are entirely separate forms of liability. For the latter form of liability causation logically cannot be a requirement.[281] With respect to the former case the Trial Chamber in *Čelebići*, with which the Appeals Chamber in *Blaškić* agreed,[282] said that it:

> found no support for the existence of a requirement of proof of causation as a separate element of superior responsibility ... This is not to say that, conceptually, the principle of

---

276 *Bemba Gombo* para. 438.

277 *Orić* ICTY T. Ch. II 30.6.2006 para. 336; see also *Halilović* ICTY T. Ch. 16.11.2005 paras. 97–100.

278 *Hadžihasanović* 2008 Appeal para. 33.

279 *Ibid.*, paras. 149–55. As this case notes though, *ibid.*, if matters are referred on, it will not always be determinative that those authorities do not take sufficient action.

280 See generally Otto Triffterer, 'Causality, a Separate Element of the Doctrine of Superior Responsibility as Expressed in Article 28 of the Rome Statute?' (2002) 15 *LJIL* 179.

281 *Orić* ICTY T. Ch. II 30.6.2006 para. 338.

282 *Blaškić Appeal* paras. 75–7. See also *Halilović* ICTY T. Ch. 16.11.2005 para. 77.

causality is without application to the doctrine of command responsibility insofar as it relates to the responsibility of superiors for their failure to prevent the crimes of their subordinates. In fact, a recognition of a necessary causal nexus may be considered to be inherent in the requirement of crimes committed by subordinates and the superior's failure to take the measures within his powers to prevent them. In this situation, the superior may be considered to be causally linked to the offences, in that, but for his failure to fulfil his duty to act, the acts of his subordinates would not have been committed.[283]

In the *Orić* case the Trial Chamber was certain that there was no requirement of causation for either type of superior responsibility, as 'even with regard to the superior's failure to prevent, a requirement of causation would run counter to the very basis of this type of superior responsibility as criminal liability of omission'.[284] Whether or not this reflects the law, this appears to misunderstand the idea of negative causation, where an omission permits something to occur. Leaving a window open allows the rain in, even if it does not cause a change in the weather. Still, the Appeals Chamber in the 2008 *Hadžihasanović* Appeal reaffirmed its view that no causation requirement exists.[285]

The ICC Statute, by imposing the general requirement for liability that the crimes occur as a result of a failure to supervise subordinates, excludes liability where there is no form of causation, even in the expanded sense that a failure to prevent may facilitate commission. The first decision on point in the ICC posited a low threshold for causation, accepting that there is some connection between the failure to exercise control and the offences, but saying that it only applied to failure to prevent crimes,[286] and:

> There is no direct causal link that needs to be established between the superior's omission and the crime committed by his subordinates. Therefore, the Chamber considers that it is only necessary to prove that the commander's omission increased the risk of the commission of the crimes charged in order to hold him criminally responsible under article 28(a) of the Statute.[287]

15.8.5 The nature of superior responsibility

The nature of responsibility attributed to a superior under this principle of liability is controversial.[288] Some domestic legislation (including that of the UK, which follows

---

283 *Čelebići* ICTY T. Ch. II 16.11.1998 paras. 398–9.
284 *Orić* ICTY T. Ch. II 30.6.2006 para. 338.
285 *Hadžihasanović* 2008 Appeal para. 39.
286 *Ibid.*, para. 38. This was in part on the basis that the Chamber treated violation of the duty to control as being, in essence, the same as failure to take reasonable and necessary steps, as required in Art. 28(a)(ii), rather than a violation of the more general duty to control subordinates. The distinction was proposed in *Halilović* ICTY T. Ch. 16.11.2005 para. 80 but criticized by the Appeals Chamber in that case as it 'fosters confusion', *Halilović* Appeal para. 62. It might be more applicable in the ICC given the wording of Art. 28, but the Pre-Trial Chamber in *Bemba Gombo* did not take this route.
287 *Bemba Gombo* paras. 424–5.
288 See *Halilović* ICTY T. Ch. 16.11.2005 paras. 42–54.

Article 28 almost verbatim), criminalizes superior responsibility as a form of complicity.[289] Others believe,[290] and the Canadian and German legislation imply, that it is a separate offence of omission, on the grounds that it would be unfair to hold a person vicariously liable for the serious crimes of another based on a relaxed mental element. On this view, command responsibility is in essence a more serious form of a dereliction of duty charge.[291] There was confusion about the basis of liability in the Secretary-General's report relating to the ICTY Statute, which said that command responsibility is a form of 'imputed responsibility or criminal negligence'.[292]

In *Hadžihasanović* Judge Shahabuddeen challenged the idea that command responsibility is a form of complicity, opining that 'Command responsibility imposes responsibility on a commander for failure to take corrective action in respect of a crime committed by another; it does not make the commander party to the crime committed by that other.'[293] As he accepted, the ambit of superior responsibility is intrinsically linked to its conceptualization.[294] Relying, in part, on Judge Shahabuddeen's opinion, the Trial Chamber in *Halilović* asserted that:

> command responsibility is responsibility for an omission. The commander is respon-
> sible for the failure to perform an act required by international law. This omission is
> culpable because international law imposes an affirmative duty on superiors to prevent
> and punish crimes committed by their subordinates. Thus 'for the acts of his subordi-
> nates' as generally referred to in the jurisprudence of the Tribunal does not mean that
> the commander shares the same responsibility as the subordinates who committed the
> crimes, but rather that because of the crimes committed by his subordinates, the
> commander should bear responsibility for his failure to act. The imposition of respon-
> sibility upon a commander for breach of his duty is to be weighed against the crimes of
> his subordinates; a commander is responsible not as though he had committed the crime
> himself, but his responsibility is considered in proportion to the gravity of the offences
> committed.[295]

This is consistent with the fact that the ICTY considers that Articles 7(1) and 7(3) provide distinct categories of criminal liability which exclude cumulative convictions for the same count based on the same facts.[296] Such views have also gained support in the Appeals Chamber. In *Krnojelac*, that Chamber, in an entirely unreasoned, rather 'throwaway' line,

---

289 International Criminal Court Act 2001, s. 65.
290 Kai Ambos, 'Superior Responsibility' in Cassese, *Commentary*, 850–5.
291 On the 'general duty to prevent' on superiors, see *Halilović* ICTY T. Ch. 16.11.2005 paras. 81–8.
292 Report of the Secretary-General Pursuant to Paragraph 2 of Security Council Resolution 808, UN Doc. S/25704 para. 56.
293 *Hadžihasanović* Appeal, Judge Shahabuddeen, para. 33. See also *Orić* ICTY T. Ch. II 30.6.2006 para. 294.
294 *Hadžihasanović* Appeal para. 33.
295 *Halilović* ICTY T. Ch. 16.11.2005 para. 54.
296 *Blaškić* Appeal para. 91; but see *Čelebići* Appeal paras. 745–6.

said '[i]t cannot be overemphasised that, where superior responsibility is concerned, an accused is not charged with the crimes of his subordinates but with his failure to carry out his duty as a superior to exercise control'.[297] In the 2008 *Hadžihasanović* Appeal the Chamber 'took into consideration' the views expressed in *Halilović* that command responsibility is a *sui generis* form of omission liability.[298] Most recently, in the *Orić* Appeal, Judge Shahabuddeen, with whom Judges Shomburg and Liu basically agreed, reasserted his view from the earlier *Hadžihasanović* decision, that command responsibility was not liability for the underlying offences.[299] As they decided in that case not to overturn the majority decision in the earlier case, the matter cannot be considered settled,[300] not least as the preponderance of case law until recently has supported the view that it is a form of liability in the underlying crimes.

Under the ICC Statute, command responsibility is treated as a form of liability for the underlying offences. Although some elements of Article 28 of the ICC Statute could be read as creating a dereliction of duty-type offence,[301] it quite clearly imputes the crimes of the subordinates to the superior,[302] which is more consistent with a form of complicity. Where there is a duty to intervene, and knowledge of an offence, it can be more easily seen that there is a complicity base for liability on the basis of traditional aiding/abetting ideas.[303]

Whichever way it is formulated in international criminal law, command responsibility is unnuanced, covering many different forms of liability under one heading. It moves from deliberate failures to intervene despite a duty to do so, which fall close to traditional complicity ideas, to, in essence, conduct which is close to, if not the same as negligent dereliction of duty.[304] This is recognized by the German law relating to the subject, which deals separately with failure to know of offences in dereliction of duty, failure to report an offence, and knowing tolerance of an offence when there is a duty and ability to intervene to prevent it.[305] By running all these concepts together, like joint criminal enterprise, the concept of superior responsibility can be criticized from the point of view of the principle of fair labelling, and on the basis that it 'display[s] a measure of insensitivity to the degree of

---

297 *Prosecutor* v. *Krnojelac*, ICTY A.Ch. 13.9.2003, para. 171.

298 *Hadžihasanović* 2008 Appeal para. 39.

299 *Orić* Appeal, Judge Shahabuddeen, paras. 18–19; Separate and Partially Dissenting Opinion of Judge Shomburg, para. 12; Separate and Partially Dissenting Opinion of Judge Liu, para. 27.

300 For a contrary view see Mettraux, *Command Responsibility*, ch. 4.

301 Ambos, 'Superior Responsibility', 850–5.

302 Article 28 provides that the commander 'shall be criminally responsible for crimes within the jurisdiction of the Court committed by forces under his or her effective command and control'. See *Bemba Gombo* para. 405.

303 See the German *Code of Crimes Against International Law*, s. 4.

304 See Mirjan Damaška, 'The Shadow Side of Command Responsibility' (2001) 49 *American Journal of Comparative Law* 455, 460–71. See generally the symposium at (2007) 5 *JICJ* 599–682.

305 German *Code of Crimes Against International Law*, ss. 13, 14.

the actor's own personal culpability',[306] and provides for the negligent commission of intentional offences.[307]

The fact that on occasion the ICTY and ICTR have accepted that command responsibility can lead to a conviction for genocide if the superior knew or had reason to know that subordinates were committing or about to commit genocide,[308] has led some commentators to express a corresponding concern about diluting the seriousness of the label 'genocide'.[309] In the ICC the Tribunals' case law will presumably be followed, unless the Court is willing to rely on the 'unless otherwise provided' phrase in Article 30 to eliminate the application of 'negligent' command responsibility for genocide.[310]

Further reading

There are helpful symposia on joint criminal enterprise and command responsibility at (2007) 5 *JICJ* 67–244 and (2007) 5 *JICJ* 599–682 respectively.

Kai Ambos, 'General Principles of Law in the Rome Statute' (1999) 10 *CLF* 1.

Kai Ambos, 'Superior Responsibility' in Cassese, *Commentary*, 823.

Kai Ambos, *Der Allgemeine Teil des Völkerstrafrechts: Ansätze einer Dogmatisierung* (Berlin, 2004).

Roberta Arnold and Otto Triffterer, 'Article 28' in Triffterer, *Observers' Notes*, 795.

Ilias Bantekas, *Principles of Direct and Superior Responsibility in International Humanitarian Law* (Manchester, 2002).

Gideon Boas, James Bischoff and Natalie Reid, *Forms of Responsibility in International Criminal Law* (Cambridge, 2007).

Robert Cryer, *Prosecuting International Crimes: Selectivity and the International Criminal Law Regime* (Cambridge, 2005) ch. 6.

Guénaël Mettraux, *The Law of Command Responsibility* (Oxford, 2009).

Darryl Mundis, 'Crimes of the Commander: Superior Responsibility Under Article 7(3) of the ICTY Statute' in Gideon Boas and William A. Schabas (eds.), *International Criminal Law Developments in the Case Law of the ICTY* (The Hague, 2003) 239.

Héctor Olásolo, *The Criminal Responsibility of Senior Political and Military Leaders as Principals to International Crimes* (Oxford, 2009).

---

306 See Damaška, 'The Shadow Side', 456; Chantal Meloni, 'Command Responsibility: Mode of Liability for Subordinates or Separate Offence of the Superior?' (2007) 5 *JICJ* 619; Volker Nerlich, 'Superior Responsibility Under Article 28 of the Rome Statute: For Exactly What is the Superior Held Responsible?' (2007) 5 *JICJ* 665.
307 William A. Schabas, 'General Principles of Criminal Law in the International Criminal Court Statute (Part III)' (1998) 6 *European Journal of Crime, Criminal Law and Criminal Justice* 400, 417.
308 See, e.g. *Blagojević and Jokić* ICTY T. Ch. 17.1.2005 para. 686.
309 See, prior to *Blagojević and Jokić* ICTY T. Ch. 17.1.2005, and in relation to earlier suggestions along the same lines, Mettraux, *International Crimes*, 261–4.
310 See William A. Schabas, 'The *Jelisić* Case and the Mens Rea of Genocide' (2001) 14 *LJIL* 125 at 132.

Per Saland, 'International Criminal Law Principles' in Lee, *The Making of the Rome Statute*, 189.

William Schabas, 'Hate Speech in Rwanda: The Road to Genocide' (2000) 46 *McGill Law Journal* 141.

William Schabas, *The UN International Criminal Tribunals: The former Yugoslavia, Rwanda and Sierra Leone* (Cambridge, 2006) ch. 9.

Elies van Sliedregt, *The Criminal Responsibility of Individuals for Violations of International Humanitarian Law* (The Hague, 2003).

16

Defences/Grounds for Excluding Criminal Responsibility

16.1 Introduction

Defences (or in the terminology of the ICC Statute 'grounds for excluding criminal responsibility')[1] are an oft-forgotten aspect of international criminal law. Jurisprudence from the international criminal Tribunals on the matter is sparse, and not always satisfactory. There are a number of reasons for this, one of which also at least partially explains the relative lack of scholarly attention given to most defences in international criminal law.[2] This is the tendency towards a lack of sympathy for defendants in international criminal proceedings. As Albin Eser has said, there are 'certain psychological reservations toward defences. By providing perpetrators of brutal crimes against humanity . . . with defences for their offences, we have effectively lent them a hand in finding grounds for excluding punishability.'[3] Other reasons include the fact that in international Tribunals, the Prosecutor's choice of defendants rarely includes those who have plausible claims of defences recognized by the law. Defences are, however, a fundamental part of criminal law, and reflect important limitations on the proper scope of punishable conduct. It is the purpose of this chapter to set out and critique the law relating to defences, in both treaty-based and customary international law. This chapter is primarily concerned with substantive defences to international crimes, it does not deal with issues such as immunity, youth, *ne bis in idem* or limitation periods. These are not defences for conduct, but pleas as to the jurisdiction or right of a court to try a person, both of which are separate matters.

16.1.1 The types of defences

At the outset, certain terminological and conceptual matters ought to be clarified. In the common law world, it is usual to speak of 'defences' in the omnibus sense whereas in civil

---

1 Although this chapter uses 'defences' it is not to be taken as representing a position on the doctrinal controversies about the choice of terminology.
2 Superior orders are an exception to this trend.
3 Albin Eser, 'Defences in War Crimes Trials' in Yoram Dinstein and Mala Tabory (eds.), *War Crimes in International Law* (The Hague, 1996) 251.

law jurisdictions a firm distinction is drawn between types of defences, in particular between justifications and excuses.[4] Justifications, broadly speaking, are pleas that the conduct of the defendant was acceptable, and thus necessarily lawful. It is difficult, for example, to argue that a person acting in self-defence has done anything which the law seeks to prevent. 'Excuses', painting again with something of a broad brush, do not seek to defend the conduct of the defendant per se, but seek to say that, in the particular instance, the defendant ought not be blamed for what he or she did. The boundary between the different types of defences is not especially clear, however,[5] even though the classification does have important consequences, at least in national law. For example, there may be no secondary liability for aiding and abetting justified conduct; the same may not be the case for excused conduct. Also, justifications tend to exclude liability for the conduct in private law, whereas excuses do not necessarily do so.[6] It is not clear that there was agreement on the distinction at Rome, hence the neutral terminology of the ICC Statute, 'grounds for excluding criminal responsibility' rather than 'defences', 'justifications' or 'excuses'. The distinction remains, nonetheless, useful for understanding the appropriate ambit of some defences.[7]

There is another set of 'defences', however, which also require treatment. These are what can be termed 'failure of proof defences'.[8] These defences are usually denials that a person can be held responsible on the basis that the prosecution has failed to show a fundamental element of the offence. As a result, some national legal systems do not treat these issues as defences. These pleas often relate to the presence or otherwise of *mens rea*.[9] Consent is a notable example in relation to offences to which it is relevant. Such defences, depending on the circumstances, may also operate across the excuse/justification divide.[10] They are dealt with in this chapter, as the ICC Statute impliedly treats them as defences.[11] A final introductory point is that defences here are those that serve, as the ICC Statute puts it, to 'exclude criminal responsibility'. Mitigating factors, such as inexperience or pressure not amounting to duress are merely mitigating factors, which go to sentencing rather than responsibility.[12]

---

4 See generally Antonio Cassese, 'Justifications and Excuses in International Criminal Law' in Cassese, *Commentary*, 951. The distinction is not entirely unknown to the common law, however.

5 See A. P. Simester and G. R. Sullivan, *Criminal Law: Theory and Doctrine*, 3rd edn (Oxford, 2007) 609–13; George Fletcher, *Rethinking Criminal Law* (New York, 1978) 759ff; Kent Greenawalt, 'The Perplexing Borders of Justification and Excuse' (1984) 84 *Columbia Law Review* 1897.

6 See Cassese, 'Justifications', 952–4. As he notes though, so far international criminal law has yet to make any practical distinction between the two.

7 See, e.g. Kai Ambos, 'Other Grounds for Excluding Criminal Responsibility' in Cassese, *Commentary*, 1003, 1036–7; Illan Rua Wall, 'Duress, International Criminal Law and Literature' (2006) 4 *JICJ* 724.

8 Simester and Sullivan, *Criminal Law*, 613–7.

9 Alibi is sometimes seen as a type of this claim, in that the assertion is that the person did not undertake the conduct, as he or she was not there. In fact it is slightly different, in that it is a denial of any of the conduct at all.

10 Cassese, 'Justifications', 953–4 treats some such defences as excuses, but others (consent) as a justification.

11 See, e.g. ICC Statute, Art. 32.

12 See section 19.3.1.

16.2 The ICC Statute and defences

Although the ICC Statute is neither a complete, nor an entirely accurate, statement of defences as they exist in international criminal law, it is the first treaty that attempts to deal with defences in any systematic way.[13] Its provisions were the outcome of compromises between a large number of States, some of which came from the common law tradition, and some from their civil law counterparts. While the provisions therefore leave something to be desired from a criminal law point of view, they provide a sensible structure within which to investigate defences in international criminal law. Article 31 sets out a reasonable proportion of the defences which are applicable to international crimes, providing for defences of insanity, intoxication, self-defence (including defence of others or, exceptionally, property), duress and necessity.

Certain points ought to be noted at the outset. First, as Article 31(1) makes clear, it is not intended to be exhaustive. There are other parts of the Statute (in particular Articles 32 and 33, which deal with mistakes of fact and law and the defence of superior orders respectively) that are also relevant. Second, as the definitions of defences given in the Statute are the outcome of difficult negotiations, Article 31(2)) provides that 'the Court shall determine the applicability of the grounds for excluding criminal responsibility provided for in this Statute to the case before it'. It has been argued, by one of its drafters, that this provision recognizes that the ICC has a residual power to refuse to apply a defence to an individual case even where the text of the ICC Statute might require it.[14] This might be criticized on the basis that a person ought to be able to rely on the defences that the Statute ostensibly sets down without the risk that they will be set aside in an individual case. A better way to interpret this provision may be that the ICC has discretion to determine the factual applicability of a defence before entering into serious discussion of it at trial. In other words, the Court may require an 'air of reality' of a defence to be established before permitting detailed argument and evidence to be tendered.[15]

On the other side, Article 31(3) of the ICC Statute recognizes that there are defences applicable to international crimes which it does not enumerate. Article 31(3) reads:

> At trial, the Court may consider a ground for excluding criminal responsibility other than those referred to in paragraph 1 where such a ground is derived from applicable law as set forth in Article 21.[16]

Pursuant to this Article a defendant may plead defences before the ICC which have their basis outside the ICC Statute, i.e. in other applicable treaties, customary law and general

---

13 See Albin Eser, 'Article 31' in Triffterer, *Observers' Notes*, 863, 865–6.
14 Per Saland, 'International Criminal Law Principles' in Lee, *The Making of the Rome Statute*, 189, 208–9.
15 This is particularly relevant where evidence, such as of consent in sexual offences, is sensitive and examination of witnesses can be distressing. See ICC RPE, r. 72.
16 Other than the ICC Statute, the Elements of Crimes and RPE, Art. 21 provides for the use of applicable treaties, principles and rules of international law (i.e. custom) and 'failing that' general principles of law.

principles of law.[17] There are a number of such defences, to which we will return. However, owing to the hierarchy of sources established in Article 21 (which places the statute at the apex of authority), arguments that defences contained within Article 31 are narrower than those available under customary law are not admissible under this head, although they may have purchase in arguments about the appropriate application of Article 31(2).

16.3   Mental incapacity[18]

Insanity is a defence which often (although not always) amounts to a claim of lack of proof. It ought to be distinguished from the procedural plea of unfitness to plead.[19] Article 31(1)(a) of the ICC Statute is the first codification of a defence of insanity in international law, and applies when:

> The person suffers from a mental disease or defect that destroys that person's capacity to appreciate the unlawfulness or nature of his or her conduct, or capacity to control his or her conduct to conform to the requirements of law;

Although parts of the provision are quite restrictive, Article 31(1)(a) is a fairly uncontroversial formulation of the defence. It encompasses three situations. The first is the *locus classicus* of a mental incapacity plea, which is when a person is unable to understand the nature of his or her conduct. The usual example given to explain this situation is a person who cuts the victim's throat delusionally thinking that it is a loaf of bread.[20] There is no point convicting such a person, who is in need of treatment rather than prison. Article 31(1)(a) also covers the situation where a person is incapable of understanding the unlawfulness of his or her conduct. Such a person may well deserve exemption from liability, but this is not quite the same as exemption under the first head, at least as appreciation of unlawfulness may involve a more subtle analysis than the concept that the drafters were probably trying to codify, which is that the person was incapable of understanding the wrongfulness of the conduct. The final concept recognized by Article 31(1)(a) is that of the 'irresistible impulse', where a person understands the nature and wrongfulness of the conduct, but is unable, owing to mental illness, to stop from acting as he or she did.[21] There is no requirement that insanity is permanent. It is sufficient that the person's capacity was destroyed at the time of

---

17 If seeking to do so the Defence must inform the Trial Chamber and Prosecutor in advance, giving them sufficient time to prepare on point: ICC RPE, r. 80.

18 See generally, Peter Krug, 'The Emerging Mental Incapacity Defense in International Criminal Law: Some Initial Questions of Implementation' (2000) 96 *AJIL* 317.

19 On which see Albin Eser, 'Article 31' in Triffterer, *Observers' Notes*, 863, 873.

20 This is, of course, also a mistake of fact, but it would essentially be impossible to persuade a fact-finder that this belief was honestly held without proof of mental incapacity.

21 In such an instance, the claim stands on the border of denial of proof (of voluntary action (i.e. *actus reus*)) and excuse.

the impugned conduct. As with the other forms of the defence, such a plea will require expert evidence from both sides.[22]

It is notable that Article 31(1)(a) requires destruction, rather than impairment, of ability. This is a high standard, albeit one which is consistent with the way most domestic jurisdictions deal with the matter. Diminished, as opposed to absent, ability to comprehend the nature or unlawfulness of conduct, or comply with the law is no defence in the ICC Statute, nor is it in the jurisprudence of the ad hoc Tribunals, which treat any such matter as one of mitigation of sentence.[23] This is similar to the way the issue was treated in the post-Second World War trials in which it was raised,[24] and in the ICC Rules of Procedure and Evidence.[25]

One unfortunate aspect of Article 31(1)(a) is its failure to provide for a special verdict in the eventuality of a person being acquitted on the basis of mental incapacity. This is important; in domestic systems, a person who is acquitted on the basis of lack of mental capacity is necessarily liable to some other form of order, which provides for psychiatric evaluation and treatment.[26] It is to be hoped that some arrangements may be found with the mental health authorities in States supportive of the ICC that will provide for those who have been acquitted by the ICC, but are in need of treatment or confinement on the basis of their disorder.[27]

16.4 Intoxication

There is a considerable history of commission of international crimes by the intoxicated. In the Second World War the *Sonderkommandos*, who were forced to work in the concentration camps they were held in, were frequently given intoxicants. Many of the participants in Rwanda's genocide were drunk.[28] Child soldiers are often given drugs or alcohol as a control mechanism, to loosen their inhibitions and increase their ferocity.[29] After the Second World War, at least one case accepted the existence of a partial defence of intoxication, although it was rejected on the facts.[30]

---

22 See Krug, 'The Emerging Mental Incapacity Defense'. In the ICTY, the Defence bears the burden of proof (on the balance of probabilities) with respect to this defence, see *Delalić, Mučić, Delić and Landžo* ICTY A. Ch. 20.2.2001 (the *Čelebići* case) para. 582.

23 See *ibid.*, paras. 580–90. The Trial Chamber in *Vasiljević* ICTY T. Ch. I 29.11.2002 paras. 282–3 defined diminished responsibility as 'an impairment to his capacity to appreciate the unlawfulness of or the nature of his conduct or to control his conduct so as to conform to the requirements of the law'. In *Jelisić* ICTY T. Ch. 14.12.1999 para. 125 'personality disorders ... [and] ... borderline, narcissistic and anti-social characteristics' were insufficient to diminish responsibility.

24 *Gerbsch* XIII LRTWC 131, 132, 137. See also Antonio Cassese, *International Criminal Law*, 2nd edn (Oxford, 2008) 263–6.

25 ICC RPE, r. 145(2).

26 In the UK see, e.g. the Criminal Procedure (Insanity and Unfitness to Plead) Act 1991.

27 See William Schabas, *Genocide in International Law*, 2nd edn (Cambridge, 2008) 399.

28 *Ibid.*, 398.

29 Matthew Happold, *Child Soldiers in International Law* (Manchester, 2004) 16–17.

30 *Chusaburo* III LRTWC 76, 78.

Although it might be queried if those most responsible for international crimes, who are likely to be the defendants before the ICC, will have much resort to the defence,[31] intoxication is dealt with in Article 31(1)(b) of the ICC Statute, which provides for the exclusion of responsibility when:

> The person is in a state of intoxication that destroys that person's capacity to appreciate the unlawfulness or nature of his or her conduct, or capacity to control his or her conduct to conform to the requirements of law, unless the person has become voluntarily intoxicated under such circumstances that the person knew, or disregarded the risk, that, as a result of the intoxication, he or she was likely to engage in conduct constituting a crime within the jurisdiction of the Court;

At the outset it ought to be noted that chronic alcoholism or addiction to drugs might also lead to a defence under Article 31(1)(a).[32] The nature of the plea is that, owing to the intoxication, the mental element is not formed; thus it is a plea of failure of proof. However, debate on the defence in Rome was awkward, as some delegations were opposed to its inclusion at all, considering intoxication as an aggravating factor rather than a possible defence.[33] As a result of this, the scope of the defence in Article 31(1)(b) is narrow.

16.4.1 Voluntary and involuntary intoxication

The primary focus of the text of the Article is involuntary intoxication, that is to say when a person unwittingly becomes intoxicated owing to inadvertent consumption of drugs or alcohol. Voluntary intoxication is only a defence when a person did not realize that he or she might engage in conduct prohibited by the Statute, and was not at fault by disregarding such a risk.[34] Taking drink or drugs to gain 'Dutch courage' will not provide the basis for a defence under this provision as the person will know of at least the risk (and almost inevitably more) that he or she will commit the offence.[35]

16.4.2 Destruction of capacity

The intoxication must have destroyed the person's capacity to understand the nature or unlawfulness of the conduct, or ability to conform to the law's dictates. Impairment, even of

---

31 Ambos, 'Other Grounds', 1031.

32 Geert-Jan Knoops, *Defences in Contemporary International Criminal Law* (New York, 2001) 123.

33 Saland, 'Principles', 209; Ambos, 'Other Grounds', 1029–30. Most (although not all) domestic systems provide for some form of defence of involuntary intoxication, but some States refuse to accept voluntary intoxication as a defence, on policy grounds. The ICTY has said that 'in contexts where violence is the norm and weapons are carried, intentionally consuming drugs or alcohol constitutes an aggravating rather than a mitigating factor': *Kvočka* ICTY T. Ch. I 2.11.2001 para. 706; *Kvočka* ICTY A. Ch. 28.2.2005 paras. 707–8.

34 Where someone is at fault in failing to realize, his or her liability is said to rest on this prior fault.

35 Eser, 'Article 31', 877.

a substantial nature, is insufficient to exclude a person's liability.[36] On the language of Article 31(1)(b), it appears that the person must be incapable of understanding or controlling his or her conduct; it does not appear sufficient that the person simply did not do so owing to the intoxication, although it is uncertain if this was the intention of the drafters.

It is not clear precisely how specific the risk of conduct has to be to exclude the defence. 'Conduct constituting a crime within the jurisdiction of the court' could be broad, simply meaning any physical act or omission prohibited in the Statute, for example killing, engaging in inhumane treatment, or inflicting serious injury. Or it could be interpreted more narrowly, meaning that the person must have known or disregarded the risk that he or she would engage in the specific conduct for which he or she is being prosecuted. Also there is ambiguity about whether the reference to 'conduct' includes the relevant circumstantial elements (for example that there was an armed conflict, there was a widespread or systematic attack on the civilian population, or a manifest pattern of similar events), although given the phrasing of Article 30 of the ICC Statute, they would appear to be included.[37] Still, it is difficult to see the ICC acquitting someone on such a basis.

16.4.3 A complete defence

In common law systems such as the UK, intoxication is only a defence to certain crimes (known, rather unfortunately, as crimes of 'specific intent').[38] Pleas that *mens rea* is not established owing to voluntary intoxication are not admissible in crimes of 'basic intent', which tend to be less serious versions of crimes of 'specific intent' (for example murder is a crime of specific intent, manslaughter is a crime of basic intent). The result of a plea of intoxication is thus usually a conviction for a less serious offence.[39] The ICC Statute does not adopt such a position. Thus a drunk offender could entirely escape criminal responsibility on the basis of this provision, although the strict terms of the defence mean that it will be difficult to sustain such a plea.

16.5 Self-defence, defence of others and of property[40]

It has never been questioned that people have the right to defend themselves. Indeed (non-mistaken) self-defence is often considered a paradigmatic justification of conduct.[41] There

---

36 See Elies van Sliedregt, *The Criminal Responsibility of Individuals for Violations of International Humanitarian Law* (The Hague, 2003) 249.

37 Eser, 'Article 31', 878 (who considers contextual elements to be included); Gerhard Werle, *Principles of International Criminal Law* (Cambridge, 2005) 162.

38 See generally, Simester and Sullivan, *Criminal Law*, 629–36. The term could cause confusion owing to its use in international criminal law, in particular when referring to the intention required for genocide.

39 In civilian systems, there is often a crime of committing an offence whilst intoxicated; see, e.g. German Criminal Code §323a.

40 See generally, van Sliedregt, *Criminal Responsibility*, 254–67.

41 See, e.g. George Fletcher, *The Grammar of Criminal Law* (Oxford, 2007), vol. I, pp. 23–7, 50–1.

were a number of cases in which this justification was raised after the Second World War.[42] The Trial Chamber in *Kordić and Čerkez* accepted that customary law recognized self-defence,[43] an uncontroversial finding made more contentious by the fact that the Chamber asserted that the formulation found in the ICC Statute represented customary law.[44] Article 31(1)(c) provides for an acquittal when:

> The person acts reasonably to defend himself or herself or another person or, in the case of war crimes, property which is essential for the survival of the person or another person or property which is essential for accomplishing a military mission, against an imminent and unlawful use of force in a manner proportionate to the degree of danger to the person or the other person or property protected. The fact that the person was involved in a defensive operation conducted by forces shall not in itself constitute a ground for excluding criminal responsibility under this subparagraph.

16.5.1 Imminent, unlawful use of force

Defence here ought not to be confused with self-defence by States under Article 51 of the UN Charter.[45] In addition, this defence is not available in relation to *any* threat. It is limited to action in response to 'an imminent and unlawful use of force'.[46] What is imminent is a matter of appreciation, although Article 31(1)(c) does make clear that a person must not wait for someone else to strike the first blow.[47] 'Unlawful' means that there is no right to defend against someone who is acting lawfully. However, this should not be interpreted as meaning 'criminally'. There have been some suggestions that there is no right to defend against those covered by any of the grounds in Article 31(1).[48] However, at the domestic level, defence against the insane or highly intoxicated is acceptable, and there seems to be no reason to doubt that the same would apply here. Some assistance might usefully be drawn here from the distinction between justifications and excuses. Justified actors are not acting unlawfully, whereas those who are merely excused (the insane and the very intoxicated are two examples of such actors) are acting unlawfully, and thus can be defended against.

The expansion of defence, with respect to war crimes, to protect 'mission essential property'[49] was controversial in the negotiations at Rome. According to Cassese 'this extension is manifestly outside the *lex lata* and may generate quite a few misgivings'.[50]

---

42 See *Tessmann (Willi)* XV LRTWC 177.
43 *Kordić and Čerkez* ICTY T. Ch. 26.2.2001 paras. 448–52.
44 *Ibid.*
45 *Martić* ICTY A. Ch. 8.10.2008 para. 268. See also Werle, *Principles*, 142–3.
46 *Kordić and Čerkez* ICTY T. Ch. 26.2.2001 para. 451.
47 Eser, 'Article 31', 881 defines imminent as 'immediately antecedent, presently exercised or still enduring'.
48 Werle, *Principles*, 141.
49 Property essential to the survival of a person may be different here.
50 Antonio Cassese, 'The Rome Statute of the International Criminal Court: Some Preliminary Reflections' (1999) 10 *EJIL* 144, 154–5.

Given that many States have limited rights to use force to protect, for example, nuclear installations, and UN Rules of Engagement often provide for defence of mission essential property, this criticism may be a little harsh.[51] On the other hand, Belgium considered this provision contrary to *jus cogens* and therefore issued a declaration on point at the time of its ratification.[52] Nonetheless fears that aspects of the provision are open to abuse have some foundation.[53] As the Article clarifies, however, the simple fact that a State is acting in self-defence is not enough in itself to invoke this provision. There does not appear to be any acceptance in this provision for a defence when a person reasonably (but wrongly) believes that there is such an attack.[54]

16.5.2 Reasonable and proportionate response

Not every reaction to an attack is acceptable. For a response to be defended on the basis of Article 31(1)(c), it must be reasonable to resort to force, and the level of force must be 'proportionate to the degree of danger' faced. Proportionality is not a test which can be set down with scientific precision in advance. However, in applying the test, 'such considerations as the nature of the weapon in the hands of the accused, the question whether the assailant had any weapon, and so forth, have to be considered'.[55] 'Eagle-eye' hindsight is to be avoided when appraising proportionality, as a person does not have the luxury of time to weigh things very carefully when there is an imminent or ongoing attack. Article 31(1)(c) does not create a duty to retreat[56] or any specific rules on what the response must be, other than setting down the test of proportionality to the level of danger. This test is to be applied by the court; the defendant's view is not determinative. The language of the Article (the person 'acts ... to defend') implies that the person must intend to act in defence.[57]

16.6 Duress and necessity

Situations in which international crimes are committed tend to be ones in which there is group activity, and therefore some level of coercion of an offender by colleagues is often to

---

51 It might be questioned if a civilian stealing a truck full of small arms ought to be protected in this situation, although in that situation it is quite possible the person would be considered (or reasonably believed) to be taking an active part in hostilities, thus forfeiting their protection.

52 See   http://untreaty.un.org/ENGLISH/bible/englishinternetbible/partI/chapterXVIII/treaty11.asp.   Although incorrect as a matter of law, this is State practice, accompanied by *opinio juris*, thus relevant for the determination of customary law, as well as interpretation of the ICC Statute.

53 See Ambos, 'Other Grounds', 1033.

54 Eser, 'Article 31', 882, and see section 16.7.1 on mistake of fact.

55 *Tessmann (Willi)* XV LRTWC 177.

56 *Tessman (ibid.)* could be read as requiring this.

57 See also Werle, *Principles*, 142.

be expected.[58] Also in such situations painful choices have at times to be made. Article 31(1)(d), the first codification at the international level of necessity and duress, decidedly controversially,[59] treats the two together, providing for a defence when:[60]

> [t]he conduct which is alleged to constitute a crime within the jurisdiction of the Court has been caused by duress resulting from a threat of imminent death or of continuing or imminent serious bodily harm against that person or another person, and the person acts necessarily and reasonably to avoid this threat, provided that the person does not intend to cause a greater harm than the one sought to be avoided. Such a threat may either be:
>
> (i) Made by other persons; or
> (ii) Constituted by other circumstances beyond that person's control.

Although this was the first codification of these defences, one of the most plausible explanations of the way in which the Nuremberg IMT dealt with its provision on superior orders[61] is that it laid down a test for duress.[62] There was also considerable jurisprudence on duress and necessity in other post-Second World War cases,[63] such as *Krupp*,[64] *Flick*,[65] *Krauch*[66] and *von Leeb*.[67] Much of this jurisprudence was canvassed in the ICTY in one of its few fully reasoned decisions on defences, *Prosecutor* v. *Erdemović*.[68] In this case, a bare majority of the Appeals Chamber decided that although there was a defence of duress in international law, it did not apply to cases involving the killings of innocents.[69] In particular, as two of the judges determined the matter on avowedly policy-based grounds, and there were strong dissents from two other judges,[70] the finding was controversial.[71] Notably, this

---

58 Such colleagues may, of course, become liable themselves for offences they encouraged, assisted or participated in.
59 Claus Kreß, 'War Crimes Committed in Non-International Armed Conflicts and the Emerging System of International Criminal Justice' (2000) 30 *Israel Yearbook on Human Rights* 103, 152ff.
60 And has been criticized for doing so, not least as duress is an excuse, and most examples of necessity are justifications: see Eser, 'Article 31', 883.
61 See section 16.8.
62 See Yoram Dinstein, *The Defence of 'Obedience to Superior Orders' in International Criminal Law* (The Hague, 1965) 147–56.
63 See Commentary, XV LRTWC 170–5.
64 X LRTWC 69, 156.
65 IX LRTWC 1, 19.
66 X LRTWC 1, 54, 57.
67 XII LRTWC 1, 144, 149.
68 *Erdemović* ICTY A. Ch. 7.10.1997.
69 *Ibid.*, Separate Opinion of Judge Li, paras. 1–12; Separate Opinion of Judges McDonald and Vohrah, paras. 32–89.
70 *Ibid.*, Dissenting Opinion of Judge Stephen, paras. 23–67; Dissenting Opinion of Judge Cassese, paras. 11–51.
71 See, e.g. Peter Rowe, 'Duress as a Defence to War Crimes After Erdemović: A Laboratory for a Permanent Court?' (1998) 1 *YIHL* 210; David Turns, 'The International Criminal Tribunal for the Former Yugoslavia: The *Erdemović* Case' (1998) 47 *ICLQ* 461; Claus Kreß, '*Zur Methode der Rechtsfindung im Allgemeinen Teil des Völkerstrafrechts. Die Bewertung von Tötungen im Nötigungsnotstand durch die Rechtsmittelkammer des*

aspect of the decision in *Erdemović* was not taken up in the ICC Statute. The requirements of the defence in the ICC Statute are probably customary.[72]

16.6.1 Imminent threat beyond the control of the accused

The first requirement is that there is a threat of 'imminent death or of continuing or imminent serious bodily harm'. Thus it is clear that blackmail or other threats not involving imminent serious violence will not suffice. For the criminal law to permit a person to excuse himself or herself from liability on the basis of threats, those threats must be very serious. Also, the threats must be of imminent danger. It is by no means clear that imminent means the same thing here as in Article 31(1)(c). The threats may be against the accused or others; there is no requirement that there be any particular relationship between the accused and the people threatened. The threat must be real, however, and not simply believed to exist by the defendant.[73]

As recognized by Article 31(1)(d)(ii), the threat must be outside the control of the defendant. The use of the term 'other' in that part of the Article implies that this condition also applies to duress in (i). This would exclude the situation where a person had 'courted' the threats by others, such as in the instance where a person had joined a group notorious for its criminality. This condition was considered a part of customary law by Judges Cassese and Stephen in *Erdemović*,[74] and is consistent with national practice.[75]

16.6.2 Necessary and reasonable actions

As with self-defence, pressure, be it from another or by virtue of circumstance, does not suffice to defend *any* reaction. The reactions of the person seeking to use the defence must be both necessary and reasonable in the circumstances to avoid the threat. The test is similar to

---

Internationalen Straftribunals für das ehemalige Jugoslawien im Fall Erdemović' (1999) 111 *Zeitschrift für die gesamte Strafrechtswissenschaft* 597; Robert Cryer, 'One Appeal, Four Opinions, Two Philosophies and a Remittal' (1998) 2 *Journal of Armed Conflict Law* 193. Aaron Fichtelberg, 'Liberal Values In International Criminal Law: A Critique of *Erdemović*' (2008) 6 *JICJ* 3. For a rare example of support of the majority, see Yoram Dinstein, 'Defences' in Gabrielle Kirk McDonald and Olivia Swaak-Goldman (eds.), *Substantive and Procedural Aspects of International Criminal Law* (The Hague, 2000) 367, 376.

72 There has been an implication that fighting on the 'right side' might be relevant to necessity, (*Fofana and Kondewa* SCSL T. Ch. 2.8.2007, Partially Dissenting Opinion of Judge Thompson, paras. 66–8. However, this must be regarded as incorrect, and inconsistent with the equal applicability of humanitarian law, see Valerie Oosterveld and Andrea Marlowe, '*Prosecutor* v. *Kamara et al.* and *Fofana and Kondewa*' (2007) 101 *AJIL* 848, 856–7.

73 The *Krupp* case may have seen things differently, *Krupp* X LRTWC 69 at 148. See also Commentary, XV LRTWC 174.

74 *Erdemović* ICTY A. Ch. 7.10.1997, Opinion of Judge Cassese, para. 16; Opinion of Judge Stephen, para. 68.

75 See, e.g. Simester and Sullivan, *Criminal Law*, 672–3. See also Werle, *Principles*, 147–8.

that of proportionality in self-defence.[76] This includes the question of whether a reasonable person would have given in to the threats.[77] One issue that does arise, however, is what can be expected of soldiers, who, although frequently in very stressful situations,[78] have undergone military training, and are expected to put themselves in harm's way to protect others,[79] with respect to this aspect of the test. In such circumstances, the test is perhaps best formulated as what would be considered necessary and reasonable by a servicemember of the experience and rank of the defendant. Such a nuance to the test is not unreasonable (after all, the test of reasonableness always begs the question of reasonable to whom?) and finds some support in Judge Cassese's interpretation of the existing jurisprudence on point in *Erdemović*.[80]

16.6.3 Causation

It is an express requirement that the threats caused the impugned conduct. If a person would have acted as he or she did anyway, he or she will not be able to take advantage of this defence. Article 31(1)(d) is silent on whether the threats have to be the sole cause of the defendant's conduct, or whether they only need to be one of a number of causes. This also means, though, that there is nothing in the Article that would require the ICC to take the view that the relevant threat needs to be the sole cause of the conduct.

16.6.4 Mental element

As can be seen from Article 31(1)(d), the intention of the person seeking to rely on either defence must be to bring about the lesser of the two evils. In the words of the *Krupp* case, 'if, in the execution of the illegal act, the will of the accused be not thereby overpowered but instead coincides with the will of those from whom the alleged compulsion emanates, there is no necessity justifying the original conduct'.[81] Owing to the formulation of the mental aspect of this defence in the ICC Statute, 'provided that the person does not intend to cause a greater harm than the one sought to be avoided', it is not absolutely clear whether a distinction between actions undertaken to avoid the harm and their consequences is created.[82] If there is a distinction, then unintended excessive consequences of necessary and reasonable reactions are not to be taken into account. If there is no distinction, then the

---

76 The test is described in proportionality terms in *Erdemović* ICTY A. Ch. 7.10.1997, Opinion of Judge Cassese, para. 16; Opinion of Judges McDonald and Vohrah, para. 37. See also Eser, 'Article 31', 886–7.
77 Eser, 'Article 31', 885–6.
78 See Larry May, *War Crimes and Just War* (Cambridge, 2007) ch. 13.
79 See, e.g. the comments in *R* v. *Dudley and Stevens* (1884–85) LR 14 QBD 273, 287.
80 *Erdemović* ICTY A. Ch. 7.10.1997, Opinion of Judge Cassese, para. 45.
81 *Krupp* X LRTWC 69 at 149.
82 Against any distinction, see Ambos, 'Other Grounds', 1040.

consequences, as well as the actions of the accused, must be necessary and reasonable. Basing himself on post-Second World War case law, Judge Cassese in the *Erdemović* case took the latter view.[83]

16.7 Mistake of fact and law[84]

Mistakes of fact and law are issues which tend to be dealt with differently by civil and common law systems. Civil law jurisdictions tend to be more generous with regard to mistakes of law, allowing for defences where there are reasonable mistakes relating to various aspects of crimes or defences.[85] Although there might be a trend away from this, in common law systems mistakes generally only provide an excuse when they serve to undermine *mens rea*, making the plea one of failure of proof.[86] Article 32 of the ICC Statute appears to adopt the common law approach. Article 32 provides that:

1. A mistake of fact shall be a ground for excluding criminal responsibility only if it negates the mental element required by the crime.
2. A mistake of law as to whether a particular type of conduct is a crime within the jurisdiction of the Court shall not be a ground for excluding criminal responsibility. A mistake of law may, however, be a ground for excluding criminal responsibility if it negates the mental element required by such a crime, or as provided for in article 33.

16.7.1 Mistake of fact

Article 32(1) is unequivocal. A mistake of fact is only relevant to liability if it serves to show that the defendant did not have the *mens rea*. For example, if a person bombed a civilian bunker believing it was a military command centre, there would not be liability on the basis of this provision. Interestingly, Article 32(1) does not contain any express requirement that the mistake be a reasonable one.[87] One practical limitation, though, is that the person must prove that he or she was honestly mistaken, the less reasonable a belief is, the less likely it is that a claim that a person honestly held that belief will be accepted. Questions may arise about the situation where a person is at fault in making the mistake, such as if he or she was drunk or reckless when he or she decided what he or she believed.

---

83 *Erdemović* ICTY A. Ch. 7.10.1997, Opinion of Judge Cassese, para. 16.
84 See generally Albin Eser, 'Mental Elements – Mistake of Fact and Mistake of Law' in Cassese, *Commentary*, 889 at 934–46. Otto Triffterer, 'Article 32' in Triffterer, *Observers' Notes*, 895. Also there is a 'grey zone' in which it is difficult to separate off mistakes of fact and law: see Thomas Wiegend, 'The Harmonization of General Principles of Criminal Law: The Statutes and Juruisprudence of the ICTY, ICTR and the ICC: An Overview' (2004) 19 *Nouvelles Etudes Pénales* 319, 333.
85 See George Fletcher, *Rethinking Criminal Law* (New York, 1978) 683–91.
86 In relation to mistakes of law, these are relevant, for example, in relation to the requirement of dishonesty in theft.
87 Cassese, *International Criminal Law*, 290 considers that any mistake must be reasonable to found a defence under Art. 32(1).

From its terms, it seems that mistakes of fact which, if they were true, would provide the basis of a defence do not fall under Article 32, as they do not relate to *mens rea*.[88] Earlier cases allowed such mistakes to negate responsibility.[89] Furthermore, certain of the Elements of Crimes[90] (and the Statute itself, in Article 28, on command responsibility) exclude mistakes of fact where the person should have known of the relevant facts.[91]

16.7.2 Mistake of law

Like mistakes of fact, mistakes of law, with one exception (which as we shall see, occurs with respect to superior orders), must negate *mens rea*. This defence does not include mistakes (or ignorance) about whether conduct is criminalized by the ICC Statute,[92] or whether a defence exists in law.[93] Nor does it deal with errors about the ambit of defences. The only acceptable mistake in Article 32(2) is where an element of a crime requires a legal evaluation, and the mistake relates to this, for example, where a person takes property under a mistaken belief that he or she was its owner. It has been suggested that when the defence is made out, the use of 'may' in Article 33(2) implies that the ICC may convict the defendant nonetheless.[94] However, the fact that this defence is a plea of failure of proof (of *mens rea* in this instance), means the argument cannot be correct as it would involve convicting someone despite an element of the offence not being proved by the prosecution.

16.8 Superior orders

The defence of superior orders has a lengthy history,[95] and reflects a basic tension between the importance of the principles of international law and those of military discipline.[96] Originally, the tendency was to accept that orders amounted to a defence for those who

---

88 Eser, 'Mental Elements', 945 argues that Art. 32(1) ought to apply by analogy to mistakes relating to justifications (as opposed to excuses), but the terms of Art. 32(1) do not provide particularly fertile soil for such arguments. See also Werle, *Principles*, 151.

89 See, e.g. *US* v. *List* VIII LRTWC 1, 69.

90 See, e.g. EoC Art. 8(2)(b)(xxvi).

91 Although the distinction ought to have relevance when it comes to describing the relevant conduct of the accused and determining the sentence of any convicted person.

92 Such a point was made expressly in *Lubanga Dyilo*, PT Ch. 29.1.2007 para. 302. See Thomas Weigend, 'Intent, Mistake of Law and Co-Perpetration in the *Lubanga* Decision on Confirmation of Charges' (2008) 6 *JICJ* 471, 474–6.

93 See Neil Boister, 'Reflections on the Relationship Between the Duty to Educate in Humanitarian Law and the Absence of a Defence of Mistakes of Law in the Rome Statute' in Richard Burchill, Nigel White and Justin Morris (eds.), *International Conflict and Security Law* (Cambridge, 2005) 32, 38–43.

94 See *ibid.*, 39; Eser, 'Mental Elements', 942.

95 See Dinstein, *Superior Orders*, 93–103.

96 See, e.g. Martha Minow, 'Living Up to Rules: Holding Soldiers Responsible for Abusive Conduct and the Dilemma of the Superior Orders Defence' (2007) 52 *McGill Law Journal* 1.

carried them out, and thus that liability accrued to the person who ordered the offence, rather than the one who carried that order out.[97] This was not the clearly accepted position, though; even by the late nineteenth century there was significant evidence that the *respondeat superior* principle (that is to say a complete defence of superior orders) had been replaced by the rule that orders only protected a subordinate if they were not manifestly unlawful.[98] Such a position crystallized after the First World War, if not before.[99] The position seemed to change, however, with Article 8 of the Nuremberg IMT Statute, which read: 'the fact that the defendant acted pursuant to an order of his government or of a superior shall not free him from responsibility, but may be considered in mitigation of punishment if the Tribunal determines that justice so requires'.[100] The Nuremberg IMT explained that provision as follows:

> The provisions of this article are in conformity with the law of all nations. That a soldier was ordered to kill or torture in violation of the international law of war has never been recognised as a defence to such acts of brutality, though, as the Charter here provides, the order may be urged in mitigation of punishment. The true test, which is found in various degrees in the criminal law of most nations, is not the existence of the order, but whether moral choice was in fact possible.[101]

After this, and General Assembly Resolution 95(I),[102] which affirmed the Nuremberg Charter and Judgment, it might be thought that international law no longer permitted superior orders as a defence. However, case law and practice on the point from the period up to the creation of the ICTY was more equivocal.[103] The Genocide Convention, and the Geneva Conventions for example, contain no provision on superior orders, although the Torture Convention excludes reliance on them.[104] Article 7(4) of the ICTY Statute (and Article 6(4) of the ICTR Statute) essentially repeated Article 8 of the Nuremberg IMT Statute. The ICC Statute, on the other hand, takes a different track, largely returning to the 'manifest illegality' test.[105] The ICC Statute has been criticized for this, although such critiques rely on the controversial assertion that the Nuremberg IMT Charter reflects

---

97 Lassa Oppenheim, *International Law* (London, 1906), vol. II, 264–5.

98 William Winthrop, *Military Law and Precedents* (Washington, 1896) 446–7.

99 See, e.g. *Llandovery Castle* (1922) 16 *AJIL* 708.

100 Charter of the International Military Tribunal, annex to the London Agreement on the Prosecution and Punishment of the major War Criminals of the European Axis Powers 82 UNTS 279, Art. 8. Art. 6 of the Tokyo IMT Charter is largely the same: see Special Proclamation: Establishment of an International Military Tribunal for the Far East, 19 January 1946 TIAS no. 1589.

101 'Nuremberg IMT: Judgment' (1947) 41 *AJIL* 172, 221.

102 UN Doc. A/64/Add.1.

103 Paula Gaeta, 'The Defence of Superior Orders: The Statute of the International Criminal Court Versus Customary International Law' (1999) 10 *EJIL* 172; *contra* Charles Garraway, 'Superior Orders and the International Criminal Court: Justice Delivered or Justice Denied?' (1999) 836 *International Review of the Red Cross* 785.

104 Torture Convention 1984, Art. 2.

105 Art. 6(4) of the SCSL Statute returns to the Nuremberg/Tokyo/ICTY/ICTR standard.

customary law.[106] Also, it must be remembered that the person giving the order will be responsible for his or her part in the crime whether or not the defence applies. Article 33 also adopts a narrow view of the applicability of superior orders as a defence:

1. The fact that a crime within the jurisdiction of the Court has been committed pursuant to an order of a government or of a superior, whether military or civilian, shall not relieve that person of criminal responsibility unless:
   (a) That person was under a legal obligation to obey orders of the government or the superior in question;
   (b) The person did not know that the order was unlawful; and
   (c) The order was not manifestly unlawful.
2. For the purposes of this article, orders to commit genocide or crimes against humanity are manifestly unlawful.

As can be seen, Article 33 provides that superior orders are not a defence unless the three cumulative conditions are fulfilled.[107]

16.8.1 Obligation to obey

For the defence to apply, the person obeying the order must be under a legal obligation to obey orders in domestic law. This will be the case for soldiers in all countries, but civilians may be in a different position in different States. The reference in Article 33(1)(a) to 'orders' is deliberate. In some States the obligation is only to obey *lawful* orders[108] and it was necessary to generalize the reference (to 'orders') as otherwise in those States at any time the defence could apply, there would be no obligation to obey the particular order. There have been suggestions that a superior/subordinate relationship is required.[109] This is only correct in so far as it could be an aspect of the requirement that there must be a legal obligation on the person to obey orders. This requirement creates an interesting question about the status of orders from rebel authorities and commanders. Owing to the requirement that there be a legal obligation to obey orders, it appears that such orders cannot form the basis of a defence of obedience.[110] Furthermore, it has been asserted that if a person mistakenly believes himself or herself to be under an obligation to obey an order, a defence of mistake of law may be pleaded.[111] However, according to Article 32, mistakes of law only exculpate if they

---

106 Cassese, *International Criminal Law*, 270; Gaeta, 'Defence of Superior Orders'. It might be noted that the ILC adopted the position in 1996 that the Nuremberg provision was the relevant standard, see the Draft Code Crimes against the Peace and Security of Mankind 1996, Art. 5.
107 The order must also have a causal link to the commission of the offence: van Sliedregt, *Criminal Responsibility*, 324.
108 In the UK, see the Army Act 1958, s. 34.
109 Andreas Zimmermann, 'Superior Orders' in Cassese, *Commentary*, 957, 968.
110 *Ibid.*, 969; and see van Sliedregt, *Criminal Responsibility*, 323–4.
111 See Otto Triffterer, 'Article 33' in Triffterer, *Observers' Notes*, 915, 920–1, although see 926–7.

negate *mens rea* (or as provided in Article 33), and, since such a mistake would not do so, this would not apply here.

16.8.2 Knowledge of unlawfulness

The nature of the defence in the ICC Statute is, as implied by Article 32(2), an expanded form of a mistake of law defence.[112] Therefore, if a person knows that an order is unlawful, he or she cannot use that order as a defence. This undermines one asserted explanation of the defence, namely that a subordinate is placed in a dilemma with respect to an unlawful order: obey and run the risk of criminal liability for an international crime, or disobey and face liability for a military offence of disobedience.[113] For a person to be placed in such a situation, they would have to know that the order is unlawful, and so would be prohibited from relying on superior orders. It is not always easy to determine what the person knew about the legality of the order, however.

16.8.3 Manifest illegality

Ignorance of the unlawfulness of the order is not enough to exempt a subordinate from liability. That ignorance must, in essence, be forgivable or, to put it another way, the subordinate must not be at fault in not knowing that the order was unlawful. The manifest illegality test now exists to help evaluate if a defendant was culpably ignorant of the illegality of the order.[114] If an order is manifestly illegal, there is no defence that can be based on it, irrespective of whether or not the subordinate knew it was unlawful. It must be remembered though that 'no sailor and no soldier can carry with him a library of international law, or have immediate access to a professor in that subject'.[115] Some cases have attempted to provide a definition of manifest illegality. The *Eichmann* case, for example stated that:

> [t]he distinguishing mark of a 'manifestly unlawful order' should fly like a black flag above the order given ... [n]ot formal unlawfulness, hidden or half-hidden, nor unlawfulness discernible only to the eyes of legal experts, but a flagrant and manifest breach of the law.[116]

The High Command case, however, framed the test as whether the order was 'criminal on its face'.[117] The *Finta* case in Canada said an order could not be relied upon if it was 'so

---

112 But not a plea of failure of proof. See Kreß, 'War Crimes', 150.
113 Where the obligation to obey orders is not limited to lawful orders.
114 Earlier cases sometimes used the test to determine if, in fact, the person knew the order was unlawful; see Dinstein, *Superior Orders*, 26–37.
115 *Peleus* 13 ILR 248, 249.
116 *A-G of Israel* v. *Eichmann* 36 ILR 277.
117 *Von Leeb* XII LRTWC 1, 74.

outrageous as to be manifestly unlawful'.[118] It might be questioned, however, if any of these formulations provide a clear standard. The question remains (analogously to the test of reasonableness in duress): manifest to whom?[119] A different standard may be expected, for example, of fully trained army lawyers or high-ranking officials from that of young, low-ranking soldiers who are on their first tour of duty. The role of culture, propaganda and 'common knowledge' may also be relevant to the extent to which unlawfulness is manifest.[120] Whether or not such considerations are appropriately integrated into the manifest illegality test, and if they are to be, to what extent, is not without controversy, as in many circumstances succumbing to ideas that international criminal law finds fundamentally objectionable is in itself wrongful.[121] The Canadian War Crimes and Crimes Against Humanity Act attempts to deal with this difficulty by providing that:

> An accused cannot base their defence … [of superior orders] … on a belief that an order was lawful if the belief was based on information about a civilian population or an identifiable group of persons that encouraged, was likely to encourage or attempted to justify the commission of inhumane acts or omissions against the population or group.[122]

16.8.4 Genocide and crimes against humanity

Article 33(2) was intended to ensure that superior orders could be pleaded in cases involving war crimes (or, possibly, aggression) but not genocide or crimes against humanity. The wording, however, is unfortunate, as it focuses on 'orders to commit genocide or crimes against humanity' rather than focusing on the perpetrator's *mens rea*.[123] It also, illegitimately, assumes that every example of a war crime will necessarily be less serious than every example of a crime against humanity, and (perhaps more legitimately) every example of genocide.[124]

16.8.5 The relationship of superior orders to other defences

The existence of superior orders may also give rise to other defences, in particular mistake of fact and duress. If an order contains a factual assertion, such as 'bomb the enemy arms cache

---

118 *R* v. *Finta* 104 ILR 285, 322.
119 For a discussion of one State's cases on point, see Ziv Bohrer, 'Clear and Obvious? A Critical Examination of the Superior Orders Defense in Israeli Case Law' (2005–2006) 2 *Israel Defence Force Law Review* 197. See also Larry May, *Crimes Against Humanity: A Normative Account* (Cambridge, 2005) 185–7.
120 See, e.g. Mark Osiel, *Mass Atrocity, Ordinary Evil and Hannah Arendt: Criminal Consciousness in Argentina's Dirty War* (New Haven, 2001).
121 Arne J. Vetlesen, *Evil and Human Agency, Understanding Collective Evildoing* (Cambridge, 2005) ch. 5.
122 2000, c. 24, s. 14(3).
123 See further Robert Cryer, 'Superior Orders in the International Criminal Court' in Burchill, White and Morris (eds.), *Conflict and Security*, 49, 63–7.
124 Zimmermann, 'Superior Orders', 972; Triffterer, 'Article 33', 928. See also s. 3 of the German Code of Crimes Against International Law, which applies the manifest illegality principle to all crimes.

at' particular coordinates, and it turns out that the building at those coordinates is a hospital, the order forms the factual underpinning for a defence of mistake of fact, rather than superior orders, as the factual basis asserted in the order would undermine *mens rea*. Duress may be relevant because, as President Cassese stated in *Erdemović*:

> Superior orders may be issued without being accompanied by any threats to life or limb. In these circumstances, if the superior order is manifestly illegal under international law, the subordinate is under a duty to refuse to obey the order. If, following such a refusal, the order is reiterated under a threat to life or limb, then the defence of duress may be raised, and superior orders lose any legal relevance.[125]

The way in which Article 33 of the Rome Statute is framed renders the defence in the ICC an expanded form of a mistake of law defence. It is expanded as it does not require a mistake of legality to undermine *mens rea*.[126]

16.9   Other 'defences'

There are other defences that may apply in international criminal law which are not directly enumerated in the ICC Statute. The three main defences falling under this head are consent and (more controversially) reprisals and military necessity.[127] If aggression is added to the jurisdiction of the ICC, it is possible that other defences may be added to the statute, although this is, currently, speculative.

16.9.1 Consent

Certain offences, in particular sexual offences, are subject to 'defences' of consent.[128] Indeed, the absence of consent is a definitional aspect of some international crimes. However, as many situations in which international crimes occur are inherently coercive, especially when people are confined, the reality of any consent must be carefully investigated,[129] and assumptions

---

125 *Erdemović* ICTY A. Ch. 7.10.1997, Separate and Dissenting Opinion of Judge Cassese, para.15. Although orders lose their legal relevance, they retain an evidential one.

126 Cryer, 'Superior Orders', 58–60.

127 *Tu quoque*, a plea that others (in particular, prosecuting States) have committed similar offences, is not a defence in law: *Kupreškic et al.* ICTY T. Ch. II 14.1.2000 paras. 515–20; *Kunarac* A. Ch. 12.6.2002 para. 87; although, admittedly, it can affect the legitimacy of proceedings. See, e.g. Robert Cryer, *Prosecuting International Crimes: Selectivity and the International Criminal Law Regime* (Cambridge, 2005) ch. 4.

128 See, e.g. William Schabas, *The UN International Criminal Tribunals* (Cambridge, 2006) 341–3. Outside this context, Art. 52 of Geneva Convention III also only allows certain forms of work to be undertaken by PoWs if they consent.

129 *Naletilić and Martinović* ICTY T. Ch. I 31.3.2003 para. 519 saw the test as being of 'true' or 'real' consent. In *Kunarac, Kovač and Vuković* ICTY A. Ch. 12.6.2002 paras. 132–3 the Chamber notes that in the circumstances of the victim's detention, 'the circumstances ... were so coercive as to negate any possibility of consent', although it appeared (*ibid.*, para. 131) to consider that consent was not an element of the offence. In about autonomy that are the norm in domestic law are not necessarily applicable in international criminal law.[130]

The ICTY has been sceptical of claims of consent in the circumstances that surround international crimes, in particular with respect to sexual offences.[131] In the *Kunarac* case, for example, the Appeals Chamber has said that 'the circumstances giving rise to the present appeal and that prevail in most cases charged as either war crimes or crimes against humanity will be almost universally coercive. That is to say, true consent will not be possible.'[132] The ICTR has held that the prosecution must prove that consent was not present.[133] However, owing to the nature of international crimes, it added that 'the Trial Chamber is free to infer non-consent from the background circumstances, such as an ongoing genocide or the detention of the victim' rather than the specific relationship between the defendant and the victim.[134] Similarly, rather than proving that the accused did not know of the lack of consent, it suffices that 'the accused was aware, or had reason to be aware, of the coercive circumstances that undermined the possibility of genuine consent'.[135]

In relation to sexual offences, the ICC Elements of Crimes vitiate any purported consent where certain offences are committed 'by force, or by threat of force or coercion, such as that caused by fear of violence, duress, detention, psychological oppression or abuse of power, against such person or another person, or by taking advantage of a coercive environment, or the invasion was committed against a person incapable of giving genuine consent'.[136] Owing to the sensitivity of evidence relating to consent, the ICC Rules of Procedure and Evidence set up a special regime for when and how the court is to hear it.[137] This is a careful balance of the facts that almost inevitably surround international crimes, and the (remote) possibility that a defendant might genuinely believe in the existence of consent. Outside this context, the ICC has rejected the defence of consent with respect to the charge of use of child

---

most cases relating to international crimes it is difficult to think of situations in which consent would be a genuine issue. See Wolfgang Schomburg and Ines Peterson, 'Genuine Consent to Sexual Violence Under International Criminal Law' (2007) 101 *AJIL* 121, 128–31. More generally, see Noëlle Quinevet, *Sexual Offences in Armed Conflict and International Law* (The Hague, 2005).

130 Schomburg and Peterson, 'Genuine Consent', 125ff.
131 *Ibid.* See also Catherine MacKinnon, 'The ICTR's Legacy on Sexual Violence' (2008) 14 *New England Journal of International and Comparative Law* 101.
132 *Kunarac, Kovać and Vuković* ICTY A. Ch. 12.6.2002 para. 130.
133 *Gacumbitsi* A. Ch. 7.7.2006 para. 153.
134 *Ibid.*, para. 155.
135 *Ibid.*, para. 157; see also Schomburg and Peterson, 'Genuine Consent', 137–8. In relation to the crime of forced marriage which is not, according to the Special Court for Sierra Leone, inherently a sexual offence, consent was an issue which was, in the circumstances, necessarily excluded: *AFRC, Prosecutor* v. *Brima Kamara and Kanu* SCSL A. Ch. 22.2.2008 paras. 187–203.
136 Elements of Crimes, Art. 8(2)(b)(xxii-1), this includes, 'natural, induced or age-related incapacity'. Other elements also note that 'genuine consent' can be vitiated through deception, see e.g. Elements of Crimes, Art. 8(2)(b)(xxii-5).
137 Rr. 70–2. See also ICTY and ICTR Rr. 96.

soldiers.[138] Given the soft paternalist justification of the criminalization of child soldiers, which is not inherently illiberal,[139] this is supportable.

16.9.2 Reprisals

Reprisals are responses to violations of humanitarian law that would themselves otherwise amount to violations of that law.[140] They are a crude and dangerous form of law enforcement, but remain lawful in limited situations, and subject to a number of stringent requirements. The ICTY summed up those restrictions as being:

> (a) the principle whereby they must be a last resort in attempts to impose compliance by the adversary with legal standards (which entails, amongst other things, that they may be exercised only after a prior warning has been given which has failed to bring about the discontinuance of the adversary's crimes); (b) the obligation to take special precautions before implementing them (they may be taken only after a decision to this effect has been made at the highest political or military level; in other words they may not be decided by local commanders); (c) the principle of proportionality (which entails not only that the reprisals must not be excessive compared to the precedent unlawful act of warfare, but also that they must stop as soon as that unlawful act has been discontinued); and (d) 'elementary considerations of humanity'.[141]

There are prohibitions on reprisals against the wounded, sick and shipwrecked, prisoners of war, interned civilians and those in occupied territories,[142] which are considered customary.[143] The prohibitions on reprisals against other civilians and against cultural property, laid down in Articles 51.6 and 53(c) AP I, are of a more dubious customary status.[144] The ICTY, in the *Kupreškić* case, asserted that they were customary; however, this conclusion has been the subject of significant academic critique,[145] and the UK Military manual expressly disavows this conclusion.[146] Another ICTY Trial Chamber, in the *Martić* case, did not follow the *Kupreškić* decision on point, and was implicitly upheld on point by the Appeals Chamber, which appraised the relevant actions with reference to the criteria

---

138 *Lubanga Dyilo* ICC PT. Ch. 29.1.2007 para. 247.

139 I.e. intervention to trump the choices of a person who is not fully autonomous (e.g. a child). See, e.g. Joel Feinberg, *Harm to Self* (Oxford, 1986).

140 As such, there is no evidence that reprisals could be a defence to crimes against humanity or genocide.

141 *Kupreškić et al.* ICTY T. Ch. II 14.1.2000 para. 535.

142 Geneva Convention I, Art. 46; Geneva Convention II Art. 47; Geneva Convention III, Art. 13; Geneva Convention IV, Art. 33.

143 Henckaerts & Doswald-Beck, *ICRC Customary Law*, 519–20.

144 *Kupreškić et al.* ICTY T. Ch. II 14.1.2000 paras. 527–35.

145 Christopher Greenwood, 'Belligerent Reprisals in the Jurisprudence of the International Criminal Tribunal for the Former Yugoslavia' in Horst Fischer, Claus Kreß and Sascha Rolf Lüder (eds.), *International and National Prosecution of Crimes Under International Law* (Berlin, 2001) 359. See also Kreß, 'War Crimes', 153ff.

146 Ministry of Defence, *Manual of the Law of Armed Conflict* (Oxford, 2004), 421.

applicable to lawful reprisals rather than relying upon a customary ban on all such reprisals.[147]

16.9.3 Military necessity[148]

Military necessity is no longer, if it ever was, a general defence. As was said in the Hostages case, 'Military necessity or expediency do not justify a violation of positive rules ... [which are] ... superior to military necessities of the most urgent nature except where the regulations themselves specifically provide to the contrary.'[149] Thus it is only a defence where rules expressly incorporate it as, for example, Article 8(2)(a)(iv) of the ICC Statute does. It is difficult to define in the abstract what is or is not a matter of military necessity, but two things are reasonably clear: neither mere expediency[150] nor political necessity[151] is sufficient.

Further reading

Antonio Cassese, *International Criminal Law*, 2nd edn (Oxford, 2008) chs. 12–13.

Roger Clark, 'The Mental Element in International Criminal Law: The Rome Statute of the International Criminal Court and the Elements of Offences' (2002) 12 *Criminal Law Forum* 291.

Robert Cryer, *Prosecuting International Crimes: Selectivity and the International Criminal Law Regime* (Cambridge, 2005) ch. 6.

Yoram Dinstein, 'Defences' in Gabrielle Kirk McDonald and Olivia Swaak-Goldman (eds.), *Substantive and Procedural Aspects of International Criminal Law* (The Hague, 2000), vol. I, 367.

Albin Eser, 'Article 31' in Triffterer, *Observers' Notes* 863.

Leslie Green, *Superior Orders in National and International Law* (Leyden, 1976).

Frits Kalshoven, *Belligerent Reprisals* (Leyden, 1976).

Matthew Lippman, 'Conundrums of Armed Conflict: Criminal Defences to Violations of the Humanitarian Law of War' (1996) 15 *Dickinson Journal of International Law* 1.

Larry May, *Crimes Against Humanity: A Normative Account* (Cambridge, 2005) ch. 10.

Larry May, *War Crimes and Just War* (Cambridge, 2007) ch. 13.

Mark Osiel, *Obeying Orders: Atrocities, Military Discipline and the Law of War* (New Brunswick, 1999).

---

147 *Martić* ICTY T. Ch. 12.7.2007 paras. 464–8; *Martić* A. Ch. 8.10.2008 paras. 263–7.
148 See further van Sliedregt, *Criminal Responsibility*, 295–8.
149 *List* VIII LRTWC 66–9.
150 Geoffrey Best, *Humanity in Warfare* (London, 1983) 64.
151 Commentary, XV LRTWC 176.

Massimo Scaliotti, 'Defences Before the International Criminal Court' Parts 1 and 2 (2001) 1 *International Criminal Law Review* 111 and (2002) 2 *International Criminal Law Review* 1.

William Schabas, *The UN International Criminal Tribunals* (Cambridge, 2006) 325–47.

Otto Triffterer, 'Article 33' in Triffterer, *Observers' Notes*, 915.

17

Procedures of International Criminal Investigations and Prosecutions

17.1 International criminal procedures

17.1.1 Introduction

From the Nuremberg trials and onwards, the need to develop a new procedural system for any new international criminal tribunal has been acknowledged. Such a procedural system would be *sui generis* in the sense that it would depart from any one domestic system or legal tradition. But, inevitably, it would have elements from the major domestic legal systems of the world, also enhancing the perceived legitimacy of the tribunal and its proceedings. In this chapter we will focus on the procedures that have developed for the ICTY, ICTR and ICC and consider how they blend elements from different legal traditions.

17.1.2 Different legal traditions

There is a significant distinction between the criminal procedures of two major domestic legal traditions: the common law tradition (or Anglo-American tradition) and the civil law tradition (or Continental or Romano-Germanic tradition). While these traditions go beyond the system of criminal procedures,[1] the common law model is said to be 'adversarial' or 'accusatorial' and the civil law model 'inquisitorial'. No domestic system represents a pure model,[2] however, and there are considerable differences between systems belonging to the same tradition. Moreover, some systems, e.g. in Scandinavia, do not really belong to either of the two traditions. In spite of shortcomings,[3] we will here use the terms 'adversarial' and 'inquisitorial' to describe in a general sense differences

---

[1] Not only legal but also sociological and cultural differences are espoused by the different legal traditions.

[2] Regarding Europe, see e.g. Mireille Delmas-Marty and John R. Spencer (eds.), *European Criminal Procedure* (Cambridge, 2002).

[3] See, e.g. Kai Ambos, 'International Criminal Procedure: "Adversarial", "Inquisitorial" or Mixed?' (2003) 3 *ICLR* 1 (noting that modern systems depart from the traditional 'inquisitorial' model, where the prosecutor and judge was one and the same, and that both models are 'accusatorial' in nature).

attributed to the two traditions, but also, on occasion, resort to the common law and civil law labels.

The fundamental difference between the procedural models is the role of the parties and of the judges. While both systems aim at finding the truth,[4] the means and methods vary. The 'adversarial' model, as the term suggests, is premised on two adversarial parties each bringing its case to court, the prosecution and the defence. Hence, the two parties conduct their own investigations and the role of the judge at trial is (traditionally) like a referee, mainly deciding procedural issues raised by the parties; a system that fits well with jury trials. In the 'inquisitorial' model, on the contrary, State agencies are obliged to carry out objective criminal investigations and prosecutions and, essentially, only one case is presented to the court. Defence interests are looked after in the investigation and there is judicial supervision, often by an examining judge (*juge d'instruction*). The prosecutor and the examining judge instruct the police and a 'dossier' is assembled for the entire case. The trial judge is different from the examining judge, but will have access to the 'dossier'. The judge plays a much more active and intervening role at trial, with an explicit task to 'seek the truth'. These differences have effects throughout the proceedings and have led to different procedures.

Ideally, elements from different domestic legal systems should be incorporated in international procedural rules with a view to creating a coherent whole, providing for fair and yet effective proceedings. But blending elements from different legal traditions is not without its problems and adversarial and inquisitorial features are not always compatible. Furthermore, political considerations (and perhaps nationalistic pride) require compromises, which in turn may result in untested solutions or overly flexible rules; procedural efficiency and fair trial rights could thereby be affected.

Apart from the need to achieve broad acceptance there are other reasons for a mixed model. Adversarial principles are generally attractive for fulfilling the fair trial rights of the accused as laid down in international human rights instruments.[5] On the other hand, procedures that require the suspect or accused to conduct his or her investigation in preparation of a separate case may prove difficult, or even impossible, in international criminal proceedings dependent upon State cooperation.[6] Moreover, the focus on objective

---

4 It is sometimes said that the civil law system aims at establishing 'objective truth', as a necessary precondition for a just decision, and the common law system rather seeks 'procedural truth', with an emphasis on a just settlement of dispute; see, e.g. Salvatore Zappalà, *Human Rights in International Criminal Proceedings* (Oxford, 2003) 16.

5 Indeed, the detailed minimum guarantees laid down in Art. 14 of the ICCPR are based on the Anglo-Saxon common law tradition of 'due process of law'; see Manfred Nowak, *U.N. Covenant on Civil and Political Rights – CCPR Commentary*, 2nd edn (Kehl/Strasbourg/Arlington, 2005) 305.

6 This may work both ways, however, and sometimes the accused will have much better access to State archives and other information than the international prosecutor (e.g. in the Former Yugoslavia). But in other instances, e.g. after a regime change (e.g. in Rwanda), the accused could be completely barred from access to the State where the investigation is to be conducted.

truth-finding in inquisitorial systems may better serve, for example, the aim of creating an 'accurate historical record'. A less two party-centred process also allows the crime victims a more pronounced role and increased judicial control may enhance the efficiency of the proceedings and the acceptance of broad prosecutorial powers.

17.1.3 International criminal tribunals and courts

Special criminal procedures were established for the Nuremberg and Tokyo IMTs. Basic provisions concerning the powers of each tribunal and the conduct of the trial, the judgment and sentences, and certain fair trial rights for the defendants, were laid down in the respective Charters.[7] In addition, the Charters provided for Rules of Procedure to be established by each tribunal.[8] The procedures were influenced by domestic procedural principles, primarily from the Anglo-American adversarial system. Adversarial features included the defendant's right to a detailed indictment, to conduct his or her own defence or to have assistance of counsel, as well as to present evidence and cross-examine witnesses. The examination of witnesses at trial was also left to the parties. But the Nuremberg procedures also had some inquisitorial elements, such as allowing trials *in absentia*, giving the defendant a right to explain himself or herself at a preliminary hearing, relaxed rules on admissibility of evidence, and trial by a panel of judges instead of a jury. When assessed by the standards of the day, the criminal procedures were essentially fair.[9] Measured against today's standards, however, the protections were minimal and did not include, for example, a right to remain silent or to appeal against a conviction.

The subsequent trials in Germany under Control Council Law No. 10 were conducted under criminal procedures established by the commanders of the different zones of occupation.[10] Except for some general principles, the criminal procedures of the Military Tribunals after the Second World War were mainly judge-made law.

The ICTY and ICTR Statutes, adopted by the Security Council, include only a few basic procedural provisions; further detail was left to the judges to establish in the form of Rules of Procedure and Evidence (RPE). The approach was that the RPE had to reflect 'concepts that

---

7 Arts. 16 (fair trial rights), 17–25 (powers and trial procedures) and 26–29 (judgment and sentence) of the Nuremberg Charter and Arts. 9–10 (fair trial), 11–15 (powers and trial procedures), and 16–17 (judgment and sentence) of the Tokyo Charter.

8 Art. 13 of the Nuremberg Charter and Art. 7 of the Tokyo Charter. The Nuremberg Rules, adopted on 29 October 1945, contained a few more detailed procedural provisions.

9 The argument has also been made that the trials as such contravened the principle of legality, but such criticisms are directed more against the substantive law than the criminal procedures.

10 Art. III.2 of Control Council Law No. 10. In the United States zone of occupation, general criminal procedures, e.g., were set forth in Ordinance No. 7 of Military Government for Germany, United States Zone, and more specific provisions were adopted by the established Military Tribunals, e.g. the Rules of Procedure of Military Tribunal I, adopted on 2 November 1946 and later amended. Later Uniform Rules of Procedure were adopted for all Military Tribunals in the US zone.

are generally recognized as being fair and just in the international arena'[11] and an early ICTY Trial Chamber decision[12] explained that the procedures were a 'unique amalgam of common and civil law features' and did not 'strictly follow the procedure of civil law or common law'. In fact, however, the ICTY procedures were mainly adversarial in nature. The RPEs for the Tribunals were experimental[13] and have been amended many times, leading to criticism regarding legal certainty and fairness.[14] Many of the amendments have been in an inquisitorial direction, inter alia increasing the judges' controlling powers with the aim to reduce the length of the proceedings.[15] In addition to written law, the ICTY and ICTR judges have resorted to the so-called 'inherent powers' of the Tribunal in seeking out procedures.[16] Notable examples are a decision in *Tadić*[17] on the competence to ascertain the Tribunal's jurisdiction and one in *Blaškić*[18] regarding the issuance of binding orders to States. Inherent powers have also been resorted to for more routine matters such as the withdrawal of counsel[19] and ordering disclosure.[20]

The ICC Statute is a treaty negotiated by States. The ILC draft Statute, much inspired by the procedural law of the ICTY and ICTR, reflected a basically adversarial approach. But during the negotiations more inquisitorial features were proposed and incorporated[21] partly as a reaction against the ICTY and ICTR procedures. Huge efforts were made towards finding solutions satisfactory to the different legal traditions, resulting in agreement on important 'bridges' between the two traditions such as a pre-trial chamber and the procedure in case of admission of guilt. In addition to the very detailed procedural regime they negotiated in the ICC Statute, the States also reserved for themselves the powers to

---

11 *Annual Report of the International Tribunal for the Prosecution of Persons Responsible for Serious Violations of International Humanitarian Law Committed in the Territory of the Former Yugoslavia Since 1991*, UN Doc. A/49/342–S/1994/1007, para. 53 (hereafter First ICTY Report to the UN, 1994).

12 *Tadić* ICTY T. Ch. II 5.8.1996 para. 14. Similarly, *Delalić et al.* ICTY T. Ch. II 1.5.1997 para. 15.

13 See also the First ICTY Report to the UN, 1994, para. 54 (stressing that the Tribunal had little by way of precedent to guide it when drafting the RPE).

14 On 24.7.2009, the 43rd revised version of the ICTY RPE was adopted, and on 14.3.2008 version 17 of the ICTR RPE. For a critical view see, e.g. Andreas O'Shea, 'Changing the Rules of the Game in the Middle of Play: The Dilemma of Procedural Development in the Rwanda Tribunal' (2001) 14 *South African Journal of Criminal Justice* 233.

15 E.g. Daryl Mundis, 'From "Common Law" Towards "Civil Law": The Evolution of the ICTY Rules of Procedure and Evidence' (2001) 14 *LJIL* 367.

16 E.g. Louise Symons, 'The Inherent Powers of the ICTY and ICTR' (2003) 3 *ICLR* 369.

17 *Tadić* ICTY A. Ch. 2.10.1995 paras. 14–20 (a power often referred to as '*Kompetenz-Kompetenz*' or '*la compétence de la compétence*').

18 *Blaškić* ICTY T. Ch. II 18.7.1997 paras. 30–40, and A. Ch. 29.10.1997 paras. 25–31 (also explaining that 'inherent powers' is preferably used for functions that are judicial in nature, while 'implied powers' is often used in relation to expanded competencies).

19 E.g. *Delalić et al.* ICTY A. Ch. 24.6.1999.

20 E.g. *Tadić* ICTY A. Ch. 15.7.1999 para. 322.

21 On the ICC negotiations, see Silvia Fernàndez de Gurmendi, 'International Criminal Law Procedures: The Process of Negotiations' in Lee, *The Making of the Rome Statute*, 217–27, and Silvia Fernàndez de Gurmendi and Håkan Friman, 'The Rules of Procedure and Evidence of the International Criminal Court' (2000) 3 *YIHL* 289.

formulate the RPE.[22] This departs from the practice of other international courts and tribunals where the adoption of procedural law is left to the judges, a practice that promotes flexibility but may cause principled objections.[23] The ICC judges were, however, given the power to adopt Regulations of the Court,[24] which in practice also regulate procedural matters of substantive importance. Together with other normative texts, the procedural law of the ICC has become voluminous, multi-layered and complex.

17.1.4 International and domestic procedural law

The relationship between international and domestic criminal procedures is complex. While influenced by domestic procedures, the ICTY, ICTR and ICC all have mixed systems with adversarial as well as inquisitorial elements. At least to an extent, the traditional common law and civil law divide has been overcome.[25] Nonetheless, the procedures are primarily adversarial in nature and the procedures of the ICTY and ICTR more so than those of the ICC.

Seen as a whole each procedural system is unprecedented and may be considered as unique (*sui generis*).[26] But some lawyers are uneasy about the hybrid systems created, which depart from the mature and carefully structured balance of domestic systems.[27] The fact that they are unique and, in the case of the ICC, the avoidance of 'technical terms' with a special meaning in domestic systems, creates uncertainties.[28] In any case, domestic notions, legal constructs and terms of art should not be 'mechanically imported into international

---

22 Art. 51 of the ICC Statute (which allows the judges to adopt amendments to the RPE under certain conditions, but only on a provisional basis and subject to the approval of the ICC States Parties).

23 E.g. Claus Kreß, 'The Procedural Texts of the International Criminal Court' (2007) 5 *JICJ* 537 at 538. See also David Hunt, 'The International Criminal Court: High Hopes, "Creative Ambiguity" and an Unfortunate Mistrust in International Judges' (2004) 2 *JICJ* 56.

24 Art. 52 of the ICC Statute.

25 But whether this reflects a real development towards a new, fused procedural tradition more generally or is just the result of the political wish to establish the ICC is a debated issue; see, e.g. Mark Findlay, 'Synthesis in Trial Proceedings? The Experience of International Criminal Tribunals' (2001) 50 *ICLQ* 26.

26 E.g. *Delalić et al.* ICTY T. Ch. II 1.5.1997 para. 15. See, e.g. Patrick Robinson, 'Ensuring Fair and Expeditious Trials at the International Criminal Tribunal for the Former Yugoslavia' (2000) 11 *EJIL* 569 at 574 (the ICTY procedures are 'neither common law accusatorial nor civil law inquisitorial, nor even an amalgam of both; it is *sui generis*'). Similarly, Ambos, 'International Criminal Procedure', 34–5, and Gabrielle Kirk McDonald, 'Trial Procedures and Practice' in Gabrielle Kirk McDonald and Olivia Swaak Goldman (eds.), *Substantive and Procedural Aspects of International Criminal Law: The Experience of International and National Courts* (Kluwer, 2000) 556. Cf. Maxime Langer, 'The Rise of Managerial Judging in International Criminal Law' (2005) *American Journal of Comparative Law* 835 (claiming that the ICTY's procedures are neither unique nor represent an undefined hybrid system).

27 E.g. Vladimir Tochilovsky, 'International Criminal Justice: Strangers in the Foreign System' (2004) 15 *CLF* 319.

28 See Kai Ambos and Dennis Miller, 'Structure and Function of the Confirmation Procedure before the ICC from a Comparative Perspective' (2007) 7 *ICLR* 335, 337–40.

proceedings'; they must be understood against the object and purpose of the international proceedings.[29] Additionally, domestic procedures are so diverse that it is often difficult to argue customary law status, and only to a limited extent are principles conceived so uniformly that domestic law analogies are relevant. Meaningful conclusions require extensive comparative research, something the Chambers rarely have time or resources to do.

These institutions serve as models for international criminal justice and a source of inspiration for the development of domestic proceedings.[30] It is important to bear in mind, however, that these international criminal procedures were never devised to be adopted by States and have been framed against the specific circumstances applicable to the international jurisdictions; they might not always represent 'best practice' for States.

17.2 International criminal proceedings and human rights

17.2.1 International human rights standards

It is to be expected that an international criminal jurisdiction should adhere to internationally recognized human rights standards. In his report on the establishment of the ICTY, the UN Secretary-General underlined, as axiomatic, that such standards regarding the rights of the accused be fully respected at all stages of the proceedings.[31] Apart from the argument of principle, this is also a necessary requirement for allowing an international court to prosecute individuals, a matter that is normally intrinsically linked to State sovereignty.[32] Adherence to international human rights standards is also important in order to obtain cooperation by States having obligations under international law to respect human rights.

Nevertheless, the international criminal courts and tribunals are not parties to, and therefore are not formally bound by, international human rights treaties nor the jurisprudence developed by international human rights courts and other organs. These are directed to States. Instead, some human rights principles are set out in the Statutes and RPEs, and are thus directly applicable in the proceedings. Being a global treaty with a large number of ratifications, the ICCPR has served as the model.[33] Such principles have also entered into the legal framework more indirectly as principles of the UN or as enshrined in customary

---

29 See Judge Cassese's dissenting opinion in *Erdemović* ICTY A. Ch. 7.10.1997 paras. 1–6.
30 E.g. Göran Sluiter, 'The Law of International Criminal Procedure and Domestic War Crimes Trials' (2006) 6 *ICLR* 605. The ICTY, ICTR and ICC procedures have also influenced the so-called 'internationalized criminal courts', e.g. the Special Court for Sierra Leone; see Chapter 9.
31 Report of the Secretary-General pursuant to Paragraph 2 of Security Council resolution 808 (1993) para. 106.
32 Antonio Cassese, 'Opinion: The International Criminal Tribunal for the Former Yugoslavia and Human Rights' (1997) 4 *European Human Rights Law Review* 329 at 332.
33 Particularly Art. 14 of the ICCPR. One should remember, however, that some States made far-reaching reservations with respect to that Article; see Nowak, *UN Covenant*, 306–7.

international law or general principles of law, regarding which human rights treaties and jurisprudence may serve as authoritative evidence.[34]

After some initial reluctance[35] the ICTY and ICTR now frequently make reference to international human rights treaties and case law in their decisions.[36] Nevertheless, in some instances the Tribunals have departed from a strict adherence to human rights standards, as developed for domestic proceedings. The Tribunals' unique structure, status, and subject matter jurisdiction have been regarded as justification for this departure. But even when the outcome can be defended, the method used may be criticized.[37] The ICC Statute, on the other hand, contains provisions reflecting international human rights law and directs that the Court must apply applicable treaties and the principles and rules of international law as sources of law; additionally, the application and interpretation of the law 'must be consistent with internationally recognized human rights'.[38] Many commentators claim that the ICC represents a clear improvement in the codification of human rights, sometimes going further than international human rights law, and the Court often resorts to such law in practice; but there is also criticism that the Court has been too reluctant to act as a supervisor of national law and practice.[39]

17.2.2 Independence and impartiality

All human rights treaties require an institutional guarantee in the form of an independent and impartial tribunal or court established by law. This is an integral part of the accused's right to a fair trial and a general principle of law recognized by all legal systems of the world. Independence requires an institutional and functional separation from the executive and legislative powers as well as from the parties.[40] One problem for the international criminal jurisdictions is their dependence on cooperation by States and others. The difficulties were described in the *Barayagwiza* case, after suspension by the government of Rwanda of

---

34 E.g. *Kajelijeli* ICTR A. Ch. 23.5.2005 para. 209 (customary international law is reflected, inter alia, in the ICCPR).
35 E.g. *Tadić* ICTY T. Ch. II 10.8.1995 paras. 17–30 (interpretations of human rights standards made by other judicial bodies were considered, by the majority, to be of limited value due to the Tribunal's unique procedures).
36 E.g. *Delalić et al.* ICTY T. Ch. II 28.4.1997 para. 27 (decisions on provisions of the ICCPR and the ECHR were found 'authoritative and applicable'); see also *Kajelijeli* ICTR A. Ch. 23.5.2005 para. 209. Generally, see Antonio Cassese, 'The Influence of the European Court of Human Rights on International Criminal Tribunals: Some Methodological Remarks' in Morten Bergsmo (ed.), *Human Rights and Criminal Justice for the Downtrodden: Essays in Honour of Asbjørn Eide* (Leiden, 2003) 19–52.
37 E.g. Gabrielle McIntyre, 'Defining Human Rights in the Arena of International Humanitarian Law: Human Rights in the Jurisprudence of the ICTY' in Gideon Boas and William Schabas (eds.), *International Criminal Law Developments in the Case Law of the ICTY* (Dordrecht, 2003) 193–238.
38 Art. 21(1)(b) and (3) of the ICC Statute. See e.g. *Lubanga Dyilo* ICC A. Ch. 14.12.2006 paras. 36–9.
39 E.g. Göran Sluiter, 'Human Rights Protection in the ICC Pre-Trial Phase' in Stahn and Sluiter, *Emerging Practice*, 459–75. Nonetheless, a thorough analysis of national seizure measures was conducted in *Lubanga Dyilo* ICC PT. Ch. I 29.1.2007 paras. 62–90 (admissibility of evidence).
40 E.g. *Ringeisen v. Austria*, ECtHR 16.7.1971 para. 95 Series A No. 13.

cooperation with the ICTR, though well aware of the fact that most of the evidence that the Tribunal needed was located in Rwanda.[41]

The impartiality requirement also relates to the judge who must be both personally and institutionally impartial. The ICTY Statute and ICTR Statute expressly require the impartiality of judges but do not address the independence of the Tribunal.[42] Their status as judicial institutions established by the Security Council has led to some discomfort regarding their institutional independence.[43] However, domestic courts are also subject to the exercise of executive and legislative powers, for example as regards budgets, and appointments, and this alone does not rule out independence. In an objective sense, the ICTY and ICTR are institutionally and functionally independent. For example, both Tribunals have addressed the legality of their creation[44] and there are no provisions allowing the Security Council to interfere in individual cases. In *Furundžija* the ICTY Appeals Chamber addressed the question of impartiality of the judges. Taking into account ECtHR jurisprudence and domestic practice, the Chamber established a standard for the assessment of impartiality.[45] Actual bias or an unacceptable appearance of bias – certain interests or circumstances that would lead 'a reasonable observer, properly informed, to reasonably apprehend bias' – reflect partiality and, hence, the judge should be disqualified.[46]

The ICC is an independent, treaty-based body and its more comprehensive Statute explicitly addresses the independence and impartiality of the judges and the Prosecutor (and Deputy Prosecutors), as well as the right of the accused to a 'fair hearing conducted impartially'.[47] The Statute provides for both personal and institutional impartiality. With respect to the Security Council, the relationship is essentially of a legal nature, but some have expressed concerns regarding the Council's power to request a deferral of an investigation or prosecution.[48] The non-renewable term in office of the judges and prosecutors is one way of ensuring independence and impartiality. While the Prosecutor's institutional

---

41 *Barayagwiza* ICTR A. Ch. 3.11.1999 and 31.3.2000 (particularly the separate opinions by Judges Vohrah and Nieto-Navia).

42 Art. 13 of the ICTY Statute and Art. 12 of the ICTR Statute. See also Rules 14–15 of the ICTY RPE and ICTR RPE (solemn declaration and disqualification of judges).

43 E.g. José Alvarez, 'Nuremberg Revisited: The Tadić Case' (1996) 7 *EJIL* 245 at 253–4.

44 E.g. *Tadić* ICTY A. Ch. 2.10.1995, and *Kanyabashi* ICTR T. Ch. II 18.6.1997.

45 *Furundžija* ICTY A. Ch. 21.7.2000 paras. 177–91. See also *Rutaganda* ICTR A. Ch. 26.5.2003 paras. 39–49. Other interesting decisions on disqualification are *Sesay et al.* SCSL A. Ch. 13.3.2004, and *Norman et al.* SCSL A. Ch. 28.5.2004.

46 In one case before the ICTR, the appearance of bias regarding one judge extended to the whole Trial Chamber and the Chamber was reconstituted: *Karemera et al.* ICTR A. Ch. 28.9.2004 and 22.10.2004 paras. 62–8 (two judges dissenting).

47 Arts. 36 (qualifications and election of judges), 40 (independence of judges), 41 (excusing and disqualification of judges), 42(5)–(8) (independence, impartiality and disqualification of the Prosecutor), 45 (solemn undertaking), and 67(1) (fair trial rights) of the ICC Statute. See also rr. 5–6 and 33–5 of the ICC RPE, which include, inter alia, a duty for a judge or Prosecutor to request to be excused if he or she 'has reason to believe that a ground for disqualification exists in relation to him or her' (r. 35).

48 See further section 8.9.

independence and large functional autonomy under the law are adversarial features, the prescribed impartiality is more inquisitorial in nature and indicates a role as 'an officer of justice' rather than a partisan party to the proceedings. There is a case for disqualification when the impartiality of a judge or the Prosecutor 'might reasonably be doubted'.

17.2.3 Presumption of innocence

Another fundamental principle set forth in human rights instruments, and also generally accepted and often constitutionally protected by States, is that the accused shall be presumed innocent until proven guilty according to law.[49] As phrased in those instruments, the principle applies only to an 'accused' and the same restriction is expressed in the ICTY and ICTR Statutes.[50] However, a widely shared opinion is that the presumption should also extend to the investigative stage. The ICC Statute indeed affords this right to 'everyone' and this wording, in spite of the provision being placed in the part dealing with trials, may suggest that it is of general application.[51] This is also reflected in the cautious approach not to pre-judge guilt when establishing who is a 'victim' in relation to victim participation in the early stages of the process.[52]

The presumption of innocence has many implications. A corollary right is to remain silent and not be compelled to incriminate oneself or confess guilt, which, broadly interpreted, applies throughout the proceedings. Indeed, this right is provided for 'suspects' at the ICTY and ICTR and generally at the ICC.[53] Silence may not be used as evidence to prove guilt and may not be interpreted as an admission.[54] Another consequence is that an accused refusing to express an opinion as to his or her guilt or innocence shall be considered as not having admitted any guilt; in the system with formal pleadings at the ICTY and ICTR, the judge shall enter a 'plea of not guilty' on behalf of the accused.[55]

Another important effect is that the prosecution must prove the defendant's guilt and in case of doubt the accused must be found not guilty (*in dubio pro reo*).[56] Hence, the prosecutor has the burden of proof. National systems take different approaches as to the scope of the prosecutor's burden. In common law and other adversarial systems the standard is referred to as 'guilt beyond a reasonable doubt' and in civil law systems often 'the judge's innermost conviction' (*l'intime conviction du juge*). The ICTY and ICTR have themselves

---

49 Some countries, however, interpret the principle as 'not presumed guilty', e.g. the Italian Constitution.
50 Art. 21(3) of the ICTY Statute and Art. 20(3) of the ICTR Statute.
51 Art. 66(1) of the ICC Statute (in Part 6 'The Trial'). See also *Bemba Gombo* ICC PT. Ch. II 14.8.2009 para. 37.
52 See Chapter 18.
53 Rule 42(A)(iii) of the ICTY RPE and ICTR RPE; Art. 55(1)(a) and (2)(b) of the ICC Statute.
54 Arts. 55(2) and 67(1)(g) of the ICC Statute. See, e.g. also *Brđanin* ICTY T. Ch. II 1.9.2004 para. 24.
55 Rule 62 of the ICTY RPE and ICTR RPE.
56 An interesting question is whether the principle applies only to questions of fact or also to questions of law: see declarations by Judges Shahabuddeen (both) and Schomburg (facts only) in *Limaj et al.* ICTY A. Ch. 27.9.2007.

adopted a common law-inspired approach whereby the Prosecutor is required to prove guilt 'beyond a reasonable doubt',[57] but the onus to establish a defence rests with the accused.[58] In relation to the charges, the accused need only bring evidence 'to suggest a reasonable possibility' in order to induce a reasonable doubt, while the proof required for other issues which the accused might raise has been declared as 'on the balance of probabilities'.[59]

In spite of domestic differences, the States agreed that the ICC Statute should establish the Prosecutor's onus and a 'beyond a reasonable doubt' standard for a conviction, but also a right for the accused 'not to have imposed on him or her any reversal of the burden of proof or any onus of rebuttal'.[60] What this right will mean in practice is not entirely clear and it may create problems, for example with respect to the generally accepted presumption of a person's sanity. But some (civil law-inspired) commentators go further, claiming a burden on the prosecution to disprove defences.[61]

17.2.4 Public, fair and expeditious proceedings

The principle of a public hearing allows a public scrutiny of the judicial proceedings and thus a protection against unfairness and arbitrary action by the courts. This principle also applies at the ICTY, ICTR and ICC. The respective Statutes provide for public hearings and delivery of the judgment in public.[62] As in domestic proceedings there are exceptions, however, and the provisions of the ICTY and ICTR RPEs are inspired by the exceptions set out in the ICCPR and ECHR; closed sessions are allowed for reasons of: public order or morality, safety, security or non-disclosure of the identity of a protected victim or witness, and the protection of the interests of justice.[63] The ICC Statute provides for two exceptions: protection of the accused, victims and witnesses, and protection of confidential or sensitive evidence.[64] It has been argued that these exceptions should be interpreted in strict accordance with human rights law.[65] In practice, however, the extensive use of protective measures constitutes infringements of the principle.

---

57 Rule 87(A) of the ICTY RPE and ICTR RPE.
58 E.g. *Delalić et al.* ICTY A. Ch. 20.2.2001 para. 582.
59 E.g. *ibid.*, para. 603.
60 Arts. 66(2)–(3) and 67(1)(i) of the ICC Statute. Cf. Art. 21 of the ICTY Statute and Art. 20 of the ICTR Statute, which simply refer to the accused being proven guilty 'according to the provisions of the present Statute'. The reasonable doubt standard was also defeated with respect to Art. 14 of the ICCPR.
61 E.g. Salvatore Zappalà, 'The Rights of the Accused' in Cassese, *Commentary*, 1346.
62 Arts. 21(2) and 23(2) of the ICTY Statute, Arts. 20(2) and 22(2) of the ICTR Statute, and Arts. 64(7), 67(1) and 74(5) of the ICC Statute. See also rr. 78 and 98*ter* of the ICTY RPE and r. 78 of the ICTR RPE.
63 R. 79 of the ICTY RPE and ICTR RPE, to be compared with Art. 14(1) of the ICCPR and Art. 6(1) of the ECHR.
64 Art. 64(7) of the ICC Statute, referring to Art. 68 concerning the protection of the accused, victims and witnesses. See also Art. 72(5)(d) (national security information) and rr. 72 (relevance or admissibility of evidence in cases of sexual violence) and 87–8 (protective and special measures).
65 E.g. Christoph Safferling, *Towards an International Criminal Procedure* (Oxford, 2001) 238–9.

To provide for a 'fair trial' is a fundamental aim for any criminal procedures, including international ones. But although the principle is recognized as such as a general principle of international law, it is subject to different interpretations. Consequently, the standards laid down in international human rights instruments are drafted in quite general terms and implemented quite differently domestically. Nonetheless, the international criminal jurisdictions require specific rules and not merely general principles.

A fundamental element of a fair trial, and a general principle of law, is the principle of equality of arms; a principle that should not be confused with the principle of equality before the law, or non-discrimination.[66] Equality of arms is more significant in adversarial proceedings and requires opportunities for each party to prepare and present its case, both on law and on facts, and to respond to the opponent's case. The Tribunals argue a broad interpretation,[67] but also establish limitations. A judicial body must ensure that neither party is put at a disadvantage when presenting its case[68] but the application is less far-reaching with respect to preparations. The accused's right to have adequate time and facilities to prepare the defence should be ensured under conditions that do not place him or her at a substantial disadvantage vis-à-vis the Prosecutor, but does not imply ensuring parity of resources between the parties, such as the material equality of financial or personal resources.[69] The ICC may well take a similar legal stance, but in practice a number of measures have been introduced to minimize unequal resources.[70] Other aspects of the equality of arms are the accused's rights to prompt and detailed information about the charges, to disclosure of and access to the Prosecutor's evidence, to defence counsel, to examine witnesses against him or her, and to call witnesses under equal conditions.[71] The right to call witnesses has been interpreted as placing a positive duty upon the Tribunal to assist the accused with summonses, safe conducts and other measures necessary for obtaining the testimony.[72]

Each Statute provides the accused with the right to be tried without 'undue delay'; a right also reflected in all major human rights instruments.[73] The ICTY and ICTR, and already the ICC, are

---

66 Art. 21(1) of the ICTY Statute, Art. 20(1) of the ICTR Statute, and Art. 67(1) of the ICC Statute. See also Arts. 14(1) and 26 of the ICCPR. For a discussion, see Stefania Negri, 'The Principle of "Equality of Arms" and the Evolving Law of International Criminal Procedure' (2005) 5 *ICLR* 513.

67 E.g. *Tadić* ICTY A. Ch. 15.7.1999 paras. 44 and 52.

68 *Ibid.*, para. 48.

69 E.g. *Kayishema and Ruzindana* ICTR A. Ch. 1.6.2001 paras. 67–9, and *Kordić and Čerkez* ICTY A. Ch. 17.12.2004 paras. 175–6 (referring to an earlier decision in the same case: A. Ch. 11.9.2001 paras. 5–9).

70 E.g. Marc Dubuisson et al., 'Contribution of the Registry to greater respect for the principles of fairness and expeditious proceedings before the International Criminal Court' in Stahn and Sluiter, *Emerging Practice*, 565–84.

71 These rights are also specifically provided for: Art. 21(4) of the ICTY Statute, Art. 20(4) of the ICTR Statute, and Art. 67(1) of the ICC Statute.

72 E.g. *Tadić* ICTY T. Ch. II 26.6.1996, and *Kupreškić et al.* ICTY T. Ch. II 6.10.1998.

73 Art. 21 of the ICTY Statute, Art. 20 of the ICTR Statute, and Art. 67 of the ICC Statute. See also Art. 14(3) of the ICCPR. In addition, Art. 64(3)(c) of the ICC Statute obliges the Trial Chamber to: 'confer with the parties and adopt such procedures as are necessary to facilitate the fair and expeditious conduct of the proceedings'.

often criticized for excessively long proceedings[74] and many challenges have been launched by accused claiming violations of this right. To no surprise, many critics are coloured by their own legal tradition; common law observers would, for example, question the relaxed practice on admissibility of evidence,[75] and civil law observers argue in favour of even more judicial intervention in the investigation and, based on a dossier, at trial.[76] In response, the ICTY and ICTR have amended their practice and rules to achieve more expeditious proceedings but they still remain very long in most cases. Quite apart from the fact that the resources are limited, the main reason is that international investigations and prosecutions are very complex, factually, legally and politically, and therefore more time-consuming than most domestic ones. Hence, procedural reforms and practices can only do so much to reduce the length of the proceedings.

17.3   Actors in the proceedings and their roles

The organs of the ICTY, ICTR and ICC are all organized in a similar way and the organs have been described briefly in Chapters 7 and 8. Their functions and powers are set out in the applicable Statute and RPE.

17.3.1   Judges

The role of the judges at the ICTY and ICTR was from the outset inspired by the adversarial nature of the proceedings; to an extent they act as umpires. But some provisions allow them a more active role, for example to order the parties to present additional evidence and *ex officio* to summon a witness. Over time the judges have become more active in controlling the proceedings as a whole, rather than simply the trial. The introduction of pre-trial judges in the ICTY and more stringent provisions for both Tribunals on preparations for trial mark this development.

The role of the ICC judges, on the other hand, is already by statute more interventionist in nature. Apart from activities regarding preparations for trial and submission of evidence, judges have a certain limited role to play in the criminal investigation. It may be a far cry from the role of an investigative judge in a civil law system, but it reflects additional inquisitorial elements in the criminal procedures. Early judicial involvement helps ensure the rights of the suspect or accused, and the protection of other interests, such as the interests of victims or States. It may also assist in obtaining State cooperation. But finding the appropriate role is difficult and the early practice has exposed palpable tensions between the judges and the prosecution.

---

74 Reference is sometimes made to the Nuremberg trials which lasted some ten months and covered all of the Second World War in the Western theatre, but this comparison is not entirely relevant due to the development of fair trial rights since the 1940s, including the right to appeals.
75 E.g. Ian Bryan and Peter Rowe, 'The Role of Evidence in War Crimes Trials: The Common Law and the Yugoslav Tribunal' (1999) 2 *YIHL* 307.
76 E.g. Stéphane Bourgon, 'Procedural Problems Hindering Expeditious and Fair Justice' (2004) 2 *JICJ* 526.

17.3.2 Prosecutor

True to adversarial principles, the international Prosecutor enjoys a high degree of independence, albeit under a varying degree of judicial supervision. The supervision is greater in the ICC than in the ICTY and ICTR and the rather interventionist approach adopted by the ICC judges has prompted an intensive discussion concerning judicial control and supervision versus prosecutorial discretion.[77] One crucial difference is in the extent of the Prosecutor's powers flowing from the more limited geographical and temporal jurisdiction of the Tribunals compared with the ICC.[78] Each Prosecutor decides on the commencement of the investigation, the conduct of the investigation and any prosecution of a crime. The onus to prove the guilt of the accused rests with the Prosecutor. However, the scope of the investigation obligations differs and the prosecutorial role to represent the public interest of prosecuting and punishing the perpetrators of crimes under its jurisdiction is tempered at the ICC by a more active truth-seeking duty.[79]

One must not underestimate the difficult role of an international prosecutor in practice. In the words of a former SCSL Prosecutor:

> In conclusion, in order to successfully execute the initial prosecutorial plan, a prosecutor must be visible, focused, situationally aware, and flexible. That prosecutor operates daily in a legal, diplomatic, political, and real world. The decisions made affect not only the prosecutorial strategy, but the very security of the region.[80]

17.3.3 Defendant and defence counsel

At the ICTY and ICTR, a 'suspect' is a person concerning whom the Prosecutor possesses reliable information which tends to show that he or she may have committed a crime over which the Tribunal has jurisdiction; the 'suspect' becomes an 'accused' upon the confirmation of an indictment.[81] The ICC Statute and RPE avoid the term 'suspect', which creates unnecessary ambiguities, and the term 'accused' applies to someone against whom charges have been confirmed.[82] The Statutes and RPE provide for some fundamental rights for those

---

77 See section 17.8.1.

78 Although the temporal jurisdiction of the ICTY is open-ended, in reality there will be an end to its operations as clearly set out in the so-called 'completion strategy', see Chapter 7.

79 Generally, see Christopher Keith Hall, 'The Powers and Role of the Prosecutor of the International Criminal Court in the Global Fight against Impunity' (2004) 17 *LJIL* 121.

80 David Crane, 'Dancing with the Devil: Prosecuting West Africa's Warlords: Building Initial Prosecutorial Strategy for an International Tribunal After Third World Armed Conflicts' (2005) 37 *Case Western Reserve Journal of International Law* 1, 8.

81 Rr. 2 and 47(H)(ii) of the ICTY RPE and ICTR RPE.

82 Art. 55(2) of the ICC Statute refers to '[w]here there are grounds to believe that a person has committed a crime within the jurisdiction of the Court', which is the equivalent of a 'suspect'. See Art. 61 of the ICC Statute regarding the 'accused' (cf. 'the person charged' or 'the person'). See also Ambos and Miller, 'Structure and Function', 339–40.

suspected or accused of a crime. Among the rights of the suspect are the right to remain silent, to legal assistance during questioning, and to interpretation and translations.[83] More extensive rights, reflecting international human rights instruments, are prescribed for the 'accused'.[84] These and other rights are further developed in more detailed statutory provisions and in the jurisprudence.

The adversarial nature of the ICTY and ICTR proceedings presupposes that the defendant may put forward his or her own 'defence case'. In turn, this requires a separate investigation conducted by the defence. The Appeals Chamber in *Tadić* stressed the importance of 'equality of arms' and concluded that the principle must be given a more liberal interpretation than at domestic courts, due to the difficulties encountered by the parties in tracing and gaining access to evidence.[85]

Under these circumstances the assistance of a defence counsel is particularly important. Almost all defendants at the ICTY and ICTR have been or are represented by counsel, normally appointed and paid for by the Tribunal. However, two political leaders (both also lawyers) indicted by the ICTY have demanded to conduct their own defences, which have highlighted the question whether legal assistance could be imposed against the will of the accused. One may note, however, that mandatory representation is accepted in civil law systems,[86] but contrary to the practice in common law systems this does not mean that the accused is prevented from participating actively at the trial. The ICTY has tried different approaches, such as *amicus curiae* (friend of the court) to assist the court[87] and 'stand-by counsel',[88] but has in the end concluded that the right to self-representation is not absolute and has imposed counsel.[89] More recently, the ICTY has allowed self-representation in two high-profile cases, including a right to legal aid which pays for 'legal assistance', but in one case counsel was later imposed 'in the interests of justice'.[90]

---

83 In particular, Art. 18(3) of the ICTY Statute and Art. 17(3) of the ICTR Statute, r. 42 of the ICTY RPE and ICTR RPE, and Art. 55(2) of the ICC Statute.

84 Primarily, Art. 21 of the ICTY Statute, Art. 20 of the ICTR Statute, and Art. 67 of the ICC Statute. At the ICC, these rights are applicable, in principle, from the first appearance before the Court, see r. 121(1) of the ICC RPE. Compare with Art. 14 of the ICCPR.

85 *Tadić* ICTY A. Ch. 15.7.1999 para. 52. See section 17.2.4.

86 See Mirjan Damaška, 'Assignment of Counsel and Perceptions of Fairness' (2005) 3 *JICJ* 3.

87 *Milošević* ICTY T. Ch. III 30.8.2001. Subsequently, Milošević identified some lawyers as 'legal associates' and was granted privileged communications with them.

88 *Šešelj* ICTY T. Ch. II 9.5.2003.

89 *Milošević* ICTY A. Ch. 1.11.2004, and *Šešelj* ICTY T. Ch. I 21.8.2006. Similarly, *Norman et al.* SCSL T. Ch. 8.6.2004 paras. 8 and 27. See r. 45*ter* of the ICTY RPE, r. 45*quater* of the ICTR RPE, Art. 67(1)(d) of the ICC Statute and reg. 76(1) of the ICC Regulations.

90 See *Šešelj* ICTY A. Ch. 8.12.2006 and *Karadžić* ICTY T. Ch. 28.1.2009 and T. Ch. III 5.11.2009. The decisions and the trial management in *Šešelj* have been strongly criticized, e.g. Göran Sluiter, 'Compromising the Authority of International Criminal Justice: How Šešelj Runs His Trial' (2007) 5 *JICJ* 529. For self-representation on appeals (with amicus counsel), see *Krajišnik* ICTY A. Ch. 11.5.2007 (including dissenting opinions).

The ICC Statute also recognizes the right to legal representation of the suspect's or accused's own choosing, and if necessary free of cost.[91] As in the Tribunals, the Registrar is to establish and maintain a list of counsel from which counsel are to be chosen, but the ICC RPE also allows a counsel not on the list to be chosen if that counsel meets the required qualifications and is willing to be included in the list.[92] The ICC has also established a system with public defence counsel to assist in the very early stages of an investigation.[93]

17.3.4 Victims and witnesses

Victims are afforded a substantially stronger role at the ICC than in the ICTY and ICTR processes, which includes an independent right to participate in the proceedings and to claim reparations.[94] In all these jurisdictions, however, victims also appear as witnesses. The term 'witness' is not defined in the rules of the ICTY, ICTR or ICC but there is a distinction between 'expert witnesses'[95] and other witnesses. Generally, adversarial and inquisitorial systems view the role of the witness differently. The ICTY and ICTR have primarily opted for an adversarial approach whereby the parties have the primary responsibility for the evidence and, accordingly, each party may call witnesses, who will be therefore either 'prosecution witnesses' or 'defence witnesses'.[96] A more inquisitorial element, however, is the power of the judges to summon witnesses or order their attendance.[97] Such witnesses are sometimes called 'court witnesses'.[98] Similar provisions apply to the ICC.[99] The accused may also give testimony as a witness, but only in his or her own defence.

A witness giving testimony under solemn declaration (a neutral term for 'oath') is obliged to speak the truth and does so with criminal liability for a false testimony.[100] A protection against self-incrimination is provided for.[101] Certain witness privileges

---

91 Arts. 55(2) and 67(1)(d) of the ICC Statute.

92 R. 22 of the ICC RPE and regs. 69–76 of the ICC Regulations. See also r. 45 of the ICTY RPE and ICTR RPE. Regarding qualifications, see r. 44 of the ICTY RPE and ICTR RPE, r. 22 of the ICC RPE and regs. 67–8 of the ICC Regulations.

93 Reg. 77 of the ICC Regulations.

94 See Chapter 18.

95 R. 94*bis* of the ICTY RPE and ICTR RPE, and r. 140(3) of the ICC RPE (see also rr. 91 and 191 of the ICC RPE).

96 E.g. r. 65*ter* of the ICTY RPE and ICTR RPE.

97 R. 98 of the ICTY RPE and ICTR RPE.

98 E.g. *Milošević* ICTY T. Ch. III 18.2.2004. There are also examples where the Trial Chamber has considered all witnesses as 'witnesses of justice', and not of either of the parties, once they have made the solemn declaration, e.g. *Jelisić* ICTY T. Ch. I 11.12.1998.

99 Arts. 64(6)(b) and 69(3) of the ICC Statute, and rr. 76 and 79 of the ICC RPE.

100 Rr. 90 and 91 of the ICTY RPE and ICTR RPE; Arts. 69(1) and 70 of the ICC Statute and r. 66 of the ICC RPE.

101 R. 90(E) of the ICTY RPE and ICTR RPE, and rr. 65, 74–5 of the ICC RPE (which also covers incrimination of family members). However, the witness may be compelled to answer incriminating questions under an assurance that the information will not be used for prosecution against him or her.

apply.[102] The ICTY and ICTR Trial Chambers may issue a *subpoena ad testificandum* when it is 'necessary for the purpose of an investigation or for the preparation or conduct of the trial'.[103] The ICC Trial Chambers may 'require the attendance and testimony of a witness'.[104] But the enforcement of such orders differs, see Chapter 20.

Both in the Tribunals and in the ICC, the protection of victims and witnesses is provided for and has been widely applied in practice.[105]

17.3.5 States, international organizations and others

An international criminal jurisdiction will inevitably take decisions which affect State interests, for example decisions regarding the exercise of jurisdiction or State cooperation. Hence, there are certain possibilities for States to intervene in the proceedings. In the ICTY, States 'directly affected' by a decision have a right to request a review and this right has been exercised with respect to, inter alia, an order to a State to provide documents,[106] an order to NATO (and SFOR) to provide reports and documents,[107] a request for arrest and surrender,[108] and disclosure of confidential information.[109]

Due to their origin, the Tribunals have a particular relationship with the UN Security Council. But while the Tribunals report to the Security Council, it is important to note that there are no provisions allowing the Security Council to intervene in their proceedings. As to other international organizations, the ICTY and ICTR have directed binding orders for cooperation to such organizations, but have also concluded that they are not, formally

---

102 R. 97 of the ICTY RPE and ICTR RPE (lawyer–client). Further privileges have evolved in practice, e.g. for a former employee of the ICRC (*Simić et al.* ICTY T. Ch. III 27.7.1999), employees and functionaries of the Tribunals (*Delalić et al.* ICTY T. Ch. II 8.7.1997), and a war correspondent (*Brđanin and Talić* ICTY A. Ch. 11.12.2002, reversing the decision by a Trial Chamber of 7.6.2002). See also r. 73 of the ICC RPE (a more general formula for privilege and special provisions regarding the ICRC). Privileges also apply for confidential (national security) information: r. 70 of the ICTY RPE and ICTR RPE, and Art. 72 of the ICC Statute; see also e.g. *Milošević* ICTY A. Ch. 23.10.2002 (interpretation of r. 70) and the subsequent application by the Trial Chamber of 30.10.2003. See further, Emily Ann Herman, 'In Pursuit of Accountability: The Red Cross, War Correspondents, and Evidentiary Privileges in International Criminal Tribunals' (2005) 80 *New York University Law Review* 241. Cf. the interesting decision by the SCSL whereby an international human rights worker was refused witness privileges: *Brima et al.* SCSL T. Ch. II 16.9.2005.
103 R. 54 of the ICTY RPE and ICTR RPE. See Chapter 20.
104 Art. 64(6)(b) of the ICC Statute. In addition, the Pre-Trial Chamber has a general power to issue necessary orders at the request of the Prosecutor or the defence: Art. 57(3)(a)–(b) of the ICC Statute.
105 See Chapter 18.3.
106 *Blaškić* ICTY A. Ch. 29.10.1997 (Croatia against a *subpoena duces tecum*), and *Kordić and Čerkez* ICTY A. Ch. 26.3.1999.
107 *Simić et al.* ICTY A. Ch. 27.3.2001 (the motions became moot after the prosecution and the accused entered into a plea agreement).
108 *Bobetko* ICTY A. Ch. 29.11.2002. Cf. *Gotovina et al.* ICTY A. Ch. 17.1.2008 (Croatia's request for review of decision to deny provisional release was rejected).
109 *Milošević* ICTY A. Ch. 23.10.2002.

speaking, obliged to cooperate.[110] The organization as such may also request a review.[111] As previously noted,[112] the ICRC is afforded special privileges.

At the ICC, States are given an even greater scope for intervention which is partly due to the principle of complementarity.[113] A referring State (or the Security Council) may request a review of the Prosecutor's decision not to investigate or to prosecute.[114] Certain decisions may be appealed by an affected State[115] and States may also seek a ruling on the legality of a request for cooperation and intervene in procedures regarding a failure to cooperate.[116] Of course, the Security Council's power to require the deferral of an investigation or prosecution is a substantive form of intervention.[117]

Additionally, the Chambers of both the Tribunals and the ICC may allow States, organizations or individuals to make *amicus curiae* (friend of the court) submissions on legal or other issues.[118]

17.4 Jurisdiction and admissibility procedures

The Tribunals have established their authority to determine the legality of their creation.[119] Challenges to the Tribunals' jurisdiction, of which there have been many in practice, are dealt with as preliminary motions and carry a right to interlocutory appeal.[120]

The procedures for establishing jurisdiction and admissibility were an important component in reaching an agreement in the ICC negotiations.[121] The main rule is that the Court must satisfy itself that it has jurisdiction and it may also, on its own motion, determine the admissibility of a case.[122] This will not be relevant at every stage of the proceedings. In relation to the issuance of arrest warrants, for example, the *proprio motu* power to determine admissibility should only be exercised exceptionally in order to preserve the interests of the suspect.[123] In practice, however, the Pre-Trial Chambers have regularly found reasons to

---

110 E.g. *Simić et al.* ICTY T. Ch. III 27.7.1999 para. 78 (Art. 29 of the ICTY Statute does not apply to international organizations). See Chapter 20.

111 *Milutinović et al.* ICTY A. Ch. 15.5.2006 para. 11.

112 See n. 102 above.

113 Arts. 18–19 of the ICC Statute.

114 *Ibid.*, Art. 53(3).

115 *Ibid.*, Art. 82(1)(d) and (2).

116 Regs. 108–9 of the ICC Regulations.

117 See Chapter 8.

118 R. 74 of the ICTY RPE and ICTR RPE, and r. 103 of the ICC RPE.

119 See section 7.2.4.

120 R. 72 of the ICTY RPE and the ICTR RPE.

121 See Chapter 8.

122 Art. 19(1) of the ICC Statute.

123 *Situation in the DRC* ICC A. Ch. 13.7.2006 (169) paras. 50–3 (requiring that, e.g., 'an ostensible cause' or 'self-evident factor' impel the exercise of the discretion). Cf. *Lubanga Dyilo* ICC PT. Ch. I 10.2.2006 paras. 17–20 (admissibility determination when deciding to issue an arrest warrant).

exercise this discretionary power, including when general information indicated that there was a domestic intention to institute prosecutions and to set up alternative justice mechanisms as part of the peace process in Uganda.[124] The Prosecutor must also consider these issues when deciding whether to proceed with an investigation or prosecution.[125] Upon the commencement of an investigation, the Prosecutor must notify all States with jurisdiction, so that they may if they wish seek a deferral of the ICC investigation while they undertake national proceedings.[126] But this notification procedure does not apply when the Security Council has referred the situation to the Court.

At the ICC, challenges to the jurisdiction or to the admissibility of a case may be raised at any time prior to the commencement of the trial, and exceptionally thereafter.[127] A right to challenge is afforded to: (1) the accused or a person for whom a warrant of arrest or a summons to appear has been issued, (2) any State with concurrent jurisdiction over the crimes and where investigation or prosecution has been commenced, and (3) any State from which acceptance of jurisdiction is required.[128] Certain provisions seek to make the scheme manageable, for example that States must make their challenge at the earliest opportunity and that a person or a State may make a challenge only once.[129] Still, these proceedings might be many and time-consuming.[130] In order to avoid a complete standstill the Pre-Trial Chamber may authorize the Prosecutor to perform specific investigative measures in spite of a deferral or a State challenge.[131] The decisions are subject to interlocutory appeal and the Prosecutor may seek review of a decision declaring the case inadmissible.[132] A question yet to be resolved is the allocation of the burden of proof for the questions of unwillingness or inability as well as the factual circumstances concerning domestic investigations, prosecutions and jurisdiction. The Statute and RPE are silent and different solutions have been advanced.[133]

While at the Tribunals a challenge may also relate to the exercise of jurisdiction in the particular case (see section 17.7.3), the ICC does not consider a request that the Court

---

124 E.g. *Kony et al.* ICC PT. Ch. 10.3.2009 (including a survey in paras. 15–19).

125 See sections 17.5 and 17.8.1.

126 Art. 18 of the ICC Statute and rr. 52–7 of the ICC RPE.

127 Art. 19(4) of the ICC Statute; see also Arts. 17(1)(c) and 20(3) and rr. 58–60 of the ICC RPE. On the meaning of 'prior to or at the commencement of the trial', see *Katanga and Ngudjolo Chui* ICC HT. Ch. II 16.6.2009 paras. 29–50.

128 Art. 19(2) of the ICC Statute. In addition, the Prosecutor may seek a ruling from the Court: *ibid.*, Art. 19(3).

129 *Ibid.*, Art. 19(4)–(5).

130 They have been described as a 'complex and burdensome procedural regime', likely to impede the functioning of the ICC; see Leila Sadat and Richard Carden, 'The New International Criminal Court: an Uneasy Revolution' (2000) 88 *Georgetown Law Journal* 381 at 417.

131 Arts. 18(6) and 19(7)–(8) of the ICC Statute and rr. 57 and 61 of the ICC RPE.

132 Art. 19(6) of the ICC Statute and r. 60 of the ICC RPE: Art. 19(10) and r. 62.

133 E.g. Simon Young, 'Surrendering the Accused to the International Criminal Court' (2001) 71 *BYBIL* 317, 334; Markus Benzing, 'The Complementarity Regime of the International Criminal Court: International Criminal Justice between State Sovereignty and the Fight Against Impunity' (2003) *Max Planck Yearbook of United Nations Law* 591; Megan Fairlie, 'Establishing Admissibility in the International Criminal Court: Does the Buck Stop with the Prosecutor, Full Stop?' (2005) 39 *International Lawyer* 817.

decline jurisdiction due to 'abuse of process' to constitute a challenge to the jurisdiction of the Court.[134] The relationship between admissibility and a 'case' is further discussed in section 17.6.

17.5 Commencement and discontinuance of a criminal investigation

The ICTY and ICTR have clear jurisdictional mandates where the substantive (crimes), personal (nationality of the individual), territorial and temporal parameters are provided in the respective Statutes (see Chapter 7). Within these parameters, the Prosecutor initiates investigations *ex officio* or on the basis of information obtained from any source, assesses the information received and decides whether there is 'sufficient basis to proceed'.[135] No permission from a judge is required and the Prosecutor has discretion to decide whether to commence a particular investigation. This discretion means, unlike the situation in many civil law jurisdictions, that there is no real obligation placed upon the Prosecutor to investigate all crimes that fulfil the jurisdictional criteria.

The first indictments at the ICTY were directed against lower-level perpetrators, prompted by the interest in showing concrete results as soon as possible. To continue with this approach would have been unsustainable, however, and the ICTY Prosecutor soon adopted a strategy focusing on those most responsible for the most serious violations of international humanitarian law, that is to say persons of authority or leadership.[136] A clear example of this strategy was the indictment against Karadžić and Mladić in 1996. More recently the prioritization has been further sharpened in light of the completion strategy.[137] The ICTR applies a similar prosecutorial strategy, and here the need for selectivity was even more pronounced considering that more than 100,000 suspects were held in Rwandan prisons.

At the ICC, the requirements for the commencement of an investigation are more complex. Unlike the Tribunals the ICC will potentially have global jurisdiction and specified 'trigger mechanisms' are therefore required for bringing a 'situation' before the Court.[138] Regardless of trigger mechanisms, however, the Prosecutor must determine whether an investigation may be initiated in accordance with set criteria: a reasonable suspicion of a crime under the Court's jurisdiction,[139] the admissibility of the case, in

---

134 *Lubanga Dyilo* ICC A. Ch. 14.12.2006 para. 24. Cf. *Karadžić* ICTY T. Ch. III 8.7.2009 paras. 41–4.

135 Art. 18(1) of the ICTY Statute and Art. 17(1) of the ICTR Statute.

136 See ICTY's annual report to the United Nations regarding the period from 1 August 1996 to 31 July 1997, UN Doc. A/52/375 – S/1997/729 of 18.9.1997, para. 58. This followed an intervention by the ICTY judges, see Antonio Cassese, 'The ICTY: A Living and Vital Reality' (2004) 2 *JICJ* 585 at 586–8.

137 See Chapter 7.

138 See section 8.6.

139 This requirement also includes respecting any applicable reservations concerning jurisdiction over war crimes (Art. 124 of the ICC Statute).

accordance with the complementarity principle and the requirement of 'sufficient gravity', and an assessment of the 'interests of justice'.[140] A process of information gathering and analysis thus precedes the criminal investigation.[141] Similar to the ICTY and ICTR, the ICC Prosecutor has made public a prosecutorial policy focusing on those bearing the greatest responsibility for the crimes;[142] this may comprise commanders and other superiors, but also others who are implicated in particularly serious or notorious crimes.

Upon a referral of the situation, the decision whether to start an investigation rests with the Prosecutor and is not subject to judicial review.[143] A decision not to investigate may be reviewed by the Pre-Trial Chamber only if it is solely based on the 'interests of justice' criterion.[144] Where there is no referral, the investigation is always subject to approval by the Pre-Trial Chamber, which in turn requires 'a reasonable basis to proceed with an investigation' and a preliminary assessment of jurisdiction.[145] Hence, a system of checks and balances between the Prosecutor and the judiciary has been built into the ICC Statute regarding the sensitive issue of the commencement of an investigation. Critics argue, however, that this is far from enough and that extended judicial control is required.[146]

An ICC investigation depends upon a positive decision by the Prosecutor and does not follow automatically from the referral of a situation. Although the drafting of Article 53 ('shall initiate … unless …') indicates a duty to go ahead if the conditions are met, the conditions in reality provide for a high degree of discretion. Such discretion is known in common law jurisdictions, but foreign to civil law systems where instead the duty approach applies. The solution provides necessary flexibility to set strategies and focus resources, but may be criticized on principled and other grounds, and has led to a debate in the literature.[147] The 'interests of justice' criterion is particularly contentious and complex and it is not defined. However, the text and purpose of the ICC Statute clearly favour the pursuit of investigations and prosecutions when the conditions concerning the evidentiary threshold

---

140 Art. 53(1) of the ICC Statute and r. 48 of the ICC RPE.

141 Procedures have been established as to how to handle referrals and communications from different sources, see the Regulations of the Office of the Prosecutor 23.4.2009 (ICC-BD 05-07-09).

142 *Paper on some policy issues before the Office of the Prosecutor*, ICC Office of the Prosecutor, September 2003 (available at: www.icc-cpi.int). See Chapter 8.

143 When the Prosecutor was challenged with inaction concerning the referral of one situation, the Pre-Trial Chamber merely concluded that the preliminary examination 'must be completed within a reasonable time' and requested the Prosecutor to inform the referring State about the current status of his examination: *Situation in CAR* ICC PT. Ch. III 30.11.2006.

144 Art. 53(3) of the ICC Statute.

145 *Ibid.*, Art. 15(4). See also reg. 49 of the ICC Regulations regarding the Prosecutor's request for authorization.

146 E.g. Carsten Stahn, 'Judicial Review of Prosecutorial Discretion: On Experiments and Imperfections' in Sluiter and Vasiliev, *International Criminal Procedure*, 239–71.

147 See section 17.8.1.

and admissibility are met. Hence, declining to proceed due to 'interests of justice' should be an exceptional decision.

17.6 The criminal investigation

At the ad hoc Tribunals as well as at the ICC, the Prosecutor is in charge of the criminal investigation.[148] Each investigation is conducted by a multidisciplinary team (lawyers, investigators, analysts and others) and led by a senior trial attorney. Hence, lawyers are directing the investigation, which departs from the traditional approach in many common law jurisdictions but corresponds to some other domestic jurisdictions.[149]

As a general rule, each Prosecutor is given the authority to take necessary measures in the investigation.[150] A specific feature of the ICC Statute is the functions of the Pre-Trial Chamber with respect to the investigation. Limited but important judicial intervention in the investigation, inspired by civil law systems, is provided for a so-called 'unique investigative opportunity', whereby the Chambers may take measures to ensure the efficiency and integrity of the proceedings and protect the rights of the defence.[151] In addition, the Chamber has certain general functions which also apply during the investigation.[152] As already stated, the Chambers have explored these powers in practice.

Another important question is the scope of the Prosecutor's investigation. In the ICTY and ICTR, the Prosecutor is not required actively to investigate circumstances and collect evidence that speak in favour of the suspect.[153] Only if such evidence emerges anyway during the investigation must it be considered and disclosed. The ICC Prosecutor, on the contrary, is under an obligation to 'investigate incriminating and exonerating circumstances equally' (a 'principle of objectivity').[154] It has been argued that this mechanism, properly operated, has the potential to narrow the scope of the case, reducing the number of charges,

---

148 In the ICC Office of the Prosecutor, one of the two Deputy Prosecutors was the head of the investigation division and the other was in charge of the prosecution division.

149 On different approaches in some European systems, see e.g. Eric Mathias, 'The Balance of Power Between the Police and the Public Prosecutor' in Delmas-Marty and Spencer, *European Criminal Procedure*, 459–87.

150 R. 39(ii) of the ICTY RPE and ICTR RPE, and Art. 54(1)(b) of the ICC Statute.

151 Art. 56 of the ICC Statute. See also *Situation in the DRC* ICC PT. Ch. I 26.4.2005.

152 Article 57(3) of the ICC Statute. These functions include, inter alia, protection and privacy of victims and witnesses, preservation of evidence, protection of persons who have been arrested or appeared in response to a summons, and protection of national security information (para. 3(c)). In order to fulfil its functions, the Pre-Trial Chamber may request the Prosecutor to provide information: reg. 48 of the ICC Regulations.

153 One ICTY Trial Chamber, however, has referred to the Prosecutor as not only a party to adversarial proceedings, but also 'an organ of the Tribunal and an organ of international criminal justice whose object is not only to secure a conviction but to present the case for the Prosecution, which includes not inculpatory evidence, but also exculpatory evidence, in order to assist the Chamber discover the truth in a judicial setting': *Kupreškić et al.* ICTY T. Ch. II 21.9.1998.

154 Art. 54(1)(a) of the ICC Statute.

and possibly the length of the subsequent trial;[155] the traditional division in adversarial proceedings between a 'prosecution case' and a 'defence case' could be reduced.

The investigation includes the questioning of individuals (suspects, victims, witnesses, experts and others) and the collection of written and other material. In some cases, extensive and resource-intense exhumation of mass graves and other forensic measures are required. The Prosecutor is responsible for the retention, storage and security of the information and material collected.[156] Without an international police force to carry out the investigation and to enforce court orders, the investigation depends very much on the cooperation of States and other entities such as peace-keeping forces.[157] The Prosecutor is entitled to seek cooperation from States and others in the investigation.[158] A Chamber may also issue necessary orders and warrants.[159] The defence may by this means seek a request for cooperation by a State and arguably, at least in the ICC,[160] an order directed to the Prosecutor regarding specific investigative measures.

As far as possible, the Court's own investigators will conduct, or at least participate in, the investigative measures. This is important in order to ensure various rights and to secure the collection of evidence that can later be used in the proceedings and, sometimes, to secure the confidence and cooperation of victims and witnesses. The ICTY and ICTR Prosecutors have a statutory right to conduct on-site investigations.[161] For the ICC, this right is circumscribed by specific conditions and confined to non-coercive measures.[162] Exceptionally, however, the ICC Pre-Trial Chamber may authorize the Prosecutor 'to take specific investigative steps within the territory of a State without having secured the cooperation of that State'.[163] This requires the complete or partial collapse of the functions of the State in question.

A suspect who is questioned has to be given certain information and has rights to silence, the presence of legal assistance, and interpretation.[164] The circumstances surrounding the

---

155 See, e.g. informal expert paper: *Measures available to the International Criminal Court to reduce the length of proceedings*, ICC Office of the Prosecutor, 2003, paras. 22–30.

156 R. 41 of the ICTY RPE and ICTR RPE, and r. 10 of the ICC RPE.

157 See further in Chapter 20.

158 Art. 18(2) of the ICTY Statute, Art. 17(2) of the ICTR Statute, and Art. 54(2)(c) of the ICC Statute, as well as provisions in the respective RPE.

159 R. 54 of the ICTY RPE and ICTR RPE, and Art. 57(3) of the ICC Statute. One form of assistance is an order to a State for production of documents, which requires a sufficient level of specificity and a 'fishing expedition' is not allowed; see *Blaškić* ICTY A. Ch. 29.10.1997 para. 32, subsequently codified in r. 54*bis* of the ICTY RPE. See also r. 116 of the ICC RPE. See further Chapter 20.

160 Cf. *Kabiligi* ICTR T. Ch. 1.6.2000 para. 20 (no legal basis for the Chamber to intervene and order supplementary investigations by the Prosecutor, as requested by the defence).

161 Art. 18(2) of the ICTY Statute and Art. 17(2) of the ICTR Statute.

162 Art. 99(4) of the ICC Statute.

163 Arts. 54(2) and 57(3)(d) of the ICC Statute and r. 115 of the ICC RPE. For these (controversial) cases there is no explicit restriction to non-coercive measures.

164 Art. 18(3) of the ICTY Statute, Art. 17(3) of the ICTR Statute, r. 42 of the ICTY RPE and ICTR RPE, and Art. 55(2) of the ICC Statute.

interview may affect the use at trial of the statement obtained.[165] The ICC provisions apply also when national authorities conduct the questioning on behalf of the Court. This is not explicitly provided for the ICTY and ICTR, but a statement given to national authorities could be declared inadmissible as evidence if the suspect is not afforded equivalent rights.[166] Additionally, the ICC Statute provides for certain fundamental rights of any person[167] – concerning self-incrimination, coercion, duress and threat, interpretation and translations, and deprivation of liberty – which reflect generally accepted human rights and, as such, will be observed also by the ICTY and ICTR. An important but difficult task, shared by the prosecution and Chambers, is to provide for protection of victims and witnesses.[168]

The ICC's practice thus far has been to commence investigations of entire 'situations', which means that formally the scope is extremely broad.[169] In practice, however, the actual investigations within the situation are much more targeted. At some point a more specific 'case' arises, but it is a matter of dispute as to when this is and also what the decisive elements of the 'specificity test' are.[170] There are indications, however, that a 'case' arises first with an arrest warrant or summons to appear.[171] Certainty as to when a 'case' exists is critical not least for admissibility determinations in accordance with the complementarity principle, since admissibility is clearly linked to a 'case'. As noted in section 17.4, admissibility considerations are already relevant at the time when commencement of an investigation is being considered.[172] But at this early stage the prosecution has a case hypothesis rather than a 'case'. Due to the broad scope of the investigation, moreover, early assessments as to whether the same person and the same conduct are subject both to international and national processes will be virtually impossible to make for anyone but the Prosecutor, who will then play the primary role in ensuring that what is investigated is not inadmissible in complementarity terms. In order to ensure a coherent system, a settled view on the understanding of 'situations' and 'cases' is thus very important.

17.7   Coercive measures

17.7.1   Coercive measures in general

In all criminal investigations and proceedings it must be possible to resort to coercive measures of various kinds. Due to the relationship between the international criminal

---

165 E.g. *Halilović* ICTY A. Ch. 19.8.2005.
166 *Delalić et al.* ICTY T. Ch. II 2.9.1997 para. 55.
167 Art. 55(1) of the ICC Statute.
168 See section 18.3.
169 Cf. Ambos and Miller, 'Structure and Function', 338, arguing that a 'case' exists, at the latest, with a decision under Art. 53 of the ICC Statute, i.e. that the investigation should relate to a 'case'.
170 An attempt to explain the distinction is provided in *Lubanga Dyilo* ICC PT. Ch. I 17.1.2006 para. 65. See further, Rod Rastan, 'What is a "Case" for the Purpose of the Rome Statute?' (2008) 19 *CLF* 435.
171 E.g. *Situation in the DRC* ICC PT. Ch. I 9.11.2005.
172 See Arts. 15(4) and 53(1) of the ICC Statute and rr. 48 and 55(2) of the ICC RPE.

jurisdictions and domestic jurisdictions, the international Prosecutor will primarily have to resort to the cooperation of States or sometimes other entities, mainly international military or police forces. The ICC Statute gives the Prosecutor powers to conduct measures on-site only in so far as they are non-coercive, although coercive measures could arguably be authorized by the Pre-Trial Chamber in case of a failed State (see section 17.6). The powers of the ICTY and ICTR Prosecutors to conduct an on-site investigation are provided for in more general terms and there are examples where persons representing the Prosecutor have executed a seizure on the territory of a State.[173] In *Blaškić*,[174] the ICTY Appeals Chamber concluded that the Prosecutor was entitled to undertake coercive measures directly on the territory of a State, that is to say without turning to the national authorities of that State, when authorized to do so by national legislation or special agreement. This also applies, regardless of legislation or special agreement, to the States and entities of the Former Yugoslavia, which was considered an inherent power, necessary for the discharge of the Tribunal's fundamental functions, including guaranteeing the accused a fair trial.

In domestic systems, coercive measures which infringe on the rights and freedoms of individuals are generally subject to judicial review, either before the measure is taken or afterwards. The Chambers of the ICTY, ICTR and the ICC have explicit powers to issue necessary warrants and orders,[175] which may also concern coercive measures. On-site measures by the ICTY and ICTR without the assistance of national authorities have been conducted pursuant to such warrants.[176] But a debated issue is whether international warrants may, or even should, also be issued in connection with a request for cooperation.[177] At the ICC, evidence obtained in contravention of the Statute or internationally recognized human rights may be declared inadmissible, which applies also to items seized by national authorities or international peacekeepers.[178]

17.7.2 Deprivation or restriction of liberty and surrender of suspects

Deprivation or restriction of liberty infringes on the fundamental rights of the person concerned and is at the same time an essential mechanism for the effective operation of criminal justice systems. These matters are therefore regulated in relative detail for the international criminal tribunals.

---

173 *Kordić and Čerkez* ICTY T. Ch. III 25.6.1999 (the investigation, resulting in the seizure of certain material, 'was perfectly within the powers of the Prosecution provided for in the Statute').
174 *Blaškić* ICTY A. Ch. 29.10.1997 para. 55.
175 R. 54 of the ICTY RPE and ICTR RPE, and Art. 57(3) of the ICC Statute.
176 E.g. *Kordić and Čerkez* ICTY T. Ch. III 25.6.1999, *Naletilić and Martinović* ICTY T. Ch. 1A 14.11.2001, and *Karadžić* ICTY T. Ch. (Duty Judge) 11.9.2003. See section 20.8.3.
177 See section 20.8.4.
178 Art. 69(7) of the ICC Statute. See also *Lubanga Dyilo* ICC PT. Ch. I 29.1.2007 paras. 62–94.

At the ICTY and ICTR, the arrest warrant must be issued by a judge following confirmation of the indictment in whole or in part.[179] The warrant is accompanied by the indictment and a statement of the accused's rights and, unless under seal, copies must be transmitted to States for execution.[180] The linkage to a confirmed indictment means that the judge must be convinced that a prima facie case exists (see section 17.9.1). Based on the warrant, the accused must be arrested and surrendered to the Tribunal. In urgent cases the Prosecutor may request any State to arrest the suspect provisionally without an arrest warrant, but the subsequent transfer to and provisional arrest at the Tribunal require an order issued by a judge.[181]

The ICTY and ICTR rules provide for mandatory detention of the accused upon being transferred to the Tribunal.[182] This common law inspired model is balanced by provisions on provisional release, which become even more important in order to respect the fundamental principle that liberty is the general rule and detention the exception.[183] The Trial Chamber may order provisional release if it is satisfied that the accused will appear for trial and, if released, will not pose a danger to any victim, witness or other persons.[184] But the accused must prove that the conditions are met[185] and provisional release is a discretionary power of the Chamber; even if the explicit conditions are met, release will be ordered only when appropriate in the particular case.[186] An earlier requirement of 'extraordinary circumstances' was the major obstacle to release, but it was abandoned by the Tribunals after extensive internal debates and external criticism.[187] The requirement, which was said to turn the general principle of liberty on its head, was motivated by the extremely serious crimes and the lack of independent resources to enforce an arrest (or re-arrest) or release conditions. Subsequent to this amendment, the ICTY has released numerous accused while the ICTR has yet to order the first provisional release; improved State cooperation vis-à-vis the ICTY has been a decisive factor for this development.

---

179 Rr. 47(H)(i) and 54 of the ICTY RPE and ICTR RPE.

180 The ICTY and ICTR rules are similar but not identical and the ICTY RPE (r. 55*bis*) contain provisions on general circulation to all States.

181 R. 40*bis* of the ICTY RPE and ICTR RPE. Regarding the Prosecutor's obligations, see *Kajelijeli* ICTR A. Ch. 23.5.2005 paras. 218–33.

182 R. 64 of the ICTY RPE and ICTR RPE.

183 See Art. 9(3) of the ICCPR, Art. 5(1) of the ECHR, Art. 6 of the ACHPR, and Art. 7(1) of the ACHR.

184 R. 65 of the ICTY RPE and ICTR RPE. On the cumulative nature of the conditions, see e.g. *Rukundo* ICTR T. Ch. III 15.7.2004 para. 19. Generally, see Fergal Gaynor, 'Provisional Release in the Law of the International Criminal Tribunal for the Former Yugoslavia' in Doria, *Legal Regime*, 183–207.

185 E.g. *Prlić et al.* ICTY A. Ch. 8.9.2004 paras. 27–8.

186 E.g. *Brđanin and Talić* ICTY T. Ch. II 25.7.2000 para. 22.

187 See the dissenting opinion by Judge Patrick Robinson in *Krajišnik and Plavšić* ICTY T. Ch. III 8.10.2001. See also A.-M. La Rosa, 'A Tremendous Challenge for the International Criminal Tribunals: Reconciling the Requirements of International Humanitarian Law with those of Fair Trial' (1997) 321 *International Review of the Red Cross* 635, and Safferling, *International Criminal Procedure*, 143–7.

The ICC Statute provides a quite different regime. Every request for a person's arrest must be based on an arrest warrant issued by the Pre-Trial Chamber.[188] A separate procedure applies for issuance of an arrest warrant and the warrant is independent of, and would normally precede, the indictment. Specific requirements must be satisfied for a warrant to be issued: 'reasonable grounds to believe' that the person has committed a crime and additional prerequisites regarding a risk that the suspect absconds, obstructs or endangers the investigation or court proceedings, or continues to commit the crime in question or a related crime.[189] The same prerequisites must also be assessed when the ICC decides upon a request for interim release pending trial and if any criterion is not met, the person is to be released, with or without conditions.[190] Unlike the Tribunals, the ICC is also given the option to issue a summons to appear, instead of an arrest warrant, when this is considered sufficient to ensure the person's appearance before the Court.[191] The summons may be combined with conditions restricting the person's liberty. In sum, the conditions for deprivation of liberty are stricter than at the Tribunals.

Interestingly, the test for provisional release at the Tribunals does not include an assessment of the strength of the suspicion and Chambers have refused to review the evidentiary basis for a challenged arrest.[192] But since the decision to confirm the indictment is not subject to a separate appeal[193] and no periodic review of detention is required, the practice prevents the accused from challenging the lawfulness of the arrest with respect to the requirement of a 'reasonable suspicion'. Hence, some ICTY Trial Chambers have allowed a review of the evidence 'in a cursory manner' in order to ascertain whether the detention of the accused remains lawful.[194] At the ICC, on the other hand, prosecution evidence is required and is already assessed when the issuance of the warrant is considered.[195] Additionally, the ICC Pre-Trial Chamber is required to review its rulings on release or detention periodically, on its own motion or at the request of a party,[196] and the Prosecutor retains the obligation to show that the conditions for an arrest warrant are still met. In addition, the Pre-Trial Chamber has a responsibility to ensure that detention does not last

---

188 Arts. 58(5), 91 (arrest and surrender) and 92 (provisional arrest) of the ICC Statute.
189 *Ibid.*, Art. 58(1). The admissibility of the case is *not* a substantive pre-requisite: *Situation in the DRC* ICC A. Ch. 13.7.2006 (169) para. 42.
190 Art. 60(2) of the ICC Statute and r. 118 of the ICC RPE. Regarding conditional release, see r. 119 of the ICC RPE.
191 Art. 58(7) of the ICC Statute. See also r. 119 of the ICC RPE. See *Abu Garda* ICC PT. Ch. I 7.5.2009; cf. *Harun and Al Kushayb* ICC PT. Ch. 27.4.2007 paras. 108–24.
192 E.g. *Brđanin and Talić* ICTY T. Ch. II 8.12.1999 para. 16, and T. Ch. II 10.12.1999.
193 E.g. *Bagosora and 28 Others* ICTR A. Ch. 8.6.1998.
194 E.g. *Delalić et al.* ICTY T. Ch. II 25.9.1996 para. 24. See also McIntyre, 'Defining Human Rights', 211–14.
195 E.g. *Lubanga Dyilo* ICC PT. Ch. I 10.2.2006 paras. 7–15.
196 Art. 60(3) of the ICC Statute and r. 118(2) of the ICC RPE. See e.g. *Lubanga Dyilo* ICC A. Ch. 13.2.2007 paras. 94–100, 134; *Katanga and Ngudjolo Chui* ICC A. Ch. 9.6.2008 paras. 12, 26–7 (the issue of detention must be assessed anew against the material presented to the Chamber); *Bemba Gombo* ICC A. Ch. 16.12.2008 (defence access to documents is essential in order to challenge the lawfulness of detention effectively).

'for an unreasonable period prior to trial due to inexcusable delay by the Prosecutor', which means that a properly detained person may be released.[197] The first interim release was ordered in *Bemba Gombo*, but unlike the Tribunals where a State guarantee is considered a condition for release, the Pre-Trial Chamber merely postponed the release pending a decision as to in which State he would be released.[198] The Appeals Chamber reversed the decision, however, concluding that it must specify the appropriate conditions that make conditional release feasible, identify the State and assess whether the State would be able to enforce the conditions.[199]

The ICC Statute, but not the rules of the ICTY and ICTR, provides for compensation to wrongfully arrested or convicted persons.[200] Such compensation is considered very differently in domestic jurisdictions; some have a general right to compensation when deprivation of liberty is not followed by a conviction and others restrict compensation to unlawful arrests. International human rights instruments reflect this divide and require compensation only for 'unlawful arrests'.[201] The ICC provisions go further and they represent a breakthrough for broader compensation rights.[202]

17.7.3 Legality of the arrest and violations of procedural rights

The Statutes of the ICTY, ICTR and ICC make no explicit provision for challenges to the legality of deprivation of liberty of the kind which are available under the common law remedy of *habeas corpus*.[203] Nonetheless, in *Barayagwiza* the ICTR Appeals Chamber concluded that a detained individual must have recourse to a court to challenge the lawfulness of his detention,[204] a conclusion that has been upheld in subsequent ICTY and ICTR decisions where *habeas corpus* motions have been heard.[205] The Chamber found support in the ICTR Statute and RPE and noted that such a right to a judicial review is also enshrined in

---

197 Art. 60(4) of the ICC Statute. See e.g. *Lubanga Dyilo* ICC A. Ch. 13.2.2007 paras. 118–24.

198 *Bemba Gombo* ICC PT. Ch. II 14.8.2009. Indeed, all States asked had expressed objections and concerns about receiving the accused, but a State guarantee was not considered a condition for release, *ibid.*, paras. 88–90; cf. *Rukundo* ICTR T. Ch. III 15.7.2004 para. 19, but also *Katanga and Ngudjolo Chui* ICC T. Ch. II 17.3.2009 para. 8.

199 *Bemba Gombo* ICC A. Ch. 2.12.2009.

200 Art. 85 of the ICC Statute and rr. 173–5 of the ICC RPE. See also *Rwamakuba* ICTR A. Ch. 13.9.2007 para. 10 (compensation refused for having been prosecuted and acquitted).

201 E.g. Art. 9(5) of the ICCPR. See also Art. 5(4) of the ECHR.

202 See also Stuart Beresford, 'Redressing the Wrongs of the International Justice System: Compensation for Persons Erroneously Detained, Prosecuted, or Convicted by the Ad Hoc Tribunals' (2002) 96 *AJIL* 628.

203 The writ of *habeas corpus* is a fundamental feature of the common law jurisdiction, deriving its origins from Magna Carta, and has long been used domestically as a means of testing the validity of executive committals. However, this judicial remedy is peculiar to certain national jurisdictions – and nominally a precept of a sovereign or a head of State (a 'writ') – but not applicable, as such, in international criminal proceedings.

204 *Barayagwiza* ICTR A. Ch. 3.11.1999 para. 88.

205 E.g. *Brđanin and Talić* ICTY T. Ch. II 8.12.1999, and *Kanyabashi* ICTR T. Ch. II 23.5.2000.

international human rights instruments.[206] Violations of other rights may be challenged, such as the rights to be promptly informed of the reasons for the arrest, brought promptly before a judge, assisted by counsel during questioning, and an initial appearance.[207] The Appeals Chamber may also intervene *proprio motu*.[208]

A challenge of this kind must be heard and ruled upon without delay.[209] However, if the objection is not pursued by the appellant with due diligence[210] or raised only a long time after the arrest,[211] the violation of the appellant's rights may not require a remedy. When the violation of the accused's rights is considered 'serious and egregious', the *Barayagwiza* decision established that there is a discretionary power, based on the so-called abuse of process doctrine, to decline to exercise jurisdiction and hence to dismiss the case.[212] This is an exceptional measure, however, and other more proportionate remedies would be a reduction of an imposed sentence or, if acquitted, compensation.[213]

The arrest requires the involvement of both the international and domestic jurisdictions and a difficult question is how far the international jurisdiction should go in the exercise of its powers to review the legality of the deprivation of liberty. Could the Tribunal also review the legality of domestic measures and, if so, which legal standard should be applied? Furthermore, abductions and the abuse of process doctrine are not merely concerned with violations of individual rights, but may also relate to a violation of rights of another State and thus a breach of international law. One view is that such a breach is always a reason to decline jurisdiction,[214] another that this should be done only if the custodial State colluded in the abduction.[215]

The Tribunals have reviewed domestic measures, by applying the Tribunal's own legal requirements and international human rights standards when the possible violation, at least to some extent, could be attributed to that Tribunal.[216] In addition, the ICTR Appeals Chamber in *Barayagwiza* did not feel barred from addressing the question of violations of

---

206 See Art. 8 of the Universal Declaration of Human Rights, Art. 9(4) of the ICCPR, Art. 5(4) of the ECHR, Art. 7(6) of the ACHR and Art. 7(1)(a) of the ACHPR. See also, Separate Opinion of Judge Robinson in *Simić et al.* ICTY T. Ch. III 18.10.2000.

207 E.g. *Kajelijeli* ICTR A. Ch. 23.5.2005 paras. 251–3.

208 *Ibid.*, para. 208.

209 *Semanza* ICTR A. Ch. 31.5.2000 paras. 112–13.

210 *Ibid.*, paras. 119 and 121.

211 *Nyiramasuhuko* ICTR T. Ch. II 20.2.2004.

212 *Barayagwiza* ICTR A. Ch. 3.11.1999 para. 74. See also *Dragan Nikolić* ICTY T. Ch. II 9.10.2002 para. 114, and A. Ch. 5.6.2003 paras. 28–30, and *Karadžić* ICTY T. Ch. III 8.7.2009 paras. 80–8.

213 E.g. *Kajelijeli* ICTR A. Ch. 23.5.2005 paras. 206, 254–5, 320.

214 E.g. the South African Supreme Court in *State* v. *Ebrahim* 1991 (2) SA 553.

215 Regarding British law, see Colin Warbrick, 'Judicial Jurisdiction and Abuse of Process' (2000) 49 *ICLQ* 489. See also *Öcalan* v. *Turkey* ECtHR 12.5.2005, paras. 83–90.

216 E.g. *Barayagwiza* ICTR A. Ch. 3.11.1999, and *Kajelijeli* ICTR A. Ch. 23.5.2005. See also *Delalić et al.* ICTY T. Ch. II 2.9.1997, confirmed on appeal, A. Ch. 20.2.2001 paras. 528–64.

the rights of the accused when these were also attributable to a State;[217] the Prosecutor and the State often have overlapping responsibilities. As clarified in *Kajelijeli*, however, the Tribunal is not competent to pronounce on the responsibility of the State for any violations, only on faults attributable to the Tribunal.[218]

Similarly, the ICTY has had to consider these issues in cases where the accused was subject to a sealed indictment and apprehended through irregular practices by the prosecution ('luring'),[219] or in the abduction of fugitives from Serbia by unknown individuals and delivery to SFOR, with which the Prosecutor had a confidential cooperation agreement.[220] Regarding setting aside jurisdiction because of a violation of State sovereignty, the Appeals Chamber concluded in *Nikolić* that State practice differed but that sovereign rights (and international human rights) must be weighed against the interest of bringing those accused of 'universally condemned offences' to justice – an 'Eichmann exception'.[221] But a minor intrusion, particularly when the violated State is in default of its cooperation obligations and has not complained, was not sufficient to decline jurisdiction. Moreover, the Chamber questioned whether abductions carried out by private individuals without being instigated, acknowledged or condoned by a State, international organization, or other entity, violate State sovereignty at all.

On the legality of the arrest warrant, the ICC law explicitly provides for both challenges and *proprio motu* reviews;[222] a challenge may be launched after the arrest but before the person is surrendered to the Court.[223] The Statute also provides that the legality of the arrest process in the custodial State is, at least primarily, a matter for domestic courts.[224] In *Lubanga*, the Appeals Chamber found the doctrine of abuse of process applicable by referring to internationally recognized human rights (Article 21(3) of the ICC Statute) and the Court's task to see that domestic law was duly followed and the rights of the arrestee properly respected.[225] In the same case, and also based on Article 21(3) and the responsibility to ensure the fairness of the proceedings, a conditional stay of the proceedings was considered to be an appropriate remedy when disclosure of exculpatory evidence was

---

217 *Barayagwiza* ICTR A. Ch. 3.11.1999 para. 73.

218 *Kajelijeli* ICTR A. Ch. 23.5.2005 paras. 219–21, 252.

219 *Dokmanović* (see *Mrkšić et al.*) ICTY T. Ch. II 22.10.1997. For a critical view, see Michael Scharf, 'The Prosecutor v. Slavko Dokmanović: Irregular Rendition and the ICTY' (1998) 11 *LJIL* 369.

220 E.g. *Simić et al.* ICTY T. Ch. III 18.10.2000 (proceedings which were later abandoned due to a plea bargaining arrangement).

221 *Dragan Nikolić* ICTY A. Ch. 5.6.2003 paras. 24–7. Regarding the *Eichmann* case, see Chapter 3. See also section 5.4.7.

222 Art. 60 of the ICC Statute. See section 17.7.2.

223 R. 117(3) of the ICC RPE.

224 Art. 59(2)(c) of the ICC Statute. The domestic court is not allowed, however, to consider the legality of the ICC arrest warrant: Art. 59(4).

225 *Lubanga Dyilo* ICC A. Ch. 14.12.2006 paras. 36–7, 41. One may note, however, that the ICC, when deciding on the relevance or admissibility of evidence collected by a State, is not allowed to rule on the application of that State's national law: Art. 69(8) of the ICC Statute.

prevented by the provider of the material; but unconditional release of the accused was held not to be an inevitable consequence of such a stay.[226]

17.8 Prosecution and indictment

17.8.1 Decision whether to prosecute

The determination whether to prosecute follows adversarial principles, in that the Prosecutor is the only one who may initiate a trial by submitting an indictment; a judge or a victim cannot do so. Furthermore, the ultimate responsibility for the content of the indictment rests with the Prosecutor. However, there are also different forms of judicial review. One review common to all international jurisdictions is the confirmation of the indictment (see section 17.9.1).

At the ICTY and ICTR, the Prosecutor must prepare an indictment and transmit it to a judge of a Trial Chamber '[u]pon the determination that a prima facie case exists'.[227] In practice, this has not been interpreted as an obligation to prosecute and the general prosecution strategy (to focus on those bearing the greatest responsibility) has guided the decisions.[228] Judicial screening of new indictments was introduced as part of ICTY's completion strategy.[229]

The provisions of the ICC Statute are different, stating the conditions under which there can be no prosecution.[230] The conditions relate to a suspicion of crime sufficient for an arrest warrant, the admissibility of the case, and an assessment of 'the interests of justice'. A decision not to prosecute is subject to judicial review by the Pre-Trial Chamber under the same terms as a decision not to commence an investigation.[231] The Prosecutor may reconsider a decision not to prosecute.[232] Here too, the decision whether to prosecute is subject to discretion and no obligation to prosecute is prescribed. The prosecutorial strategy regarding cases to pursue applies.

The question of prosecutorial discretion, including its limits and judicial supervision, has been the subject of considerable debate, often with reference to domestic practice.[233] The

---

226 *Lubanga Dyilo* ICC T. Ch. I 13.6.2008 (1401) and A. Ch. 21.10.2008 (1486). On the issue of release, see A. Ch. 21.10.2008 (1487). Cf. *Kony et al.* ICC PT. Ch. II 31.10.2008 (request for stay was denied).

227 Art. 18(4) of the ICTY Statute and Art. 17(4) of the ICTR Statute.

228 Indeed, Trial Chambers have accepted the withdrawal of indictments in cases where the statutory conditions for the indictment were met but the case did not fall under the (new) prosecutorial strategy, e.g. *Sikirica et al.* ICTY T. Ch. 5.5.1998.

229 R. 28(A) of the ICTY RPE; see further Chapter 7. For a critical view, see Daryl Mundis, 'The Judicial Effects of the "Completion Strategies" on the Ad Hoc International Criminal Tribunals' (2005) 99 *AJIL* 142.

230 Art. 53(2) of the ICC Statute.

231 *Ibid.*, Art. 53(3); see section 17.5.

232 *Ibid.*, Art. 53(4).

233 Generally, see Robert Cryer, *Prosecuting International Crimes* (Cambridge, 2005). See also, e.g. Allison Marston Danner, 'Enhancing the Legitimacy and Accountability of the Prosecutorial Discretion at the International Criminal Court' (2003) 97 *AJIL* 510; Luc Côte, 'Reflections on the Exercise of Prosecutorial question of improperly exercised (selective) discretion was raised in *Delalić et al.*[234] The Appeals Chamber concluded that the ICTY Prosecutor has a broad discretion concerning initiation of investigations and preparations of indictments, but also that there are limitations, particularly the statutory requirements of prosecutorial independence and equality before the Tribunal (that is to say the law). Since it was not established that the Prosecutor had any discriminatory or otherwise unlawful or improper motive, the challenge was dismissed. At the ICC, the issue of prosecutorial inaction has been raised by request for Pre-Trial Chamber intervention in the various 'situations'. But while Pre-Trial Chambers have shown preparedness to intervene, and have convened 'status conferences', they have refrained from interfering substantively in the Prosecutor's exercise of discretionary powers. For example, one Chamber did not consider that decisions to prosecute certain individuals included an implicit decision not to prosecute others within the same situation, which could be subject to review.[235]

17.8.2 Amendments to and withdrawal of the indictment

As in domestic criminal proceedings, an international indictment may be amended or withdrawn.[236] In accordance with adversarial principles, these measures are, generally, the Prosecutor's prerogative in the ICTY, ICTR and ICC, but the principles and procedures vary. Amendments and clarifications are common at the ICTY and ICTR and the required judicial approval has normally been granted; the main consideration is whether the amendment will cause unfair prejudice to the accused.[237] A 'new charge' requires a new confirmation and to be supported by evidence. Amendments may also be made during trial,[238] but not on appeal.[239]

Post-confirmation, the ICC Prosecutor may amend the charges only with permission of the Pre-Trial Chamber; a new confirmation is required if the Prosecutor 'seeks to add additional charges or to substitute more serious charges'.[240] But without a formal hierarchy of crimes,[241] the notion of 'more serious charges' will cause difficulties in practice.

Discretion in International Criminal Law' (2005) 3 *JICJ* 162; Alexander Greenawalt, 'Justice Without Politics? Prosecutorial Discretion and the International Criminal Court' (2007) 39 *New York University Journal of International Law and Politics* 583, and contributions by various authors in Stahn and Sluiter, *Emerging Practice*, chs. 11–15.

234 *Delalić et al.* ICTY A. Ch. 20.2.2001 paras. 596–618.
235 E.g. *Situation in the DRC* ICC PT. Ch. I 26.9.2007.
236 Rr. 50–1 of the ICTY RPE and ICTR RPE; see also, e.g. *Dragan Nikolić* ICTY T. Ch. II 20.10.1995 para. 32; Art. 61(4) of the ICC Statute.
237 E.g. *Naletilić and Martinović* ICTY T. Ch. I 14.2.2001. Regarding other circumstances to consider, such as delays, see e.g. *Kovačević* ICTY A. Ch. 2.7.1998, and *Karemera et al.* ICTR A. Ch. 19.12.2003.
238 *Akayesu* ICTR A. Ch. 1.6.2001 para. 120.
239 *Niyitegeka* ICTR A. Ch. 9.7.2004 para. 196.
240 Art. 61(4) and (9) of the ICC Statute.
241 See further in Chapter 19.

Moreover, the provisions refer only to amendments 'before the trial has begun' and thus beg the question whether any amendments may be made thereafter. Different interpretations are possible. A complete ban on amendments at trial could result in acquittals on 'technical' grounds, although this may be counteracted by the chamber's power to 'modify the legal characterization' of the facts (see section 17.8.4).

17.8.3 The indictment

Framing an indictment is often a routine task in domestic criminal systems, but not so in the international jurisdictions; the crimes and further requirements for criminal responsibility are not very well defined in law and the indictments often cover multiple alleged perpetrators and events. The form of the indictment and the relationship between the charges and a subsequent judgment vary in different domestic legal systems. Hence, the principles for and form of the indictment have been subject to much confusion and many challenges in the ICTY and ICTR. True to adversarial trial principles, however, the Chambers have been unwilling, although empowered thereto, to check the form of the indictment *ex officio*.[242] Over time a relatively consistent practice has been established,[243] which is relevant also to the ICC.

The form of the indictment is important in order to uphold the rights of the accused to a fair hearing, to be informed promptly and in detail of the nature and cause of the charges, and to have adequate time and facilities for the preparation of the defence.[244] The 'nature' of the charge relates to the legal characterization of the charge, that is to say the alleged offence and form of criminal liability, and the 'cause' to the factual basis or description of the charge.

Nonetheless, the statutory requirements for the Tribunals are very general in nature and instead a rich case law has developed.[245] The indictment must include the 'material facts' underpinning the charges, but not the evidence by which such material facts are to be proven. The material facts must be given with enough detail to inform the defendant clearly of the charges and allow him or her to prepare the defence. What constitutes a material fact, however, depends on the nature of the case at hand, and the specificity, such as the identity of the victims, mainly on the nature of the alleged criminal conduct. Direct perpetration requires a higher degree of precision than more indirect conduct such as aiding or abetting. With the experiences and case law of the Tribunals in mind, the ICC Regulations are more detailed.[246]

---

242 E.g. *Brđanin and Talić* ICTY T. Ch. II 20.2.2001 para. 23.

243 For a survey of the principles as developed in case law, see e.g. *Blaškić* ICTY A. Ch. 29.7.2004 paras. 207–21, and *Ntakirutimana* ICTR A. Ch. 13.12.2004 paras. 21–9 and 469–77.

244 Art. 21(2) and (4)(a)–(b) of the ICTY Statute, Art. 20(2) and (4)(a)–(b) of the ICTR Statute, and Art. 67(1) (a)–(b) of the ICC Statute. The text of the ICC Statute is different, however, and speaks of, inter alia, the 'nature, cause, and content' of the charges.

245 Art. 18(4) of the ICTY Statute and Art. 17(4) of the ICTR Statute, r. 47(C) of the ICTY RPE and ICTR RPE. See also, e.g. *Milutinović et al.* ICTY T. Ch. III 22.3.2006 (with references).

246 Reg. 52 of the ICC Regulations. See, e.g. *Bemba Gombo* ICC PT. Ch. II 15.6.2009 paras. 65–70.

Defects may be cured by amendments of the indictment or subsequent information and minor ones may be ignored, as long as the fair trial rights of the accused are not affected. A fundamental defect, however, can result in the Trial Chamber disregarding the charge or the Appeals Chamber reversing a conviction.[247]

17.8.4 The charge and its relationship to the judgment

The indictment is the primary accusatory instrument and establishes the frame for the criminal trial; only what is properly charged may lead to a conviction. Hence, the judges of the Tribunals and the ICC are required to identify, assess and pronounce on each charge (or count) of the indictment, and the ICC Statute clarifies that the judgment 'shall not exceed the facts and circumstances described in the charges and any amendment to the charges'.[248]

Other questions are how the legal classification of facts – the nature of the charge – in the indictment should be understood and how Trial Chambers should act in the case of an erroneous legal classification. All the Statutes and RPE are silent on these matters and different legal traditions take different approaches. Common law jurisdictions place the emphasis on the 'offence' as categorized by the prosecutor in the indictment. This means that the legal characterization made for a charge is binding on the trial court; after all, it is against the crime charged that the accused raises the defence. An exception, however, is that the court may, without amendment, convict for a lesser included offence. As a consequence, the indictment will often present numerous counts in order to avoid an acquittal when all the factual and legal requirements for a conviction are met but the court finds a crime different from the one charged. The ICTY has opted to follow this model.[249]

In many civil law jurisdictions and mixed jurisdictions, the conduct – the acts or omissions – is instead decisive, not the legal categorization of the 'offence'. The principle *iura novit curia* (the court knows the law) applies and, therefore, the prosecutor's legal characterization is not binding but merely a theory (a recommendation). The ICTY Trial Chamber in *Kupreškić et al.* discussed the possible application of this principle but concluded that it should not be applied.[250] In the ICC, however, an expression of the *iura novit*

---

247 E.g. *Krnojelac* ICTY A. Ch. 17.9.2003 paras. 138–42, and *Muhimana* ICTR A. Ch. 21.5.2007 paras. 217–18, 224–6 (cf. dissenting opinion by Judge Schomburg).

248 R. 87 of the ICTY RPE and ICTR RPE, Art. 74(2) of the ICC Statute (where 'charges' is used instead of the term 'indictment', see also Art. 61 of the ICC Statute).

249 *See Kupreškić et al.* ICTY T. Ch. 14.1.2000 paras. 728–48 (including a survey of domestic law in different countries).

250 *Ibid.*, para. 740. The Chamber was prepared to apply a lesser included offence theory and gave some examples which, however, require an established hierarchy of offences and of modes of criminal liability (crimes against humanity more serious than war crimes, perpetration more serious than aiding or abetting, etc.): paras. 744–6. The issue was raised but not considered in *Aleksovski* ICTY A. Ch. 24.3.2000 para. 55. Cf. *Karemera et al.* ICTR T. Ch. III 13.2.2004 para. 47, where the Trial Chamber indicated that it would apply the principle of *iura novit curia* at the close of the proceedings. Similarly, *Ntagerura et al.* ICTR T. Ch. 25.2.2004 paras. 36–8.

curia principle has been established in the Regulations, allowing a chamber to 'modify the legal characterization' of the facts;[251] that is, to determine that the facts and circumstances pleaded in the charges should be characterized as a different crime or a different form of participation from that which the Prosecutor has chosen. Indictments with a large number of counts and acquittals on 'technical grounds' can hereby be avoided.

Very controversially, the *Lubanga* Pre-Trial Chamber applied the modification provisions when confirming the charges and substituted charges of war crimes in a non-international armed conflict for the same offences in an international armed conflict.[252] This is difficult to reconcile with Article 61(7) of the ICC Statute.[253] It resulted in the Prosecutor prosecuting something other than he planned to do (based on the evidence available to him) and the Trial Chamber having to determine at the trial to what extent the confirmation findings were binding or not. The Trial Chamber did not consider itself competent to annul or amend the confirmed charges, but provided the procedural solution of allowing the parties to present evidence relating to both classifications of the conflict.[254] It might be that the Trial Chamber will have to recharacterize the charges again to set things right. In the meantime, the Trial Chamber has announced the possible application of the modification provision on a different point, whereby the majority and minority views expose conceptual differences concerning 'amendments' of the charges which stem from different domestic legal traditions.[255] The decision was reversed, however, and the Appeals Chamber concluded that the modification provisions, while compatible with the ICC Statute and the defendant's right to a fair trial, had been incorrectly applied by the majority of the Trial Chamber in that they may not be used to exceed the facts and circumstances described in the charges or any amendment thereto.[256]

17.8.5 Concurrence of offences – alternative and cumulative charges

International crimes are more complex than most crimes under domestic law. Multiple acts by many perpetrators and over a long period of time are often the case. Overlapping crimes are also common; the same killing or rape could, depending on the surrounding (contextual)

---

251 Reg. 55 of the ICC Regulations. Any such recategorization is subject to safeguards ensuring the participants, particularly the accused, an opportunity to respond and make preparations. The accused may also, if necessary, examine again a previous witness or call new evidence. See further Carsten Stahn, 'Modification of the Legal Characterization of Facts in the ICC System: A Portrayal of Regulation 55' (2005) 16 *CLF* 1.

252 *Lubanga Dyilo* ICC PT. Ch. I 29.1.2007. Requests for leave to appeal the decision were later denied.

253 See, e.g. Michaela Miraglia, 'Admissibility of Evidence, Standard of Proof, and Nature of the Decision in the ICC Confirmation of Charges in Lubanga' (2008) 6 *JICJ* 489, 501–3, and Rastan, 'What is a "case"' 444–6. Cf. Ambos and Miller, 'Structure and Function', 358–60 (putting forward arguments for the PT. Ch. position). For the better solution of requesting the Prosecutor to reconsider the charges, see *Bemba Gombo* ICC PT. Ch. III 3.3.2009.

254 *Lubanga Dyilo* ICC T. Ch. I 13.12.2007. The T. Ch. later ordered an amended document containing the charges (T. Ch. I 9.12.2008).

255 *Lubanga Dyilo* ICC T. Ch. I 14.7.2009 (minority opinion of 17.7.2009).

256 *Lubanga Dyilo* ICC A. Ch. 8.12.2009; see also T. Ch. I 8.1.2010.

facts, simultaneously be considered as genocide, crimes against humanity and war crimes. This concurrence of offences (*concursus delictorum*) gives rise to both theoretical and practical difficulties,[257] but the Statutes and RPE provide little assistance and here too the common law and civil law approaches vary.

The ICTY and ICTR have long accepted cumulative charges and, when challenged, the Trial Chambers have concluded that this is a matter to be resolved at trial, particularly in sentencing.[258] In turn, this triggers the question of cumulative convictions and after some initial uncertainty consistent principles now apply in both Tribunals. The Appeals Chamber in *Delalić et al.* concluded that only distinct crimes justify multiple convictions.[259] Cumulative convictions entered under different statutory provisions but based on the same conduct are permissible only if both statutory provisions involved have a materially distinct element not contained within the other. An element is materially distinct from another if it requires proof of a fact not required by the other element.[260] If this test is met, cumulative convictions must be imposed; this is not a discretionary decision.[261] If not, a single conviction must be entered; the more specific offence is to have preference over the more general one (a *lex specialis* principle). The contextual elements for the different crimes are also to be taken into account, meaning that cumulative convictions for the same conduct, for example murder/killing, are permissible as different crimes (under different articles of the Statute). The test becomes more complicated for different charges for the same conduct under the same Article. For example, cumulative convictions are not permitted for persecution as a crime against humanity and other underlying crimes against humanity, unless each offence has a materially distinct element which the ICTY Appeals Chamber has concluded that many of them have.[262]

When cumulative charges and cumulative convictions are allowed there is little need for alternative charges. However, different forms of criminal responsibility cannot be imposed for the same conduct and thus these forms may be pleaded in the alternative in the ICTY and ICTR.[263] For example, superior responsibility is subsidiary to other modes of liability, and commission excludes a conviction for also planning the crime; a superior position or participation in planning will instead be factors in sentencing.[264]

---

257 See Carl-Friedrich Stuckenberg, 'Multiplicity of Offences: Concursus Delictorum' in Horst Fischer, Claus Kreß and Sascha Rolf Lüder (eds.), *International and National Prosecution of Crimes Under International Law* (Berlin, 2001) 559–604.

258 E.g. *Delalić et al.* ICTY T. Ch. II 2.10.1996 para. 24, and *Kanyabashi* ICTR T. Ch. II 31.5.2000 paras. 5.5–5.7. See section 19.3.2.

259 *Delalić et al.* ICTY A. Ch. 20.2.2001 paras. 412–13. See also *Musema* ICTR A. Ch. 16.11.2001 paras. 358–70. But cf. *Kupreškić et al.* ICTY T. Ch. II 14.1.2000 paras. 637–748.

260 This test serves two purposes: to ensure that the accused is convicted only for distinct offences and that the convictions fully reflect his or her criminality: *Kordić and Čerkez* ICTY A. Ch. 17.12.2004 para. 1033.

261 E.g. *Strugar* ICTY A. Ch. 17.7.2008 para. 324.

262 *Kordić and Čerkez* ICTY A. Ch. 17.12.2004 paras. 1039–44.

263 E.g. *Stanisić* ICTY T. Ch. II 19.7.2005 para. 6.

264 E.g. *Blaškić* ICTY A. Ch. 29.7.2004 para. 91, and *Kajelijeli* ICTR A. Ch. 23.5.2005 para. 81.

The pleading practice of the ICC – alternative or cumulative charges – is still in its infancy, but it is already clear that the practice will be influenced by the provisions allowing the Trial Chamber to 'modify the legal characterization' of the facts (see section 17.8.4).

17.9   Pre-trial proceedings – preparations for trial

17.9.1   First appearance and confirmation of charges

As with many domestic jurisdictions, a formal first appearance hearing is held at the ICTY, ICTR and ICC as soon as the suspect has arrived at the Tribunal or Court.[265] The Chamber will check that the person has been served with the indictment (ICTY/ICTR) or arrest warrant (ICC) and that certain rights are respected. At the ICTY and ICTR, one main function is to charge the accused formally and allow him or her to enter a plea to the charges (immediately or at a further appearance). A date for trial will be set in case of a plea of not guilty, whereas a guilty plea leads to simplified trial proceedings (see section 17.11). In the ICC proceedings, on the other hand, it is not required that the person is formally charged at this stage and the main purpose, apart from the assurance of rights, is instead to set a date for the confirmation of charges.

Another common feature of many, but not all, domestic systems is a judicial pre-trial review of the indictment to assess that charges concern criminal acts and that there is evidence of sufficient strength for prosecution. Judicial confirmation of the indictment (in the ICC Statute called 'charges') is also required at the ICTY, ICTR and ICC.[266] It is intended to protect suspects against unsubstantiated prosecutions, which is particularly important when the crimes are inherently very serious and the proceedings often attract public attention.[267]

The Tribunal proceedings are *ex parte* while the ICC Statute provides for an adversarial process with a hearing in the presence of the prosecution and defence.[268] In both cases the Prosecutor must support the charges with sufficient evidence, at this stage normally documentary or summary evidence. But in the ICC process the accused is also entitled to challenge the Prosecutor's evidence and to present his or her own evidence, which has prompted concerns that the proceedings could lead to an additional 'mini-trial' without sufficient control by the Pre-Trial Chamber. The Tribunals apply a prima facie test and the ICC Statute requires 'substantial grounds to believe' that the person has committed the crime charged.[269] The primary purpose is to test whether the evidentiary requirements for committing the case to trial are met. The judge or Chamber is to consider each charge and either confirm or dismiss it. Upon confirmation, a case at the ICC is transferred from the Pre-Trial Chamber to the Trial

---

265   R. 62 of the ICTY RPE and ICTR RPE, Art. 60(1) of the ICC Statute and r. 121 of the ICC RPE.

266   Art. 19 of the ICTY Statute, Art. 18 of the ICTR Statute, and Art. 61 of the ICC Statute.

267   The indictment (and any subsequent amendment to it) is to be served upon the accused: r. 53*bis* of the ICTY RPE and ICTR RPE, and r. 121 of the ICC RPE.

268   Art. 61 of the ICC Statute and r. 121 of the ICC RPE.

269   See e.g. *Milošević* ICTY (Judge May) 22.11.2001; Art. 61(6)–(7) of the ICC Statute.

Chamber. In practice, ICC confirmation hearings have run over a number of days, with a few witnesses being examined, and have resulted in very long and detailed decisions; the latter may be criticized for potentially affecting the impartiality of the trial judges.[270]

In general, the confirmation of the indictment at the ICTY and ICTR precedes the arrest and surrender of the accused, while the opposite is scheduled to apply at the ICC. But the actual apprehension and surrender of the suspect or accused is a serious obstacle to international criminal proceedings. Therefore, special confirmation proceedings *in absentia* have been introduced.[271] In the Tribunals, these rather controversial proceedings[272] relate to indictments that have already been confirmed with a view to issuing an international arrest warrant to all States. Moreover, the Trial Chamber in *Karadžić and Mladić* expressed the view that the proceedings have stigmatizing and reparative effects and contribute to a true historical record.[273] While the first two results are true, the third is debatable since only the prosecution case is presented and the accused could be unrepresented. At the ICC, on the other hand, confirmation *in absentia* is neither a second (more extensive) proceeding, nor a precondition for an international arrest warrant, and its value is questionable. Indeed, a confirmation *in absentia* does not substitute for a trial and cannot result in a verdict. Moreover, the conclusions reached in a decision of this kind can only be preliminary in nature and cannot prevent different conclusions at trial.[274]

The general principle is that ICTY and ICTR indictments are to be made public, but it is possible to keep the indictment under seal, inter alia to facilitate an arrest or protect confidential information.[275] This was for a long time standard practice at the ICTY and disclosure took place first when the indictment had been served on the accused. This is not an issue for the ICC since the indictment is not a prerequisite for the arrest warrant and the warrant need not be made public.[276]

17.9.2 Preparations for trial

The preparations for trial include the resolution of many legal issues, such as challenges[277] to jurisdiction, matters relating to evidence, protective measures and, in the ICC, the

---

270 E.g. Miraglia, 'Admissibility of Evidence', 498–501.
271 R. 61 of the ICTY RPE and ICTR RPE, as well as Art. 61(2) of the ICC Statute and rr. 123–6 of the ICC RPE.
272 See, e.g. Mark Tieroff and Edward Amley, 'Proceeding Justice and Accountability in the Balkans: The International Criminal Tribunal for the Former Yugoslavia and Rule 61' (1998) 23 *Yale Journal of International Law* 231; Shuichi Furuya, 'Rule 61 Procedure in the International Criminal Tribunal for the Former Yugoslavia: A Lesson for the ICC' (1999) 12 *LJIL* 635.
273 *Karadžić and Mladić* ICTY T. Ch. I 11.7.1996 para. 3.
274 Christopher Greenwood, 'The Development of International Humanitarian Law by the International Criminal Tribunal for the Former Yugoslavia' (1998) 2 *Max Planck Yearbook of United Nations Law* 97 at 113.
275 Rr. 52–3 of the ICTY RPE and ICTR RPE.
276 *Situation in Uganda* ICC PT. Ch. II 13.10.2005.
277 See rr. 54, 72 and 73 of the ICTY RPE and ICTR RPE.

admissibility of a case. A controversial issue, where the different legal traditions provide different answers, is whether the parties may prepare witnesses in substance before giving evidence ('witness proofing'). Whereas it is allowed in ICTY and ICTR, an ICC Pre-Trial Chamber has prohibited the Prosecutor from this practice.[278] However, so-called 'witness familiarization' is accepted by all. Another important issue is the joinder or severance of trials against multiple accused,[279] which has been ordered in many ICTY and ICTR cases concerning crimes committed in the course of 'the same transaction'.[280] Joint trials may promote judicial economy, avoid duplication of evidence and repeated witness appearances, and ensure the consistency of verdicts, but a concern is prejudice to the accused.[281]

Much time and effort has been devoted to such issues at the Tribunals and the ICC. In the interest of efficiency, the ICTY, ICTR and ICC have developed different procedural tools, such as pre-trial (or pre-appeal) judges,[282] status conferences,[283] and pre-trial and pre-defence conferences.[284] The ICC also has a detailed pre-confirmation scheme.[285] A common feature is that the judges have assumed an increasingly active and controlling role. This even includes powers to restrict, inter alia, the number of witnesses at trial and the time available to the respective party for presenting evidence at trial.[286]

17.9.3 Disclosure of evidence

A fundamental feature of a fair trial – a manifestation of 'equality of arms' – is the disclosure of the prosecutor's evidence to the accused, allowing the latter to prepare for trial. In an inquisitorial system, this is done easily since all the material collected during the investigation – incriminating and exonerating – is collected in a 'dossier' which, in principle, is

---

278 *Lubanga Dyilo* ICC PT. Ch. I 8.11.2006 (see also T. Ch. I 23.5.2008); cf. *Limaj et al.* ICTY T. Ch. III 10.12.2004, *Milutinović et al.* ICTY T. Ch. III 12.12.2006 and *Karemera et al.* ICTR A. Ch. 11.5.2007 para. 7 (the two latter reacting to the ICC decision). See also Sergey Vasiliev, 'Proofing the Ban on "Witness Proofing": Did the ICC Get it Right?' (2009) 20 *CLF* 193, and Kai Ambos, '"Witness Proofing" before the ICC: Neither legally admissible nor necessary' in Stahn and Sluiter, *Emerging Practice*, 599–614.
279 Rr. 48, 49 and 82 of the ICTY RPE; rr. 48, 48*bis*, 49 and 82 of the ICTR RPE; Art. 64(5) of the ICC Statute and r. 136 of the ICC RPE.
280 R. 2 of the ICTY RPE and ICTR RPE; see also *Milošević* ICTY A. Ch. 18.4.2002 para. 20. Concerning the ICC, see *Katanga and Ngudjolo Chui* ICC PT. Ch. I 10.3.2008 and A. Ch. 9.6.2008.
281 For a review of the jurisprudence, see *Popović et al.* ICTY T. Ch. III 21.9.2005. For a critical view on the joinder decision in *Milošević*, see Gideon Boas, *The Milošević Trial* (Cambridge, 2007) 115–21.
282 Rr. 65*ter* and 108*bis* of the ICTY RPE; Arts. 39(2)(b)(iii) and 57(2)(b) of the ICC Statute, r. 7 of the ICC RPE, and reg. 47 of the ICC Regulations.
283 R. 65*bis* of the ICTY RPE and ICTR RPE; r. 132 of the ICC RPE and reg. 54 of the ICC Regulations.
284 Rr. 73*bis* and 73*ter* of the ICTY RPE and ICTR RPE; reg. 54 of the ICC Regulations.
285 R. 121 of the ICC RPE.
286 E.g. *Milošević* ICTY A. Ch. 16.5.2002 (time limit etc. for the prosecution case), and T. Ch. III 25.2.2004 (time limit etc. for the defence case). See also T. Ch. III 17.9.2003 (time for preparation of the defence case), upheld on appeal, A. Ch. 20.1.2004, and T. Ch. III 17.10.2003 (time limits for examination of a witness). Regarding limitations, however, see *Orić* ICTY A. Ch. 20.7.2005.

available to the accused. In an adversarial system, however, disclosure is more complicated and premised on separate prosecution and defence cases. While the prosecutor normally has extensive disclosure obligations, including for material that is favourable to the accused, defence disclosure is more restricted and is often postponed until the prosecutor has presented his or her evidence at trial. The defendant has the right to remain silent. Another difference is the extent to which the evidence should be disclosed to the court before the trial. Such disclosure allows the judges to prepare and control the trial more actively, as well as fulfilling a truth-finding function, but could taint the court's impartiality (or at least be perceived to do so). Where a 'dossier' is collected, the material is also made available to the court.

The ICTY and ICTR procedures are primarily adversarial in nature and disclosure is regulated against this background. The Prosecutor has extensive, and continuous, obligations concerning pre-trial disclosure: the material supporting the indictment, copies of statements of all witnesses whom the Prosecutor intends to call to testify at trial, and copies of all statements offered in evidence in lieu of a witness testimony.[287] The defence must also be permitted to inspect the prosecutor's material.[288] The obligation to disclose also extends to exculpatory and other relevant material within the custody or control of the Prosecutor,[289] a provision which has triggered numerous claims of violations at both Tribunals. However, certain information and material are exempt from disclosure[290] and, in addition, the Trial Chamber may allow non-disclosure of specific information. Defence disclosure is also provided with respect to a defence of alibi or any special defence (for example diminished or lack of mental responsibility) at the ICTR before the commencement of the trial, but at the ICTY full disclosure is provided only once the prosecution has closed its case at trial.[291] Failure by the defence to disclose does not prevent it from raising a defence or presenting evidence.

The Trial Chamber also exerts a certain control over disclosure; the Prosecutor may seek clarifications on disclosure from the Chamber[292] and the accused may obtain an order to the Prosecutor to meet the disclosure obligations. In the case of violations, the trial may be reopened in order to allow the presentation of additional evidence,[293] and sanctions may be

---

287 Rr. 66, 92*bis* and 94*bis* of the ICTY RPE and ICTR RPE. Generally, see Vladimir Tochilovsky, 'Prosecution Disclosure Obligations in the ICC and Relevant Jurisprudence of the Ad Hoc Tribunals' in Doria, *Legal Regime*, 843–62.

288 At the ICTR, the Prosecutor has a reciprocal right to inspect material within the custody or control of the accused and intended to be used as evidence at trial: r. 66(B) of the ICTR RPE. An equivalent provision was repealed from the ICTY RPE.

289 R. 68 of the ICTY RPE and ICTR RPE. See also *Blaškić* ICTY A. Ch. 29.7.2004 paras. 263–9.

290 R. 70 of the ICTY RPE and ICTR RPE.

291 R. 67 of the ICTY RPE and ICTR RPE. Regarding the timing of the defence disclosure, see also r. 65*ter* of the ICTY RPE.

292 E.g. *Krajišnik and Plavšić* ICTY T. Ch. III 1.8.2001.

293 See *Furundžija* ICTY T. Ch. II 10.12.1998 para. 22.

imposed.[294] A controversial question is whether the evidence should also be disclosed to the Trial Chamber. Some Chambers have required such disclosure by the Prosecutor, but others have refused, and the ICTY Appeals Chamber has established that this is a discretionary matter for the Trial Chamber.[295]

Disclosure is briefly touched upon in the ICC Statute and further developed in the RPE and jurisprudence. Controversial questions in the negotiations were whether full disclosure of the evidence for trial should take place before or after the confirmation hearing and whether the Chambers should have access to a 'dossier'.[296] The Rules leave room for different interpretations. But it is important to note that the confirmation and the trial serve different purposes and that the evidentiary requirements differ, which is also reflected in the rules on pre-confirmation disclosure.[297]

The Chambers play a significant role in the disclosure process and are empowered to order disclosure for the purpose of the confirmation of charges. The Trial Chamber is also empowered to provide for disclosure of documents and information not previously disclosed.[298] Disclosure takes place between the parties and there has not (so far) been any all-embracing 'dossier'. The Statute places an important obligation upon the Prosecutor to disclose evidence that is exculpatory, mitigating, or which may affect the credibility of prosecution evidence.[299] The RPE contain provisions on disclosure by the prosecution and, regarding material offered in evidence, by the defence as well as on inspection by the other party of material subject to disclosure.[300] Exceptions from disclosure are also available,[301] and many have been made for protection purposes. Regarding disclosure of exculpatory evidence, the Prosecutor may in *ex parte* proceedings seek a ruling from the relevant Chamber and it is clear that such disclosure is an interest with priority status.[302]

17.10 Evidentiary rules

At the ICTY, ICTR and ICC the procedures are adversarial in the sense that the parties are primarily responsible for putting evidence before the court, although the judges may provide

---

294 Rr. 46 and 68*bis* of the ICTY RPE and r. 46 of the ICTR RPE; e.g. *Krštić* ICTY A. Ch. 19.4.2004 paras. 210–15, and *Blaškić* ICTY A. Ch. 29.7.2004 para. 295.

295 *Blagojević et al.* ICTY A. Ch. 8.4.2003 paras. 11–19.

296 For opposing views, see contributions by Helen Brady and Gilbert Bitti in Fischer et al., *International and National Prosecution*, 261–88.

297 Regarding the confirmation hearing, see Art. 61(5) of the ICC Statute and r. 121(3) of the ICC RPE.

298 Arts. 61(3) (Pre-Trial Chamber) and 64(3)(c) (Trial Chamber) of the ICC Statute. Extensive instructions for disclosure were issued in *Lubanga Dyilo* ICC PT. Ch. I 15.5.2006 and 19.5.2006.

299 Art. 67(2) of the ICC Statute.

300 Rr. 76–9 of the ICC RPE.

301 *Ibid.*, rr. 81–2.

302 *Ibid.*, r. 83. See section 17.7.3 on the problems in the *Lubanga* case. See also Ambos and Miller, 'Structure and Function', 341–4, and Sabine Swoboda, 'The ICC Disclosure Regime – A Defence Perspective' (2008) 19 *CLF* 449.

for additional evidence. Issues concerning the burden and standard of proof, the ro
witnesses and disclosure, have already been discussed (see sections 17.2.3, 17.3
17.9.3).

Domestic systems provide for rules on evidence, particularly rules regarding t
sion and exclusion of evidence. While many adversarial systems, particularly
jury trials, tend to have strict and technical provisions, inquisitorial systems do not and
instead admit most evidence to be presented at trial.[303] The former approach seeks to protect
the fact-finder from unreliable or improper evidence. The latter places the emphasis on the
court weighing the totality of the evidence (a principle of 'free evaluation of evidence') and
providing the findings in a reasoned opinion. Regardless of the system, however, a high
evidentiary standard is important for the legitimacy of any court; in *Kupreškić et al.* the Trial
Chamber stated: 'we have had to shoulder the heavy burden of establishing incredible facts
by means of credible evidence'.[304]

The approach to evidence at the Tribunals has been described as flexible, liberal and
unhindered by technical rules found in national and particularly common law systems.[305]
Professional judges try both fact and law and there is no need to protect jurors from lay
prejudice. The same is true for the ICC. The complex factual situations, large amount of
evidence, and difficulties in obtaining it, are all reasons for flexibility, but this also raises
issues of fairness and efficiency of the proceedings.[306] *See footnote*

There are a few rules for the Tribunals but a rich jurisprudence,[307] which have also
influenced the ICC law. The Trial Chambers are not to be bound by national rules of
evidence.[308] Instead, the Tribunals are instructed to apply the rules 'which will best favour
a fair determination of the matter' and 'are consonant with the spirit of the Statute and the
general principles of law'.[309] They have the discretion to 'admit any relevant evidence
which it deems to have probative value' and to exclude evidence 'if its probative value is
substantially outweighed by the need to ensure a fair trial'.[310] In order to be relevant (to an
allegation or issue in the trial) and probative (whether it tends to prove an issue) the evidence
must be 'reliable', which in turn depends upon many circumstances, for example the origin,

---

[303] E.g. Mirjan Damaška, 'Free Proof and Its Detractors' (1995) 43 *American Journal of Comparative Law* 343.

[304] *Kupreškić et al.* ICTY T. Ch. II 14.1.2000 para. 758; see also A. Ch. 23.10.2001 paras. 34–40 (on domestic principles).

[305] Richard May and Marieke Wierda, 'Evidence before the ICTY' in Richard May et al. (eds.), *Essays on ICTY Procedure and Evidence* (The Hague, 2001), 251.

[306] In particular, commentators with a common law background have been critical of the relaxed regime of the Tribunals, e.g. Patricia Wald, 'To Establish Incredible Events by Credible Evidence: The Use of Affidavit Testimony in Yugoslavia War Crimes Tribunal Proceedings' (2001) 42 *Harvard International Law Review* 535.

[307] Instructive are the 'guidelines' issued in *Brđanin and Talić* ICTY T. Ch. II 15.2.2002.

[308] R. 89(A) of the ICTY RPE and ICTR RPE; Art. 69(8) of the ICC Statute and r. 63(5) of the ICC RPE.

[309] R. 89(B) of the ICTY RPE and ICTR RPE.

[310] R. 89(C)–(D) of the ICTY RPE. Cf. the ICTR RPE which only set out the first part on admission: r. 89(C).

content, corroboration, truthfulness, voluntariness, and trustworthiness of the evidence.[311] The ICC Statute is less extensive but provides a few exclusionary rules. Generally, the 'probative value of the evidence and any prejudice that such evidence may cause to a fair trial or to a fair evaluation of the testimony of a witness' are decisive factors for a ruling on admissibility or relevance.[312] Additionally, evidence before the Tribunals as well as the ICC may be excluded because of the means by which it was obtained.[313]

With legally trained judges only, and an obligation to provide reasons for the factual findings, a presumption in favour of admission of evidence exists in the Tribunals and the ICC; the evidence should rather be assessed at trial than weeded-out beforehand.[314] For example, the Tribunals have usually accepted hearsay evidence.[315]

With respect to certain evidence in cases of sexual assault the opposite presumption applies or the evidence is banned altogether.[316] The issue of 'consent' with respect to crimes of sexual violence committed in coercive circumstances requires special attention; in such a situation, a claim of consent is rarely credible. But the issue is difficult both in substance and with respect to the conflation of material (element of the crime) and procedural aspects. The Tribunals have established that consent must be given voluntarily and be assessed in the context of the circumstances, but that it is not necessary to show the use of force by the perpetrator, nor is it necessary to prove resistance by the victim.[317] From national jurisprudence has been drawn a principle of presumed non-consent in certain situations such as between detainees and captors.[318] Similarly, the ICC RPE provide that consent cannot be inferred from silence or lack of resistance, nor can it be inferred from words or conduct of a victim incapable of giving genuine consent.[319] It is against this interpretation of the law that the special evidentiary rules, which also aim to protect the victims from spurious lines of questioning, are to be understood.

Another issue that has provoked much debate and litigation is the use of written witness statements in lieu of oral testimony, which is now allowed at the ICTY and ICTR regarding 'proof of a matter other than the acts and conduct of the accused as charged in the indictment'.[320] Other rules address depositions, evidence of a consistent pattern of conduct and

---

311 E.g. *Tadić* ICTY T. Ch. II 5.8.1996 paras. 15–19, and *Musema* ICTR T. Ch. I 27.1.2000 paras. 38–42.

312 Art. 69(4) of the ICC Statute.

313 R. 95 of the ICTY RPE and ICTR RPE; Art. 69(7) of the ICC Statute. See section 17.7.2 (on exclusion of evidence in *Lubanga Dyilo*).

314 On general considerations concerning the evaluation of evidence, see e.g. *Brđanin* ICTY T. Ch. II 1.9.2004 paras. 20–36.

315 E.g. *Aleksovski* ICTY A. Ch. 16.2.1999 para. 15, and *Ndindabahizi* ICTR A. Ch. 16.1.2007 para. 115.

316 R. 96 of the ICTY RPE and ICTR RPE, and rr. 70–2 of the ICC RPE. See further Donald Piragoff, 'Evidence' in Lee, *Elements and Rules*, 369–91.

317 E.g. *Kunarac et al.* ICTY A. Ch. 12.6.2002 paras. 127–9.

318 *Ibid.*, para. 131.

319 R. 70 of the ICC RPE.

320 R. 92*bis* of the ICTY RPE and ICTR RPE.

judicial notice of notorious facts and adjudicated facts or documentary evidence from other proceedings.[321] Similarly, the ICC may also permit video-recorded or audio-recorded testimony, documents and written transcripts;[322] but how the Court will deal with already adjudicated facts and material from other proceedings is a matter for jurisprudence.[323] While there is still a preference for oral testimony in principle, the ICTY in particular has been prepared to depart from this in the interest of shorter trials.[324]

17.11 Admission of guilt, guilty pleas, plea bargaining

Common law and civil law systems take very different approaches when the accused confesses the crimes charged. The law of the ICTY and ICTR, on the one hand, and the ICC, on the other, reflect these differences. The Tribunals have adopted the common law approach of a formal review of the 'guilty plea' and, if accepted by the Chamber, a finding of guilt and a move to a sentencing hearing, that is to say simplified proceedings.[325] The test is whether it was a voluntary, informed and unequivocal plea, and whether there is a sufficient factual basis for the crime and the participation of the accused in it. The crucial difference between the common law and civil law view is whether the court must accept the facts as the parties have agreed them or whether it will conduct a further inquiry and perhaps require additional evidence. Although the ICTY and ICTR Chambers are required to satisfy themselves as to the facts, the factual basis is often limited and the Chambers are reluctant to call for additional evidence. Recent ICTY practice, however, reveals a more thorough examination of the agreed facts and the consistency with the admitted crimes.[326]

This approach leaves room for agreements between the parties regarding matters of guilt and sentencing – 'plea bargaining' – as is the case in many common law jurisdictions.[327] The idea is that the dispute between the parties may be resolved in this way too. It is a

---

321 *Ibid.*, rr. 71, 93 and 94.

322 Art. 69(2) of the ICC Statute and rr. 47, 67 and 68 of the ICC RPE. See e.g. *Lubanga Dyilo* ICC T. Ch. I 13.6.2008 (1399) (written evidence) and 15.1.2009 (prior recorded witness statements).

323 There are, however, provisions on judicial notice of facts of common knowledge and on agreements between the parties regarding evidence: Art. 69(6) of the ICC Statute and r. 69 of the ICC RPE.

324 Compare r. 89(F) of the ICTY RPE and r. 90.1 of the ICTR RPE; the ICTY, but not the ICTR, has departed from the primary reliance on oral testimony. See also *Milošević* ICTY T. Ch. III 21.3.2002 (general requirements for r. 92*bis*), and A. Ch. 30.9.2003 (relationship between rr. 89 and 92*bis*; including a dissenting opinion). See further, Steven Kay, 'The Move from Oral Evidence to Written Evidence' (2004) 2 *JICJ* 495.

325 Rr. 62*bis* and 62*ter* of the ICTY RPE, and rr. 62 and 62*bis* of the ICTR RPE. Cf. Art. 20(3) of the ICTY Statute and Art. 19(3) of the ICTR Statute, which direct that, regardless of the plea, there be a 'trial'.

326 See e.g. *Babić* ICTY A. Ch. 18.7.2005 paras. 8–10, and *Deronjić* ICTY A. Ch. 20.7.2005 paras. 12–19. Cf. *Jelisić* ICTY A. Ch. 5.7.2001 para. 87 (unless cogent reasons indicate otherwise, the sentence should be based on the agreed facts).

327 One should note, however, that not all common law jurisdictions allow plea bargaining and that among those allowing the practice there are important differences.

debated matter, however, and while proponents often highlight the judicial economy of plea bargaining, opponents focus instead on inequality before the law and the risk of materially incorrect verdicts.[328]

The ICTY and ICTR have long accepted plea bargaining, but the attraction of this tool depends on a predictable outcome for the accused, particularly a sentencing rebate, and here the jurisprudence is inconsistent.[329] While it is clear that the Chamber is not bound by any agreement between the parties, many sentencing recommendations have been accepted and the Trial Chamber in *Todorović* concluded that a timely plea would normally result in a rebate.[330] But in later decisions, ICTY Trial Chambers have departed from such recommendations and the Appeals Chamber has avoided giving express support to a rebate.[331]

During the ICC negotiations, the issue of guilty pleas was extensively discussed. As a compromise, the Statute provides a formula more towards the civil law view that a confession is merely one piece of evidence, but it still allows simplified proceedings in case of 'an admission of guilt'.[332] The assessment of the 'admission of guilt' by the Trial Chamber is similar to that of the Tribunals but with a stronger focus on the submitted facts and any evidence. The Chamber may also, in 'the interests of justice', decide on a more complete presentation of the facts of the case by requesting the Prosecutor to present additional evidence or ordering a trial under the ordinary trial procedures. The question of plea bargaining was also a hotly contested issue in the negotiations and some expressed strong reservations. A provision was inserted in the Statute that no agreement between the parties is to be binding on the Court. But the provision does not prevent plea bargaining as such and certain powers of the Prosecutor, albeit under certain Court control, could leave room for such agreements.[333] Whether the ICC will accept the practical necessity of some form of plea bargaining in spite of the principled concerns and likely criticism is not yet known. But, as one commentator suggests, it would be desirable to conduct as many trials as possible, and resort to bargaining only when absolutely necessary.[334]

---

328 See *Erdemović* ICTY A. Ch. 7.10.1997 paras. 17–21, and the dissenting opinion by Judge Cassese. See further, e.g. Michael Bohlander, 'Plea-Bargaining before the ICTY' in May et al., *Essays on ICTY Procedure*, 151–63; Nancy Amoury Combs, 'Copping a Plea to Genocide: The Plea Bargaining of International Crimes' (2002) 151 *University of Pennsylvania Law Review* 1; Henri Bosly, 'Admission of Guilt before the ICC and in Continental Systems' (2004) 2 *JICJ* 1040; Julian Cook, 'Plea Bargaining at the Hague' (2005) 30 *Yale Journal of International Law* 473; Mark Harmon, 'Plea Bargaining: The Uninvited Guest at the International Criminal Tribunal for the Former Yugoslavia' in Doria, *Legal Regime*, 163–82.

329 On concerns regarding such rebates, see section 19.3.1.

330 *Todorović* ICTY T. Ch. I 31.7.2001 para. 80.

331 See *Dragan Nikolić* ICTY A. Ch. 4.2.2005 paras. 55–6.

332 Art. 65 of the ICC Statute and r. 139 of the ICC RPE.

333 Art. 54(3)(d) of the ICC Statute, on agreements with individuals, as well as Arts. 53(3) and 61(4) and (9), relating to decisions not to pursue a prosecution.

334 Mirjan Damaška, 'Negotiated Justice in International Criminal Courts' (2004) 2 *JICJ* 1018.

17.12 Trial and judgment

Generally, the trial hearings before the Tribunals have been lengthy. In part this is due to the adversarial nature of the trial whereby the prosecution and the defence present separate 'cases'. The parties have been allowed to make different dispositions and adapt their evidence depending on the development of the trial, with little intervention by the Chambers. This has changed over time, however, and the preparations are now much more rigorous and under stricter judicial control (see section 17.9).

Unlike many civil law jurisdictions, neither the ICTY and ICTR nor the ICC may proceed with the trial in the absence of the accused (trials *in absentia*).[335] While some criticize this choice, particularly in light of the difficulties of apprehending the accused, others consider this to be a fundamental precondition for a fair trial and the issue was much discussed in the ICC negotiations.[336] Nonetheless, the compromise was to allow for confirmation hearings *in absentia* (see section 17.9.1).

In principle, the trial is to be public but closed sessions are allowed for specified reasons: public order and morality, safety and security of a victim or witness, protection of confidential or sensitive information, or the protection of the interests of justice.[337] Disruptive persons, including the accused, may be removed from the courtroom.[338]

The trial itself follows a straightforward scheme: opening statements, presentation of evidence, closing arguments, deliberations, and judgment.[339] Sentencing and reparations proceedings are discussed in Chapters 18 and 19. In the ICTY and ICTR this follows the two-case model, prosecution first and defence thereafter. This will not necessarily be the case at the ICC, however, where the presiding judge has broad powers to give directions for the conduct of the proceedings. The considerable discretion could result in fundamentally different approaches being taken in different cases, and in turn affect the perceived fairness of the Court proceedings and the right of all accused to equal treatment, but this risk could be reduced by practice directives or harmonization in other forms.[340]

Unless the Trial Chamber decides otherwise, the presentation of evidence in Tribunal trials follows a true adversarial model: prosecution evidence, defence evidence,

---

335 Art. 21(4)(d) of the ICTY Statute, Art. 20(4)(d) of the ICTR Statute, and Art. 63 of the ICC Statute.

336 See Håkan Friman, 'Rights of Persons Suspected or Accused of a Crime' in Lee, *The Making of the Rome Statute*, 255–61, and William Schabas, 'In Absentia Proceedings Before International Criminal Courts' in Sluiter and Vasiliev, *International Criminal Procedure*, 335–80.

337 Rr. 78 and 79 of the ICTY RPE and ICTR RPE, and Arts. 63 and 64(7) of the ICC Statute.

338 R. 80 of the ICTY RPE and ICTR RPE, and Arts. 63(2) and 71 of the ICC Statute.

339 Rr. 84–7 of the ICTY RPE, rr. 84–8 of the ICTR RPE; Art. 64(8) of the ICC Statute and rr. 140–2 of the ICC RPE.

340 See Reinhold Gallmetzer, 'The Trial Chamber's discretionary power to devise the proceedings before it and its exercise in the trial of Thomas Lubanga Dyilo' in Stahn and Sluiter, *Emerging Practice*, 501–24.

prosecution evidence in rebuttal, defence evidence in rejoinder, evidence ordered by the Chamber, evidence regarding sentencing.[341] In each case, examination-in-chief, cross-examination, and re-examination are to be allowed and the judge may ask questions at any stage.[342] The Chamber is to exercise control over the mode and order of interrogating witnesses, with a view to efficiency, and the cross-examination is limited in scope.[343] The ICC scheme, on the other hand, leaves room for a different approach inspired by inquisitorial principles: less of a distinction, or none at all, between prosecution and defence witnesses, and a less strict scheme for examination beginning with a free statement and questions by the judges, not the parties. There are some minimum rules, however, which provide for an examination model quite similar to that of the Tribunals.[344] The first ICC trial, however, has not exposed any substantive departure from Tribunal practice in this respect.

Before the Tribunals and the ICC, the accused may appear as a witness in his or her own defence, which departs from the practice in civil law jurisdictions. In addition, both the ICTY and ICC allow the accused to make unsworn statements at trial.[345]

In line with the adversarial two-case model at the ICTY and ICTR, there is room for the accused to request a judgment after the presentation of the prosecution case, a so-called mid-trial acquittal.[346] The Chamber may also enter such a judgment *proprio motu*. The rationale is that the accused has 'no case to answer' due to insufficient evidence, but the assessment of evidence at mid-trial could potentially affect the perception of the judges' impartiality. Attempting to overcome this, the test is explained as: 'whether there is evidence (if accepted) upon which a reasonable tribunal of fact *could* be satisfied beyond reasonable doubt of the guilt of the accused on the particular charge in question'.[347] No similar provisions are provided for the ICC but it is possible that the Court, like early ICTY decisions,[348] will argue an 'inherent power' to dismiss charges due to insufficient evidence.

The judgment must contain reasons, which allows a subsequent review of the legal and factual findings.[349] As majority decisions are permitted, both majority and minority opinions are to be included.

---

341 R. 85 of the ICTY RPE and ICTR RPE.

342 In particular the cross-examination is considered a cornerstone for the common law trial model, sometimes even called 'the greatest legal engine ever invented for the discovery of truth', see John H. Wigmore, *A Treatise on the Anglo-American System of Evidence at Trials in Common Law*, 3rd edn (Boston, 1940) 29, § 1367.

343 R. 90 of the ICTY RPE and ICTR RPE.

344 R. 140 of the ICC RPE.

345 R. 84*bis* of the ICTY RPE and Art. 67(1)(h) of the ICC Statute.

346 R. 98*bis* of the ICTY RPE and ICTR RPE.

347 E.g. *Delalić et al*. ICTY A. Ch. 20.2.2001 para. 434.

348 *Tadić* ICTY T. Ch. II 13.9.1996.

349 Art. 23 of the ICTY Statute and r. 98*ter* of the ICTY RPE; Art. 22 of the ICTR Statute and r. 88 of the ICTR RPE; Art. 74 of the ICC Statute and r. 144 of the ICC RPE.

17.13 Appeals proceedings

17.13.1 Appeal against judgment and sentence

The Nuremberg and Tokyo Tribunals did not provide for appeals, but today anyone convicted of a crime is entitled to a review of the conviction and sentence by a higher court.[350] The ICTY, ICTR and ICC all allow appeals.[351] Like many civil law jurisdictions, appeals are not restricted to convictions or sentences, but also extend to acquittals. In many common law jurisdictions, on the contrary, acquittals are considered final immediately and are not subject to appeal. The latter model stresses a protection of the individual against repeated charges by the State,[352] the former is more concerned with achieving a materially correct verdict.

On appeal, the Appeals Chamber may affirm, reverse or revise the appealed decision.[353] Alternatively, it may set aside the judgment and order a new trial before a different trial chamber.[354] Detailed procedures are set forth for each jurisdiction.[355]

A safeguard in domestic jurisdictions where acquittals are subject to appeals is a prohibition against *reformatio in peius* (worsening of an earlier verdict), which safeguard prevents changes regarding the verdict or sentence to the detriment of the accused if only he or she appeals; such a change requires the prosecutor to appeal. The ICC Statute sets out this principle and the Tribunals have applied it too.[356] In practice, however, the principle will be straightforward concerning penalties but hard to apply regarding convictions since no formal hierarchal order has been established between the different crimes (see section 19.3).

17.13.2 Grounds of appeal and standard of review

At the ICTY and ICTR, appeals against trial judgments, as appeals against sentencing judgments, are appeals *stricto sensu*, that is to say of a corrective nature, and not new trials

---

350 E.g. Art. 14(5) of the ICCPR.

351 Art. 25 of the ICTY Statute, Art. 24 of the ICTR Statute, and Art. 81 of the ICC Statute.

352 In the common law jurisdictions an appeal against an acquittal would contravene the principle of protection against double jeopardy, at least if it relates to facts established by a jury, but exceptions also exist; see, e.g. Rafael Nieto-Navia and Barbara Roche, 'The Ambit of the Powers under Article 25 of the ICTY Statute: Three Issues of Recent Interest' in May et al., *Essays on ICTY Procedure*, 473–94.

353 Art. 25(2) of the ICTY Statute, Art. 24(2) of the ICTR Statute, and Art. 81(2) of the ICC Statute.

354 Art. 81(2) of the ICC Statute. At the ICTY, cases have been remitted to the Trial Chamber when a guilty plea was invalid (*Erdemović* ICTY A. Ch. 7.10.1997) or for resentencing subsequent to the reversal of acquittals (*Tadić* ICTY A. Ch. 10.9.1999). At the ICTR, a retrial was ordered because of insufficient reasoning in the trial judgment (*Muvunyi* ICTR A. Ch. 29.8.2008). See also r. 117(C) of the ICTY RPE and r. 118(C) of the ICTR RPE.

355 Rr. 107–18 of the ICTY RPE, rr. 107–19 of the ICTR RPE, rr. 149–58 of the ICC RPE and regs. 57–65 of the ICC Regulations.

356 Art. 83(2) of the ICC Statute; *Bralo* ICTY A. Ch. 2.4.2007 para. 85; and *Muvunyi* ICTR A. Ch. 29.8.2008 para. 170.

(trials *de novo*).[357] Hence, the process is limited to correcting errors of law invalidating the decision and errors of fact resulting in a 'miscarriage of justice'. The threshold for intervening in factual determinations is high and requires that the Trial Chamber's conclusion is one 'which no reasonable trier of fact could have reached',[358] leading to a 'grossly unfair outcome in judicial proceedings, as when the defendant is convicted despite a lack of evidence on an essential element of the crime'.[359]

Against this limited scope of the appeals process, the ICTY and ICTR Appeals Chambers have also established an inherent power, deriving from their judicial function, to ensure that justice is done by assuming a discretionary power to correct an error of law on their own motion if the interests of justice so require.[360] Consequently, the burden of proof on appeals is not absolute regarding points of law, but the party must at least identify the alleged error, present arguments and explain how the error invalidates the decision.[361]

In earlier decisions, the ICTY Appeals Chamber has avoided assuming the role of trier of fact after having established an error of law, and instead ordered a retrial by a Trial Chamber. But increasingly being faced with additional evidence on appeal,[362] and mindful of the long trials and limited resources, the Appeals Chamber has become less hesitant. Hence, in *Blaškić* it decided not only to correct errors of law but also to apply the correct legal standard to the case at hand.[363] Critics would argue, however, that the parties are thereby deprived of the right to appeal the subsequent factual findings.

As to sentencing, both Tribunals have taken the view that the Appeals Chamber should not revise the sentence unless the Trial Chamber has committed a 'discernible error' in exercising its discretion or has failed to follow applicable law.[364]

The ICC Statute lists the grounds of appeal as procedural error, error of fact, and error of law, and, as an additional ground in case of conviction, 'any other ground that affects the fairness or reliability of the proceedings or decision'.[365] Regarding sentences, the main ground of appeal is disproportion between the crime and the sentence.[366] In addition, however, a reversal, amendment or remittal to a new trial before a Trial Chamber requires that the 'proceedings were unfair in a way that affected the reliability of the decision or sentence' or that 'the decision or sentence . . . was materially affected by error of fact or law

---

357 Art. 25 of the ICTY Statute and Art. 24 of the ICTR Statute; also e.g. *Kupreškić et al.* ICTY A. Ch. 23.10.2001 para. 408.
358 E.g. *Tadić* ICTY A. Ch. 15.7.1999 para. 64, and *Akayesu* ICTR A. Ch. 1.6.2001 para. 178.
359 *Furundžija* ICTY A. Ch. 21.7.2000 para. 37.
360 E.g. *Delalić et al.* ICTY A. Ch. 8.4.2003 para. 16, and *Kambanda* ICTR A. Ch. 19.10.2000 para. 98.
361 E.g. *Krnojelac* ICTY A. Ch. 17.9.2003 para. 10.
362 R. 115 of the ICTY RPE and ICTR RPE.
363 *Blaškić* ICTY A. Ch. 29.7.2004 para. 24. See also *Kordić and Čerkez* ICTY A. Ch. 17.12.2004 para. 24.
364 E.g. *Tadić* ICTY A. Ch. 26.1.2000 para. 22, and *Musema* ICTR A. Ch. 16.11.2001 para. 395.
365 Art. 81(1) of the ICC Statute; see also Christopher Staker, 'Article 81' in Triffterer, *Observers' Notes* 1466.
366 Arts. 81(2) and 83(3) of the ICC Statute.

or procedural error'.[367] Hence, the standard of review is further qualified. The Appeals Chamber is not restricted by the appeals and may also on its own motion raise the question to set aside a conviction or reduce a sentence, that is only to the benefit of the convicted person.[368]

The nature of the appeals review at the ICC is less clear and the Statute leaves the Appeals Chamber with broad discretion; the Appeals Chamber has all the powers of the Trial Chamber and evidence may be presented in the appeals proceedings.[369] Although it could be argued that the scheme leaves room for a trial *de novo*, the enumerated grounds for an appeal rather point towards a corrective procedure with a possibility of admitting additional evidence.[370] So far, the Appeals Chamber has dealt only with interlocutory appeals, primarily on procedural issues.

17.13.3 Interlocutory appeals

Interlocutory appeals are not provided for in the ICTY and ICTR Statutes, but they were soon accepted in practice[371] and are now provided for in the RPE.[372] Such appeals are also allowed at the ICC.[373] But since interlocutory appeals are time- and resource-consuming, only certain decisions are subject to such review. Decisions on jurisdiction, traditionally quite strictly defined in ICTY and ICTR jurisprudence,[374] and in the ICC also decisions concerning the admissibility of the case, are always subject to separate appeals. The ICC Statute also allows interlocutory appeals against decisions concerning provisional release and certain Pre-Trial Chamber-ordered measures during the investigation. All other decisions require leave of appeal (or certification) by the Chamber issuing the challenged decision. In turn, a leave to appeal normally requires that the decision 'involves an issue that would significantly affect the fair and expeditious conduct of the proceedings or the outcome of the trial' and for which 'an immediate resolution by the Appeals Chamber may materially advance the proceedings'.[375]

---

367 *Ibid.*, Art. 83(2).
368 *Ibid.*, Art. 81(2); similarly, see *Erdemović* ICTY A. Ch. 7.10.1997 para. 39 (exercising an 'inherent power').
369 Art. 83(1)–(2) of the ICC Statute; see also r. 149 of the ICC RPE.
370 See Helen Brady, 'Appeal and Revision' in Lee, *The Making of the Rome Statute*, 585–6, and Alphons Orie, 'Accusatorial v. Inquisitorial Approaches in International Criminal Proceedings Prior to the Establishment of the ICC and in the Proceedings Before the ICC' in Cassese, *Commentary*, 1490–1.
371 E.g. *Tadić* ICTY A. Ch. 2.10.1995 paras. 4–6.
372 Rr. 72 and 73 of the ICTY RPE and ICTR RPE.
373 Art. 82 of the ICC Statute and rr. 154–8 of the ICC RPE.
374 However, a more generous practice is discernible in more recent decisions, e.g. *Boškoski and Tarčulovski* ICTY A. Ch. 22.7.2005 para. 5.
375 Rr. 72(B)(ii) and 73(B) of the ICTY RPE and ICTR RPE, and Art. 82(1)(d) of the ICC Statute. At least initially, the ICC has adopted a very restrictive approach to granting leave, e.g. *Situation in Uganda* ICC PT. Ch. II 19.8.2005.

The ICTY and ICTR have adopted a restrictive approach to reviews of the Trial Chamber's exercise of discretionary powers, restricting it to whether the discretion was correctly exercised, but not to whether the Appeals Chamber agrees in substance.[376] A matter determined in an interlocutory decision is not open for reconsideration unless 'a clear error of reasoning has been demonstrated or if it is necessary to do so to prevent an injustice'.[377]

The early practice of the ICC gives only limited guidance concerning interlocutory appeals. By addressing the 'admissibility of an appeal' the Appeals Chamber has explained the requirements for such an appeal, both concerning the matters specifically mentioned in Article 82(1) of the ICC Statute and the 'issues' that may be appealed if leave for appeal is granted.[378] The standard of review is not yet fully clarified. As to leave for appeal, the applied standard is rather strict, but inconsistent approaches to various procedural issues have prompted a more generous practice, allowing the Appeals Chamber to provide authoritative determinations.[379]

17.14 Revision

The Statutes of the ICTY, ICTR and ICC make provision for review proceedings,[380] an exceptional remedy against miscarriage of justice, which goes beyond mere errors of fact or law. There are some important differences between the ICTY and ICTR on the one hand and the ICC on the other. While the Tribunals allow either party to seek revision, thus allowing the Prosecutor to apply in relation to an acquittal,[381] revision at the ICC applies only to a conviction or sentence.[382] Moreover, the Tribunals have extended the scope to all final decisions, not only those which include a verdict of conviction or acquittal but also, for example, final decisions resulting in the dismissal of the case with prejudice to the Prosecutor.[383]

The strict requirements for a review by the ICTY or ICTR are: (1) a 'new fact'; (2) the new fact was not known to the applicant at the time of the original proceedings; (3) the failure to

---

376 E.g. *Milošević* ICTY A. Ch. 1.11.2004 paras. 9–10.

377 E.g. *Kajelijeli* ICTR A. Ch. 23.5.2005 paras. 201–7.

378 E.g. *Situation in the DRC* ICC A. Ch. 13.7.2006 (168; on Art. 82(1)(d)) (169; on Art. 82(1)(a)). See Franziska Eckelmans, 'The First Jurisprudence of the Appeals Chamber of the ICC' in Stahn and Sluiter, *Emerging Practice*, 527–52.

379 For a critical view, see Håkan Friman, 'Interlocutory Appeals in the Early Practice of the International Criminal Court' in Stahn and Sluiter, *Emerging Practice*, 553–61.

380 Art. 26 of the ICTY Statute, Art. 25 of the ICTR Statute, and Art. 84 of the ICC Statute.

381 The Prosecutor may seek revision within one year after the final judgment; for the convicted person there is no time limit: r. 119 of the ICTY RPE and r. 120 of the ICTR RPE.

382 Art. 84(1) of the ICC Statute.

383 E.g. *Barayagwiza* ICTR A. Ch. 31.3.2000 paras. 45–50 and *Delalić et al.* ICTY A. Ch. 25.4.2002 para. 5. See Jean Galbraith, 'New Facts in ICTY and ICTR Review Proceedings' (2008) 21 *LJIL* 131.

discover the new fact was not due to the applicant's lack of due diligence; and (4) the new fact could have been a decisive factor in reaching the original decision.[384] In extraordinary circumstances, however, review may be granted by the Tribunal although the fact was known to or discoverable by the applicant; this is in order to prevent a miscarriage of justice.[385] Similarly, revision at the ICC requires that 'new evidence', which was not available at the time of the trial by reasons not wholly or partially attributable to the moving party, is sufficiently important so that the verdict is likely to have turned out differently. In addition, however, the ICC Statute allows revision when decisive evidence at trial turns out to be false, forged or falsified, or in case of serious misconduct or breach of duty by a participating judge.

The procedures also differ.[386] At the Tribunals, both admissibility of the application for revision and any review of the earlier decision are normally adjudicated by the original Chamber. At the ICC, however, a two-step approach applies whereby the Appeals Chamber first determines admissibility and, if the application succeeds, the revision itself is conducted by this or another Chamber.

17.15 Offences against the administration of justice

The ICTY, ICTR and ICC all have provisions on prosecution and punishment of offences directed against the administration of justice. Since the ICTY and ICTR Statutes are silent on the matter, this is considered an inherent power derived from the judicial function of the Tribunals.[387] For the ICC, however, the power is laid down in the Statute.[388] Another important difference is that prosecution and punishment of these offences is a shared responsibility between the ICC and the States Parties.[389]

At the Tribunals, the rules refer to 'contempt of court' and specify the criminal offences, penalties and the procedures. The ICC provisions, however, make a distinction between 'offences against the administration of justice' – with a broader scope than the Tribunals' contempt provisions – and lesser 'misconduct before the Court'. The maximum penalty for offences against the administration of justice is a prison sentence, a fine, or a combination of the two; misconduct at the ICC may lead to a fine and other measures.[390] Separate provisions apply for misconduct of counsel.[391]

---

384 *Barayagwiza* ICTR A. Ch. 31.3.2000 para. 41, and *Delalić et al.* ICTY A. Ch. 25.4.2002 para. 8.

385 *Barayagwiza* ICTR A. Ch. 31.3.2000 para. 65, and *Tadić* ICTY A. Ch. 30.7.2002 para. 27.

386 Rr. 119–22 of the ICTY RPE; rr. 120–3 of the ICTR RPE; Art. 84(2) of the ICC Statute, rr. 159–61 of the ICC RPE, and reg. 66 of the ICC Regulations.

387 R. 77 of the ICTY RPE and ICTR RPE. See also, e.g. *Tadić* ICTY A. Ch. 31.1.2000 para. 13.

388 Arts. 70 and 71 of the ICC Statute; see also rr. 162–72 of the ICC RPE.

389 Art. 70(4) of the ICC Statute.

390 In addition, the ICC may also order forfeiture: r. 166(2) of the ICC RPE.

391 R. 46 of the ICTY RPE and ICTR RPE; concerning the ICC, see Arts. 30–44 of the *Code of Professional Conduct for Counsel* (ICC-ASP/4/Res.l) of 2.12.2005.

17.16 Some observations

A comprehensive assessment of the procedural law of the international criminal jurisdictions is a huge task and beyond the scope of this book. Remarks of a more principled nature are made throughout the chapter; many of them, however, stem from the dichotomy between the different legal traditions, or adversarial and inquisitorial features. Indeed, most, if not all, qualitative assessments of the international criminal procedures are coloured by the commentator's own domestic legal background. Another common yardstick is international human rights standards and principles, which again are subject to different interpretations and preferences as how best to be implemented. The particular circumstances and challenges that exist, not least concerning international cooperation, must also be considered. Hence, international procedures will always be faced with critical comments and amendments, just as in a domestic setting, although there the calls for dramatic shifts are more rare.

Some further selected observations should be made. The ICTY and ICTR, beginning with very little guidance, have shown that international criminal proceedings can be conducted in accordance with high procedural and human rights standards, including extensive protection of the rights of the accused. However, a major problem, due to internal and external circumstances, is the length of the proceedings. The major internal remedy has been a shift from purely adversarial principles to stronger and more invasive intervention by the judges. On the whole, the primary roles and responsibilities of the parties are still respected and the victims are afforded only a very limited role.

For the ICC the inquisitorial features and the role of victims were present from the outset, a novel set-up to which neither the Tribunals nor most domestic analogies provide real guidance. Some would argue that these procedures are more fair, others that they are less so and instead rather confusing. Clearly the proper distribution of roles and powers between the judges and the prosecution has not been settled. Still also outstanding is a more conclusive stance on important elements such as the distinction between 'situations and cases', admissibility assessments, restrictions on disclosure, and participation of victims. In practice, the pre-trial process has turned into 'a gigantic enterprise, with an almost unmanageable amount of documentation, filings and litigation'.[392] The confirmation process, with separate disclosure and a hearing, has also turned out to be complex and time-consuming. The sustainability and precedential value of meticulously detailed and lengthy confirmation decisions can also be questioned. The first case of a new jurisdiction must, of course, be allowed more time to settle matters, but the ICC process has proved to be particularly difficult and the pre-trial period in the *Lubanga case*, from arrest to the trial hearing, was considerably longer than the first trials of the ICTY (*Tadić*), ICTR (*Akayesu*) and SCSL (*Norman et al.*). Although the pre-trial process in the subsequent ICC cases appears to be

---

[392] William Schabas and Carsten Stahn, '(Symposium) Introductory Note: Legal Aspects of the Lubanga Case' (2008) 19 *CLF* 431, 432.

shorter, the procedural regime should be continuously evaluated and adjusted in the light of actual experience. Creating a good international code of criminal procedure is, to be sure, a daunting task.

Further reading

Gideon Boas, *The Milošević Trial* (Cambridge, 2007).

Michael Bohlander, Roman Boed and Richard Wilson (eds.), *Defence in International Criminal Proceedings* (New York, 2005).

Antonio Cassese, Paolo Gaeta and John R. W. D. Jones (eds.), *The Rome Statute of the International Criminal Court* (Oxford, 2002) chs. 28–38.

Rodney Dixon and Karim Kahn (eds.), *Archbold International Criminal Courts – Practice, Procedure and Evidence*, 2nd edn (London, 2005).

Silvia Fernándes de Gurmendi and Hakan Friman, 'The Rules of Procedure and Evidence and the Regulations of the Court' in Doria, *Legal Regime*, 797–824.

Horst Fischer, Claus Kreß and Sascha Rolf Lüder (eds.), *International and National Prosecution of Crimes Under International Law* (Berlin, 2001).

John R. W. D. Jones and Steven Powles, *International Criminal Practice*, 3rd edn (New York, 2003).

Roy Lee et al. (eds.), *The International Criminal Court – Elements of Crimes and Rules of Procedure and Evidence* (New York, 2001).

Richard May et al. (eds.), *Essays on ICTY Procedure and Evidence* (The Hague, 2001).

Christoph Safferling, *Towards an International Criminal Procedure* (Oxford, 2001).

William A Schabas, *The UN International Criminal Tribunals: The Former Yugoslavia, Rwanda and Sierra Leone* (Cambridge, 2006) chs. 10–13.

Göran Sluiter and Sergey Vasiliev (eds.), *International Criminal Procedure: Towards a Coherent Body of Law* (London, 2009).

Carsten Stahn and Göran Sluiter (eds.), *The Emerging Practice of the International Criminal Court* (Leiden, 2009).

Salvatore Zappala, *Human Rights in International Criminal Proceedings* (Oxford, 2003).

18

Victims in the International Criminal Process

18.1 Introduction

Traditionally, the accused is at the very centre of the criminal process and he or she is afforded rights and protection in order to ensure a fair process. The opposite party is the prosecutor, in modern criminal systems primarily a public prosecutor representing the public interest in prosecuting crimes. But where does that leave the victim who, to be sure, also has interests in the process? Domestic systems address this issue in different ways.[1] Generally speaking, an adversarial process, based upon two opposing parties before a neutral court, leaves little room for providing the victim with a strong and independent participatory role. Also, where private prosecutions are allowed if the public prosecutor is not pursuing the case, or where victims may play a subsidiary prosecutorial role when a public prosecution is instituted, the two-party process is basically retained. On the other hand, the more active role of the judge in an inquisitorial process, and consequently a less clear-cut two-party design, leaves a greater scope for victims to participate in their own right. Regardless of the system, however, victims play an important role as witnesses in the criminal process,[2] a role that may be compromised if the victim also has an independent function in the same process.

Domestic systems also vary with respect to the victim's right to obtain compensation from the perpetrator of the crime. Often this is considered as a civil claim to be pursued in a separate civil process, but there are also examples where such claims can be handled within the criminal proceedings.[3] Quite apart from this, certain criminal sanctions may be of a compensatory nature, for example orders for restitution of property.

---

1 For examples (France, the Netherlands, Germany and the UK), see Claude Jorda and Jérome de Hemptinne, 'The Status and Role of the Victim' in Cassese, *Commentary*, 1401–2. See also Mikaela Heikkilä, *International Criminal Tribunals and Victims of Crimes* (Åbo, 2004) 43–56, and generally, Mireille Delmas-Marty and John R. Spencer (eds.), *European Criminal Procedure* (Cambridge, 2002).

2 In most domestic systems the victim will be treated as other witnesses, including being required to give evidence under oath. But in some systems, for example in Sweden, where the accused may not be heard under oath, a sworn statement by the victim is also not allowed for fairness sake.

3 Again, Sweden may serve as an example.

Internationally, an increasing focus on the role of victims of crime is discernible. But opinions differ and different schools of thought are more, or less, victim-friendly; retributive and utilitarian thinking tends to place the accused at the forefront, while restorative justice theories allow for a greater role for the victims.[4] A milestone was the UN Victims Declaration, adopted by the UN General Assembly in 1985.[5] Twenty years later, the General Assembly adopted the so-called 'Van Boven/Bassiouni Principles' on victims' right to a remedy and to reparation for gross violations of international human rights and international humanitarian law.[6] Guidelines on child victims and witnesses of crime have been adopted by ECOSOC.[7] Regional instruments have also been developed, for example within the Council of Europe[8] and the European Union.[9]

When the international criminal jurisdictions were established, different models were contemplated. Clearly, one important objective behind the creation of these jurisdictions was to provide redress to the victims of atrocities. However, redress may take different forms and be provided in different forums, not necessarily by the international criminal jurisdictions. The procedures of the ICTY and ICTR were from the outset clearly adversarial in nature and thus the role of the victims was rather limited; the primary function is to give evidence as a witness. They are not even parties to the proceedings with respect to restitution of property.[10] This largely auxiliary role has been criticized as insufficient if, as France stated at the time of adoption of the ICTY Statute, one of the rationales behind the institution is to bring justice to the victims.[11]

Hence, the relatively extensive scheme provided for victims in the ICC Statute – protection, participation and reparations – was not inevitable. On the contrary, the issues and how best to address them were rather controversial matters during the negotiations.[12] The

---

4 E.g. Heikkilä, *International Criminal Tribunals*, 23–42.
5 *Declaration of Basic Principles for Victims of Crime and Abuse of Power* UNGA res. 40/34 of 29.11.2005.
6 *Basic Principles and Guidelines on the Right to a Remedy and Reparations for Victims of Gross Violations of International Human Rights Law and Serious Violations of International Humanitarian Law*, UNGA res. 2005/35 of 16.12.2005. See also Marten Zwanenburg, 'The Van Boven/Bassiouni Principles: An Appraisal' (2006) 24 *Netherlands Quarterly of Human Rights* 641.
7 *Guidelines on Justice in Matters involving Child Victims and Witnesses of Crime* of 22.7.2005.
8 See, e.g. the *European Convention on the Compensation of Victims of Violent Crimes* of 24.11.1983 (ETS 116), and *Recommendation of the Committee of Ministers to Member States on the Position of the Victim in the Framework of Criminal Law and Procedure* of 28.6.2005 (R(85)11).
9 See, e.g. *Council Framework Decision on the standing of victims in criminal proceedings* (2001/220/JHA of 15.3.2001) and *Council Framework Decision on combating trafficking in human beings* (2002/629/JHA of 19.7.2002); both currently in the process of being amended.
10 R. 105 of the ICTY RPE and ICTR RPE (the question of restitution may be raised by the prosecutor or by the trial chamber *proprio motu*).
11 E.g. Jorda and de Hemptinne, 'Status and Role of the Victim', 1387–98. Generally, see Eric Stover, *The Witnesses: War Crimes and the Promise of Justice in The Hague* (Philadelphia, 2007).
12 On the negotiations, see Christopher Muttukumaru, 'Reparations to Victims' in Lee, *The Making of the Rome Statute*, 262–70, and Gilbert Bitti and Håkan Friman, 'Participation of Victims in the Proceedings' in Lee, *Elements and Rules*, 456–74.

comments by observers have been mixed too. Many have hailed the victims-related provisions as a substantial advance when compared with the law and practice of the predecessors of the ICC.[13] The scheme has been described as representing a move away from the exercise of purely retributive justice.[14] But there are also critics, some of whom warn that the scheme for victims, particularly their rights to participate, is a potentially harmful experiment in a still fragile system.[15]

It has very wisely been argued that while the ICC procedures should indeed allow for effective victim participation, the limitations on restoring every victim's sense of self-respect should be honestly acknowledged in order to avoid false expectations.[16] In fact, an ambition that the ICC should provide justice to individual victims[17] could easily cause unrealistic expectations, since it would most likely be unattainable in practice. However, the ICC should not be seen as the only forum for redress for the victims of atrocities. Just because the Court is there, that does not mean it can take on all the roles undertaken at the national level by large parts of government structures. Other initiatives, whether national or international, could also, and perhaps even better, serve interests such as establishing a historical record and promoting reconciliation; criminal proceedings clearly have limitations in this sense. The Court has adopted a strategic plan for outreach activities and a comprehensive strategy in relation to victims is under way.

Later internationalized courts also recognize victims' rights.[18] The Extraordinary Chambers in the Courts of Cambodia (ECCC) underline reconciliation as an important aim and provide for extensive victim participation in the proceedings and a right to claim moral and collective reparations.[19] Moreover, the Special Tribunal for Lebanon Statute contains provisions on victim participation, which are based on the ICC Statute, but here

---

13 See, e.g. Theo van Boven, 'Victims' Rights and Interests in the International Criminal Court' in Doria, *Legal Regime*, 895–906.

14 See, e.g. Silvia Fernández de Gurmendi and Håkan Friman, 'The Rules of Procedure and Evidence of the International Criminal Court' (2001) 3 *YIHL* 289 at 312.

15 See, e.g. Alexander Zahar and Göran Sluiter, *International Criminal Law* (Oxford, 2007) at 75–6.

16 Emily Haslam, 'Victim Participation at the International Criminal Court: A Triumph of Hope over Experience?' in Dominic McGoldrick et al. (eds.), *The Permanent International Criminal Court* (Oxford, 2004) 319. See also *Victim Participation before the International Criminal Court*, American University Washington College of Law, War Crimes Research Office, International Criminal Court Legal Analysis and Education Project (Washington DC, November 2007) at 44–6.

17 See, e.g. David Donat-Cattin, 'The Role of Victims in ICC Proceedings' in F. Lattanzi and W. Schabas (eds.), *Essays on the Rome Statute of the International Criminal Court* (il Sirente, 1999), vol. I, 252.

18 Apart from those mentioned in the text, the courts in East Timor (UNTAET Reg. 2000/30 on Transitional Rules of Criminal Procedure) and Kosovo (Provisional Criminal Procedure Code) also allow victim participation in the proceedings.

19 See Brianne McGonigle, 'Two for the Price of One: Attempts by the Extraordinary Chambers in the Courts of Cambodia to Combine Retributive and Restorative Justice Principles' (2009) 22 *LJIL* 127. See also *Nuon Chea* ECCC PT. Ch. 20.3.2008.

civil claims for reparations are to be placed before ordinary national courts.[20] In both cases, the principles have support in domestic (French influenced) law.

18.2 Definition of victims

The ICC Rules include a general definition of 'victims', which is influenced by the 1985 UN Victims Declaration and intended for all purposes (protection, participation and reparations).[21] It distinguishes between 'natural persons' and 'organizations or institutions'.

A victim is someone who has suffered 'harm', but this notion is not defined and may be understood in a number of different ways. The Court has resorted to the Van Boven/ Bassiouni Principles for guidance,[22] and also to the practice of international human rights courts. 'Harm' to natural persons[23] denotes hurt, injury and damage and the definition covers material, physical and psychological (or emotional) harm, but only insofar as the harm is suffered personally by the victim ('personal harm').[24] Although the harm must be suffered personally, not only 'direct victims' but also 'indirect victims', such as family members of someone killed or of a child soldier, are covered by the definition.[25] The harm must relate to a crime within the jurisdiction of the Court in substantive, territorial and temporal terms; the question of nexus between the 'harm' and a crime actually investigated or prosecuted by the Court is addressed below in relation to participation. What evidence may be sufficient will be determined on a case-by-case basis.[26]

Legal persons may qualify as victims too, but the definition requires that they have sustained direct harm and that this relates to certain property such as a hospital or a school.

18.3 Protection of victims and witnesses

Protection of victims and witnesses is a difficult and demanding task for any criminal jurisdiction, and particularly so for the international criminal jurisdictions. Apart from a great reliance upon live evidence, the nature of the crimes and the fact that the Tribunals are international and highly public, necessitated the development of thorough victim/witness

---

20 Arts. 17 and 25 of the STL Statute.
21 Rule 85 of the ICC RPE. See generally, Silvia Fernández de Gurmendi, 'Definition of Victims and General Principle' in Lee, *Elements and Rules*, 427–34.
22 *Lubanga Dyilo* ICC T. Ch. I 18.1.2008 para. 92 (cf. Judge Blattmann's dissent, paras. 4–5), and A. Ch. 11.7.2008 paras. 20 and 33.
23 Practice varies concerning whether deceased persons are included or not: see *Situation in Darfur* ICC PT. Ch. I 14.12.2007 para. 36 (excluded) and *Bemba Gombo* ICC PT. Ch. III 12.12.2008 para. 40 (included).
24 *Lubanga Dyilo* ICC A. Ch. 11.7.2008 paras. 31–2. Hence, personal harm, not collective harm, is decisive for the right to participate: *ibid.*, paras. 35 and 37.
25 *Ibid.*, para. 32 (cf. Judge Pikis dissent, para. 3). See also *Lubanga Dyilo* ICC T. Ch. I 18.1.2008 para. 91, and T. Ch. I 8.4.2009.
26 *Kony et al.* ICC A. Ch. 23.2.2009 para. 38.

protection regimes. In addition, the ICC conducts its first investigations during ongoing violent conflicts, which makes the question of protection even more important and challenging. But these institutions have a more limited range of possible protective measures than national authorities; the international jurisdictions do not have their own police forces and are dependent upon State authorities, peacekeeping forces or others in order to offer the more robust forms of protection.[27]

The protection of victims and witnesses is regulated in the Statutes and Rules[28] and a rich jurisprudence has developed. While the granting of protective measures is primarily a responsibility of the Chambers at the Tribunals, the Prosecutor and the Chambers, and also the Registrar and Registry, share the responsibility at the ICC; the Pre-Trial Chambers have been particularly active, including during the investigation.[29] Special units for victim and witness issues, including protective measures and security arrangements, are also established in the respective Registries.[30] In order to avoid 'secondary victimization', specialized Registry units also provide support measures that are similar to social welfare services.[31]

Factors such as the victim's age, gender, health, and the nature of the crime, particularly sexual crimes, may add to his or her vulnerability and thus require protective measures.[32] But in practice the need for protective measures goes far beyond that. Most of the crimes, as well as the circumstances within which the Tribunals and Court operate, are such that witnesses and victims are very anxious and may refuse to collaborate unless various protective measures are taken. Coercing a person to appear and give evidence is seldom a realistic option.[33] Hence, there is abundant use of protective measures.

The protection may be motivated by security or privacy reasons.[34] Protective measures which are to be enforced out of court are possible only to a limited extent; witness protection programmes, including relocation, require assistance by States and others and must be used sparingly. A cheaper, and perhaps more effective, alternative is to develop prosecutorial investigation plans and practices whereby contacts with vulnerable witnesses and victims are avoided to the greatest possible extent. In the proceedings, measures may be taken to

---

27 See Chapter 20.

28 Arts. 20(1) and 22 of the ICTY Statute, Arts. 19(1) and 21 of the ICTR Statute, rr. 39(ii), 69, 75 and 79 of the ICTY RPE and ICTR RPE, Arts. 54(1)(b) and (3)(f), 57(3)(c), 64(6)(e) and 68 of the ICC Statute, and rr. 87–8 of the ICC RPE.

29 See Håkan Friman, 'Protection of victims and witnesses' in André Klip and Göran Sluiter (eds.), *Annotated Leading Cases of International Criminal Tribunals* (Antwerp, 2010), vol. XXIII, 297–302.

30 R. 34 of the ICTY RPE and ICTR RPE, Arts. 43(6) and 68(4) of the ICC Statute, and rr. 16–19 of the ICC RPE.

31 See, e.g. Stover, *The Witnesses*, 79–91.

32 See Art. 60(1) of the ICC Statute.

33 See section 20.2.3.

34 The ICTY, ICTR and ICC have concluded special (confidential) agreements with States for the purpose of witness protection.

prevent disclosure to the public (screening, voice or image distortion, pseudonyms and photo prohibition), and postponed disclosure, closed sessions and testimony by video-link may be employed. Apart from the actual witnesses, family members and even potential witnesses may also be afforded protection.[35] By an extensive interpretation of non-disclosure provisions, the ICC Appeals Chamber extended the application of protection measures to 'persons at risk on account of the activities of the Court' and thus to identification of 'innocent third parties' and Court staff.[36]

Protection programmes must be available to both the prosecution and the defence and be perceived as neutral. Hence, the responsibility for these matters, including relocation, is placed upon special units with the Registry. The ICC Appeals Chamber rejected the Prosecutor's attempt to 'preventively relocate' witnesses unilaterally and concluded that the relevant Chamber was the final arbiter in case of disagreement between the Prosecutor and the Registry unit.[37]

Clearly, all these measures infringe on important fair trial principles and a careful balancing of interests is required.[38] Protection from public identification deviates from the principle of a public trial. Even worse are measures withholding the identity from the accused, which must be construed so that rights such as having adequate time and facilities for the preparation of the defence and examining witnesses are respected. A particularly controversial measure is the use of anonymous witnesses, that is to say witnesses whose identity is not known to both parties. An early ICTY decision allowed this practice, clearly influenced by the Tribunal's impotence concerning physical protection, but it was sharply criticized, particularly by proponents of adversarial procedures,[39] and the practice has not been repeated. At the ICC it is clear that the identity of witnesses may be withheld from disclosure to the defence, but different interpretations are possible as to whether witnesses may remain anonymous at trial.[40] The better view, however, is that the identity may be withheld only 'prior to the commencement of the trial'.[41] For example,

---

35 See, e.g. *Ngirabatware* ICTR T. Ch. II 6.5.2009.
36 *Katanga* ICC A. Ch. 13.5.2008 (Judge Pikis dissenting).
37 *Katanga and Ngudjolo Chui* ICC A. Ch. 26.11.2008.
38 For a critical view of ICTR practice, see Göran Sluiter, 'The ICTR and the Protection of Witnesses' (2005) 3 *JICJ* 962; similar criticisms can be raised against the ICTY and ICC as well.
39 *Tadić* ICTY T. Ch. II 10.8.1995 (Judge Stephen dissenting). See also Monroe Leigh, 'The Yugoslav Tribunal: Anonymity is Inconsistent with Due Process' (1996) 90 *AJIL* 235 (and (1997) 99 *AJIL* 80); Christine Chinkin, 'Due Process and Witness Anonymity' (1997) 99 *AJIL* 75; Olivia Swaak-Goldman, 'The ICTY and the Right to a Fair Trial: A Critique of the Critics' (1997) 10 *LJIL* 215; and Natasha Affolder, 'Tadić, the Anonymous Witness and the Sources of International Procedural Law' (1998) 19 *Michigan Journal of International Law* 445.
40 On non-disclosure see, e.g. *Lubanga Dyilo* ICC A. Ch. 11.7.2008. See also Claus Kreß, 'Witnesses in Proceedings Before the International Criminal Court: An Analysis in the Light of Comparative Criminal Procedure' in Horst Fischer et al. (eds.), *International and National Prosecutions of Crimes Under International Law* (Berlin, 2001) 309 at 364–82 (arguing that the ICC judges are left with a policy choice).
41 Art. 68(5) of the ICC Statute and r. 81(4) of the ICC RPE.

during the confirmation process identities may be withheld, although on an exceptional basis only.[42]

Quite another matter is to what extent participating victims, who are not witnesses but at least sometimes could be considered as 'accusers', may have their identities protected from the prosecution and defence. Such anonymity has not been ruled out.[43]

18.4   Victim participation in ICC criminal proceedings

Unlike the ICTY and ICTR, the ICC Statute and Rules provide for victim participation in pursuance of their own personal interests, both in certain specific instances and generally, although the latter is a right with explicit caveats.[44] Importantly, the exercise of this right – where, when and how – is to be firmly controlled by the relevant Chamber, thus having the challenging task of balancing the victims' rights so that a 'second prosecution' to the detriment of the accused and the prosecution is avoided. Victims in the ICC are not given a status like that of a *partie civile* known to many civil law systems. It is also necessary to find practical and pragmatic solutions in light of the potentially very large number of affected victims. Hence, jurisprudence in this area is particularly important and eagerly awaited. In practice, these issues have occupied, and continue to occupy, considerable time and effort on the part of everyone involved in the process.

This general right of participation should be distinguished from participation with respect to protective measures and reparations.[45] On such matters victims may initiate proceedings themselves and hence are parties to them, including a right to appeal decisions. Beyond that, and in relation to the general right to participate, victims are not considered parties and their rights as 'participants' are more confined. Discussion of the conditions and the evolving practice of the Court follows.

The early decisions, and comments concerning them,[46] relate primarily to victim participation in the investigation and pre-trial stages. The first and very influential decision by a Pre-Trial Chamber was handed down in January 2006 in the *Situation in the Democratic Republic of the Congo*,[47] soon to be followed by several other Pre-Trial Chamber decisions.

---

42 *Lubanga Dyilo* ICC A. Ch. 13.10.2006 paras. 34–9.
43 E.g. *Lubanga Dyilo* ICC T. Ch. I 18.1.2008 paras. 130–1.
44 Arts. 15(3), 19(3) and 68(3) of the ICC Statute. See also rr. 89–93 of the ICC RPE.
45 See *Situation in the DRC* ICC A. Ch. 19.12.2008 para. 50.
46 See, e.g. Carsten Stahn, Hector Olásolo and Kate Gibson, 'Participation of Victims in the Pre-Trial Proceedings of the ICC' (2006) 4 *JICJ* 219; Christine Chung, 'Victims' Participation at the International Criminal Court: Are Concessions of the Court Clouding the Promise?' (2008) 6 *Northwestern Journal of International Human Rights* 459; Sergey Vasiliev, 'Article 68(3) and personal interests of victims in the emerging practice of the ICC' in Stahn and Sluiter, *Emerging Practice*; and Håkan Friman, 'The International Criminal Court and Participation of Victims: A Third Party to the Proceedings?' (2009) 22 *LJIL* 485.
47 *Situation in the DRC* ICC PT. Ch. I 17.1.2006.

The first decision concerning trial proceedings was made by the Trial Chamber in the subsequent *Lubanga* case in January 2008.[48] Being interlocutory matters, the decisions on victim participation require leave for appeal and a very restrictive practice meant that for a long time the Appeals Chamber was prevented from addressing the issues beyond the question of victim participation in the appeals proceedings as such.[49] The practice of the different Chambers, however, became inconsistent, and leave to appeal was granted for a few decisions, among them the *Lubanga* trial decision.[50]

18.4.1 Purposes of participation

The purposes behind the participatory rights afforded to victims are not explicitly laid out in the ICC Statute and must therefore be established by the Court. Ideally, the answer should inform when and how, and perhaps where, participation ought to take place, as well as guide the substantive content of participation. The objectives should be realistic, possible to implement and achieve in practice, and conform with the rights of the defence and the overall procedural system. But so far no comprehensive and consistent analysis has been presented by the Court.

Obvious purposes would be to contribute to the prosecution and obtain restitution or reparation and various forms of satisfaction.[51] But participatory rights may have further aims: fairness to the victim who has suffered harm, avoiding secondary victimization and victim alienation, treating the victim with dignity and respect, and ensuring that the truth is exposed and that a just punishment is imposed.[52] It could contribute to making the offender more conscious of the serious injury and suffering inflicted on others. Even broader restorative and reconciliatory aims could also be claimed in which the interest of bringing the process closer to those who have suffered could be an important component. Hence, merely linking the participatory rights to interests in seeking a conviction and obtaining reparations is arguably too narrow an approach; after all, the explicit general purpose is to enable the victims to present their 'views and concerns'.[53]

18.4.2 Conditions for participation and legal representation

Article 68(3) of the ICC Statute provides for victim participation as a right. Nonetheless, the ICC Chambers have considerable discretion regarding when and how this may be done. The

---

48 *Lubanga Dyilo* ICC T. Ch. I 18.1.2008.
49 See, e.g. *Lubanga Dyilo* ICC A. Ch. 13.6.2007. For a critical view, see e.g. Håkan Friman, 'Interlocutory appeals in the early practice of the International Criminal Court' in Stahn and Sluiter, *Emerging Practice*, 553–61.
50 *Lubanga Dyilo* ICC T. Ch. I 26.2.2008.
51 See, e.g. Salvatore Zappalà, *Human Rights in International Criminal Proceedings* (Oxford, 2003) 221.
52 See Heikkilä, *International Criminal Tribunals*, 141–2 (with further references). See also *Katanga and Ngudjolo Chui* ICC PT. Ch. I 13.5.2008 paras. 31–44.
53 Article 68(3) of the ICC Statute.

assessment encompasses whether: (1) those seeking participation are 'victims'; (2) their 'personal interests' are affected; (3) the participation is 'appropriate'; and (4) the manner of participation is not prejudicial to or inconsistent with the rights of the accused and a fair and impartial trial. In practice, the Chambers have adopted a rather cumbersome two-step process with, first, an authorization of the individual victim's right to participate in a 'situation' or a 'case' and, secondly, applications and determinations concerning the actual participation. The burden to satisfy the Chamber that the conditions are met rests with the victim and the Court has been at pains to make the task a reasonable one. The evidentiary standard has been described differently by different Chambers, but it now seems to be a combination of a prima facie test and a freer assessment (similar to the French *intime conviction*).[54] For certain facts, such as identity, a higher standard may be required.[55]

A 'victim' must meet the criteria of the definition (see section 18.2) and thus be a natural person (or a legal person as specified in the definition) and have suffered 'harm' which ensued from a crime within the jurisdiction of the Court.[56] Moreover, a causal link between the crime and the harm is required, which may be difficult to establish; in the early stages of the process only the Prosecutor knows which incidents are being investigated, and at a later stage the assessment of the linkage could affect the presumption of innocence. A relaxed evidentiary standard and an explicitly preliminary and non-prejudicial determination of this causal link have not satisfied all critics.[57] One problem is that a victim of a particular offence which is neither investigated nor prosecuted may participate in the proceedings regarding the 'situation'. Once a 'case' is identified, the nexus must be between the 'harm' and the crime that the perpetrator is actually suspected or accused of (in the arrest warrant or indictment). The *Lubanga* Trial Chamber's decision to construe 'personal interests' without requiring such a link was rejected by the Appeals Chamber.[58]

The notion of 'personal interests' is decisive for participation and should be closely linked to the rationale behind the participation scheme as such. Yet no guidance is given as to the interpretation of this term. Furthermore, the interests may shift during the course of the process. During the 'situation' phase, the interests are considered as quite general and primarily having 'their crimes' investigated and the perpetrator identified.[59] To

---

54 See, e.g. *Katanga and Ngudjolo Chui* ICC PT. Ch. I 2.4.2008 at 8–9.

55 See, e.g. *Kony et al.* ICC A. Ch. 23.2.2009 paras. 35–8.

56 See, e.g. *Situation in the DRC* ICC PT. Ch. I 17.1.2006 para. 79.

57 *Ibid.*, paras. 94–101. For example, some argue that the Court should refrain from an adjudication of harm in the participation process: American University Washington College of Law, *Victim Participation*, 63.

58 *Lubanga Dyilo* ICC T. Ch. I 18.1.2008 paras. 93–5 (Judge Blattmann dissenting) and A. Ch. 11.7.2008 paras. 58–66.

59 See, e.g. *Situation in the DRC* ICC PT. Ch. I 17.1.2006 paras. 63–4 and 72. See also *Bemba Gombo* ICC PT. Ch. III 12.12.2008 para. 90 (noting, inter alia, that the victims' and prosecution's interests do not always coincide).

confine the interests to receiving reparations is clearly too narrow.[60] Another possible, albeit not uncontroversial, interest could be with respect to sentencing.[61] But there are limitations and the Appeals Chamber has emphasized that the interests of the victims must not be regarded as the same as those belonging to the role assigned to the Prosecutor.[62] The suggestion that victim participation may be used by the judges to 'exert some pressure on the Prosecutor to proceed with an investigation' is thus highly doubtful.[63]

Participation of victims must be 'appropriate'. This issue should be considered primarily against the objectives of participation. Other circumstances may also be relevant; one Pre-Trial Chamber found participation inappropriate due to the current security situation.[64] In most cases, however, the issue has been assessed with respect to the manner in which participation may take place,[65] which in fact relates to the fourth condition of safeguarding the rights of the accused and the fairness of the proceedings. This last requirement presupposes a delicate balancing act. A number of defence rights might be affected, not least the right to be tried without undue delay.[66] Preserving the equilibrium between the prosecution and the defence is also a challenge. Another difficulty is reconciling the roles of a participating victim who is also a witness.[67]

Legal representation is both a stick and a carrot; common legal representation may be necessary in order to make a large number of victims manageable but counsel is also guaranteed more extensive participation than an unrepresented victim.[68] A Chamber may direct that victims be legally represented and the Office of Legal Counsel for victims has been established.[69]

---

60 *Lubanga Dyilo* ICC T. Ch. I 18.1.2008 para. 98. Cf. *Lubanga Dyilo* ICC A. Ch. 16.5.2008 paras. 42–6 (highlighting protection and reparations as examples of personal interests) and separate opinions by Judges Pikis and Song.

61 See, e.g. Elisabeth Baumgartner, 'Aspects of victim participation in the proceedings of the International Criminal Court' (2008) 90:870 *International Review of the Red Cross* 409, 434–7.

62 *Lubanga Dyilo* ICC A. Ch. 19.12.2008 paras. 52–3.

63 See Jérôme de Hemptinne and Francesco Rindi, 'ICC Pre-Trial Chamber allows Victims to Participate in the Investigation Phase of Proceedings' (2006) 4 *JICJ* 342, 346.

64 *Lubanga Dyilo* ICC PT. Ch. I 20.10.2006 paras. 10–11.

65 See, e.g. *Lubanga Dyilo* ICC PT. Ch. I 17.1.2006 paras. 56–60. For a better elaboration of 'appropriateness', see Judge Blattmann's Separate and Dissenting Opinion in *Lubanga Dyilo* ICC T. Ch. I 18.1.2008.

66 See, e.g. Jorda and de Hemptinne, 'Status and Role of the Victim', 1393, and Heikkilä, *International Criminal Tribunals*, 152.

67 See, e.g. *Lubanga Dyilo* ICC T. Ch. I 5.6.2008. For the view that the dual status of victim and witness should not be allowed, see Jorda and de Hemptinne, 'Status and Role of the Victim', 1409.

68 R. 91 of the ICC RPE.

69 *Ibid.*, r. 90 and Regs. 79–82 of the ICC Regulations. See also *Katanga and Ngudjolo Chui* ICC T. Ch. II 22.7.2009.

18.4.3 Participation in different stages of the process

Victim participation is not confined to any particular stage of the process but is likely to have substantive differences at the different stages. To establish the modalities is fully within the domain of judicial discretion. Victims may provide the Prosecutor with information for the purpose of a criminal investigation, but this is not a formal report of a crime (*notitia criminis*) which automatically triggers an investigation. The information may, however, contribute to the Prosecutor seeking authorization to commence an investigation under Article 15 of the ICC Statute and participation in the Pre-Trial Chamber's authorization process is explicitly spelled out. Victims may also apply to participate in any review, in accordance with Article 53(3), of the Prosecutor's decision not to investigate or prosecute, but they are not competent to seek such a review.[70]

Although Article 68(3) refers to participation in 'the proceedings', it was established early on that participation in the investigation stage is possible.[71] But the conduct of the investigation falls under the Prosecutor's authority and participation at this stage is therefore confined to judicial proceedings, including when these affect the investigation; they, however, relate to the investigation as such.[72] A better approach than allowing participation generally during the investigation of a situation would therefore be to address the matter with respect to particular procedural activities, but the Pre-Trial Chambers have rejected this 'casuistic approach'.[73] In practice the nature of the participation has been framed in vague terms 'to be heard' and 'to file documents'[74] and the added value of this, compared with not seeking a formal authorization to participate, is questionable. But early indications by Pre-Trial Chambers that participation may also take very far-reaching forms, such as requesting specific proceedings or requesting the Prosecutor to provide information on 'the status of the investigation',[75] run contrary to the statutory scheme and more recent Appeals Chamber decisions.

Once a suspect is identified and a 'case' established, which is normally when a warrant of arrest or summons to appear is issued, many assessments become more straightforward. As already mentioned, a nexus between the harm and the crimes alleged or charged is required. The participation is continuous but the Chambers generally require discrete applications for participation in specific procedural activities. Arrest proceedings, confirmation hearings and the trial are instances where typically victims' interests are at stake and participation thus

---

70 The presumed interest of victims to take part in such reviews is indicated by the notification requirements in r. 92(2) of the ICC RPE.

71 *Lubanga Dyilo* ICC PT. Ch. I 17.1.2006 paras. 28–54.

72 *Situation in the DRC* ICC A. Ch. 19.12.2008 paras. 45 and 52–6 (reversing the PT. Ch. decision). See also *Situation in Darfur* ICC A. Ch. 2.2.2009.

73 See, e.g. *Katanga and Ngudjolo Chui* ICC PT. Ch. I 13.5.2008 paras. 45–51. See also Friman, 'Participation of Victims', 223–6.

74 See, e.g. *Lubanga Dyilo* ICC PT. Ch. I 17.1.2006 para. 71.

75 *Ibid.*, para. 75 and *Situation in the DRC* ICC PT. Ch. I 26.9.2007.

takes place. The ICC Statute specifically provides that victims may submit observations in proceedings with respect to jurisdiction or admissibility.[76]

The ICC Rules provide only limited guidance as to what the participation right might entail. Apart from notifications from the Court and possible invitations to submit observations, there is a presumption that unrepresented victims are confined to written interventions, while a more active participation (attending hearings, making oral interventions etc.) is foreseen for legal representatives.[77] But a much more ambitious scheme for participation has been worked out by the Chambers in practice, which includes access to documents (including confidential ones), making submissions, attending public and sometimes closed sessions, making oral and written interventions, and even examination of witnesses.[78] A right to pose questions to witnesses at trial is laid down in the ICC Rules, inspired by judicial economy and the wish to avoid recalling witnesses to subsequent reparations proceedings, but this has been extended through jurisprudence to a right to tender and examine evidence pertaining to guilt or innocence, as well as to challenge the admissibility of evidence.[79] In another controversial ruling, the majority of the *Lubanga* Trial Chamber admitted a request by victim representatives to consider a legal recharacterization of the charges in accordance with Regulation 55 of the ICC Regulations. Although only an 'early notice' of the possibility of the Chamber taking this course of action, the application should have been dismissed, as the strong dissent by one judge concluded, and later also the Appeals Chamber.[80]

Victims are entitled to appeal decisions on matters that they may initiate, in particular on reparations and possibly also protective measures. In other appeals proceedings the general provisions on victim participation apply and the key question is whether their 'personal interests' are affected by the matter under appeal. For example, a limited right of participation was granted in the appeal against a decision to refuse interim release.[81]

---

76 Art. 19(3) of the ICC Statute. Observations by victims were provided when the admissibility of the case was challenged in *Katanga and Ngudjolo Chui* (ICC T. Ch. II 16.6.2009), but not in *Kony et al.* (ICC PT. Ch. II 10.3.2009) where instead two NGOs made *amicus curiae* submissions under r. 103 of the ICC RPE.

77 Rr. 91–3 of the ICC RPE.

78 A comprehensive analysis is provided in *Katanga and Ngudjolo Chui* ICC PT. Ch. I 13.5.2008 paras. 127–45. The Pre-Trial Chamber distinguished between anonymous and non-anonymous victims (*ibid.*, paras. 182–4), granting the former more limited rights, but this distinction has not been upheld by other Chambers; see, e.g. *Bemba Gombo* ICC PT. Ch. III 12.12.2008 paras. 99, 103–5.

79 R. 91(3) of the ICC RPE. *Lubanga Dyilo* ICC T. Ch. I 18.1.2008 paras. 108–9, 119–22, upheld by the majority of the A. Ch. 11.7.2008 para. 93 (Judges Pikis and Kirsch recording strong dissents). See also *Katanga and Ngudjolo Chui* ICC PT. Ch. I 13.5.2008 paras. 30–44, 101–3 (concluding a right for victims to call evidence, but not evidence not furnished by the parties for the purpose of confirmation of charges). For analysis and criticism see, e.g. Friman, 'International Criminal Court and Participation of Victims', 492–8.

80 *Lubanga Dyilo* ICC T. Ch. I 14.7.2009 and Minority opinion (dissent) by Judge Fulford 17.7.2009, and A. Ch. 8.12.2009. See also section 17.8.4.

81 See *Lubanga Dyilo* ICC A. Ch. 13.2.2007; also concluding that a new application must be made and thus that the right to participate does not automatically transfer to the appeals proceedings (*ibid.*, paras. 38–43: cf. the dissenting opinion of Judge Song).

18.5 Reparations to victims

The ICTY and ICTR Statutes do not provide for reparations to victims and the rule on compensation in the RPE relates to domestic proceedings.[82] The ICC, however, does have the power to order reparations directly to, or in respect of, victims;[83] a contentious matter in political as well as in legal terms.[84] Reparations may include restitution, compensation and rehabilitation. It is left to the judges to establish principles and determine the scope and extent of any damage, loss or injury; so far no general principles have been established and it appears that this will occur on a case-by-case basis. The Van Boven/Bassiouni Principles may provide guidance on the principles and the different forms of reparations.[85]

While it could be argued that reparations are a penal sanction – as they presuppose a conviction – they are rather of a civil nature;[86] an order will normally follow upon a request, albeit that the ICC in exceptional circumstances may act upon its own motion. Both individual and collective awards are foreseen and a special trust fund will likely be the main conduit for the latter.[87] In addition, the trust fund itself may provide support for physical or psychological rehabilitation or material support for the benefit of victims or their families, although this must not be inconsistent with the judicial activities of the Court and is thus subject to the relevant Chamber's approval.[88]

Reparations are subject to separate proceedings including appeals.[89] In order to secure future reparations, the Court may request States to freeze assets.[90] The Pre-Trial Chambers have regularly, and on their own motion, made such requests when issuing arrest warrants.[91] No reparations awards have yet been made but at the start of the *Lubanga* trial, the Registry

---

82 R. 106 of the ICTY RPE and ICTR RPE, which also provide that the judgment of the Tribunal 'shall be final and binding as to the criminal responsibility of the convicted person for such injury'. However, whether this provision binds States is debatable, see, e.g. Zappalà, *Human Rights*, 227–8.

83 Art. 75 of the ICC Statute. See also rr. 94–9 of the ICC RPE.

84 See, e.g. Muttukumaru, 'Reparations to Victims', 262–70.

85 Although guidance from 'soft law' was controversial, the Rome Conference Working Group referred explicitly to the Van Boven/Bassiouni Principles in its report; footnote 5 to Article 73 in doc. A/CONF/F.183/C.1/WGPM/L.2/Add.7 of 13.7.1998. See also Peter Lewis and Håkan Friman, 'Reparations to Victims' in Lee, *Elements and Rules*, 477–8. Successive ICTY Presidents have noted the lack of compensation to victims as a shortcoming and have proposed, inter alia, the establishment of a claims commission.

86 Cf. Birte Timm, 'The Legal Position of Victims in the Rules of Procedure and Evidence' in Horst Fischer et al. (eds.), *International and National Prosecution of Crimes Under International Law* (Berlin, 2001) 306–8.

87 Arts. 75(2) and 79 of the ICC Statute and rr. 98 and 221 of the ICC RPE. A board of directors has been appointed and Regulations of the Trust Fund for Victims (ICC-ASP/4/Res.3 of 3.12.2005) have been adopted.

88 Reg. 50 of the Trust Fund Regulations. See *Situation in Uganda* ICC PT. Ch. II 19.3.2008 (approval of proposed trust fund activities in Uganda). See also Anne-Marie de Brouwer and Marc Groenhuijsen, 'The Role of Victims in International Criminal Proceedings' in Sluiter and Vasiliev, *International Criminal Procedure*, 190–5.

89 Arts. 76(3) and 82(4) of the ICC Statute; rr. 91(4) and 94–7 of the ICC RPE.

90 Art. 57(3)(e) of the ICC Statute.

91 See, e.g. *Lubanga Dyilo* ICC PT. Ch. I 10.2.2006 paras. 130–41. See further section 20.7.

notified the Chamber of seven applications with claims for reparations. The management of the reparations process will be a challenge and other international or national mass claims processes may give valuable pointers.[92]

18.6   An assessment

The focus on victims is far greater in the ICC than in the ICTY and ICTR, and this trend has continued in subsequent internationalized courts. An assessment of the fundamental issue of whether this is valuable, or instead a detraction from the 'core mandate' of prosecuting international crimes, goes back to the question of the objectives of international criminal justice.[93] Apart from the element of restorative justice that victims' rights encompass, some would add that this involvement could boost the legitimacy of the international criminal process and thus of the relevant court. But such effects will occur only if both scheme and expectations are well managed. A proper balancing vis-à-vis the rights of the accused is also necessary. A further complication, which must be taken into account, is that not all victims share the same interests; a general assumption that they all support prosecution would be an oversimplification. For the ICC, the policy choice was made when its Statute was adopted and it is now up to the Court to implement the scheme in the best possible way.

Although there are domestic systems that combine far-reaching victims' rights with a basically adversarial criminal process, from which the Court may seek inspiration, the ICC victim participation scheme is a novel feature that must be developed gradually. This is a daunting and resource-intensive task that has resulted in a very large number of decisions. Difficulties have included large numbers of victims, detailed application requirements and assessments, and multiple decisions in the same 'situation' or 'case', some of them early on and rather hypothetical in nature. While the prosecution, defence counsel and Appeals Chamber have been more restrained, most Pre-Trial and Trial Chambers have taken a more radical approach with the apparent aim of providing for meaningful forms of victim participation. The emerging practice is not entirely consistent and serious questions may be raised concerning the role of the victims and its relationship to the parties, the rights of the accused, and trial efficiency, and also whether the participatory rights in practice are more than merely symbolic. It may also be asked to what extent individual victims, and not only more lawyers, ought to and do get involved in the judicial process. It is always difficult to backtrack from a laid course, but in order to find a workable system the Court will need to test different options and allow the scheme to evolve progressively. It is too early to assess whether the scheme produces restorative justice effects that motivate the time and efforts

---

92 Marc Henelin, Veijo Heiskanen and Guénaël Mettraux, 'Reparations to Victims before the International Criminal Court: Lessons from International and National Mass Claims Processes' (2006) 17 *CLF* 317.
93 See Chapter 2.

spent by many and the procedural challenges that arise, but it is already clear that the Court is set to take this matter seriously.

The ICC reparations regime is also an unprecedented and often praised restorative justice element in international criminal law. But the scheme is not yet fully developed and it requires further elaboration. It is not intended to prejudice any other international or domestic reparations options that may exist. Whether an individual right to compensation from the State exists for violations of international human rights law or international humanitarian law, is a hotly contested issue, but good arguments can be made in support of such a right.[94] In any case, the resources available for reparations will most likely be small and one challenge for the Court is to avoid the reparations regime being perceived as nothing more than an illusion.

As for protective measures for victims and witnesses, their extensive use of is an unfortunate necessity in all international criminal jurisdictions. But it is important to be vigilant so that they do not become merely routine, and to ensure that the rights of the accused are respected.

Further reading

Useful reviews and analysis of ICC practice concerning victims are provided in a series of reports by the American University Washington College of Law, War Crimes Research Office: http://www.wcl.american.edu/warcrimes/icc/icc_reports.cfm.

Elisabeth Baumgartner, 'Aspects of victim participation in the proceedings of the International Criminal Court' (2008) 90/870 *International Review of the Red Cross* 409.

Gilbert Bitti and Håkan Friman, 'Participation of Victims in the Proceedings' in Lee, *Elements and Rules*, 456–74.

Helen Brady, 'Protective and Special Measures for Victims and Witnesses' in Lee, *Elements and Rules*, 434–56.

Pascale Chifflet, 'The Role and Status of the Victim' in Gideon Boas and William Schabas (eds.), *International Criminal Law Developments in the Case Law of the ICTY* (Leiden, 2003) 75–111.

Christine Chung, 'Victims' Participation at the International Criminal Court: Are Concessions of the Court Clouding the Promise?' (2008) 6 *Northwestern Journal of International Human Rights* 459.

Anne-Marie De Brouwer, 'Reparations to Victims of Sexual Violence: Possibilities at the International Criminal Court and at the Trust Fund for Victims and Their Families' (2007) 20 *LJIL* 207.

---

94 See Roland Bank and Elke Schwager, 'Is there a Substantive Right to Compensation for Individual Victims of Armed Conflicts against a State under International Law?' (2006) 49 *German Yearbook of International Law* 367.

Carla Ferstman, 'The Reparation Regime of the International Criminal Court: Practical Considerations' (2002) 15 *LJIL* 667.

Håkan Friman, 'Participation of Victims before the ICC: A Critical Assessment of the Early Developments' in Sluiter and Vasiliev, *International Criminal Procedure*, 205–36.

Håkan Friman, 'The International Criminal Court and Participation of Victims: A Third Party to the Proceedings?' (2009) 22 *LJIL* 485.

Sam Garakawe, 'Victims and the International Criminal Court: Three major issues' (2003) 3 *ICLR* 345.

Emily Haslam, 'Victim Participation at the International Criminal Court: A Triumph of Hope Over Experience?' in Dominic McGoldrick et al. (eds.), *The Permanent International Criminal Court* (Oxford, 2004) 315–34.

Mikaela Heikkilä, *International Criminal Tribunals and Victims of Crimes* (Åbo, 2004).

John R. W. D. Jones, 'Protection of Victims and Witnesses' in Cassese, *Commentary*, 1355–70.

Claude Jorda and Jérôme de Hemptinne, 'The Status and Role of Victims' in Cassese, *Commentary*, 1387–419.

Peter Lewis and Håkan Friman, 'Reparations to Victims' in Lee, *Elements and Rules*, 474–91.

Carsten Stahn, Hector Olásolo and Kate Gibson, 'Participation of Victims in the Pre-Trial Proceedings of the ICC' (2006) 4 *JICJ* 219.

Theo van Boven, 'Victims' Rights and Interests in the International Criminal Court' in Doria, *Legal Regime*, 895–906.

Sergey Vasiliev, 'Article 68(3) and personal interests of victims in the emerging practice of the ICC' in Stahn and Sluiter, *Emerging Practice*, 635–90.

19

Sentencing and Penalties

19.1 International punishment of crimes

International humanitarian law and criminal law treaties provide for individual criminal responsibility for certain violations, but they give virtually no guidance as to applicable penalties or other sentencing issues. For example, the Genocide Convention merely provides that penalties shall be 'effective' and the Torture Convention that the penalties shall be 'appropriate' and take into account the 'grave nature' of the offence.[1] However, the principle of legality includes a prohibition against retroactive creation of punishments (*nulla poena sine lege*)[2] and for that reason an international criminal jurisdiction regulation is required; an effort that is fraught with difficulties since States take very different views on penalties. Consequently, international provisions on penalties and sentencing are rather general, leaving a tribunal with wide discretion, again triggering concerns regarding the legality principle.[3]

The Nuremberg and Tokyo Tribunals had the power to impose 'death or such other punishment as shall be determined by it to be just'.[4] At Nuremberg, twelve of the accused were sentenced to death (by hanging), three to life imprisonment and four to fixed-term prison sentences. The Tokyo trial produced seven sentences of death, eleven of life imprisonment and two of fixed-term imprisonment. The national military tribunals operating in Germany (under Control Council Law No. 10) and in the Far East had the same sentencing powers.[5] To dispel concerns about retroactivity, the penalties were considered rooted in

---

1 Art. 5 of the 1948 Genocide Convention; Art. 4(2) of the 1984 Torture Convention. The requirement of effective punishment is also reflected elsewhere, e.g. the 1949 Geneva Conventions (Art. 49 of GC I; Art. 50 of GC II; Art. 129 of GC III; Art. 146 of GC IV).
2 See Kai Ambos, 'Nulla Poena Sine Lege in International Criminal Law' in Roelof Haveman and Olaoluwa Olusanya (eds.), *Sentencing and Sanctioning in Supranational Criminal Law* (Antwerp, 2006) 17.
3 On the discussions concerning the ICTY, see William Schabas, 'Sentencing by International Tribunals: A Human Rights Approach' (1997) 7 *Duke Journal of Comparative & International Law* 461.
4 Art. 27 of the Nuremberg Charter and Art. 16 of the Tokyo Charter. In addition, the Nuremberg Tribunal could deprive the convicted person of stolen property: Art. 28 of the Nuremberg Charter.
5 On the Far East, see Neil Boister and Robert Cryer, *The Tokyo International Military Tribunal: A Reappraisal* (Oxford, 2008) ch. 9.

customary international law.[6] None of these Tribunals developed sentencing guidelines of use for later tribunals. In fact, sentencing considerations occupied very little room in the judgments and, even then, only briefly on mitigating factors.[7]

When the ICTY and ICTR were established, the development of international human rights standards in general, and the gradual international rejection of capital punishment in particular, had an impact. Capital punishment is highly controversial and State practice ranges from extensive use to complete abolition. This divide is also reflected in international human rights treaties. The ICCPR and ECHR restrict, but do not prohibit, the penalty, while additional protocols to those treaties provide for prohibitions which, by way of reservations, may be set aside in time of war;[8] however, Protocol No. 13 to the ECHR prohibits capital punishment in all circumstances. States may therefore be treaty-bound to abolish the death penalty and an emerging abolitionist norm in customary international law is asserted,[9] but a universally accepted prohibition does not exist today.

The only applicable penalty for the core crimes at the Tribunals is a term of imprisonment, for life or time-limited.[10] In response to concerns regarding the principle of legality, the Statutes provide that the respective Tribunal shall have recourse to the general practice regarding prison sentences in the courts of the Former Yugoslavia and Rwanda. In practice, however, both Tribunals have established that there is no obligation to conform to the national practice, only to take it into account and give reasons for any departure.[11] The principle also applies when the domestic law prescribes a less severe penalty than the law of the Tribunal.[12] Nonetheless, the Tribunals have addressed the principle of legality with reference to more severe penalties (capital punishment) in domestic law.[13] In the case of the

---

6 For a critical view, see, e.g. William Schabas, 'War Crimes, Crimes Against Humanity, and the Death Penalty' (1997) 60 *Albany Law Review* 733 at 735.

7 See Bradley Smith, *Recalling Judgment at Nuremberg* (New York, 1977) chs. 7–9. As to the Tokyo judgment, Judge Röling developed his views in his dissenting opinion; see Bernard Röling and Antonio Cassese, *The Tokyo Trial and Beyond* (Oxford, 1993) 64.

8 Art. 6 ICCPR and Art. 2 ECHR; Second Optional Protocol to the ICCPR 15.12.1989, and Protocol No. 6 to the ECHR 28.4.1983.

9 See, e.g. William Schabas, *The Abolition of the Death Penalty in International Law*, 3rd edn (Cambridge, 2002).

10 Art. 24 of the ICTY Statute, Art. 23 of the ICTR Statute, and r. 101 of the ICTY RPE and ICTR RPE. The Tribunals may also order the return of property and proceeds of crime to their rightful owners, but this penalty has not yet been applied. For contempt of court, fines may also be imposed: r. 77 of the ICTY RPE and ICTR RPE.

11 See, e.g. *Kunarac et al.* ICTY T. Ch. II 22.2.2001 para. 829, *Krstić* ICTY A. Ch. 19.4.2004 para. 260, and *Semanza* ICTR A. Ch. 20.5.2005 para. 377. It has also been noted in this context that very important differences often exist between international and national prosecutions, particularly concerning the nature, scope and scale of the offences.

12 See, e.g. *Dragan Nikolić* ICTY A. Ch. 4.2.2005 paras. 77–86, and *Semanza* ICTR A. Ch. 20.5.2005 para. 393.

13 See, e.g. *Tadić* ICTY T. Ch. II 14.7.1997 para. 9. For a critical view, see, e.g. Dirk Van Zyl Smit, *Taking Life Imprisonment Seriously in National and International Law* (The Hague, 2002) 180–3.

Former Yugoslavia, however, the death penalty had already been abolished in the early 1990s, and replaced by a maximum of forty years imprisonment, and in Rwanda it was replaced by life imprisonment in 2007.[14]

The issue of applicable penalties was also controversial in the ICC negotiations.[15] Some States, a number of them strong supporters of the Court generally, insisted on the death penalty as a prerequisite for the Court's credibility and its deterrent functions, but many other States could not accept this penalty, not the least because of other treaty commitments. Life imprisonment represented a compromise solution. But again, concerns were raised from a human rights perspective, some States also referring to constitutional prohibitions. The solution was imprisonment for a fixed term not exceeding thirty years or, when justified by the extreme gravity of the crime and the individual circumstances of the convicted person, life imprisonment.[16] An aspect of the compromise was the insertion of a provision to ensure that the penalties which the ICC may impose will not affect any powers by States to impose penalties that are allowed in their national law, penalties either more lenient or more severe than those applicable at the ICC.[17] This is a step away from the idea of a more coherent international criminal justice system with harmonized penalties for international crimes as one element.[18]

The ICC may also impose a fine and may order forfeiture of proceeds, property and assets derived directly or indirectly from the crime. It is noteworthy that forfeiture does not include instrumentalities of crime; for example, forfeiture of military equipment would be very sensitive. While forfeiture is a post-conviction measure, the ICC may also seek to obtain, from a State, provisional measures for the purpose of forfeiture;[19] victims may ultimately benefit if the money or other property is subsequently forfeited and transferred to the trust fund for victims.

19.2   Purposes of sentencing

The purposes of sentencing, and indeed the purposes of punishment as such, are a relatively undeveloped aspect of international criminal law. Classical objectives in municipal systems are retribution, deterrence, public protection (incapacitation), rehabilitation and social integration of the offender. As discussed in Chapter 2, however, the objectives of punishment in general, and for the purpose of international criminal justice in particular,

---

14 See, e.g. *Milutinović et al.* ICTY T. Ch. III 26.2.2009 paras. 1159–60, and *Kanyarukiga* ICTR T. Ch. 6.6.2008 paras. 94–6.

15 See, e.g. Rolf Einar Fife, 'Penalties' in Lee, *The Making of the Rome Statute*, 319–43.

16 Art. 77 of the ICC Statute. Offences against the administration of justice may be punished by a maximum five-year sentence, or a fine, or both; *ibid.*, Art. 70(3).

17 *Ibid.*, Art. 80.

18 See, e.g. M. Cherif Bassiouni, *Introduction to International Criminal Law* (New York, 2002) 682.

19 Arts. 57(3)(e) and 93(1)(k) of the ICC Statute, and r. 99 of the ICC RPE.

are the subject of very different opinions. All of them have their strengths and pitfalls, particularly in the context of international criminal justice. Some consider that retribution (or 'just desert') is the appropriate philosophical and policy ground for international punishment.[20] Others dispute this, however, advocating a more restorative approach in international sentencing and arguing that this will better serve peace and reconciliation efforts.[21] Deterrence presents special difficulties in this context. Broader aims such as rehabilitation and social integration are difficult to pursue; the range of penalties is limited and the enforcement is outsourced to States. In the absence of consensus regarding the objectives of punishment and how to balance different objectives against each other, the ICTY, ICTR and ICC are provided with very little guidance as to the purposes of sentencing.

As primary purposes for sentencing, the ICTY and ICTR have consistently emphasized retribution and general deterrence,[22] although retribution appears to be considered most important.[23] Retribution should be seen as 'just desert' and not as revenge or vengeance.[24] But other objectives are also emphasized, such as special deterrence (concerning the defendant),[25] rehabilitation,[26] 'protection of society, stigmatization and public reprobation',[27] and reconciliation.[28] However, as the ICTY has said:

> [t]he other three aims that sentencing usually promotes, namely, rehabilitation, social defence and restoration have not yet achieved the same dominance as retribution and deterrence in the sentencing history of this Tribunal, even though, in the opinion of the Trial Chamber, they are important for achieving the goals of this Tribunal. Such factors have tended to be dealt with as mitigating or aggravating factors, with social defence intermingling with the understanding that this Tribunal has of the aim of deterrence.[29]

---

20 See, e.g. Bassiouni, *Introduction to International Criminal Law*, 681.

21 See, e.g. Ralph Henham, 'Some Issues for Sentencing in the International Criminal Court' (2003) 52 *ICLQ* 81.

22 See, e.g. *Delalić et al.* ICTY A. Ch. 20.2.2001 para. 806 and *Serushago* ICTR T. Ch. I 5.2.1999 para. 20. On deterrence, see section 2.2.2.

23 See Mark Drumbl, 'Collective Violence and Individual Punishment: The Criminality of Mass Atrocity' (2005) 99 *Northwestern University Law Review* 539.

24 See section 2.2.1 and *Kordić and Čerkez* ICTY A. Ch. 17.12.2004 para. 1075.

25 *Ibid.*, paras. 1076–7; cf. *Dragan Nikolić* ICTY A. Ch. 4.2.2005 paras. 45–7 (may be considered but is merely one factor in sentencing).

26 But rehabilitation should not be given 'undue weight', see, e.g. *Delalić et al.* ICTY A. Ch. 20.2.2001 para. 806; cf. *Kunarac et al.* ICTY T. Ch. 22.2.2001 para. 844 (questioning rehabilitation as a sentencing purpose). Cf. *Erdemović* ICTY T. Ch. I 29.11.1996 para. 111 (considering the 'corrigible personality' as a mitigating factor), and see section 2.2.4.

27 See section 2.2.5 and *Ntakirutimana* ICTR T. Ch. I 21.2.2003 paras. 881–2; cf. *Kunarac et al.* ICTY T. Ch. 22.2.2001 para. 843 (protection of society not very relevant).

28 *Kamuhanda* ICTR T. Ch. II 22.1.2004 paras. 753–4 and A. Ch. 19.9.2005 para. 351 (see also the preamble to the ICTR Statute); *Momir Nikolić* ICTY T. Ch. I 2.12.2003 para. 93.

29 *Brđanin* ICTY T. Ch. II 1.9.2004 para. 1092.

Inconsistency in sentencing exists, revealing an absence of agreed principles, and could affect the legitimacy of the judicial institution.[30] It has also been noted that the pragmatic rationales behind plea bargaining in the Tribunals are at odds with the general purposes of punishment; sentencing rebates depart from the idea of punishment based on the gravity of the crime (retribution) and could weaken its deterrent function.[31] Another source of criticism is that the sentences are lenient when compared with domestic practice, but this comparison relates to ordinary crimes such as murder and domestic sentencing practice differs greatly.[32]

19.3 Sentencing practice

The ICTY and ICTR have emphasized that sentencing is an essentially discretionary responsibility; no sentencing scales for the different crimes are provided. Consequently, the ICTY Appeals Chamber has repeatedly refused to set down a definite list of sentencing guidelines.[33] While emphasizing the principle of equal treatment, that is to say consistency, the Appeals Chamber has also concluded that a comparison with the sentences imposed in other cases before the Tribunal is often of limited assistance; the previous decision must relate to the same offence and the circumstances be substantially similar.[34]

Most important for sentencing at the Tribunals is the gravity of the offence, including considerations regarding the form and degree of the participation of the accused in the crimes and the circumstances of the case.[35] Lacking any formal hierarchy of crimes, advocated by some as necessary for sentencing,[36] the Tribunals have taken a case-by-case approach. Due to the special *mens rea* requirement, however, genocide has generally been regarded as more serious than crimes against humanity and war crimes.[37] Similarly, persecution has been considered 'inherently very serious', justifying a more severe

---

30 See, e.g. Ralph Henham, *Punishment and Process in International Criminal Trials* (Aldershot, 2005) 16–24.

31 See, e.g. Ralph Henham and Mark Drumbl, 'Plea Bargaining at the International Criminal Tribunal for the Former Yugoslavia' (2005) 16 *CLF* 56–9.

32 See, e.g. Mark Harmon and Fergal Gaynor, 'Ordinary Sentences for Extraordinary Crimes' (2007) 5 *JICJ* 683; cf. Marisa Bassett, 'Defending Sentencing: Past Criticism to the Promise of the ICC' (2009) 16 *Human Rights Brief* 22. On difficulties with domestic analogies, see also section 2.2.1.

33 See, e.g. *Furundžija* ICTY A. Ch. 21.7.2000 para. 238; *Delalić et al.* ICTY A. Ch. 20.2.2001 para. 715; and *Krštić* ICTY A. Ch. 19.4.2004 para. 242.

34 See, e.g. *Delalić et al.* ICTY A. Ch. 20.2.2001 paras. 719–20; *Kamuhanda* ICTR A. Ch. 19.9.2005 paras. 361–2; *Momir Nikolić* ICTY A. Ch. 8.3.2006 paras. 38–54; and *Strugar* ICTY A. Ch. 17.7.2008 paras. 336 and 348.

35 Art. 24(2) of the ICTY Statute and Art. 23(2) of the ICTR Statute; and see, e.g. *Delalić et al.* ICTY A. Ch. 20.2.2001 paras. 731 and 741; and *Blaškić* ICTY A. Ch. 29.7.2004 para. 683.

36 See, e.g. Allison Marston Danner, 'Constructing a Hierarchy of Crimes in International Criminal Law Sentencing' (2001) 87 *Virginia Law Review* 415.

37 See, e.g. *Kambanda* ICTR T. Ch. I 4.9.1998 paras. 16 and 42; *Krštić* ICTY T. Ch. I 2.8.2001 para. 700 and A. Ch. 19.4.2004 paras. 36–7 and 275. Cf. *Serushago* ICTR T. Ch. I 5.2.1999 paras. 13–14 (considering genocide and crimes against humanity to be of an equally grave nature).

penalty.[38] Although not uncontroversial, crimes against humanity and war crimes are seen by the Tribunals as equally serious in principle.[39] This has led to much debate and some argue that there is a hierarchy based upon the inherent gravity of the different crimes, while others consider that other circumstances, such as the quantum of suffering inflicted, are more important than the characterization of the offence.[40] However, the Tribunals' broad acceptance of cumulative convictions reduces the legal importance of a hierarchy of crimes.[41] The form of responsibility is also important and, for example, both Tribunals have established that aiding and abetting generally warrants lower sentences than co-perpetration.[42] But an abstract ranking and comparison are not decisive; the punishment always depends on the facts of the case. Additionally, the Tribunals are required to take into account the individual circumstances of the accused and give credit for time already spent in detention.[43] Similar provisions and principles are applicable to the ICC, although the RPE give some further direction.[44]

The sentencing practice of the ICTY and ICTR has not been consistent, neither within the same Tribunal nor between them.[45] In spite of the general seriousness of the crimes, the final sentences imposed by the ICTY and ICTR have had a very broad span from three years to life. Life sentences have been meted out in a number of ICTR cases regarding genocide and more rarely by the ICTY for crimes against humanity.[46] Nonetheless, a recent study concludes that ICTY sentencing is fairly structured and logical, and exposes certain patterns: high-ranked perpetrators in influential positions receive longer sentences; more extensive criminal activities are punished more severely than isolated, single acts; crimes against

---

38 See, e.g. *Blaškić* ICTY T. Ch. I 3.3.2000 para. 785; *Todorović* ICTY T. Ch. I 31.7.2001 para. 31.

39 See, e.g. *Tadić* ICTY A. Ch. 26.1.2000 para. 69; and *Kayishema and Ruzindana* ICTR A. Ch. 1.6.2001 para. 367. Earlier decisions, however, considered crimes against humanity as more serious and carrying a higher penalty than war crimes, see, e.g. *Tadić* ICTY T. Ch. II 14.7.1997 para. 73; *Erdemović* ICTY A. Ch. 7.10.1997 (majority) paras. 20–6; and *Kambanda* ICTR T. Ch. I 4.9.1998 para. 14.

40 For proponents of a hierarchy see, e.g. Jan Christoph Nemitz, 'The Law of Sentencing in International Criminal Law: The Purposes of Sentencing and the Applicable Method for the Determination of the Sentence' (2001) 4 *YIHL* 87, and Olaoluwa Olusanya, 'Do Crimes against Humanity Deserve a Higher Sentence than War Crimes?' (2004) 4 *ICLR* 431. Against, see, e.g. Mark Harmon and Fergal Gaynor, 'Ordinary Sentences for Extraordinary Crimes' (2007) 5 *JICJ* 683.

41 See section 17.8.5.

42 See, e.g. *Vasiljević* ICTY A. Ch. 25.2.2004 para. 182 and *Kajelijeli* ICTR T. Ch. II 1.12.2003 para. 963.

43 Art. 24(2) of the ICTY Statute, Art. 23(2) of the ICTR Statute, and r. 101 of the respective RPE.

44 Art. 78 of the ICC Statute and r. 145 of the ICC RPE.

45 For examples, see John R. W. D. Jones and Steven Powles, *International Criminal Practice*, 3rd edn (Oxford, 2003) 778–80. For the contrary view, see Frederik Harhoff, 'Sense and Sensibility in Sentencing – Taking Stock of International Criminal Punishment' in Ola Engdahl and Pål Wrange (eds.), *Law at War: The Law as it Was and the Law as it Should Be* (Leiden, 2008) 121, 134–7.

46 See, e.g. *Akayesu* ICTR A. Ch. 1.6.2001; *Stakić* ICTY T. Ch. II 31.7.2003 (life imprisonment replaced on appeal by a fixed-term sentence of forty years: A. Ch. 22.3.2006); *Galić* ICTY A. Ch. 30.11.2006 paras. 455–6 (a twenty-year sentence increased after appeal to life imprisonment); and *Lukić and Lukić* ICTY T. Ch. 20.7.2009.

humanity generate longer sentences than war crimes;[47] and instigators are punished harder than all other participants in the atrocities.[48]

19.3.1 Aggravating and mitigating circumstances

While the ICTY and ICTR Trial Chambers are required to consider any aggravating and mitigating circumstances in passing sentence, neither the Statutes nor the RPE exhaustively define those factors.[49] Instead, both the factors and their relative weight are left for judicial discretion. The RPE of the ICC, although inspired by Tribunal case law, are more detailed.[50] In the Tribunals, and most likely in the ICC, the Prosecutor must establish any aggravating circumstances; proof 'beyond a reasonable doubt' is required.[51] The defendant is required to prove mitigating circumstances on a lower – 'balance of probabilities' – standard.[52]

The aggravating factors developed by the ICTY and ICTR in the jurisprudence include[53] the scale of the crimes, the length of time during which it continued, the age, number and suffering of the victims, the nature of the perpetrator's involvement, premeditation and discriminatory intent, abuse of power and position as a superior. The main rule is that only circumstances directly related to the offence may be considered as aggravating.[54] But a factor may not be aggravating if it forms an element of the actual crime or has been taken into account as an aspect of the gravity of the crime (no 'double-counting').[55] Similarly, the ICC RPE mention abuse of power or official capacity, particularly defenceless victims, multiple victims, particular cruelty, and discrimination; relevant prior convictions must also be taken into account.[56]

The only mitigating circumstance expressed in the ICTY and ICTR RPE is substantial cooperation with the Prosecutor before or after conviction.[57] A related issue is whether and to what extent a guilty plea should be a mitigating factor.[58] Usually such pleas have been

---

47 Interestingly, this finding runs counter to the rhetorical position on the abstract relationship between the two crimes.
48 B. Hola, A. L. Smeulers and C. C. J. H. Bijleveld, 'Is ICTY Sentencing Predictable? An Empirical Analysis of ICTY Sentencing Practice' (2009) 22 *LJIL* 79.
49 R. 101 of the ICTY RPE and ICTR RPE. See, e.g. *Musema* ICTR A. Ch. 16.11.2001 para. 395.
50 R. 145(2) of the ICC RPE.
51 See, e.g. *Delalić et al.* ICTY A. Ch. 20.2.2001 para. 763 and *Kajelijeli* ICTR A. Ch. 23.5.2005 para. 294.
52 The circumstance must be 'more probable than not': see, e.g. *Delalić et al.* ICTY A. Ch. 20.2.2001 para. 590 and *Kajelijeli* ICTR A. Ch. 23.5.2005 para. 294.
53 See, e.g. *Blaškić* ICTY A. Ch. 29.7.2004 para. 686.
54 See, e.g. *Stakić* ICTY T. Ch. II 31.7.2003 para. 911 and *Simba* ICTR A. Ch. 27.11.2007 para. 82; cf. *Delalić et al.* ICTY A. Ch. 20.2.2001 paras. 780–9 (also conduct at trial, indicating a lack of remorse, was considered as an aggravating factor).
55 *Blaškić* ICTY A. Ch. 29.7.2004 para. 693; *Deronjic* ICTY A. Ch. 20.7.2005 paras. 106–7; *Momir Nikolić* ICTY A. Ch. 8.3.2006 paras. 57–67; *Simba* ICTR A. Ch. 27.11.2007 para. 320.
56 R. 145(2) of the ICC RPE.
57 R. 101(B)(ii); see, e.g. *Jokić* ICTY T. Ch. I 18.3.2004 paras. 93–6 and A. Ch. 30.8.2005 paras. 87–9; and *Zelenović* ICTY A. Ch. 31.10.2007 para. 24 (the cooperation need not be substantial for mitigation).
58 See further section 17.11.

linked to an agreement between the accused and the prosecution, which may include non-binding recommendations to the court as to the sentence. In order to encourage guilty pleas – for reasons of judicial economy, concerns for victims, or otherwise – it is important that the accused can expect a sentencing discount. While guilty pleas have generally been considered in mitigation, the Chambers have avoided declaring a guaranteed discount and have instead adopted an individualized approach to the mitigating effect of the plea.[59] Hence, there are examples where the Tribunal has found that the aggravating circumstances outweighed the mitigating effect of a guilty plea[60] and also, more recently, departed from the sentencing recommendations.[61]

Other mitigating factors include[62] an expression of remorse,[63] voluntary surrender, assistance to detainees or victims, and personal circumstances such as good character,[64] age, comportment in detention, and family circumstances, but only exceptionally poor health. Hence, many mitigating circumstances relate to conduct subsequent to the crime, and this is also acknowledged when a Tribunal has attached significant weight to the contributions of the accused to peace.[65] But factors directly related to the crime in question are also of importance, such as indirect or limited participation[66] and circumstances falling short of constituting grounds for excluding criminal liability (duress and diminished mental responsibility); again, 'double-counting' is not allowed (see above in this section).[67] Similar factors apply for the ICC.[68] Importantly, the ICTR has also established that the sentence may be reduced as a remedy for violations of the convicted person's fundamental rights during the proceedings.[69]

The relative significance of the role of the accused may have an impact on the penalty. But the Tribunals have stated that a high position should not automatically aggravate, nor should a low rank or subordinate function mitigate, the sentence.[70] In fact, a superior position as

59 See Henham & Drumble, 'Plea Bargaining'.
60 See, e.g. *Kambanda* ICTR T. Ch. I 4.9.1998 paras. 60–2 and A. Ch. 19.10.2000 paras. 125–6.
61 See, e.g. *Dragan Nikolić* ICTY T. Ch. II 18.12.2003 and A. Ch. 4.2.2005 (a sentence of twenty-three years imposed when the recommendation was fifteen years; reduced to twenty years on appeal). For more on these issues, see the symposia in (2004) 2 *JICJ* 1018–81 and (2005) 3 *JICJ* 649–94.
62 See, e.g. *Blaškić* ICTY A. Ch. 29.7.2004 para. 696.
63 To be understood in the context of reconciliation, see, e.g. Alan Tieger, 'Remorse and Mitigation in the International Criminal Tribunal for the Former Yugoslavia' (2003) 16 *LJIL* 777, and Henham & Drumble, 'Plea Bargaining'.
64 Generally of limited importance, see, e.g. *Semanza* ICTR A. Ch. 20.5.2005 para. 398. Cf. *Tadić* ICTY T. Ch. II 14.7.1997 para. 59 (good character was considered to aggravate more than mitigate: 'for such a man to have committed these crimes requires an even greater evil will on his part than for a lesser man').
65 See, e.g. *Krajišnik and Plavšić* ICTY T. Ch. III 27.2.2003 paras. 85–94 and *Babić* ICTY A. Ch. 18.7.2005 paras. 55–9.
66 See, e.g. *Babić* ICTY A. Ch. 18.7.2005 paras. 39–40.
67 See, e.g. *Limaj et al.* ICTY A. Ch. 27.9.2007 para. 143.
68 R. 145(2) of the ICC RPE.
69 *Semanza* ICTR A. Ch. 31.5.2000 and 20.5.2005 para. 389 and *Kajelijeli* ICTR A. Ch. 23.5.2005 paras. 320–4.
70 See, e.g. *Delalić et al.* ICTY A. Ch. 20.2.2001 para. 847 and *Krstić* ICTY T. Ch. I 2.8.2001 para. 709. See further, Guénaël Mettraux, *International Crimes and the ad hoc Tribunals* (Oxford, 2005) 353–5.

such is not an aggravating factor, since this may constitute an element of the crime, but the abuse of such a position may well be.[71] But the fact that the accused otherwise had a high level of authority, or the status of being known and respected, such as a priest, may be considered aggravating.[72]

It is not clear whether, and if so to what extent, the accused's motive may influence the sentence. Interestingly, a SCSL Trial Chamber considered a political motive, namely to support the democratically elected regime, as an important mitigating factor and the accused also received relatively short prison terms. The Appeals Chamber disagreed, holding that allowing a 'just cause' to mitigate the sentence would contravene the sentencing purpose of affirmative prevention, and thus it avoided the conflation of *ius in bello* with *ius ad bellum* that was the result of the Trial Chamber's determination.[73]

19.3.2 Cumulative or joint sentences

As we have seen in section 17.8.5, the ICTY and ICTR allow cumulative charges and convictions based on the same underlying conduct; this practice ought not to prejudice the accused, and therefore raises the question of sentencing. The jurisprudence of both Tribunals establishes that a Chamber has discretion to impose sentences which are either global, concurrent or consecutive; this has subsequently also been clarified in the ICTY RPE.[74] Consequently, the practice is not consistent. Regardless of method, however, the final or aggregated sentence should reflect the totality of the culpable conduct in a just and appropriate way.

The ICC Statute provides that a separate sentence is to be pronounced for each crime, together with a joint sentence specifying the total period of imprisonment.[75] The joint sentence must not be less than the highest individual sentence or exceed the maximum sentence according to the Statute.

19.4 Sentencing procedures

Initially the ICTY Trial Chambers addressed sentencing separately and subsequent to conviction.[76] Thereafter the RPE have been amended and guilt and sentencing may be

---

71 See, e.g. *Kayishema and Ruzindana* ICTR A. Ch. 1.6.2001 paras. 358–9; *Stakić* ICTY A. Ch. 22.3.2006 para. 411.
72 See, e.g. *Rugambarara* ICTR T. Ch. II 16.11.2007 para. 26 and *Seromba* ICTR A. Ch. 12.3.2008 para. 230.
73 *Fofana and Kondewa* SCSL T. Ch. I 9.10.2007 paras. 80 and 86, and A. Ch. 28.5.2008 paras. 533–4 (concurring with *Kordić and Čerkez* ICTY A. Ch. 17.12.2004 para. 1082). Moreover, the Sierra Leonean judges of both Chambers dissented and voted to acquit on the same ground. See discussion in section 12.1.3.
74 R. 87(C) of the ICTY RPE; see *Delalić et al.* ICTY A. Ch. 20.2.2001 para. 429 and *Kambanda* ICTR A. Ch. 19.10.2000 paras. 102–12 (interpreting r. 101 of the respective RPE).
75 Art. 78(3) of the ICC Statute.
76 See, e.g. *Erdemović* ICTY T. Ch. I 29.11.1996 and *Tadić* ICTY T. Ch. II 14.7.1997.

determined in a single judgment,[77] which is now the practice in both Tribunals. The ICC Statute also provides for unified trials, but a bifurcated trial will be conducted if either party so requests;[78] reparations claims should normally be heard at a sentencing or separate hearing. A unified trial means that the defendant cannot apply a different strategy for the purpose of sentencing. In case of an accepted guilty plea at the Tribunals or admission of guilt at the ICC, the case will move to a sentencing hearing.[79]

A sentence may be appealed separately both at the Tribunals and at the ICC,[80] and an appeal against a conviction or acquittal may also lead to the revision of the sentence. Due to the corrective nature of the ICTY and ICTR appeals proceedings, the normal test will be whether the Trial Chamber has committed a 'discernible error' in the exercise of its sentencing discretion, something that the appellant must demonstrate.[81] If a conviction or acquittal is revised on appeal, however, the Appeals Chamber will either refer the matter back to the Trial Chamber for sentencing[82] or itself impose a new sentence.[83] At the ICTY and ICTR, time-limited sentences have been replaced by life imprisonment.[84] A different test applies for the ICC – whether 'the sentence is disproportionate to the crime' – and the determination of a new sentence on appeal is a matter for the Appeals Chamber unless a retrial is ordered.[85]

19.5   Pardon, early release and review of sentence

The prisoner may be eligible for pardon, commutation of the sentence or early release in the State where it is served (see section 19.6) but the Tribunal stays in control of the sentence and therefore retains the final say on the matter.[86] Although not provided in the Statute or the RPE, the Tribunals apply the same rules to prisoners who have not been transferred to a State but still remain in the Tribunal's detention centre in The Hague or

---

77 Rr. 85 and 87 of the ICTY RPE and ICTR RPE. The Tokyo IMT was also criticized for its unified trial, see Boister and Cryer, *Tokyo Tribunal*, 250.

78 Art. 76 of the ICC Statute and r. 143 of the ICC RPE. In addition, the Trial Chamber on its own motion may decide to hold a separate sentencing hearing.

79 Rr. 62*bis* and 100 of the ICTY RPE, rr. 62(B) and 100 of the ICTR RPE, and (indirectly) Art. 76(2) of the ICC Statute.

80 See section 17.13.

81 See, e.g. *Delalić et al.* ICTY A. Ch. 20.2.2001 para. 725, and *Semanza* ICTR A. Ch. 20.5.2005 para. 374.

82 See, e.g. *Tadić* ICTY A. Ch. 15.7.1999 para. 27.

83 See, e.g. *Blaškić* ICTY A. Ch. 29.7.2004 para. 726.

84 *Gacumbitsi* ICTR A. Ch. 7.7.2006 para. 206 and *Galić* ICTY A. Ch. 30.11.2006 paras. 454–5; in both cases, judges presented dissenting opinions and separate opinions on this matter.

85 Art. 83 of the ICC Statute.

86 Art. 28 of the ICTY Statute, Art. 27 of the ICTR Statute, rr. 123–5 of the ICTY RPE, and rr. 124–6 of the ICTR RPE. See also ICTY, *Practice Direction on the Procedure for the Determination of Applications for Pardon, Commutation of Sentence and Early Release of Persons Convicted by the International Tribunal* (IT/146, 7 April 1999). See, e.g. *Furundžija* ICTY President 29.7.2004.

Arusha.[87] The Tribunal will consider, inter alia, the gravity of the crimes, the prisoner's demonstration of rehabilitation, any substantial cooperation with the Prosecutor, and personal circumstances.

As part of the compromise reached at the Rome Conference regarding applicable penalties, the ICC Statute makes provision for an automatic review of sentences.[88] The review must take place when two-thirds of the sentence has been served, or twenty-five years of life imprisonment, and a decision not to reduce the sentence must be reviewed at regular intervals. The grounds for reduction of sentence relate to post-conviction cooperation or change of circumstances and the mechanism serves essentially the same purpose as an early release or a pardon.

19.6   Enforcement

A sentence imposed by a Tribunal or the ICC will be served in a State which has declared its willingness to enforce the sentence.[89] This is a voluntary undertaking by States and may have conditions attached, for example regarding the nationality of the prisoner, acceptance of only a limited number of prisoners, or retention of a right to accept or reject in each individual case. Separate enforcement agreements with States have been concluded. The Tribunal President or the (collective) ICC Presidency designates the State of enforcement in the individual case.[90] While the ICC will seek and take into account the views of the convicted person, no such role is afforded him or her at the Tribunals.[91]

The enforcing State may not modify the length of the sentence. Consequently, the State may not release the convicted person due to pardon, commutation of sentence and early release, without the approval of the Tribunal or Court.[92] Disapproval of an impending domestic measure may cause a transfer of the enforcement to another State.[93] The conditions of imprisonment will be in accordance with domestic law, but subject to the supervision of

---

87 In accordance with *Practice Directions*, the respective President takes a decision, which is not subject to appeal; see, e.g. *Simić et al.* ICTY President 21.1.2004, and *Rutaganira* ICTR A. Ch. 24.8.2006 (where an appeal against the President's decision was dismissed).

88 Art. 110 of the ICC Statute and rr. 223–4 of the ICC RPE.

89 Art. 27 of the ICTY Statute, Art. 26 of the ICTR Statute, and Art. 103 of the ICC Statute. While the ICTY convicts serve their sentences in a number of European States, the ICTR prisoners have been transferred to Mali and Benin. The enforcement of sentences and their oversight was also a big issue concerning the Nuremberg and Tokyo Tribunals; see, e.g. Boister and Cryer, *Tokyo Tribunal*, 261–9.

90 R. 103 of the ICTY RPE and ICTR RPE, rr. 198–206 of the ICC RPE and regs. 113–15 of the ICC Regulations.

91 R. 203 of the ICC RPE; cf. *Kvočka et al.* ICTY President 31.5.2006.

92 Art. 28 of the ICTY Statute, Art. 27 of the ICTR Statute, and Arts. 105(1) and 110(1) of the ICC Statute. Hence, Art. 103(2) of the ICC Statute, and the Tribunal enforcement agreements, provide for notifications and consultations on matters which could affect the terms or extent of the imprisonment.

93 See Art. 104 of the ICC Statute and rr. 209–10 of the ICC RPE. Transfer for this reason may also be ordered by the ICTY and ICTR but is not explicitly provided for in the Statutes or RPEs.

the respective Tribunal or Court.[94] The ICC Statute additionally requires compliance with 'widely accepted international treaty standards governing treatment of prisoners' and no better or worse treatment than other prisoners convicted of similar offences.[95]

The ICC Statute also provides for the obligatory enforcement of fines, forfeiture orders and reparation orders by national authorities at the request of the Court.[96] Here too, the State of enforcement must not modify the fines or orders. Enforcement by national authorities is also foreseen concerning restitution of property or the proceeds thereof to victims at the ICTY and ICTR.[97]

The ICC Statute distinguishes between international cooperation (Part 9) and enforcement (Part 10) in spite of the close relationship between the two. While enforcement of prison sentences differs in that it is voluntary, enforcement of the other specified orders is not and it has been argued that certain cooperation provisions of Part 9 should apply by analogy to obligations regarding the latter too.[98]

Further reading

Penalties and sentencing

Stuart Beresford, 'Unshackling the Paper Tiger – The Sentencing Practices of the Ad Hoc International Criminal Tribunals for the Former Yugoslavia and Rwanda' (2001) 1 *ICLR* 33.

Andrea Carcano, 'Sentencing and the Gravity of the Offence in International Criminal Law' (2002) 51 *ICLQ* 583.

Rolf Einar Fife, 'Penalties' in Lee, *The Making of the Rome Statute*, 319–43.

Rolf Einar Fife, 'Penalties' in Lee, *Elements and Rules*, 555–73.

Frederick Harhoff, 'Sense and Sensibility in Sentencing – Taking Stock of International Criminal Punishment' in Ola Engdahl and Pål Wrange (eds.), *Law at War: The Law as it Was and the Law as it Should Be: Lieber Amoricum Ove Bring* (Leiden, 2008) 121–40.

Mark Harmon and Fergal Gaynor, 'Ordinary Sentences for Extraordinary Crimes' (2007) 5 *JICJ* 683.

Ralph Henham, 'Some Issues for Sentencing in the International Criminal Court' (2003) 52 *ICLQ* 81.

Ralph Henham and Mark Drumbl, 'Plea Bargaining at the International Criminal Tribunal for the Former Yugoslavia' (2005) 16 *CLF* 49.

---

94 Art. 27 of the ICTY Statute, Art. 26 of the ICTR Statute, and Art. 106 of the ICC Statute.

95 Art. 106(2) of the ICC Statute. Similarly, a standards requirement is included in the Tribunal enforcement agreements.

96 *Ibid.*, Arts. 75 and 109. See also rr. 212, 217–22 of the ICC RPE and reg. 116 of the ICC Regulations.

97 R. 105 of the ICTY RPE and ICTR RPE.

98 See further Claus Kreß and Göran Sluiter, 'Enforcement' in Cassese, *Commentary*, 1752 and 1831.

Jan Christoph Nemitz, 'The Law of Sentencing in International Criminal Law: The Purposes of Sentencing and the Applicable Method for the Determination of the Sentence' (2001) 4 *IYHL* 87.

Olaoluwa Abiola Olusanya, 'Do Crimes against Humanity Deserve a Higher Sentence than War Crimes?' (2004) 4 *ICLR* 431.

William A. Schabas, 'Sentencing by International Tribunals: A Human Rights Approach' (1997) 7 *Duke Journal of Comparative & International Law* 461.

William A. Schabas, 'Penalties' in Cassese, *Commentary*, 1497–534.

William A. Schabas, *The UN International Criminal Tribunals: The Former Yugoslavia, Rwanda and Sierra Leone* (Cambridge, 2006) ch. 14.

Dirk Van Zyl Smit, *Taking Life Imprisonment Seriously in National and International Law* (The Hague, 2002) ch. 5.

Dirk Van Zyl Smit, 'International Imprisonment' (2005) 54 *ICLQ* 357.

Enforcement of penalties

Claus Kreß and Göran Sluiter, 'Enforcement' in Cassese, *Commentary*, chs. 43–5.

Róisín Mulgrew, 'On the Enforcement of Sentences Imposed by International Courts' (2009) 7 *JICJ* 353.

David Tolbert and Åsa Rydberg, 'Enforcement of Sentences' in Richard May et al. (eds.), *Essays on ICTY Procedure and Evidence – In Honour of Gabrielle Kirk McDonald* (The Hague, 2001) 533–43.

PART F

Relationship Between National and International Systems

20

State Cooperation with the International Courts and Tribunals

20.1 Characteristics of the cooperation regimes

State cooperation with the Tribunals and the ICC – the 'external part' of the judicial process – departs in many important ways from State-to-State cooperation in criminal matters (see Chapter 5). The obligations vis-à-vis the international jurisdictions are more far-reaching[1] since these jurisdictions are created by the international community to investigate and prosecute the most serious crimes of international concern. As regards the Tribunals, and Security Council referrals of situations to the ICC, they also explicitly form part of international efforts to preserve or restore international peace and security. In addition, traditional restrictions on cooperation can be renounced since the international jurisdictions must act in accordance with the highest international standards of procedures and protection of individual rights.

The successful operation of these institutions is completely dependent upon international cooperation. They may not and cannot themselves implement their decisions, such as an arrest warrant, on the territory of a State, and they do not have their own police force.[2] As the ICTY Appeals Chamber concluded in its landmark decision in *Blaškić*, enforcement powers must be expressly provided and cannot be regarded as inherent in an international criminal tribunal.[3] Cooperation is therefore at the heart of effective international criminal proceedings, but this dependence has led to many difficulties in practice.[4]

The *Blaškić* decision found that inter-State and State-Tribunal cooperation follows different models;[5] the former is 'horizontal' and the latter 'vertical' in nature. This

---

1 Compare, however, the SCSL which cannot demand that any State, except Sierra Leone, cooperate unless the State has entered into a separate cooperation agreement with the Court.
2 Of course, this was not the case for the Nuremberg and Tokyo IMTs, which were established by occupying powers.
3 *Blaškić* ICTY A. Ch. 29.10.1997 para. 25.
4 See Mark Harmon and Fergal Gaynor, 'Prosecuting Massive Crimes with Primitive Tools: Three Difficulties Encountered by Prosecutors in International Criminal Proceedings' (2004) 2 *JICJ* 403, and Yolanda Gamarra and Alejandra Vicente, 'United Nations Member States' Obligations Towards the ICTY: Arresting and Transferring Lukić, Gotovina and Zelenenović' (2008) 8 *ICLR* 627.
5 *Blaškić* ICTY A. Ch. 29.10.1997 paras. 47 and 54.

characterization is now commonly used. The distinction is based on the stricter obligations to the international jurisdictions, non-reciprocity, and the right of the requesting party (that is, the Court or Tribunal) unilaterally to interpret and determine the duties of cooperation.[6]

The ICC is the creation of all States Parties and acceptance of even stricter obligations to cooperate than with respect to the Tribunals could therefore be expected. But in fact the opposite is true. The general duty to cooperate set out in the ICTY and ICTR Statutes[7] is binding on all UN Member States by virtue of Chapter VII of the UN Charter and it contains no qualifications or exceptions: a truly vertical scheme. The State-negotiated ICC scheme, on the other hand, also contains a duty to cooperate but it is in some respects closer to inter-State cooperation. In particular, the regime is based on requests instead of orders, certain grounds for postponement or refusal exist, and the scope for on-site investigations and compelling individuals to give evidence is limited. The weaknesses of the ICC cooperation regime, sometimes referred to as a middle ground between a vertical and a horizontal model, are often criticized.[8]

20.2   Obligation to cooperate

20.2.1   States

The ICTY and ICTR are subsidiary organs of the Security Council, and thus of the UN, but being judicial institutions they are of 'a special kind' and have been given powers by the Security Council to make decisions that are binding on sovereign States.[9] The duty to cooperate is explicitly laid down in the Statutes (see section 20.1) and corresponds to the general principle that the Tribunals have primacy over national courts. In accordance with the principle that an international treaty cannot impose obligations on third States without their consent (*pacta tertiis non nocent*),[10] this duty is confined to UN Member States and other States that have accepted obligations of cooperation. But the ICTY has gone further and decided, inter alia, that self-proclaimed and non-recognized entities which exercise governmental functions must also cooperate.[11] In addition there are duties of cooperation under the Dayton Peace Agreement and other agreements: the Dayton Agreement imposes on the signatories, States of the Former Yugoslavia and the Bosnian Serb entity, obligations

---

6 See Göran Sluiter, *International Criminal Adjudication and the Collection of Evidence: Obligations of States* (Antwerp, 2002) 82–8.

7 Art. 29 of the ICTY Statute and Art. 28 of the ICTR Statute, which derive their authority from SC Res. 827 (1993) and 955(1994). According to the wording, the Tribunal may choose between issuing an 'order' or a 'request', both being equally binding on the States; see Sluiter, *International Criminal Adjudication*, 147–50.

8 See, e.g. Bert Swart, 'General Problems' in Cassese, *Commentary*, 1589–605, and Hans-Peter Kaul and Claus Kreß, 'Jurisdiction and Cooperation in the Statute of the International Criminal Court: Principles and Compromises' (1999) 2 *YIHL* 143 at 158–61.

9 *See Blaškić* ICTY T. Ch. II 18.7.1997 paras. 18–23.

10 Art. 35 of the 1969 Vienna Convention on the Law of Treaties.

11 E.g. *Karadžić and Mladić* ICTY T. Ch. I 11.7.1996 para. 98. See also r. 2 of the ICTY RPE regarding the definition of a 'State'. For a critical view, see Sluiter, *International Criminal Adjudication*, 54–5.

supplementary to the ICTY Statute on important issues such as unrestricted access to areas over which the signatory exercises control.

The Tribunal Statutes provide a non-exhaustive list, which means that the duty is not confined to particular forms of cooperation. Grounds for refusal traditional to inter-State cooperation are not permitted.[12] The Tribunal decides the scope of the duty in the particular case and it may issue binding orders to States and, as we shall see in section 20.2.3, to individuals, 'as may be necessary for the purposes of an investigation or for the preparations or conduct of the trial'.[13] The Appeals Chamber in *Blaškić* concluded that the term 'binding order' should be used with respect to States, not 'subpoena' which requires that the injunction is accompanied by a threat of penalty.[14] The assistance will normally be provided in accordance with national law; the Tribunals sometimes make clear that there is a certain discretion as to how the State is to meet a specific request.[15]

The ICC is an independent and autonomous intergovernmental organization with international legal personality and powers to request cooperation from the States Parties.[16] The Statute explicitly requires these States to 'cooperate fully with the Court' and to ensure that national law allows all specified forms of cooperation.[17] The provisions should serve as general interpretive principles for the specific obligations set out in the Statute.[18] The duty to 'cooperate fully' is explicitly confined to cooperation in accordance with the provisions of the Statute, which means that the ICC cannot demand cooperation beyond what the Statute requires. However, there is a catch-all provision at the end of the list of measures for assistance other than arrest and surrender.[19] States may also provide additional cooperation voluntarily. The duty of implementation requires that States make any necessary domestic changes so that they are able to provide all the required forms of cooperation, but allows the States Parties to design the procedures in keeping with their legal and constitutional systems (see section 20.9). Some grounds for refusal are explicitly laid down in the Statute; in the light of the negotiating history these should be considered as exhaustive.[20] There may be additional obligations to cooperate in other agreements, including those concluded by the Court with individual States to enhance cooperation.[21]

---

12 See Chapter 5.
13 R. 54 of the ICTY RPE and ICTR RPE.
14 *Blaškić* ICTY A. Ch. 29.10.1997 para. 25.
15 See, e.g. *Gotovina et al.* ICTY T. Ch. I 16.9.2008.
16 Art. 4 and Part 9 of the ICC Statute.
17 *Ibid.*, Arts. 86 and 88.
18 Claus Kreß, 'Penalties, Enforcement and Cooperation in the International Criminal Court' (1998) 6 *European Journal of Crime, Criminal Law and Criminal Justice* 442 at 450.
19 Art. 93(1)(l) of the ICC Statute.
20 See Phakiso Mochochoko, 'International Cooperation and Judicial Assistance' in Lee, *The Making of the Rome Statute*, 305–17.
21 See Art. 54(3)(d) of the ICC Statute and reg. 107 of the ICC Regulations; and see *Report of the International Criminal Court for* 2005–2006 (UN Doc. A/61/217 of 3.8.2006) paras. 52–6.

Although not beyond dispute, the duty to cooperate with the ICC (and Part 9 of the Statute) is triggered first when an investigation is formally commenced.[22] It thereafter covers subsequent proceedings; certain obligations apply after the final verdict, for example the temporary transfer of a prisoner to the Court for testimony.[23]

20.2.2 Conflicting international obligations of States

Another important aspect of the different regimes is the relationship between the State's cooperation duties towards the Tribunal or Court and other international obligations. Since the duties vis-à-vis the Tribunals have their legal force in the UN Charter, these will normally prevail over the State's obligations under other international agreements, at least agreements between UN Member States.

The situation is more complex regarding the ICC. If the Security Council imposes cooperation obligations when referring a situation to the Court, and thus acts under Chapter VII of the UN Charter, the equivalent primacy over other international obligations should apply.[24] This is how the ICC has interpreted the not entirely clear cooperation provisions in the Security Council resolution concerning the *Situation in Darfur, Sudan.*[25] In other instances general international principles for contradictory treaty obligations will apply, such as *lex posterior* (the treaty later in time prevails) and *lex specialis* (the more specific treaty prevails). To what extent such interpretations favour the Court will depend on the circumstances. Hence, the obligations vis-à-vis the ICC do not have a general primacy. Two types of conflicts are addressed in the Statute: competing requests for cooperation, and immunities and similar obstacles. On competing requests the Statute sets out a complex system whereby the existence of an admissibility decision by the Court (on the grounds of complementarity) and the origin of the competing request (from a State Party or third State) are important factors for the resolution of the conflict.[26]

The provision on conflicts regarding immunities (for example state immunity, diplomatic immunity, or safe conduct) and similar obstacles (for example exclusive jurisdiction in Status of Forces Agreements or conditioned re-extradition in extradition agreements) is

---

22 See Informal Expert Paper: *Fact-finding and investigative functions of the Office of the Prosecutor, including international cooperation* (2003) paras. 22–9, available at the ICC webpage: www.icc-cpi.int.
23 R. 193 of the ICC RPE.
24 See also, e.g. Dan Sarooshi, 'The Peace and Justice Paradox: The International Criminal Court and the UN Security Council' in Dominic McGoldrick et al. (eds.), *The Permanent International Criminal Court: Legal and Policy Issues* (Oxford, 2003) 95 at 104.
25 SC res. 1593(2005) of 31.3.2005; *Situation in Darfur* (*Al Bashir* arrest warrant case) ICC PT. Ch. I 4.3.2009 paras. 244–7; see also Matthias Neuner, 'The Darfur Referral of the Security Council and the Jurisdiction of the International Criminal Court' (2005) 8 *YIHL* 320 and Robert Cryer, 'Sudan, Resolution 1593, and International Criminal Justice' (2006) 19 *LJIL* 195.
26 Art. 90 of the ICC Statute. See also Art. 93.9 on other forms of cooperation.

Article 98; it has turned out to be controversial.[27] From a cooperation perspective, however, it is important to note that the provision, as drafted, is directed to the ICC: '[t]he Court may not proceed with a request' unless a waiver of immunity or consent for surrender has been obtained. Hence, the requested State may raise the issue of conflicting obligations before the Court,[28] but the conflict is not a ground for refusal if the Court still insists on the request.[29] If the requested State continues to resist, however, the issue may be subject to adjudication by the Court in non-compliance proceedings.[30] Besides, nothing prevents a non-State Party from seeking a remedy against a violation by the requested State of the agreement between them. When issuing an arrest warrant against the President of Sudan, the Pre-Trial Chamber did not address the issue of Article 98 although the request for arrest and surrender was sent to numerous States and thus issues of immunity or conflicting treaty obligations could possibly arise.[31]

20.2.3 Individuals

The Tribunals have on occasion issued binding orders to individuals to appear and give evidence. These orders are 'subpoenas' (*subpoena ad testificandum*) since non-compliance may result in liability for contempt. Lacking explicit support in the Statutes, the practice has been based on 'inherent powers'.[32] By jurisprudence, and now also in the Rules, it is clarified that such orders may only be issued by a Chamber.[33] The orders, as well as any sanctions, must be enforced by national authorities and most States will require that a domestic order be issued. Some States attribute direct effect to the order issued by the Tribunal, meaning that the Tribunal order serves as the basis for a domestic compulsory process. According to the Appeals Chamber in *Blaškić* States have a duty, when requested, to arrest, compel under threat of a domestic penalty to surrender evidence, or bring a witness to the Tribunal to testify.[34] These are far-reaching obligations that depart from the general practice among States, which does not recognize a duty to testify across national borders.[35] In practice, however, only a few States have introduced legislation providing for forcible

---

27 See sections 8.11.3 and 21.5.3.

28 R. 195 of the ICC RPE.

29 See also Art. 119(1) of the ICC Statute which provides: 'Any dispute concerning the judicial functions of the Court shall be settled by the direction of the Court'.

30 Reg. 109 of the ICC Regulations.

31 *Al Bashir* arrest warrant case ICC PT. Ch. I 4.3.2009. See section 21.5.4.

32 *Blaškić* ICTY A. Ch. 29.10.1997 paras. 47 and 55. See Anne-Laure Chaumette, 'The ICTY's Power to Subpoena Individuals, to Issue Binding Orders to International Organisations and to Subpoena Their Agents' (2004) 4 *ICLR* 357.

33 R. 54 of the ICTY RPE and ICTR RPE. See, e.g. *Mrkšić et al.* ICTY A. Ch. 30.7.2003 and *Krštić* ICTY A. Ch. 1.7.2003.

34 *Blaškić* ICTY A. Ch. 29.10.1997 para. 27.

35 A special scheme exists among the Nordic countries, however, but it does not include effective sanctions in case of non-compliance by the witness.

transfer of witnesses to the Tribunals, and the Tribunals have framed their requests for State assistance in very cautious terms.[36]

Here the traditional act of State doctrine is to be observed and the Tribunal may not address binding orders to State officials for cooperation in their official capacity; such orders must instead be made to the State.[37] The orders may, however, be addressed to officials when acting in their 'private capacity', but still the Tribunal will normally proceed via national authorities and only exceptionally address itself directly to the individual.[38] An unqualified immunity of this kind could go too far,[39] however, and subsequently the 'State official' exception has been further restricted to apply 'only in relation to the production of documents in their custody in their official capacity'; it does not cover what the official has seen or heard in the course of exercising official functions.[40] The Tribunals have dismissed claims of immunity, inter alia, regarding the then British Prime Minister Blair and German Chancellor Schröder, and have issued a subpoena to the Rwandan Defence Minister.[41] Members of international peacekeeping or peace-enforcing forces with a UN mandate are also compellable.[42]

The ICC Statute gives conflicting messages as to whether the Court may compel an individual to cooperate, the suspect or accused of course being excluded. The cooperation obligation of Part 9 does not extend to private individuals. But another provision authorizes the Trial Chamber to 'require the attendance and testimony of witnesses', although the RPE restrict the 'compellability of witnesses' to those who actually appear before the Court.[43] Read together with the provision that States are required to assist with the 'voluntary appearance' of witnesses and experts,[44] it appears that the ICC might have the power to order a witness to appear before the Court but cannot demand that a State deliver a witness who does not comply. The Court might request non-voluntary transfer of a witness under the catch-all provision. But this requires that no 'existing fundamental legal principle of general application' in the requested State would be violated, which could well be argued to preclude coercive measures without an explicit authorization in national law.

---

36 See Sluiter, *International Criminal Adjudication*, 253–68.
37 *Blaškić* ICTY A. Ch. 29.10.1997 paras. 39–44.
38 *Ibid.*, paras. 46–51 and 53–6.
39 For criticism see, e.g. Susan Lamb, 'The Powers of Arrest of the International Criminal Tribunal for the Former Yugoslavia' (1999) 70 *BYBIL* 165 at 217–18.
40 *Krstić* ICTY A. Ch. 1.7.2003 paras. 24, 26–8.
41 *Milošević* ICTY T. Ch. III 9.12.2005 and *Bagosora et al.* ICTR T. Ch. I 11.9.2006. Cf. the SCSL which avoided the issue of immunity when refusing to subpoena the President of Sierra Leone: *Norman et al.* SCSL A. Ch. 11.9.2006 paras. 40–4 (but Judge Robertson, dissenting, addressed the issue). For further discussion of immunities, see Chapter 21.
42 See, e.g. *Simić et al.* ICTY T. Ch. I 18.10.2000 paras. 62–3 and *Bagosora et al.* ICTR T. Ch. III 14.7.2006.
43 Art. 64(6)(b) of the ICC Statute and r. 65 of the ICC RPE.
44 Art. 93(1)(e) of the ICC Statute.

As in ordinary inter-state regimes, the Tribunal or Court, instead of issuing a subpoena, may order the temporary transfer of a witness who is already detained in a State.[45] If a subpoena fails to secure the appearance of the witness, for example when the non-appearance is because of a medical condition, compelled testimony by video-link can be an alternative.[46]

20.3 Non-States Parties and international organizations

In practice, cooperation with non-States Parties has not been much of an issue for the Tribunals owing to the practically universal membership of the UN; Switzerland, a non-member at the time of the Tribunals' creation, declared that it would cooperate voluntarily. Neither has the application of the duty of cooperation, laid down in the ICTY Statute to the newly independent States after the break-up of the Former Yugoslavia, been challenged with reference to non-membership in the UN, which would have involved difficult issues of State succession.[47] All but one of these States were UN members when the ICTY was established; Serbia and Montenegro considered itself the successor State, although this was not accepted by the UN with respect to membership.[48]

The explicit duty to cooperate set out in the ICC Statute is confined to States Parties, but special provisions authorize the Court to invite non-States Parties to cooperate in accordance with separate arrangements.[49] In addition, non-States Parties which accept the jurisdiction of the ICC in individual cases must also cooperate with the Court in accordance with Part 9 of the ICC Statute.[50] Finally, the Security Council may, when referring a situation to the ICC, require that UN Member States cooperate with the Court, regardless of whether those States are parties to the ICC Statute or not. This was done with respect to Sudan (Darfur).[51] Quite apart from this, it has been argued that there may be a customary law duty to ensure compliance with international humanitarian law, which in turn could translate into a duty to

---

45 R. 90*bis* of the ICTY RPE and ICTR RPE and Art. 93(1)(f) and (7) of the ICC Statute. See, e.g. *Karemera et al.* ICTR T. Ch. III 9.4.2009.

46 See, e.g. *Haradinaj et al.* ICTY T. Ch. I 14.9.2007. See also Art. 69(2) of the ICC Statute.

47 These issues were raised, however, with respect to the ICTY's jurisdiction over crimes committed in Kosovo, see *Milutinović et al.* ICTY T. Ch. III 6.5.2003.

48 The question of the UN membership of Serbia and Montenegro was extraordinarily complicated and was described as a 'rather confused and complex state of affairs': see ICJ in *Case Concerning Legality of Use of Force (Serbia and Montenegro* v. *United Kingdom)* 15.12.2004 paras. 53–77. See also ICJ in *Case Concerning the Application of the Convention on the Prevention and Punishment of the Crime of Genocide (Croatia* v. *Serbia)* 18.11.2008 paras. 43–51.

49 Art. 87(5) of the ICC Statute.

50 *Ibid.*, Art. 12(3).

51 SC res. 1593 (2005) of 31.3.2005.

cooperate with the ICC in a given case,[52] although such an argument has by no means been universally accepted.[53]

The cooperation of entities other than States has proved indispensable in practice. For example, international forces have carried out most of the arrests for the ICTY. Such action was controversial and there was initial resistance to authorizing, let alone requiring, IFOR to arrest indicted war criminals.[54] Nonetheless, an authorization to arrest was given to IFOR, but only under restrictive conditions, and it took some time before the first arrest was made. Contributing to this increased willingness to assist was a practice of 'sealed indictments' which reduced the risks to troops effectuating the arrests.[55] It has been debated whether the ICTY Statute allows arrest by bodies other than States and whether IFOR (later SFOR) has a duty to arrest:[56] ICTY itself has given an affirmative answer to the former question[57] and a negative to the latter.[58] Arrest warrants have sometimes been issued directly to non-State entities instead of States.[59] It is truly an anomaly, however, that the international community imposed a duty on States to cooperate with the ICTY but provided the relevant international forces (IFOR/SFOR and KFOR) with only a permission to do so.

Due mainly to US opposition to the Court, the mandate of the UN peacekeeping forces in the Democratic Republic of Congo (MONUC) did not refer to the ICC; more robust assistance in arresting war criminals was only to be provided to Congolese authorities and courts. More recently, however, MONUC was given an explicit mandate to cooperate with international efforts to bring perpetrators to justice.[60] But MONUC has for a long time been involved in the arrest of suspects in the *Situation of the DRC*, including in one instance where there were no domestic proceedings but solely an ICC arrest warrant. In Sudan, on the contrary, any links between the ICC and the international peacekeeping mission (UNAMID)

---

52 Claus Kreß and Kimberly Prost, 'Article 87' in Triffterer, *Observers' Notes*, 1061–2; Zhu Wenqi, 'On Co-operation by States Not Party to the International Criminal Court' (2006) 88:861 *International Review of the Red Cross* 87.

53 Henckaerts & Doswald-Beck, *ICRC Customary Law*, 618–21.

54 See Richard Holbrook, *To End a War*, 2nd edn (New York, 1998) 221–2.

55 See Gary Jonathan Bass, *Stay the Hand of Vengeance: The Politics of War Crimes Tribunals* (Princeton, 2000) 265–7.

56 See, e.g. John R. W. D. Jones, 'The Implications of the Dayton Peace Agreement for the International Criminal Tribunals for the Former Yugoslavia' (1996) 7 *EJIL* 226; Gary Sharp, 'International Obligations to Search for and Arrest War Criminals: Government Failure in the Former Yugoslavia' (1997) 7 *Duke Journal of Comparative & International Law* 411; Paolo Gaeta, 'Is NATO Authorized or Obliged to Arrest Persons Indicted by the International Criminal Tribunal for the Former Yugoslavia?' (1998) 9 *EJIL* 174; Lamb, 'Powers of Arrest', 165–244; and Han-Ru Zhou, 'The Enforcement of Arrest Warrants by International Forces' (2006) 4 *JICJ* 202.

57 See r. 59*bis* of the ICTY RPE.

58 (1996) *Yearbook of the ICTY* 229.

59 See, e.g. *Dokmanović* ICTY T. Ch. II 22.10.1997 para. 3 (arrest warrant issued to the United Nations Transitional Administration for Eastern Slavonia, Baranja and Western Sirmium, UNTAES).

60 Cf. SC res. 1565(2004) of 1.10.2004 and 1856(2008) of 22.12.2008.

have been avoided and UNAMID's mandate contains no reference to international criminal investigations or prosecutions.[61]

Intergovernmental organizations may have international legal personality, separate from that of the constituent States. Regardless of this, the ICTY, by using a 'purposive interpretation' of its Statute, has found itself competent to issue binding orders to such organizations. In *Simić et al.*, for example, such an order was issued not only to the participating States of SFOR but also to SFOR, as a collective State enterprise, and its responsible authority, the North Atlantic Council.[62] Binding orders have also been directed to others.[63] The ICC, on the other hand, applies the same scheme to intergovernmental organizations as to non-States Parties, and cooperation thus depends on a voluntary commitment.[64] For example, a cooperation agreement has been concluded with the European Union.[65] A special relationship exists between the ICC and the United Nations and matters having an impact on cooperation are addressed in a Relationship Agreement.[66] A separate agreement was concluded concerning MONUC.[67] The difficult issue of how to deal with confidentiality is discussed in section 20.8.2. One organization, the ICRC, has been granted special treatment, motivated by the special status drawn from its mandate under the Geneva Conventions. In *Simić et al.*, the ICTY found that in order to discharge its mandate the ICRC must have a right not to disclose information relating to its activities.[68] The ICC has followed suit with an absolute privilege provision.[69] The ICRC may thus prevent disclosure of information or testimonies by present and past ICRC officials or employees.

20.4 Non-compliance

The ICTY and ICTR Statutes do not address the issue of non-compliance with the duty of cooperation, but again the *Blaškić* decision provides answers. The Appeals Chamber found

---

61 SC res. 1769(2007) of 31.7.2007; the earlier African Union mission (AMIS) also had no mandate to cooperate with the ICC.

62 ICTY T. Ch. III 18.10.2000 paras. 46–9, 58. One should note, however, that SFOR is different from regular UN peacekeeping forces since it consists of different State-led forces remaining under the control of their respective governments.

63 See, e.g. *Kordić* ICTY T. Ch. III 4.8.2000 (the European Community Monitoring Mission) and *Haradinaj et al.* ICTY A. Ch. 10.3.2006 (UNMIK); cf. *Kovačević* ICTY T. Ch. II 23.6.1998 (refusal to issue an order to the OSCE). See also Chaumette, 'The ICTY's Power to Subpoena', 413–7.

64 Art. 87(6) of the ICC Statute.

65 Agreement between the International Criminal Court and the European Union on Cooperation and Assistance of 10.4.2006 (ICC-PRES/01–01–06).

66 Art. 2 of the ICC Statute and the Relationship Agreement between the International Criminal Court and the United Nations of 4.10.2004 (ICC-ASP/3/Res.1).

67 *Memorandum of Understanding between the UN and the ICC Concerning Co-operation between MONUC and the ICC* 8.11.2005. See Rod Rastan, 'Testing Co-operation: The International Criminal Court and National Authorities' (2008) 21 *LJIL* 444–6.

68 *Simić et al.* ICTY T. Ch. III 27.7.1999 paras. 72–4 (but with one judge dissenting).

69 R. 73(4) of the ICC RPE.

that an international tribunal must have powers to make all judicial determinations that are necessary for the exercise of its primary jurisdiction, including making a finding of non-compliance and reporting this to the Security Council.[70] But the Tribunal may not recommend or suggest how the Security Council could or should address the matter. Similarly, the ICC may make a finding of non-compliance and refer the matter to the Assembly of States Parties or, when the Security Council has referred the underlying situation, to the Security Council.[71] A breach by a non-State Party of a legally binding cooperation agreement or arrangement may also be reported. Having the power to make findings of non-cooperation is important for the credibility of the institution, but also a sensitive matter for States, and the potential consequences are not spelled out at all. Measures such as public condemnation and even collective economic sanctions could be contemplated, but other considerations, such as the need to maintain support for the international jurisdiction, may well prevail.[72] Moreover, the State might cooperate partially and a finding of non-cooperation is likely to close the door to further cooperation and inhibit positive developments in that respect.

In practice, the Security Council has failed to respond effectively to reports of non-compliance by the ICTY; collective action by States, such as threats to withhold financial aid, has been more successful.[73] Although Slobodan Milošević was at last surrendered to the Tribunal in 2001 and Karadžić in 2008, two high-profile indicted persons still remain at large. The ICTR has also experienced instances of non-cooperation, including at times by the Government of Rwanda.[74] But the potential tools available are manifold[75] and international pressure and Security Council action toward the arrest and surrender to the SCSL of the former Liberian President, Charles Taylor in 2006 show that if there is a will there is also hope.[76] However, the Council's response so far to the ICC Prosecutor's report of May 2008 that Sudan has failed to comply with its cooperation obligations in accordance with Security Council resolution 1593(2005) was merely a Presidential Statement urging the Government of Sudan and others to cooperate fully with the Court.[77]

---

70 *Blaškić* ICTY A. Ch. 29.10.1997 paras. 33–7.

71 Art. 87(7) of the ICC Statute.

72 See Bruce Broomhall, *International Justice and the International Criminal Court* (Oxford, 2003) 156–7.

73 Gabrielle Kirk McDonald, 'Problems, Obstacles and Achievements of the ICTY' (2004) 2 *JICJ* 558 at 562–7.

74 See, e.g. Erik Møse, 'Main Achievements of the ICTR' (2005) 3 *JICJ* 920 at 939–40.

75 See Michael Scharf, 'The Tools for Enforcing International Criminal Justice in the New Millennium: Lessons from the Yugoslav Tribunal' (2000) 49 *DePaul Law Review* 925.

76 See SC res. 1638(2005) of 11.11.2005.

77 *Seventh Report of the Prosecutor of the International Criminal Court to the UN Security Council pursuant to UNSCR 1593(2005)* of 5.6.2008, repeated in subsequent reports to the Council; Presidential Statement of 16.6.2008 (S/PRST/2008/21).

20.5   Cooperation and the ICC complementarity principle

The ICC cooperation regime is influenced by the fundamental complementarity principle; domestic investigations and prosecutions have priority in principle. The regulation of issues such as competing requests (see section 20.2.2), challenges concerning *ne bis in idem* (or double jeopardy),[78] and simultaneous proceedings in the requested State concerning other crimes,[79] bear evidence of this. Generally, a decision by the Court on admissibility is decisive of the matter since that decision determines whether the Court will go ahead with its investigation or prosecution. A complementarity challenge by a State has the effect that the Prosecutor must suspend the investigation. However, authority to take certain measures may be sought from the Chamber; in addition, the State's duty to cooperate remains in effect until the Court orders otherwise, as does an arrest warrant.[80] In line with this, a *ne bis in idem* challenge before a national court may cause the requested State to postpone surrender pending an admissibility decision by the ICC, but the execution of the arrest warrant may not be postponed.[81]

The Statute also provides for some, limited, assistance that the ICC may grant a State, which is a logical consequence of the complementarity principle.[82] Moreover, the ICC may transfer the suspect or accused to a State that has made a successful admissibility challenge, but only with the approval of the originally surrendering State.[83] Clearly, the negotiating States were more hesitant about transferring information and suspects to other States than to the ICC. Nonetheless, cooperation among States is truly important for the prosecution of the Statute crimes where there is more than one State willing and able to take jurisdiction, a situation that will often arise with the growth of universal jurisdiction. This is not, however, addressed by the Statute.

20.6   Authority to seek cooperation and defence rights

As in inter-State cooperation, there is a certain inequality between the powers of the prosecution and the defence to seek cooperation, and this is a source of criticism.[84] While the Prosecutor has certain powers to seek cooperation independently on behalf of the

---

78 Art. 89(2) of the ICC Statute.

79 *Ibid.*, Arts. 89(4) and 94.

80 *Ibid.*, Arts. 19(7)–(9) and 58(4).

81 *Ibid.*, Art. 89(2). See Informal Expert Paper: *Fact-finding and investigative functions*, paras. 45–7; but cf. Bert Swart, 'Arrest and Surrender' in Cassese, *Commentary*, 1694–5.

82 Art. 93(10) of the ICC Statute. See Federica Gioia, '"Reverse Cooperation" and the Architecture of the Rome Statute: A Vital Part of the Relationship Between States and the ICC?' in Maria Chiara Malaguti (ed.), *ICC and international cooperation in light of the Rome Statute* (Lecce, Italy, 2007) 75–101.

83 R. 185 of the ICC RPE.

84 See, e.g. Mark Ellis, 'Achieving Justice Before the International War Crimes Tribunal: Challenges for the Defence Counsel' (1997) 7 *Duke Journal of Comparative and International Law* 519 at 533–6.

international jurisdiction, including provisional arrest and seizure of evidence in urgent cases,[85] the defence is directed to go through a judge.[86] Such court orders have been issued by all the international criminal jurisdictions and some States even require them in order to provide assistance in accordance with national law.[87] The problem is more pronounced in adversarial proceedings where each party prepares its case, than in inquisitorial ones where the prosecution has a duty to investigate exonerating circumstances actively.[88] Hence, this could be less of a problem at the ICC than in the Tribunal proceedings.[89]

In addition, the Prosecutor may turn to the relevant Chamber for the grant or authorization of necessary warrants or orders.[90] The ICTY judges may issue an arrest warrant directly to the Prosecutor.[91] In the same vein, it has been suggested that the ICC Prosecutor may retain the right to determine where and when to request an arrest, although the underlying arrest warrant will always be issued by the Pre-Trial Chamber.[92] But in practice the Chambers have rejected such an argument and instead made the requests themselves.[93]

Another issue is to what extent fair trial rights and other procedural standards must be respected by national authorities when acting on behalf of the Tribunal or Court and what remedies are available when such rights or standards are violated. This is discussed in more detail in Chapter 17, but it should now be noted that the ICC Statute lays down some procedural rights relating to the questioning of a suspect which are also explicitly applicable when it is being conducted by national authorities.[94]

20.7   Arrest and surrender

The duty to assist with arrest and surrender is explicitly mentioned in the ICTY and ICTR Statutes and further reinforced in the respective RPE. The basis is normally an arrest warrant issued by a Tribunal judge, but in urgent cases the Prosecutor may request provisional arrest

---

85 Rr. 39(iii) and 40(A) of the ICTY RPE and ICTR RPE; Art. 54(3)(c)–(d) of the ICC Statute.

86 R. 54 of the ICTY RPE and ICTR RPE; Art. 57(3)(b) of the ICC Statute and r. 116 of the ICC RPE.

87 See, e.g. *Setako* ICTR T. Ch. I 31.3.2009 para. 4.

88 See sections 17.3.2 and 17.6.

89 See *Katanga and Ngudjolo Chui* ICC PT. Ch. I 25.4.2008, where the majority found the defence request partially unnecessary since the documents were available from the prosecution; cf. the dissenting opinion of Judge Ušacka).

90 R. 54 of the ICTY RPE and ICTR RPE; Art. 57(3)(a) of the ICC Statute.

91 R. 59*bis* of the ICTY RPE.

92 Informal Expert Paper: *Fact-finding and investigative functions*, para. 82.

93 See, e.g. *Situation in Uganda* ICC PT. Ch. II 8.7.2005 and *Lubanga Dyilo* ICC PT. Ch. I 24.2.2006. For a critical view, see Håkan Friman, 'Cooperation with the International Criminal Court: Some Thoughts of Improvements Under the Current Regime' in Mauro Politi and Federica Gioia (eds.), *The International Criminal Court and National Jurisdictions* (Aldershot, 2008) 93–102. See also Rastan, 'Testing Co-operation', 447–9.

94 Art. 55(2) of the ICC Statute.

to be followed up by a judge-made order for surrender.[95] The special confirmation proceedings *in absentia* at the Tribunals are provided with a view to issuing an international arrest warrant to all States.[96] Both an international and, according to case law, a regular arrest warrant may be combined with an order to freeze the assets of the accused.[97]

In spite of the lack of grounds for refusal, States have sometimes refused cooperation on grounds of national law. For example, a US court refused to extradite an accused to the ICTR claiming that there was no extradition treaty, as required by national law.[98] The Federal Republic of Yugoslavia initially refused to transfer indictees to the ICTY on the basis of a constitutional prohibition against extradition of nationals.[99] Moreover, some domestic implementation laws contain double criminality requirements.[100] But such traditional grounds for refusing extradition are not compatible with the Tribunal cooperation regime.[101]

The fact remains that the national law of many States prohibits 'extradition' under certain circumstances, most notably concerning nationals in many civil law jurisdictions. These strongly held exceptions were advanced in the ICC negotiations and in order to create a regime which excludes any explicit grounds for refusal, compromises were required. One element of the agreed regime was to distinguish between 'surrender' (to the Court) and 'extradition' (to a State), and thereby avoid a potential application of ordinary extradition principles and national requirements (see section 20.9).[102] Another element was to satisfy the evidentiary requirements that apply to extradition in many common law States. While the judicial authorities of the requested State may not examine the legality of the warrant itself or rule on a *habeas corpus* challenge, the Statute indirectly acknowledges that the State, as part of its surrender procedures, may test evidence and that the Court must support its request with documents, statements or information to meet the requirements.[103] But the Statute also requires that national requirements for surrender should not be more burdensome, and should if possible be less burdensome, than those applicable to inter-State extradition. A State that normally applies evidentiary requirements for extradition but has made exceptions concerning requests from certain States, will therefore arguably be prevented from applying such requirements vis-à-vis the ICC.

---

95 Rr. 40 and 40*bis* of the ICTY RPE and ICTR RPE.

96 So-called 'Rule 61 proceedings': see section 17.9.1.

97 R. 61(D) of the ICTY RPE and ICTR RPE; *Milošević* ICTY (Judge Hunt) 24.5.1999 paras. 26–9.

98 See Göran Sluiter, 'To Cooperate or not to Cooperate?: The Case of the Failed Transfer of Ntakirutimana to the Rwanda Tribunal' (1998) 11 *LJIL* 383 and Mary Coombs, 'International Decisions: In Re Surrender of Ntakirutimana' (2000) 94 *AJIL* 171.

99 ICTY Report to the United Nations 1997, UN Doc. A/52/375 and S/1997/729 para. 189.

100 See section 5.3.2.

101 See r. 58 of the ICTY RPE and ICTR RPE.

102 Art. 102 of the ICC Statute. See Michael Plachta, '"Surrender" in the context of the International Criminal Court and the European Union' (2004) 19 *Nouvelles études pénales* 465.

103 Art. 91(2) and (4) of the ICC Statute; see Kaul and Kreß, 'Jurisdiction and Cooperation', 165–6.

Other issues were resolved in the Statute by introducing postponements or consultations.[104] By containing these detailed provisions, the Statute may satisfy any national requirement that there must be an extradition treaty before a person may be transferred.

For the ICC, arrest and surrender or provisional arrest will always be based on an arrest warrant issued by the Pre-Trial Chamber. National authorities will enforce the request by applying national procedures, but the Statute sets forth some minimum requirements concerning the national arrest proceedings, and prescribes a division of competences, consultations regarding provisional release, and speedy execution of the request.[105] In practice, most decisions to issue arrest warrants have been lengthy and included a detailed assessment of the various matters, including the alleged crimes, jurisdiction and, in some, the complementarity principle.[106] An arrest warrant may be combined with a request for identification, tracing, and seizing or freezing assets and property belonging to the suspect, which has regularly been done and sometimes also led to assets being frozen.[107]

Somewhat surprisingly, in view of the strictly limited subject matter jurisdiction of the ICC, there was strong support for including the rule of specialty in the ICC Statute.[108] Hence, if there are amendments to the charges a waiver may have to be obtained from the surrendering State.[109] The consent of the person surrendered is not required. The Tribunals, on the other hand, have rejected the rule by reference to the fact that States cannot refuse surrender on any ground.[110] The same argument could be made for the ICC, but still the specialty rule applies explicitly and may create practical problems.

20.8   Other forms of legal assistance

As already mentioned, the cooperation obligation of the ICTY and ICTR Statutes are not restricted to specified forms of cooperation; it is up to the Tribunal to decide what is required for the case at hand. Requests and orders for various measures have been issued and the Tribunals have established some general principles. For example, a request for an order to

---

104 Art. 89(2) (*ne bis in idem* challenge), Art. 89(4) (domestic proceeding concerning other crimes), and Art. 95 (general provision on postponement) of the ICC Statute.

105 *Ibid.*, Arts. 89(1), 58 and 59.

106 However, the issue of admissibility should only exceptionally be addressed in connection to the issuance of an arrest warrant, see *Situation in the DRC* ICC A. Ch. 13.7.2006 (169) paras. 53–4; see section 17.4.

107 Art. 57(3)(e) of the ICC Statute; *Lubanga Dyilo* ICC PT. Ch. I 24.2.2006 paras. 130–41. In one case, a bank account was seized and frozen in Portugal but since most of the money seemed to have disappeared, the Court requested national authorities to investigate the matter; see *Bemba Gombo* ICC PT. Ch. III 17.11.2008.

108 Art. 101 of the ICC Statute.

109 Unlike most extradition instruments, however, the provision is drafted in such a way that it only targets a different 'conduct or course of conduct' but does not apply to a different legal qualification of the charged facts: see Peter Wilkitzki, 'Article 101' in Triffterer, *Observers' Notes*, 1638.

110 *Kovačević* ICTY A. Ch. 2.7.1998 para. 37. However, the rule of specialty might apply if the case and accused are later referred from the Tribunal to a national jurisdiction; see *Milan Lukić* ICTY Referral Bench 5.4.2007 para. 45. See also Gamarra and Vicente, 'UN Member States' Obligations', 644–6.

produce documents must be relatively specific, explain why the documents are relevant for trial, not be unduly onerous, and allow sufficient time for compliance.[111]

Article 93 of the ICC Statute, on the other hand, sets out various forms of assistance that are to be provided, and measures other than those listed are available under the 'catch-all' provision (see section 20.2.1). The drafting of the Statute, and indeed early practice, suggests that the Court makes the requests and the requested State thereafter performs the investigative acts or other measures on behalf of the Court.

20.8.1 Grounds for refusal

No grounds for refusal are provided with respect to cooperation with the Tribunals. Apart from the national security exception (see section 20.8.2), only one ground for refusal for 'other forms' of assistance was retained in the ICC regime: if the requested measure is prohibited on the basis of 'an existing fundamental legal principle of general application' in the requested State.[112] Arguably, a strict interpretation should apply and it may even be that the principle must be of a constitutional character.[113] But all other grounds for declining assistance that normally apply in inter-State cooperation,[114] such as a double criminality requirement, are disallowed. Nevertheless, the requested State may seek consultation, modification or postponement of the cooperation, and thus cause disruption and delays, on a number of additional grounds, such as a competing request, an ongoing domestic case, lack of information or immunity.

20.8.2 National security objections

Orders or requests directed to States or individuals may give rise to national security concerns; the question arises whether the relevant national law of a State should constitute an obstacle to cooperation. Clearly, a national security exception can jeopardize efficient cooperation and even the rights of the accused (if the information is exculpatory in nature). But it is at the same time unrealistic to believe that a State will readily reveal sensitive secrets, or even admit to their existence, even though the information could be indispensable to the case.[115] Hence, both the ICTY RPE and the ICC Statute contain compromise solutions in order to protect national security interests.

The Appeals Chamber in *Blaškić* rejected Croatia's claim that it is for the State to determine its national security needs and that such needs may serve as a ground for refusal.

---

111 *Blaškić* ICTY A. Ch. 29.10.1997 para. 32.
112 Art. 93(3) of the ICC Statute; on national security, see Art. 93(4).
113 See Kreß, 'Penalties, Enforcement and Cooperation', 456–7.
114 See further Chapter 5.
115 See Grant Dawson and Joakim Dungel, 'Compulsion of Information from States and Due Process in Cases before the International Criminal Tribunal for the Former Yugoslavia' (2007) 20 *LJIL* 115.

The Chamber decided that a right to refuse by reference to *ordre public*, which is a general cooperation principle, would therefore not be 'fully in keeping with the Statute'.[116] But since national security concerns may well be legitimate, the Chamber devised a number of mechanisms to protect sensitive information in the Tribunal proceedings,[117] which have later been codified.[118] They apply also when the information is provided in the form of testimony.[119] For information provided by international organizations, their relationship to Member States and others comes into play. For example, the ICTY has ruled that NATO is not required to divulge intelligence information provided to it by States and other entities without the provider's consent.[120]

The ICC Statute allows a State to deny cooperation on national security grounds.[121] The State itself determines when such interests are affected, but it must comply with detailed procedures that are inspired by the *Blaškić* scheme and aimed at ensuring sufficient protection so that the information can be made available. Nevertheless, it is ultimately the Chamber that determines whether a State has complied with its duty to cooperate, and if it decides that it has not, the Court may refer the matter to the Assembly of States Parties or the Security Council. Apart from this, the Chamber may make certain inferences at trial.[122]

As with the Tribunals, sensitive information may also be transmitted to the Court on the condition that it be used solely for the purpose of generating new evidence and, thus, not be subject to disclosure without the consent of the provider.[123] This may cause difficulties with respect to the rights of the accused. A telling example is the *Lubanga Dyilo* case where the conflict between the provider's confidentiality requirement and the accused's right to exculpatory disclosure led the Trial Chamber to stay the proceedings and order the release of the accused.[124] The prosecution was found to have entered into confidentiality agreements, routinely and in inappropriate circumstances, with the United Nations and others.[125] The matter was finally resolved after arrangements were made to allow the judges to review the material and make an assessment in accordance with Art. 67(2) of the ICC Statute. But the Appeals Chamber also held that the confidentiality agreement must be respected and hence that other counter-balancing measures must be considered if the provider does not

---

116 *Blaškić* ICTY A. Ch. 29.10.1997 paras. 61–6.

117 *Ibid.*, paras. 67–9.

118 Rr. 54*bis* and 70 of the ICTY RPE.

119 *Milošević* ICTY A. Ch. 23.10.2002.

120 *Milutinović et al.* ICTY A. Ch. 15.5.2006 paras. 16 and 19–20, reversing the opposite conclusion by the T. Ch. (T.Ch. III 17.11.2005).

121 Arts. 72, 73 and 93(4)–(6) of the ICC Statute. See further Donald Piragoff, 'Protection of National Security Information' in Lee, *The Making of the Rome Statute*, 270–94.

122 Art. 72(7) of the ICC Statute.

123 *Ibid.*, Arts. 54(3)(e) and 93(8).

124 *Lubanga Dyilo* ICC T. Ch. I 13.6.2008 (1401) (staying the proceedings) and 3.9.2008 (refusing to lift the stay), A. Ch. 21.10.2008 (1486) (confirming the stay), and T. Ch. I 18.11.2008 (lifting the stay).

125 *Lubanga Dyilo* ICC T. Ch. I 13.6.2008 (1401) para. 72.

agree to disclosure.[126] At the Tribunals the opposite approach applies and the exculpatory disclosure rules are explicitly made subject to confidentiality provisions vis-à-vis the information provider.[127]

20.8.3 On-site investigations

On-site investigations can be crucial for the criminal investigation and not only when the State is uncooperative. Having direct access to sites, victims and witnesses will generally be conducive to an effective and complete investigation. For example, potential witnesses may be reluctant to speak in the presence of national authorities in view of their recent experience; to be meaningful the questioning would have to be conducted by the international investigators alone. Their involvement on site will also offer an assurance that the investigative measures are taken in accordance with international standards and procedures, which in turn may preclude later challenges by the accused.

In the Tribunals, the Prosecutor's power to conduct on-site investigations is expressly laid down in the Statutes;[128] the Prosecutor may seek assistance from State authorities, but the consent of the State is not required. Coercive measures may be taken, such as search and seizure.[129] In practice, however, State permission or other involvement will often be sought and one may note that only a few domestic implementation laws authorize the Prosecutor to act independently on national territory.[130]

The ICC Statute contains provisions empowering the ICC Prosecutor to undertake certain measures on the territory of a State Party without making a request for assistance by State authorities. But being controversial, this power is normally confined to non-compulsory measures, for example taking voluntary witness statements, and may require consultations and sometimes adherence to reasonable, State-imposed conditions.[131] Exceptionally, the Pre-Trial Chamber may also authorize specific on-site measures to be taken without securing cooperation in the case of a 'failed State' that is clearly unable to execute a request;[132] arguably these also include coercive measures. But considering the importance of on-site investigations, the scope under the Statute is very narrow and reflects the horizontal approach to cooperation; the ICC is seen as a separate entity, not an extension of the national jurisdiction, and the Court's activities on the State territory are therefore an intrusion on the sovereignty of the State. However, it is not ruled out that the Prosecutor may make a request

---

126 *Lubanga Dyilo* ICC A. Ch. I 21.10.2008 (1486) paras. 3, 43–8.
127 R.68 of the ICTY RPE and (less explicit) r.68 of the ICTR RPE.
128 Art. 18(2) of the ICTY Statute and Art. 17(2) of the ICTR Statute.
129 See, e.g. *Kordić and Čerkez* ICTY T. Ch. III 25.6.1999.
130 See, e.g. German, Norwegian and Swiss law (but special permission is required). Also without legislation, some States, e.g. Sweden, allow certain measures to be taken, such as obtaining voluntary witness statements.
131 Art. 99(4) of the ICC Statute.
132 *Ibid.*, Art. 57(3)(d), and r. 115 of the ICC RPE.

for assistance in the form of an on-site investigation which goes further than what is explicitly set out in the Statute.[133]

20.8.4 Assistance regarding coercive measures

An issue of controversy is whether the ICC may, or should, issue a warrant in connection with a request to national authorities for assistance involving coercive measures. The basic principle is that the request must be executed in accordance with national procedures in the requested State, while procedures prescribed in the request must also be followed.[134] Normally, domestic law will require a judicial warrant for coercive measures, or a judicial review, and this should be sufficient. But there could be instances where there is no such judicial supervision or a review that departs from international human rights standards and the standards applicable to the international jurisdiction in question. Some therefore argue that all coercive measures taken on behalf of an international criminal tribunal or court ought to be subject to a warrant issued by that tribunal or court, or, in urgent cases, a subsequent review of the measure.[135] In Tribunal practice, judge-made warrants for coercive measures other than arrest have sometimes been issued when the measures were to be taken without the assistance of national authorities,[136] including ordering the State to permit the measures to be taken.[137] However, no general requirement of international warrants or reviews in case of State cooperation has been adopted in written law or in practice.[138] Instead, the major forms of judicial supervision by the Tribunal or Court are conducted *ex post facto* with respect to an alleged abuse of process or admissibility of evidence (see further in Chapter 17).

20.9　Domestic implementation

When international law creates obligations for States, it is not permissible to raise the objection that national law, constitutional or otherwise, prevents the honouring of the obligations.[139] Therefore, States must make sure that national law allows them to comply

---

133 See Informal Expert Paper: *Fact-finding and investigative functions*, para. 57.

134 Art. 99(1) of the ICC Statute.

135 See Sluiter, *International Criminal Adjudication*, 125–8. See also Christoph Safferling, *Towards an International Criminal Procedure* (Oxford, 2001) 108–14, 125–8 and Karel de Meester, 'Coercive Measures, Privacy Rights and Judicial Supervision in International Criminal Investigations: In Need of Further Regulation?' in Sluiter and Vasiliev, *International Criminal Procedure*, 273–309.

136 See, e.g *Kordić and Čerkez* ICTY T. Ch. III 25.6.1999 and *Naletilić and Martinović* ICTY T. Ch. IA 14.11.2001.

137 See, e.g. *Karadžić* ICTY T. Ch. (Duty Judge) 11.9.2003.

138 Both principled and practical objections could be advanced. Pre-authorization may not be possible or be time-consuming and post-authorization could be sensitive if it involves international judicial supervision of domestic measures, including the application of national law and perhaps even its compliance with international human rights standards.

139 See *Blaškić* ICTY T. Ch. II 18.7.1997 para. 84.

with their international obligations, either by direct application of international rules or by implementing legislation. This is required with respect both to the Tribunals and the ICC;[140] a request cannot be refused with reference to the absence of procedures under national law.[141] It also corresponds with the principle that requests be executed in accordance with domestic procedures. But while national law may govern procedures, it will lead to violations of the respective Statutes if it inhibits the cooperation required.[142] Cooperation with the ICC must also be provided in the manner specified in the request, unless this is specifically prohibited by national law.[143]

In practice, however, only a few States have introduced implementing legislation or concluded that the cooperation rules have direct effect in the domestic system. Such legislation, where it exists, provides a basis, inter alia, for arrest and surrender, assistance concerning evidence and witnesses, and enforcement of penalties; but the scope of cooperation and the means for providing assistance vary and States have often resorted to inter-State practices and principles.[144] The lack of domestic legislation may create serious problems in practice. Reliance on the ordinary law on extradition and mutual legal assistance to other States may not be sufficient, in the light of the significant differences between the cooperation rules and normal inter-State practice. Special legislation could also speed up the process considerably.[145] With respect to the ICC, various efforts are being made to encourage and assist States to legislate.[146] It has been suggested that the ICC itself should provide such assistance, but great care is required since the Court is the counter-party and may have to assess compliance with the cooperation duties under the Statute.[147] It should be noted that States have provided substantive assistance also without domestic legislation on cooperation; for example, a number of African States have arrested and handed over accused persons to the ICTR.[148]

The ICC Statute is a complex instrument and domestic implementation is a challenging task. Apart from legal and technical issues, the cooperation obligations have triggered questions concerning national constitutional compatibility.[149] The debates have mainly

---

140 SC Res. 827(1993) and 955(1994), and Art. 88 of the ICC Statute.

141 See, e.g. Claus Kress and Kimberly Prost, 'Article 88' in Triffterer, *Observers' Notes*, 1534.

142 See Broomhall, *International Justice*, 155.

143 See Rastan, 'Testing Co-operation', 434–5.

144 For criticism, see e.g. Antonio Cassese, 'On Current Trends Towards Criminal Prosecution and Punishment of Breaches of International Humanitarian Law' (1998) 9 *EJIL* 2 at 13–14.

145 On the Spanish process to surrender Gotovina to the ICTY (three days after his arrest), see Gamarra and Vicente, 'UN Member States' Obligations', 648–9.

146 For a collection of such legislation, see http://www.legal-tools.org.

147 See Informal Expert Paper: *Fact-finding and investigative functions*, para. 16.

148 See Broomhall, *International Justice*, 154.

149 See Helen Duffy, 'Overview of Constitutional Issues and Recent State Practice' in Claus Kreß, Bruce Broomhall, Flavia Lattanzi and Valeria Santori (eds.), *The Rome Statute and Domestic Legal Orders* (Baden-Baden, 2005), vol. II, 498–514; Darryl Robinson, 'The Rome Statute and Its Impact on National Law' in taken place concerning the ICC, but many of the same issues are also relevant with respect to the Tribunals. Common problems relate to extradition of nationals and constitutional immunities, in relation to the obligation to arrest and surrender suspects to the Tribunal or the ICC.[150] Other areas of controversy are the powers to conduct on-site investigations, life imprisonment, national amnesties and pardons. Importantly, the States cannot avoid such problems by making reservations to their obligations of cooperation.[151] On the other hand, constitutional amendments are often difficult politically, if indeed they are possible at all, and require lengthy processes. A few States, such as France, Germany and Mexico, have amended their constitutions before ratifying the ICC Statute, but most States have not and have instead interpreted the international instruments and the constitution as compatible with each other.

20.10 An assessment

The dependence upon cooperation by States and others has led to the metaphorical description of each Tribunal as a 'giant without arms or legs'.[152] The distinction between 'horizontal' and 'vertical' cooperation schemes depicts a fundamental difference in approach; the 'vertical' model attributes greater powers to the international jurisdiction and imposes greater duties on the States. The scheme of the tribunals is more 'vertical' than that of the ICC and the latter is weaker on issues such as arrest by peacekeeping forces, investigations on site and powers to bring witnesses before the Court. But although it contributes to explaining the normative framework, the distinction does little to explain why cooperation is successful or not in practice. Both models currently provide for indirect rather than direct enforcement and compliance with the cooperation obligations depends primarily upon factors that are unrelated to the judicial functions of the Tribunal or Court. In view of the difficulties of conducting international investigations and trials, and the weak sanctions regimes, neither system can be effective unless States are truly willing (and able) to assist. A breach of international obligations may come with a price, but the alternative price for complying may be higher and more direct (for example in domestic public opinion).

Both the Tribunals and the ICC are faced with instances of non-compliance or a bare minimum of cooperation. For example, the relationship between the ICTR and the Government of Rwanda has been troubled at times, with Rwanda suspending the cooperation when the Tribunal ordered the release of an accused.[153] In the Former Yugoslavia, the

Cassese, *Commentary*, 1849–60; and the Venice Commission, *Report on Constitutional Issues Raised by the Ratification of the Rome Statute of the International Court*, 45th Plenary Meeting on 15–16.12.2000.
150 See, e.g. Zsuzsanna Deen-Racsmány, 'Lessons of the European Arrest Warrant for Domestic Implementation of the Obligation to Surrender Nationals to the International Criminal Court' (2007) 20 *LJIL* 167.
151 See Art. 120 of the ICC Statute.
152 Cassese, 'On Current Trends', 13.
153 The decision in *Barayagwiza* ICTR A. Ch. 3.11.1999 was subsequently reversed (A. Ch. 31.3.2000): see sections 17.2.2 and 17.7.3.

willingness to cooperate with the ICTY has varied over time but more recent changes of government have improved the cooperation. The ICTY still has two outstanding arrest warrants against high-profile accused, the ICTR has thirteen. Over time, however, the Tribunals have been rather successful in obtaining cooperation.[154]

The ICC encounters an even more complex situation: schematically it has been described as the Democratic Republic of Congo being unable, Sudan unwilling, and Uganda in the middle of a peace process.[155] It operates in conflicts which are still ongoing and this complicates all forms of cooperation. As an example, four years after the issuance of arrest warrants in the *Situation in Uganda* all suspects remain at large. Although the current practice of 'self-referrals' of situations by States[156] includes a particular commitment to cooperate with the Court, something that the ICC Prosecutor has stressed as important,[157] practical and other circumstances may prevent effective cooperation. Moreover, the ICC's activities, and hence the need for cooperation, will in many cases occur when the State most concerned is unwilling or unable to take appropriate action itself; a paradoxical effect of the complementarity principle. How could one then expect any constructive assistance from that State? The refusal to cooperate with respect to Darfur by the Sudanese Government, concerning both the investigations and the surrender of suspects, is a telling example.

In practice, the international tribunals and courts are often cautious not to rush to depict States as uncooperative.[158] They have no real influence over and should not expect much visible action from the bodies that could impose sanctions. Instead, strong political support and more informal forms of pressure tend to be more important and effective. Hence, the decision of the African Union not to cooperate with the ICC concerning the arrest warrant against Al Bashir is potentially very damaging;[159] it is politically hazardous in spite of the fact that the linkage made between non-cooperation, Article 98, and the Security Council's non-action on the AU's request for a deferral in accordance with Article 16 of the ICC Statute, is nonsensical from a legal point of view.

The ICC cooperation regime may be strengthened and improved over time, but it is unrealistic to expect that the indirect model for enforcement will be replaced and it will therefore remain the weakest link of the Court's procedural framework.

---

154 See, e.g. Viktor Peskin, *International Justice in Rwanda and the Balkans: Virtual Trials and the Struggle for State Cooperation* (Cambridge, 2008) 237.
155 Rod Rastan, 'The responsibility to enforce – Connecting justice with unity' in Stahn and Sluiter, *Emerging Practice*, 163–82.
156 See section 8.7.4, which also notes risks arising from self-referrals.
157 Remarks by ICC Prosecutor, Luis Moreno-Ocampo at the 27th meeting of the Committee of Legal Advisers on Public International Law (CADHI), Strasburg, 18–19.3.2004.
158 Although non-compliance has been reported, for example by the ICTY; see Gabrielle Kirk McDonald, 'Problems, Obstacles and Achievements of the ICTY' (2004) 2 *JICJ* 558 at 562–7.
159 Decision by the 13th Ordinary Session of the AU Assembly 3.7.2009, doc. Assembly/AU/13(XIII).

Further reading

Antonio Cassese, Paolo Gaeta and John R. W. D. Jones (eds.), *The Rome Statute of the International Criminal Court: A Commentary* (Oxford, 2002) chs. 39–42.

Yolanda Gamarra and Alejandra Vicente, 'United Nations Member States' Obligations Towards the ICTY: Arresting and Transferring Lukić, Gotovina and Zelenenović' (2008) 8 *ICLR* 627.

Thomas Henquet, 'Mandatory Compliance Powers vis-à-vis States by the Ad Hoc Tribunals and the International Criminal Court: A Comparative Analysis' (1999) 12 *LJIL* 969.

Claus Kreß, Bruce Broomhall, Flavia Lattanzi and Valeria Santori (eds.), *The Rome Statute and Domestic Legal Orders* (Baden-Baden, 2005), vol. II.

Roy S Lee (ed.), *States' Responses to Issues Arising From the ICC Statute: Constitutional, Sovereignty, Judicial Cooperation and Criminal Law* (New York, 2005).

Valerie Oosterveld, Mike Perry and John McManus, 'The Cooperation of States with the International Criminal Court' (2002) 25 *Fordham International Law Journal* 767.

Viktor Peskin, *International Justice in Rwanda and the Balkans: Virtual Trials and the Struggle for State Cooperation* (Cambridge, 2008).

Rod Rastan, 'Testing Co-operation: The International Criminal Court and National Authorities' (2008) 21 *LJIL* 431.

Göran Sluiter, *International Criminal Adjudication and the Collection of Evidence: Obligations of States* (Antwerp, 2002).

Dagmar Stroh, 'State Cooperation with the International Criminal Tribunals for the Former Yugoslavia and for Rwanda' (2001) 5 *Max Planck Yearbook of United Nations Law* 249.

Triffterer, *Observers' Notes*.

21

Immunities

21.1 Introduction

21.1.1 Overview

The international law of immunities has ancient roots, extending back not hundreds, but thousands, of years.[1] In order to maintain channels of communication and thereby prevent and resolve conflicts, societies needed to have confidence that their envoys could have safe passage, particularly in times when emotions and distrust were at their highest. Domestic and international law developed to provide for inviolability of a foreign State's representatives and immunities from the exercise of jurisdiction over those representatives.

While immunities are valuable in preventing interference with representatives, and thereby maintaining the conduct of international relations, they can also frustrate prosecutions for very serious crimes. In recent decades, with the advent of the human rights movement, States have taken stronger and stronger steps to prosecute international criminals. This emboldened State practice has brought to the fore many hidden or unresolved questions as to the boundaries between principles of accountability and immunity.

While international priorities are shifting in favour of justice and accountability, it would be an oversimplification to assume that international criminal law has simply superseded immunities law. Commentators have at times assumed that no immunity of any kind may be raised in response to allegations of genocide, crimes against humanity or war crimes.[2] However, such a view overlooks different kinds of immunities, and is contradicted by the

---

1 Linda S. Frey and Marsha L. Frey, *The History of Diplomatic Immunity* (Columbus, 1999); J. Craig Barker, *The Abuse of Diplomatic Privileges and Immunities: A Necessary Evil?* (Dartmouth, 1996) 14–31; Montell Ogdon, *Juridical Bases of Diplomatic Immunity* (Washington DC, 1936) 8–20; Grant V. McLanahan, *Diplomatic Immunity* (New York, 1989) 18–25.

2 See, e.g. Andrea Bianchi, 'Immunity versus Human Rights: The Pinochet Case' (1999) 10 *EJIL* 237. See also the comprehensive study by Amnesty International, *Universal Jurisdiction: The Duty of States to Enact and Implement Legislation*, Sept. 2001, AI Index IOR 53/2001, ch. 14.

great bulk of State practice and jurisprudence.[3] Even the landmark precedents narrowing immunities explicitly affirm that there are still some immunities which apply even with regard to allegations of serious international crimes.[4]

A recurring argument against immunity is that the prohibitions of international crimes are *ius cogens*, and therefore any immunities must give way to the 'higher value' of ensuring prosecution.[5] Such arguments have been considered and rejected in an extensive line of national cases in various countries as well as at the European Court of Human Rights and the International Court of Justice.[6] As was recently observed by the House of Lords in the *Jones* case,[7] the argument depends on a false conflict – *ius cogens* prohibits *committing* the crimes; it does not mean that all international laws regarding *prosecution* cease to apply.[8]

As was explained by three judges of the ICJ, the principle that serious crimes must be punished:

> ... does not *ipso facto* mean that immunities are unavailable whenever impunity would be the outcome ... [I]mmunities serve other purposes which have their own intrinsic value and ... [i]international law seeks the accommodation of this value with the fight against impunity, and not the triumph of one norm over the other. A State may exercise the criminal jurisdiction which it has under international law, but in doing so it is subject to other legal obligations ...[9]

Thus, a more sophisticated approach is needed in order to understand this area of law. It will be necessary to appreciate the underlying principles and protected values, to distinguish between 'functional' immunity and 'personal' immunity and to distinguish between national and international courts.

The interplay of international criminal law and immunities is complex, and the jurisprudence and authorities have been described as perplexing, contradictory, confused or

---

3 See sections 21.3 and 21.4.

4 Art. 27 of the ICC Statute is often cited as declaring that there are no immunities, yet Art. 98 explicitly contemplates that some persons will not be surrendered to the ICC because of their immunities, unless a waiver is obtained. In the *Pinochet* decision, each one of the seven law lords emphasized that had Pinochet been a *current* head of State, he would have received absolute immunity *ratione personae*, even against charges of torture or crimes against humanity.

5 See, e.g. Bianchi, 'Immunity', 265.

6 See, e.g. *Al-Adsani* v. *United Kingdom* App. No. 35763/97, (2002) 34 EHRR 11; *Tachiona* v. *Mugabe*, 169 F. Supp. 2d 259 (SDNY, 2001); *Jones* v. *Kingdom of Saudi Arabia* [2006] UKHL 26, [2006] 2 WLR 1424, considering and rejecting arguments based on *ius cogens*, as well as the ICJ *Yerodia* decision, discussed in section 21.4.2.

7 *Jones* v. *Kingdom of Saudi Arabia* [2006] UKHL 26, [2006] 2 WLR 1424 at paras. 24–8 and 43–63.

8 Hazel Fox, *The Law of State Immunity* (Oxford, 2004); Lee Caplan, 'State Immunity, Human Rights and Jus Cogens: A Critique of the Normative Hierarchy Theory' (2003) 97 AJIL 741; Andrea Gattini, 'War Crimes and State Immunity in the *Ferrini* Decision' (2005) 3 *JICJ* 224. But see Lorna McGregor, 'Torture and State Immunity: Deflecting Impunity, Distorting Sovereignty' (2007) 18 *EJIL* 903 noting that formalistic arguments should not obscure the fact that upholding immunity can lead to impunity.

9 Joint Separate Opinion of Judges Higgins, Kooijmans and Buergenthal, para. 79, in the *Yerodia* judgment, discussed in section 21.4.2.

incoherent.[10] However, if one keeps in mind the above-mentioned distinctions and the underlying purposes of the rules, one will find that a fairly consistent and coherent set of rules is emerging. The fact that the law reflects a balance means that this balance may of course continue to shift over time.

This chapter discusses the immunities of individuals in relation to criminal prosecution for international crimes, in national and international courts. Personal immunities in civil proceedings and questions of State immunity are not discussed here. Nor does this chapter deal with immunities of heads of State or high officials in their own countries, which are governed primarily by national law.

21.1.2 Functional and personal immunity

With respect to immunity from prosecution, a fundamental distinction must be made between 'functional immunity' (also known as immunity *ratione materiae*) and 'personal immunity' (also known as immunity *ratione personae*).

Functional immunity protects *conduct* carried out on behalf of a State. It is linked to the maxim that a State may not sit in judgment on the policies and actions of another State, since they are both sovereign and equal. If a State could bring criminal proceedings against the individual officials who carried out official functions of another State, the State would be doing indirectly what it cannot do directly, namely, acting as the arbiter of the conduct of another State. Functional immunity attaches to a comparatively large class of officials – all who carry out State functions. Significantly, functional immunity does not provide complete protection of the person, it only covers conduct that was an official act of a State. Thus, for example, criminal activity carried out in a private capacity remains subject to prosecution. As will be discussed below, an exception to functional immunity has emerged whereby international crimes may also be prosecuted.

Personal immunity is not limited to any particular conduct; it provides complete immunity of the *person* of certain office-holders while they carry out important representative functions. Personal immunity is granted only to a comparatively small set of people, such as heads of State and diplomats accredited to a host country. It is temporary, in that it lasts only for as long as the person is serving in that representative role. There is no exception based on the seriousness of the alleged crime, or whether the acts were private or official, because the rationale is unconnected to the nature of the charge. The rationale was stated in 1740 by Wicquefort:

> ... if Princes had the Liberty of Proceeding against the Embassador who negotiates with them on any Account, or under any Colour whatsoever, the Person of the Embassador

---

10 Rosanne van Alebeek, 'The Pinochet Case: International Human Rights Law on Trial' (2001) 71 *BYBIL* 29 at 47; J. Craig Barker, 'The Future of Former Head of State Immunity After *Ex Parte Pinochet*' (1999) 48 *ICLQ* 937 at 938.

> would never be in Safety; because those who should have a Mind to make away with Him would never want a Pretext.[11]

In other words, personal immunity is absolute, but it attaches to a limited set of official roles and it endures only while the person enjoys the official position which attracts the immunity. Conversely, functional immunity protects only conduct carried out in the course of the individual's duties, but does not drop away when a person's role comes to an end, since it protects the conduct, not the person. For both types of immunity, the purpose is not to benefit the individual,[12] but to protect official acts (functional immunity) or to facilitate international relations (personal immunity). It is the State which is the real beneficiary of the immunity, and it is the State which may waive it, irrespective of the wishes of the person claiming the immunity.

The existence of immunity does not mean that there is a lack of substantive legal responsibility, but rather that a foreign State is procedurally prevented from bringing proceedings against the alleged offender. Thus immunities are not a 'defence' as such.[13] As merely procedural bars, immunities may be waived by the State concerned.

21.1.3 Examples of immunities

The most well-developed and well-defined area of immunities is that of diplomatic immunities. Centuries of State practice with diplomatic relations have produced considerable precision as to the rules. The law is now codified in the Vienna Convention on Diplomatic Relations 1961. While serving in a host country, diplomatic agents enjoy personal immunity: they are immune from criminal jurisdiction, their person is inviolable and they may not be arrested or detained.[14] Diplomats also enjoy immunity in third States while in transit between their sending State and host State.[15] After their term of service in the host country has ended, diplomats continue to enjoy functional immunity for acts in the exercise of their functions.[16] If the diplomat commits a serious crime, the recourse available to the host State is to request a waiver of immunity from the sending State[17] or to declare the

---

11 A. van Wicquefort, *The Embassador and his Functions*, 2nd edn (London, 1740) (translated into English by John Digby) 251, quoted in Ogdon, *Juridical Bases*, 128–9.
12 Vienna Convention on Diplomatic Relations ('VCDR') 1961, preamble, paras. 2–4.
13 A claim to functional immunity may also bring with it a claim under the 'act of State doctrine', under which national courts of one State may decline to examine the acts of another State. This is a matter of substantive law and, along with the fact that it applies only to particular conduct, probably explains why functional immunity is sometimes referred to as a substantive defence: Hazel Fox, *The Law of State Immunity*, 2nd edn (Oxford, 2008) 93–7.
14 Arts. 29 and 31 of the VCDR.
15 *Ibid.*, Art. 40.
16 *Ibid.*, Art. 39(1).
17 *Ibid.*, Art. 32.

diplomat *persona non grata*.[18] After the diplomat's term is over (and after a reasonable time for departure has elapsed), the diplomat enjoys only functional immunity, and thus the host authorities may prosecute the diplomat for any crimes committed in a non-official capacity, if they can acquire custody of him or her. Other members of a diplomatic mission enjoy lesser degrees of immunity,[19] as do consular officials.[20]

The contours of head of State immunity are less well defined. There is no codifying convention and State practice on point is limited. The lack of State practice is probably in part a reflection of the immunity and in part due to the reluctance of States to interfere with heads of State.[21] Even the conceptual foundations of the immunity are unclear.[22] It is widely accepted however that heads of State enjoy at least the same immunities as ambassadors: absolute personal immunity while in office[23] and afterwards, functional immunity for official acts carried out while in office.[24]

While head of State immunity is well established, the position of heads of government and other ministers has not always been so clear.[25] In *DRC* v. *Belgium*, the International Court of Justice upheld personal immunity for ministers of foreign affairs, analogous to that of heads of State.[26] This conclusion is understandable in that the post fulfils similar representative roles. Similar principles undoubtedly apply to a head of government, such as a prime minister – whose representative function is more sensitive than a minister of foreign affairs and, in many systems, the head of State.[27] As will be discussed in section 21.4.2, it is unclear whether other ministers enjoy this immunity as well.[28]

---

18 *Ibid.*, Art. 9.

19 *Ibid.*, Art. 37(3).

20 Vienna Convention on Consular Relations 1963.

21 In a recent exception, French authorities issued a witness summons to the head of State of Djibouti, a matter brought to the ICJ by Djibouti in *Certain Questions of Mutual Assistance in Criminal Matters (Djibouti* v. *France)* 4.6.2008. The Court held that as the summons was only an invitation, there was no violation by France of its obligations to Djibouti.

22 Some treat it as a type of State immunity and others as a type of diplomatic immunity, but neither of these analogies is entirely apt, so it seems most accurate to regard head of State as a separate category. Diplomatic immunity provides the closer analogy, although a head of State is not posted in the host State. See, e.g. Jerrold Mallory, 'Resolving the Confusion Over Head of State Immunity: The Defined Right of Kings' (1986) 86 *Columbia Law Review* 169; Jürgen Bröhmer, *State Immunity and the Violation of Human Rights* (Martinus Nijhoff, 1997) 29–32.

23 Charles Lewis, *State and Diplomatic Immunity*, 3rd edn (Lloyd's of London Press, 1999) 125; *R.* v. *Bow Street Metropolitan Stipendiary Magistrate ex parte Pinochet Ugarte (No. 3)* [1999] 2 All ER 97, HL at 111, 119–20, 152, 168–9, 179 and 181.

24 Lord Gore Booth (ed.), *Satow's Guide to Diplomatic Practice*, 5th edn (Longman, 1979) 9.

25 Arthur Watts, 'The Legal Position in International Law of Heads of State, Heads of Government and Foreign Ministers' (1994–III) 247 *Hague Recueil* 97–113.

26 See section 21.4.2.

27 Watts, 'Legal Position', 97–113.

28 See discussion of *Yerodia* in section 21.4.2; and see the *Mofaz* case, concluding that a Minister of Defence enjoys personal immunity but expressing doubts with respect to several other types of minister, reproduced (2004) 53 *ICLQ* 769.

State representatives travelling to participate in meetings of international organizations enjoy immunities provided in the relevant treaties, which typically include personal immunity.[29] In addition, when a State hosts a major summit or meeting outside the context of an international organization (such as a G8 summit), it is typical practice to extend immunity to visiting delegates.[30] The Convention on Special Missions (1969) sought to provide a general regime for visits of officials to another State, with the consent of that State, 'for the purpose of dealing with it on specific questions or performing in relation to it a specific task'.[31] That convention has not been widely ratified.[32]

Certain officials of international organizations, such as the United Nations or the International Criminal Court, enjoy immunities as provided in specific conventions.[33] In general, personal immunity is granted sparingly and reserved for the highest officials. Most officials receive only functional immunity even while on official missions.[34]

While this chapter is focused on criminal proceedings, a brief word should be offered with respect to State immunity from civil proceedings. Under the customary law principle of State immunity, a State (and hence its assets) may not be subjected to civil proceedings in foreign courts, unless it chooses to submit to such courts. However, this immunity is subject to many exceptions. For example, a State is not immune in relation to its commercial activities, or for acts causing death or injury that are committed in the territory of the forum State. There have been many proposals for a 'human rights' or 'international crime' exception to State immunity, although such proposals have met with little success at this time.[35]

---

29 See, e.g. in the context of the UN, the Convention on the Privileges and Immunities of the United Nations 1946, 1 UNTS 15.

30 See, e.g. a typical Canadian regulation, the G8 Summit Privileges and Immunities Order, 2002, PC 2002–828.

31 Convention on Special Missions 1969, Art. 1(a).

32 The immunities are analogous to those in the VCDR: Convention on Special Missions 1969, Arts. 29 and 31. While some commentators believe that aspects of it may reflect customary law (Watts, 'Legal Position', 38), others have concluded that it goes beyond State practice in the extent of immunity it confers: *United States* v. *Sissoko* (1997) 121 IR 599.

33 See, e.g. Convention on the Privileges and Immunities of the United Nations 1946; Agreement on Privileges and Immunities of the International Criminal Court 2002.

34 See, e.g. Convention on the Privileges and Immunities of the United Nations 1946, Art. V, ss. 18–19, granting full diplomatic immunities to the Secretary-General and Assistant Secretary-Generals and functional immunity to other staff.

35 *Princz* v. *Federal Republic of Germany* 26 F. 3d 1166 (DC Cir. 1994); *Al-Adsani* v. *Government of Kuwait* (1996) 107 ILR 536, England CA; *Al-Adsani* v. *United Kingdom* App. No. 35763/97, (2002) 34 EHRR 11; *Tachiona* v. *Mugabe*, 169 F. Supp. 2d 259 (SDNY, 2001); *Jones* v. *Kingdom of Saudi Arabia* [2006] UKHL 26, [2006] 2 WLR 1424; but see the anomalous Greek case concerning the Distomo massacre, discussed in Ilias Bantekas, 'Prefecture of Voiotia v. Federal Republic of Germany' (1998) 92 *AJIL* 765, which was doubted in subsequent Greek cases and rejected by the German Supreme Court in *Distomo Massacre* (2003) 42 ILM 1030. Italian cases, such as *Ferrini*, have, however, held that they could set aside the immunities of Germany; Germany has now brought the question before the ICJ in *Jurisdictional Immunities of the State (Germany* v. *Italy)*, which at the time of writing has yet to be considered by the Court. State immunity was also addressed in the United Nations Convention on Jurisdictional Immunities of States and Their Property, UN. Doc A/59/508, adopted 2.12.2004, not yet in force; it has been noted that the Convention contains no 'human rights' exception to State immunity.

21.1.4 *Underlying rationales and values*

Historically, various rationales have been put forward in support of immunities. Some of these were legal fictions, such as 'extraterritoriality' (the fiction that the premises of the mission represented an extension of the sending State's territory), 'personal representation' (that the ambassador is equivalent to his or her head of State), or 'personification' (that the head of State personifies the State).[36] Respect for the 'dignity' of the head of State or the sending State has also been a major consideration,[37] as has political expediency – the desire to avoid controversy with other nations.[38]

In the last century, and especially in recent decades, there has been a considerable demystification in this area, such that legal fictions are no longer plausible bases for immunities.[39] Moreover, with increasing emphasis on human rights, neither dignity nor political expediency is a compelling reason to preclude *a priori* accountability for serious international crimes.

With respect to functional immunity, the remaining rationale is the principle that one State may not sit in judgment on another State (also known as *par in parem non habet iudicium*). This is an attribute of sovereign equality. This is why international law insists that disputes between States may only be brought to appropriate forums with the agreement of States. If a State could prosecute officials for acts of another State, it would indirectly be passing judgment on another State, and could even use prosecutions to force changes in policies of the other State. As is discussed below, however,[40] an exception has emerged for some or all serious international crimes.

The rationale for personal immunity is its value in facilitating international relations. The ICJ has described the inviolability of diplomatic envoys as the most fundamental prerequisite for the conduct of relations between States.[41] The institution of diplomacy is 'an instrument essential for effective co-operation in the international community, and for enabling States, irrespective of their differing constitutional and social systems, to achieve mutual understanding and to resolve their differences by peaceful means'.[42] The existing system of diplomatic relations has made possible global summits, the creation of international organizations, and development of treaties creating today's corpus of laws. It has enabled diplomats to work in antagonistic States to protect nationals and to avert or end escalating conflicts. It also enables UN human rights rapporteurs and international

---

36 See Ogdon, *Juridical Bases*, 63–165; Robert Jennings and Arthur Watts, *Oppenheim's International Law*, 9th edn (London, 1992) 1034.
37 See *Schooner Exchange* v. *M'Fadden* 11 US 116 (1812) 137.
38 See, e.g. *Tachiona* v. *Mugabe*, 169 F. Supp. 2d 259 (SDNY, 2001) 290–1.
39 See, e.g. Watts, 'Legal Position', 35–6.
40 Section 21.2.
41 *United States Diplomatic and Consular Staff in Iran* (*US* v. *Iran*), Merits, 1980 ICJ Rep 3 para. 91.
42 *Ibid.*

prosecutors to carry out their work in States that might welcome pretexts to frustrate their work.[43]

On the other hand, immunities have also had many perverse effects, shielding persons responsible for spectacular abuses and crimes. This has often led to public outcry. Recently, with the increased prioritization of human rights and the rule of law, governments have become more assertive and immunities have rightly come under scrutiny and pressure.

Two main methods have been employed to rebalance the goals served by immunities with the goal of ending impunity. Both methods were foreshadowed by the Nuremberg Charter, but it is only recently that international practice has followed up on these ideas. The first method was to declare that functional immunity, which protects State conduct from scrutiny, does not extend to international crimes (21.2 and 21.3). That solution is not transposable to personal immunity, because such immunity is not based on any authorization of the act, but rather the need to enable international discourse by precluding any pretext to interfere with high representatives (see section 21.4). However, Nuremberg serves as a precedent on how to deal with this problem as well: the creation of international criminal tribunals authorized to set aside even personal immunity (see section 21.5). After many decades of neglect, the international community has rather suddenly started to make impressive strides in both of these avenues.

21.2 Functional immunity and national courts

The question of immunities in respect of the prosecution of international crimes may arise before national courts in different ways. A State may wish to prosecute a current or former official of another State, may wish to request extradition, or may receive a request for extradition.[44] Traditionally, national governments and courts were so cautious and deferential in the area of immunities that controversial efforts at prosecution simply did not arise; in recent times, this has begun to change.[45]

21.2.1 The Pinochet precedent

In 1998, Senator Augusto Pinochet, former head of State of Chile, was visiting the UK when Spain issued a request for his extradition. The charges included torture and conspiracy to torture. Pinochet was arrested by British authorities. He applied to have the warrants quashed, inter alia, on the ground that as a former head of State he was entitled to immunity.

---

43 See, e.g. *Difference Relating to Immunity from Legal Process of a Special Rapporteur of the Commission on Human Rights*, Advisory Opinion, 1999 ICJ Rep 100.

44 Examples of the first scenario are the *Mugabe* and *Qaddafi* cases (see section 21.4.1); an example of the second scenario is the Belgian case against Yerodia (see section 21.4.2), and the *Pinochet* case (see section 21.2.1) is an example of the third scenario.

45 Michael Byers, 'The Law and Politics of the Pinochet Case' (2000) 10 *Duke Journal of Comparative and International Law* 415.

In the first hearing of the immunity issue, at the level of the Divisional Court, three judges, applying a classically deferential approach to immunities, unanimously upheld Senator Pinochet's claim and quashed the warrant.[46] The court applied the established proposition that a former head of State 'ceases to enjoy any immunity in respect of *personal or private* acts but continues to enjoy immunity in respect of *public* acts performed by him as head of State'.[47] Since Pinochet was charged 'not with personally torturing or murdering victims or causing their disappearance, but with using the power of the State of which he was head to that end',[48] the judges concluded that they could hardly be described as 'private' acts and therefore had to be official acts. They rejected the argument that serious international crimes could not be functions of a head of State.[49] Immunity from criminal jurisdiction must include criminal conduct, as such immunity would otherwise be entirely pointless.[50] The court considered the possibility of an exception restricted to serious international crimes, but rejected it as it would be unclear where to draw the line.[51] The Nuremberg Charter, ICTY Statute and ICTR Statute were distinguished on the grounds that 'these were international tribunals, established by international agreement. They did not therefore violate the principle that one sovereign State will not implead another in relation to its sovereign acts.'[52]

At the first House of Lords hearing, following the intervention of *amici curiae* and a more detailed review of developments in international law, three out of five judges were persuaded that former head of State immunity did not cover such serious international crimes.[53] The essence of the decision was that the commission of certain serious international crimes, contrary to *ius cogens*, is condemned by all States as illegal and therefore cannot also be protected by international law as an 'official function'. However, a rehearing was necessitated by the possible appearance of bias of one of the judges in the first hearing, who had some (fairly slender) affiliations with Amnesty International, one of the intervenors.[54]

At the third and final House of Lords hearing (the second appeal hearing on the merits of the claim for immunity), six out of seven judges confirmed that the immunity of a former head of State did not prevent his extradition for torture.[55] Each of the judges in

---

46 *Re Pinochet Ugarte* [1998] All ER (D) 629; [1998] EWJ No. 2878 (QB Div Ct 1998) (Quicklaw).

47 *Ibid*., at para. 56 (Quicklaw citation) (emphasis added).

48 *Ibid*., at para. 58.

49 *Ibid*., at paras. 63–5 and 80.

50 *Ibid*., at para. 63.

51 *Ibid*.

52 *Ibid*., at para. 68.

53 *R. v. Bow Street Metropolitan Stipendiary Magistrate and others ex parte Pinochet Ugarte (No. 1)* [1998] 4 All ER 897, HL.

54 *R. v. Bow Street Metropolitan Stipendiary Magistrate and others ex parte Pinochet Ugarte (No. 2)* [1999] 1 All ER 577, HL.

55 *R. v. Bow Street Metropolitan Stipendiary Magistrate and others ex parte Pinochet Ugarte (No. 3)* [1999] 2 All ER 97, HL (hereafter '*Pinochet 3*').

the third hearing issued a separate opinion, and the reasoning within each opinion was not always clear. As a result, the judgment is one of those gems of the common law system in which, however important the decision, it is difficult to identify the *ratio decidendi*. Commentators tend to emphasize different passages and offer different interpretations, and thereby arrive at different views as to the basis of the decision. It is beyond the scope of this introductory text to provide a detailed analysis, but the following observations illustrate the open questions concerning the rationale as well as the scope of the decision.

The most cautious interpretation, restricted to the terms of the 1984 Torture Convention, is that, where official involvement is a necessary element of a crime, there cannot be immunity by reason of official involvement; otherwise the crime would be vacated of content.[56] As noted by Lord Millett, '[t]he offence is one which could only be committed in circumstances which would normally give rise to the immunity ... International law cannot be supposed to have established a crime having the character of *ius cogens* and at the same time to have provided an immunity which is co-extensive with the obligation it seeks to impose.'[57] Support for this reading can be found in the opinions of Lords Browne-Wilkinson, Saville and Phillips.[58]

Another reading is that international crimes cannot constitute 'official functions' and hence do not give rise to functional immunity. Such a reading may be supported from passages of Lord Browne-Wilkinson and Lord Hutton.[59] However, the approach of denying the official character of the acts does not appear to find support among a majority of the judges. Several judges noted that the mere fact that conduct is criminal does not per se change its governmental character.[60] In any event, such an approach would create contradictions, given that for the crime of torture, official participation is an element of the crime, so official character would have to be asserted in order to gain jurisdiction and then denied in order to avoid immunity. To say such crimes are not 'official' is also counter-factual when the crimes are in fact committed through the apparatus of the State; moreover such an approach could obscure State responsibility for the act.[61]

---

56 See, e.g. Colin Warbrick, Elena Martin Salgado and Nicholas Goodwin, 'The Pinochet Cases in the United Kingdom' (1999) 2 *Yearbook of International Humanitarian Law* 91; Barker, 'Future of Former Head of State Immunity'; Eileen Denza, '*Ex Parte Pinochet*: Lacuna or Leap?' (1999) 48 *ICLQ* 949; van Alebeek, 'Pinochet Case'; Dapo Akande, 'International Law Immunities and the International Criminal Court' (2004) 98 *AJIL* 407 at 415.

57 *Pinochet 3* at 179.

58 *Ibid.*, at 114–15 (Browne-Wilkinson), 169 (Saville) and 190 (Phillips).

59 *Ibid.*, at 113 (Browne-Wilkinson) and 166 (Hutton).

60 *Ibid.*, at 172 (Millett), 147 (Hope), 119 (Goff) and 187 (Phillips).

61 Antonio Cassese, 'When May Senior State Officials Be Tried for International Crimes? Some Comments on the *Congo* v. *Belgium* Case' (2002) 13 *EJIL* 853; Marina Spinedi, 'State Responsibility v. Individual Responsibility for International Crimes: *Tertium Non Datur?*' (2002) 13 *EJIL* 895; Barker, 'Future of Former Head of State Immunity', 943 and 948.

A more sophisticated variation on that reading is that international crimes are not a type of official conduct that attracts functional immunity.[62] Functional immunity protects certain conduct, but it would be contradictory for international law to protect conduct and at the same time condemn it and require its prosecution.[63] On this view, one would interpret the speeches of Lords Browne-Wilkinson and Hutton not as denying any official character of the acts, but as indicating that these acts 'could not rank *for immunity purposes* as perform-ance of an official function' (emphasis added).[64] Lord Phillips appears to come into this camp: 'where international crime is concerned, that principle [that one State cannot judge another] cannot prevail'; 'no immunity *ratione materiae* could exist for … a crime contrary to international law'.[65] Lord Hope may also be interpreted as not permitting functional immunity for serious international crimes: 'the obligations which were recognised by customary law in the case of such serious international crimes … are so strong as to override any objection … on the ground of immunity *ratione materiae*'.[66] Passages by Lord Millett may also fall within this camp, as he cites with approval the *Eichmann* case as authority that official authority is no bar to the exercise of jurisdiction for certain interna-tional crimes, and then refers to *ius cogens* crimes on a large scale, including murder.[67]

In addition to these differing interpretations of the *legal basis* for loss of immunity, there are differing possibilities as to the *scope* of the rule. On the first approach mentioned above, the scope would be limited to torture and other crimes specifically requiring official participation as an element of the crime;[68] on the latter approaches, the rule is broader, potentially covering all serious international crimes.

There are also many possible different readings as to whether the result flows from treaty, from general customary international law or, more specifically, from *ius cogens*, because all three concepts were referenced extensively. Most of the judges found that the entry into force of the Torture Convention 1984 (or its ratification by Chile or the UK, or its incorporation into UK law) was significant, although one may discern many possible reasons for this significance: creating an obligation upon Chile, authorizing UK courts to act or establishing dual criminality.[69] At the same time, the judges also referred extensively

---

62 See, e.g. Christine Chinkin, 'Regina v. Bow Street Stipendiary Magistrate, Ex Parte Pinochet Ugarte (No. 3)' (1999) 93 *AJIL* 703; Steffen Wirth, 'Immunities, Related Problems, and Article 98 of the Rome Statute' (2001) 12 *CLF* 429; Claus Kreß, 'War Crimes Committed in Non-International Armed Conflict and the Emerging System of International Criminal Justice' (2000) 30 *Israel Yearbook on Human Rights* 103 at 158–9.
63 Note that such reasoning would not apply to personal immunity, because personal immunity does not protect '*conduct*', it protects persons in particular high representative *roles* from interference on any grounds.
64 *Pinochet 3* at 114 (Browne-Wilkinson), 166 (Hutton).
65 *Ibid.*, at 190.
66 *Ibid.*, at 152.
67 *Ibid.*, at 176–7.
68 Warbrick et al., 'The Pinochet Cases', 113–14.
69 See, e.g. *Pinochet 3* at 144 (Hope), 164 (Hutton); but see 178 (Millet) and see discussion in Bruce Broomhall, *International Justice and the International Criminal Court: Between Sovereignty and the Rule of Law* (Oxford, 2003) 133ff.

to customary international law and *ius cogens*, and the reasoning they employed would encompass not only torture under the Torture Convention but other crimes as well.

Some judges indicated that a single act of torture would not suffice to override functional immunity, and that it would have to constitute a crime against humanity, that is to say 'widespread or systematic torture as an instrument of State policy'.[70] At least one judge felt that a single act of torture would suffice (presumably with respect to States Parties to the Torture Convention).[71]

The basis of the *Pinochet* decision, and thus the extent of its implications, remains shrouded in some uncertainty. For the purposes of UK law the decision has been interpreted in a subsequent House of Lords case as standing only for the narrower proposition;[72] that does not mean that other States have to regard it as exhaustive of international law on the matter, which is discussed in the next section.

21.2.2 The scope of the exception to functional immunities

A considerable body of international cases, national cases, other State practice and academic commentary supports the view that functional immunity does not preclude prosecution for serious international crimes, which is consistent with the broader reading of *Pinochet*. However, as will be discussed in this section, the failure of the ICJ to mention the principle, as well as a few outlying cases, means that the proposition is not free from doubt.

Authorities indicating no functional immunities for core crimes

As the Nuremberg Judgment observed:

> The principle of international law which, under certain circumstances, protects the representative of a State cannot be applied to acts which are condemned as criminal by international law. The authors of these acts cannot shelter themselves behind their official position in order to be freed from punishment ... [I]ndividuals have duties which transcend the national obligations of obedience imposed by the individual State. He who violates the laws of war cannot obtain immunity while acting in pursuance of the authority of the State, if the State in authorizing action moves outside its competence under international law.[73]

The legal theory underlying this proposition is compelling. First, functional immunity protects State conduct from scrutiny, but it would be incongruous for international law to protect the very conduct which it criminalizes and for which it imposes duties to prosecute. Second, the State cannot complain that its sovereignty is being restricted or that a policy is

---

70 *Pinochet 3* at 144–5 and 150–1 (Hope); see also 177 (Millet), 188 (Phillips).
71 *Ibid.*, at 166 (Lord Hutton).
72 See *Jones* v. *Kingdom of Saudi Arabia* [2006] UKHL 26, [2006] 2 WLR 1124, paras. 19 and 79–81.
73 Judgment of the International Military Tribunal (Nuremberg) 41 *AJIL* (1947) 172 at 221.

being imposed on it, when the prohibited conduct is recognized by all as an international crime. Third, from the perspective of the perpetrator, State agents are normally able to pass responsibility for dubious activities to the State that authorized them, but in the case of serious international crimes, 'individuals have international duties which transcend the national obligations of obedience',[74] and hence they are rightly held to account. Finally, it is also sound in terms of balancing the underlying values; where an individual possesses only functional immunity, international law already reflects that such an individual is no longer playing a high representative role which necessitates absolute immunity.

The proposition was endorsed by the International Law Commission and the General Assembly as principle III of the Nuremberg principles[75] and has subsequently been reconfirmed by the International Law Commission.[76]

The principle was applied in subsequent national cases. In *Eichmann*, the Israeli Supreme Court rejected a plea by Eichmann that he was carrying out official activities and held that:

> There is no basis for the doctrine when the matter pertains to acts prohibited by the law of nations, especially when they are international crimes of the class of 'crimes against humanity' (in the wide sense). [S]uch acts ... are completely outside the 'sovereign' jurisdiction of the State that ordered or ratified their commission, and therefore those who participated in such acts must personally account for them and cannot shelter behind the official character of their task or mission ...[77]

More recently, in *Bouterse*, the Amsterdam Court of Appeal held with respect to the former head of State of Suriname that serious international crimes such as crimes against humanity did not constitute 'official functions' for the purpose of functional immunity.[78] A Belgian court in the *Sharon* case, Spanish authorities requesting extradition of Pinochet, and a Spanish court in the *Castro* case all indicated that there was no functional immunity for serious international crimes, as did a committee of jurists appointed by the African Union recommending prosecution of Hassan Habré, former head of State of Chad.[79]

---

[74] Trial of the Major War Criminals before the International Military Tribunal, vol. I, Nuremberg 1947, page 223.

[75] Affirmation of the Principles of International Law recognized by the Charter of the Nuremberg Tribunal, Resolution 95 (I) of the United Nations General Assembly, 11 December 1946; Principles of the Nuremberg Tribunal, Report of the International Law Commission Covering its Second Session, 5 June–29 July 1950, Document A/1316, pp. 11–14 and commentaries in *Yearbook of the International Law Commission*, 1950, vol. II, pp. 374–8.

[76] See, e.g. Draft Code of Crimes against the Peace and Security of Mankind, *Yearbook of the International Law Commission*, 1996, vol. II (Part Two), Article 7.

[77] *A.G of Israel* v. *Eichmann* (1968) 36 ILR 277 at 308–10. The discussion was in the context of 'act of State' but, as noted by Lord Millet in *Pinochet 3*, the principles are the very same (*Pinochet 3* at 176).

[78] *Bouterse* (2000) 51 *Nederlandse Jurisprudentie* 302. An appeal was granted by the Supreme Court on other, jurisdictional, grounds.

[79] See 'Immunity of State officials from criminal jurisdiction, memorandum by the Secretariat', UN Doc. A/CN.4/596, 31 March 2008 at paras. 180–90; Antonio Cassese, 'The Belgian Court of Cassation v. The International Court of Justice: The *Sharon and Others* Case' 1 *JICJ* (2003) 437 at 443–50.

The proposition has also been supported by international criminal tribunals. For example, in *Blaškić*, the ICTY recognized functional immunity as a 'well-established rule of customary international law', with the exception that those responsible for 'war crimes, crimes against humanity and genocide ... cannot invoke immunity from national or international jurisdiction even if they perpetrated such crimes while acting in their official capacity'.[80]

The proposition is also supported in the literature.[81]

An open question?

While the trend of these authorities seems clear, there are a few judgments that leave a possibility of doubt. The most important of these is the failure of the ICJ to mention such an exception in the *DRC* v. *Belgium* case (discussed in section 21.4). In a paragraph of *obiter dicta*, the ICJ mentioned that a former foreign minister may be tried for acts committed during his or her period of office in a *private capacity*.[82] This appears to omit the exception that former officials can also be tried for any acts which constitute serious international crimes, whether in a 'private capacity' or not. The omission was conspicuous, and it was extensively criticized by commentators.[83] The omission was also puzzling in that both parties to the dispute – DRC and Belgium – agreed that functional immunity is not a bar to prosecution for international crime.[84] As already discussed (in section 21.2.1), one solution might be to say that international crimes are not 'official' acts but rather 'private' acts,[85] but such a solution raises its own problems.[86] As the paragraph was merely *obiter dicta*, providing a series of examples rather than a closed list, most subsequent national decisions have continued to assert an exception for international crimes.[87]

---

80 *Blaškić* ICTY A. Ch. 24.10.1997 para. 41. See also *Furundžija* ICTY T. Ch. II 10.12.1998 para. 140.

81 See, e.g. *Princeton Principles on Universal Jurisdiction* (Princeton University, 2001) 48–50; Paola Gaeta, 'Official Capacity and Immunities' in Cassese, *Commentary*, 981; Cassese, 'Senior State Officials'; Steffen Wirth, 'Immunity for Core Crimes? The ICJ's Judgment in the *Congo* v. *Belgium* Case' (2002) 13 *EJIL* 877; Hugh King, 'Immunities and Bilateral Agreements: Issues Arising from Articles 27 and 98 of the Rome Statute', (2006) *New Zealand Journal of Public and International Law* 269; Watts, 'Legal Position', 4.

82 *Case Concerning the Arrest Warrant of 11 April 2000 (Democratic Republic of Congo* v. *Belgium)* ICJ Rep 2002 at para. 61.

83 See, e.g. Cassese, 'Senior State Officials'; Wirth, 'Immunity for Core Crimes?'; David Koller, 'Immunities of Foreign Ministers: Paragraph 61 of the *Yerodia* Judgment as it Pertains to the Security Council and the International Criminal Court' (2004) 20 *American University International Law Review* 7; Paolo Gaeta, '*Ratione Materiae* Immunities of Former Heads of State and International Crimes: The *Hissène Habré* Case' (2003) 1 JICJ 186; Chanakra Wickremasinghe, 'Arrest Warrant of 11 April 2000' (2003) 52 *ICLQ* 775; King, 'Immunities and Bilateral Agreements'.

84 Cassese, 'Senior State Officials', 872.

85 The Joint Separate Opinion of Judges Higgins, Kooijmans and Buergenthal in the *Yerodia* case (see footnote 104 below) at para. 85, suggests that international crimes should not be seen as 'official acts'.

86 See section 21.2.1.

87 Examples are listed above in this section.

Nonetheless, in 2007 French authorities decided not to proceed with torture allegations against Donald Rumsfeld, citing advice from the Ministry of Foreign Affairs that under 'rules of customary law established by the International Court of Justice', immunity for official functions continues after termination of their functions.[88] The case may be authority against the exception for international crimes. On the other hand, observers have suggested that the decision was not entirely untouched by politics, given that the position taken in relation to Rumsfeld is irreconcilable with the earlier French request for the extradition of Pinochet.

Another case raises possible doubts about the parameters of the exception. An Italian case, *Lozano*, dealt with a US serviceman in Iraq who opened fire on a car speeding toward a checkpoint, killing an Italian agent and wounding another officer and a reporter.[89] The Court specifically affirmed a general exception that functional immunity does not prevail against international crimes.[90] The significant finding was that Lozano's conduct was not a war crime, given the car's rapid approach to the checkpoint.[91] Because of high thresholds suggested by that court, it is possible to interpret the decision as requiring that war crimes be 'odious or inhuman', involving scale or planning, to fall outside of functional immunity, but the better view is that the Court simply misstated the elements of war crimes.[92]

21.3   Functional immunity and international courts

The reasoning in the foregoing authorities is based on the nature of functional immunity, and not on the nature of the jurisdiction trying the crime. Thus the same reasoning would apply in any forum, including international courts. The ICTY has confirmed that international law offers no functional immunity for genocide, crimes against humanity or war crimes.[93]

In addition to benefiting from any inherent inapplicability of functional immunity to international crimes, international tribunals are also granted certain powers to set aside immunities, as is discussed in section 21.5.

21.4   Personal immunity and national courts

21.4.1   State practice and jurisprudence

While inroads have been made into *functional* immunity, State practice and jurisprudence have consistently upheld *personal* immunity, regardless of the nature of the charges. For

---

88 See UN, 'Immunity of State officials', para. 188.
89 Antonio Cassese, 'The Italian Court of Cassation Misapprehends the Notion of War Crimes' (2008) 6 *JICJ* 1077.
90 *Ibid.*, at 1082.
91 *Ibid.*, at 1084.
92 *Ibid.*, at 1085–8. Such a requirement would not be entirely unprecedented; several passages in *Pinochet* arguably required 'widespread or systematic' crimes: see section 21.2.
93 See, e.g. *Blaškić* ICTY A. Ch. 24.10.1997 para. 41.

example, even in the *Pinochet* decision, all of the Law Lords agreed that if Pinochet were still a serving head of State, he could not be arrested; a serving head of State has personal immunity and, '[t]he nature of the charge is irrelevant; his immunity is personal and absolute'.[94] 'He is not liable to be arrested or detained on any ground whatever.'[95]

To understand the divergent treatment of functional and personal immunity, one must recall their purposes. Functional immunity relates to the conduct and its authorization by a State, whereas personal immunity flows from a completely different rationale, unconnected with the alleged conduct. Its purpose is to preclude any pretext for interference with a State representative, in order to allow international relations between potentially distrustful States. Thus personal immunity cannot be set aside without the consent of the relevant State.

The possibility of creating exceptions to personal immunity was considered and rejected even in situations of great pressure or incentive to prosecute, including cases of espionage, drug smuggling, murder,[96] and plots against monarchs.[97] In each case, the conclusion reached was that, despite all of the problems with immunities, the benefits of upholding the existing system of diplomatic immunities and diplomatic communication outweighed the disadvantages.[98]

Judicial decisions have confirmed that there is no exception to personal immunity. In 1946, a Canadian case held that a foreign diplomat could not be arrested or detained even after threatening the security of the State, because '[i]f the diplomat violates the law of nations, it does not follow that the other State has the right to do likewise'.[99]

This view has been upheld in recent cases in the context of serious international crimes. In March 2001, the French *Cour de cassation* held in the *Qaddafi* case that a serving head of State is immune from prosecution in national courts in relation to serious acts of terrorism.[100] The Spanish *Audienco Nacional* reached a similar conclusion with respect to allegations of international crimes by Fidel Castro,[101] and the same result was reached in a UK court in a case against President Mugabe.[102] Recent State practice has adhered to the

---

94 *Pinochet 3* at 179 (Millett).

95 *Ibid.*, at 171 (Millett).

96 The murder of policewoman Yvonne Fletcher in the UK in 1984 provoked a massive outcry and a parliamentary review of diplomatic immunities. The review concluded, however, that attempts to renegotiate the Vienna Convention would create more problems than they would solve. See Barker, *A Necessary Evil?*, 135–52.

97 In 1571 and in 1584, when ambassadors in England were detected in plots against the Crown, some urged that foreign ambassadors should lose their immunity for treason and high crimes. In the end, these arguments did not prevail and the diplomats were expelled. Similar practices were followed in other countries. See Ogdon, *Juridical Bases*, 56–9.

98 In the United States, proposals for legislation to remove diplomatic immunity for drunk driving and violent crimes have been rejected, on the grounds that complete immunity is essential for diplomatic relations, as otherwise other States could bring false charges. See Barker, *A Necessary Evil?*, 232.

99 *Rose* v. *R.* [1947] 3 DLR 618 at 645.

100 *Qadaffi* (2001) 125 ILR 456.

101 *Castro* (1999) 32 ILM 596.

102 Reproduced in Colin Warbrick, 'Immunity and International Crimes in English Law' (2004) 53 *ICLQ* 769.

same line. For example, when lobbied by NGOs to arrest the serving Israeli ambassador, Carmi Gillon, on allegations that he was previously responsible for torture, Denmark refused, on the basis of its obligation to respect diplomatic immunity.[103]

21.4.2 The ICJ Yerodia decision

In April 2000, a Belgian judge issued an international arrest warrant against Abdulaye Yerodia Ndombasi, who was at the time serving as the minister for foreign affairs for the Democratic Republic of Congo (DRC). The DRC brought the matter to the ICJ, arguing that Belgium had failed to recognize the immunity of a serving minister of foreign affairs. The ICJ held, by thirteen votes to three, that Belgium had breached its international legal duties to the DRC 'in that they failed to respect the immunity from criminal jurisdiction and the inviolability which the incumbent Minister for Foreign Affairs of the Democratic Republic of the Congo enjoyed under international law'.[104] The personal immunity enjoyed by a foreign minister could not be set aside by a national court by charging him or her with war crimes or crimes against humanity.[105] The ICJ examined the non-immunity provisions of the Nuremberg Charter, and the Statutes of the ICTY, ICTR and ICC, and found that these did not suggest any exception in customary international law in regard to national courts.[106]

The judgment emphasized that the temporary status of personal immunity did not mean *impunity* for serious crimes. First, persons may be tried in their home courts; second, they may be prosecuted if the State waives the immunity; third, they may be prosecuted, once they cease to hold office, for crimes committed in a private capacity; and fourth, they may be prosecuted before international criminal courts where such courts have jurisdiction.[107]

The outcome of the decision is consistent with the line of national decisions and State practice upholding absolute personal immunity. Nevertheless, there are elements of the decision which have been questioned. First, by observing that former high officials may be tried for 'private' acts once they cease to hold office, the ICJ seemed to omit the exception that serious international crimes may also be prosecuted.[108] Second, in the view of some commentators, it unjustifiably extended head of State immunity to what may be a wide range of ministers, without sufficient argument or reference to authority.[109] Third, the ICJ asserted that such ministers enjoy personal immunity even when on 'private visits', without a demonstration that State practice supports such a view.

---

103 Jacques Hartmann, 'The Gillon Affair' (2005) 45 *ICLQ* 745.
104 *Case Concerning the Arrest Warrant of 11 April 2000 (Democratic Republic of Congo* v. *Belgium)*, Judgment, 14 Febratry 2002; ICJ Rep 2002 (hereafter '*Yerodia*') at para. 75.
105 *Yerodia* paras. 56–8.
106 *Ibid.*, para. 58.
107 *Ibid.*, para. 61.
108 Discussed in section 21.2.2.
109 Akande, 'International Law Immunities', 412.

Which ministers enjoy personal immunity?

The ICJ recognized immunity for heads of State, heads of government and ministers of foreign affairs, and left a door open for other ministers. Jurisprudence has to date been cautious in extending personal immunity to other ministers. In the *Mofaz* case, a UK court found that the role of a minister of defence was one attracting personal immunity, but expressed doubt that ministers of culture, sport or education would qualify.[110] Other cases indicate that neither Solicitors-General nor ministers of State qualify, nor do leaders of provinces and sub-States.[111]

Are personal immunities established for private visits?

The *Yerodia* judgment indicated that personal immunity must be recognized even on private visits, on the grounds that the consequences of being arrested for the performance of one's functions would be the same.[112] There are reasons to doubt whether this observation is sufficient to prove personal immunities in customary international law. Curiously, the ICJ did not conduct its usual review of State practice and *opinio iuris*, instead it purported to deduce the law from a one-paragraph analysis of the functions of a foreign minister. A review of State practice might have led to more nuanced conclusions. First, it is doubtful that State practice supports a sweeping rule relating to private visits; the sparse authorities refer to such immunities *on an official visit*.[113] If analogy is drawn from the law of diplomatic immunities (where usages have been worked out and defined over the centuries), personal immunity is not accorded during holidays in third countries, but only when *en poste* and during transit between the home country and the host country.[114]

Second, where a host State has invited or consented to an official visit, it may be argued that there is an undertaking that full immunity will be bestowed,[115] as was recognized even in the arrest warrant issued by Belgium:

> [I]mmunity from enforcement must, in our view, be accorded to all State representatives welcomed as such onto the territory of Belgium (on 'official visits') . . . [S]uch welcome includes an undertaking by the host State and its various components to refrain from taking any coercive measures against its guest and the invitation cannot become a pretext for ensnaring the individual concerns in what would then have to be labelled a trap.[116]

---

110 *Mofaz*, reproduced (2004) 53 *ICLQ* 769.
111 UN, 'Immunity of State officials', paras.132–6.
112 *Yerodia* para. 55.
113 Convention on Special Missions 1969, Art. 21; US Restatement (Third) of Foreign Relations Law § 464, note 14.
114 VCDR 1961, Art. 40.
115 R. Y. Jennings and A. Watts (eds.), *Oppenheim's International Law*, 9th edn (Essex, 1992) 1034.
116 Quoted in *Yerodia* at para. 68.

Where the host State has not invited or consented to the visit, this consideration is absent. On the ICJ approach, where a high official arrives *incognito* or without announcing official status, the host State has no opportunity to decline to have a person on its territory but outside its enforcement jurisdiction.

Third, the extension of full immunity to private visits is not supported by the rationale on which the ICJ founded its decision, which was that exposure to proceedings 'could deter the Minister from travelling internationally *when required to do so for the purposes of the performance of his or her official functions*' (emphasis added).[117] This rationale is inapplicable to holiday travel. The ICJ reasoned that being arrested on holiday travel would impede one's functions, but this falls short of proving that high officials may travel anywhere they wish for personal reasons and receive personal immunity. The concern about arrest during holiday travel can be addressed more simply; an official fearful of such an arrest could be well advised to curtail his or her holiday travel, particularly to countries where he or she may be under indictment. The ICJ's approach grants more importance to the holiday travel of high officials than to States' jurisdiction over their territories. Such jurisdiction may understandably be displaced for high officials on mission, because of the need to maintain international relations, but this does not pertain to private travel.

The comments were *obiter dicta* and, given that many judges dissented from or distanced themselves from this particular finding, it seems not to have commanded a majority.[118] Thus, this issue is still open for clarification in State practice; it may be for example that only heads of State are entitled to personal immunity during non-official visits, but State practice is unsettled even on that point.[119]

21.5   Personal immunity and international courts

As may be seen from the foregoing, authorities have consistently rejected any exception to personal immunity in domestic courts based on the nature of the charges. For personal immunity, the nature of the charge is irrelevant; the purpose is to guarantee safe passage for certain office-holders charged with the conduct of international relations. Personal immunity may only be overcome through consent of the State concerned. This raises the unsettling prospect of an accountability gap with respect to such persons while they are in office. Fortunately, States have devised means of reducing this accountability gap: to create international tribunals and to empower them to supersede even their personal immunities.

---

117 *Yerodia* para. 55.
118 Seven out of thirteen judges dissented from or expressed doubts about this finding. See Darryl Robinson, 'The Impact of the Human Rights Accountability Movement on the International Law of Immunities' (2002) 40 *Canadian Yearbook of International Law* 151 at 188–9.
119 Watts, 'Legal Position', 72–4; Salvatore Zappala, 'Do Heads of State in Office Enjoy Immunity from Jurisdiction for International Crimes? The *Ghaddafi* Case Before the French *Cour de Cassation*' (2001) 12 *EJIL* 595 at 606; Koller, 'Immunities of Foreign Ministers', 15–16; UN, 'Immunities of State officials', para. 128.

In the case of the Nuremberg and Tokyo Tribunals, both Japan and Germany had surrendered. Hence the Allies stood in the position of national legislators and, in that position, they could legislate away immunity before the Tokyo and Nuremberg Tribunals. In the case of the ad hoc Tribunals, immunities are relinquished by virtue of the paramount obligation to comply with Chapter VII decisions of the Security Council. In the case of the ICC, States Parties relinquish their immunities by treaty.

Section 21.5.1 examines an alternative theory raised in the *Taylor* case, that international courts are able to supersede personal immunity not because of the relinquishment of such immunity, but because the international character of such courts makes such immunity inapplicable. The remaining sections examine specific issues arising before the ad hoc Tribunals and the ICC, especially following the ICC's arrest warrant against Omar Al Bashir, President of Sudan.

21.5.1 *The* Taylor *theory: personal immunity is irrelevant before international courts*

In June 2003, the Special Court for Sierra Leone (SCSL) issued a warrant for the arrest of Charles Taylor, who at the time was the President of Liberia, engaged in peace talks in Ghana. Ghana allowed Taylor to return to Liberia. (In August 2003, Taylor accepted an offer from Nigeria to grant him asylum if he stepped down as head of State and stopped participating in Liberian politics. Following repeated breaches of the latter undertaking, Taylor was eventually arrested in 2006 and transferred to the custody of the SCSL.)

In July 2003, lawyers for Charles Taylor made an application to declare the warrant null and void, on the grounds that he was a serving head of State, enjoying absolute immunity; that exceptions to this immunity can only be derived from other rules of international law such as Security Council resolutions under Chapter VII; and that the SCSL did not have Chapter VII powers.

In May 2004, the SCSL issued its decision, holding that the SCSL was an 'international court' and as such not barred from prosecuting serving heads of State.[120] The SCSL relied on passages in *Pinochet* and *Yerodia* which made reference to the possibility of prosecution before international courts. For example, the ICJ, in explaining that immunity did not necessarily lead to impunity, noted that 'an incumbent ... Minister for Foreign Affairs may be subject to criminal proceedings before certain international courts, where they have jurisdiction'.[121]

The question is what those passages meant. Were they simply observing that there are international courts with the power to supersede personal immunities in accordance with known principles of law (for example relinquishment through treaty or Chapter VII powers)? Or were they positing a general rule that all personal immunities are eliminated

---

120 *Taylor* SCSL A. Ch. 31.05.2004 (hereafter '*Taylor*') paras. 51–3.
121 *Yerodia* para. 61.

before any court that may be characterized as 'international'? If the latter, what is the legal origin of this exception?

The SCSL adopted the latter interpretation, that personal immunities are simply inapplicable before any tribunal that can be characterized as 'international'. Although the Security Council imposed no Chapter VII obligations upon States to cooperate with the SCSL, the SCSL held that it was created by an agreement between the UN and Sierra Leone, and therefore it was an 'international' court,[122] and hence personal immunity was no barrier to prosecution.

This legal assessment has been accepted by some[123] and doubted by many.[124] Can the reasoning in support of such a rule be supported?

The SCSL argued that personal immunity is rooted in the 'principle that one sovereign State does not adjudicate on the conduct of another State', which 'has no relevance to international criminal tribunals which are not organs of a State but derive their mandate from the international community'.[125] Several flaws in this assertion are apparent. Most importantly, the Court incorrectly identified the rationale for personal immunity. The principle *par in parem non habet iudicium* is the basis for *functional* immunity, not personal immunity. Personal immunity exists to protect international relations by precluding any basis to interfere with high representatives without consent of their sending State.

In addition, it is rather facile to assert that a tribunal is not a State and hence the principle is inapplicable. An international tribunal is a creation of States. The obligations of States cannot be sidestepped by simply creating an institution to do what they cannot. If neither State A nor State B has the power to ignore the personal immunity of State C without consent, then the two together cannot create an international court and bestow upon it a power that they do not possess. The problem remains whether it is two States, or twenty, or sixty: they cannot bestow a power that they do not possess.[126]

The theory supporting *Taylor* emphasizes that international courts are in a 'vertical relationship' with States, ranking hierarchically above States and hence not subject to the same limitations.[127] However, international courts only acquire that vertical relationship (the ability to issue orders to States) insofar as States grant them that position, by treaty or other means such as Chapter VII.[128] A claim that one is acting 'on behalf of the international community', which is a rather amorphous concept, does not expand one's powers.

---

122 *Taylor* paras. 34–42.
123 Paola Gaeta, 'Does President Al Bashir Enjoy Immunity from Arrest?' (2009) 7 *JICJ* 315; UN, 'Immunities of State officials', para. 87.
124 Zsuzsanna Deen-Racsmány, 'Prosecutor v. Taylor: The Status of the Special Court for Sierra Leone and its Implications for Immunity' (2005) 18 *LJIL* 299; Micaela Frulli, 'The Question of Charles Taylor's Immunity' (2004) 2 *JICJ* 1118; Koller, 'Immunities of Foreign Ministers'; King, 'Immunities and Bilateral Agreements'.
125 *Taylor* para. 51.
126 *Nemo dat quod non habet.*
127 Gaeta, 'President Al Bashir', 320–2.
128 Note that this is a very different question from jurisdiction. To acquire jurisdiction over the nationals of a State does not require the consent of the State. See Chapter 8. There are many possible bases on which

The *Taylor* judgment also emphasized that international courts have limited jurisdiction and safeguards against abuse, and that their collective judgment reduces the potential destabilizing effects of unilateral action.[129] These are indeed good *policy* arguments as to why such an exception might be desirable, but it does not explain the *legal* basis or origin for the alleged exception. As one commentator has noted, not only does this purported exception 'violate the principle of *pacta tertiis*, but it also ignores the fact that fairness [of the tribunal] has nothing to do with the creation of immunities'.[130] The safeguards and stability may help explain why States are willing to relinquish immunities, but they do not in themselves override immunities.

State practice seems to have been predicated on the need for relinquishment of personal immunity (hence the existence of Article 98 in the ICC Statute and the emphasis on the Chapter VII powers of the ad hoc Tribunals, as discussed in the following sections).[131]

The SCSL would have been on much sounder ground if it had simply observed that Taylor was no longer a head of State at the time of the decision, having stepped down in August 2003, and hence that he no longer enjoyed personal immunity and was liable to arrest and prosecution for international crimes.

For the reasons given above, the more plausible view is that under existing international law, 'it is not the international nature of the court as such but the waiver by the parties (and the Security Council's Chapter VII powers …) that accounts for the irrelevance of immunities before it'.[132] Nonetheless, if State practice and *opinio iuris* consistently begin to support the proposition that personal immunity is no barrier before international courts, then such an exception could certainly emerge in customary law by virtue of that practice and *opinio iuris*.

21.5.2 Relinquishment by Security Council decision

The UN Charter grants the Security Council a broad discretion to determine what measures are appropriate to maintain or restore international peace and security, whether involving use of force (Article 42) or not (Article 41). When the Council decides upon measures under Chapter VII, all UN Member States are obliged to carry out such measures (Articles 25 and 48).[133]

---

jurisdiction may be acquired; we deal here with the separate question of obtaining authority to set aside immunities.

129 See, e.g. *Taylor* para. 51; similar possibilities are suggested in Ryszard Piotrowicz, 'Immunities of Foreign Ministers and their Exposure to Universal Jurisdiction' (2002) 76 *Austin Law Journal* 290 at 293.

130 Koller, 'Immunities of Foreign Ministers', 32.

131 Another indicator of State practice is national legislation such as the UK International Criminal Court Act 2001, s. 23(1) and (2). The legislation of some other countries (such as Canada) is consistent with this position but defers the issue entirely to the ICC.

132 Deen-Racsmány, 'Prosecutor v. Taylor', 318; see also King, 'Immunities and Bilateral Agreements'.

133 For further discussion on the power of the Security Council to create Tribunals, see Chapter 7.

When creating the ad hoc Tribunals, the Security Council incorporated the principle that the official position of a defendant is no bar before the tribunals,[134] and ordered all States to comply with requests from the Tribunals, including requests for surrender. No exception was created for surrender requests relating to persons otherwise enjoying immunities. A State's obligation to the Security Council is paramount over all other obligations.[135] Thus, a UN member State receiving a request for the surrender of a person is obliged to comply with that request, even if the request conflicts with a duty to respect immunities. By the same token, the State otherwise enjoying the immunities is estopped from raising those immunities as a shield, by virtue of its obligations under the UN Charter.[136] The legal analysis is the same where the Security Council orders States to cooperate with the ICC, as will be discussed in section 21.5.4.

The situation is less straightforward with respect to the Federal Republic of Yugoslavia (FRY), the recipient of orders to surrender its head of State, because it was not recognized as a UN Member State. However, it was a party to the Dayton Accords, which imposed an obligation to cooperate with the ICTY.[137]

Both Tribunals have carried out proceedings with respect to high governmental officials. In 1998, the ICTR convicted former Prime Minister Jean Kambanda, sentencing him to life imprisonment for genocide and crimes against humanity.[138] In 1999, the ICTY issued the first indictment against a serving head of State, Slobodan Milošević.[139] Although Slobodan Milošević died of a heart attack before the completion of his trial,[140] his indictment, arrest and trial remain a valuable precedent on the authority of a Security Council tribunal over heads of State.

In *Karadžić*, the accused argued that, under an alleged agreement with US envoy Richard Holbrooke, he had been promised immunity from prosecution if he retired from public life.[141] The issue arose in the context of a disclosure motion, which the Chamber dismissed due to lack of specificity. The Chamber noted in passing that it was 'well established that any immunity agreement in respect of an accused indicted for genocide, war crimes and/ or crimes against humanity before an international tribunal would be invalid under

---

134 ICTY Statute, Art. 7(2); ICTR Statute, Art. 6(2).
135 See UN Charter, Arts. 25, 41, 49 and esp. 103: 'In the event of a conflict between the obligations of the Members of the United Nations under the present Charter and their obligations under any other international agreement, their obligations under the present Charter shall prevail.'
136 Koller, 'Immunities of Foreign Ministers' 35–6; Gaeta, 'Official Capacity and Immunities', 989.
137 Dayton Peace Accords, 21 November 1995, Art. IX. On approaches to this question, as well as the interpretation that the UN Charter is of a *sui generis* character that binds third party States, see Chapter 7.
138 *Kambanda* ICTR T. Ch. I 4.9.1998.
139 *Milošević* Indictment ICTY (Judge Hunt) 24.5.1999; *Milošević* Decision on Preliminary Motion ICTY T. Ch. 8.11.2001 paras. 26–53.
140 See Chapter 7.
141 *Karadžić*, ICTY T. Ch. III 17.12.2008.

international law'.[142] Although the Chamber appeared to treat the issue as one of immunity, the claim was not based on the official character of acts (functional immunity) nor on a high representative role (personal immunity). In a later motion, the Chamber more correctly characterized the matter as an alleged promise of non-prosecution, but dismissed the claim as Holbrooke had neither actual nor ostensible authority to bind the Tribunal or the Security Council for any such agreement.[143]

21.5.3 Relinquishment through accession to the ICC Statute

The ICC Statute offers another solution to the problem of personal immunity. In the present stage of development of international relations, States are apparently unwilling to recognize a general exception to personal immunities that would allow other States to prosecute their highest officials; however, a great many States have been willing to create an impartial international court with jurisdiction over serious international crimes, and to relinquish even their personal immunities to that court.

ICC States Parties are obliged to cooperate with the ICC and to surrender individuals in accordance with the terms of the Statute, without reservation.[144] Article 27(2) specifies that '[i]mmunities or special personal rules which may attach to the official capacity of a person ... shall not bar the Court from exercising its jurisdiction ...'.[145] Thus, States Parties accept that the immunities their officials may enjoy under international law will not bar prosecution before the ICC. This provision has required many States to amend domestic legislation and even their constitutions in order to ratify the ICC Statute.[146]

However, that is not the only provision on immunities in the ICC Statute. Article 98(1) provides that the ICC will not proceed with requests for surrender:

> which would require the requested State to act inconsistently with its obligations under international law with respect to the State or diplomatic immunity of a person or property of a third State, unless the Court can first obtain the cooperation of that third State for the waiver of the immunity.[147]

---

142 *Ibid.*, para. 25.

143 *Karadžić*, ICTY T. Ch. III 8.7.2009.

144 ICC Statute Art. 86 (obligation to cooperate), Art. 89 (surrender of persons to the court), Art. 120 (no reservations).

145 *Ibid.*, Art. 27(1): 'official capacity as a Head of State or Government, a member of a Government or parliament, an elected representative or a government official shall in no case exempt a person from criminal responsibility under this Statute'. See Otto Triffterer, 'Article 27' in Triffterer, *Observers' Notes*, 501.

146 See, e.g. Claus Kreß and Flavia Lattanzi (eds.), *The Rome Statute and Domestic Legal Orders* (Rome, 2000), vol. I; Darryl Robinson, 'The Rome Statute and its Impact on National Laws' in Cassese, *Commentary*, 1849.

147 Similarly, Art. 98(2) of the ICC Statute respects obligations under international agreements pursuant to which the consent of a sending State is required to surrender a person of that State to the court. The controversy over the interpretation of Art. 98(2) is discussed in Chapter 8. See generally Kimberly Prost and Angelika Schlunck, 'Article 98' in Triffterer, *Observers' Notes*, 1131.

Article 27 and Article 98(1) must be read together to understand the Statute regime.[148] At first glance, they appear contradictory, with one rejecting immunities and the other upholding immunities.[149] The provisions apply at different stages. Article 98(1) deals with a specific situation where a State Party (or other State obliged to cooperate[150]) is requested to surrender a person, but that person is protected by immunities bestowed by a third State. In such a case, the requested State would be placed in a position of conflicting obligations: for example, either to breach a duty to carry out ICC requests or to breach a duty to respect immunities of a State not party to the ICC Statute.

The interplay of Articles 27 and 98(1) therefore creates a regime wherein States Parties agree to relinquish all immunities in relation to ICC requests concerning their own nationals, representatives or officials, while still respecting the existing immunities of States which have not joined the ICC Statute system. It is worth recalling here that the only relevant immunities would be personal immunities, since functional immunity does not protect conduct which amounts to a core crime.[151]

In relation to a request for surrender of a State's own nationals, Article 98(1) does not apply, since it refers to obligations to a 'third State'. The State is obliged to cooperate without reservation (Article 86).

If the request for surrender relates to a person who enjoys immunities bestowed by *another* State Party, it is generally accepted that it would not be necessary for the requested State first to obtain the waiver of the other State Party.[152] Interestingly, there are different interpretive routes by which this conclusion is reached. Some interpret 'third State' in Article 98(1) as referring only to non-party States. However, this view overlooks that the Statute consistently uses the term 'State not party to this Statute' to describe non-party States, and that 'third State' is routinely used in cooperation treaties to refer to a State other than the requesting and requested State. Thus a more convincing view is that ICC States Parties have already relinquished any immunities against ICC proceedings by virtue of ratifying the Statute and being bound by Articles 27 and 88, and hence there are no 'obligations under international law' hindering surrender.[153]

---

148 Triffterer, 'Article 27', 509.
149 Gaeta, 'Official Capacity', 992–6.
150 States may undertake duties to cooperate through accession (Art. 125) or through unilateral declarations (see, e.g. Arts. 12(3), 87(5) of the ICC Statute). As discussed in section 21.5.4, duties to cooperate may also be imposed by the Security Council under Chapter VII.
151 See section 21.2 and 21.3.
152 The relationship between Arts. 27 and 98 was discussed in informal meetings at the ICC Preparatory Commission, on the basis of an informal paper by Canada and the UK, with the conclusion being reached that: 'Having regard to the terms of the Statute, the Court shall not be required to obtain a waiver of immunity with respect to the surrender by one State Party of a head of State or government, or diplomat, of another State Party.' See Broomhall, *International Justice*, 144.
153 See Broomhall, *International Justice*, 144–5; Wirth, 'Immunities, Related Problems', 456–7; Gaeta, 'Official Capacity', 993–5.

In relation to a request concerning an official enjoying immunities of a *non-State Party*, Article 98(1) requires respect for any immunities existing under international law. This does not mean there can be no prospect for surrender. First, prosecution is possible if the non-State Party agrees to waive the immunity. Second, once the official is no longer serving in a capacity that entails personal immunity, he or she will only have functional immunity, and hence be liable to prosecution for core crimes. Third, even non-States Parties will lose their immunity if the Security Council under Chapter VII orders full cooperation, as will be discussed in section 21.5.4.

21.5.4 Decisions by the Security Council requiring cooperation with the ICC

The remaining scenario deals with personal immunity bestowed by a State not party to the Rome Statute, where the Security Council has acted under Chapter VII. An example of this has already arisen. Sudan is not party to the Rome Statute, but it is a UN member State, and the situation in Darfur was referred to the Court by a Security Council resolution under Chapter VII. In March 2009, a Pre-Trial Chamber of the ICC issued an arrest warrant against Omar Al Bashir, President of Sudan.[154] The Chamber referred to Sudan's obligations of cooperation under Chapter VII and sent a request for arrest and surrender to Sudan, all ICC States Parties and all members of the UN Security Council.[155] The development has triggered a vigorous international legal debate about the status of immunities in such a situation.

Some commentators argue that the ICC Statute is simply a treaty, and hence its provisions, including Article 27, only bind States Parties. In this vein, it has been argued that the Statute does not provide that a Security Council referral imposes obligations on all UN member States; thus a non-party to the Rome Statute retains the personal immunities of its officials vis-à-vis the Court.[156]

This argument is correct as far as it goes, but it misses the basis for the legal obligation imposed on non-party States. Such an obligation arises not from the Statute, but from the UN Charter, and the fact that the Security Council, acting under Chapter VII, expressly orders the State to cooperate fully.[157] In doing so, the Security Council creates the same situation as was described in section 21.5.2: UN member States have a paramount obligation to comply with Chapter VII resolutions, which can include relinquishing immunities and surrendering persons.[158] The obligation to cooperate fully imposes obligations identical to those of a State

---

154 *Situation in Darfur* (*Al Bashir* arrest warrant case) ICC PT. Ch. I 4.3.2009.

155 *Ibid.*, paras. 240–8 and the dispositive provisions at the end of the judgment.

156 Gaeta, 'President Al Bashir', 322–5.

157 Dapo Akande, 'The Legal Nature of Security Council Referrals to the ICC and its Impact on Al Bashir's Immunities' (2009) 7 JICJ 333 at 341–2.

158 Marko Milanovic, 'ICC Prosecutor charges the President of Sudan with genocide, crimes against humanity and war crimes in Darfur' (2008, 28 July) 12 *ASIL Insights* accessible at www.asil.org/insights.cfm.

Party, but the legal compulsion flows not from the Statute but from the UN Charter obligation to comply with Chapter VII decisions. The Council can impose obligations on member States which may be identical to those found in a treaty.[159]

Some counter-arguments might be ventured against this conclusion. First, one might argue that the Security Council can only order States to relinquish immunities vis-à-vis Tribunals of its own creation but not vis-à-vis a treaty creation such as the ICC.[160] However, no such limitation may be found in Articles 41 or 42 of the Charter. Further, such arguments, which would require reversion to costly and redundant Tribunals to address immunities, contradict a major purpose of the Court, which was to avoid the need for the Council to create new ad hoc Tribunals from scratch for each situation.[161] Instead the Council can compel member States to cooperate with the Court under Chapter VII, just as it required cooperation with Tribunals.[162]

More convincing counter-arguments are that the obligation to 'cooperate fully' is not sufficient to entail a loss of personal immunity. In this vein it could be argued that Part 9 of the Rome Statute is imposed on a State by the Council decision, but that Article 27 is not, and hence the combination of commitments described in section 21.5.3 is not satisfied. A related argument might be that a State is obliged to waive its immunities under the Council resolution, but that if it fails to do so, other States still face conflicting obligations. Such issues will only be resolved conclusively through future practice. It may be noted in response that 'cooperate fully' was precisely the term that was used in the resolutions creating the ICTY and ICTR, and these were considered sufficiently clear to remove immunities.[163] Furthermore, in the context of the ICC, the most obvious interpretation of 'cooperate fully' is that a State must cooperate, in accordance with the terms of the Statute, to the same extent as if it were a State party.[164] It is conceivable that 'cooperate fully' might mean cooperation *less* than that required of a State party, but then it would be profoundly unclear what that lesser extent of cooperation might be.[165] Moreover it would seem

---

159 See, e.g. Security Council resolution 1373 (2001). The Council can also impose obligations on member States overriding any that arise from a treaty; see, e.g. *Case Concerning Questions of Interpretation and Application of the 1971 Montreal Convention Arising from the Aerial Incident at Lockerbie* (*Libya* v. *USA*), Request for Provisional Measures, ICJ, 14.4.1992, para. 42.

160 Gaeta, 'President Al Bashir', 326, 330.

161 Lionel Yee, 'The International Criminal Court and the Security Council' in Lee, *The Making of the Rome Statute*, 146.

162 Claus Kreß and Kimberly Prost, 'Article 87' in Triffterer, *Observers' Notes* at 1523 and 1525. The Statute expressly contemplates that the facility of the Court is available to the Security Council and that a Council reference of a situation to the Court can entail a wider personal and territorial jurisdiction, further cooperation and different arrangements for funding: Arts. 13, 53(3), 87(5)(b), 87(7), 115.

163 Resolution 827(1993) para. 4, Resolution 935(1994) para. 2, both of which have been read in conjunction with the relevant Statute provisions denying immunities.

164 Akande, 'Legal Nature of Security Council Referrals', 342.

165 On the potential vagaries of 'cooperate fully' see Göran Sluiter, 'Obtaining Cooperation from Sudan – Where is the Law?' (2008) 6 *JICJ* 871.

incompatible with the adverb '*fully*'. Thus, if the Council-imposed obligation to 'cooperate fully' entails the same obligations of a State Party, then the analysis in section 21.5.3 applies, and immunity is not opposable against surrender to the ICC.

A third possible counter-argument is to concede that the above analysis may be correct where the Security Council orders *all* member States to cooperate fully, but that in the Darfur situation the Council did not do so.[166] Because of US concerns about the ICC, the Security Council in resolution 1593 did not issue an order to all member States; instead it only ordered 'the Government of Sudan and all other parties to the conflict in Darfur' to cooperate fully, and 'urged' other States and organizations to cooperate fully.[167] Nonetheless, if the analysis given above is correct, the narrower focus of the obligation does not change the outcome. If a State Party were requested to surrender Al-Bashir to the Court, Sudan would qualify as a 'third State' under Article 98(1), but because of the Chapter VII order to Sudan to cooperate, Sudan would have the same obligations as a State Party and hence would not have an immunity under international law opposable to the surrender request.[168]

One final complication arises because of the narrow wording of resolution 1593: what is the legal position if President Al Bashir travels to the territory of a *non-party State*? Non-party States are merely 'urged' to cooperate fully with the Court; they have no *obligation* to arrest Al Bashir or surrender him to the Court. Would a non-party State be *permitted* to do so? The most plausible view is that the above analysis would still apply: Sudan has no immunity opposable to the ICC by virtue of the Council resolution, and thus arrest and surrender would not be a wrongful act about which Sudan could complain.[169]

These questions are certainly complex and controversial, and it will be valuable to have them clarified through practice and jurisprudence.

21.6 Conclusion

The shift in the law toward the narrowing of immunities is readily seen. Many authorities recognize that functional immunity does not protect conduct that amounts to a serious international crime. Personal immunity has proved more resilient, allowing no exception based on the nature of the crimes alleged. States have, however, relinquished personal immunity to some international jurisdictions; for example, by ratifying the ICC Statute, or by virtue of their obligations to the Security Council under Chapter VII of the UN Charter. An alternative view is that personal immunity is never opposable to an 'international court'.

As priorities continue to shift, there may be further developments to limit the negative effects of immunities. Possibilities include increased ratification of the ICC Statute, more

---

166 Gaeta, 'President Al Bashir', 330–1.
167 Resolution 1593(2005) para. 2.
168 The UK International Criminal Court (Darfur) Order 2009 (SI 2009/699) appears to support this view.
169 Akande, 'Legal Nature of Security Council Referrals', 344–5.

assertive Security Council action, such as referrals to the ICC imposing duties of cooperation on all States, and more robust national action, including requesting waivers of immunity or pressing for national prosecution. International law might be developed or clarified so that personal immunity is clearly limited to official visits and a smaller range of ministers and officials. The day may come when States agree to exceptions even for personal immunity before national courts. After all, as was noted by three judges in *Yerodia*, the law reflects a balancing of different community interests, and therefore is in constant evolution, with a discernible trend to limiting immunity and strengthening accountability.[170]

Further reading

Dapo Akande, 'International Law Immunities and the International Criminal Court' (2004) 98 *AJIL* 407.

Dapo Akande, 'The Legal Nature of Security Council Referrals to the ICC and its Impact on Al Bashir's Immunities' (2009) 7 *JICJ* 332.

Bruce Broomhall, *International Justice and the International Criminal Court: Between Sovereignty and the Rule of Law* (Oxford, 2003) ch. 7.

J. Craig Barker, *The Abuse of Diplomatic Privileges and Immunities: A Necessary Evil?* (Dartmouth, 1996).

J. Craig Barker, 'The Future of Former Head of State Immunity After *Ex Parte Pinochet*' (1999) 48 *ICLQ* 937.

Antonio Cassese, 'When May Senior State Officials Be Tried for International Crimes? Some Comments on the *Congo* v. *Belgium* Case' (2002) 13 *EJIL* 853.

Zsuzsanna Deen-Racsmány, 'Prosecutor v. Taylor: The Status of the Special Court for Sierra Leone and its Implications for Immunity' (2005) 18 *LJIL* 299.

Eileen Denza, 'Ex Parte Pinochet: Lacuna or Leap?' (1999) 48 *ICLQ* 949.

Linda S. Frey and Marsha L. Frey, *The History of Diplomatic Immunity* (Columbus, 1999).

Micaela Frulli, 'The Question of Charles Taylor's Immunity' (2004) 2 *JICJ* 1118.

Paola Gaeta, 'Official Capacity and Immunities' in Cassese, *Commentary*, 975.

Paola Gaeta, 'Does President Al Bashir Enjoy Immunity from Arrest?' (2009) 7 *JICJ* 315.

David Koller, 'Immunities of Foreign Ministers: Paragraph 61 of the Yerodia Judgment as it Pertains to the Security Council and the International Criminal Court' (2004) 20 *American University International Law Review* 7.

Rosanne Van Alebeek, *The Immunities of States and Their Officials in International Criminal Law and International Human Rights Law* (Oxford, 2008) ch. 5.

Colin Warbrick, 'Immunity and International Crimes in English Law' (2004) 53 *ICLQ* 769.

Colin Warbrick, Elena Martin Salgado and Nicholas Goodwin, 'The Pinochet Cases in the United Kingdom' (1999) 2 *Yearbook of International Humanitarian Law* 91.

---

170 *Yerodia*, Joint Separate Opinion of Judges Higgins, Kooijmans and Buergenthal para. 75.

Arthur Watts, 'The Legal Position in International Law of Heads of State, Heads of Government and Foreign Ministers' (1994–III) 247 *Hague Recueil.*

Steffen Wirth, 'Immunities, Related Problems, and Article 98 of the Rome Statute' (2001) 12 *CLF* 429.

Steffen Wirth, 'Immunity for Core Crimes? The ICJ's Judgment in the *Congo* v. *Belgium* Case' (2002) 13 *EJIL* 877.

22

Alternatives and Complements to Criminal Prosecution

22.1 Introduction

It is probably fair to say that most international criminal lawyers have an expressed or unexpressed preference for criminal prosecutions as the default response to the commission of international crimes. It is also the case that there has been a swing away from the 'politics of impunity' in international law.[1] However, many people hold out greater goals for international criminal justice than prosecutions for their own sake, and as was seen in Chapter 2, there is truth in the proposition that '[c]riminal prosecution ... does some things rather well, other things only passably well, and makes an utter hash of still others'.[2] Thus it is unsurprising that there have been other models suggested for dealing with international crimes, on the basis that they are said to fulfil more completely at least some of the purposes of trials, and incur fewer of the problems. Not all of them are mutually exclusive.[3] This chapter will provide an overview of them, alongside some of their positive and negative features.[4]

None of the mechanisms discussed in this chapter are in and of themselves perfect. Each has 'incompleteness and inescapable inadequacy' as a response to international crimes.[5] Just

---

[1] See, e.g. Leila Sadat, *The International Criminal Court and the Transformation of International Law: Justice for the New Millennium* (New York, 2002) ch. 3; *Case Concerning the Arrest Warrant of 11 April 2000 (Democratic Republic of Congo* v. *Belgium)* ICJ Rep 2002 p. 3, 14.2.2002, Separate Opinion of Judges Higgins, Kojimans and Buergenthal, para. 51; *Case Concerning Questions Relating to the Obligation to Extradite or Prosecute (Belgium* v. *Senegal)*, Request for the Indication of Provisional Measures Order of 29 May 2009, ICJ General List 144, Dissenting Opinion of Judge Cançado Trindade, paras. 30–45.

[2] Mark Osiel, 'Ever Again: Legal Remembrance of Administrative Massacre' (1995) 144 *University of Pennsylvania Law Review* 463 at 700.

[3] Obviously, amnesties and prosecutions are inconsistent, although amnesties do not have to cover all people or all offences.

[4] See further, e.g. W. Michael Reisman, 'Institutions and Practices for Restoring and Maintaining Public Order' (1995) 6 *Duke Journal of International and Comparative Law* 175; Martha Minow, *Between Vengeance and Forgiveness* (Boston, 1998); Ruti Teitel, *Transitional Justice* (New York, 2002).

[5] Minow, *Between Vengeance*, 5. See also Katherine Francke, 'Gendered Subjects of Transitional Justice' (2006) *Columbia Journal of Gender and Law* 813: 'Transitional justice will always be both incomplete and messy' (*ibid.*, 813).

because other mechanisms perform certain roles in a fashion that prosecutions cannot, does not mean that they are necessarily the most appropriate response to international crimes in any particular situation. The circumstances that attend decisions about that are too varied to take a 'one size fits all' approach to what ought to be done.[6] The political, economic, cultural and religious aspects of each situation have affected each response, and the outcomes of the approaches taken.[7] Care must therefore be taken when transposing 'lessons' from one context to another.

In appraising the way in which international crimes are dealt with, it must be remembered that when decisions are being made about what to do about international crimes, practical limits, such as funding, political possibility and the available infrastructure, are important.[8] This is particularly the case for transitional societies or those emerging from conflicts. As was said in relation to the South African transition (which was itself by no means uncontroversial):

> the Constitution seeks to ... facilitate the transition to a new democratic order, committed to 'reconciliation between the people of South Africa and the reconstruction of society'. The question is how this can be done effectively with the limitations of our resources and the legacy of the past ... The families of those whose fundamental human rights were invaded by torture and abuse are not the only victims who have endured 'untold suffering and injustice' in consequence of the crass inhumanity of apartheid which so many have had to endure for so long. Generations of children born and yet to be born will suffer the consequences of poverty, of malnutrition, of homelessness, of illiteracy and disempowerment generated and sustained by the institutions of apartheid and its manifest effects on life and living for so many. The country has neither the resources nor the skills to reverse fully these massive wrongs ... Those negotiators of the Constitution and leaders of the nation who were required to address themselves to these agonising problems must have been compelled to make hard choices. They could have chosen to direct that the limited resources of the state be spent by giving preference to the formidable delictual claims of those who had suffered from acts of murder, torture or assault perpetrated by servants of the state, diverting to that extent, desperately needed funds in the crucial areas of education, housing and primary health care ... They were entitled to permit the claims of ... school children and the poor and the homeless to be preferred.[9]

6 See Mark Drumbl, *Atrocity, Punishment and International Law* (Cambridge, 2007).

7 See on one aspect, e.g. Thomas Brudholm and Thomas Cushman, *The Religious in Responses to Mass Atrocity* (Cambridge, 2009).

8 See Secretary-General's Report on The Rule of Law and Transitional Justice in Post-Conflict Societies, 23 August 2004, S/2004/616, para. 3; Jon Elster, *Closing the Books: Transitional Justice in Historical Perspective* (Cambridge, 2004) ch. 7; Stanley Cohen, 'State Crimes of Previous Regimes: Knowledge, Accountability and the Policing of the Past' (1995) 20 *Law and Social Inquiry* 7 at 8.

9 *Azanian People's Organization (AZAPO) and others* v. *President of the Republic of South Africa* (1996) 4 SA 562 (CC) paras. 42–5 (hereinafter *AZAPO*).

This is an important point. Equally, however, it must be noted that the language of necessity, appropriateness or feasibility is open to abuse,[10] and it often ignores the broader aspects of international crimes. One of the reasons which may justify a separate regime of international criminal accountability is that crimes which are thought to affect all humanity need to be dealt with sensitively as to both the national and international effects of such crimes. The international community of States has, at least at the level of rhetoric, affirmed the unacceptability of impunity for such crimes.[11] It must also be remembered that transitional societies are not the only societies that need to deal with issues relating to international criminal law. It is all too easy to assume that international criminal law is only an issue for such States. Many stable, democratic States also have nationals, including State officials, who have committed international crimes.

22.2 Amnesties

Probably the most well-known, and controversial, alternatives to prosecutions are amnesties.[12] Amnesties are conferred under law that blocks criminal action against people in the State in which it is passed. They can also block civil claims. Amnesties have a lengthy history in international law. The Treaty of Westphalia, which was considered by many to usher in the modern era in international law and order, contained an amnesty.[13] More recently, they were frequently employed in Latin America during and after the military dictatorships, often as the price paid for the leaders of those dictatorships to hand over power to civilian governments.[14] Probably the most famous amnesty is the South African one.[15]

There are various types of amnesties, which go from those granted by regimes to themselves, such as that in Chile, to those which are voted upon by the population. Although the latter are usually thought, with some justification, to have greater legitimacy than the former, it must also be said that the consent of the population in such instances is often coerced, as the alternative is the continuation in power of an abusive regime.[16] A further distinction must be made between 'blanket' amnesties, which prevent legal proceedings against all persons without distinction, and those, such as the South African amnesty

---

10 Susan Dwyer, 'Reconciliation for Realists' (1999) 13 *Ethics and International Affairs* 81.
11 See, e.g. Security Council Resolutions 1012 (28.8.1995), 1545 (21.5.2004), 1556 (11.6.2004), 1564 (18.9.2004); General Assembly Resolution 60/147.
12 For a detailed study, see Louise Mallinder, *Amnesty, Human Rights and Political Transitions: Bridging the Peace and Justice Divide* (Oxford, 2008).
13 Scott Veitch, 'The Legal Politics of Amnesty' in Emilios Christodoulidis and Scott Veitch (eds.), *Lethe's Law: Justice, Law and Ethics in Reconciliation* (Oxford, 2001) 33.
14 For discussion, see Elster, *Closing the Books*, 62ff.
15 Which has generated a huge literature; see, e.g. Charles Villa-Vincencio and Erik Doxtader, *The Provocations of Amnesty* (Cape Town, 2003).
16 Mark Osiel, *Mass Atrocity, Collective Memory and the Law* (New Brunswick, 1997) 138.

legislation, which required certain conduct (often full confession of crimes) and/or certain motivations for the crimes (usually political ones) before an amnesty was granted.[17]

22.2.1 International law and amnesties

There are a number of claims that amnesties for international crimes are always unlawful.[18] One claim is that amnesties are contrary to the duty to prosecute international crimes. The question of whether or not there is a duty to prosecute all international crimes was canvassed in Chapter 4. In brief, however, leaving aside treaty-based obligations to prosecute international crimes, it is difficult to prove a duty to prosecute every instance of an international crime on the basis of customary law, human rights obligations, or the *jus cogens* prohibitions that are encapsulated in parts of international criminal law.[19]

The question of duties to prosecute does not quite exhaust that of the legality of amnesties, although the issues are closely related. The question is whether there is an exception to any existing duty to prosecute when an amnesty is said to be necessary to re-establish peace.[20] Human rights bodies have not been very sympathetic to such claims. The Human Rights Committee has said that amnesties for State officials for torture were 'generally incompatible' with obligations to investigate, prosecute and prevent human rights violations, although the word 'generally' introduces some doubt into the matter.[21] The ICTY has gone further, asserting that the *jus cogens* prohibition on torture also delegitimizes any amnesty for torture.[22] This was also part of the decision of the European Court of Human Rights in *Ould Dah*, where the Court agreed that amnesties for torture are generally incompatible with the international prohibition of that crime.[23] In any event, domestic amnesties do not affect the jurisdiction of other States.

The Inter-American Human Rights Court and Commission have been the most strident in declaring amnesties unlawful.[24] The high-water mark of its practice was the *Barrios Altos*

---

17 See, e.g. Veitch, 'The Legal Politics of Amnesty', 37–8.

18 Diane Orentlicher, 'Settling Accounts, The Duty to Prosecute Human Rights Violations of a Former Regime' (1991) 100 *Yale Law Journal* 2537.

19 See further, section 4.3.

20 See, e.g. Anja Siebert-Fohr, *Prosecuting Serious Human Rights Violations* (Oxford, 2009) 37ff.

21 General Comment 20, Compilation of General Comments and General Recommendations Adopted by Human Rights Treaty Bodies, UN Doc. HRI\GEN\1\Rev. 1 at 30 (1994).

22 *Furundžija* ICTY Ch. II 10.12.1998 para. 155. See also *Karadžić* ICTY T. Ch. 17.12.08, and Benjamin Brockman-Hawe, 'Decision on the Accused's Second Motion for Inspection and Disclosure: Immunity Issue' (2009) 58 *ICLQ* 726 at 730–2.

23 *Ould Dah* v. *France*, Decision No. 13113/03, European Court of Human Rights, 17 March 2009, at 17.

24 See, e.g. Inter-American HR Commission El Salvador Report, 'State's responsibility for 1983 Las Hajas massacre', Report No. 26/92 24 September 1992 para. 169. See generally Siebert-Fohr, *Prosecuting*, ch. 3.

case.[25] In this case the Inter-American Court of Human Rights expressly said that the amnesty granted to state agents by the Peruvian government was invalid, and that:

> This Court considers that all amnesty provisions, provisions on prescription and the establishment of measures designed to eliminate responsibility are inadmissible, because they are intended to prevent the investigation and punishment of those responsible for serious human rights violations such as torture, extrajudicial, summary or arbitrary execution and forced disappearance, all of them prohibited because they violate non-derogable rights recognized by international human rights law.[26]

This is a strong statement, and the case has been interpreted by some as sounding the death knell for all amnesties.[27] This may overstate what is probably the most assertive of all the international courts' decisions on point, and it has not been adopted by other international courts. The case ought to be read against the backdrop of the nature of the (self)amnesties that were granted, the fact that they were not aimed at reconciliation, related to developed States, and did not involve mass participation in international crimes.[28]

At first sight one international treaty provision, Article 6(5) of Additional Protocol II relating to non-international armed conflict, appears to argue in favour of amnesties. It reads as follows:

> At the end of hostilities, the authorities in power shall endeavour to grant the broadest possible amnesty to persons who have participated in the armed conflict, or those deprived of their liberty for reasons related to the armed conflict, whether they are interned or detained.

But in 1999, when interpreting this provision, the ICRC asserted that it was not intended to cover international crimes, in spite of the fact that this was not clear in 1977 when the Protocol was drafted.[29]

Claims that amnesties are always contrary to international law are therefore probably in advance of the current law, although UN policy is now formally against amnesties for international crimes.[30] The current position on amnesties in international law was summed up by the Special Court for Sierra Leone in the *Kallon and Kamara* decision:

---

25 *Barrios Altos Case (Chumbipuma Aguierre et al.* v. *Peru)* Judgment of 14 March 2001; Series C No. 75 [2001] IACHR 5.

26 *Ibid.*, para. 41.

27 Lisa LaPlante, 'Outlawing Amnesty: The Return of Criminal Justice to Transitional Justice Schemes' (2008–2009) 48 *Virginia Journal of International Law* 915.

28 Siebert-Fohr, *Prosecuting*, 109; Robert Cryer, 'Accountability in Post-Conflict Societies: A Matter of Judgment, Practice or Principle?' in Nigel White and Dirk Klaasen (eds.), *The United Nations and Human Rights Protection in Post-Conflict Situations* (Manchester, 2005) 267 at 269–70.

29 Mallinder, *Amnesty*, 125–6.

30 UN practice since the late 1990s (but not before) has been to say that amnesties are not acceptable: see *Report of the Secretary-General on the Establishment of a Special Court for Sierra Leone* UN Doc. S/2000/915, 4 October 2000 para. 24.

that there is a crystallising international norm that a government cannot grant amnesty for serious violations of crimes under international law is amply supported by materials placed before the Court [but the view] that it has crystallised may not be entirely correct ... it is accepted that such a norm is developing under international law.[31]

As time goes by, though, the scope for lawful amnesties appears to be narrowing.[32] As was said by Judge Robertson in his separate opinion in *Kondewa*:

> What can ... be detected, in what may be the development of an interim position is a focus on major malefactors, the intellectual or commanding 'authors' of torture and genocide, who will not be permitted to escape through a pardon that exonerates their underlings. The mesh of the international law dragnet may be excessively loose at this rudimentary stage of its development, but it nonetheless serves to entangle the biggest fish – those who can credibly be accused of bearing the greatest responsibility for international crimes.[33]

22.2.2 The International Criminal Court and amnesties[34]

The preamble of the ICC Statute affirms 'that the most serious crimes of concern to the international community as a whole must not go unpunished', and that States Parties are 'determined to put an end to impunity for the perpetrators of such crimes'; it recalled 'that it is the duty of every State to exercise its criminal jurisdiction over those responsible for international crimes'.[35] Although these provisions do not create legal obligations, a failure to do anything about crimes committed by nationals of, or on the territory of, States Parties to the ICC Statute could well lead to the ICC exercising its powers to prosecute offenders itself.[36] A domestic amnesty does not bind the ICC nor its Prosecutor. The early practice of the ICC, in particular in relation to Uganda, has raised the issue of amnesties.[37] The Prosecutor has taken a tough line in this regard, refusing to take the possibility of an amnesty into account. Although there is the possibility of the Prosecutor deciding to take account of amnesties in his assessment of whether the 'interests of justice' require him to refrain from prosecution,[38] the Prosecutor seems not to have taken that approach. He has taken the view

---

31 *Prosecutor* v. *Kallon and Kamara* SCSL A. Ch. 13.3.2004 para. 82.
32 Although see Christine Bell, *On the Law of Peace: Peace Agreements and the Lex Pacificatoria* (Oxford, 2008) at 240–1.
33 *Kondewa*, SCSL A. Ch. 25.5.2004 para. 48.
34 See generally, Mallinder, *Amnesty*, 279–91 and section 8.6.5.
35 ICC Statute, preambular paras. 4–6.
36 See section 8.6.5.
37 See section 8.12 and William W. Burke-White and Scott Kaplan, 'Shaping the Contours of Domestic Justice: The International Criminal Court and an Admissibility Challenge in the Uganda Situation' in Stahn and Sluiter, *Emerging Practice*, 79.
38 See, e.g. Darryl Robinson, 'Serving the Interests of Justice: Amnesties, Truth Commissions and the International Criminal Court' (2003) 14 *EJIL* 481; Michael P. Scharf, 'The Amnesty Exception to the Jurisdiction of the International Criminal Court' (1999) 32 *Cornell International Law Journal* 507.

that such matters are rarely, if ever, to be taken into account, stating that the drafters of the Rome Statute clearly chose prosecution as the appropriate response to international crimes.[39] Hence, when the Prosecutor is dealing with a matter '[t]he issue is no longer about whether we agree or disagree with the pursuit of justice in moral or practical terms: it is the law', and non-prosecution is a 'last resort'.[40]

While the reason that many assert for the necessity of amnesties is the so-called 'peace versus justice' dilemma,[41] the Prosecutor has stated his view that the 'interests of justice' are not the same as the interests of peace, and his mandate does not cover the latter. They are, to the Prosecutor, the domain of the political organs of the UN, in particular the Security Council, which has the power to defer (for renewable one-year periods) investigations and prosecutions under Article 16 of the Rome Statute.[42] Whether this is an abdication of responsibility, or a sensible means of ensuring that the ICC is seen as being apolitical, is perhaps an open question.[43]

22.2.3 Domestic jurisdictions and amnesties

Domestic amnesties do not bind States other than the granting State in their exercise of extraterritorial jurisdiction; legislation in one State does not alter the jurisdiction of another.[44] It was in part for this reason that the Special Court for Sierra Leone declared that it was not unlawful for the United Nations to refuse to accept the amnesty contained in the 1999 Lomé Peace Accord and thus grant the Court jurisdiction over international crimes from 1996:

> Where jurisdiction is universal, a State cannot deprive another of its jurisdiction to prosecute the offender by the grant of amnesty. It is for this reason unrealistic to regard as universally effective the grant of an amnesty by a State in regard to grave international crimes in which universal jurisdiction exists. A State cannot bring into oblivion and forgetfulness a crime, such as a crime against international law, which other States are entitled to keep alive and remember.[45]

---

39 ICC Office of the Prosecutor, Policy Paper on the Interests of Justice, September 2007, at 3–4.

40 *Ibid.*, at 4, 8–9.

41 See section 2.3.1.

42 See section 8.9.

43 See, e.g. Jens David Ohlin, 'Peace, Security and Prosecutorial Discretion' in Carsten Stahn and Göran Sluiter (eds.), *The Emerging Practice of the International Criminal Court* (Leiden, 2009) 185; Steven Roach, *Politicizing the International Criminal Court: The Convergence of Politics, Ethics and Law* (New York, 2006). It bears remembering that, as Martti Koskenniemi has said, institutions enact, rather than replace politics: Martti Koskenniemi, *The Gentle Civilizer of Nations: The Rise and Fall of International Law 1870–1960* (Cambridge, 2002) 177. The Prosecutor's point is, however, that the politics have been, and are still to be, determined by others, not the ICC.

44 In *Ould Dah* (see footnote 23 above) the European Court of Human Rights decided that a Mauritanian amnesty for torture occurring in Mauritania did not prevent France from prosecuting torture there; see section 22.2.1.

45 *Prosecutor* v. *Kallon and Kamara* SCSL A. Ch. 13.3.2004 para. 67.

The Court had, as mentioned above (see section 22.2.1), noted that amnesties were not contrary to customary law, but took the view that it was not an abuse of process for the Court to ignore the amnesty given its perilous status under international law and the fact that the Court was not a Sierra Leonean court.[46]

The extent to which amnesties granted within a jurisdiction preclude action by municipal courts in that jurisdiction depends, inter alia, on the status of international law in the domestic legal order, and the consistency or otherwise of the amnesty with international law.[47] Although it must be said that it is a trend rather than a rule, judges in some countries are increasingly unlikely to accept amnesties. For example, there are a number of examples of domestic courts, after many years of accepting amnesties, coming around to the view that they are unconstitutional, not relevant to the particular charge, or otherwise inapplicable. For example, in 2005 the Argentine Supreme Court declared the amnesties relating to the 'Dirty War' in the 1970s and 1980s to be unconstitutional.[48] In this case, although the Congress had already repealed the amnesty, the Supreme Court, relying on international law, made clear that the amnesty was also unlawful. In other examples, courts have restrictively interpreted amnesties. For example, in Chile, the Supreme Court has determined that neither amnesties nor statutes of limitation apply to offences involving disappearances, since they are 'continuing' offences, and therefore not susceptible to being amnestied.[49] Against this, though, it ought to be noted that the majority of domestic decisions on point have upheld amnesties early after their passage, only later becoming willing to challenge or limit them.[50]

22.2.4 Appraisal of amnesties

Amnesties are controversial both in law and policy. Those who speak in their favour often claim that it is necessary to have amnesties to bring to an end conflicts, and that to insist on anything more is to condemn others to death or other serious human rights violations, as combatants and others will refuse to relinquish their weapons or power without promises of amnesties.[51] Others see the grant of amnesties as giving in to blackmail,[52] and fostering a

---

46 *Ibid.* And see José Doria, 'The Work of the Special Court for Sierra Leone Through its Jurisprudence' in José Doria et al. (eds.), *The Legal Regime of the International Criminal Court. Essays in Honour of Igor Blishchenko* (The Hague, 2009) 229 at 243.

47 Mallinder, *Amnesty*, 204. For a detailed survey of court decisions on point see *ibid.*, ch. 4.

48 *Simón*, Decision of 14 June 2005, Case No.17.768. See Christine Bakker, 'A Full Stop to Amnesty in Argentina' (2005) 3 *JICJ* 1106.

49 *Sepúlveda*, 17 November 2004. See Fannie Lafontaine, 'No Amnesty or Statute of Limitation for Enforced Disappearances: The *Sandoval* Case Before the Supreme Court of Chile' (2005) 3 *JICJ* 469. For an example of a narrow reading from an internationalized tribunal, see *Sary*, Decision on Appeal Against Provisional Detention Order of Ieng Sary, ECCC P.T. Ch. 17.10.2008 para. 61.

50 Mallinder, *Amnesty*, 206.

51 Anonymous, 'Human Rights in Peace Negotiations' (1996) 18 *Human Rights Quarterly* 249.

52 Mallinder, *Amnesty*, 1–2.

culture of impunity which encourages the future commission of international crimes.[53] It has also been said that amnesties do not lead to peace, and that 'warlords and political leaders capable of committing human rights atrocities are not deterred by amnesties obtained, but emboldened'.[54] Granting amnesties, therefore, is considered by many to undermine the deterrent function of international criminal law (to the extent that it has one),[55] and to represent an ugly political compromise. Sometimes this compromise is also seen as one between elites who bargain away the rights of victims with little regard for them.[56] In part, this has led to calls for 'transitional justice from below', where the calls of those outside political elites are given greater respect,[57] although it is accepted that this can also be exclusionary.[58]

As a result, many approach amnesties with a deeply sceptical, raised eyebrow. Still, even if the time for 'blanket' amnesties may now be over, there are other forms of amnesty, such as the South African amnesty, that are accompanied by other processes that may render them more acceptable, and it is important not to treat all amnesties as the same. Conditional amnesties, that require truth telling, or apply to the less responsible, or are democratically legitimated in the State that passes them, are more likely to be acceptable than those that do not.[59]

It is often said (but not empirically proved) that amnesties promote reconciliation between previously antagonistic parties, and allow populations to 'move on' from the past.[60] However, on the other side it is argued that 'it is difficult to imagine how society can liberate itself from a past in which impunity, lawlessness and abuse of power have prevailed, unless respect for the basic principle of individual criminal responsibility is resurrected'.[61] This is often reduced to the phrase 'no peace without justice' (or more recently, 'no lasting peace without justice'). Whether this is empirically true is a matter of contention.

---

53 See Anja Sibert-Fohr, *Prosecuting Serious Human Rights Violations* (Oxford, 2009) 281–2.

54 Leila Nadya Sadat, 'The Effect of Amnesties Before Domestic and International Tribunals: Morality, Law and Politics' in Edel Hughes, William Schabas and Ramesh Thakur (eds.), *Atrocities and International Accountability: Beyond Transitional Justice* (Tokyo, 2007) 225 at 227.

55 See Mallinder, *Amnesty*, at 17.

56 Richard A. Wilson, *The Politics of Truth and Reconciliation in South Africa: Legitimizing the Post-Apartheid State* (Cambridge, 2001); Richard Burchill, 'From East Timor to Timor-Leste: A Demonstration of the Limits of International Law in the Pursuit of Justice' in Doria, *Legal Regime*, 255 at 288–9. Desmond Tutu's response is that the delegations which negotiated the amnesty in South Africa included victims, who were entitled to speak on behalf of the victims: Desmond Tutu, *No Future Without Forgiveness* (London, 1999) 52–4.

57 See Kieran McEvoy and Lorna McGregor, *Transitional Justice from Below: Grassroots Activism and the Struggle for Change* (Oxford , 2008).

58 Kieran McEvoy and Lorna McGregor, 'Transitional Justice from Below: An Agenda for Research, Policy and Praxis' in McEvoy and McGregor, *Transitional Justice*, 9–10.

59 See Mallinder, *Amnesty*, chs. 2–4, 10; John Dugard, 'Dealing With the Crimes of a Past Regime, Is Amnesty Still an Option?' (1999) 12 *LJIL* 1001.

60 Andreas O'Shea, *Amnesty for Crime in International Law and Practice* (The Hague, 2002) 23–33.

61 Lyal S. Sunga, 'Ten Principles for Reconciling Truth Commissions and Criminal Proceedings' in Doria, *Legal Regime*, 1071.

The matter is made more complex by loose talk about reconciliation (often from perpetrators, rather than victims).[62] Reconciliation is not a simple notion.[63] For example, it is often assumed that reconciliation is a social process, whereas it is at least as much an individual one, between victim and perpetrator.[64] Also, it must be acknowledged that reconciliation, and its partner, forgiveness, often draw upon religious (often, although by no means exclusively, Christian) notions, which are not necessarily universalizable.[65] Indeed, some question the philosophical appropriateness of forgiveness at all.[66] What is certain is that reconciliation, like friendship, cannot be forced upon people, and some victims will not wish to be reconciled with their persecutors, in particular in the absence of remorse.[67] Equally, there is no doubt that forgiveness has accompanied amnesties in certain circumstances.[68]

Alongside forgiveness, there is also the possibility of forgetfulness, in particular, of victims. After all, the term amnesty, as is often pointed out, shares a common Latin root, *amnestia*, with forgetfulness – amnesia.[69] With this comes the risk of increased denial or relativization of international crimes.[70] Not all amnesty processes provide for revelations about what has been done, and as such, can lead to a refusal to acknowledge the suffering of victims, or the extent of wrongdoing. This can be non-accidental, as Stanley Cohen has said: 'social control is ... possible by transforming ... or obliterating the past ... not by opening the past to scrutiny, but closing it and deliberately setting up barriers to memory. This mode of policing the past calls not for the recovery of memory, but its eradication,'[71] or by simple 'slippage' when things are not acknowledged.[72] This strategy is not necessarily effective, in particular where, as in South America, long-standing victims' rights advocates have kept the suffering of the victims visible, and as time has gone on, amnesties and the like have been repealed.[73]

---

62 Stanley Cohen, *States of Denial: Knowing About Atrocities and Suffering* (Cambridge, 2001) 238–9.

63 See, e.g. Laura Olson, 'Provoking the Dragon on the Patio: Matters of Transitional Justice: Penal Repression vs Amnesties' (2006) 88 *IRRC* 275, 277.

64 Arne J. Vetlesen, *Evil and Human Agency, Understanding Collective Evildoing* (Cambridge, 2005) 272–81.

65 Thomas Brudholm, 'On the Advocacy of Forgiveness after Mass Atrocities' in Brudholm and Cushman, *The Religious*, 124. For a more sanguine view see Daniel Philpott, 'When Faith Meets History: The Influence of Religion on Transitional Justice' in *ibid.*, 174.

66 See the discussion in Brudholm and Cushman, *The Religious*.

67 Antje du Bois-Pedain, *Transitional Amnesty in South Africa* (Cambridge, 2007) 232–43, 286–93; Brudholm, and Cushman, *The Religious*, 132–5; Olson, 'Provoking the Dragon', 277.

68 For examples in South Africa, see Tutu, *No Future*.

69 See, e.g. Mallinder, *Amnesty*, 4.

70 For examples, see Mallinder, *Amnesty*, 243.

71 Cohen, *States of Denial*, 243.

72 *Ibid.*, 222.

73 LaPlante, 'Outlawing Amnesty', 950–6. On an African analogue, in relation to Hissene Habré, see Dissenting Opinion of Judge Cançado Trindade in *Belgium* v. *Senegal* (footnote 1 above) paras. 30–45.

Still, international law has not yet developed so far as to prohibit all amnesties in all situations. There is also political support for them in some States; for example, prior to the Iraq war in 2003, the US offered Saddam Hussein exile and non-prosecution if he were to stand down as President of Iraq.[74] There are, in spite of the fact that the language of forgiving and forgetting comes easier to the mouths of perpetrators than victims, possible defences of amnesties as necessary measures in post-conflict situations, at least with respect to lower-ranking offenders, and where resources outstrip the level of offending have been made.[75] As a result, amnesties are likely to continue to be a (contested) feature of responses to international crimes.

22.3 Truth commissions

In part because of the possibility that amnesties will lead to forgetfulness or denial, one of the activities which often accompany them is the setting up of a truth commission.[76] These are often defined as bodies that '(1) investigate the past, (2) . . . investigate a pattern of abuses over a period of time, rather than a specific event, (3) . . . [are] temporary . . . completing . . . [their] . . . work with the submission of a report, and (4) . . . are officially sanctioned, authorized or empowered by the State'.[77] They are often set up as an alternative to prosecutions, especially where the clandestine nature of many of the offences means that they are difficult, if not impossible, to prove to the relevant criminal standard. They are also a means of attempting to get beyond the 'closing of ranks' that can make prosecution of offences by those in close-knit groups, such as particular regiments or teams, so difficult, The idea behind many truth commissions is that people will be more willing to tell about their activities if they are not to be prosecuted for them. This can be important, for example when people have 'disappeared' and relatives of the victims are caught in limbo, not knowing the fate of their family members. Truth commissions can also enable more victims to be able to tell their story than is possible in a court, with all its procedural restrictions. Some commissions, such as the Guatemalan commission, have the authority to make recommendations for reforms, although they are not always taken up.[78]

74 See Mallinder, *Amnesty*, ch. 8.

75 *Ibid.*, *passim*.

76 Albie Sachs, *The Strange Alchemy of Life and Law* (Oxford, 2009) 84. On truth commissions see generally Priscilla Hayner, *Unspeakable Truths: Confronting State Terror and Atrocity* (London, 2001); Priscilla Hayner, 'Fifteen Truth Commissions – A Comparative Study' (1994) 16 *Human Rights Quarterly* 597; Minow, *Between Vengeance*, ch. 4.

77 Hayner, *Unspeakable Truths*, 14. Mark Freeman, *Truth Commissions and Procedural Fairness* (Cambridge, 2006) 18 defines them as 'an *ad hoc*, autonomous, and victim centred commission of inquiry set up in and authorized by a state for the primary purposes of (1) investigating and reporting on the principal causes and consequences of broad and relatively recent patterns of severe violence or repression that occurred in the state during determinate periods of abusive rule or conflict, and (2) making recommendations for their redress and future prevention'.

78 Hayner, *Unspeakable Truths*, ch. 10.

The terms of reference setting up a commission will define the time frame and sometimes the kinds of conduct to be investigated. The terms of reference are usually the outcome of negotiations between the relevant parties, and can reflect their relative power. One of the main purposes of truth commissions is to acknowledge the harm that was done to the victims, by writing an official report setting out the violations of their rights. This is thought not only to counter later denials,[79] but also to provide a form of healing for victims,[80] and provide the basis for societal reconciliation. The South African Truth and Reconciliation report named names, whilst the Argentinean commission did not have the authority to do so.[81] Where names are named, it is more important to have some form of procedural protection for those giving evidence or admitting crimes.[82] For example, some truth commissions that identified perpetrators gave them advance notice of this and a chance to respond.[83]

There are other possible limits on the reports they issue. The South African report, for example, only had the mandate to deal with political violence. It could not, thus, deal with issues such as land dispossessions, forcible transfers and other aspects of apartheid.[84] As a result it could only tell part of the story of apartheid. It could not deal with the use and abuse of the legal and political system in creating and maintaining the apartheid system. In contrast, the Liberian Truth and Reconciliation Commission, although intended to focus primarily on the post-1979 history of that country's conflict, also looked into issues such as corruption, misgovernment and the role of third party States.[85]

The quality of the report depends in part on how good the information available to the commission is. It can be difficult to persuade perpetrators to come forward to testify about their role in repressions, or victims to speak about sensitive matters such as sexual offences committed against them.[86] The confessions of perpetrators can also be framed in a manner which amounts, in fact, to a form of denial.[87] This was, in part, avoided in South Africa by making amnesty applications contingent on attending the commission and telling the full story. There have been some prosecutions for those who refused to testify, or who did not completely disclose their actions.[88] However, some important witnesses such as ex-President P. W. Botha refused to testify before the commission.

The evidence-taking engaged in by a commission often requires people to incriminate themselves and, therefore, truth commissions often stand in place of prosecutions. This does

---

79 Cohen, *States of Denial*, ch. 10.
80 Minow, *Between Vengeance*, 66–74.
81 Hayner, *Unspeakable Truths*, ch. 8.
82 See Freeman, *Truth Commissions*.
83 Freeman, *Truth Commissions*, ch. 7.
84 *Ibid.*, 73–4.
85 Truth and Reconciliation Commission of Liberia, Final Report, vol. II (available at https://www.trcofliberia.org/reports/final) ch. 6, 261, 243–51.
86 Hayner, *Unspeakable Truths*, 77–8.
87 Cohen, *States of Denial*, ch. 4.
88 Sachs, *Strange Alchemy*, 78.

not, however, have to be the case.[89] For example the Truth and Reconciliation Commission in Sierra Leone took place at the same time as the Special Court for Sierra Leone.[90] Relations between the two were strained, however, and the Commission was critical of the Special Court in its report, in particular of the fact that the Special Court was not willing to allow Sam Hinga Norman, being tried before that court, to testify before the Commission in the manner it preferred.[91] The Liberian Truth and Reconciliation Commission's final report recommended prosecutions of some of those responsible for gross violations of human rights or serious violations of humanitarian law,[92] although whether these will materialize is unclear at present.

There are questions about the extent to which the reports of truth commissions can reflect any form of 'objective truth', if such a concept exists, and whether they can lead to an agreed history between old enemies.[93] Given the orientation of truth commissions towards victims, they do not have the rules of procedure and evidence that are considered necessary in courts to ensure reliability and verification of testimony. Whilst this is understandable and correct, it may impact upon the truth that the report seeks to set out.[94]

It has also been questioned if truth-telling does lead to reconciliation,[95] or an ability to move beyond the past.[96] Similarly, it has been doubted if truth and reconciliation are congruent goals.[97] Most, though, accept that truth has a role to play in reconciliation, although few would say that truth alone can achieve such a goal.[98] Much again can depend on what is reported on; commissions which exclude the roles of bystanders and of those who benefited from the system that committed such crimes have been criticized on the basis that they cannot provide for reconciliation, as they exclude a large part of society from their gaze.[99]

89 See Sunga, 'Ten Principles'.

90 See generally William Schabas, 'Internationalized Courts and their Relationship with Alternative Accountability Mechanisms: The Case of Sierra Leone' in Cesare Romano et al. (eds.), *Internationalized Criminal Courts* (Oxford, 2004) 157.

91 *Witness to Truth: Report of the Truth and Reconciliation Commission for Sierra Leone* (Accra, 2004), vol. 3b, ch. 6; *Norman* SCSL A. Ch. 28.11.2003.

92 TRC Liberia, Final Report, vol. II, 268. It also recommended non-prosecution (but not amnesty) for some perpetrators, on the basis that they had cooperated fully with the TRC: *ibid.*, 268–9, 288.

93 François du Bois, 'Nothing But the Truth: The South African Alternative to Corrective Justice in Transitions to Democracy' in Christodoulidis and Veitch, *Lethe's Law*, 91.

94 Anne Orford, 'Commissioning the Truth' (2006) 15 *Columbia Journal of Gender and Law* 851 at 859–60.

95 Hayner, *Unspeakable Truths*, 155–61.

96 It is possible that the idea that truth allows people to move on is at least in part a religious notion, see e.g. the Gospel according to St John 8:23 'And ye shall know the truth, and the truth shall make you free' (New Testament, Bible). It is notable that the South African Truth and Reconciliation Commission often began its hearings with prayers (Sachs, *Strange Alchemy*, 75). See also Minow, *Between Vengeance*, 55.

97 Hayner, *Unspeakable Truths*, 155.

98 See, e.g. Minow, *Between Vengeance*, 79–83.

99 Rama Maini, 'Does Power Trump Morality? Reconciliation or Transitional Justice?' in Hughes, Schabas and Thakur, *Atrocities*, 27 at 36.

Sometimes, as occurred in South Africa, as part of the attempt to promote reconciliation and help provide victims with some form of healing, victims are given the opportunity to attend the hearings and discuss the revelations made by the perpetrators. Some scholars are of the view that truth commissions are particularly well suited to provide healing for victims.[100] Much depends on the attitude of perpetrators, and the engagement that they have with the process ranges from the full to the essentially grudging and formal. Albie Sachs writes of the South African Truth and Reconciliation hearings that:

> instead of coming forward and speaking from the heart and crying and being open, most of the perpetrators came in neatly pressed suits, expressing tight body language, with their lawyers next to them, and read prepared statements as though they were in a court of law. Their admissions were important but tended to be limited to a factual acknowledgement of unlawful conduct coupled with a rehearsed apology, rather than encompassing an emotional and convincing acknowledgement of wrongdoing.[101]

Others have used truth and reconciliation hearings as political platforms.[102] Rather like in the case of testifying in criminal proceedings, the extent to which victims are assisted by the process depends on individual reactions, and these are not easily extrapolated into general statements about victims as a whole. Some victims in South Africa issued a court challenge to the truth and reconciliation commission and the amnesty process, although it was rejected by the South African Constitutional Court.[103]

Truth commissions, as has been said, are both high risk and 'inherently political enterprises'.[104] They are set up for reasons that are both good and bad. They may well be created in some circumstances to ensure that victims are given acknowledgement of their suffering, or as a means of attempting to prevent the recurrence of the crimes.[105] In others, though, 'a cynical government may hope that a truth commission will help exhaust public interest in greater measures of political and legal accountability'.[106] Such critiques have been made in relation to the recommendation of the East Timor Truth and Reconciliation Commission that there be no further prosecutions.[107] Truth commissions are considered by some to be an ersatz response to international crimes. This is a harsh evaluation: truth commissions do not always replace prosecutions, and can go at least part of the way to fulfilling goals that prosecutions cannot, particularly for victims.[108] Much, of course, depends on how well the

---

100 Minow, *Between Vengeance*, 61–79.
101 Sachs, *Strange Alchemy*, 86–7. A similar problem was noted by the TRC Liberia, Final Report, vol. II, v.
102 Minow, *Between Vengeance*, 83.
103 See *AZAPO* (footnote 9 above).
104 Freeman, *Truth Commissions*, 37.
105 *Ibid.*, 38.
106 *Ibid.*, 37.
107 Burchill, 'From East Timor', 289.
108 Minow, *Between Vengeance*, 55–90.

process is designed and implemented, and 'a poorly executed truth commission may be worse than no truth commission at all'.[109]

22.4 Lustration

One way of dealing with large-scale administrative complicity in international crimes is lustration, i.e. purging of public servants who are thought to be responsible for international crimes.[110] This was a frequently used mechanism in Eastern Europe after the collapse of Communism there in the late 1980s. There are elements of this approach to international crimes in the removal of members of the Ba'ath party from the Iraqi public service and judiciary. Lustration may be seen as a means of removing corrupt or inefficient staff, but the main purpose is often a form of punishment. Although it can deal in some ways with large-scale complicity, the fact that it is a form of punishment (or is intended to be) is problematic, because it involves serious consequences for people, but is almost always done on a mass basis, without individual hearings to determine what precise responsibility a lustrated person bears. In many totalitarian societies, party membership is necessary for a career in the civil service, and many join essentially as an administrative convenience, and are not personally involved in wrongdoing. As a result, it is questionable whether lustration is consistent with human rights law, in particular the right to have rights and duties at law determined by a judicial process.[111] Punishment is only appropriate following a criminal proceeding.[112] Notwithstanding this, the Liberian Truth and Reconciliation Commission recommended that people whom it had found responsible for grave crimes ought to be barred from public office.[113] The United Nations has undertaken vetting proceedings, for example in Kosovo; however, these are designed as individuated processes, where individuals are identified who have engaged in wrongdoing and are given opportunities to answer allegations against them. This is to ensure that the processes are compatible with international human rights law standards.[114]

---

109 Maini, 'Does Power Trump Morality?', 34. The Secretary-General's Report on the Rule of Law and Transitional Justice (see footnote 8 above), para. 51, takes the view that truth commissions are best formed through consultative processes on mandates and commissioner selection and that, to be successful, they must enjoy real independence and have credible commissioner criteria and processes, strong public information and communication strategies, be gender and victim sensitive and provide for reparations. They also need international support.

110 See generally, Teitel, *Transitional Justice*, ch. 5; Stanley Cohen, 'State Crimes of Previous Regimes: Knowledge, Accountability and the Policing of the Past' (1995) 20 *Law and Social Inquiry* 7.

111 ICCPR, Art. 14; *Casanovas* v. *France* Human Rights Committee (441/90).

112 Joel Feinberg, *Doing and Deserving* (1970) 95–118, reprinted in Antony Duff and David Garland (eds.), *A Reader on Punishment* (Oxford, 1994) 71.

113 TRC Liberia, Final Report, vol. II, 269–70.

114 Secretary General's Report on the Rule of Law and Transitional Justice (see footnote 8 above), paras. 52–3.

22.5   Reparations and civil claims

International crimes, where attributable to States, have been the subject of reparations. Germany, for example, has paid over $60billion to victims in reparations for the Holocaust. Reparations have also been given to some of those who were the victims of the Argentinean junta in the 1970s and 1980s.[115] There is a human right to a remedy for violations of human rights, which may involve some form of financial recompense.[116] The levels of such reparations are often controversial, however, and many societies in which international crimes are committed do not have large funds to finance reparations programmes. Even so, the symbolic function of reparations can be important.[117]

There may also be the possibility of bringing private civil actions against those responsible for international crimes, either in the State where the activity occurred, or in a third State.[118] The US is perhaps the most well known of those third States, owing to its Alien Tort Claims Act and the *Filartiga* jurisprudence on it, which permit non-US nationals to bring tort actions against certain violators of international law.[119] In other countries such claims may be excluded through lack of jurisdiction or because of immunities attaching to State officials. Civil claims may mean quite a lot to victims, as the continued attempts by 'comfort women' to obtain compensation from Japan show.[120] The problem with such claims, even where they succeed, is that it is difficult to enforce the judgments,[121] and they rely on the person sued having money. Evidence gathering is also difficult, and bringing such claims can be expensive. In the absence of a legal aid programme, or lawyers willing to work *pro bono*, such actions can be beyond the means of victims. Also, financial measures may not bring the same satisfaction to victims as would the criminal prosecution of the offenders.

22.6   Local justice mechanisms

In part because of the increasing acceptance of cultural diversity in relation to the implementation of international criminal law,[122] there has been an increase in interest in local justice mechanisms. Local justice has been said to have 'three key attributes, (1) it focuses on groups rather than individuals, (2) it seeks compromise and community

---

115 See Hayner, *Unspeakable Truths*, ch. 11; Teitel, *Transitional Justice*, ch. 4.
116 ICCPR, Art. 2(3).
117 Minow, *Between Vengeance*, 100, 102–5.
118 Although amnesties may limit the possibility of civil actions in the *locus delicti*.
119 *Filartiga* v. *Pena-Irala* 630 F. 2d 876 (1980); *Sosa* v. *Alvarez-Machain* 542 US 692 (2004).
120 Kelly Askin, 'Comfort Women – Shifting Blame and Stigma from Victims to Victimizers' (2001) 1 *International Criminal Law Review* 5.
121 Which may be disappointing for victims expecting to obtain anything other than moral satisfaction from the proceedings.
122 See section 2.4.

"harmony", and (3) it emphasizes restitution over other forms of punishment'.[123] The practices of local justice are probably too varied to be defined easily in such a way, however, as they run the gamut of responses from the *gacaca* trials in Rwanda, which are in essence a form of semi-formal court proceeding, to the ceremonial reintegration ceremony *mato oput* in Northern Uganda which involves the drinking of a bitter root-based drink. It is possible to see the South African Truth and Reconciliation Commission as being in part inspired by local justice ideas, in particular the concept of humaneness and community known in South Africa as *ubuntu*. The Commission has frequently been defended on this basis.[124]

Local justice mechanisms are supported by many, on the basis that they 'may have greater legitimacy and capacity than devastated formal systems, and they promise local ownership, access and efficiency'.[125] In addition, some take the view that such local justice mechanisms can provide a more comprehensive and individuated response to conflicts.[126] Support for local justice mechanisms is often linked to calls for the ICC to show respect for their activities, to avoid being seen as culturally insensitive.[127] In his paper on the interests of justice the ICC Prosecutor has recognized a role for local justice mechanisms.[128] However, care must be taken not to accept uncritically, or 'sentimentalize',[129] local justice mechanisms, which can in fact be government-led, questionable on human rights grounds, and can reproduce local hierarchies rather than respond to the needs of all.[130] Some may also not be appropriate for international crimes, as they were not developed for such serious offences, or their procedures cannot be invoked, for example when the victims (or perpetrators) are dead or unknown.[131] At the same time 'in exploring the relationship between indigenous processes and formal justice mechanisms, the debate should not regress to a stark neo-colonialist versus cultural relativism stand-off ... [and] ... in considering options for transitional justice, the choice between local and international approaches should not be viewed as exclusive'.[132]

---

123 Lars Waldorf, 'Mass Justice for Mass Atrocity: Rethinking Local Justice as Transitional Justice' (2006) 79 *Temple Law Review* 1 at 9.
124 See, e.g. Minow, *Between Vengeance*, 51.
125 Waldorf, 'Mass Justice', 4.
126 Lorna McGregor, 'International Law as a Tiered Process: Transitional Justice at the Local, National and International Level' in McEvoy and McGregor, *Transitional Justice*, 47 at 61.
127 Drumbl, *Atrocity*, ch. 5 and 187–94.
128 See p. 8 of ICC office of the Prosecutor, Policy Paper on the Interests of Justice, available at http://www.icc-cpi.int/.
129 Drumbl, *Atrocity*, 148.
130 McGregor, 'International Law', 61–3; Mark Drumbl, 'Collective Violence and Individual Punishment: The Criminality of Mass Atrocity' (2005) 99 *Northwestern University Law Review* 539 at 549; Tim Allen, *Trial Justice: The International Criminal Court and the Lord's Resistance Army* (London, 2007) ch. 6.
131 Lino Owor Ogora, *Moving Forward: Traditional Justice and Victim Participation in Northern Uganda* (Wynberg, 2009) 9–10.
132 McGregor, 'International Law', 72.

Further reading

M. Cherif Bassiouni (ed.), *Post-Conflict Justice* (Ardsley, 2002).

Christine Bell, *On the Law of Peace: Peace Agreements and the Lex Pacificatoria* (Oxford, 2008) ch 12.

Antonio Cassese, 'On the Current Trend towards Criminal Prosecution and Punishment of Breaches of International Humanitarian Law' (1998) 9 *EJIL* 2.

Stanley Cohen, *States of Denial* (Cambridge, 2001).

David Dyzenhaus, *Judging Judges, Judging Ourselves: Truth, Reconciliation and the Apartheid Legal Order* (Oxford, 1998).

Neil Kritz, *Transitional Justice: How Emerging Democracies Reckon With Former Regimes* (Washington DC, 1995).

Louse Mallinder, *Amnesty, Human Rights and Political Transitions: Bridging the Peace and Justice Divide* (Oxford, 2008).

Juan Méndez, 'National Reconciliation, Transnational Justice and the International Criminal Court' (2001) 15 *Ethics and International Affairs* 25.

Carlos Nino, 'The Duty to Punish Past Abuses of Human Rights Put Into Context: The Case of Argentina' (1991) 100 *Yale Law Journal* 2619.

Laura Olsen, 'Measures Complementing Prosecution' (2002) 84 *International Review of the Red Cross* 173.

Steven Ratner, 'New Democracies, Old Atrocities: An Inquiry in International Law' (1999) 87 *Georgetown Law Journal* 707.

Paul Roberts, 'Restoration and Retribution in International Criminal Justice' in Andrew von Hirsch et al. (eds.), *Restorative Justice and Criminal Justice: Competing or Reconcilable Paradigms?* (Oxford, 2004) 115.

Naomi Roht-Arriaza, 'State Responsibility to Investigate and Prosecute Grave Human Rights Violations in International Law' (1990) 78 *California Law Review* 449.

Carsten Stahn, 'United Nations Peace-Building, Amnesties and Alternative Forms of Justice: A Change in Practice?' (2002) 845 *International Review of the Red Cross* 191.

23

The Future of International Criminal Law

23.1 Introduction

International criminal law has developed at an unprecedented rate since the early 1990s. It is therefore too early for us to issue any final judgments but it is the purpose of this chapter to evaluate recent developments as far as possible, and to look tentatively to the future of international criminal law.

23.2 International courts and tribunals

It is a commonplace, because it is largely correct, that the catalyst for the revival of international criminal law was the creation of the ad hoc Tribunals by the Security Council in the early to mid 1990s. Although the project for an international criminal court had received some increased attention since its reinclusion on the General Assembly's agenda in 1989, this was not seen as likely to bear fruit. The creation of the ad hoc Tribunals, on the other hand, showed that such tribunals could be established in a reasonably short time, and the focus of debate shifted from the question whether such tribunals were a realistic possibility to how they could be improved.

The ad hoc Tribunals have been criticized almost from the start as being expensive and bureaucratic,[1] as well as producing what some consider to be show trials.[2] Nonetheless, these experiments (as that is what they were at their beginnings)[3] have to be credited not only with a reasonable level of success in their own proceedings,[4] but also with providing the impetus for the creation of what many thought was a near impossibility in the international legal order, a permanent international criminal court.[5]

---

1 Ralph Zacklin, 'The Failings of the *ad hoc* Tribunals' (2004) 2 *JICJ* 541 at 542–3.
2 See the discussion in Martti Koskenniemi, 'Between Impunity and Show Trials' (2002) 6 *Max Planck Yearbook of United Nations Law* 1.
3 Which many thought would never get beyond the paper stage, see Antonio Cassese, 'The ICTY: A Living and Vital Reality' (2004) 2 *JICJ* 585 at 585–6.
4 See sections 7.2.5 and 7.3.5.
5 Ian Brownlie, *Principles of International Law*, 5th edn (Oxford, 1998) 568.

The progression from Nuremberg to the ICC has been described as a long road ending in the triumph of the Rome Conference, hence the frequent use of the title 'From Nuremberg to The Hague' in writings on international criminal law.[6] It has often been claimed that the ICC will lead to the 'end of impunity' and it has been hailed as something of a panacea for international ills.[7] But the euphoria which accompanied the adoption of the ICC Statute has given way to a hard-headed, sometimes cynical, realism about what can be achieved by an international court. The Rome Statute does not create a supranational criminal law enforcement regime. It does not create a self-contained police force to investigate international crimes or to enforce its arrest warrants. As such, the investigations and prosecutions before the ICC may often occur against the backdrop of situations of extreme practical and political difficulty.[8] Furthermore, the ICC Statute has not been universally ratified and a number of States are either ambivalent about or opposed to the ICC. Although the US has become more supportive of the Court, some African States appear to be cooling in their relationship with it.[9]

That said, given the inertia that frequently attends treaty ratification, most supporters of the ICC would not have dared to predict that about 110 States would have ratified the ICC Statute by 2010. Early fears that only stable Western democracies would ratify, leaving the Court with little to investigate, have also proved unfounded. The first trials are proceeding and there is anecdotal evidence that they are having a deterrent effect.

23.3   Developments in national prosecutions of international crimes

It ought not to be forgotten that the site of most international criminal law enforcement is not intended to be international courts. International tribunals have arisen because of the failure, or the absence, of national justice efforts, but they are not meant to replace them. One of the major roles which international judicial mechanisms have is the promotion of the more effective use of national criminal justice systems. The international courts and tribunals cannot deal with any but a handful of cases, and national systems must take a greater part in the prosecution of international crimes if international criminal law is to be effectively enforced.

This is particularly the case for the ICC. Owing to the principle of complementarity,[10] it is sometimes said that the ICC will have succeeded if it never has to prosecute anyone itself.[11] Such assertions are overstated: if all the Court did was to oversee domestic jurisdictions it

---

6 Koskenniemi, 'Between Impunity', 34–5.

7 On this discussion, see Bruce Broomhall, *International Justice and the International Criminal Court: Between Sovereignty and the Rule of Law* (Oxford, 2003) 1–2.

8 Paper on Some Policy Issues Before the Office of the Prosecutor, September 2003, 1–2 (hereafter 'Policy Paper').

9 See section 8.11.

10 See section 8.6.

11 Policy Paper, 4; and see section 8.6.

would rapidly be seen as an extremely expensive way of doing so. Nonetheless, there is a great deal of truth in the claim that a major role of the ICC is to ensure that domestic jurisdictions act against international crimes. The role of the Prosecutor is structured so that the Court can act as a considerable incentive to States in ensuring that they prosecute international crimes and, where it is appropriate, assist them in doing so. This includes the passing of evidence and expertise. The Prosecutor has stated that the policy of the Office of the Prosecutor is to engage with governments to ensure prosecution of crimes within the jurisdiction of the ICC.[12] In addition, ratification of the ICC Statute has prompted a reasonable number of States (although not enough) to adopt domestic criminal legislation covering the core international crimes.[13] Against a background of States traditionally failing to implement international crimes into their domestic law,[14] this in itself is a development worthy of note.

Universal jurisdiction has come under attack in recent years, and this has led, to some extent, to a retrenchment of universal jurisdiction in theory and in practice.[15] Nonetheless, this retrenchment has occurred because of, with notable exceptions such as the *Eichmann* case, a move for universal jurisdiction from the warmth of the greenhouse of suggestion to the cold light of day-to-day international law. Universal jurisdiction, in some form or another, has been implemented into more States' domestic law than was the case in 1998. The existence of such jurisdiction and its possible exercise have plausibly had some impact on other States, which have looked to prosecute the commission of international crimes by their own nationals, in part to pre-empt such claims. There have also been some significant exercises of universal jurisdiction at the domestic level, which are sometimes forgotten in the debate over the precise ambit of the permission which international law grants to States to assert it.[16] But as the 2009 statement of the African Union criticizing the 'abuse' of universal jurisdiction shows, the political controversies about the exercise of universal jurisdiction have not gone away.[17]

The problems which States have in cooperating with one another in prosecuting international crimes may, it is hoped, become less significant with the conclusion of new and more effective agreements on inter-State cooperation, including those at the regional level. The situation at present, though, cannot be described as satisfactory.[18]

---

12 Policy Paper, 3.

13 See section 4.4.

14 Menno Kamminga, 'Final Report on the Exercise of Universal Jurisdiction in Relation to Gross Human Rights Abuses' in International Law Association, *Report of the Sixty-Ninth Conference* (London, 2000) 403 at 412–14.

15 See section 3.5.4.

16 *Ibid*.

17 Decision on the Report of the Commission on the Abuse of Universal Jurisdiction (Assembly/AU/14/ (XI)), annexed to Letter from the AU Permanent Observer to the President of the Security Council, UN Doc. S/2008/465.

18 See Chapters 5 and 20.

As shown, inter alia, by the angry reaction of the African Union to the indictment of President Al Bashir,[19] one continued area of controversy is that of immunities. The ICJ in the *Yerodia* case has shown that international criminal law is still subject to aspects of the law on immunity.[20] Therefore, national (and international) courts have recognized that certain immunities still exist under general international law[21] and this limits the possibilities for prosecuting international crimes in some instances, especially on the basis of extraterritorial jurisdiction. Immunities, which reflect some aspects of the international legal order, show that international criminal law has not established itself as a trump card in international law.[22] As a result triumphalism about international criminal law would be misplaced.

23.4   The trend towards accountability

In a statement released just after the Rome Conference, which adopted the Statute for the ICC, Amnesty International claimed:

> [t]he true significance of the adoption of the Statute may well lie, not in the actual institution itself in its early years, which will face enormous obstacles, but in the revolution in legal and moral attitudes towards the worst crimes in the world. No longer will these crimes be simply political events to be addressed by diplomacy at the international level, but crimes which all states have a duty to punish themselves, or, if they fail to fulfil this duty, by the international community in accordance with the rule of law.[23]

This assertion contains more than a grain of truth. The creation of the ICC reflects, and contributes greatly to, a significant cultural turn to accountability. Fifteen years ago, most of those accused of international crimes could sleep soundly, fairly sure that they would not be required to stand trial for their conduct. It is unlikely that Augusto Pinochet or Hissene Habré thought that international law would be brought to bear upon them. Both of them, to different extents, have been proved wrong, even if, on the basis of what had occurred since Nuremberg and Tokyo, their opinion had an empirical basis.

The ad hoc international criminal tribunals may well have been created out of motives that were, at best, mixed,[24] but the idea they contained, that of accountability for international crimes, was one which caught on. Ideas are important in international relations,[25] and this

---

19 Decision of the African States Parties to the Rome Statute of the International Criminal Court (Assembly/ AU/13 (XIII)).
20 On the ambit of these, see Chapter 21.
21 *Ibid.*
22 As Judge ad hoc Van den Wyngaert noted, the majority opinion in *Yerodia* did not even use the term: *Case Concerning the Arrest Warrant of 11 April 2000 (DRC v. Belgium)* 14.2.2002, ICJ Rep 2002, Dissenting Opinion of Judge ad hoc Van den Wyngaert, para. 6.
23 Quoted in William Pace and Mark Thieroff, 'Participation of Non-Governmental Organizations' in Lee, *The Making of the Rome Statute*, 396.
24 See section 2.4.
25 See Alexander Wendt, *Social Theory of International Relations* (Cambridge, 1999).

one caught the eye both of States and many non-governmental actors. As has been said, '[w]hat started out in 1993 as mostly a public relations ploy, namely to create an *ad hoc* tribunal to appear to be doing something about human rights violations in Bosnia without major risk, by 1998 had become an important global movement for international criminal justice'.[26]

The existence of international criminal law is now challenging States to determine the place of justice in their foreign relations policy. It is notable that criminal justice has been structured into the work of the relevant UN agencies, and whenever the UN has a say in a post-conflict situation, accountability for international crimes appears on the agenda. This does not guarantee a particular response, but the fact that justice weighs in the scales is a transformation from the politics of impunity from which even the UN was not immune as recently as 1994.[27] The importance of international justice has been accepted by what some consider to be the primary international organ of *realpolitik*, the Security Council. For example, in Resolution 1265(1999) the Security Council emphasized 'the responsibility of States to end impunity and to prosecute those responsible for genocide, crimes against humanity and serious violations of international humanitarian law ... and [the Security Council] acknowledge[d] the historic significance of the adoption of the ICC Statute of the International Criminal Court'. It must be conceded, by way of reminder, that 'present signals are not universally positive'[28] and the power of ideas is not always determinative. Nor should the capacity for States to maintain a distinction between their public rhetoric and private positions be underestimated.

States have had to engage with the peace and justice dilemma in relation to the early cases at the ICC; on occasion there has been a lack of enthusiasm for the enforcement of arrest warrants if that is perceived, rightly or wrongly, to pose a threat to peace processes. The apparently conflicting requirements of peace and justice have been seen in the ICC warrants against the LRA leaders and those in Sudan and this has led to criticisms of the Prosecutor or the Court as a whole. But this is a matter which the international community as a whole must address, and if there is in reality an instance when prosecutions should temporarily give way to justice, it should be for the Security Council to seek a deferral.

However, many of the criticisms of international criminal prosecution which bedevilled it before, especially that of 'victor's justice', have been blunted, if not eradicated. It is true that selectivity remains a problem in international criminal law, and the perception of bias against Africa has caused some concern, but selectivity is probably less pronounced than before.[29] Also, selective justice is probably preferable to no justice at all, even though the

---

26 David Forsythe, *Human Rights in International Relations* (Cambridge, 2000) 221.
27 See Michael Scharf, 'Swapping Amnesty for Peace, Was There a Duty to Prosecute International Crimes in Haiti?' (1996) 31 *Texas International Law Journal* 1.
28 Broomhall, *International Justice*, 3.
29 Robert Cryer, *Prosecuting International Crimes: Selectivity and the International Criminal Law Regime* (Cambridge, 2005) 327–30.

legitimacy of international criminal law will be ensured only when it is clear that such crimes are prosecuted wherever, and by whomever, they are committed. The more States that ratify the ICC Statute, the less this critique will have purchase in relation to the applicability of the substantive law of the ICC.[30]

Having asserted the importance of international criminal law, States and others may, and will, according to a constructivist account, begin to internalize the values they have espoused, even if initially only rhetorically, and act upon them.[31] Once States prosecute international crimes, even if it is on the basis that if they do not do so the ICC will or that they will be criticized internationally or domestically, this will have an effect on the way they perceive their interests. The more that international crimes are prosecuted, the more that doing so becomes normalized and States are likely to do so simply on the basis that it is what is done in relation to international crimes.[32]

There have been suggestions that the current trend towards international criminal liability runs the risk of removing focus for liability from States.[33] There are a number of answers to such critiques. Where the conduct of those committing international crimes is attributable to a State, through the normal rules of State responsibility,[34] such responsibility is concurrent, rather than exclusive.[35] Pragmatically speaking, the reason for the rise of individual liability is also that State responsibility has not proved efficacious in achieving any of the specific aims of international criminal law; hence Leila Sadat's view that individual criminal liability has been revived, at least as much as for any other reason, out of a frustration with other mechanisms of ensuring accountability.[36] Such a view is more than adequately supported by the classic statement of the Nuremberg IMT that 'crimes against international law are committed by men, not abstract entities, and only by punishing individuals who commit such crimes can the provisions of international law be enforced'.[37] In the end, the critique ought to be seen not as undermining the importance of individual liability, but a reminder that it is not the only form of responsibility relevant to international crimes.

---

30 Although on the limitations of this law see *ibid.*, chs. 4–6.

31 Robert Cryer, 'State Sovereignty vs International Criminal Law: Another Round?' (2005) 16 *EJIL* 979 at 994–6.

32 *Ibid.*

33 See the careful case made in Hazel Fox, 'The ICJ's Treatment of Acts of the State, and in Particular, the Attribution of Acts of Individuals to the State' in Nisuke Ando, Edward McWhinney and Rüdiger Wolfrum (eds.), *Liber Amoricum Shigeru Oda* (The Hague, 2001) 147.

34 Which is frequently, although not inevitably, the case. For details on such rules see James Crawford, *The International Law Commission's Articles on State Responsibility: Introduction, Text and Commentaries* (Cambridge, 2002).

35 See, e.g. André Nollkaemper, 'Concurrence Between Individual Responsibility and State Responsibility in International Law' (2003) 52 *ICLQ* 615.

36 Leila Sadat, *The International Criminal Court and the Transformation of International Law: Justice for the New Millennium* (New York, 2002) ch. 3.

37 Nuremberg IMT: Judgment and Sentences (1947) 41 *AJIL* 221.

23.5   The development of international criminal law

International criminal law is a relatively new discipline and it does not pretend to be a complete system of criminal law. It is not intended to be a replacement for the totality of domestic criminal law; and there is no reason why it ought to be. It has inconsistencies and incoherencies that are the result of its formation in political negotiations.[38] Furthermore, within the parameters of international criminal law the ICC Statute is not the final word. Some have presented it as something close to definitive, even where it is controversial,[39] but Article 10 of the Statute itself recognizes that the law may continue to develop. There is scope for further development, within limits, by courts including the ICC, although the ICC's interpretive mandate is more 'hemmed in' than others have been.[40]

These considerations raise the possibility that different bodies of international criminal law will apply before different tribunals and there will be consequent problems not only of coherence but also in determining the precise customary position on controversial parts of international criminal law. This problem arises both with the criminal tribunals and in the International Court of Justice in the context of State responsibility.[41] There are already areas of divergence on substantive law between the founding documents of the ad hoc Tribunals and the ICC Statute,[42] and, although the ICC has shown respect towards the jurisprudence of the ad hoc Tribunals, there are already some significant differences with respect to substantive international criminal law on, for example genocide, joint criminal enterprise and superior responsibility.[43] There are also differences between international law and some national laws.[44] This is unfortunate, although it must be said that there is far more evidence

---

38 Broomhall, for example, correctly notes that '[b]ecause the judgement of states, individually and collectively, is subject to diverse extra-legal influences, the process of international criminalization will always be less orderly than its conceptual formulation' (Broomhall, *International Justice*, 39).

39 Robert Cryer, 'Of Custom, Treaties, Scholars and the Gavel: The Impact of the International Criminal Tribunals on the ICRC Customary Law Study' (2006) 11 *Journal of Conflict and Security Law* 239 at 257–62.

40 See William Schabas, 'Interpreting the Statutes of the ad hoc Tribunals' in Lal Chand Vohrah et al. (eds.), *Man's Inhumanity to Man: Essays in Honour of Antonio Cassese* (The Hague, 2003) 847 at 887.

41 For discussion of the different rulings of the ICJ (in the *Nicaragua* case) and ICTY (in *Tadić*) on the meaning of 'effective' or 'overall' control for the purpose of responsibility for the acts of others, see Report of the Study Group of the ILC, 'Fragmentation of International Law: Difficulties Arising from the Diversification and Expansion of International Law' (GAOR A/CN.4/L.682 13 April 2006) paras. 49–52. The ICJ has reiterated its support for the *Nicaragua* test and criticized the ICTY on point; see *Case concerning the Application of the Convention on the Prevention and Punishment of the Crime of Genocide (Bosnia and Herzegovina* v. *Serbia and Montenegro)* ICJ 26.2.2007, paras 402–6.

42 Compare, for example Art. 7 of the ICC Statute with Art. 5 of the ICTY Statute, Art. 3 of the ICTR Statute and Art. 2 of the SCSL Statute.

43 On genocide compare *Situation in Darfur (Al Bashir* arrest warrant case) ICC PT. Ch. I 4.3.2009 paras. 117–33 with *Krstić* ICTY A. Ch. 19.4.2004 para. 224. On command responsibility see *Bemba Gombo* ICC PT. Ch. I 15.6.2009 paras. 432–4. As seen in Chapter 15, the ICC has preferred co-perpetration to joint criminal enterprise in its early practice.

44 See, e.g. Australia and the International Criminal Court (Consequential Amendments) Act 2002, s. 268.115.

in support of propositions of customary international law than was previously the case. Some of the remaining problems can be mitigated by careful study of the law, which involves an appreciation of the relative authoritativeness of the various sources and evidences of custom on point.

This issue arises perhaps most clearly with respect to the question of the extent to which the law of non-international armed conflict ought to be assimilated to that applicable in international armed conflict. Some take a very broad approach to the extent to which the two have already coalesced.[45] The ICTY has implied such a view, by suggesting that:

> elementary considerations of humanity and common sense make it preposterous that the use by States of weapons prohibited in armed conflicts between themselves be allowed when States try to put down rebellion by their own nationals on their own territory. What is inhumane, and consequently proscribed, in international wars, cannot but be inhumane and inadmissible in civil strife.[46]

On the other hand, not all of the rules applicable to international armed conflict are easily applied to their civil war counterparts,[47] as the ICTY, in the same case averred:

> only a number of rules and principles governing international armed conflicts have gradually been extended to apply to internal conflicts; and ... this extension has not taken place in the form of a full and mechanical transplant of those rules to internal conflicts; rather, the general essence of those rules, and not the detailed regulation they may contain, has become applicable to internal conflicts.[48]

Where it is possible to do so, however, the case for unifying the law relating to international and non-international armed conflicts, both in treaty and customary international law, is very strong.[49]

Another area of international criminal law where suggestions have been made for change is the distinction between war crimes and crimes against humanity. An eminent authority in the area, Leslie Green, has suggested that the two crimes ought to be amalgamated.[50] The fact that the contextual elements for the two crimes reflect different (if overlapping) situations militates against the advisability of this position.[51] Still, there may be room for harmonization of the physical elements of similar offences, such as unlawful confinement and arbitrary imprisonment. The expansion of international criminal law into some areas

---

45 See Henckaerts and Doswald-Beck, *ICRC Customary Law*.
46 *Tadić* ICTY A. Ch. 2.10.1995 para. 119.
47 Marco Sassoli and Laura Olsen, 'Prosecutor v. Tadić' (1999) 93 *AJIL* 571 at 575–7.
48 *Tadić* ICTY A. Ch. 2.10.1995 para. 126.
49 Colin Warbrick and Peter Rowe, 'The International Criminal Tribunal for Yugoslavia: The Decision of the Appeals Chamber on the Interlocutory Appeal on Jurisdiction in the *Tadić* Case' (1996) 45 ICLQ 691 at 698.
50 Leslie Green, 'Grave Breaches or Crimes Against Humanity?' (1997–1998) 8 *US Air Force Academy Journal of Legal Studies* 19.
51 William Fenrick, 'Should Crimes Against Humanity Replace War Crimes?' (1999) 37 *Columbia Journal of Transnational Law* 767.

that it does not adequately cover, such as the intentional or reckless creation of mass starvation, would also seem appropriate,[52] and go some way to accepting the reality of structural as well as direct violence. That said, further expansion should be supported by credible legal methods, and one must also recall that 'there might be a fundamental incompatibility between the political agendas of States and the process of codifying, in a progressive manner ... [international criminal law]'.[53]

Another area in which there may be further development is that of corporate liability for criminal conduct. The ad hoc Tribunals and the ICC have jurisdiction only over natural persons; there was strong support at the Rome Conference for including legal entities, but it did not prove possible to reach agreement.[54] Financial gain – whether from the acquisition of natural resources or from arms trading – may be either the cause of atrocities committed in conflicts or the reason for their continuation, and accountability would be increased if it were possible to prosecute directly the companies participating in such atrocities. This is an area which deserves more study in relation to both international and national jurisdictions.[55]

As we approach the first Review Conference of the ICC in 2010 there is a possibility of adding new crimes to the ICC Statute. This represents an opportunity to improve the substantive law included in the ICC Statute but, at the risk of being confounded by developments (and international criminal law has a history of overshooting as well as falling short of hopes and expectations), it is unlikely that significant changes will be made to the substantive law of the ICC Statute at the review conference.[56] There is little more agreement on the ambit of terrorism than there was in 1998.[57] The question of including aggression within the jurisdiction of the ICC will probably prove controversial, in spite of the efforts of the Special Working Group on the Crime of Aggression.[58] Even if there were to be agreement on additions to the ICC Statute, the heavy strictures of the amendment provisions of the Statute[59] will make rapid expansion of the jurisdiction of the ICC highly unlikely.

23.6   The path forward (or back?)

In one respect, international criminal law has probably reached the end of an era. That era is the era of ad hoc international tribunals. The critiques of ad hoc tribunals, not least of having

---

52 So long as it is carefully defined. See David Marcus, 'Famine Crimes in International Law' (2004) 97 *AJIL* 245.

53 Sadat, *Justice for the New Millennium*, 261; see also Broomhall, *International Justice*, 18, 131.

54 See Per Saland, 'International Criminal Law Principles' in Lee, *The Making of the Rome Statute*, 199.

55 See the workshop in (2008) 6 *JICJ* 899.

56 There may, however, be a successful move to delete Art. 124.

57 See section 14.2.3. For a view to the contrary, see Antonio Cassese, 'Terrorism as an International Crime' in Andrea Bianchi (ed.), *Enforcing International Law Norms Against Terrorism* (Oxford, 2004) 213.

58 See section 13.1.2. There is also a proposal for the Review Conference to make the weapons-based war crimes applicable to international armed conflicts also apply to non-international armed conflicts.

59 ICC Statute, Arts. 121, 122.

to reinvent, to various extents, the wheel, have taken hold. The referral of the situation in Darfur to the International Criminal Court rather than setting up an ad hoc tribunal at the global or local level represents a watershed, if an ambiguous one. Nevertheless, we may not have seen the end of internationalized courts, where the input from the international community is less, though still significant.

As the ICC Statute only entered into force in July 2002, it is too early to assess its work critically at a general level. The ICC's first trial has begun, and a number of indictees are in the custody of the Court, even if some high-profile indictees, such as Ahmed Harun and President Al Bashir are not. As yet, the ICC has yet to issue significant decisions on fundamental aspects of its law equivalent to the seminal *Tadić* and *Blaškić* decisions of the ICTY.[60] In some ways, the environment, both political and practical, which the ICC faces for its work is worse than that faced by the ad hoc Tribunals. It does not have the strong powers and the clear (if at times rhetorical) support of the Security Council which the ad hoc Tribunals had at their outset. On the other hand, the ICC operates against a background of increased acceptance of international criminal law, far greater than existed in 1993.

An optimistic forecast for the ICC would look to the diminution of opposition to the Court in the next decade or so, as it proves that it is able to deal with some of the world's greatest atrocities, and fears of political prosecutions die down in the light of experience. This will require, inter alia, careful but objectively justifiable action on the part of the ICC Prosecutor and sound reasoning by its judicial chambers. Procedures must be applied in a manner that is perceived as fair, yet efficient, and representing a proper balance of sometimes competing interests.[61] An outcropping of such action would, it could be hoped, lead to States trusting the Court, thus becoming more willing to cooperate with it. The Court is, to a very considerable extent, reliant on the willingness of States to assist the Court in every form of cooperation and enforcement, including provision of intelligence, arrest of suspects and acceptance of convicted persons for imprisonment.[62] The ICC will fail unless it is properly resourced.[63] If it is to make any difference, the role of the Court and its needs and capabilities will have to become a part of the general policy of States in strengthening or restoring international peace and security.

The ICC should not, however, be the cynosure of international criminal law. Domestic proceedings have many advantages over international ones, including the benefit for the victims of having the trial in their own country, and local enforcement mechanisms such as

---

60 See sections 7.2.4 and 20.1.
61 See Chapter 17.
62 See, e.g. Hans-Peter Kaul, 'Construction Site for More Justice: The International Criminal Court After Two Years' (2005) 99 *AJIL* 370 at 383.
63 A serious failure in this respect is the refusal of the Security Council to allow UN funding of the Darfur referral; see Robert Cryer, 'Sudan, Resolution 1593 and International Criminal Justice' (2006) 19 *LJIL* 195 at 206–8.

police and prison systems; but domestic proceedings may need the legitimacy that an international imprimatur can ensure. The best way forward for international criminal law, in our view, is for there to be a synergy between international and domestic efforts to ensure accountability for international crimes.[64] International assistance for national prosecutions of international crimes will continue and, it is to be hoped, lead to further entrenchment of international criminal law in the area, and maybe even globally.

Too much should not be claimed for international criminal law. The purposes of an international trial which are sometimes advanced – for example, recording history, reconciling communities, telling the victims' story – may sometimes run counter to the interests at the centre of a criminal trial, namely to determine guilt or innocence while respecting the rights of the accused; further, history may actually be distorted in the process.[65] The necessary selection of serious cases also means that ambitions of this kind will only partially be satisfied. There are additional approaches to bringing reconciliation in conflict situations and post-conflict societies.[66] More work needs to be done on the particular difficulties of delivering non-judicial forms of justice and how to calibrate criminal justice mechanisms with other forms of justice. The broader aspects of this programme require a detailed examination of the complex causes of mass crimes, including the role of those financing and profiting from atrocities.[67] This will not be a simple task.

International courts and tribunals operate in an international legal system which is made up of sovereign States. Just as it is still only an aspiration that all States should accept the rule of law in international relations generally (and thus, for example, subordinate their policy on the use of force to international law), so there are still huge difficulties in achieving the rule of law in international criminal justice, in the sense of the consistent and impartial enforcement of the law.[68] That would require more States accepting that their policy be shaped 'on a basis that is less responsive to geopolitical realism, and more in line with legal/moral factors and a genuine commitment to global humane governance as a long-term goal'.[69] In many ways the development of international criminal law is a metonym for the extent to which an international community can be said to exist.[70] The evidence of whether international society has developed into an international community is mixed.[71]

---

64 See also William W. Burke-White, 'A Community of Courts: Toward a System of International Criminal Law Enforcement' (2002) 24 *Michigan Journal of International Law* 1.

65 Mark Osiel, *Mass Atrocity, Collective Memory, and the Law* (New Brunswick, 1997).

66 Section 2.3.

67 For acceptance of such a view see, e.g. Security Council Resolution 1306 (2000) on 'blood diamonds'.

68 Broomhall, *International Justice*, 53–4.

69 Richard Falk, 'Telford Taylor And The Legacy Of Nuremberg' (1999) 37 *Columbia Journal of Transnational Law* 693 at 716.

70 Frédéric Mégret, 'Epilogue to an Endless Debate, The International Court's Third Party Jurisdiction and the Looming Revolution of International Law' (2001) 12 *EJIL* 247.

71 See Hedley Bull, *The Anarchical Society: A Study of Order in World Politics*, 2nd edn (London, 1995).

All that said, between the late 1940s and the early 1990s international criminal law was a field of law which was rarely seen as relevant by many international lawyers or governments, and which was rarely studied or written on, let alone taught as a separate subject.[72] Now it is a major area of study and practice. Twenty years ago few would have thought that a textbook like this would be useful, or necessary, even less would it have been thought that developments in international criminal law would warrant a second edition in less than half a decade. It is our hope that, by aiding understanding of the law, this book will contribute in a small way to the objectives of international criminal law as a whole, the bringing to justice, and finally the deterrence, of those responsible for the atrocities that continue to plague our world.

---

[72] The most notable exception to this trend were the voluminous writings on the subject by M. Cherif Bassiouni.

Index

uniforms, misuse, 307
United Kingdom
  Boer Wars, 65
  command responsibility, 397
  cooperation, statutory limitations, 90
  Declaration on Armenia (1915), 230
  def

  e

aggression, 314–15, 321–5
cooperation, Model Treaties, 86, 99
crimes against humanity, 232
emblems, perfidious use, 306, 307
Friendly Relations Declaration (1970), 315
GA powers, 329
genocide and, 203, 205, 220
Human Rights Committee, amnesties
      564
    , 536
    575
    Principles, 113, 543
    ing forces
    tion with Tribunals, 516–17
    mor, 189
    o, 189
    la, 136
    Leone, 182
    of conflicts, 281
    Council. *See* United Nations
      Security Council
    uperior orders, 416
    m
    definition, 339, 340
    han rights and, 349
    s
    n Boven/Bassiouni Principles, 479,
      481, 490
    ictims Declaration (1985), 479, 481
    Crimes Commission, 53
    xtermination, 247
    rking Group on Arbitrary Detention, 251
    d Nations Security Council
    countability and, 583
  TR
    completion strategy, 139
    cooperation obligations, 510
    creation, 136
    staffing, 138, 139
    war crimes in internal conflicts, 277
ICTY
    completion strategy, 131
    cooperation obligations, 510
    creation, 123–4, 126–8
International Criminal Court and
    aggression jurisdiction, 316, 329–31
    deferral of investigations/prosecutions,
      169–70
    enforcement of decisions, 171
    independence, 432
    initiation of proceedings, 163–4, 166

DATE DUE FOR RETURN

An Introduction to
Law and Procedure

This market-leading textbook
and focuses on what the s
national courts and tribun
prosecution of those crime
yet sophisticated, approach
of teaching the subject, an
Court (ICC) and the Rom
international criminal law
ICC and victims' rights al
mented by an extensive
which offers convenient ac
reading, problems and que
and simulations.

ROBERT CRYER is Profe
Birmingham.

HÅKAN FRIMAN is Visitin

DARRYL ROBINSON is a
Canada.

ELIZABETH WILMSHURST
at University College Lon

The loan period may be shortened if the item is requested.